EXPORT/IMPORT PROCEDURES and DOCUMENTATION

FIFTH EDITION

DONNA L. BADE

HarperCollins
Leadership

AN IMPRINT OF HarperCollins

Export/Import Procedures and Documentation

© 2022 Donna L. Bade

Published by HarperCollins Leadership, an imprint of HarperCollins Focus LLC.

Bulk discounts available. For details visit:
www.harpercollinsleadership.com/bulkquotes
Email: customercare@harpercollins.com

ISBN 978-1-4002-4239-9 (TP)

Contents

Contents

Contents

Contents

Contents

Part III
Importing: Procedures and Documentation

Contents

Contents

Contents

Part IV
Global Customs Considerations

Contents

Part V
Specialized Exporting and Importing

Contents

Preface

The world of international trade changes daily and staying current with those changes is complex. Unrest in the Ukraine and the Middle East results in sanctions by the United Nations, the United States, and the European Union. Tensions ease in countries formerly sanctioned by the United States and new general licenses are issued. Defense articles previously controlled by the Department of State are transferred to the Department of Commerce with new licensing requirements or in some cases no licenses required at all. New free trade agreements between countries allow for raw materials to transfer from one country to another duty free, making the cost of the manufacturing less expensive, but the record-keeping to support the duty-free claim is vital. Keeping all the balls in the air for trade compliance, supply chain efficiency, and financial competitiveness is challenging. For the experienced international trade professional, it is all about staying abreast of the changes and implementing them into their supply chain as quickly and efficiently as possible. For the startup or domestic company that is first venturing abroad, complying with the rules and regulations for the numerous government agencies in the United States and in other countries can be daunting.

This book provides guidance for the novice to the basic import and export requirements, both from the perspective of the United States, but it also discusses the universality of many compliance requirements established by the World Customs Organization of the World Trade Organization. It is also a handy resource for experienced international traders to review an area that may be unfamiliar to them or to just review the exact language on a specific Customs document.

My career path in international trade was all about making lemonade out of lemons. Having no job in a recession led me to a career first as a customs broker and then as an international trade attorney, and I never looked back. It is precisely the fact that my world is in constant change that keeps me intrigued. It is the variety of commodities and services that my clients offer; the problems they encounter in the countries they import from and export to; the constant evolution of international agreements; the revised focus of each new administration; and the broad spectrum of agencies that regulate the movement of goods in and out of countries that make this business an ongoing challenge.

Preface

I am a member of Sandler, Travis & Rosenberg, P.A., co-chair of the firm's Import and Export Practice Group, and manage the firm's Chicago office. I feel like one of the elder statesmen these days when I realize that I have been working in this field for more than 40 years. I have lectured extensively on import and export trade regulations at meetings, seminars, and webinars. I have actively participated in many organizations dedicated to this industry and even spent a few years as an adjunct professor teaching lawyers the basics of importing and exporting in the LLM program in International Trade at The John Marshall Law School.

I am very fortunate to have worked with many extremely knowledgeable professionals in this field and have learned from their experience, intelligence, and humor over the years, and in some cases all you can do is laugh. My gratitude goes out to many of them, including Thomas Johnson, the former author and co-author of this book on whose shoulders I stand, Lee Sandler, Len Rosenberg, Tom Travis, Jack Cline, Al D'Amico, Chet Wilson, and many others too numerous to name.

I wish to acknowledge and express my appreciation for the assistance, patience, and moral support provided by Nicole Kehoskie, Mark Segrist, Michelle Mejia, Aman Ansari, and Joey Martinez of the Chicago STR office while I put this edition together. I also wish to thank my editor, James Bessent, for turning what I originally put in writing into something that is both readable and understandable. Finally, my deepest appreciation goes to my family, Thomas, Lindsey, and Tom, for their ongoing love and support.

The information contained herein is accurate as far as I am aware and is based on sources available to me. Nevertheless, it is not legal advice, and specific legal advice based upon the facts and circumstances of the reader's own situation should be sought in making export or import decisions.

Any comments or suggestions for the improvement of this book will be gratefully accepted.

Donna L. Bade
Sandler, Travis & Rosenberg, P.A.
Chicago, Illinois

Acknowledgments

The author gratefully acknowledges the courtesy of the following for inclusion of their forms in this book:

United States Council for International Business – www.uscib.org

Roanoke Trade Services, Inc. – www.roanoketrade.com

Unz & Co. – www.unzco.com

Tops Business Forms – www.tops-products.com

First National Bank of Chicago – www.nndb.com

Shipping Solutions, a division of Intermart, Inc. – www.shipsolutions.com

SGS North America – www.sgs.com

About the Author

Donna L. Bade is a partner in the international trade law firm of Sandler, Travis & Rosenberg, P.A., and manages the firm's Chicago office. Her practice is focused on import and export trade law, trade regulations and customs law, regulatory law, and transportation law.

Ms. Bade is a licensed customs broker, has extensive experience advising companies in the areas of tariff classification, valuation, country of origin marketing, and utilization of preference programs. She has represented clients before U.S. Customs and Border Protection on focused assessments and before other government agencies with responsibilities over import and export transactions. She also helps companies develop internal compliance programs. She worked as a customs broker and freight forwarder for many years in the ports of Detroit, St. Louis, and Chicago, and brings that experience to her understanding of the supply chain and important process.

In addition, Ms. Bade has extensive experience assisting clients with export control, licensing, commodity jurisdiction, and compliance issues. She has represented companies before the Bureau of Industry and Security, the Office of Foreign Assets Control, and the Department of State. She has also worked with companies to establish export management systems and has provided training to foreign branches and subsidiaries on U.S. export controls.

Ms. Bade also counsels customs brokers and freight forwarders regarding licensing and other issues before CBP and the Federal Maritime commission.

Ms. Bade has lectured extensively on issues pertaining to import and export law and procedures on behalf of various organizations. She has taught import and export law as an adjunct professor and served on the board of advisors to the John Marshall Law School's LLM program in international business and trade.

Part I

Organizing for Export and Import Operations

Chapter 1

Organizing for Export and Import Operations

When a company makes the decision to begin marketing its products outside the United States or to source raw materials from abroad, it generally assigns the compliance task to someone in the supply chain group with little to no background in the complexities of regulatory compliance. Very few people set out on a career path to develop an expertise in the import/export compliance field, but it is a highly necessary and valued position in today's global environment.

Companies must have a smooth, efficient, and compliance-oriented (and, therefore, profitable) exporting and/or importing program and it requires that some personnel must have specialized knowledge. The personnel involved and their place in the business organization vary from company to company, and sometimes the same personnel have roles in both exporting/importing and other functions within the company. In small companies, one person may perform all of the relevant functions, while in large companies or companies with a large amount of exports or imports, the number of personnel dedicated to the compliance responsibilities may be large. In addition, as a company decides to perform in-house the work that it previously contracted with outside companies (such as customs brokers, freight forwarders, consultants, packing companies, and others) to perform, the export/import department may grow. As business increases, specialties may develop within the department, and the duties performed by any one person may become narrower.

A. Export Compliance Department

For a company to grow by marketing its products abroad, it must be compliant with both U.S. export controls and foreign import regulations. This compliance-first attitude must be driven from the top by the President or CEO. To be compliant, every employee must be aware of his own role in the process. Violations may result in penalties of $250,000 per violation, bad publicity and even a denial of export privileges. It is critical to the bottom line of any company to be compliant. One of the key responsibilities of an export compliance person is the ability to say "Stop the Shipment" and have the support of management to enforce that dictate. It is far better to stop a shipment than try to explain later when a subpoena arrives or when an enforcement agent shows up at your door why the company exported products in violation of the law.

For many companies, the export department begins in the sales or marketing department. That department may develop leads or identify customers located in other countries. Inquiries or orders may come from potential customers through the company's web site. When such orders come in, the salespeople need to determine what steps are different from its domestic sales in order to fill those export orders. For example, how do they arrange for the shipment; how will they guarantee payment; who is responsible for insurance; etc. Often the exporter's first foreign sales are to Canada or Mexico. Because the export order may require special procedures in manufacturing, credit checking, insuring, packing, shipping, and collection, it is likely that a number of people within the company will have input on the appropriate way to fill the order. In addition, if the customer is expecting to take advantage of the North American Free Trade Agreement, the products must meet certain criteria to be eligible. Determining the eligibility should be done before marketing the product and the process can be complicated, but without ensuring the product is eligible, all duty-free privileges will be denied and the Company may lose a customer. As export orders increase (for example, as a result of an overseas distributor having been appointed or through an expansion of Internet sales), the handling of such orders should become more routine and the assignment of the special procedures related to an export sale should be given to specific personnel. It will be necessary to interface with freight forwarders, couriers, banks, packing companies, steamship lines, airlines, translators, government agencies, domestic transportation companies, and attorneys. Because most manufacturers have personnel who must interface with domestic transportation companies (traffic or logistics department), often additional personnel will be assigned to that department to manage export shipments and interface with other outside services. Some of this interface, such as with packing companies and steamship lines, and possibly government agencies and banks, may be handled by a freight forwarder, but the ultimate responsibility lies with the exporter, so knowledgeable oversight of the supply chain partnerships including, freight forwarder oversight is critical. The number of personnel needed and the assignment of responsibilities depend upon the size of the company and the volume of exports involved. A chart for a company with a large export department is shown in Figure 1–1. The way in which an export order is processed at the time of quotation, order entry, shipment, and collection is shown in Figures 1–2, 1–3, 1–4, and 1–5, respectively. Smaller companies will combine some of these functions into tasks for one or more persons.

B. Import Department

A manufacturer's import department often grows out of the purchasing department, whose personnel have been assigned the responsibility of procuring raw materials or components for the manufacturing process or out of the supply chain department, because the responsibility of that group is managing the international transportation. It is important that the personnel responsible for the import compliance receive proper training.

For importers or trading companies that deal in finished goods, the import department may begin as the result of being appointed as the U.S. distributor for a foreign manufacturer or from purchasing a product produced by a foreign manufacturer that has U.S. sales potential. Because foreign manufacturers often sell their products ex-factory or FOB plant, a U.S. company that intends to import such products must familiarize itself with ocean shipping, insurance, U.S. Customs clearance, and other procedural matters. Increasingly, a number of U.S. manufacturers are moving their manufacturing operations overseas to cheaper labor regions and importing products they formerly manufactured in the United States. That activity will also put them in contact with foreign freight forwarders, U.S. customs brokers, banks, the U.S. Customs and Border Protection, marine insurance companies, and other service companies.

Once again, import compliance is key to ensuring a smooth import process and all parties in an organization must be aware of the compliance role they play in meeting those requirements. Compliance begins at the time a product is in the design stages for manufacture either abroad or in the U.S. in order to be able to take advantage of import opportunities for finished goods or components and to ensure that there is no misunderstanding regarding the classification, duty rate, availability of certain free trade agreements duty reduction programs, proper valuation, county of origin marking, etc. There are potential penalties and seizures available to the U.S. Customs and Border Protection, so compliance must be first and foremost at all times.

Figure 1–1. Export organization chart.

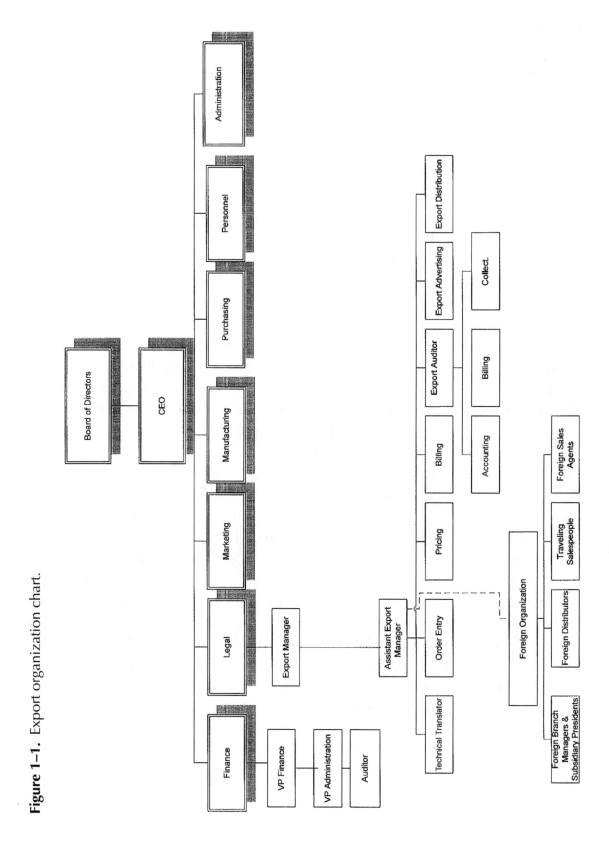

Figure 1–2. Export order processing—quotation.

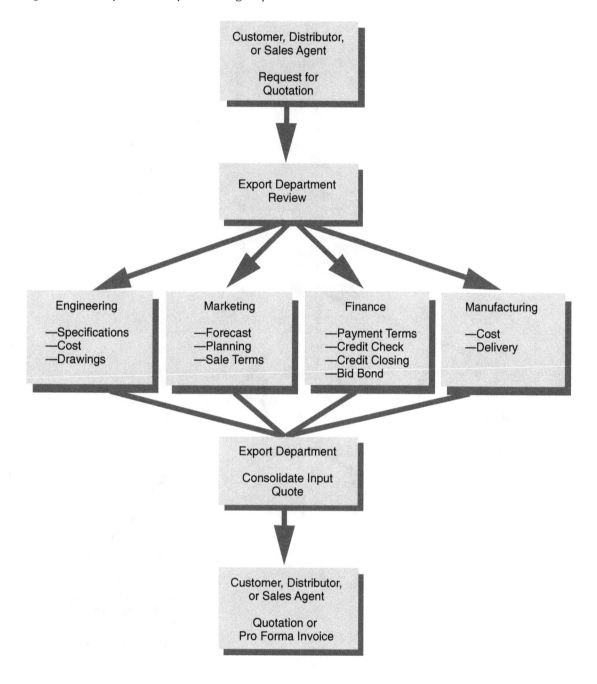

Figure 1–3. Export order processing—order entry.

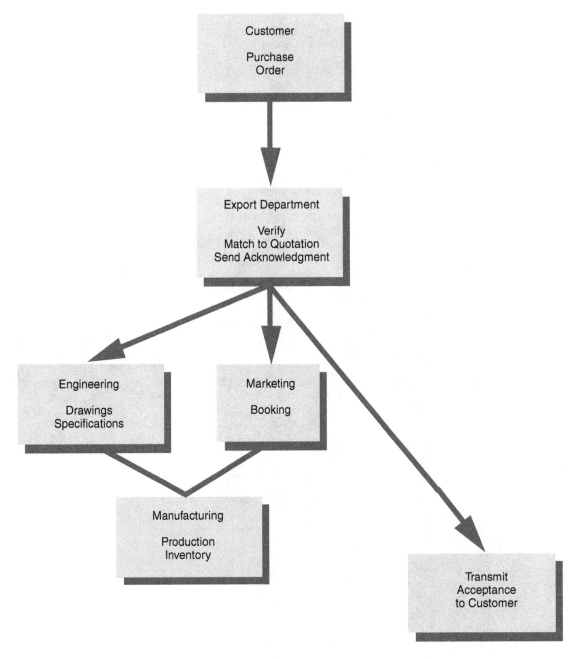

Figure 1–4. Export order processing—shipment.

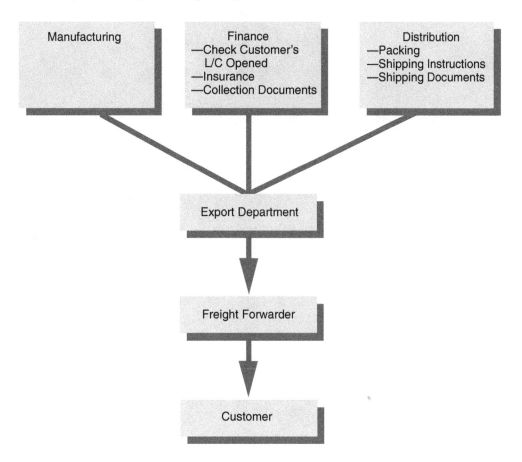

C. Combined Export and Import Departments

In many companies, some or all of the functions of the export and import departments are combined in some way. In smaller companies, where the volume of exports or imports does not justify more personnel, one or two persons may have responsibility for both export and import procedures and documentation. As companies grow larger or the volume of export/import business increases, these functions tend to be separated more into export departments and import departments as each develops a specialized expertise in their areas. A diagram of the interrelationships between the export and import personnel in the company and outside service providers is shown in Figure 1–6.

Figure 1–5. Export order processing—collection.

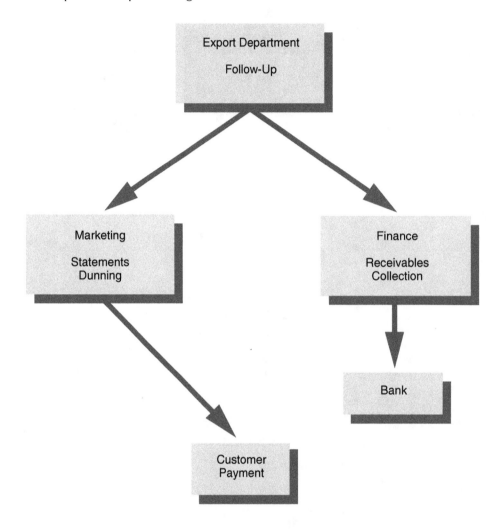

D. Manuals of Procedures and Documentation

It is often very helpful for companies to have a manual of procedures and documentation for their export and import departments particularly as personnel changes. Such manuals serve as a reference tool for smooth operation and as a training tool for new employees. Moreover, since the Customs Modernization Act, such manuals *are required* to establish that the importer is using "reasonable care" in its importing operations, and they have become essential in the mitigation of penalties for violations of the import and export laws administered by the U.S. Customs and Border Protection; the Bureau of Industry & Security, Department of Commerce; and the Office of Foreign Assets Control, Department of Treasury and Directorate of Defense

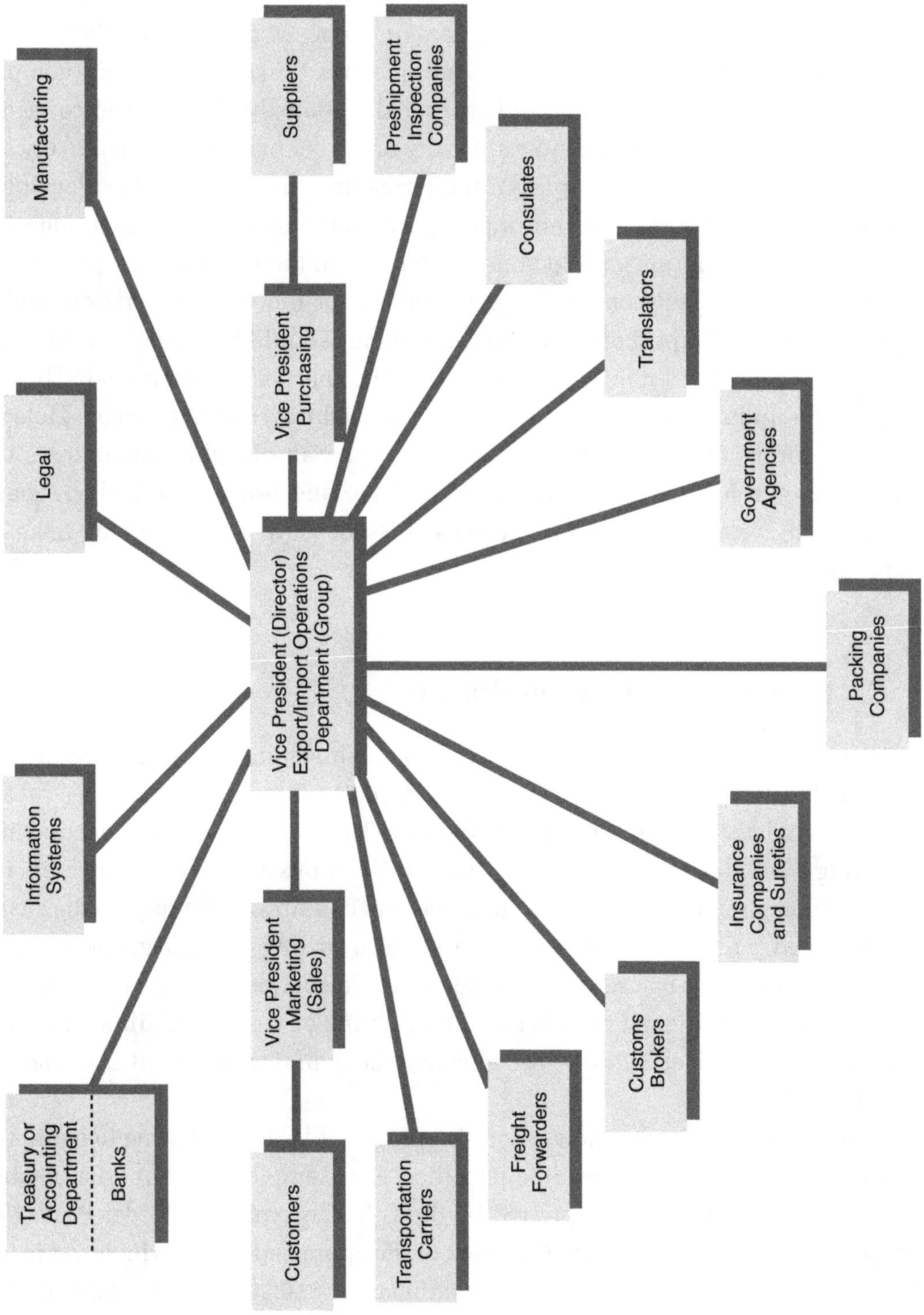

Figure 1–6. Interrelationships with outside service providers.

Trade Control, Department of State. Such manuals should be customized to the particular company and kept up-to-date. A good manual should describe the company's export and import processes. It should contain names, telephone numbers, and contact persons at the freight forwarders and customs brokers, steamship companies, packing companies, and other services that the company has chosen to utilize as well as government agencies required for the import or export of the company's commodities. It should contain copies of the forms that the company has developed or chosen to use in export sales and import purchases and transportation, identify the internal routing of forms and documentation within the company for proper review and authorization, and contain job descriptions for the various personnel who are engaged in export/import operations. The manuals should be kept electronically and disseminated via hard copy or the company intranet to key personnel. The manuals *must* be updated as changes in policies, procedures, contact persons, telephone numbers, forms, or government regulations occur. Sample tables of contents for export and import manuals are shown in Figures 1–7 and 1–8, respectively. A company manual that is stagnant, unread and unused is not viewed favorably by the government agencies.

E. Record-Keeping Compliance

Exporters and importers have always had an obligation to maintain records relating to their international trade transactions. Recently, however, these obligations have become mandatory due to changes in the law. The use of electronic documentation including emailing or web purchasing and confirmations as well as the invoices makes it all the more important to identify the terms and conditions and require the customer to either send confirmation of acceptance either in writing through an email or by having a mandatory link before the transaction can be complete. Almost all government agencies have transitioned to either electronic filing or web-based filing of important documentation. It doesn't, however, alleviate the exporter or import from hard-copy record-keeping.

Each of the agencies has new record-keeping standards and failing to maintain the proper documentation may result in penalties. For example, if an importer or exporter fails to provide documents requested by the U.S. Customs and Border Protection, it can be fined up to $100,000 (or 75 percent of the appraised value, whichever is less) if the failure to produce a document is intentional, or $10,000 (or 40 percent of the appraised value, whichever is less) if it is negligent or accidental.

Figure 1–7. Export manual table of contents.

I. Statement of Manual's Purpose
   - Company Policies Relating to Export
II. The Export Department
   - Role
   - Function/Operation Statement
   - Organization Chart—Positions; Export Compliance Manager
   - Job Descriptions and Responsibilities
   - Initial and Periodic Training Requirements
   - Procedures for Disseminating Current Regulatory Developments Information
III. Export Legal Procedures
   - Preliminary Considerations
   - Formation of Sales Agreement
   - Understanding the Incoterms® (i.e. FOB, FCA, DDP)
   - Determining Where Title Will Transfer
   - Specifying the Particulars of the Agreement
   - List of Existing Agents and Distributors
   - List of Approved Freight Forwarders, Steamship Companies, Insurance Brokers, Packing Companies, Attorneys
   - Collections and Banking Procedures (Drafts, Letters of Credit)
   - Record-Keeping Compliance
IV. Export Documents (Samples of Company-Approved Standard Forms)
   - Quotations, Costing Sheets
   - Purchase Order Acknowledgments
   - Purchase Order Acceptances
   - Terms and Conditions
   - Invoices (Commercial, Pro Forma, and Special Customs)
   - Payment Terms
   - Electronic Export Information (Shipper's Export Declaration), Automated Export System Records
   - Powers of Attorney
   - Shipper's Letter of Instructions
   - Bills of Lading

(continues)

Figure 1–7. (*continued*)

- Packing Lists
- Inspection Certificates
- Insurance Certificates
- Dock and Warehouse Receipts
- Consulate Invoices
- Certificates of Origin
- Delivery Instructions
- Declarations for Dangerous Goods (if applicable)

V. Export Licenses

- Process for Screening Restricted Parties for Current and New Customers
- Procedures for Determining Export Commodity Classification Number
- Procedures for Applying for Bureau of Industry Determination of Classification
- Procedures for Determining Applicability of Export Administration Regulations Based on:
  - ECCN Classification
  - Bases for Restrictions
  - Identification of Country
  - Any Applicable Exemptions
- Procedures for Applying for Export Licenses with Bureau of Industry or Security
- Procedures for Monitoring Embargoed Countries and Areas of Concern
- Determining U.S. Munitions List Applicability for Defense Articles
- Determining "Specially Designed"
- Annual Registration with Directorate of Defense Trade Controls as Needed
- Procedures for Obtaining a License through D-Trade
- Obtaining a Manufacturing License Agreement, Technology Transfer Agreement, or Distribution Agreement as Needed
- Procedures for Ensuring Shipment in Accordance with License Requirements
- Procedures for Reporting or Other Compliance in Accordance with License Provisos

Figure 1–8. Import manual table of contents.

I. Statement of Manual's Purpose
- Company Policies Relating to Import

II. The Import Department
- Role
- Function/Operation Statement
- Organization Chart—Positions; Import Compliance Manager
- Job Descriptions and Responsibilities
- Procedures for Disseminating Current Regulatory Developments Information

III. Import Procedures
- Preliminary Considerations
- Formation of Purchase Agreement
- Understanding the Incoterms (e.g., FOB, FCA, DDP)
- Specifics of the Transaction
- List of Existing Suppliers
- List of Approved Customs Brokers, Foreign Freight Forwarders, Steamship Companies, Airlines, Insurance Brokers, Inland Carriers, Attorneys
- Payment and Banking Procedures (Drafts, Letters of Credit)
- Record-Keeping Compliance

IV. Import Documents (Samples of Company-Approved Standard Forms, Customs Forms)
- Requests for Quotations
- Purchase Orders
- Terms and Conditions
- Invoices (Commercial, Pro Forma)
- Bills of Lading
- Packing Lists
- Inspection Certificates
- Customs Broker's Letter of Instructions
- Customs Entries (CF3461 Entry/Immediate Delivery and CF7501 Entry Summary)

(continues)

Figure 1–8. (*continued*)

- Certificates of Origin (NAFTA, other FTA)
- Other Government Agency Required Documentation
- Liquidation Information
- Notices of Redelivery, Request for Information, and Notices of Action and Responses
- Requests for Reliquidation
- Protests, Petitions, Post-Entry Amendments
- Reconciliation Entries
- Summons, Warrants, Subpoenas, Seizure Notices
- Prepenalty and Penalty Notices
- Liquidated Damages Notices
- ITC Questionnaires
- Surety Bond Information

Other laws, such as the Export Administration Act, the Foreign Trade Statistics Regulations, the North American Free Trade Agreement, and the various other free trade agreements, also impose record-keeping requirements on exporters. For companies that engage in both exporting and importing, it is important to establish a record-keeping compliance program that maintains the documents required by all the laws regulating international trade. In general, U.S. export and import laws require that the records be kept for a period of five years from the date of import or export (or three years from date of payment on drawback entries). However, other laws—for example, state income tax laws or foreign laws—may require longer periods.

U.S. Customs and Border Protection has issued a *Recordkeeping Compliance Handbook* describing in detail its interpretation of the proper record-keeping responsibilities for importers. This *Handbook* states that Customs expects each importer to designate a manager of record-keeping compliance who can act as the point of contact for all document requests from Customs and who is responsible for managing and administering the record-keeping compliance within the company. The manager, as well as all employees involved in importing (and exporting), is expected to receive regular training on compliance with the customs laws and on documentation and record-keeping requirements. Each company is expected to maintain a procedures manual to ensure compliance with all customs laws and record-keeping requirements.

F. Software

Many companies offer software programs for managing the export process, including order taking, generation of export documentation, compliance with export control regulations, calculation of transportation charges and duties, and identification of trade leads including leading business software companies. Not all software programs are the same so it is important to review various different programs to determine which one is right for your current and future business as well as the ability to stay current. The use of software enables companies to process import and export documentation more efficiently, but the legal burden of accuracy always remains with the importer or exporter.

G. Federal, State, International, and Foreign Law

The Constitution of the United States specifically provides that the U.S. Congress shall have power to regulate exports and imports (Art. 1, §8). This means that exporting or importing will be governed primarily by federal law rather than state law.

On the other hand, the law of contracts, which governs the formation of international sales and purchase agreements and distributor and sales agent agreements, is almost exclusively governed by state law, which varies from state to state. As discussed in Chapter 3, Section B.2.m, and Chapter 7, Section B.2.l, a number of countries, including the United States, have entered into an international treaty that governs the sale of goods and will supersede the state law of contracts in certain circumstances. Finally, in many circumstances, the laws of the foreign country will govern at least as to that portion of the transaction occurring within its borders, and in certain situations, it may govern the international sales and purchase agreements as well. Most of the procedures and forms that are used in exporting and importing have been developed to fulfill specific legal requirements, so that an exporter or importer should disregard such procedures and forms only after confirming that doing so will not subject the company to legal risks or penalties.

Part II
Exporting: Procedures and Documentation

Chapter 2

Exporting: Preliminary Considerations

This chapter will discuss the preliminary considerations that anyone intending to export should consider. Before beginning to export and on each export sale thereafter, a number of considerations should be addressed to avoid costly mistakes and difficulties. Those companies that begin exporting or continue to export without having addressed the following issues will run into problems sooner or later.

A. Products

Initially, the exporter should think about certain considerations relating to the product it intends to export. For example, is the product normally utilized as a component in a customer's manufacturing process? Is it sold separately as a spare part? Is the product a raw material, commodity, or finished product? Is it sold singly or as part of a set or system? Does the product need to be modified—such as the size, weight, or color to be salable in the foreign market? Is the product new or used? (If the product is used, some countries prohibit importation or require independent appraisals of value, which can delay the sale.) Often the appropriate methods of manufacturing and marketing, the appropriate documentation, the appropriate procedures for exportation, and the treatment under foreign law, including foreign customs laws, will depend upon these considerations.

Some products are subject to special export limitations and procedures. In addition to the general export procedures discussed in this part, exporters of munitions; narcotics and controlled substances; nuclear equipment, materials, and waste; watercraft; natural gas; electric power; hazardous substances; biological products; consumer products not conforming to applicable product safety standards; adulterated or misbranded food, drugs, medical devices, and cosmetics; endangered species; ozone-depleting chemicals; flammable fabrics; precursor chemicals; tobacco seeds and plants; fish and wildlife; crude oil; certain petroleum-based chemicals and products; and pharmaceuticals intended for human or animal use must give notices or apply for special licenses, permits, or approvals from the appropriate U.S. government agency before exporting such products.

B. Volume

What is the expected volume of export of the product? Will this be an isolated sale of a small quantity or an ongoing series of transactions amounting to substantial quantities? Small quantities may be exported under purchase orders and purchase order acceptances. Large quantities may require more formal international sales agreements; more secure methods of payment; special shipping, packing, and handling procedures; the appointment of sales agents and/or distributors in the foreign country; or after-sales service (see the discussion in Chapter 3).

C. Country Market and Product Competitiveness Research

On many occasions, a company's sole export sales business consists of responding to orders from customers located in foreign countries without any active sales efforts by the company. However, as a matter of successful exporting, it is imperative that the company adequately evaluate the various world markets where its product is likely to be marketable. This will include a review of macroeconomic factors such as the size of the population and the economic development level and buying power of the country, and more specific factors, such as the existence of competitive products in that country. The United Nations publishes its *International Trade Statistics Yearbook* (http://comtrade.un.org/), and the International Monetary Fund (IMF) publishes its *Direction of Trade Statistics Yearbook* (http://www.imf.org/external/) showing what countries are buying and importing all types of products. The U.S. Department of Commerce, Bureau of Census gathers and publishes data to assist those who are interested in evaluating various country markets, including its International Data Base and Export and Import Trade Data Base (http://www.census.gov/foreign-trade/statistics/country/index.html). It has also compiled detailed assessments of the international competitiveness of many U.S. products and information on foreign trade fairs to identify sales opportunities for such products. Another useful tool for evaluating the political and commercial risk of doing business in a particular country is the Country Limitation Schedule published periodically by the Export-Import Bank of the United States (http://www.exim.gov/tools/country/country_limits.cfm). The Department of Commerce's web site is Export.gov (http://www.export.gov/exportbasics/index.asp). It provides information about the basics of exporting, Frequently Asked Questions, and information on marketing, finance, and logistics. Of course, other private companies also publish data, such as those contained in the Dun & Bradstreet *Exporters Encyclopedia* or BNA's *Export Reference Manual*. With limited personnel and resources, all companies must make strategic decisions about which countries they will target for export sales and how much profit they are likely to obtain by their efforts in various countries.

D. Identification of Customers: End Users, Distributors, and Sales Agents

Once a company has evaluated the countries with the best market potential and the international competitiveness of its products, the specific purchasers, such as end users of the products, sales agents who can solicit sales in that country for the products, or distributors who are willing to buy and resell the products in that country, must be identified. This is a highly important decision and some of the worst experiences in exporting result from not having done adequate homework in selecting customers, sales agents, and distributors. It is far more efficient and profitable to spend significant amounts of time evaluating potential customers, sales agents, and distributors than to have to start over again because such customers, sales agents, or distributors turn out to be unable to pay, unable to perform, or difficult to work with. The U.S. Department of Commerce International Trade Administration offers a number of services and publications, such as overseas trade missions and fairs, business matchmaking services, market intelligence, background reports, trade counseling, international partner search, in country promotions all designed to assist U.S. companies in identifying possible customers.

Once potential customers have been identified, if an ongoing relationship is contemplated, a personal visit to evaluate the customer is essential. One efficient way is to arrange a schedule of interviews at its foreign offices where representatives of the U.S. company could meet with numerous potential customers, sales agents, and distributors in that country in the course of a two- or three-day period. Based on such meetings, one or more distributors or sales agents can be selected, or the needs of a customer can be clearly understood.

In evaluating potential customers, sales agents, and distributors, it is important to obtain a credit report. Credit reports are available from Dun & Bradstreet, www.dnb.com; Teikoku Data Bank America, Inc. [Japan], http://www.tdb.co.jp/english/index.html; Owens Online, http://www.owens.com; and local offices of the U.S. Department of Commerce (International Company Profiles), http://www.export.gov/salesandmarketing/ism_market_research.asp.

E. Compliance With Foreign Law

Prior to exporting to a foreign country or even agreeing to sell to a customer in a foreign country, a U.S. company should be aware of any foreign laws that might affect the sale. Information about foreign law often can be obtained from the customer or distributor to which the U.S. company intends to sell. However, if the customer or distributor is incorrect in the information that it gives to the exporter, the exporter may pay dearly for having relied solely upon the advice of the customer. Incorrect information about foreign law may result in the prohibition of importation of the exporter's product, or it may mean that the customer cannot resell the products profitably as expected. Unfortunately, customers often overlook those things that may be of the greatest concern to the exporter. Although, in most foreign countries, someone within the country such as the buyer or delivery party must act as the Importer of Record for the import compliance, it may be necessary for the U.S. exporter to confirm its customer's advice with third parties, including attorneys, banks, or government agencies, to feel confident that it properly understands the foreign law requirements. Some specific examples are as follows:

1. *Industry Standards*

Foreign manufacturers and trade associations often promulgate industry standards that are enacted into law or that require compliance in order to sell successfully there. It may be necessary to identify such standards even prior to manufacture of the product that the company intends to sell for export or to modify the product prior to shipment. Or, it may be necessary to arrange for the importing customer to make such modifications. Sometimes compliance with such standards is evidenced by certain marks on the product, such as "JIS" (Japan), "CSA" (Canada), and "UL" (Underwriters Laboratories—U.S.).

All countries are concerned about import safety and have been enacting new laws regulating standards. Of particular concern is the area of consumer products, including foods, toys, children's wear, etc. One type of foreign safety standard that is becoming important is the "CE" mark required for the importation of certain products into the European Community. The European Community has issued directives relating to safety standards for the following important products: food, chemicals, toys, simple pressure vessels, telecommunications terminal equipment, machinery, gas appliances, electromagnetic compatibility, low-voltage products, and medical devices (see www.efsa.europa.eu, http://echa.europa.eu/web/guest/regulations/reach and www.newapproach.org). Products not conforming to these directives are subject to seizure and the assessment of fines, not to mention associated bad publicity that might result from these actions. The manufacturer may conduct its own conformity assessment and self-declare compliance in most cases. For some products, however, the manufacturer is required (and in all cases may elect) to hire an authorized independent certifying service company to conduct the conformity assessment. The manufacturer must maintain a Technical Construction File to support the declaration and must have an authorized representative located within the European Community to respond to enforcement actions.

The International Organization for Standards (ISO) is an independent, non-governmental organization that works to create technical standardization. With 161 member countries, it provides a consistency critical to a global marketplace. Technical commodities develop the standards that are codified into voluntary agreements. Ensuring your product meets these standards will make entry into the marketplace of the member countries much easier. (http://www.iso.org/iso/home/standards.htm.)

Other resources for exporting products to consumers include the United Nations Guidelines for Consumers (http://unctad.org/en/docs/poditcclpm21.en.pdf) and NSF International, which develops public health standards in a variety of industries. (http://www.nsf.org.)

Helpful sources of information in the United States include the National Center for Standards and Certification Information, a part of the Department of Commerce National Institute of Standards and Technology (www.nist.gov), which maintains collections of foreign government standards by product; the National Technical Information Service (ww.ntis.gov); the Foreign Agricultural Service of the Department of Agriculture (www.fas.usda.gov); and the American National Standards Institute (www.ansi.org), which maintains over 100,000 worldwide product standards on its NSSN network, also collect such information. Canada has the Standards Council (www.scc.ca); and Germany has the Deutsches Institut für Normung (DIN) (http://www.din.de/cmd?level=tpl-home&languageid=en).

2. Foreign Customs Laws

Uniformity of Customs laws is significantly progressing with more and more countries joining the World Trade Organization (WTO). Under the WTO, is the World Customs Organization (WCO), which works to establish uniformity of practice among the member countries, while still allowing some "opt-outs" for a period of years after joining. As a result member countries use the Harmonized Tariff Schedules for classification purposes, the World Customs Organization Valuation Agreement (formerly known at the General Agreement on Tariffs and Trade Valuation Code); and it is currently working to unify the origin standards. This uniformity allows for a greater transparency in international trade and certainly a goal for the WCO; however, interpretation of the laws is left to the Member States which still results in discrepancies and many issues are simply not addressed at the WCO level. Also the allowance of "opt-out" clauses for a number of years, allow developing countries to bring their own programs into compliance.

It is important to identify the amount of customs duties that will be assessed on the product, which will involve determining the correct tariff classification for the product under foreign law in order to determine whether the tariff rate will be so high that it is unlikely that sales of the product will be successful in that country, and to evaluate whether a distributor will be able to make a reasonable profit if it resells at the current market price in that country. The countries of export destination may have absolute quotas on the quantity of products that can be imported. Importation of products in excess of the quota will be prohibited. It is especially important to confirm that there are no antidumping, countervailing, or other special customs duties imposed on the products (see more on this in Chapter 10). These duties are often much higher than regular *ad valorem* duties, and may be applied to products imported to the country even if the seller was not subject to the original antidumping investigation.

Another problem is "assists." If the buyer will be furnishing items used in the production of merchandise, such as tools, dies, molds, raw materials, or engineering or development services, to the seller, the importer of record (whether that is the buyer or the seller through an agent) may be required to pay customs duties on such items, and the seller may be required to identify such items in its commercial invoices. (More information about valuation and assists can be found in Chapter 10.)

Many countries have severe penalties for import violations that may include fines or seizure, so it is important to be familiar with these provisions. See Appendix J listing web sites for foreign customs agencies and tariff information.

In any case, where there is doubt as to the correct classification or valuation of the merchandise, duty rate, or existence of assists, the importer (whether buyer or seller) may wish to seek an administrative ruling from the foreign customs agency. This will usually take some period of time, and the seller and buyer may have to adjust their production and delivery plans accordingly. (A more thorough understanding of the types of considerations that the buyer may have to take into account under its customs laws can be gained by reviewing the similar considerations for a U.S. importer discussed in Chapter 6, Section F.)

3. *Government Contracting*

Sales to foreign governments, government agencies, or partially government owned private businesses often involve specialized procedures and documentation. Public competitive bidding and compliance with invitations to bid and acquisition regulations, and providing bid bonds, performance bonds, guarantees, standby letters of credit, and numerous certifications may be required. Commissions may be prohibited, or the disclosure of commissions paid may be required. Government purchases may qualify for customs duty, quota, or import license exemptions. Barter or countertrade may be necessary.

Foreign government agencies often promulgate regulations that are designed to give preferential treatment to products supplied by manufacturers in their own country. This may consist of an absolute preference, or it may be a certain price differential preference. Determining whether such laws or agency regulations exist for your company's products is mandatory if government sales are expected to be important.

The United States has entered into numerous Free Trade Agreements with various countries and each of the Agreements has reciprocal government procurement provisions which allow for U.S. products to be treated as the equivalent of domestic goods in government procurement contracts. There are rules of origin to determine when third country components are substantially transformed into a U.S. origin good eligible for these government procurement bids. (See more on origin in Chapter 11.)

4. *Exchange Controls and Import Licenses*

Unlike the United States, many foreign governments have policies and procedures designed to regulate economic stability by establishing currency exchange controls. Common controls include restrictions on the amount of currency that can be imported or exported; fixed exchange rates; and banning certain currencies. These nations may require that an import license from a central bank or the government be obtained in order for customers in that country to pay for imported products. For a U.S. exporter who wishes to get paid, it is extremely important to determine (1) whether an exchange control system exists and an import license is necessary in the foreign country, (2) what time periods are necessary to obtain such licenses, and (3) the conditions that must be fulfilled and documentation that must be provided in order for the importer to obtain such licenses. (See www.imf.org.)

5. Value-Added Taxes

Many countries impose a value-added tax on the stages of production and distribution. Such taxes usually apply to imported goods, so that the importer, in addition to paying customs duties, must pay a value-added tax based, usually, on the customs value plus duties. When the importer marks up and resells the goods, it will collect the tax from the purchaser, which it must remit to the tax authorities after taking a credit for the taxes due on importation. The amount of value-added tax can be significant, as it is usually higher than traditional sales taxes, and, therefore, whether the product can be priced competitively in the foreign market is a matter of analysis.

6. Specialized Laws

Foreign countries often enact specialized laws prohibiting the importation of certain products except in compliance with such laws. In the United States, there are many special laws regulating the domestic sale and importation of a wide variety of products. Some U.S. laws regulate all products manufactured in the United States; others do not apply to products being manufactured for export. In any case, like the United States, foreign countries often have special laws affecting certain products or classes of products, and the existence of such regulation should be ascertained prior to manufacture, prior to entering into an agreement to sell, and even prior to quoting prices or delivery dates to a customer.

F.   Export Controls and Licenses

This subject is treated in detail in Chapter 5. However, it is a very important preliminary consideration because if an export license from the U.S. Department of Commerce, Bureau of Industry and Security, the Office of Foreign Assets Control, or the Department of Defense Trade Controls is required, and such license is not obtained by the exporter, U.S. Customs and Border Protection will detain the shipment, and the sale cannot be completed. Even if the exporter sells ex-factory and the buyer is technically responsible for U.S. inland transportation, export, and ocean shipment, the buyer may file a lawsuit if the exporter does not inform the customer that an export license is necessary and the shipment is detained. The method for determining whether an export license is required for a particular product is discussed in Chapter 5.

G. Patent, Trademark, and Copyright Registrations and Infringements

These rights are sometimes called intellectual or industrial property rights. This topic includes two common problems. First, a U.S. company that invents and manufactures a product may secure a patent, trademark, or copyright in the United States, but might not apply for any registration of its rights in a foreign country. In many countries, if the U.S. rights are not filed there within a specific period, such as one year after filing in the United States, they are forever lost and are part of the public domain in the foreign country. This means that without registering its rights in that country, an exporter cannot prevent copying, pirating, and the marketing of imitation products.

Second, without conducting a patent, trademark, or copyright search, a U.S. company cannot know whether the product that it is exporting will infringe a patent, trademark, or copyright that has been filed in a foreign country. Unfortunately, in many foreign countries, the first person to file a patent, trademark, or copyright will be the legal owner, even if the product was previously invented and used by someone in another country. Consequently, it is not uncommon for foreign competitors, distributors, or customers to register a U.S. company's patents, trademarks, or copyrights, so that if the U.S. company exports to the foreign country, this would result in an infringement of the intellectual property rights that the foreign entity now owns in that country. Thus, in order for the U.S. company to export its products to that country, it may have to negotiate to obtain a license and pay a royalty to the foreign company or to purchase back the intellectual property rights that have been registered there. In sales documentation commonly used in the United States, the U.S. manufacturer will give a warranty, or it will automatically be implied under the Uniform Commercial Code, that the product does not infringe any person's intellectual property rights. A U.S. exporter may be using the same type of documentation for export sales. If the U.S. exporter has not searched the foreign intellectual property registrations, and the product does infringe a foreign registration, the U.S. exporter will be in breach of warranty and may be unable to perform its sales agreement with its customer.

H. Confidentiality and Non-Disclosure Agreements

As a preliminary consideration, before exporting products to foreign countries or providing samples to potential customers, it is important to ask the foreign company to sign a confidentiality and non-disclosure agreement. In many countries, especially if the U.S. company has no patent registration there, the ability of the U.S. company to prohibit copying and piracy by reverse engineering is virtually nil. Some measure of protection can be obtained by requiring the foreign company to sign a confidentiality and non-disclosure agreement that commits it to not reverse engineer the product or engage in its manufacture itself or through third parties. Such agreements are not unusual, and any potential customer who refuses to sign one should be suspect.

I. Antiboycott Compliance

If you plan to make sales in the Middle East or you receive an order from a customer located there, before proceeding to accept and ship the order, you should be aware of the U.S. antiboycott regulations. Certain countries in the Middle East maintain international boycotts, usually of Israel, although there are times when other boycotts are in place. The Treasury Department updates the list of countries that participate in international boycotts on a quarterly basis. U.S. law prohibits any U.S. company from refusing or agreeing to refuse to do business pursuant to an agreement or request from a boycotting country or to discriminate on the basis of race, religion, sex, or national origin. The antiboycott restrictions are discussed in more detail in Chapter 5.

J. Employee Sales Visits to Foreign Countries—Immigration and Customs Compliance

In the course of developing export sales, it is likely that sales employees of the U.S. company will visit foreign countries to identify customers and evaluate markets. Another common export sales activity is exhibiting products in trade fairs sponsored by U.S. or foreign government agencies or trade associations. It is important that the U.S. company satisfy itself that its sales employees traveling to foreign countries comply with the immigration and customs laws of those countries. In particular, many countries require that individuals entering their country to engage in business activities obtain a different type of visa (which is stamped in the U.S. passport) to enter the country. Entering the country on a visitor's visa or engaging in activities inconsistent with the visa that has been issued can subject an employee to serious penalties and delay. With regard to the U.S. company's employees bringing samples of its products into a foreign country for display or sale, it is necessary that the regular customs duties be paid on the samples or that salespeople arrange for compliance with the local temporary importation procedures. Most countries have a temporary importation procedure whereby a bond must be posted to guarantee that the product that is being imported will be exported at a later time. For employees visiting a number of countries on sales visits, posting temporary importation bonds in a number of countries can be burdensome and must be arranged significantly in advance.

1. Carnets

One solution to this problem is the ATA Carnet developed by the Customs Cooperation Council and administered by the International Chamber of Commerce. In effect, the carnet is both a customs entry and a temporary importation bond that is honored by 83 countries and territories and that permits temporary entry of samples for order solicitation, display, and exhibition for generally up to six months for the Exhibitions and Fairs carnet and up to one year for other temporary eligible uses abroad. Products entered by carnet must be exported and not sold without the payment of the bond premium. The carnet is obtained by applying through one of the carnet services with such expertise and posting cash or a bond generally for 40 percent of the value with them. The carnet is shown in Figure 2–1. Additional information about carnets can be obtained from the U.S. Council for International Business in New York City, (www.uscib.org) or Boomerang Carnets (www.atacarnet.com). Applications for carnets can be filed online. In order to avoid having to pay duties at the time of import, the carnet should be signed off by the Customs authorities both at the time of export and the time of import.

K. Utilization of Freight Forwarders and Foreign Customs Brokers

A competent freight forwarder can handle routing, inland and international transportation, containerization, scheduling of carriers, transshipments, bills of lading, consular certifications, legalizations, inspections, export licenses, marine and air insurance, warehousing, and export packing, either itself or through its agents. Unless the U.S. company is large enough to have a number of personnel who can perform the

Figure 2–1. ATA Carnet.

Issuing Association
Association émettrice

USCIB

INTERNATIONAL GUARANTEE CHAIN
CHAÎNE DE GARANTIE INTERNATIONALE

ICC W.C.F.

A.T.A. CARNET FOR TEMPORARY ADMISSION OF GOODS
CARNET A.T.A. POUR L'ADMISSION TEMPORAIRE DE MARCHANDISES
CUSTOMS CONVENTION ON THE A.T.A. CARNET FOR THE TEMPORARY ADMISSION OF GOODS
CONVENTION DOUANIERE SUR LE CARNET A.T.A. POUR L'ADMISSION TEMPORAIRE DE MARCHANDISES
CONVENTION ON TEMPORARY ADMISSION / *CONVENTION RELATIVE À L'ADMISSION TEMPORAIRE*
(Before completing the Carnet, please read Notes on cover page 3 / *Avant de remplir le carnet, lire la notice en page 3 de la couverture*)

ATA CARNET / CARNET ATA

A. HOLDER AND ADDRESS / *Titulaire et adresse*
Sandler, Travis & Rosenberg
225 West Washington Street
Suite #1550
Chicago, IL, IL 60606

G. FOR ISSUING ASSOCIATION USE / *Réservé à l'association émettrice*
FRONT COVER / *Couverture*

a) A.T.A. CARNET No. / *Carnet A.T.A. N°* US 89/09-SAMPLE

Number of continuation sheets: / *Nombre de feuilles supplémentaires:* 0

B. REPRESENTED BY* / *Représenté par**
D.Bade, Corp. for Int'l Business 800-282-2900, Freight Forwarder's And/Or Any Authorized Representatives

b) ISSUED BY / *Délivré par*
United States Council for International Business

C. INTENDED USE OF GOODS / *Utilisation prévue des marchandises*
Commercial Samples,Exhibitions and Fairs,Professional Equipment

c) VALID UNTIL / *Valable jusqu'au*

2010	3	1
year / *année*	month / *mois*	day (inclusive) / *jour (inclus)*

P. This Carnet may be used in the following countries/customs territories under the guarantee of the associations listed on page 4 of the cover:
Ce carnet est valable dans les pays/territoire douaniers ci-après, sous la garantie des associations reprises en page quatre de la couverture:

EUROPEAN UNION

AUSTRIA (AT)	FINLAND (FI)	LATVIA (LV)	ROMANIA (RO)
BELGIUM (BE)	FRANCE (FR)	LITHUANIA (LT)	SLOVAKIA (SK)
BULGARIA (BG)	GERMANY (DE)	LUXEMBOURG (LU)	SLOVENIA (SI)
CYPRUS (CY)	GREECE (GR)	MALTA (MT)	SPAIN (ES)
CZECH REPUBLIC (CZ)	HUNGARY (HU)	NETHERLANDS (NL)	SWEDEN (SE)
DENMARK (DK)	IRELAND (IE)	POLAND (PL)	UNITED KINGDOM (GB)
ESTONIA (EE)	ITALY (IT)	PORTUGAL (PT)	

OTHER COUNTRIES

ALGERIA (DZ)	ICELAND (IS)	MONGOLIA (MN)	SINGAPORE (SG)
ANDORRA (AD)	INDIA (IN)	MONTENEGRO (ME)	SOUTH AFRICA (ZA)
AUSTRALIA (AU)	ISRAEL (IL)	MOROCCO (MA)	SRI LANKA (LK)
BELARUS (BY)	IVORY COAST (CI)	NEW ZEALAND (NZ)	SWITZERLAND (CH)
CANADA (CA)	JAPAN (JP)	NORWAY (NO)	THAILAND (TH)
CHILE (CL)	KOREA (KR)	PAKISTAN (PK)	TUNISIA (TN)
CHINA (CN)	LEBANON (LB)	RUSSIA (RU)	TURKEY (TR)
CROATIA (HR)	MACEDONIA (MK)	SENEGAL (SN)	UKRAINE (UA)
GIBRALTAR (GI)	MALAYSIA (MY)	SERBIA (RS)	UNITED STATES (US)
HONG KONG, CHINA (HK)	MAURITIUS (MU)		

The Holder of this Carnet and his representative will be held responsible for compliance with the laws and regulations of the country/customs territory of departure and the countries/customs territories of importation. / *A charge pour le titulaire et son représentant de se conformer aux lois et règlements du pays/territoire douanier de départ et des pays/territoire douaniers d'importation.*

H. CERTIFICATE BY CUSTOMS AT DEPARTURE
Attestation de la douane, au départ

a) Identification marks have been affixed as indicated in column 7 against the following items No(s). of the General List
Apposé les marques d'identification mentionnées dans la colonne 7 en regard du (des) numéro(s) d'ordre suivant(s) de la liste générale

b) GOODS EXAMINED* / *Vérifié les marchandises**
Yes / *Oui* ☐ No / *Non* ☐

c) Registered under Reference No.*
*Enregistré sous le numéro**

d) ______ ______ / / ______
Customs Office / *Bureau de douane* Place / *Lieu* Date (year/month/day) / *Date (année/mois/jour)* Signature and Stamp / *Signature it timbre*

I. Signature of authorized official and Issuing Association stamp / *Signature du délégué et timbre de l'association émettrice*
Curt Wilson
Barrington 2009 / 3 / 2
Place and Date of Issue (year/month/day)
Lieu et date d'émission (année/mois/jour)

J.

X ______ X
Signature of Holder / *Signature du titulaire*

*If applicable / **S'il y a lieu*

N1 (11/3/08)

THIS CARNET IS THE PROPERTY OF USCIB. AFTER FINAL USE, RETURN IT TO USCIB.
1212 AVENUE OF THE AMERICAS, NEW YORK, NY 10036
(A RETOURNER A LA CHAMBRE EMETTRICE IMMEDIATEMENT APRES UTILISATION)

US89/09-SAMPLE

Figure 2–1. (*continued*)

CONTINUATION SHEET GENERAL LIST No. ....0. FEUILLE SUPPLEMENTAIRE LISTE GENERALE N°				CARNET No. Carnet N°.	US 89/09-SAMPLE	

Item No. N° d'ordre	Trade description of goods and marks and numbers, if any / Désignation commerciale des marchandises et, le cas échéant, marques et numéros	Number of Pieces Nombre de Pièces	Weight or Volume Poids ou Volume	Value* Valeur*	**Country of Origin *Pays d'origine	For Customs Use Réservé à la douane Identification marks / Marques d'identification
1	2	3	4	5	6	7
1	Trade Show Booth	1		$10,000.00	US	
2	Professional Equipment, s/n:1234	1		$25,000.00	US	
3	Commercial Samples	5		$500.00	US	
	Totals	7		$35,500.00		

NO CHANGES OR ADDITIONS ABOVE OR BELOW THIS LINE

TOTAL or CARRIED OVER / TOTAL ou À REPORTER	7		$35,500.00	

(09/04)

Commercial value in country/customs territory of issue and in its currency, unless stated differently.   / Valeur commerciale dans le pays/territoire douanier d'émission et dans sa monnaie, saul indication contraire.

** Show country of origin if different from country/customs territory of issue of the Carnet, using ISO country codes.   /** Indiquer le pays d'origine s'il est différent du pays/territoire douanier d'émission du carnet, en utilisant le code international des pays ISO.

Figure 2–1. (*continued*)

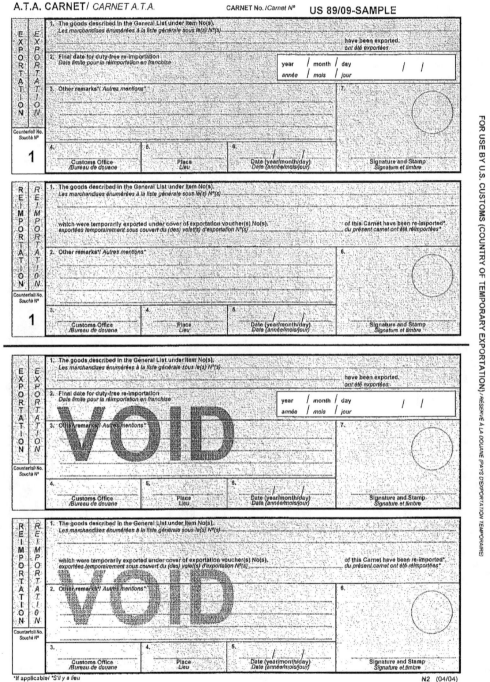

Figure 2–1. (*continued*)

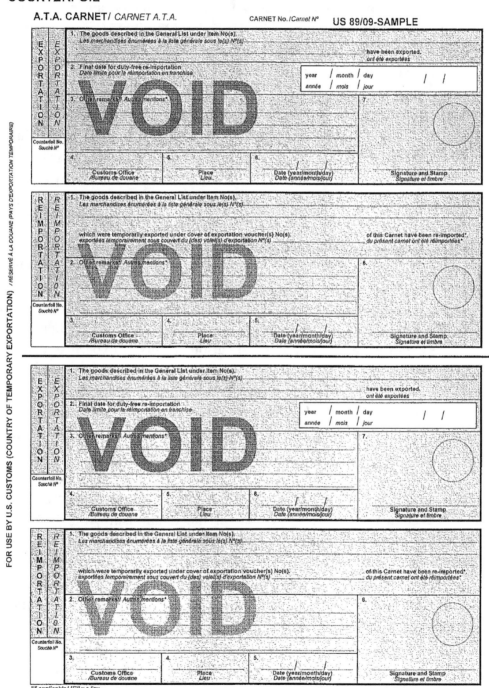

COUNTERFOIL

DO NOT REMOVE FROM THE CARNET / *NE PAS DÉTACHER DU CARNET*

services in-house that are offered by freight forwarders, it is likely that the U.S. company will have to select and interface with a freight forwarder on export sales (and possibly a foreign customs broker on landed, duty-paid sales) in exporting its products to foreign countries. Most freight forwarders handle both air and ocean exports; however, for ocean exports they must be licensed by the Federal Maritime Commission. Freight forwarders and Non-Vessel Operating Common Carrier's (NVOCCs) are collectively called Ocean Transportation Intermediaries (OTIs) in the United States The licensing process which requires the freight forwarder to have a "qualifying individual" on staff overseeing the export activities as well as a surety bond as proof of financial stability. A qualifying individual must have a minimum of three years freight forwarding experience in the United States. The FMC investigates and conducts a business background check before issuing the license. Although not required to be licensed by any particular government agency, air freight forwarders have extensive requirements under the Transportation Security Administration to ensure the safety of air cargo which involve security checks and fines if the proper and sensitive procedures are not followed.

Ocean transportation carriers are allowed to pay compensation (commissions) only to licensed freight forwarders for booking shipments. Freight forwarders have inherent conflicts of interest because they receive compensation from carriers and also receive freight-forwarding fees from shippers. Selection of the right freight forwarder is no small task, as freight forwarders have various levels of expertise, particularly in regard to different types of products and different country destinations. Some of the things that should be considered include reputation, size, financial strength, insurance coverage, fees, and automation. References should be checked. A list of licensed ocean freight forwarders can be obtained from the FMC at http://www2.fmc.gov/oti/ or ocean and air freight forwarders may be obtained from the National Customs Brokers and Freight Forwarders Association of America in Washington, D.C., www.ncbfaa.org. Before selecting a freight forwarder, a face-to-face meeting with alternative candidates is recommended. At the outset of the relationship, the U.S. exporter will be asked to sign an agreement appointing the freight forwarder as its agent and giving it a power of attorney. It is important that the U.S. exporter ask its attorney to review such an agreement and make appropriate changes. (A simple sample power of attorney is shown in Figure 4–1.) Some exporters prefer to quote terms of sale where the exporter is responsible for the transportation and to control delivery by selection of and payment to their own freight forwarder. In other cases, the buyer selects the freight forwarder, known as a "routed export' 'transaction. The U.S. exporter should be aware that a freight forwarder and any foreign customs broker selected by it or by the freight forwarder are the exporter's agents, and any mistakes that they make will be the exporter's responsibility as far as third parties and government agencies are concerned. This is not always understood by companies that pay significant amounts of money to hire such persons. Where a freight forwarder is responsible for some loss or damage and refuses to make a reasonable settlement, the exporter may be able to proceed against the surety bond or even raise an action through the FMC administrative review process for certain ocean freight forwarding issues. They may even seek cancellation of the forwarder's Federal Maritime Commission license. Where the forwarder is bankrupt and has failed to pay transportation carriers amounts paid by the exporter, the exporter may be required to pay twice. See more on Freight Forwarders and NVOCCs in Chapter 4.

L. Export Packing and Labeling (Hazardous Materials)

It may be necessary for the U.S. company to have special packing for its products for long-distance ocean shipments. The packing used for domestic shipments may be totally inadequate for such shipping. Identification marks on the packages should be put in the packing list. Containers may be of various lengths and heights. Special types of containers may be needed, such as insulated, ventilated, open top, refrigerated ("reefers"), flat, and/or high-cube. Containerized shipments may be eligible for low insurance rates compared with breakbulk or palletized cargo. Specialized export packing companies exist and can often do the packing or can act as consultants in assisting the U.S. company with formulating packing that would be suitable for such shipments. Under the U.S. Uniform Commercial Code and the Convention on the International Sale of Goods (discussed in Chapter 3, Section B), unless expressly excluded, a seller makes a warranty that its products have been properly packaged. Under the Carriage of Goods by Sea Act, a steamship line is not responsible for damage to cargo due to insufficient packing. Improper packing can lead to disputes and claims for breach of warranty.

Under the Intermodal Safe Container Transportation Act as amended, a shipper arranging for intermodal transportation of a container or trailer carrying more than 29,000 pounds and traveling in any part by truck over the road must provide the initial carrier with a certificate of gross weight including a description of contents, which certificate must be transferred to each subsequent carrier.

All hazardous materials must be packed in accordance with the United Nations' Performance Oriented Packaging (POP) Standards. Shippers of hazardous materials must be registered with the Department of Transportation. "Hazmat employees," including those who handle, package, or transport hazardous materials and those who fill out shipping papers, must have training at least every three years (see discussion in Chapter 4, Section O). The International Civil Aviation Authority (ICAO) is an international organization made up of member states and it has technical guidelines for the handling and labeling of hazardous materials for aircraft. (www.icao.int.) Similarly, the International Maritime Dangerous Goods Code was developed by the International Maritime Organization for handling hazardous materials in ocean transportation. (http://www.imo.org/Pages/home.aspx.)

Based on Transportation Security Administration requirements, passenger air carriers and air freight forwarders are required to maintain strict controls on the receipt of merchandise and obtain a "Shippers Security Endorsement" from the shipper certifying that the shipment does not contain any unauthorized explosive or destructive devices or hazardous materials and including a consent to search the shipment. Personal identification is required from the person tendering the shipment. Any shipments from unknown shippers must undergo more thorough examination. The TSA has developed several sensitive security programs from Known Shipper Programs to the Indirect Air Carrier Management System for air freight forwarders.

Labeling is equally important. If the product is a hazardous substance, special labeling and placarding is required. Furthermore, any product labeling may require printing in the foreign country's language. The types of information and disclosures required on such labeling may be prescribed by foreign law in the country of destination and should be confirmed as part of the pre-export planning.

M. Terms of Sale

When shipping internationally it is critical to understand the terms and conditions of the international transportation. Without a true understanding of the terms it is hard to know which party bears the risk of loss if the freight is damaged during the inland transportation, which party is responsible for the customs clearance at the port of entry, or who should purchase the insurance on the cargo during the international transportation. It is for this reason that the International Chamber of Commerce first developed the INCOTERMS® (International Commerce Terminology) in 1936. The most recent version is the INCOTERMS® 2010 and became effective January 1, 2011. Even though the Incoterms have no legal basis, they are recognized by judicial bodies throughout the world as an indication of agreement by the parties. See Figure 2–2.

The Incoterms® define where risk of loss is transferred and the responsibilities of the parties in the transaction. They do NOT define where title transfers, so it is always

Figure 2–2. Examples of Incoterms® 2010 version (not all inclusive).

Incoterms® for all modes of transportation (including intermodal)

Term	Seller	Buyer	Delivery (Risk of Loss)
ExW (named factory location)	Packing & making freight available for pick-up	Loading on truck at door, foreign inland transportation, export clearance, international transportation, customs clearance domestic delivery	At seller's door
FCA (named port of export)	Packing, loading on truck, export clearance	International transportation, customs clearance, domestic delivery	At port of export loaded on board
CFR (named port of import)	Packing, inland transportation, export clearance, international transportation	Customs clearance, domestic delivery	Port of *export* loaded on board (note even though seller is paying for international transportation)
DAT (named port of import)	Packing, inland transportation, export clearance, international transportation	Customs clearance, domestic delivery	Port of import
DDP (named delivery point)	Packing, inland transportation, export clearance, international transportation, customs clearance, delivery to door	Unloading at door	Customer's door

Incoterms® for maritime shipments (only)

Term	Seller	Buyer	Delivery (Risk of Loss)
FOB (named port of export)	Packing, inland transportation to port of export, export clearance	International transportation, customs clearance, domestic delivery	At port of export when loaded on board
CIF (named port of export)	Packing, inland transportation port of export, export clearance, international transportation, international insurance in the name of the buyer	Customs clearance, domestic delivery	At port of *export* (even though shipper pays for international freight, he must purchase insurance in the name of the buyer)

important for other related documents to indicate the point at which title transfers. While many assume the title will transfer where the risk of loss transfers, that may not always be the case, for example, there may be tax implications if the buyer takes title in the seller's country.

Incoterms® should have three components to be clear: the three-letter term, a location name, and the Incoterms® version. For example: FCA LAX Incoterms® 2010 – this means that the seller is transferring the risk of loss at the Los Angeles Airport using the Incoterms® 2010 definition of FCA. It should also be noted that there are some Incoterms® that are designed for use with ocean freight only and the others can be used for all modes of transportation, including ocean freight.

In the United States, confusion regarding the Incoterms® FOB and CIF relates to the Uniform Commercial Code, which regulates domestic sales transactions. At one time, the Uniform Commercial Code had its own definitions of FOB and CIF for use in domestic sales. Those terms were dropped many years ago, but they still appear in some domestic transactions and when companies first begin to export, they do not realize that the terms have different meanings internationally.

A diagram of the Incoterms® is shown in Figure 2–3. In the author's experience, even if the parties choose to use an abbreviation to specify the way in which title will pass and delivery will be made, the author strongly recommends that the "who does what" be stated in detail in the sales agreement to avoid the possibility of a misunderstanding.

Incoterms® do not define when payment is made. Payment may be made earlier or later depending upon the agreement of the parties. Sellers should be sure that their export sales documentation distinguishes between price terms, title and risk of loss terms, and payment terms.

Figure 2–3. Diagram of the Incoterms®.

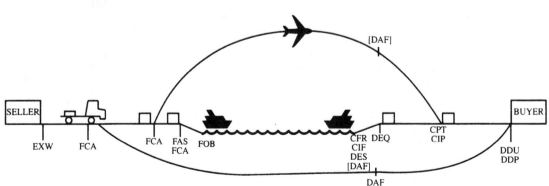

Under the Convention on the International Sale of Goods (discussed in Chapter 3, Section B.2.m), if the parties do not agree upon a place for the transfer of title and delivery in their sales agreement, title and delivery will transfer when the merchandise is delivered to the first transportation carrier.

Another consideration is tax planning. Under U.S. law, if title on the sale of inventory passes outside the U.S., foreign source income is created. In some situations, depending on the seller's tax situation, the seller can reduce its U.S. income taxes this way. It is usually advisable to ensure that title passes prior to customs clearance in the foreign country, however, to make sure the seller is not responsible for customs duties, which could include antidumping or other special duties.

In most international transactions, the buyer will be responsible for importing the products to its own country, clearing customs, and paying any applicable customs duties. This is because the importer is liable for all customs duties, even antidumping duties. However, if the seller agrees to sell landed, duty paid, or delivered to the buyer's place of business (so-called "free domicile" or "free house" delivery), the seller will be responsible for such customs duties. Ordinarily, the seller cannot act as the importer of record in a foreign country unless it obtains a bond from a foreign bonding company and appoints an agent in that country for all claims for customs duties. Generally, a seller would not want to sell delivered, duty paid, but sometimes the buyer's bargaining leverage is such or competition is such that the seller cannot get the business unless it is willing to do so. If the buyer is wary of paying duties, it may refuse to act as the importer of record. Similarly, when the seller is selling to a related buyer, such as a majority or wholly owned subsidiary, the parent company may want to sell landed, duty paid, and assume such expenses.

In general, if the seller sells ex-factory (ex-works), it will have the least responsibility and risk. The buyer will then be responsible for arranging and paying for inland transportation to the port of export, ocean transportation, and foreign importation. In many cases, an ex-factory sale can result in the buyer's being able to avoid customs duties on the inland freight from the seller's factory to the port of export. In such instances, even though the buyer will have the responsibility for complying with all U.S. export laws, such as export control licenses, filing Electronic Export Information (formerly Shipper's Export Declarations) through the Automated Export System record, arranging insurance, and complying with foreign laws, it is a shortsighted seller who does not thoroughly discuss all of these items with the buyer during the formation of the sales agreement and obtain written confirmation that the buyer will file the Electronic Export Information. If the buyer is unable to complete export or effect import, the fact that the seller is not legally responsible will be of little consolation and will lead to lawsuits, nonpayment, and loss of future business.

Even though selling ex-factory may be attractive to a seller, there are many reasons why the seller may want or need to sell on other terms. For example, the buyer may be inexperienced in arranging international shipments; the seller's competitors may be offering delivered terms; the seller may be selling to an affiliated company; the seller may need to control diversion back into the United States or other countries; the seller may be trying to assure delivery of goods subject to U.S. export controls; the seller may want to control the shipment until it is loaded on board the ship for letter of credit sales; the seller may want to control title and ownership until payment; or the seller may have warehouse-to-warehouse marine insurance under an open-cargo policy, and therefore, by agreeing to pay the insurance costs, can save the buyer some money; and sometimes the seller is in a better position to obtain lower ocean transportation or insurance rates. As already indicated, sometimes sales effected outside of the United States can lower the U.S. seller's income tax liability. For all of these reasons, a thorough discussion of the terms and conditions of sale between the seller and buyer, rather than simply following a set policy, may be advantageous.

N. Consignments

Unlike in sales transactions, where title to the merchandise transfers to the foreign buyer in the United States or sometime up to delivery in the foreign country in accordance with the terms of sale between the parties, in consignment transactions, the exporter/seller maintains ownership of the goods, and the consignee in the foreign country takes possession of the goods. The consignee then offers the goods for sale, and when a customer purchases the goods, title transfers from the exporter/seller to the importer/buyer and to the customer simultaneously. Such transactions have various procedural and documentary considerations. As the owner, the exporter/seller will be responsible for all transportation costs, insurance, filing of Electronic Export Information (Shipper's Export Declarations) through the Automated Export System, and obtaining export control licenses. While foreign customs regulations may permit the consignee to effect customs clearance, legally the goods are owned by the exporter/ seller, and the exporter/seller will be liable for the foreign customs duties. Additional taxes may be assessed, such as personal property taxes assessed on the goods while they are awaiting sale and income taxes, because title will pass to the importer/buyer at the buyer's place of business in the foreign country. In addition, to avoid the inability to take possession of the goods in case of bankruptcy of the importer/buyer or other claims by the importer's creditors, special arrangements under the buyer's law, such as chattel mortgages, conditional sale agreements, public notices, or security interests, may be required. Because the export/import transaction is not a sale at the time of entry, transaction value cannot be used—the customs authorities will assess customs duties based upon an alternative valuation method. (See also Chapter 10.)

O. Leases

In export transactions that are leases, no sales documentation should be used, although the creation of documentation for Customs purposes may be required in order to effect clearance. The ability of the exporter/lessor to retain title and ownership, repossess the goods at the end of the lease, and obtain income tax benefits depends upon using lease documentation rather than sales agreements. As with consignments, the exporter/seller is legally responsible for all exporting and importing obligations, although those obligations can be delegated to the importer in the lease agreement. For customs valuation purposes, a lease is not a sale; therefore, transaction value will not be used, and the customs duties payable will depend upon an alternative valuation method. Whether the transaction will be subject to value-added taxes or other exactions depends upon the law of the destination country.

P. Marine and Air Casualty Insurance

Marine (or ocean) and air insurance is important on export shipments. Under the Carriage of Goods by Sea Act, ocean carriers are responsible for the seaworthiness of the vessel, properly manning the vessel, and making the vessel safe for carriage of the cargo. The ocean carrier is not responsible for negligence of the master in navigating the vessel, fires, perils, dangers, accidents of the sea, acts of God, acts of war, acts of public enemies, detention or seizures, acts or omissions of shippers, strikes or lockouts, riots and civil commotions, saving or attempting to save a life or property at sea, inherent defect, quality or vice of the goods, insufficiency of packing, quarantine restrictions, insufficiency or inadequacy of marks, latent defects not discoverable by due diligence, and any other causes arising without the actual fault and privity of the ocean carrier.

Without insurance, even when the carrier can be proven liable, responsibility is limited to $500 per "package" on ocean shipments and $28 per kilogram on air shipments unless a higher value is declared in advance and a higher transportation charge is paid. The seller may be responsible for (1) obtaining and paying for such insurance with no reimbursement by the buyer, or (2) obtaining and paying for such insurance with reimbursement by the buyer. Or, the buyer may be responsible for (1) obtaining and paying for such insurance with no reimbursement by the seller, or (2) obtaining and paying for such insurance with reimbursement by the seller. Although abbreviated trade terms, such as FOB port of shipment, are designed to clarify which parties are responsible for arranging and paying for various aspects of an export shipment, often confusion and misunderstandings occur. It is extremely important to clearly determine who will pay for such insurance and who will arrange for it. It is necessary for a seller or buyer to have an "insurable interest" in the merchandise in order to obtain insurance coverage. Depending on the terms of sale, the seller may have an ownership interest up to a particular point or a financial interest in the safe arrival of the shipment up until the time it is paid.

A U.S. company can buy an open or blanket cargo marine or air insurance policy that is in continuous effect for its shipments, or a special onetime cargo policy that insures a single shipment. Alternatively, it can utilize its freight forwarder's blanket policy. There are many advantages for a company to have its own open cargo policy, but the quantity of exports must justify it; otherwise, it is probably more appropriate to utilize the freight forwarder's blanket policy. Some insurance brokers recommend that a company have its own policy when exports and/or imports reach $500,000 to $1 million. When a blanket policy is used, a separate certificate is issued by the insurance company or the holder of the policy to evidence coverage for each shipment. (A sample marine insurance policy and certificate are shown in Chapter 4, Figures 4–10 and 4–11, respectively.) Familiarizing oneself with such insurance policies is also important in the event that a casualty occurs and a claim needs to be filed. Generally, it is best to obtain "all risks" (rather than "named peril") and "warehouse-to-warehouse" (or "marine extension") coverage. Even "all risks" coverage does not include war risk or "strike, riot and civil commotion" coverage, and the seller should specifically determine whether these risks and others, such as delay in arrival and change in customs duties, should be covered by a rider and payment of an additional premium. Under the Incoterms®, it is necessary to insure the shipment at 110 percent of the invoice value; in the case of some letter of credit sales, payment cannot be obtained unless insurance in that amount has been obtained. The filing of claims is discussed in Chapter 4, Section H.

In order to get paid under letters of credit or documentary collections through banking channels, it may be necessary for the seller to furnish a certificate to the bank evidencing that insurance coverage exists.

Marine insurance companies and insurance brokers can advise on the different types of coverage available and comparative premiums. The premium will depend on the type of merchandise, its value (risk of pilferage), its packing, the type of coverage (including riders), the method of transportation, the country of destination and routing, the loss history of the insured, the carriers used, whether transshipment will occur, etc.

Q. Methods of Transportation; Booking Transportation

In determining the general method by which the U.S. company will export, or in filling a specific shipment to a particular customer, marine transportation and air transportation must be evaluated. Obviously, air transportation is much quicker but is more expensive. Large shipments cannot be shipped by air. The exporter may choose to charter a vessel to obtain lower rates for bulk commodities. Inland transportation by truck, rail, or air must be selected. The booking of steamship lines, shipping schedules, any delays necessary to load a full container, and any intermediate stops for the ship must all be considered by the U.S. company or its freight forwarder before selecting the appropriate transportation method and carrier. Companies with small quantities or those unfamiliar with shipping internationally should work with a freight forwarder or a non-vessel-operating common carrier (NVOCC). These companies can arrange and book shipments with carriers, or they can arrange to consolidate small shipments together in order to make up a full container, thus further reducing the cost of transportation rates. One aspect to consider when consolidating cargo is that any delay by Customs or some other government agency would cause delays to other cargo in the same container. NVOCCs are companies that contract with the vessel-operating common carriers (VOCCs) to guarantee the purchase of a significant quantity of containers over a period of time. In exchange for the volume, the VOCC sells to the NVOCCs at reduced costs. In turn, the NVOCCs sell that container space to shippers at a profit. NVOCCs are considered the actual carriers to the shippers and they prepare their own "house" bills of lading, but they are considered shippers to the VOCCs, who prepare the "master" bill of lading. Both the ocean freight forwarders and the NVOCCs are required to be licensed by the Federal Maritime Commission and carry adequate insurance.

Both NVOCCs and VOCCs are required to maintain lists of service charges based upon commodity classifications called "tariffs" (not to be confused with the customs duties paid to governments on imported merchandise). These tariffs are subject to change and often contain numerous exceptions and surcharges. Tariffs must be filed with the Federal Maritime Commission electronically and be made publicly available. Links to the tariffs are available at the Federal Maritime Commission's web site: www.fmc.gov. All shipments are to be made in accordance with the tariffs on file unless the shipper has entered into a Confidential Service Agreement with the carrier.

Both VOCCs and NVOCCs may enter into Service Agreements with shippers. Under these agreements, the shipper and the carriers may come to terms on rates, minimum quantities, and service commitments. Certain minimum elements of all service agreements must be made publicly available, but not the rates or service commitments. The exporter should be careful in recording quotations, dates, tariff classification numbers, rates, and the person making the quotation in order to avoid disputes over the details of the Service Agreement.

Airfreight rates are based on actual weight or dimensional weight, whichever is more. The size of the shipment (height x width x length in inches) divided by 166 equals the dimensional weight. Ocean freight rates will also be based on weight or measure, whichever is greater. Measure is calculated by multiplying the height by width by length in inches and dividing by 1,728 to get cubic feet. Sometimes the carrier's rates will be expressed in tons (short ton = 2,000 pounds, long ton = 2,240 pounds, or metric ton = 1,000 kilograms = 2,200 pounds) or in units of 40 cubic feet of volume. Containers are standardized sizes – 20', 40', 45', sometimes they are 40' high cube (which means taller than the normal 40'). They can be refrigerated for foods, pharmaceutical or other products which might require that. Miscellaneous freight shipped together is classified as "Freight All Kinds," which pays a higher rate than specific commodities. It is a violation of the Shipping Act of 1984 for a shipper to seek to obtain a lower shipping rate by misclassifying merchandise or stating false weights or measurements. Likewise, it is a violation for a steamship line to charge more or less than its publicly filed tariff rate (except under a service contract) or to pay rebates to shippers. If a shipper (exporter or importer) has satisfactory credit arrangements with a steamship line, it can ship "freight collect."

Shippers should also check into using courier services that can handle air, ground, and marine transportation for inclusive rates. Couriers also will handle the customs clearance. Unique to the courier services is that a courier will clear merchandise through customs in the country of import on its own bond, which allows it to clear merchandise more quickly. Unfortunately, the customs officials may still hold the importer responsible for declarations made by those couriers using their own bonds; therefore, importers will still be responsible for the errors of the couriers.

Smaller shippers can join "shippers' associations" and obtain similar benefits reductions in transportation costs. Shippers' associations are nonprofit transportation cooperatives. The associations arrange for domestic or international transportation for their members and the transportation costs are based on the consolidated quantities of cargo from the association which will result to lower rates for the members For more information on shippers' associations, contact the American Institute for Shippers' Associations, a trade association, at www.shippers.org.

R. Country of Origin Marking

As in the United States, many foreign countries require that the product and the product packaging be marked with the country of manufacture or production before the product can enter the foreign country. Since the shipment cannot enter the country unless such marking has been done properly, it is important to check the foreign regulations prior to manufacture and shipment. The foreign country may also have specific requirements with respect to marking based on the product, such as pharmaceuticals, food products, textiles and apparel, etc. These requirements will generally be imposed not by the foreign customs service, but by the local consumer products agency. Other countries do not require country of origin marking, but just that any marking that exists on the product must be correct. More information on country of origin and marking may be found in Chapter 11.

S. Foreign Warehousing and Free Trade Zones

Many companies use a regional distribution center (for example, in Rotterdam or Hong Kong) for re-export to various countries in the region. Shipments to such regional distribution centers can be entered into that country temporarily for repackaging, relabeling, manipulation, modification, and sometimes further manufacturing without the payment of any customs duties if the product is going to be re-exported. Foreign countries often have certain bonded warehousing and free trade zone systems that permit such activities. If the U.S. exporter wishes to avail itself of those benefits, it must carefully check and comply with those procedures in order to obtain the duty-free treatment.

T. Export Financing and Payment Insurance

A number of government agencies, U.S. and foreign, provide financing for U.S. exporters. The U.S. Export-Import (EXIM) Bank has financing available for large exporters as well as a new program for smaller exporters. The Agency for International Development under its tied aid program, the Department of Agriculture, the International Development Cooperation Agency, the International Bank for Reconstruction and Development (World Bank), the Inter-American Development Bank, the Asian Development Bank, the African Development Bank, and the Small Business Administration all have programs designed to finance exports. Some foreign countries even finance the importation of products that they are seeking to obtain. Most recently, in the United States, the federal government has encouraged states to develop export financing programs. At last count, forty-eight states, including California and Illinois, have established successful programs, and a U.S. exporter should check with its state agencies or the National Association of Development Organizations (www.nado.org) to determine the availability and terms and conditions of financing prior to manufacture and export of its products. This is an important preliminary consideration because the buyer may have to provide documentation before the exporter can apply for such financing, and there may be longer lead times in completing the sale.

Related to this subject is insurance issued by the Foreign Credit Insurance Association and marketed by the U.S. Export-Import Bank, which has offices in major U.S. cities. This association of U.S. insurance companies offers policies that can protect an exporter against default in payment due to expropriation, foreign government political risks, and customer nonpayment due to commercial reasons. Several different types of policies are available covering 90 to 95 percent of the risk. Such insurance may be required in order to obtain certain export financing.

U. Tax Incentives

Most tax incentives for export have been eliminated in the U.S.; however, there is one type of business entity that can receive some deductions for exporting. It is known as an Interest Charge-Domestic International Sales Corporation (IN-DISC). It is important to check with a tax attorney to determine whether this type of legal entity will be of assistance for the exporter.

V. Export Trading Companies, Export Trade Certificates of Review, and Export Management Companies

In 1982, Congress enacted the Export Trading Company Act (ETC), which established encourages U.S. companies to collaborate with each other in order to reduce shipping costs, increase their negotiating power, fill large orders and increase their presence in the foreign market. The Department of Commerce in conjunctions with the Department of Justice provides an Export Trade Certificate of Review which can be useful to these collaborative efforts in avoiding costly treble damage liability and expensive attorney's fees and court costs if the exporter obtains such a certificate. Certified activities often include the appointment of exclusive distributors and agents, and the imposition of restrictions on distributors, such as territories, prices, the handling of competitive products, and the termination of such distributors, all of which might normally violate U.S. antitrust laws. Furthermore, if a U.S. company wishes to cooperate with other companies in exporting, even with competitors, such activities can be protected under the certificate. However, the U.S. exporter should also check foreign law in the country of destination, as such certificates do not exempt the U.S. exporter from foreign law.

An export management company, or EMC, is usually an export intermediary located in the United States that acts as a sales agent or representative for the manufacturer for exports to certain foreign markets. Typically, EMCs are paid a commission and may be helpful where the manufacturer is new to exporting or does not have its own distributor or sales agent in that foreign country. Theoretically, the difference between the EMC and the ETC is that ETC purchase from the manufacturer, paying in advance and making their compensation through a resale markup rather than a commission. In actuality, some EMCs and ETCs do both.

W. Translation

An exporter should give sufficient forethought to the necessity of translating its advertising materials, instructions, warranties, and labeling into the language of the destination country. Not only will this be necessary in order to achieve sales, but failure to do so can lead to legal liabilities. For example, if a patent application is not properly translated, the rights may be lost. Some countries require that certain labeling be in their language. The location of a competent translator and completion of the translation may require significant lead time and, depending on the quantity of material, involve a significant expense.

X. Foreign Branch Operations, Subsidiaries, Joint Ventures, and Licensing

Sometimes the exporter will be exporting to its or its parent company's existing branch or subsidiary company in a foreign country. Or, rather than selling to an independent distributor, utilizing a sales agent, or selling directly to the end user, the exporter may decide to establish such a branch operation or subsidiary company. If personnel are available to staff the foreign branch or company, this step may increase the exporter's marketing penetration and may smooth export and import operations.

Similarly, the exporter may form a joint venture with a foreign company to manufacture or market the exporter's products in one or more foreign countries. Where laws prohibit the importation of the exporter's products or where transportation costs or delays are unreasonable, the exporter may need to license a foreign company to manufacture the product and sell it in that market in return for payment of a royalty. All of these methods of doing business will require some modifications to the sales and other export and import documentation and procedures. For example, sales to affiliated companies often raise income tax issues involving transfer pricing and the related issue of proper customs valuation. License royalties may in certain circumstances be dutiable, and licensed technology may require export control approvals. A recent problem is the inadequacy of sales and purchase documentation for export audits due to simplified electronic ordering procedures between affiliated companies.

Y. Electronic Commerce

The development of the Internet and email and the proliferation of web sites have created a revolution in electronic commerce. Because of the essentially worldwide availability of the Internet and access to web sites, new issues for cross-border exporting and importing have arisen. This has opened a new channel of direct marketing using electronic catalogs and has created conflict with the seller's traditional foreign distribution channels, such as distributors and sales agents. Sellers are more interested in marketing internationally and are forced to cope with the logistical issues that arise from purchase orders from abroad. Increasingly there are sales platforms that enable the sale of products on behalf of other companies. Some may simply take orders and pass them through to the actual exporter, but others may manage the whole export process on behalf of the exporter. Some of the more important issues that must be considered and managed include the following:

• *Validity and enforceability of electronic sales contracts.* This concern has required the consideration and development of legal terms of sale on the web site that are modified and appropriate for foreign as well as domestic customers. It has also forced the use of "click-wrap" agreements to record the purchaser's agreement to the sales terms and authentication procedures to confirm that the person purporting to place the order is actually that person. For low-price items, sellers may be willing to accept the risk of lack of enforceability of the sales contract, but for expensive items or ongoing business, this is not feasible. Many sellers have required their distributors and customers who are making ongoing purchases to sign hard-copy "umbrella" agreements at the outset of the relationship before undertaking electronic sales. This is a less satisfactory solution for onetime purchasers.

• *Delivery and logistics.* At least with direct sales to consumers, and for consumer goods, customers want and expect the convenience of direct delivery to their door. These "delivered duty paid" terms of sale are almost a necessity for this type of business. Customers also want prompt delivery, which is difficult to achieve if there is no stock of inventory in the buyer's country. For smaller products, delivery by international courier services such as UPS, Federal Express, and DHL has become more practical. In such cases, the transportation carrier is also able to act as the customs broker in the foreign country, paying customs duties and value-added taxes and billing them back to the seller. For large capital goods, however—such as in business-to-business (B2B) transactions, where the issues of containerized or other packaging, transportation booking, export licenses or permits, foreign customs clearance, and lack of skilled in-house personnel, require the use of a freight forwarder—have limited the expansion of Internet sales. Challenges continue to exist relating to establishing in-country inventory for immediate delivery without the expenses of establishing branch offices or subsidiary companies.

• *Price.* Since many customers want to have delivery to their door, when they see a price quotation on a web site, they expect to see an "all-in" (delivered duty paid) price. The difficulty of maintaining up-to-date quotations online, including freight charges, insurance, duties, quotas, and value-added taxes for multiple countries of the world, has forced many sellers to hire software companies that offer such services.

• *Payment.* For low-price consumer goods, payment by credit card or through PayPal accounts has enabled sellers to increase Internet sales. However, there are fees associated with these types of purchases and the virtual impossibility of pursuing a collection lawsuit overseas because of prohibitive cost and low pricing has limited expansion. For expensive purchases or ongoing accounts, the seller may need the security of a letter of credit or documents against payment. On the other side, buyers dislike having to pay for purchases in advance without inspection of the goods. Where the seller has done business in the past on open account, or is willing to do so in the future, Internet sales can be practical.

• *Taxation.* Although one of the great spurs to the growth of electronic commerce in the past has been the ability to avoid certain taxes in certain countries, such as sales, value-added, corporate franchise, or personal property taxes, there is an increasing demand by governments to recover those tax revenues that are being lost. It is likely that some forms of taxation will increase and sellers may have to comply with foreign tax claims.

- *Information security.* Although there has been significant progress in maintaining the confidentiality of information transmitted over the Internet, the sophistication of "hackers" has also increased. For information from credit card numbers to purchase order numbers and customer lists, confidentiality, particularly from competitors and fraud artists, is crucial. The most secure current technologies using "key" systems are cumbersome, especially for small orders and onetime sales. Furthermore, exporting such software may require an export license.

- *Export controls.* There are concerns when selling through the internet as to where the customer is located and whether there may be embargoes to the destination. So companies marketing through the Internet must have specific export controls in place that require customer interaction to ensure compliance. More on export controls in Chapter 5.

Despite the foregoing difficulties, the outlook is good for more creative ways of dealing with these problems to evolve and that Internet sales will continue to expand.

Chapter 3
Exporting: Sales Documentation

The single most important document in the export sale is the sales agreement. Repeat: The single most important document in the export sale is the sales agreement! Most of the problems that occur in exporting can be eliminated or greatly reduced by using a suitable sales agreement. Generally, different types of sales agreements are used for isolated sales transactions and for ongoing sales transactions. This chapter will discuss these as well as look at the important provisions in international sales agreements, distribution agreements, and sales agent agreements.

A. Isolated Sales Transactions

For the purposes of discussion in this chapter, isolated sales transactions are defined as situations where, for example, the customer purchases infrequently, or where sales are made on a trial basis in the anticipation of establishing an ongoing sales relationship, or when a customer is not being granted any credit until a satisfactory history of payment has been established. Sales agreements for such transactions should be in writing, and the seller and buyer may use a variety of common, preprinted forms; however, with the increase of Internet communication and sales, these formalized agreements seem to be less prominent which can lead to misunderstandings regarding the commitments of the parties. The seller should check carefully to eliminate as much as possible any conflicting provisions between the seller's forms and the forms received from the buyer.

1. Importance of Written Agreements

In some industries, for example, the commodities industry, it is common to conduct purchases and sales orally through telephone orders and acceptances. Sometimes oral agreements occur in international sales when the seller receives an order at a trade show, by telephone, or in a meeting. (Under the Convention on Contracts for the International Sale of Goods discussed in Section B.2.m, a sales agreement may be formed or modified orally.) It is highly advisable to formalize the purchase and sale agreement in a written document, even if it is in an email. There are many reasons why export sales should be embodied in a written agreement. Under the Uniform Commercial Code applicable in the United States, if the sale exceeds $500 in value, an agreement to sell, and therefore to get paid for the sale, is enforceable by the seller only if the agreement is in writing. While there are some exceptions to this law, and sometimes even informal notes will be sufficient to create an enforceable sales agreement, by far the safest practice is to formalize the sales agreement in a written document signed by the parties.

In addition to legal issues, an old Chinese proverb states: "The lightest ink is better than the brightest memory." This is one way of saying that disputes in international sales transactions often arise because the parties did not record their agreement or failed to discuss an issue and reach agreement. Written sales agreement acts both as a checklist to remind the buyer and seller what they should discuss and agree upon and as a written record of their agreement. All modifications of the agreement should also be in writing.

2.   Email Orders

While an email order and acceptance can satisfy the legal requirements of written evidence of an agreement, such sales agreements commonly contain only the specification of the quantity, usually a price, and sometimes a shipment date. There are many other terms and conditions of sale that should be inserted in a good sales agreement, and a simple acceptance by the seller of such email orders will fall far short of adequately protecting the seller in case of problems in the transaction. Consequently, acceptances of orders by email should specifically and expressly state that the sale incorporates the seller's other standard terms and conditions of sale. Those additional terms and conditions of sale should be included in the seller's email response as an attachment to the buyer with a required acknowledgement, so that there can be no argument that the buyer was not aware of such terms and conditions of sale before proceeding with the transaction.

3.   The Formation of Sales Agreements

The sales agreement is a formal contract governed by law. In general, a sales agreement is formed by agreement between the seller and the buyer and is the passing of title to and ownership of goods for a price. An agreement is a mutual manifestation of assent to the same terms. Agreements are ordinarily reached by a process of offer and acceptance. This process of offer and acceptance can proceed by the seller and the buyer preparing a sales agreement contained in a single document that is signed by both parties; by the exchange of documents such as purchase orders and purchase order acceptances; or by conduct, such as when the buyer offers to purchase and the seller ships the goods.

Particularly in light of the high-speed nature of business these days, from the point of view of clarity and reducing risks, preparation of a sales agreement contained in a single document is best. Both parties negotiate the agreement by exchanges of emails, or in person. Before proceeding with performance of any part of the transaction, both parties reach agreement and sign the same sales agreement. This gives both the seller and the buyer the best opportunity to understand the terms and conditions under which the other intends to transact business, and to negotiate and resolve any differences or conflicts. This type of sales agreement is often used if the size of the transaction is large; if the seller is concerned about payment or the buyer is concerned about manufacture and shipment; or if there are particular risks involved, such as government regulations or exchange controls, or differences in culture, language, or business customs that might create misunderstandings.

Quite often, however, the process of formation of the sales agreement is an exchange of documents that the seller and buyer have independently prepared and that, in the aggregate, constitute the sales agreement. These documents may contain differences and conflicts. Figure 3–1 shows the chronology of exchange and common documents used in many sales transactions. Although not all documents will be used in all sales transactions, these documents are in common use.

Several questions arise when a sales transaction is formed by such an exchange of documents. The first relates to the time of formation of the sales agreement. For example, a seller or buyer may send certain preliminary inquiries or information, such as a price list, without intending to actually offer to sell or place an order, but may find that the other party's understanding (or the applicable law) has created a binding sales agreement prior to the first party's intention. This can arise because under some countries' laws, an offer to sell or buy is accepted when the acceptance is dispatched, rather than when it is received. It can also arise because silence can be considered as acceptance if the parties are merchants.

The second issue that arises relates to the governing law. Contracts are often governed by the law of the country where the contract is negotiated and performed or where the offer to sell or buy was accepted. Since an international agreement may be

Figure 3–1. Formation of sales agreements.

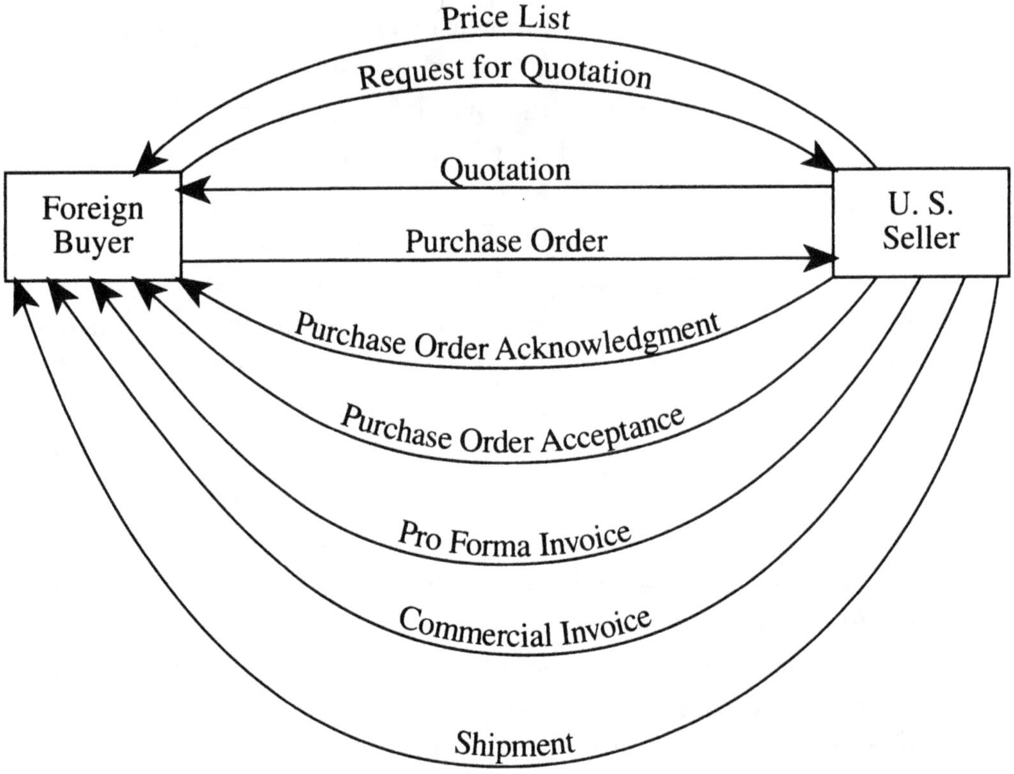

partly negotiated and partly performed in both countries, and since there may be a question as to whether the buyer accepted the offer to sell or the seller accepted the offer to purchase, situations can arise where the sales agreement is governed by the law of the buyer's country. Since foreign law may be quite different from U.S. law, the seller's rights and responsibilities may differ greatly from what she anticipated. Customary local ways of doing business, called trade usages, may unknowingly become a part of the sales agreement under the sales laws of some countries. Sellers and buyers sometimes try to resolve this problem by including a governing law term in their documents, but again, these may conflict.

A final method of formation of a sales agreement involves conduct. A simple example is where a buyer sends a purchase order and the seller, without communicating, simply ships the goods; or if the seller offers to sell the goods and the buyer simply sends payment. In such cases, the conduct in accepting the offer will include all of the terms and conditions of the offer. If the seller is not satisfied with the buyer's terms and conditions of purchase, he should send some communication to negotiate those terms before simply shipping the goods.

4. Common Forms for the Formation of Sales Agreements

There are a number of forms customarily used in the formation of sales agreements. In order to save time (and discourage changes by the other party), both buyers and sellers often purchase preprinted forms from commercial stationers, although this is not suggested as it may contain provisions that do not reflect the intentions of the parties, or develop and preprint their own forms. Not all of the same documents are used by the seller or the buyer in all sales transactions. For example, a seller may submit a quotation to a potential buyer without receiving any request for quotation, or the first communication the seller receives may be a purchase order from the buyer. However, it is important to be familiar with the various forms and the role they play in bringing the negotiations to agreement.

a. Price Lists. Sometimes a seller will send a price list to a prospective buyer as its first communication. Ordinarily, such price lists would not be considered as an offer to sell, entitling the buyer to immediately accept. However, in order to prevent the unexpected formation of a sales agreement, such price lists should specify that this is not an offer to sell and no agreement will arise until a purchase order has been received and accepted. Such price lists should also specify their expiration date and that they are subject to change. Price lists should also include the terms and conditions of the seller as this is the first opportunity for the buyer to be put on notice of those terms and conditions, should it wish to place an order.

b. Requests for Quotations. Sometimes the first document involved in the formation of a sales agreement is a request from the buyer to the seller for a quotation (RFQ). Ordinarily, such a request—whether it be informal in an email or formal in a printed form—will ask for a price quotation from the seller for a specific quantity and often a shipping date. (A sample printed form is shown in Figure 3–2.) When receiving such a request for quotation, the seller should be particularly careful to ascertain whether the request contains other terms and conditions of purchase that are incorporated by reference to another document or are contained in the fine print "boilerplate" on the front or back of the request for quotation. If other terms are referenced, the best precaution is to ask the buyer to send such terms and conditions for the seller's review before replying.

If additional terms of purchase are provided, they should be reviewed to determine if they conflict with the seller's usual terms and conditions of sale. This is particularly important in this day of email correspondence. The buyer should always request a copy of the seller's terms and conditions.

Figure 3–2. Quotation request.

QUOTATION REQUEST

From _____   Inquiry No. _____

Street Address _____   Date _____

City and State _____   Classification _____

To   ┌   ┐   **PLEASE NOTE CAREFULLY**
      ·   This inquiry implies no obligation
      ·   on the part of the buyer.
      ·   Unless otherwise specified, there is
                                                          no restriction on the number of items,
                                                          that may be ordered.
                                                              In quoting, use duplicate copy of this
      └   ┘   form provided. Fill in complete infor-
                                                          mation before returning.
                                                          Do not quote on articles you can-
THIS IS AN INQUIRY—NOT AN ORDER   **not supply.** If substitutes are offered,
                                                          make full explanation.

Delivery Point	By	☐ Parcel Post ☐ Rail Freight Line _____	If not indicated, suggest most practical way.
		☐ Express ☐ Motor Freight Line _____	

Prices Quoted F.O.B. _____   Freight Allowance _____

Shipping Point _____

Terms: _____ _____ % Discount _____ Days   Net Cash _____ Days   No charge to be made for packing, boxing crating or delivery to Transportation Co.

ITEM NO.	QUANTITY	ITEM AND SPECIFICATIONS	*	UNIT	LIST PRICE OF UNIT	DISCOUNT OFFERED	NET UNIT PRICE	ESTIMATED GROSS WT.

* Check-mark in this column indicates shipment can be made from stock.

Delivery of other items as follows: _____

Subject to withdrawal _____   Date returned _____

For Seller _____   For Buyer _____

CASCADE® L1-C2451   PRINTED IN U.S.A.

c. ***Quotations and Costing Sheets.*** In response to a request for a quotation, the seller ordinarily prepares and forwards a quotation. Before quoting a price for any specific quantity or any shipment date, it is extremely important that the seller accurately calculate its additional costs relating to an export sale and shipment before providing the quotation. The use of a costing sheet is highly recommended. (A sample costing sheet is shown in Figure 3–3.) When responding to a request for quotation, the seller should be particularly careful to ascertain whether the request contains other terms and conditions. By accurately completing the costing sheet, the seller can avoid quoting prices that will result in sales commitments with too little or no profit. In making quotations, the seller can use a printed form or prepare the quotations on a case-by-case basis. (A sample is shown in Figure 3–4.)

If this is the first communication from the seller to the buyer, the seller should be careful to ensure that it contains all of the seller's terms and conditions of sale in addition to the price, quantity, and shipment date, or the quotation should specify that the seller will not be bound until he has received a written purchase order and has issued a written purchase order acceptance. Otherwise, when the buyer receives the quotation, she may find the price, quantity, and shipment date acceptable and accept that quotation when she receives it. This means that the sales agreements may be formed at that time in the buyer's country, or it may be formed when the buyer issues her purchase order (but before the purchase order is received by the seller). This may be so whether or not the seller designates his quotation as firm, because under the laws of some countries, quotations by merchants are deemed irrevocable for a certain period of time. When the sales agreement is formed under the law of the country of the buyer, the seller's rights and responsibilities under the sales agreement may be quite different from those under U.S. law. Sometimes it is necessary or acceptable to have a sales agreement governed by foreign law, but only after the seller has investigated the differences and has made an informed choice—not a mistaken one. Moreover, unless the seller has forwarded all of his terms and conditions of sale with his first communication (the quotation), the terms and conditions included in subsequent communications from the seller may not be binding on the buyer. Once again, as a seller, it is important to clearly state all terms and conditions at the time of quotation; even by email correspondence, attach a copy to any quotation.

d. ***Purchase Orders.*** The next document that may occur in a sales transaction is a purchase order (PO) issued by the buyer. Again, the purchase order may be informal, such as in an email, or it may be on a printed form. Purchase orders are likely to contain many additional terms and conditions that the buyer wants to be a part of the sales agreement when the purchase order is accepted by the seller.

Figure 3–3. Export quotation worksheet.

EXPORT QUOTATION WORKSHEET

DATE_____   REF/PRO FORMA INVOICE NO._____
COMMODITY_____   EXPECTED SHIP DATE_____
CUSTOMER_____   PACKED DIMENSIONS_____
COUNTRY_____   PACKED WEIGHT_____
PAYMENT TERMS_____   PACKED CUBE_____

PRODUCTS TO BE SHIPPED FROM_____
                       TO_____

SELLING PRICE OF GOODS: $_____

SPECIAL EXPORT PACKING:
    $_____   quoted by_____
    $_____   quoted by_____
    $_____   quoted by_____ $_____

INLAND FREIGHT:
    $_____   quoted by_____
    $_____   quoted by_____
    $_____   quoted by_____ $_____
    Inland freight includes the following charges:
    ☐ unloading   ☐ pier delivery   ☐ terminal   ☐_____

OCEAN FREIGHT			AIR FREIGHT		
quoted by	tariff item		quoted by	spec code	
$_____	_____ #_____		$_____	_____ #_____	
$_____	_____ #_____		$_____	_____ #_____	
$_____	_____ #_____		$_____	_____ #_____	

Ocean freight includes the following surcharges:

☐ Port congestion   ☐ Heavy lift
☐ Currency adjustment ☐ Bunker
☐ Container rental   ☐ Wharfage
☐_____   ☐_____

☐ INSURANCE   ☐ includes war risk
rate:_____ per $100 or $_____

TOTAL OCEAN CHARGES $_____
notes:

Air freight includes the following surcharges:

☐ Fuel adjustment
☐ Container stuffing
☐_____

☐ INSURANCE   ☐ includes war risk
rate:_____ per $100 or $_____

TOTAL AIR CHARGES $_____ $_____
notes:

FORWARDING FEES: $_____
Includes: ☐ Courier Fees   ☐ Certification Fees   ☐ Banking Fees   ☐_____

CONSULAR LEGALIZATION FEES: $_____

INSPECTION FEES: $_____

DIRECT BANK CHARGES: $_____

OTHER CHARGES:_____ $_____
              _____ $_____

TOTAL: ☐ FOB_____   ☐ C & F_____
         ☐ FAS_____   ☐ CIF_____ $_____

Form No. 10-020 Printed and Sold by *UNZ&CO* 201 Circle Drive N, Suite 104, Piscataway, NJ 08854   (800) 631-3098 www.unzco.com   © Copyright Unz & Co. 2001

Figure 3–4. Quotation.

```
                    §2.4—Form 5

                     Quotation

                    [Face side]
                  SELLER COMPANY

          _____

          _____


                         Date: _____

BUYER COMPANY


    _____


    _____

We are pleased to quote as follows on your recent
inquiry:
_____

_____

    Quantity      Description       Price
_____


                    Very truly yours,
                    SELLER COMPANY


                    By _____
THIS QUOTATION INCLUDES ALL OF THE PROVISIONS ON
THE REVERSE SIDE HEREOF.


               [Reverse side]
                  PROVISIONS

    1. ANY PURCHASE ORDER PURSUANT TO THE ACCOMPANY-
ING QUOTATION SHALL NOT RESULT IN A CONTRACT UNTIL
IT IS ACCEPTED AND ACKNOWLEDGED BY SELLER AT SELL-
ER'S OFFICE IN ____, ____.¹
    2. Payment terms are net ten (10) days after the
rendering of seller's invoice.²
    3. Delivery terms are f.o.b. cars at seller's
```

§ 2.4—Form 5

1. See § 2.5.   2. See § 9.6.

Figure 3–4. (*continued*)

plant in ___. Dates of delivery are determined from the date of seller's acceptance of any order or orders by buyer and are estimates of approximate dates of delivery, not a guaranty of a particular day of delivery.[3] Seller shall not be liable for failure or delay in shipping goods hereunder if such failure or delay is due to an act of God, war, labor difficulties, accident, inability to obtain containers or raw materials, or any other causes of any kind whatever beyond the control of seller.[4]

4. Any tax imposed by federal, state or other governmental authority on the sale of the merchandise and service referred to in this quotation shall be paid by buyer in addition to the quoted purchase price.

5. Buyer shall in respect of goods packaged by seller in accordance with designs, processes or formulas supplied, determined or requested by buyer, defend seller at buyer's expense and pay costs and damages awarded in any suit brought against seller for infringement of any letters patent by reason of use of such designs, processes or formulas, provided seller promptly notifies buyer in writing of any claim of or suit for infringement and tenders defense thereof to buyer. Seller is entitled to be represented in any suit at its own expense.[5]

6. Except for the warranty that the goods are made in a workmanlike manner and in accordance with the specifications therefor supplied or agreed to by buyer and are made or packaged pursuant to seller's customary manufacturing procedures, SELLER MAKES NO WARRANTY EXPRESS OR IMPLIED; AND ANY IMPLIED WARRANTY OF MERCHANTABILITY OR FITNESS FOR A PARTICULAR PURPOSE WHICH EXCEEDS THE FOREGOING WARRANTY IS HEREBY DISCLAIMED BY SELLER AND EXCLUDED FROM ANY AGREEMENT MADE BY ACCEPTANCE ANY ORDER PURSUANT TO THIS QUOTATION.[6] Seller will not be liable for any consequential damages, loss or expense arising in connection with the use of or the inability to use its goods for any purpose whatever. Seller's maximum liabil-

3. See § 9.4.

4. See § 9.19.

5. See §§ 8.1, 8.9.

6. See §§ 8.2 et seq.

Figure 3–4. (*continued*)

ity shall not in any case exceed the contract price for the goods claimed to be defective or un-suitable.[7]

8. Buyer shall notify seller within ten days of receipt of merchandise of any complaint whatsoever buyer may have concerning such merchandise.[8]

9. There are no provisions with respect to this quotation which are not specified herein.[9] IF BUYER PLACES AN ORDER WITH SELLER BASED ON THIS QUOTATION, WHETHER IN WRITING OR ORALLY, THEN THIS QUOTATION AND BUYER'S ORDER AND SELLER'S ACCEPT-ANCE OR CONFIRMATION WILL CONSTITUTE THE ENTIRE CONTRACT BETWEEN BUYER AND SELLER WITH RESPECT TO THE SUBJECT MATTER OF THIS QUOTATION.[10] Any agreement so made shall be governed by the law of [state].[11]

SELLER COMPANY

COMMENT

This is a quotation, as distinguished from a firm offer. Since a quotation is only an invitation to submit an offer or to place an order, no power of acceptance is created in the addressee or recipient. See UCC § 2–205.

7. See §§ 8.12, 15.2.

8. See §§ 8.8, 9.9, 9.14, 9.15, 14.1.

9. See § 5.2.

10. See § 2.7.

11. See § 1.2.

(Samples are shown in Figures 3–5 and 3–6.) Even though the seller may expect that no sales agreement will be formed until he has received the buyer's purchase order, if he has previously sent a quotation to the buyer, the terms and conditions stated in the buyer's purchase order may govern the sales agreement. Of course, the terms and conditions contained in the buyer's purchase order are always written to be most favorable to the buyer. Another way in which the seller can try to guard against such a result is to expressly state in her quotation that the quotation is not an offer to sell and that no sales agreement will exist until such time as the seller has received a purchase order from the buyer and has issued its purchase order acceptance.

e. Purchase Order Acknowledgments, Acceptances, and Sales Confirmations. When a purchase order is received, some sellers prepare a purchase order acknowledgment form. A purchase order acknowledgment may state that the seller has received the purchase order from the buyer and is in the process of evaluating it, such as checking on the credit of the buyer or determining the availability of raw materials for manufacture, but that the seller has not yet accepted the purchase order and will issue a purchase order acceptance at a later date. In other cases, the language of the purchase order acknowledgment indicates that it is also an acceptance of the order, and no further communication is issued. Sales confirmations usually perform the same role as purchase order acceptances. The seller will normally include its detailed terms and conditions of sale in its purchase order acknowledgment or purchase order acceptance. If the buyer's request for a quotation or purchase order does not contain detailed terms and conditions of purchase, the seller can feel reasonably comfortable that its terms and conditions of sale will control if they are included in the purchase order acknowledgment or acceptance form. If the buyer has previously sent detailed terms and conditions of purchase, however, the seller is at risk that those terms and conditions will control unless it expressly states that the order is accepted and the sale is made *only* on the seller's terms and conditions of sale *and* thereafter (prior to production and shipment) the buyer confirms its acceptance of the seller's terms. (A sample purchase order acceptance is shown in Figure 3–7.) The purchase order acceptance should specify that the agreement cannot be modified except in writing signed by the seller. As many sales confirmations occur through email correspondence these days, it is important to ensure that the seller include the terms and conditions in its confirmation.

f. Pro Forma Invoices. If the buyer is in a country that has foreign exchange controls, he may need to receive a pro forma invoice from the seller in order to get government approval to make payment, and the seller may want to receive such

Figure 3–5. Purchase order.

Reprinted with permission from Bradford Stone's *West's Legal Forms,* Second Edition, copyright © 1985 by West Publishing Co.

Figure 3–6. Purchase order.

§ 2.6—Form 2

Buyer's Purchase Order—Another Form

Purchase Order No. _____
Purchase Order Number
Must Appear on Invoices,
n/l. Packages and Packing
Slips.

BUYER COMPANY

P.O. Date

IMPORTANT
READ ALL INSTRUCTIONS, TERMS
AND CONDITIONS ON FACE
AND REVERSE SIDES.
ONLY SUCH INSTRUCTIONS, TERMS
AND CONDITIONS SHALL CONSTI-
TUTE THE AGREEMENT BETWEEN
THE PARTIES.

TO:

SELLER COMPANY

Ship via	f.o.b.	terms	ship to
as per your quotation			promised delivery date at destination

Please Enter Our Purchase Order of Above No. Subject to All Instructions, Terms and Conditions
on Face and Reverse Side Hereof.

QUANTITY	DESCRIPTION	Price Per	AMOUNT

<u>TOTAL</u>

ADDITIONAL INSTRUCTIONS, TERMS AND CONDITIONS ON REVERSE SIDE
INSTRUCTIONS, TERMS AND CONDITIONS:

1. **Acceptance Copy** must be signed and returned immediately.

BUYER COMPANY

2. **Packing Slips** must be included in all shipments and last copy must state "ORDER COMPLETED."
3. **Order Number** must be shown on each package, packing slip and invoice.

By _____

4. **Invoices** must be rendered in duplicate not later than the day following shipment. Attach bill of lading or express receipt to each invoice.[1]
5. **Deliveries** must be made to Buyer's receiving room, not to individuals or departments.[2]
6. **Extra Charges.** No additional charges of any kind, including charges for boxing, packing, cartage, or other extras will be allowed unless specifically agreed to in writing in advance by Buyer.
7. **Payment.** It is understood that the cash discount period will date from the receipt of

§2.6—Form 2
1. UCC §§ 2-503, 2-504(b) and (c). See § 9.4. 2. UCC §§ 2-308, 2-309(1), 2-503. See § 9.4.

Figure 3–6. (*continued*)

the goods or from the date of the invoice, whichever is later. C.O.D. shipments will not be accepted. Drafts will not be honored.[3]

8. **Quantities.** The specific quantity ordered must be delivered in full and not be changed without Buyer's consent in writing. Any unauthorized quantity is subject to our rejection and return at Seller's expense.[4]

9. **Price.** If price is not stated in this order, it is agreed that the goods shall be billed at the price last quoted, or billed at the prevailing market price, whichever is lower. This order must not be filled at a higher price than last quoted or charged without Buyer's specific authorization.[5]

10. **Applicable Laws.** Seller represents that the merchandise covered by this order was not manufactured and is not being sold or priced in violation of any federal, state or local law.

11. **Fair Labor Standards Act.** Seller agrees that goods shipped to Buyer under this order will be produced in compliance with the Fair Labor Standards Act.[6]

12. **Warranty Specifications.** Seller expressly warrants that all the materials and articles covered by this order or other description or specification furnished by Buyer will be in exact accordance with such order, description or specification and free from defects in material and/or workmanship, and merchantable. Such warranty shall survive delivery, and shall not be deemed waived either by reason of Buyer's acceptance of said materials or articles or by payment for them. Any deviations from this order or specifications furnished hereunder, or any other exceptions or alterations must be approved in writing by Buyer's Purchasing Department.[7]

13. **Cancellation.** Buyer reserves the right to cancel all or any part of the undelivered portion of this order if Seller does not make deliveries as specified, time being of the essence of this Contract, or if Seller breaches any of the terms hereof including, without limitation, the warranties of Seller.[8]

14. **Inspection and Acceptance.** All goods shall be received subject to Buyer's right of inspection and rejection. Defective goods or goods not in accordance with Buyer's specifications will be held for Seller's instruction at Seller's risk and if Seller so directs, will be returned at Seller's expense. If inspection discloses that part of the goods received are not in accordance with Buyer's specifications, Buyer shall have the right to cancel any unshipped portion of the order. Payment for goods on this order prior to inspection shall not constitute acceptance thereof and is without prejudice to any and all claims that Buyer may have against Seller.[9]

15. **Patents.** Seller warrants the material purchased hereunder does not infringe any letters patent granted by the United States and covenants and agrees to save harmless and protect Buyer, its successors, assigns, customers and users of its product, against any claim or demand based upon such infringement, and after notice, to appear and defend at its own expense any suits at law or in equity arising therefrom.[10]

16. **Interpretation of Contract and Assignments.** This contract shall be construed according to the laws of the State of [*state*]. This contract may not be assigned by Seller without Buyer's written consent.[11]

3. UCC §§ 2-310, 2-511. See § 9.6.
4. UCC §§ 2-307, 2-601, 2-602. See §§ 9.4, 9.8 et seq.
5. UCC § 2-305. See § 2.3.
6. 29 U.S.C.A. § 215.
7. UCC §§ 2-313, 2-316. See §§ 8.2, 8.10.
8. UCC § 2-703(f); see UCC §§ 2-612, 2-719, 2-720. See §§ 9.16, 13.2, 15.2.
9. UCC §§ 2-512, 2-513, 2-601 through 2-607. See §§ 9.5, 9.7, 9.8 et seq.
10. UCC § 2-312(3). See §§ 8.1, 8.9.
11. UCC §§ 1-105, 2-210. See §§ 1.2, 6.1 et seq.

Figure 3–7. Purchase order acceptance.

§ 2.6—Form 8

Seller's Sales Order—Another Form

[Face side]

SELLER COMPANY

PRODUCT

TO: *[Buyer Company]*

GENTLEMEN:
We thank you for the order listed below which we are pleased to have accepted subject to only those terms and conditions of sale which are set forth below and on the reverse side hereof.[1]

Trusting that we have your assent to these terms and conditions we accordingly have entered your order in our mill schedules.

DATE

YOUR ORDER:

TERMS OF DELIVERY:[2]

§ 2.6—Form 8

1. UCC § 2-207(1). These terms probably will not ribbon match those on buyer's purchase order form. See discussion and forms at § 2.7 below.

2. UCC §§ 2-307, 2-308, 2-309(1), 2-319 et seq., 2-503. See § 9.4.

Figure 3–7. *(continued)*

TERMS OF PAYMENT:[3]

PLEASE ADDRESS CORRESPONDENCE RELATING TO THIS ORDER TO OUR DISTRICT SALES OFFICE AT

VERY TRULY YOURS,
SELLER COMPANY

By _____

[Manager of Sales]

[Reverse side]

TERMS AND CONDITIONS OF SALE

In accordance with the usage of trade, your assent to the terms and conditions of sale set forth below and on the reverse side hereof shall be conclusively presumed from your failure seasonably to object in writing and from your acceptance of all or any part of the material ordered.[4]

All proposals, negotiations, and representations, if any, regarding this transaction and made prior to the date of this acknowledgment are merged herein.[5]

PRICES—All prices, whether herein named or heretofore quoted or proposed, shall be adjusted to the Seller's prices in effect at the time of shipment.[6]

If transportation charges from point of origin of the shipment to a designated point are included in the prices herein named or heretofore quoted—

    (a) any changes in such transportation charges shall be for the account of the Buyer;

---

3. UCC § 2-310; see UCC § 2-511. See § 9.6.

4. See § 2.6—Form 7 and Comment. See also § 2.7.

5. UCC § 2-202. See § 5.2.

6. UCC § 2-305. See § 2.3.

Figure 3–7. (*continued*)

(b) except as otherwise stated in the Seller's quotation, the Seller shall not be responsible for switching, spotting, handling, storage, demurrage or any other transportation or accessorial service, nor for any charges incurred therefor, unless such charges are included in the applicable tariff freight rate from shipping point to the designated point.

TAXES—Any taxes which the Seller may be required to pay or collect, under any existing or future law, upon or with respect to the sale, purchase, delivery, storage, processing, use or consumption of any of the material covered hereby, including taxes upon or measured by the receipts from the sale thereof, shall be for the account of the Buyer, who shall promptly pay the amount thereof to the Seller upon demand.

DELAY—The Seller shall be excused for any delay in performance due to acts of God, war, riot, embargoes, acts of civil or military authorities, fires, floods, accidents, quarantine restrictions, mill conditions, strikes, differences with workmen, delays in transportation, shortage of cars, fuel, labor or materials, or any circumstance or cause beyond the control of the Seller in the reasonable conduct of its business.[7]

INSPECTION—The Buyer may inspect, or provide for inspection, at the place of manufacture. Such inspection shall be so conducted as not to interfere unreasonably with the manufacturer's operations, and consequent approval or rejection shall be made before shipment of the material. Notwithstanding the foregoing, if, upon receipt of such material by the Buyer, the same shall appear not to conform to the contract between the Buyer and the Seller, the Buyer shall immediately notify the Seller of such condition and afford the Seller a reasonable opportunity to inspect the material. No material shall be returned without the Seller's consent.[8]

EXCLUSION OF WARRANTIES—The Implied Warranties of Merchantability and Fitness for Purpose Are Excluded From This Contract.[9]

BUYER'S REMEDIES—If the material furnished to the Buyer shall fail to conform to this contract or to any express or implied warranty, the Seller shall replace such non-conforming material at the original point of delivery and shall furnish instructions for its disposition. Any transportation charges involved in such disposition shall be for the Seller's account.

The Buyer's exclusive and sole remedy on account or in respect of the furnishing of material that does not conform to this contract, or to any express or implied warranty, shall be to secure replacement thereof as aforesaid. The Seller shall not in any event be liable for the cost of any labor expended on any such material or for any special, direct,

7. UCC § 2-615. See § 9.19.

8. UCC §§ 2-512, 2-513. See § 9.7.

9. UCC §§ 2-314, 2-315, 2-316. See §§ 8.4, 8.5, 8.6, 8.11.

Figure 3–7. (*continued*)

indirect, incidental or consequential damages to anyone by reason of the fact that such material does not conform to this contract or to any express or implied warranty.[10]

PERMISSIBLE VARIATIONS, STANDARDS AND TOLERANCES—Except in the particulars specified by Buyer and expressly agreed to in writing by Seller, all material shall be produced in accordance with Seller's standard practices. All material, including that produced to meet an exact specification, shall be subject to tolerances and variations consistent with usages of the trade and regular mill practices concerning: dimension, weight, straightness, section, composition and mechanical properties; normal variations in surface, internal conditions and quality; deviations from tolerances and variations consistent with practical testing and inspection methods; and regular mill practices concerning over and under shipments.[11]

PATENTS—The Seller shall indemnify the Buyer against any judgment for damages and costs which may be rendered against the Buyer in any suit brought on account of the alleged infringement of any United States patent by any product supplied by the Seller hereunder, unless made in accordance with materials, designs or specifications furnished or designated by the Buyer, in which case the Buyer shall indemnify the Seller against any judgment for damages and costs which may be rendered against the Seller in any suit brought on account of the alleged infringement of any United States patent by such product or by such materials, designs or specifications; provided that prompt written notice be given to the party from whom indemnity is sought of the bringing of the suit and that an opportunity be given such party to settle or defend it as that party may see fit and that every reasonable assistance in settling or defending it shall be rendered. Neither the Seller nor the Buyer shall in any event be liable to the other for special, indirect, incidental or consequential damages arising out of or resulting from infringement of patents.[12]

CREDIT APPROVAL—Shipments, deliveries and performance of work shall at all times be subject to the approval of the Seller's Credit Department. The Seller may at any time decline to make any shipment or delivery or perform any work except upon receipt of payment or security or upon terms and conditions satisfactory to such Department.

TERMS OF PAYMENT—Subject to the provisions of CREDIT APPROVAL above, terms of payment are as shown on the reverse side hereof and shall be effective from date of invoice. A cash discount shall not be allowed on any transportation charges included in delivered prices.[13]

---

10. UCC §§ 2-508, 2-714, 2-715, 2-719. See §§ 9.17, 14.1, 14.2, 15.2.

11. UCC §§ 1-205, 2-208, 2-313, 2-314(2)(d). See §§ 5.1, 8.2, 8.4.

12. UCC § 2-312(3). See §§ 8.1, 8.9.

13. UCC §§ 2-310, 2-511. See § 9.6.

Figure 3–7. *(continued)*

COMPLIANCE WITH LAWS—The Seller intends to comply with all laws applicable to its performance of this order.[14]

RENEGOTIATION—The Seller assumes only such liability with respect to renegotiation of contracts or subcontracts to which it is a party as may be lawfully imposed upon the Seller under the provisions of any Renegotiation Act applicable to this order.[15]

NON-WAIVER BY SELLER—Waiver by the Seller of a breach of any of the terms and conditions of this contract shall not be construed as a waiver of any other breach.[16]

14. UCC § 1-103. See § 1.1.

15. See, e.g., Renegotiation Act (Renegotiation of Contracts), 50 U.S.C.A.App. §§ 1211 et seq.

16. UCC § 1-107; see UCC §§ 2-209, 1-207. See §§ 3.3, 10.2.

approval before commencing production. This is an invoice that the buyer will submit to the central bank to obtain permission and clearance to convert foreign currency into U.S. dollars in order to make payment to the seller. The seller should exert some care in preparing this invoice, because it may be extremely difficult to change the price in the final invoice due to changes in costs or specifications. Sometimes, a pro forma invoice is used as the first document sent by the seller in response to a buyer's request for quotation. (A sample pro forma invoice is shown in Figure 3–8.) It should contain the complete terms and conditions of sale. This type of pro forma invoice should not be confused with that used by an importer when the seller has not provided a commercial invoice (see Figure 8–2).

g. Commercial Invoices. Later, when manufacture is complete and the product is ready for shipment, ordinarily the seller will prepare a commercial invoice, which is the formal statement for payment to be sent directly to the buyer or submitted through banking channels for payment by the buyer. (See Figure 8-2.) Such invoices may also contain the detailed terms or conditions of sale on the front or back of the form. (A sample commercial invoice is shown in Figure 3–9.) However, if this is the first time that the seller has brought such terms to the attention of the buyer, it is likely that they will not be binding on the buyer because the seller has already accepted the buyer's order by the seller's conduct in manufacturing and/or shipping the products. (See also the discussion of commercial invoices in Chapter 4, Section C.)

h. Conflicting Provisions in Seller and Buyer Sales Documentation. It is common in international trade for sellers and buyers to use preprinted forms designed to reduce the amount of negotiation and discussion required for each sales agreement. Undoubtedly, such forms have been drafted by attorneys for each side and contain terms and conditions of purchase or terms and conditions of sale that are favorable to the buyer and seller, respectively. Consequently, it is not unusual for sellers and buyers intent on entering into a sales transaction to routinely issue such documentation with little or no thought regarding the consistency of those provisions. Afterward, if the sales transaction breaks down and either the buyer or the seller consults its attorney regarding its legal rights and obligations, the rights of the parties may be very unclear. In the worst case, the seller may find that a sales agreement has been validly formed on all of the terms and conditions of the buyer's purchase order and is governed by the law of the buyer's country. In order to reduce or eliminate this problem, often the seller's attorney drafts requests for quotations, conditions that might be contained in the buyer's request for quotation or purchase order, the seller agrees to make the sale only on its own terms and conditions. While this can be of some help, sometimes the

Figure 3–8. Pro forma invoice.

PROFORMA INVOICE/EXPORT ORDER		UNITRAK™

Copyright © 1988 UNZ & CO.

CUSTOMER:

_____

_____

_____

_____

SHIP TO (Consignee):

_____

_____

_____

_____

NOTIFY (Intermediate Consignee):

_____

_____

IN-HOUSE ORDER NO.	DATE
PRO FORMA INVOICE NO.	DATE
COMMERCIAL INVOICE NO.	DATE
CUSTOMER PURCHASE ORDER NO.	DATE
CUSTOMER ACCOUNT NO	
PURCHASER'S NAME	TITLE
SHIP VIA	EST. SHIP DATE
TELEPHONE NO.	
TELEX/FAX/CABLE NO	

PART NUMBER	UNIT OF MEASURE	QUANTITY	DESCRIPTION	UNIT PRICE	TOTAL PRICE

SPECIAL INSTRUCTIONS:

ADDITIONAL CHARGES

FREIGHT ☐ Ocean ☐ Air _____

CONSULAR/LEGALIZATION _____

INSPECTION/CERTIFICATION _____

SPECIAL PACKING _____

TERMS OF PAYMENT

☐ LETTER OF CREDIT   Bank _____

☐ DRAFT   Terms _____

☐ OPEN ACCOUNT   Terms _____

☐ OTHER _____

CURRENCY OF PAYMENT _____

Form 15-330 Printed and Sold by *UNZ®* 190 Baldwin Ave., Jersey City, NJ 07306 • (800) 631-3098 • (201) 795-5400

PROFORMA INVOICE
Reprinted with permission of Unz & Co., 190 Baldwin Ave., Jersey City, NJ 07306, USA.

Figure 3–9. Commercial Invoice.

Copyright © 1988 UNZ & CO.			COMMERCIAL INVOICE			

SHIPPER/EXPORTER

COMMERCIAL INVOICE NO.	DATE

CUSTOMER PURCHASE ORDER NO.	B/L, AWB NO.

COUNTRY OF ORIGIN	DATE OF EXPORT

CONSIGNEE

TERMS OF PAYMENT

EXPORT REFERENCES

NOTIFY: INTERMEDIATE CONSIGNEE

FORWARDING AGENT

AIR/OCEAN PORT OF EMBARKATION

EXPORTING CARRIER/ROUTE

Terms of Sale and Terms of Payment under this offer are governed by Incoterms # 322, "Uniform Rules For The Collection Of Commercial Paper" and # 400 "Uniform Customs And Practice For Documentary Credits"

PKGS.	QUANTITY	NET WT. *(Kilos)*	GROSS WT. *(Kilos)*	DESCRIPTION OF MERCHANDISE	UNIT PRICE	TOTAL VALUE

PACKAGE MARKS:

MISC. CHARGES *(Packing, Insurance, etc.)*

	INVOICE TOTAL	

CERTIFICATIONS

AUTHORIZED SIGNATURE

Form 15-320 Printed and Sold by *UNZ & CO.* 190 Baldwin Ave., Jersey City, NJ 07306 · (800) 631-3098 · (201) 795-5400

Reprinted with permission of Unz & Co., 190 Baldwin Ave., Jersey City, NJ 07306, USA.

buyer's requests for quotation and purchase orders also contain such language, and consequently, the buyer's terms and conditions may win out. If the buyer was the last to send its terms and conditions of purchase, and the seller did not object, the seller's conduct in shipping the goods can result in an agreement under the buyer's terms and conditions. In fact, the only way to be comfortable regarding the terms and conditions of sale that will govern a sales agreement is to actually review the terms and conditions contained in the buyer's forms and compare them with the terms and conditions that the seller desires to utilize. Where specific conflicts exist or where the buyer's terms and conditions of purchase differ from the seller's terms and conditions of sale, the seller should expressly bring that to the attention of the buyer, the difference should be negotiated to the satisfaction of the seller, and appropriate changes should be made in the form of a rider to the standard form or a letter to clarify the agreement that has been reached between the parties (which should be signed by both parties). In some isolated sales transactions where the quantities are small, the seller may simply choose to forgo this effort and accept the risk that the transaction will be controlled by the buyer's terms and conditions of sale. However, the seller should establish some dollar limit over which a review is to be made and should not continue a practice that might be appropriate for small sales but would be very dangerous for large sales.

i. Side Agreements. Occasionally, the buyer may suggest that the seller and buyer enter into a side or letter agreement. In some cases, the suggestion may be innocent enough, for example, where the parties wish to clarify how they will interpret or carry out a particular provision of their sales agreement. Even then, however, it is better practice to incorporate all of the agreements of the parties in a single document. Unfortunately, more often the buyer's proposal of a side agreement is designed to evade the buyer's foreign exchange control, tax, customs, or antitrust laws. Sellers should be wary of entering into such agreements unless they fully understand the consequences. Such agreements may be unenforceable, the seller may not be able to get paid on its export sale, and/or the seller may be prosecuted as a co-conspirator for violating such laws.

B. Ongoing Sales Transactions

When a customer begins to purchase on a regular basis, or when the seller desires to make regular sales to a particular end user or reseller, the seller and the buyer should enter into a more comprehensive agreement to govern their relationship. Often these types of agreements are a result of the buyer's being willing to commit to regular purchases, and, therefore, to purchase a larger quantity of the goods, in return for obtaining a lower price. Or, they may result from the buyer's desire to "tie up," that is, to obtain more assurance from the seller to commit to supply the buyer's requirements, or from the seller's desire to plan its production. The three major types of agreements used in ongoing sales transactions are (1) international sales agreements, that is, supply agreements where the seller sells directly to an end-user customer who either incorporates the seller's product as a component into a product the buyer manufactures, or consumes the product and does not resell the product; (2) distributor agreements, where the seller sells the product to a purchaser, usually located in the destination country, who resells the product in that country, usually in the same form but sometimes with modifications; and (3) sales agent or sales representative agreements, where a person, usually located in the destination country, is appointed to solicit orders from potential customers in that country. In the last case, the sale is not made to the sales agent, but is made directly to the customer, with payment of a commission or other compensation to the sales agent. In any of the three foregoing agreements, there is a correlation between the documentation used in isolated sales transactions and the documentation used in ongoing sales transactions. Furthermore, there are a number of important provisions that are not relevant to domestic sales that should be included in international sales, distributor, and sales agent agreements.

1. Correlation with Documentation for Isolated Sales Transactions

As discussed in Section A.4 above, it is common for sellers and buyers to use forms such as requests for quotation, purchase orders, purchase order acknowledgments, purchase order acceptances, sales confirmations, pro forma invoices, and invoices during the course of ordering and selling products. When an ongoing sales relationship is being established with a particular customer, it is usual to enter into an umbrella or blanket agreement that is intended to govern the relationship between the parties over a longer period of time, for example, one year, five years, or longer. Sometimes the parties will enter into a trial marketing agreement that will last for a short period of time, such as one year, before deciding to enter into a longer-term agreement. In any event, the international sales (supply) agreement, the distributor agreement, and the sales agent (representative) agreement define the rights and obligations of the parties over a fairly long period of time and commit the seller and the buyer to doing business with each other so that both sides can make production, marketing, and advertising plans and expenditures. Special price discounts in return for commitments to purchase specific quantities are common in such agreements. Such agreements may contain a commitment to purchase a specific quantity over the life of the agreement and may designate a specific price or a formula by which the price will be adjusted over the life of the agreement. To this extent, these agreements serve as an umbrella over the parties' relationship, with certain specific acts to be accomplished as agreed by the parties from time to time. For example, it is usually necessary during the term of such agreements for the buyer to advise the seller from time to time of the specific quantity that it wishes to order at that time, to be applied against the buyer's overall purchase commitment. This will be done by the issuance of a purchase order.

If the price of the product is likely to fluctuate, no price may be specified in the umbrella agreement. Instead, the price may be changed from time to time by the seller depending on the seller's price at the time the buyer submits a purchase order, perhaps with a special discount from such price because the buyer has committed to buy a substantial quantity over the life of the agreement. In such cases, depending upon whether or not a specific price has been set in the umbrella agreement, the buyer will send a request for a quotation and the seller will provide a quotation, or a purchase order will be sent describing the specific quantity the buyer wishes to order at that time, a suggested shipment date, and the price. The seller will still use a purchase order acknowledgment and/or a purchase order acceptance form to agree to ship the specific quantity on the specific shipment date at the specific price. The seller will continue to provide pro forma invoices if they are necessary for the buyer to obtain a foreign exchange license to make payment, as well as a commercial invoice against which the buyer must make payment.

In summary, where the seller and the buyer wish to enter into a longer-term agreement, they will define their overall relationship in an umbrella agreement, but the usual documentation utilized in isolated sales transactions will also be utilized to set specific quantities, prices, and shipment dates. Sometimes conflicts can arise between the terms and conditions in the umbrella agreement and the specific documentation. Usually the parties provide that in such cases, the umbrella agreement will control, but this can also lead to problems in situations where the parties wish to vary the terms of their umbrella agreement for a specific transaction.

2.   *Important Provisions in International Sales Agreements*

There are numerous terms and conditions in an international sales agreement that require special consideration different from the usual terms and conditions in a domestic sales agreement. Unfortunately, sometimes sellers simply utilize sales documentation that was developed for U.S. domestic sales, only to discover that it is woefully inadequate for international sales. A simple sample international sales agreement (export) is included as Appendix B.

a. Selling and Purchasing Entities. In entering into an international sales agreement, it is important to think about who the seller and buyer will be. For example, rather than the U.S. company acting as the seller in the international sales agreement, it may wish to structure another company as the seller, primarily for potential tax savings. There are two main structures available to take advantage of such tax savings: the commission agent structure and the buy-sell structure. In the commission agent structure, the exporter will incorporate another company (in the United States or abroad, depending upon the tax incentive being utilized) and pay that company a commission on its export sales (which is, of course, a payment to a related company). In the buy-sell structure, an exporter would sell and transfer title to a related company that it sets up (in the United States or abroad), and the related company would act as the seller for export sales in the international sales agreement. If the exporter is not manufacturing products but is instead buying from an unrelated manufacturing company and reselling to unrelated companies, such activities sometimes can be more profitably conducted if the company incorporates a subsidiary in a low-tax jurisdiction, such as the Cayman Islands or Hong Kong.

If the seller and the buyer are related entities, such as a parent and subsidiary corporation, the foreign customs treatment may be different, for example, in the valuation of the merchandise or the assessment of duties. Some transactions may be structured to involve the use of a trading company, either on the exporting side, the importing side, or both. Depending upon whether the trading company takes title or is appointed as the agent (of either the buyer or the seller), or whether the trading company is related to the seller or the buyer, the foreign customs treatment may be different. For example, commissions paid to the seller's agent are ordinarily subject to customs duties in the foreign country, but commissions paid to the buyer's agent are not.

b. Quantity. The quantity term is even more important than the price. Under U.S. law, if the parties have agreed on the quantity, the sales agreement is enforceable even if the parties have not agreed on price—a current, or market, price will be implied. When no quantity has been agreed upon, however, the sales agreement will not be enforceable.

One reason for creating a formal sales agreement is for the buyer to obtain a lower price by committing to purchase a large quantity, usually over a year or more. The seller may be willing to grant a lower price in return for the ability to plan ahead, schedule production and inventory, develop economies of scale, and reduce shipping and administrative costs. The seller should be aware that price discounts for quantity purchases may violate some countries' price discrimination laws, unless the amount of the discount can be directly related to the cost savings of the seller for that particular quantity.

Quantity agreements can be for a specific quantity or a target quantity. Generally, if the commitment is a target only, failure to actually purchase such amount will not justify the seller in claiming damages or terminating the agreement (although sometimes the buyer will agree to a retroactive price increase). Failure to purchase a minimum purchase quantity, however, will justify termination and a claim for breach.

Sometimes the buyer may wish to buy the seller's entire output or the seller may seek a commitment that the buyer will purchase all of its requirements for the merchandise from the seller. Usually such agreements are lawful, but in certain circumstances they can violate the antitrust laws, such as when the seller is the only supplier or represents a large amount of the supply, or the buyer is the only buyer or represents a large segment of the market.

c. Pricing. There are a number of considerations in formulating the seller's pricing policy for international sales agreements. In addition to the importance of using a costing sheet to identify all additional costs of exporting to make sure that the price quoted to a customer results in a net profit acceptable to the seller (see Section A.4.c), the seller has to be aware of several constraints in formulating its pricing policy.

The first constraint relates to dumping. Many countries of the world are parties to the GATT Antidumping Code or have domestic legislation that prohibits "dumping" of foreign products in their country. This generally means that the price at which products are sold for export to their country cannot be lower than the price at which such products are sold in the United States. The basis for this protective action is that by dumping products cheaply into new markets, a seller can establish themselves into the market while causing injury to domestic competitors. The mere fact that sales are made at lower prices for export does not automatically mean that a dumping investigation will be initiated or that a dumping finding will occur. Under the laws of most countries, no dumping will occur if the price to that market is above that country's current market price, even if the seller's price to that country is lower than its sales price in its own country. (See more information on antidumping in Chapter 6.)

On the other hand, there are essentially no U.S. legal constraints on the extent to which a price quoted for export can exceed the price for sale in the United States. The antitrust laws in the United States (in particular the price discrimination provisions of the Robinson-Patman Act) apply only when sales are being made in the United States. Consequently, a seller may charge a higher or lower price for export without violating U.S. law. However, if the seller is selling to two or more customers in the same foreign country at different prices, such sales may violate the price discrimination provisions of the destination country's law.

If the price is below the seller's total cost of production, there is always a risk that such sales will be attacked as predatory pricing in violation of the foreign country's antitrust laws. The accounting calculation of cost is always a subject of dispute, particularly where the seller may feel that the costs of domestic advertising or other costs should not be allocated to export sales. However, in general, any sales below total, fully allocated costs are at risk.

Another very important pricing area relates to rebates, discounts, allowances, and price escalation clauses. Sometimes the buyer will ask for and the seller will be willing to grant some form of rebate, discount, or allowance under certain circumstances, such as the purchase of large quantities of merchandise. Such price concessions generally do not, in and of themselves, violate U.S. or foreign law, but if such payments are not disclosed to the proper government authorities, both the U.S. exporter and the foreign buyer can violate various laws, and the U.S. exporter also may be charged with conspiracy to violate, or aiding and abetting the buyer's violation of those laws. For example, the U.S. exporter must file the Electronic Export Information form on most export shipments (see discussion in Chapter 4, Section T), and must declare the price at which the goods are being sold. If, in fact, this price is false (because the exporter has agreed to grant some rebate, discount, or allowance, or, in fact, does so), the U.S. exporter will violate U.S. law and be subject to civil and criminal penalties. Similarly, when the buyer imports the goods to the destination country, the buyer will be required to state a value for customs and foreign exchange control purposes in its country and will receive U.S. dollars through the central bank to pay for the goods and must pay customs duties on the value declared. In addition, the buyer will probably use that value to show a deduction from its sales or revenues as a cost of goods sold, that is, as a tax deduction. Consequently, the true prices must be used. If the buyer requests the seller to provide two invoices for different amounts or if the buyer asks the seller to pay the rebate, discount, or allowance outside of its own country (for example, by deposit in a bank account in the United States, Switzerland, or some other country), there is considerable risk that the intended action of the buyer will violate the buyer's foreign exchange control laws, tax laws, and/or customs laws. If the seller cooperates by providing any such documentation or is aware of the scheme, the seller can also be charged with conspiracy to violate those foreign laws and can risk fines, arrest, and imprisonment in those countries. Similarly, retroactive price increases (for example, due to currency fluctuations) or price increases or decreases under escalation clauses may cause a change in the final price that may have to be reported to the customs, foreign exchange, or tax authorities. Before agreeing to grant any price rebate, discount, or allowance, or before agreeing to use a price escalation clause, or to implement a retroactive price increase or decrease, or to make any payment to the buyer in any place except the buyer's own country, the seller should satisfy itself that its actions will not result in the violation of any U.S. or foreign law.

If the sale is to an affiliated company, such as a foreign distribution or manufacturing subsidiary, additional pricing considerations arise. Because the buyer and seller are related, pricing can be artificially manipulated. For example, a U.S. exporter that is taxable on its U.S. manufacturing and sales profits at a rate of 35 percent when selling to an affiliated purchaser in a country that has a higher tax rate may attempt to minimize taxes in the foreign country by charging a high price to its foreign affiliate. Then, when the foreign affiliate resells the product, its profit will be small. Or, if the foreign affiliate uses the product in its manufacturing operation, the deduction for cost of materials will be high, thereby reducing the profits taxable in that country. When the sale is to a country where the tax rate is lower than in the United States, the considerations are reversed and the transfer price is set at a low rate, in which case the U.S. profits will be low. These strategies are well known to the tax authorities in foreign countries and to the Internal Revenue Service in the United States. Consequently, sales between affiliated companies are always susceptible to attack by the tax authorities. In general, the tax authorities in both countries will require that the seller sell to its affiliated buyer at an arm's-length price, as if it were selling to an unaffiliated buyer. Often, preserving evidence that the seller was selling to its unaffiliated customers at the same price as its affiliated customers will be very important in defending a tax audit. When the U.S. seller is selling to an affiliated buyer in a country with a lower tax rate, the customs authorities in the foreign country will also be suspicious that the transfer price is undervalued, and, therefore, customs duties may be underpaid.

Another consideration in the pricing of goods for export concerns parallel imports or gray market goods. If buyers in one country (including the United States) are able to purchase at a lower price than buyers in another country, an economic incentive will exist for customers in the lower-price country to divert such goods to the higher-price country in hopes of making a profit. Obviously, the seller's distributor in the higher-price country will complain about such unauthorized imports and loss of sales. The laws of many countries, however, such as the European Community (EC) and Japan, encourage such parallel imports as a means of encouraging competition and forcing the authorized distributor to reduce its price. In the EC, attempts to prohibit a distributor from selling outside of its country (but within the EC) can violate the law. Unfortunately, maintaining pricing parity is not always easy because of floating exchange rates, not only between the United States and other countries, but among those other countries.

d. Currency Fluctuations. Related to the issue of pricing is the potential for currency fluctuations that occur between the markets of the seller and the buyer and for using those fluctuations to your advantage. If the U.S. exporter quotes and sells only in U.S. dollars, the fluctuation of the foreign currency will not affect the final U.S. dollar amount that the exporter receives as payment. However, if the buyer is a much larger company than the seller and has more negotiating and bargaining leverage, or if the seller is anxious to make the sale, it may be necessary to agree to a sale denominated in foreign currency, such as Japanese yen or European euros. In such a case, if the foreign currency weakens between the time of the price agreement and the time of payment, the U.S. exporter will receive fewer U.S. dollars than it had anticipated when it quoted the price and calculated the expected profit. In such a case, the exporter is assuming the foreign exchange fluctuation risk. Sometimes, when the term of the agreement is long, or when major currency fluctuations are anticipated, neither the seller nor the buyer is comfortable in entirely assuming such risk. Consequently, they may agree to some sharing of the risk, such as a 50/50 price adjustment for changes due to any exchange fluctuations that occur during the life of the agreement, or some other formula that attempts to protect both sides against such fluctuations.

e. Payment Methods. In a domestic sales transaction, the seller may be used to selling on open account, extending credit, or asking for cash on delivery. In international agreements, it is more customary to utilize certain methods of payment that are designed to give the seller a greater level of protection. The idea is that if the buyer fails to pay, it is much more difficult for a seller to go to a foreign country, institute a lawsuit, attempt to attach the buyer's assets, or otherwise obtain payment. When sellers are dealing with buyers who are essentially unknown to them, with whom they have no prior payment experience, or who are small or located in countries where there is significant political upheaval or changing economic circumstances, the seller may insist that the buyer pay by cash in advance. This is particularly important if the sale is of specially manufactured goods. Where a seller wants to give the buyer some credit but also to have security of payment, the seller often requires the buyer to obtain a documentary letter of credit from a bank in the buyer's country. The seller may also require that the letter of credit be confirmed by a bank in the seller's country, which guarantees payment by the buyer's bank. The seller may still sell on terms with payment to be made at the time of shipment, or the seller may give the buyer some period of time (for example, from 30 days to 180 days) to make payment, but the letter of credit acts as an umbrella obligation of the bank guaranteeing the buyer's payment. In some cases, however, the buyer will be unable to obtain a letter of credit, for example, because the buyer's bank does not feel comfortable with the buyer's financial solvency.

Furthermore, issuance of letters of credit involves the payment of bank fees, which are normally paid for by the buyer, and the buyer usually does not wish to incur such expenses in addition to the cost of purchasing the goods. In such cases, particularly if the seller is anxious to make the sale or if other competitors are willing to offer more liberal payment terms, the seller may be forced to give up a letter of credit and agree to make the sale on some other, less secure, method of payment.

The next best method of payment is by sight draft documentary collection, commonly known as documents against payment or D/P transactions. In this case, the exporter uses the services of a bank to effect collection, but neither the buyer's bank nor a U.S. bank guarantees payment by the buyer. The seller will ship the goods, and the bill of lading and a draft (that is, a document like a check in the amount of the sale drawn on the buyer—rather than a bank—and payable to the seller) will be forwarded to the seller's bank. The seller's bank will forward such documents to a correspondent bank in the foreign country (sometimes the seller or its freight forwarder sends the documents directly to the foreign bank—this is known as direct collection), and the foreign bank will collect payment from the buyer prior to the time that the goods arrive. If payment is not made by the buyer, the correspondent bank does not release the bill of lading to the buyer, and the buyer will be unable to take possession of the goods or clear customs. Although it can still be a significant problem for the seller if the buyer does not make payment and the shipment has already gone, the seller should still be able to control the goods upon arrival, for example, by asking the bank to place them in a warehouse or by requesting that they be shipped to a third country or back to the United States at the seller's expense. Direct collections are often used for air shipments to avoid delays through the seller's bank and, also, because air waybills are non-negotiable.

The next least secure payment method is to utilize a time draft, commonly known as documents against acceptance or D/A transactions. Like the sight draft transaction, the bill of lading and time draft are forwarded through banking channels, but the buyer agrees to make payment within a certain number of days (for example, 30 to 180) after she receives and accepts the draft. Normally, this permits the buyer to obtain possession of the goods and may give the buyer enough time to resell them before her obligation to pay comes due. However, documents against acceptance transactions are a significantly greater risk for the seller because, if the buyer does not pay at the promised time, the seller's only recourse is to file a lawsuit—the goods have already been released to the buyer. Where the buyer is financially strong, sometimes such acceptances can be discounted by the seller, however, permitting the seller to get immediate payment but giving the buyer additional time to pay. This discounting may be done with recourse or without recourse depending upon the size of the discount the seller is willing to accept. There may also be an interest charge to the buyer for the delay in payment, which the seller may decide to waive in order to make the sale. The buyer's bank may also agree to add its "aval." This process is primarily used in European banks where the buyer has a strong credit rating. This then becomes a bank guaranty of payment equivalent to a letter of credit.

The least secure payment method is sale on open account, where the seller makes the sale and the shipment by forwarding the bill of lading and a commercial invoice directly to the buyer for payment. Because the bill of lading is sent directly to the buyer, once it leaves the possession of the seller, the seller will be unable to control what happens to the goods and the buyer will be able to obtain the goods whether or not payment is made. When a seller agrees to sell on open account, it must look to an alternative method, for example, a security interest under foreign law (see subsection g, below), to protect its right to payment in case the buyer fails to pay at the agreed time. For this method of payment and for documents against acceptance, the seller should definitely consider obtaining commercial risk insurance through the Foreign Credit Insurance Association (see Chapter 2, Section T).

Another type of letter of credit transaction that adds security is the standby letter of credit. If a buyer opens a standby letter of credit in favor of the seller, invoices, bills of lading, and similar documentation are forwarded directly to the buyer without using a bank for collection, but the issuing bank's guaranty is there in case of default by the buyer.

Sometimes a seller will begin selling to a particular customer under letters of credit, but as the seller becomes more familiar with the customer (the customer honors its obligations, increases its purchases, or enters into an ongoing sales agreement), the seller will be willing to liberalize its payment terms.

In addition, in international transactions, the seller will have to consider alternative payment methods, such as wire transfers via banking channels, since payment by check will often involve an inordinate length of time if the check is first sent to the seller in the United States and then sent back to the foreign country to be collected from the buyer's bank. Direct telegraphic transfer from bank account to bank account is a highly efficient and useful way to deal with international payments. However, buyers may be unwilling to wire the money to the seller until they are satisfied that the goods have been sent or until after arrival and inspection. Other methods of payment, such as cash payments made by employees traveling from the buyer to the seller or vice versa, or payments made in third countries, all carry the risk of violating the buyer's foreign exchange control, tax, and/or customs laws, and should be agreed to only after detailed investigation of the possible risks. A chart comparing these various methods of payment is shown in Figure 3–10.

Another method of payment that may arise in international sales is countertrade. Countertrade describes a variety of practices, such as barter (an exchange of goods), counter-purchase (where the seller must agree to purchase a certain amount from the buyer or from another seller in the buyer's country), or offset (where the seller must reinvest some of the sales profits in the buyer's country). The risks and complications of such sales are higher. Sometimes, of course, the seller may have to agree to such arrangements in order to get the business, but specialized sales agreements adequately addressing many additional concerns must be utilized. Countertrade is further discussed in Chapter 12, Section D.

Finally, an additional method of obtaining payment is the factoring of export accounts receivable. "Factoring" is when a business sells its accounts receivables to a third party known as the "factor." Essentially, the factor advances the company 75-80 percent of the money the company is owed by its customers. While many banks and some factors are reluctant to accept receivables on foreign sales due to the greater risks and uncertainties of collection, other factors are willing to do so. This may represent an opportunity for an exporter to obtain its money immediately in return for accepting a lesser amount, some discount from the sales price. If the factor buys the accounts receivable with recourse, that is, the right to charge back or get back the money paid to the exporter in case of default in payment by the customer, the factor's charge or discount should be correspondingly lower.

f.   Export Financing. The substantive aspects of export financing were discussed in Chapter 2, Section T. If export financing is going to be utilized, it should be discussed in the international sales agreement.

The buyer will thus be clearly aware that the seller intends to use such export financing. The documentation that the buyer is required to provide in order for the seller to obtain such financing should be specified in the agreement, and the seller's obligation to sell and make shipment at specific dates should be subject to obtaining such export financing in a timely manner.

g.   Security Interest. If the seller intends to sell on open account or on documents against acceptance, the seller should carefully investigate obtaining a security interest under the law of the buyer's country to protect its rights to payment. Under the laws of most countries, unless the seller has registered its lien or security interest with a public agency, if the buyer goes into bankruptcy or falls into financial difficulties, the seller will be unable to repossess the merchandise that it sold, even if the merchandise

Figure 3-10. International credit terms/payment methods.

FIRST CHICAGO

INTERNATIONAL CREDIT TERMS/PAYMENT METHODS

TERM	DEFINITION	APPLICATION	ADVANTAGES	DISADVANTAGES
Open Account	Exporter makes shipment and awaits payment direct from importer. Any documents needed by importer sent when sale is invoiced.	1. Importer has excellent credit rating. 2. Importer is long-time, well-known customer. 3. Importer is subsidiary of exporter or vice versa. 4. Small shipments to good customers. 5. Low-risk country.	1. Simple bookkeeping for exporter. 2. Easy documentation. 3. Competitive. 4. Low cost. 5. May be insured.	1. Full brunt of financing falls on exporter. 2. In matters of dispute, no interested third party involved. 3. Problems of availability of foreign exchange. 4. Exporter assumes credit risk of importer and risk of importer's country's political condition.
Consignment or Extended Terms	Exporter makes shipment and receives payment as goods are sold or used by importer.	1. Normally used only between subsidiaries of the same company. 2. Promissory notes may be used along with trust receipts and other legal agreements.	1. Exporter may retain title until goods are sold and/or paid for. 2. Competitive.	1. Same as Open Account. 2. Subject to local laws and customs. 3. Requires periodic inventorying of goods.
Time or Date Draft, Documents against Acceptance (D/A)	Exporter makes shipment and presents draft and documents to bank with instructions that documents are to be released to importer upon importer's acceptance of the draft (importer's acknowledgment of his debt and promise to pay at a future date).	1. Importer has excellent and/or good credit rating. 2. Low-risk country. 3. Extended terms necessary to make sale.	1. Draft is evidence of indebtedness. 2. Receivable may be discountable by exporter's bank with or without recourse. 3. Gives importer time to sell goods before having to pay for them. 4. Interested third party involved in case of dispute (bank). 5. Low cost. 6. May be insured.	1. Exporter is financing shipment until maturity of draft. 2. Problems of availability of foreign exchange. 3. Exporter assumes credit risk of importer and risk of importer's country's political condition. 4. Exporter assumes risk of refused shipment.

Exporting: Sales Documentation

(continues)

87

Figure 3–10. (*continued*)

[*reverse*]

TERM	DEFINITION	APPLICATION	ADVANTAGES	DISADVANTAGES
Sight Draft, Documents against Payment (D/P), Cash against Documents	Exporter makes shipment and presents documents to bank with instructions that documents be released to importer only upon payment of draft.	1. Importer has excellent and/or good credit rating. 2. Small shipments. 3. Medium volume. 4. Low-risk country. 5. May be used in countries having foreign exchange restrictions not allowing open account purchases or sales.	1. Evidence of indebtedness. 2. Documents not released to importer before payment. (Exporter may retain title to merchandise until paid.) 3. Interested third party involved (bank). 4. Low cost. 5. May be insured.	1. Exporter must wait until draft has been received and paid. 2. Exporter assumes credit risk of importer and risk of importer's country's political condition. 3. Exporter assumes risk of refused shipment.
C.O.D.	Cash on delivery, collected by the carrier.	1. Importer's credit is excellent or good. 2. Small shipments. 3. Carrier accepts such shipments.	1. Exporter assured of payment before delivery of goods to importer by carrier.	1. Importer must have cash available. 2. Someone must pay C.O.D. charges. 3. Service not available to all countries. 4. Discourages repeat sales. 5. Exporter assumes risk of refused shipment.
Irrevocable L/C	Instrument issued by importer's bank in favor of exporter, payable against presentation to the issuing bank of specified documents.	1. Importer's credit rating may be excellent, good, fair, or unknown. 2. First-time sale. 3. Large sale. 4. Sale to country that requires L/Cs. 5. Low-risk country.	1. Exporter looks to bank for payment if documents are proper and in order. 2. Credit is irrevocable and may be amended only upon concurrence of all parties. 3. May be insured at preferred rate. 4. Banks may be willing to offer engagements to negotiate.	1. Cost of L/C. 2. Documents must be carefully prepared by exporter. 3. Exporter's credit risk is the foreign bank: foreign exchange and political risk still exist. 4. Importer exposed to possibilities of fraud.
Confirmed Irrevocable Letter of Credit	Same as above, except importer's bank asks advising bank to add its confirmation. Payable upon presentation of documents to the advising/confirming bank.	1. Importer's credit rating may be excellent, good, fair, or unknown. 2. First-time sale. 3. Large sale. 4. Country that requires L/Cs. 5. High-risk country.	1. Exporter looks to confirming bank for payment immediately upon shipment if documents are proper. 2. Credit is irrevocable and may be amended only upon concurrence of all parties. 3. Exporter's credit risk is confirming bank; confirming bank takes credit of issuing bank.	1. Cost of L/C. 2. Documents must be carefully prepared by exporter. 3. Importer exposed to possibility of fraud.
Cash in Advance	Importer sends good funds before exporter ships.	1. Importer is good, fair, or unknown credit risk. 2. One-time sale. 3. Small shipment. 4. High-risk country.	1. Exporter may use funds to prepare shipment. 2. No risk to exporter. 3. Low cost.	1. Importer bears costs of financing as well as risk of never receiving goods. 2. Uncompetitive; may preclude repeat business. 3. Some countries prohibit payment in advance.

88

is still in the possession of the buyer. Also, the seller may be unable to obtain priority over other creditors, and after such creditors are paid, nothing may remain for the seller. For example, through an attorney, the seller should investigate the availability of a security interest in the buyer's country and the requirements for establishing a security interest. The seller may need to retain title or a chattel mortgage or make a conditional sale. Then, in the international sales agreement, the fact that the buyer is granting a security interest to the seller and the documents that will be furnished by the buyer for public registration should be discussed and specified. The security interest normally should be established, including public registration, prior to delivery to the buyer, whether such transfer occurs in the United States (for example, ex-factory sales) or in the foreign country (for example, landed sales). The attorney would conduct a search of the public records in the buyer's country, and if other security interests have been granted, the seller should require the buyer to obtain a written subordination agreement from the other creditors before going forward.

h. *Passage of Title, Delivery, and Risk of Loss.* Ownership is transferred from the seller to the buyer by the passage of title. Under U.S. law, title will pass at the time and place agreed to by the parties to the international sales agreement. It can pass at the seller's plant; at the port of export; upon arrival in the foreign country; after clearance of customs in the foreign country; upon arrival at the buyer's place of business; or at any other place, time, or manner agreed to by the parties. Under the new Convention on the International Sale of Goods (discussed in subsection m), if the parties do not agree on the time and place for transfer of title and delivery, title will pass when the merchandise is transferred to the first transportation carrier. Usually the risk of loss for any subsequent casualty or damage to the products will pass to the buyer at the same time the title passes. However, it is possible to specify in the sales agreement that it will pass at a different time. Up to the point where the risk of loss passes to the buyer, the seller should be sure that the shipment is insured against casualty loss.

i. *Warranties and Product Defects.* From the seller's point of view, next to the payment provision, perhaps the most important single provision in an international sales agreement is the one that specifies the warranty terms. Under the laws of most countries and the Convention on Contracts for the International Sale of Goods (discussed in subsection m), unless the seller limits its warranty expressly in writing in its international sales agreement, the seller will be responsible and liable for foreseeable consequential damages that result to the buyer from defective products. Since such consequential damages can far exceed the profits that the seller has made on such sales, unless the seller expressly limits its liabilities, the risk of engaging in the sales transaction can be too great. The sales agreement should specify exactly what warranty the seller is giving for the products, whether the products are being sold "as is" with no warranty, whether there is a limited warranty such as repair or replacement, whether there is a dollar limit on the warranty, whether there is a time period within which the warranty claim must be made, and/or whether there is any limitation on consequential damages. In many countries, as a matter of public policy, the law prohibits certain types of warranty disclaimers or exclusions. Consequently, in drafting the warranty limitation, the seller may need to consult with an attorney to make sure that the warranty will be effective in the destination country. In addition, of course, the buyer will be seeking the strongest warranty possible, so this is an area in which the seller must be particularly careful. If the sales agreement is formed by a mere exchange of preprinted forms, as discussed in Section A.4 above, the seller may find that the buyer's terms or conditions control the sale and that no limitation of warranty has been achieved. In such cases, the seller must negotiate a warranty acceptable to both sides before going ahead with the sale. One related point is that the Magnuson-Moss Warranty Act, which prescribes certain warranties and is applicable to merchandise sold in the United States, including imported merchandise, is not applicable to export sales. However, laws in the foreign country may be applicable.

j. Preshipment Inspections. A number of countries, particularly in South America and Africa (see list in Chapter 4, Section G), require that before companies located in their country purchase products from a foreign seller, the foreign seller submit to a preshipment inspection. The ostensible purpose of such inspections is to eliminate a situation where a dishonest seller ships defective products or even crates of sawdust, but obtains payment through a letter of credit or banking channels because the seller has provided a fraudulent bill of lading and draft to the bank, and the buyer has not yet been able to inspect the goods. Even if the buyer has not paid in advance, if the products arrive in the foreign country and are defective, the buyer may be faced with substantial losses or the necessity of re-exporting the merchandise to the seller. Consequently, it is not unreasonable for a buyer to request and for a seller to agree to a preshipment inspection, but the terms and conditions of such an inspection should be specified in the international sales agreement. In particular, in recent years, some of the inspection agencies have been reviewing more than the quality of the goods and have been requiring sellers to produce documentation relating to sales of the same product to other customers to ascertain the prices at which sales were made. If the particular customer that is getting the preshipment inspection determines that the price that it is paying is higher than the prices that the seller has charged other customers, the customer may refuse to go forward with the transaction or attempt to renegotiate the price. Consequently, in an international sales agreement, if the seller simply agrees to a preshipment inspection satisfactory to the buyer, the inspection company's report may be an unfavorable one based upon price, and the buyer would be excused from going forward with the purchase. In summary, the type of preshipment inspection that will be permitted, its scope, its terms, and the consequences if the inspection is unfavorable should be specified in the international sales agreement.

The seller (and buyer) should also realize that providing for a preshipment inspection will usually delay the shipment anywhere from twenty to forty days.

k. Export Licenses. The importance of an export license was touched upon in Chapter 2, Section F, and is discussed in detail in Chapter 5. If an export license will be required in an international sales agreement, the exporter should state that it is required and should require the buyer to provide the necessary documentation to apply for the license. If the buyer fails to provide such documentation, the seller would be excused from making the export sale and could claim damages. Furthermore, in order to protect the seller from a violation of U.S. export control laws, the international sales agreement and the provisions therein relating to any export license would be evidence that the seller had fulfilled its responsibilities to inform the buyer that the products cannot be re-exported from the buyer's own country without obtaining a re-export license from the U.S. authorities. Finally, the sales agreement should provide that if the seller cannot obtain the export license, the seller's performance of the sales agreement will be excused without the payment of damages to the buyer. (Under the Incoterms®, the buyer is responsible for obtaining the export license on "ex-works" sales, but U.S. law makes the seller responsible unless the buyer has specifically agreed to such responsibility in writing and has appointed a U.S. agent.)

l. Import Licenses and Foreign Government Filings. An international sales agreement should specify that the buyer will be responsible for obtaining all necessary import licenses and making any foreign government filings. The buyer should state exactly what licenses must be obtained and what filings must be made. The sales agreement should specify that the buyer will obtain such licenses sufficiently in advance, for example, prior to manufacture or shipment, so that the seller can be comfortable that payment will be forthcoming. In regard to the applications for such licenses or any foreign government filings, the exporter should insist upon and should obligate the buyer in the international sales agreement to provide copies of those applications prior to their filing. In this way, the seller can confirm that the information in the application is correct; for example, that the prices being stated to the government agencies are the same as those that the seller is quoting to the buyer, or if there is any reference to the seller in the applications, that the seller will know what is being said about it. This will also permit the seller to know the exact time when such applications are being made and, therefore, whether the approval will delay or interfere with the anticipated sales shipment and payment schedule.

    m. *Governing Law.* In any international sales agreement, whether the agreement is formed by a written agreement between the parties or whether it is an oral agreement, the rights and obligations of the parties will be governed by either the law of the country of the seller or the law of the country of the buyer. The laws of most countries permit the seller and buyer to specifically agree on which law will apply, and that choice will be binding upon both parties whether or not a lawsuit is brought in either the buyer's or the seller's country. Of course, whenever the subject is raised, the seller will prefer the agreement to be governed by the laws of the seller's country, and the buyer will prefer it to be governed by the laws of the buyer's country. If the bargaining leverage of the parties is approximately equal, it is fair to say that it is more customary for the buyer to agree that the seller's law will govern the agreement. However, if the buyer has more bargaining leverage, the seller may have to agree that the buyer's foreign law applies. Before doing so, however, the seller should check on what differences exist between the foreign law and U.S. law so that the seller can fully appreciate the risks it is assuming by agreeing to the application of foreign law. The seller can also determine whether or not the risk is serious enough to negotiate a specific solution to that particular problem with the buyer. Frequently, however, the parties do not raise, negotiate, or expressly agree upon the governing law. This may occur as a result of an exchange of preprinted forms wherein the buyer and seller have each specified that its own law governs, which results in a clear conflict between these two provisions. It may also occur when the parties have not agreed upon the governing law, as in a situation where an oral agreement of sale has occurred, or when the email or other purchase or sale documentation does not contain any express specification of the governing law. In such cases, if a dispute arises between the parties, it will be extremely difficult to determine with any confidence which law governs the sales agreement. Often the seller believes that the law of the country where the offer is accepted will govern. However, the laws of the two countries may be in conflict on this point, and it may be unclear whether this means an offer to sell or an offer to buy and whether or not the acceptance must be received by the offeror before the formation of the sales agreement.

    An additional development relating to this issue is the Convention on Contracts for the International Sale of Goods (the Convention). On January 1, 1988, this multinational treaty went into effect among the countries that signed it, including the United States. Figure 3-11 shows the parties to the Convention as of January 2014.

Figure 3–11. Parties to the Convention on CISG.

Parties to the Convention on Contracts for the International Sale of Goods
(as of January 10, 2014)

Albania	Finland	Montenegro
Argentina	France	Netherlands
Armenia	Gabon	New Zealand
Australia	Georgia	Paraguay
Austria	Germany	Peru
Bahrain	Ghana	Poland
Belarus	Greece	Romania
Belgium	Guinea	Russian Federation
Benin	Honduras	Saint Vincent & Grenadines
Bosnia-Herzegovina	Hungary	San Marino
Brazil	Iceland	Serbia
Bulgaria	Iraq	Singapore
Burundi	Israel	Slovakia
Canada	Italy	Slovenia
Chile	Japan	South Korea
China (PRC)	Kyrgyzstan	Spain
Colombia	Latvia	Sweden
Croatia	Lebanon	Switzerland
Cuba	Lesotho	Syria
Cyprus	Liberia	Turkey
Czech Republic	Lithuania	Uganda
Denmark	Luxembourg	Ukraine
Dominican Republic	Macedonia	United States
Ecuador	Mauritania	Uruguay
Egypt	Mexico	Uzbekistan
El Salvador	Moldova	Venezuela
Estonia	Mongolia	Zambia

Notable absences are Hong Kong, India, South Africa, Taiwan and the United Kingdom. Many countries have taken reservations to certain provisions. For more information see: http://www.newyorkconvention.org/uncitral.

The Convention is a detailed listing of over one hundred articles dealing with the rights and responsibilities of the buyer and the seller in international sales agreements. It is similar in some respects to Article 2 of the Uniform Commercial Code in the United States. Nevertheless, there are many concepts, such as fundamental breach, avoidance, impediment, and nonconformity that are not identical to U.S. law.

The Convention permits buyers and sellers located in countries that are parties to the Convention to exclude the application of the Convention (by expressly referring to it) and to choose the law of either the seller or the buyer to apply to the international sales agreement. However, for companies located in any of the countries that are parties to the convention (including U.S. companies), if the seller and buyer cannot or do not agree on which law will apply, the provisions of the Convention will automatically apply. In general, this may be disadvantageous for the U.S. seller because the Convention strengthens the rights of buyers in various ways.

In summary, the seller should include provisions on governing law in its international sales agreement, and if the buyer disagrees, the seller should negotiate this provision. The seller should also determine what differences exist between the Convention and U.S. law in case the parties cannot agree and the Convention thereby becomes applicable.

n. *Dispute Resolution.* One method of resolving disputes that may arise between the parties is litigation in the courts. For a U.S. exporter, the most likely dispute to arise is the failure of the buyer to make payment. In such a case, the exporter may be limited to going to the courts of the buyer's country in order to institute litigation and seek a judgment to obtain assets of the buyer. Even if the parties have agreed that U.S. law will govern the sales agreement, there is a risk that a foreign court may misapply U.S. law, disregard U.S. law, or otherwise favor and protect the company located in its own country. Furthermore, there can be significant delays in legal proceedings (from two to five years), court and legal expenses can be high, and the outcome may be unsatisfactory. In order to reduce such risks, the exporter can specify in the international sales agreement that all disputes must be resolved in the courts of the seller's country, and that the buyer consents to jurisdiction there, and to the commencement of any such lawsuit by the simple forwarding of any form of written notice by the seller. Of course, buyers may resist such provisions, and whether or not the seller will be able to finally obtain this agreement will depend upon the negotiating and bargaining strength of the parties. The seller does need to realize that even if it obtains a judgment in the United States, if the buyer has no assets in the United States, its judgment may be of limited value.

Another form of dispute resolution that is common in international sales agreements is arbitration. In many foreign countries, buyers take a less adversarial approach to the resolution of contractual disputes, and they feel more comfortable with a less formal proceeding, such as arbitration. While arbitration can be included in an international sales agreement, an exporter should thoroughly understand the advantages and disadvantages of agreeing to resolve disputes by arbitration.

First, arbitration is unlikely to save much in expenses, and quite often may not involve a significantly shorter time period to resolve the dispute. In fact, from the point of view of expense, in some cases, if the buyer refuses to go forward with the arbitration, the seller will have to advance the buyer's portion of the arbitration fees to the arbitration tribunal; otherwise, the arbitrators will not proceed with the dispute. Furthermore, in litigation, of course, the judges or juries involved are paid at the public expense, whereas in arbitration, the parties must pay the expenses of the arbitrators, which can be very substantial.

Second, the administering authority must be selected. The International Chamber of Commerce is commonly designated as the administering authority in arbitration clauses, but the fees it charges are very high. The American Arbitration Association also handles international disputes, but the foreign buyer may be unwilling to agree to arbitration by a U.S. administering authority. Other administering authorities, such as the Inter-American Commercial Arbitration Commission, the London Court of International Arbitration, the Stockholm Chamber of Commerce Arbitration Institute, the British Columbia International Arbitration Centre, or an arbitration authority in the buyer's country, may be acceptable.

Third, the number of arbitrators should be specified. Since the parties will be paying for them, the author recommends that one arbitrator be utilized and specified in the agreement to resolve disputes of a smaller amount (a specified dollar figure) and those three arbitrators be utilized for larger disputes.

Fourth, the place of arbitration must be specified. Again, the seller and buyer will have a natural conflict on this point, so some third country or intermediate location is probably most likely to be mutually agreeable. Another variation that has developed, although its legal validity has been questioned, is an agreement that if the exporter commences the arbitration, arbitration will be conducted in the buyer's country, and if the buyer commences the arbitration, the arbitration will be conducted in the exporter's country. This has the effect of discouraging either party from bringing arbitration and forcing the parties to reach amicable solutions to their disputes.

Finally, the seller should ascertain beforehand whether an arbitral award would be enforced in the courts of the buyer's country. Over 150 countries have become parties to a multinational treaty known as the New York Convention, which commits them to enforcing the arbitral awards of other member countries. Without this assurance, the entire dispute may have to be relitigated in the buyer's country. See more information at: http://www.newyorkconvention.org/contracting-states/list-of-contracting-states.

o. Termination. Termination of an international sales agreement or distributor or sales agent agreement may prove to be much more difficult than termination of a domestic agreement. Many countries have enacted laws that as a matter of public policy are designed to protect buyers, distributors, and sales agents located in their country against unfair terminations. The rationale for these laws is generally that the U.S. seller has significant economic leverage by virtue of its position, and that after a buyer has invested a great deal of time in purchasing products or building up a market for resale of such products, the sellers should not be permitted to terminate the agreement on short notice or without payment of some compensation. Of course, such rationale may be totally inconsistent with the facts, such as when the seller is a small company or when the buyer is breaching the agreement. In any event, before engaging in an ongoing sales relationship with any customer in a foreign country or appointing a distributor or sales agent there, the seller should get specific legal advice and determine what protective legislation exists. Often, avoidance of such legislation or reduction in the amount of compensation that must be paid at the time of termination is highly dependent upon inserting in the international sales agreement at the outset certain specific provisions (which will vary from country to country) limiting the seller's termination liability. For example, the seller's right to terminate without any payment of compensation when the buyer is in breach should be specified. The right of the seller to appoint another distributor in the country and to require the former distributor to cooperate in transferring inventory to the new distributor and the right to terminate for change in control, bankruptcy, or insolvency of the buyer should be specified.

Related thereto is the term of the agreement. Often agreements will be set up for a one-year term with automatic renewal provisions. Such agreements are treated as long-term agreements or indefinite or perpetual agreements under some laws and can result in the payment of maximum termination compensation. The term of the agreement that will best protect the seller's flexibility and reduce the compensation payable should be inserted after review of the buyer's law.

C. Export Distributor and Sales Agent Agreements

In addition to the foregoing provisions, which arise in all international sales agreements, there are other, specific provisions that arise in export distributor agreements and sales agent agreements.

1. *Distinction Between Distributor and Sales Agent*

A distributor is a company that buys products from a seller, takes title thereto, and assumes the risk of resale. A distributor will purchase at a specific price and will be compensated by reselling the product at a higher price. Under the antitrust laws of most countries, the seller cannot restrict or require a distributor to resell the product at any specific price, although it may be able to restrict the customers or territories to which the buyer resells. A sales agent does not purchase from the seller. The sales agent or representative locates customers and solicits offers to purchase the product from them. In order to avoid tax liability for the seller in a foreign country, the sales agent normally will not have any authority to accept offers to purchase from potential customers in that country. Instead, the offers from the customer are forwarded to the seller for final acceptance, and shipment and billing is direct between the seller and the customer. For such services, the sales agent is paid a commission or some other type of compensation. Because no sale occurs between the seller and the sales agent, the seller can specify the price at which it will sell to customers, and the sales agent can be restricted to quoting only that price to a potential customer. Likewise, the sales agent can be restricted as to its territory or the types of customers from which it can solicit orders. Sometimes the sales agent will guarantee payment by the customers or perform other services, such as after-sales service or invoicing of the customers. A chart summarizing these differences is shown in Figure 3–12. The financial returns and accounting will differ when using a distributor versus a sales agent. The main reason is that the sales price will be direct to the customer, which will be higher than the sale price to a distributor. A comparison of these revenues and expenses is shown in Figure 3–13.

2. *Export Distributor Agreements*

As previously indicated, when a distributor agreement is utilized, such agreement will act as an umbrella agreement, and specific orders for specific quantities, shipment dates, and, possibly, prices will be stated in purchase orders, purchase order

Figure 3–12. Legal comparison of agents and distributors.

	Distributor	**Agent**
Compensation	Markup	Commission
Title	Owner	Not owner
Risk of loss	On distributor	On seller
Price control	Cannot control	Seller controls
Credit risk	On distributor	On seller
Tax liability in foreign country	On distributor	Potentially on seller if agent given authority to accept orders or if distributor maintains inventory for local delivery

Figure 3–13. Financial comparison of using distributors and sales agents.

Seller's Profit and Loss	**Distributor**	**Sales Agent**
Net sales	$2,000,000	$4,000,000
Gross profit	$1,000,000	$3,000,000
Commission (10%)		$400,000
Possible need to warehouse inventory in foreign country		$400,000
Advertising		$400,000
Customer service, after-sales service		$300,000
General, selling, and administrative	$200,000	$200,000
Operating income	$800,000	$900,000
Operating income/net sales	40%	22.5%

acceptances, and similar documentation. A checklist for negotiation issues for the appointment of a distributor is shown in Figure 3–14. The important provisions in an international distributor agreement include the following:

a. Territory and Exclusivity. The distributor will normally want to be the exclusive distributor in a territory, whereas the seller would generally prefer to make a nonexclusive appointment so that if the distributor fails to perform, it can appoint other distributors. Also, the seller may simply wish from the outset to appoint a number of distributors in that country to adequately serve the market. A possible compromise is that the appointment will be exclusive unless certain minimum purchase obligations are not met, in which case the seller has the right to convert the agreement to a nonexclusive agreement. Usually the country or part of the country that is granted to the distributor is specified. The distributor agrees not to solicit sales from outside the territory, although under the laws of some countries, it may not be possible to prohibit the distributor from reselling outside the territory. In such cases, the distributor may be prohibited from establishing any warehouse or sales outlet outside the territory.

b. Pricing. As previously indicated, normally it will be illegal to specify the price at which the foreign distributor can resell the merchandise. This may present some problems because the distributor may mark the product up very substantially, gouging end users and resulting in less sales and market penetration for the seller's products. Consequently, in some countries it is possible to restrict the maximum resale price but not the minimum resale price. In addition, because of the gray market problem, the price at which the seller sells to the distributor must be set very carefully. Depending on the price at which the distributor buys or whether or not the distributor can be legally prohibited from exporting, the distributor may resell products that will create a gray market in competition with the seller's other distributors or even the seller in its own markets. This can occur especially as a result of exchange rate fluctuations, where the distributor is able to obtain a product at a lower price in its own currency than is available in other markets where the product is being sold.

The seller must monitor currency fluctuations and retain the right to make price adjustments in the distributor agreement to make sure that the seller is fairly participating in the profits being created along the line of distribution. For example, if the U.S. seller sells a product for $1 at a time when the Japanese exchange rate is ¥250 to $1, the buyer will be paying ¥250 for the $1 product and perhaps marking it up to ¥400. However, if the yen strengthens and the buyer can purchase a $1 product by paying only ¥150, and if the buyer continues to resell at ¥400, the buyer will make inordinate profits. Sometimes the buyer will continue to ask for price reductions from

Figure 3–14. Foreign distributorship appointment checklist.

1. Appointment
   - (a) Appointment
   - (b) Acceptance
   - (c) Exclusivity
   - (d) Subdistributors
2. Territory
3. Products
4. Sales Activities
   - (a) Advertising (optional)
   - (b) Initial purchases (optional)
   - (c) Minimum purchases (optional)
   - (d) Sales increases (optional)
   - (e) Purchase orders
   - (f) Distributor's resale prices
   - (g) Direct shipment to customers
   - (h) Product specialist (optional)
   - (i) Installation and service
   - (j) Distributor facilities (optional)
   - (k) Visits to distributor premises
   - (l) Reports
   - (m) Financial condition
5. Prices
   - (a) Initial
   - (b) Changes
   - (c) Taxes
6. Acceptance of Orders and Shipment
   - (a) Acceptance
   - (b) Inconsistent terms in distributor's order
   - (c) Shipments
   - (d) No violation of U.S. laws
   - (e) Passage of title, risk of loss

(continues)

Figure 3–14. *(continued)*

---

7. Payments
   - (a) Terms
   - (b) Letter of credit
   - (c) Deposits
   - (d) Payments in dollars
   - (e) No set off by distributor
   - (f) Security interest
8. Confidential Information
9. Sales Literature
   - (a) Advertising literature
   - (b) Quantities
   - (c) Mailing lists
10. Patents, Trademarks, and Copyrights; Agency Registrations
11. No Warranty Against Infringement
12. No Consequential Damages
13. Product Warranty, Defects, Claims, Returns
14. Relationship Between Parties
15. Effective Date and Duration
    - (a) Effective date and term
    - (b) Early termination
      - (i) Breach
      - (ii) Insolvency
      - (iii) Prospective breach
      - (iv) Change in ownership or management
      - (v) Foreign protective law
      - (vi) Unilateral (reciprocal) on agreed notice (without cause)
16. Rights and Obligations Upon Termination
    - (a) No liability for seller
    - (b) Return of promotional materials
    - (c) Repurchase of stock
    - (d) Accrued rights and obligation

(continues)

Figure 3–14. *(continued)*

---

    17. Non-Competition

    18. No Assignment

    19. Government Regulation

        (a) Foreign law

        (b) U.S. export control laws

        (c) Foreign Corrupt Practices Act compliance

    20. Force Majeure

    21. Severability

    22. Waiver

    23. Notices

        (a) Written notice

        (b) Oral

---

the seller even though the buyer has had a very favorable exchange rate movement. Normally the seller's interest is that the buyer reduce the resale price (for example, to ¥250) in order to make more sales, increase volume, increase market penetration, and capture the long-term market. When the distributor will not agree to reduce its resale price, the price from the seller should be raised to make sure that part of the profits that the distributor is making on resales in its own country are recovered by the seller.

c. Minimum Purchase Quantities. In most long-term sales agreements or distributor agreements, one of the reasons for entering into such agreements is that the seller expects a commitment for a significant quantity to be purchased and the buyer is requesting some price discount for such a commitment. Consequently, before a seller agrees to give a distributor an exclusive appointment in a territory or to grant any price reductions, a provision relating to the minimum purchase quantities (which may be adjusted from time to time according to some objective formula or by agreement of the parties) should be inserted in the distributor agreement. Distributors will ordinarily be required to commit to using their best efforts to promote the sale of the merchandise in the territory, but since best efforts is a somewhat vague commitment, minimum purchase quantities (or dollar amounts) are important supplements to that commitment.

d. Handling Competing Products. Normally a seller will want a provision wherein the distributor agrees not to handle competing products. If the distributor is handling any competing products (either manufacturing them or purchasing them from alternative sources), it is likely that the distributor will not always promote the seller's products, especially if the buyer is getting larger markups or margins on the other products. In addition, if the seller grants an exclusive distribution right to the distributor, the seller has given up the opportunity to increase its sales by appointing more distributors in the territory. Under such circumstances, the distributor should definitely agree not to handle any competing products. In some countries, the distributor can be restricted from handling competing products only if an exclusive appointment is given by the seller.

 e. Effective Date and Government Review. In some countries it is necessary to file distributor or long-term sales agreements with government authorities. Sometimes there is a specific waiting period before the agreement can become effective or government review will be completed. In any event, the distributor agreement should provide that it does not become effective until government review is completed. If the distributor's government suggests changes to the agreement, for example, the elimination of minimum purchase quantities, the seller should have the opportunity to renegotiate the agreement or withdraw from the agreement without being bound to proceed. In that respect, the seller must be careful not to ship a large amount of inventory or accept a large initial order while government review is pending.

 f. Appointment of Subdistributors. Whether or not a distributor has the right to appoint subdistributors should be expressly stated in the distributor agreement. If this right is not discussed, the distributor may have the right under its own law to appoint subdistributors. This can cause various problems for the seller. Not only will the seller have no immediate direct contact with the subdistributors, but it may not even be aware of who such subdistributors are, their location, or the territories into which they are shipping. Soon the seller's products may show up in territories granted to other distributors or be imported back into the United States, or significant gray market sales or counterfeits may develop. If the right to appoint subdistributors is granted, the distributor should remain responsible for its activities, including payment for any goods sold to such subdistributors, and for providing the names of such subdistributors to the seller in advance so that the seller will have the opportunity to investigate the financial strength, creditworthiness, business reputation, and the restrictive persons lists of all persons who will be distributing its products.

 g. Use of Trade Names, Trademarks, and Copyrights. As discussed in Chapter 2, Section G, there are risks that the seller's intellectual property rights will be lost. Sometimes distributors are the biggest offenders. In an effort to protect their market position, they use the seller's name or trademark in their own business or corporate name or register the seller's intellectual property in their own country. This is a particular disadvantage for the seller, because if the distributor does not perform properly and the seller wishes to terminate the distributor and to appoint a new distributor, the past distributor may own the intellectual property rights or have a registered exclusive license to distribute the products in that country. Until the distributor consents to the assignment of the intellectual property rights to the seller or the new distributor or deregisters its exclusive license, any sales into the territory by the seller or by the new distributor will be an infringement of the intellectual property rights owned by the former distributor and cannot proceed. This puts the former distributor in a very strong bargaining position to negotiate a substantial termination compensation payment. Even when the distributor is granted an exclusive territory, the distributor agreement should provide that the distributor is granted a nonexclusive patent, trademark, and/ or copyright license to sell the products (but not to manufacture or cause others to manufacture the products), and should obligate the distributor to recognize the validity of the intellectual property rights and to take no steps to register them or to otherwise interfere with the ownership rights of the seller. Of course, the seller should register its intellectual property rights directly in the foreign country in its own name and not permit the distributor to do so on the seller's behalf or in the distributor's name.

h.   *Warranties and Product Liability.* In addition to the considerations discussed above, the seller should require the distributor to maintain product liability insurance in its own name and to name the seller as an additional insured in amounts that are deemed satisfactory by the seller. Although product liability claims are not as common overseas as they are in the United States, they are increasing substantially, and under most product liability laws, even though the distributor sold the product to the customer, the customer will have a right to sue the manufacturer (or supplier) directly. Furthermore, the fact that the manufacturer was aware that its product was being sold in that country will make it foreseeable that a defective product will be sold there and the U.S. manufacturer may be subject to the jurisdiction of the courts in that country. The seller should also make sure that the distributor does not modify or add any additional warranties in the resale of the product beyond those that the manufacturer or U.S. seller has given. Practically, this means that the distributor should be obligated to provide a copy of its warranty in advance of resale for approval by the seller. The distributor may also be authorized or required to perform after-sales service, but the seller will need an opportunity to audit the books and service records from time to time to prevent abuses and warranty compensation reimbursement claims by the distributor for service that has not actually been performed.

3. Export Sales Agent Agreements

Like distributor agreements, sales agent agreements often contain many of the same provisions included in an international sales agreement, but there are certain provisions that are peculiar to the sales agent agreement that must be considered. A checklist for negotiation issues for the appointment of a sales agent is shown in Figure 3–15.

a. Commissions. The sales agent is compensated for its activities by payment of a commission by the seller. The sales agent is appointed to solicit orders, and when such orders are accepted by the seller, the agent may be paid a commission. Sometimes payment of the commission is deferred until such time as the customer actually makes payment to the seller. Generally, the seller should not bill the agent for the price of the product (less commission) because such a practice could result in characterizing the relationship as a distributorship rather than a sales agency. Generally, any commissions payable should be made by wire transfer directly to the sales agent's bank account in the foreign country. Payments in cash, checks delivered in the United States, or payments in third countries may facilitate violation of the foreign exchange control or tax laws of the foreign country, and the seller may be liable as an aider and abettor of the violation.

b. Pricing. Because there is no sale between the seller and the sales agent, the seller can lawfully require the sales agent to quote only prices that the seller has authorized. For sellers who wish to establish uniform pricing on a worldwide basis, eliminate gray markets, and control markups, use of the sales agent appointment can be highly beneficial. However, the trade-off is that the seller will ordinarily assume the credit risk and will have to satisfy itself in regard to the ability of the customer to pay.

This sometimes presents difficulties in obtaining sufficient information, although the sales agent can be given the responsibility for gathering and forwarding such information to the seller prior to acceptance of any orders. In addition, some sales agents are willing to be appointed as del credere agents, whereby the sales agent guarantees payment by any customer from whom it solicits an order. Obviously, sales agents will require higher commissions for guaranteeing payment, but it can reduce the seller's risks in having to investigate the customer's credit while permitting the seller to specify the price that the sales agent quotes.

c. Shipment. Shipment is not made to the sales agent; it is made directly to the customer from whom the sales agent has solicited the order. Generally there will be problems associated with trying to maintain an inventory at the agent's place of business in the foreign country. Under the laws of many countries, if the seller maintains an inventory abroad in its own name or through an agent, the seller can become taxable

Figure 3–15. Foreign sales representative appointment checklist.

1. Appointment—Acceptance
   (a) Exclusivity
   (d) Subrepresentatives
2. Territory
3. Product
4. Responsibilities
   (a) Promotional efforts
   (b) Price quotations
   (c) Minimum orders (optional)
   (d) Increase in orders (optional)
   (e) Representative's facilities
5. Confidential Information
6. Reports
   (a) Operations report
   (b) Credit information
7. Visits to Representative's Premises by Supplier
8. Promotional Literature
9. Trademarks and Copyrights
10. Acceptance of Orders and Shipments
    (a) Acceptance only by supplier
    (b) No violation of U.S. laws
    (c) Direct shipment to customers
11. Commissions
    (a) Commission percentage or fee
    (b) Accrual
    (c) Refund
12. Discontinuation of Products
13. Repair and Rework
14. Relationship Between Parties
15. No Warranty Against Infringement
16. Product Warranty (to customers)

(continues)

Figure 3–15. (*continued*)

17. Effective Date and Duration
    (a) Effective date and term
    (b) Early termination
        (i) Breach
        (ii) Insolvency
        (iii) Prospective breach
        (iv) Change in ownership or management
        (v) Foreign protective law
        (vi) Unilateral (reciprocal) on agreed notice (without cause)
18. Rights and Obligations Upon Termination
    (a) No liability of supplier
    (b) Commission
    (c) Return of promotional materials
    (d) Accrued rights and obligation
19. Non-Competition
20. No Assignment
21. Government Regulation
    (a) Foreign law
    (b) U.S. law – Export Control Laws
    (c) Foreign Corrupt Practices Act compliance
22. Force Majeure
23. Severability
24. Waiver
25. Notices
    (a) Written notice
    (b) Oral notice
26. Governing Law
27. Dispute Resolution
28. Entire Agreement
    (a) Entire agreement
    (b) Modifications

on its own sales profits to customers in that country. If the customer cannot wait for shipment from the United States, or if it is important to maintain an inventory in the country, the appropriate way to do so while using sales agents must be investigated with an attorney knowledgeable in foreign law.

d. Warranties. It is important to keep in mind that product warranties should be made only to customers (purchasers). Since sales agents are not purchasers, the inclusion of warranty provisions in a sales agency agreement can cause confusion unless it is made clear that the warranty in the agreement with the sales agent is for the purpose of informing the sales agent as to what warranty it is authorized to communicate to prospective purchasers.

e. Relationship of the Parties. Although businesspersons frequently refer to intermediaries as distributors and "agents," legally, it is dangerous for a seller to enter into a principal-agent relationship. In such cases, the seller may become legally responsible for the acts and omissions of the agent. Generally, the "agent" should be an independent contractor, and that should be clearly expressed in the agreement. For this reason, it is usually better to designate the intermediary as a sales "representative." Furthermore, the seller should make clear that it does not control the day-to-day activities of the agent; otherwise, he may be deemed an agent or even an employee (if he is an individual), with corresponding liability risks and potential tax obligations.

D. Foreign Corrupt Practices Act Compliance

Another provision that should be included in the agreement relates to the Foreign Corrupt Practices Act (FCPA). In the United States, the FCPA makes it a violation of U.S. law for an agent of a U.S. exporter to pay any money or compensation to a foreign government agency, official, or political party for the purpose of obtaining or retaining business. If this occurs, the U.S. exporter will have violated the law if it knew that the foreign agent was engaged in such activities. Obviously, whether the exporter "knew" can be a matter of dispute, but if unusual circumstances occur, for instance, a distributor or agent asks for a special discount, allowance, or commission, or that payment be made to someone other than the distributor or agent, the exporter can be charged with knowledge of unusual circumstances that should have caused it to realize that something improper was occurring. One way to help avoid such liability is to specify expressly in the agreement that the agent recognizes the existence of the FCPA and commits and agrees not to make any payments to foreign government officials or political parties for the purpose of gaining business, or at least not to do so without consultation with the seller and receiving confirmation that such activity will not violate the FCPA. Distributors and agents should also be informed and agree not to make such payments to the buyer's employees, even if the buyer is not a government agency, as such payments will usually violate foreign commercial bribery laws.

To date, thirty-four countries have ratified the Organization of Economic Cooperation and Development Anti-Bribery Convention. The OECD monitors enforcement in order to ensure that all member countries continue to fight against bribery.

E. U.S. Export Control Laws

Merchandise exported from the United States, whether of U.S. or foreign origin, is covered by the U.S. export control regulations. While the laws are discussed at length in Chapter 5, it is important for the exporter to advise its distributors and sales agents that the merchandise cannot be sold, resold or transferred to embargoed destinations, restricted parties, or for a prohibited end-use. Should a U.S. exporter become subject to an investigation because its products are found to be in violation of the law, it will receive a subpoena for documentation. An export enforcement officer will want to review the exporter's files for up to the five-year statute of limitations to determine what the exporter knew with respect to its shipments and what it did to ensure that its sales agents and distributors were aware of the laws and regulations. So it is critical for U.S. exporter to put its representatives on notice as to the regulations in its contracts and its documentation.

Chapter 4

Exporting: Other Export Documentation

Although the sales agreement is by far the most important single document in an export sales transaction, there are numerous other documents with which the exporter must be familiar. In some cases, the exporter may not actually prepare such documents, especially if the exporter utilizes the services of a freight forwarder. Nevertheless, as discussed in Chapter 2, Section K, relating to the utilization of freight forwarders, the exporter is responsible for the content of the documents prepared and filed by its agent, the freight forwarder. Since the exporter has legal responsibility for any mistakes of the freight forwarder, it is very important for the exporter to understand what documents the freight forwarder is preparing and for the exporter to review and be totally comfortable with the contents of such documents. Furthermore, the documents prepared by the freight forwarder are usually prepared based on information supplied by the exporter. If the exporter does not understand the documents or the information that is being requested and a mistake occurs, the freight forwarder will claim that the mistake was due to improper information provided by the exporter.

A. Freight Forwarders

A freight forwarder is an agent that acts like a travel agent for the cargo. The freight forwarder will arrange for the best method of transportation, prepare and file the export documentation based on the exporter's instructions, make arrangements for pickup or delivery, make arrangements for inspection if necessary, provide insurance if requested, etc. There are forwarders that specialize in air freight. They are not required to be licensed by any particular U.S. agency, but the Transportation Security Agency (TSA) has authority to establish regulations over the receipt of cargo and shipping on aircraft under the Indirect Air Carrier Security Program. See more about this program in Chapter 4, Section V. Ocean freight forwarders are required to be licensed by the Federal Maritime Commission (FMC) as an "Ocean Transportation Intermediary." The FMC requires that ocean freight forwarders have a "qualified individual," which is a person who has at least three years of experience in U.S. ocean freight forwarding and must maintain a surety bond to ensure financial security. Most freight forwarders function handle both air and ocean shipments.

In order to act as the agent of the exporter, the freight forwarder may provide a form contract that specifies the services it will perform and the terms and conditions of the relationship. Among other things, the contract will contain a provision appointing the freight forwarder as an agent to prepare documentation and granting a power of attorney for that purpose. A sample power of attorney form from the Census Bureau is shown in Figure 4–1. The freight forwarder is required to have a power of attorney or other written authorization in order to prepare and file the Electronic Export Information through the Automated Export System. In many instances, the freight forwarder may only ask for the power of attorney up front, and the terms and conditions for the exporter/forwarder relationship appear on the back of its invoice received after the export has taken place. Although the Power of Attorney is the most common form of authorization the Census Bureau does allow an exporter to provide a written authorization for the forwarder to file the Electronic Export Information on its behalf. A sample written authorization is shown in Figure 4–2.

The exporter and forwarder should clearly define the extent of the services that are expected and any terms and conditions in advance of beginning their relationship together. The exporter should be sure to ask for a copy of the terms and conditions from the forwarder and review them and discuss what it is looking for in a forwarder. What will be the forwarder's role? Most companies will make freight arrangements with the freight forwarder directly or through the carrier's or the forwarder's online web sites. If booking through a web site, forwarders will generally require that the exporter "accept" the terms and conditions before accepting the freight order.

B. Shipper's Letters of Instructions

On each individual export transaction, the freight forwarder will need instructions from the exporter on how the export is to be processed. The terms or conditions of sale agreed upon between the seller and the buyer may vary from sale to sale. Consequently, in order for the freight forwarder to process the physical export of the goods and

Figure 4–1. Power of attorney (U.S. Census Bureau form).

SAMPLE FORMAT: Power of Attorney

POWER OF ATTORNEY
U.S. PRINCIPAL PARTY IN INTEREST/AUTHORIZED AGENT

Know all men by these presents, that_____, the
(Name of U.S. Principal Party in Interest (USPPI))
USPPI organized and doing business under the laws of the State or Country of
_____ and having an office and place of business
at_____hereby
(Address of USPPI)
authorizes_____, (Authorized Agent)
(Name of Authorized Agent)
of_____
(Address of Authorized Agent)
to act for and on its behalf as a true and lawful agent and attorney of the U.S. Principal Party in
Interest (USPPI) for, and in the name, place, and stead of the USPPI, from this date, in the
United States either in writing, electronically, or by other authorized means to: act as authorized
agent for export control, U.S. Census Bureau (Census Bureau) reporting, and U.S. Customs and
Border Protection (CBP) purposes. Also, to prepare and transmit any Electronic Export
Information (EEI) or other documents or records required to be filed by the Census Bureau,
CBP, the Bureau of Industry and Security, or any other U.S. Government agency, and perform
any other act that may be required by law or regulation in connection with the exportation or
transportation of any goods shipped or consigned by or to the USPPI, and to receive or ship any
goods on behalf of the USPPI.

The USPPI hereby certifies that all statements and information contained in the documentation
provided to the authorized agent and relating to exportation will be true and correct.
Furthermore, the USPPI understands that civil and criminal penalties may be imposed for
making false or fraudulent statements or for the violation of any United States laws or
regulations on exportation.

This power of attorney is to remain in full force and effect until revocation in writing is duly
given by the U.S. Principal Party in Interest and received by the Authorized Agent.

IN WITNESS WHEREOF, _____ caused these
(Full Name of USPPI/USPPI Company)
presents to be sealed and signed:

Witness: _____   Signature:_____
Capacity: _____
Date:_____

Figure 4–2. Written authorization (U.S. Census Bureau form).

Sample Written Authorization
SAMPLE FORMAT: Written Authorization

WRITTEN AUTHORIZATION TO PREPARE OR TRANSMIT ELECTRONIC EXPORT INFORMATION

I, _____ , authorize
(Name of U.S. Principal Party in Interest)

_____ to act as authorized agent for
(Name of Authorized Agent)

export control, U.S. Customs, and Census Bureau purposes to transmit such export information electronically that may be required by law or regulation in connection with the exportation or transportation of any goods on behalf of said U.S. Principal Party in Interest. The U.S. Principal Party in Interest certifies that necessary and proper documentation to accurately transmit the information electronically is and will be provided to the said Authorized Agent. The U.S. Principal Party in Interest further understands that civil and criminal penalties may be imposed for making false or fraudulent statements or for the violation of any U.S. laws or regulations on exportation and agrees to be bound by all statements of said authorized agent based upon information or documentation provided by the U.S. Principal Party in Interest to said authorized agent.

Signature: _____
(U.S. Principal Party in Interest)

Capacity: _____
Date: _____

prepare the proper documentation, it is necessary for the exporter to advise the freight forwarder as to the specific agreement between the seller and buyer for that sale, including the International Commerce Terminology (INCOTERMS®, see Chapter 2), the parties, the value, the delivery destination, inland carriers, etc. Freight forwarders often provide standard forms containing spaces to be filled in by the exporter for the information that it needs. Commercial stationers also sell forms that are designed to fit most transactions. (An example of such a form is shown in Figure 4–3.) The instructions should indicate the name of the U.S. Principal Party in Interest (see more in Chapter 4, Section T), the consignee's name and address, the Incoterms® for the shipment, the country of origin, the quantity, description, Schedule B or Harmonized Tariff Number, the value of the merchandise, the carriers, the marks and numbers on the cartons, etc. Alternatively the exporter may complete the information online or send an email with the information. As previously noted, the exporter should take special care in providing instructions to the forwarder, since any mistakes will be the basis on which the freight forwarder avoids responsibility; therefore it is important that the exporter keep a copy of the instructions.

C. Commercial Invoices

When the merchandise is ready to be shipped, the exporter must prepare a commercial invoice, which is a statement to the buyer for payment. Usually English is sufficient, but some countries require the seller's invoice to be in their language. Multiple copies are usually required, some of which are sent with the bill of lading and other transportation documents. The original is forwarded through banking channels for payment (except on open account sales, where it is sent directly to the buyer). On letter of credit transactions, the invoice must be issued by the beneficiary of the letter of credit and addressed to the applicant for the letter of credit. Putting the commercial invoice number on the other shipping documents helps to tie the documents together. The customs laws of most foreign countries require that a commercial invoice be presented by the buyer (or the seller if the seller is responsible for clearing customs), and the price listed on it is used as the value for the assessment of customs duties where the customs duties are based upon a percentage of the value (ad valorem rates). Perhaps the most important thing to note here is that many countries, like the United States, have special requirements for the information that, depending upon the product involved, must be contained in a commercial invoice. It is extremely important that, before shipping the product and preparing the commercial invoice, the

Figure 4–3. Shipper's letter of instructions.

1a. EXPORTER *(Name and address including ZIP CODE)*				

SHIPPER'S LETTER OF INSTRUCTIONS

b. EXPORTER'S EIN (IRS) NO.	c. PARTIES TO TRANSACTION ☐ Related ☐ Unrelated	2. DATE OF EXPORTATION	3. BILL OF LADING/AIR WAYBILL NO.

4a. ULTIMATE CONSIGNEE	SHIPPER'S REFERENCE

b. INTERMEDIATE CONSIGNEE

5. FORWARDING AGENT

	6. POINT (STATE) OF ORIGIN OR FTZ NO.	7. COUNTRY OF ULTIMATE DESTINATION

8. LOADING PIER *(Vessel only)*	9. MODE OF TRANSPORT *(Specify)*	**SHIPPER MUST CHECK**
10. EXPORTING CARRIER	11. PORT OF EXPORT	☐ C.O.D. $ _____ ☐ AIR ☐ OCEAN
		☐ PREPAID ☐ COLLECT ☐ DIRECT ☐ CONSOLIDATE
12. PORT OF UNLOADING *(Vessel and air only)*	13. CONTAINERIZED *(Vessel only)* ☐ Yes ☐ No	SHIPPER'S INSTRUCTIONS IN CASE OF INABILITY TO DELIVER CONSIGNMENT AS CONSIGNED
14. SHIPPER REQUESTS INSURANCE ☐ Yes ☐ No		☐ ABANDON ☐ RETURN TO SHIPPER ☐ DELIVER TO

SCHEDULE B DESCRIPTION OF COMMODITIES
- - - - - - - - - - - - - - - } *(Use Columns 17-19)*

15. MARKS AND NOS. AND KINDS OF PACKAGES

D/F (16)	SCHEDULE B NUMBER (17)	CHECK DIGIT	QUANTITY SCHEDULE B UNITS (18)	SHIPPING WEIGHT *(Kilos)* (19)	SHIPPER'S NOTE: IF YOU ARE UNCERTAIN OF THE SCHEDULE B COMMODITY NO. DO NOT TYPE IT IN - WE WILL COMPLETE WHEN PROCESSING THE 7525V.	VALUE *(U.S. dollars, omit cents)* *(Selling price or cost if not sold)* (20)

WE HAVE FORWARDED TO YOU THE SHIPMENT DESCRIBED BELOW VIA:
☐ YOUR TRUCK, OR
☐ OTHER CARRIER (LISTED BELOW)
TRUCK LINE NAME

RECEIPT (PRO) NUMBER

DECLARED VALUE FOR CARRIAGE
$

21. VALIDATED LICENSE NO./GENERAL LICENSE SYMBOL	22. ECCN *(When required)*	PLEASE SIGN THE FIRST EXPORT DECLARATION IN BOX 23 WITH PEN AND INK

23. Duly authorized officer or employee	The exporter authorizes the forwarder named above to act as forwarding agent for export control and customs purposes.	DOCUMENTS ENCLOSED

24. I certify that all statements made and all information contained herein are true and correct and that I have read and understand the instructions for preparation of this document, set forth in the "Correct Way to Fill Out the Shipper's Export Declaration." I understand that civil and criminal penalties, including forfeiture and sale, may be imposed for making false or fraudulent statements herein, failing to provide the requested information or for violation of U.S. laws on exportation (13 U.S.C. Sec. 305; 22 U.S.C. Sec. 401; 18 U.S.C. Sec. 1001; 50 U.S.C. App. 2410).

Signature	Confidential - For use solely for official purposes authorized by the Secretary of Commerce (13 U.S.C. 301 (g)).	SPECIAL INSTRUCTIONS
Title	Export Shipments are subject to inspection by U. S. Customs Service and/or Office of Export Enforcement.	
Date	25. AUTHENTICATION *(When required)*	

NOTE: The Shipper or his authorized agent hereby authorizes the above named Company, in his name and on his behalf, to prepare any export documents, to sign and accept any documents relating to said shipment and forward this shipment in accordance with the conditions of carriage and the tariffs of the carriers employed. The shipper guarantees payment of all collect charges in the event the consignee refuses payment. Hereunder the sole responsibility of the Company is to use reasonable care in the selection of carriers, forwarders, agents and others to whom it may entrust the shipment.

STF EX10026F

exporter check with an attorney, the buyer, or the freight forwarder to determine exactly what information must be included in the commercial invoice in order to clear foreign customs. In addition, often certain items, such as inland shipping expenses, packing, installation and service charges, financing charges, international transportation charges, insurance, assists, royalties, or license fees, may have to be shown separately because some of these items may be deducted from or added to the price in calculating the customs value and the payment of duties. Additional information on the proper valuation may be found in Chapter 10. Many countries in the Middle East and Latin America require that commercial invoices covering shipments to their countries be "apostilled" or legalized. This means that the country's U.S. embassy or consulate must stamp the invoice. All exports require a destination control statement to appear on the commercial invoice and on the bill of lading, air waybill, or other export documentation. For standard shipments, the following is the proper destination control statement.

> These commodities, technology or software were exported from the United States in accordance with the Export Administration Regulations. Diversion contrary to U.S. law is prohibited.

(See discussion in Chapter 5, Section J.) For defense articles, there is a different destination control statement. See Chapter 5, Section R for more information. Commercial invoices are also discussed in Chapter 3, Section A.4.g, and a sample is shown in Figure 3–9. While there is no international standard for the contents of invoices, Figure 4–4 summarizes typical requirements.

D. Bills of Lading

Bills of lading are best understood if considered as bills of loading. These documents are issued by transportation carriers as evidence that they have received the shipment and have agreed to transport it to the destination in accordance with their usual tariffs (rate schedule) or under the terms of a service agreement. Separate bills of lading may be issued for the inland or domestic portion of the transportation and the ocean (marine) or air transportation, or a through bill of lading covering all transportation to the destination may be issued. The domestic portion of the route will usually be handled by the trucking company or railroad transporting the product to the port of export. Such transportation companies have their own forms of bills of lading, and, again, commercial stationers make available forms that can be utilized by exporters,

Figure 4–4. Contents of a commercial invoice.

---

1. Full name of seller, including address and telephone number, on letterhead or printed form.

2. Full name of buyer and buyer's address (or, if not a sale, the consignee).

3. The Incoterms® including place of delivery, where the risk of loss transfers from the seller to the buyer. (For example, ex-works Nagoya Incoterms® 2010, FOB port of export Shanghai Incoterms® 2010, CIF Long Beach Incoterms® 2010). (See Chapter 2 for discussion of Incoterms®.)

4. The sale price and grand total for each item, which includes all charges to the place of delivery (#3 above). "Assists," royalties, proceeds of subsequent resale or use of the products, and indirect payments, if any, must also be included in the sale price. If it is not a sale, list the fair market value, a statement that it is not a sale, and that the value stated is "For Customs Purposes Only." (See Chapter 10 for discussion of valuation.)

5. A description of the product(s) sufficiently detailed for the foreign customs authorities to be able to confirm the correct Harmonized Tariff classification, including the quality or grade.

6. The quantities (and/or weights) of each product.

7. A date for the invoice (on or around the date of export).

8. The currency of the sale price (or value). (U.S. or foreign.)

9. The marks, numbers, and symbols on the packages.

10. The cost of packaging, cases, packing, and containers, if paid for by the seller, which is not included in the sales price and being billed to the buyer.

11. All charges paid by the seller, separately identified and itemized, including freight (inland and international), insurance, and commissions, etc., which are not included in the price and being billed to the buyer.

12. The country of origin (manufacture). (See Chapter 11.)

13. CHECK WITH THE BUYER OR IMPORTER BEFORE FINALIZING THE INVOICE TO CONFIRM THAT NO OTHER INFORMATION IS REQUIRED.

---

which generally say that the exporter agrees to all of the specific terms or conditions of transport normally contained in the carrier's usual bill of lading and tariff. The inland bill of lading should be prepared in accordance with the freight forwarder's or transportation carrier's instructions.

The ocean transportation will be covered by a marine bill of lading prepared by the exporter or freight forwarder and issued by the steamship company. Information in bills of lading (except apparent condition at the time of loading), such as marks, numbers, quantity, weight, and hazardous nature, is based on information provided to the carrier by the shipper, and the shipper warrants its accuracy. Today many bills of lading are completed online to ensure accuracy by the exporter, although generally it is the forwarder who completes the documentation which is then presented to the exporting carrier for loading notations and departure dates signed by the carrier. Making, altering, negotiating, or transferring a bill of lading with intent to defraud is a criminal offense. If the transportation is by air, the airline carrier will prepare and issue an air waybill. A freight consolidator will issue house air waybills, which are not binding on the carrier but are given to each shipper to evidence inclusion of its shipment as part of the consolidated shipment. In such cases, the freight consolidator becomes the "shipper" on the master bill of lading.

Bills of lading, whether inland or ocean, can be issued either in non-negotiable (straight) form or in negotiable form. Air waybills are issued only in a non-negotiable form. The Uniform Commercial Code for sales within the U.S. requires bills of lading to be negotiable unless the seller and buyer expressly agree otherwise. If the bill of lading is specified as non-negotiable, the transportation carrier must deliver it only to the consignee usually issued in three originals, any of which may be used by the buyer to obtain possession.

Inland bills and air waybills are issued in only one original. Where a negotiable bill of lading cannot be produced at the time of delivery, the steamship line may agree to make delivery if it receives a "letter of indemnity" from the exporter or importer (or both). Letters of credit require that before payment can be made, the exporter must furnish evidence to the bank that the goods have been loaded "on board" a steamship, and the bill of lading must be "clean." This latter term means that the steamship company has inspected the goods and found no damage to them at the time they were loaded on board. Steamship companies also issue "received for shipment" bills of lading. Steamship companies will hold such shipments in storage for some time until one of their steamships is going to the designated destination, but, until such bill of lading is stamped "on board," it is not clear when the shipment will actually depart and when it will arrive in the country of destination. When a U.S. export control license is needed for the shipment (and on some other types of shipments), a destination control statement must be put on the bill of lading. (See discussion in Chapter 5, Section J.) Samples of an inland bill of lading, an ocean bill of lading, and an air waybill are shown in Figures 4–5, 4–6, and 4–7, respectively.

E. VOCCs and NVOCCs

The Federal Maritime Commission (FMC) regulates all ocean transportation in commerce with the United States. It is governed under the statutory provisions and regulations of the Shipping Act of 1984, the Foreign Shipping Practices Act of 1988, section 19 of the Merchant Marine Act, 1920, and Public Law 89-777 and the Ocean Shipping Reform Act of 1998.

The FMC regulates the steamship lines, or the vessel-operating common carriers (VOCCs). The Shipping Act of 1916 granted immunity from the antitrust laws in order to stabilize shipping rates and services. As a result, the carriers formed conferences that were able to discuss and set rates for all ocean transportation. In exchange, the carriers were required to publish their rates with the Commission and make them available to all similarly situated shippers. With the passage of the Ocean Shipping Reform Act of 1998, steamship lines were allowed to enter into confidential service contracts with shippers and publish only limited information. The rates and service commitments remained confidential. The VOCCs now publish these tariffs on the Internet, where anyone may access them for a fee.

The FMC also regulates and licenses all ocean transportation intermediaries (OTI), which are the ocean freight forwarders, as discussed above in Section A, and the non-vessel-operating common carriers (NVOCCs). NVOCCs purchase large quantities of container space from the VOCCs on specific trade lanes, and since they buy in bulk, they obtain highly favorable rates. In turn, the NVOCCs sell that space to shippers at a higher cost. They issue their own bills of lading and are required to make their tariffs publicly available. In addition, they are able to enter into confidential service agreements with their shippers. The NVOCC plays a unique position in the transportation of goods; it is a shipper to the VOCCs and a carrier to its shippers.

F. Packing Lists

Packing lists are used to describe the way the goods are packed for shipment, such as how many packages are in the shipment, the types of packaging used, the weight of

Figure 4–5. Inland bill of lading.

STRAIGHT BILL OF LADING—SHORT FORM—ORIGINAL—NOT NEGOTIABLE

RECEIVED, subject to the classifications and tariffs in effect on the date of the issue of this Bill of Lading, the property described above in apparent good order, except as noted (contents and condition of contents of packages unknown), marked, consigned, and destined as indicated above which said carrier (the word carrier being understood throughout this contract as meaning any person or corporation in possession of the property under the contract) agrees to carry to its usual place of delivery at said destination, if on its route, otherwise to deliver to another carrier on the route to said destination. It is mutually agreed as to each

carrier of all or any of said property over all or any portion of said route to destination and as to each party at any time interested in all or any said property, that every service to be performed hereunder shall be subject to all the bill of lading terms and conditions in the governing classification on the date of shipment.
Shipper hereby certifies that he is familiar with all the bill of lading terms and conditions in the governing classification and the said terms and conditions are hereby agreed to by the shipper and accepted for himself and his assigns.

From _____

At _____ 20 ___ DESIGNATE WITH AN (X) BY TRUCK ☐ FREIGHT ☐ Shipper's No. _____

Carrier _____ Agent's No. _____
(Mail or street address of consignee—For purposes of notification only.)

Consigned to _____

Destination _____ State of _____ County of _____

Route _____

Delivering Carrier _____ Vehicle or Car Initial _____ No. _____

No. Packages	Kind of Package, Description of Articles, Special Marks, and Exceptions	*Weight (Sub. to Cor.)	Class or Rate	Check Column	

Subject to Section 7 of conditions of applicable bill of lading, if this shipment is to be delivered to the consignee without recourse on the consignor, the consignor shall sign the following statement:
The carrier shall not make delivery of this shipment without payment of freight and all other lawful charges.

Per _____
(Signature of Consignor.)

If charges are to be prepaid, write or stamp here, "To be Prepaid."

Received $ _____
to apply in prepayment of the charges on the property described hereon.

Agent or Cashier

Per _____
(The signature here acknowledges only the amount prepaid.)

Charges Advanced:

C.O.D. SHIPMENT
Prepaid ☐
Collect ☐ $ _____
Collection Fee _____
Total Charges _____

*If the shipment moves between two ports by a carrier by water, the law requires that the bill of lading shall state whether it is "Carrier's or Shipper's weight."

†Shipper's imprint in lieu of stamp: not a part of bill of lading approved by the Department of Transportation.

NOTE—Where the rate is dependent on value, shippers are required to state specifically in writing the agreed or declared value of the property.

THIS SHIPMENT IS CORRECTLY DESCRIBED. CORRECT WEIGHT IS

_____ LBS.

Subject to verification by the Respective Weighing and Inspection Bureau According to Agreement.

Per _____

TOTAL PIECES |

‡ The fibre containers used for this shipment conform to the specifications set forth in the box maker's certificate thereon, and all other requirements of Rule 41 of the Uniform Freight Classification and Rule 5 of the National Motor Freight Classification. †Shipper's imprint in lieu of stamp, not a part of bill of lading approved by the Interstate Commerce Commission.

If lower charges result, the agreed or declared value of the within described containers is hereby specifically stated to be not exceeding 50 cents per pound per article.

_____ Shipper, Per _____

_____ Agent, Per _____

This is to certify that the above-named materials are properly classified, described, packaged, marked and labeled and are in proper condition for transportation according to the applicable regulations of the Department of Transportation.

Form 35-643H Printed and Sold by *UNZ&CO* www.unzco.com • (800) 631-3098

1

Figure 4–6. Ocean bill of lading template.

Ocean Bill of Lading

Exporter	Booking Number		Document Number
	Export References		
Ultimate Consignee	Forwarding Agent		
Notify Party	Also Notify		

Pre-Carriage By	Place of Receipt	Domestic Routing
Exporting Carrier	Port of Loading	Loading Pier/Terminal
Port of Discharge	Place of Receipt on Carrier	Type of Move

Marks and Numbers	No. of Pkgs	HM	Description	Weight	Measurements

Ship Ref No. [_____] [_____]   There are: [____] pages, including attachments to this Ocean Bill of Lading

These commodities, technology or software were exported from the United States in accordance with the Export Administration Regulations. Diversion contrary to U.S. law prohibited. Carrier has a policy against payment solicitation, or receipt of any rebate, directly or indirectly, which would be unlawful under the United States Shipping Act, 1984 as amended.

FREIGHT RATES, CHARGES, WEIGHTS AND/OR MEASUREMENTS

Received by Carrier for shipment by ocean vessel between port of loading and port of discharge, and for arrangement or procurement of pre-carriage from place of receipt and on-carriage to place of delivery, where stated above, the goods as specified above in apparent good order and condition unless otherwise stated. The goods to be delivered at the above mentioned port of discharge or place of delivery, whichever is applicable.

IN WITNESS WHEREOF [____] original Bills of Lading have been signed, not otherwise stated above, one of which being accomplished the others shall be void.

DATED AT _____

BY _____
Agent

Mo.	Day	Year
B/L No.		

This document created using Shipping Solutions Professional export software, www.shipsolutions.com.

Figure 4–6. *(continued)*

BILL OF LADING–TERMS AND CONDITIONS

Figure 4–7. Air waybill.

Shipper's Name and Address | Shipper's Account Number

Not negotiable

Air Waybill

Issued by

Copies 1, 2 and 3 of this Air Waybill are originals and have the same validity

Consignee's Name and Address | Consignee's Account Number

It is agreed that the goods described herein are accepted in apparent good order and condition (except as noted) for carriage SUBJECT TO THE CONDITIONS OF CONTRACT ON THE REVERSE HEREOF. ALL GOODS MAY BE CARRIED BY ANY OTHER MEANS INCLUDING ROAD OR ANY OTHER CARRIER UNLESS SPECIFIC CONTRARY INSTRUCTIONS ARE GIVEN HEREON BY THE SHIPPER, AND SHIPPER AGREES THAT THE SHIPMENT MAY BE CARRIED VIA INTERMEDIATE STOPPING PLACES WHICH THE CARRIER DEEMS APPROPRIATE. THE SHIPPER'S ATTENTION IS DRAWN TO THE NOTICE CONCERNING CARRIERS' LIMITATION OF LIABILITY. Shipper may increase such limitation of liability by declaring a higher value for carriage and paying a supplemental charge if required.

Issuing Carrier's Agent Name and City

Accounting Information

Agent's IATA Code | Account No.

Airport of Departure (Addr. of First Carrier) and Requested Routing

to	By first Carrier	Routing and Destination	to	by	to	by	Currency	CHGS Code	WT/VAL PPD	WT/VAL COLL	Other PPD	Other COLL	Declared Value for Carriage	Declared Value for Customs

Airport of Destination	Flight/Date	For Carrier Use only	Flight/Date	Amount of Insurance	INSURANCE: If Carrier offers insurance and such insurance is requested in accordance with conditions thereof, indicate amount to be insured in figures in box marked "amount of

Handling Information

SCI

These commodities licensed by the U.S. for ultimate destination | Diversion contrary to U.S.law prohibited.

No. of Pieces RCP	Gross Weight	kg lb	Rate Class / Commodity Item No.	Chargeable Weight	Rate / Charge	Total	Nature and Quantity of Goods (incl. Dimensions or Volume)

Prepaid	Weight Charge	Collect
0.00		0.00
	Valuation Charge	
0.00		0.00
	Tax	
0.00		0.00
	Total Other Charges Due Agent	
0.00		0.00
	Total Other Charges Due Carrier	
0.00		0.00
Total Prepaid		Total Collect
0.00		0.00
Currency Conversion Rates	CC Charges in Dest. Currency	
For Carriers Use only at Destination	Charges at Destination	Total Collect Charges

Other Charges

Shipper certifies that the particulars on the face hereof are correct and that insofar as any part of the consignment contains dangerous goods, such part is properly described by name and is in proper condition for carriage by air according to the applicable Dangerous Goods Regulations.

Signature of Shipper or his Agent

Executed on (Date) at (Place) Signature of Issuing Carrier or its Agent

This document created using Shipping Solutions Professional export software, www.shipsolutions.com.

Figure 4–7. *(continued)*

NOTICE CONCERNING CARRIER'S LIMITATION OF LIABILITY

IF THE CARRIAGE INVOLVES AN ULTIMATE DESTINATION OR STOP IN A COUNTRY OTHER THAN THE COUNTRY OF DEPARTURE, THE WARSAW CONVENTION MAY BE APPLICABLE AND THE CONVENTION GOVERNS AND IN MOST CASES LIMITS THE LIABILITY OF THE CARRIER IN RESPECT OF LOSS, DAMAGE, OR DELAY TO CARGO TO 250 FRENCH GOLD FRANCS PER KILOGRAM, UNLESS A HIGHER VALUE IS DECLARED IN ADVANCE BY THE SHIPPER AND A SUPPLEMENTARY CHARGE PAID IF REQUIRED.
THE LIABILITY LIMIT OF 250 FRENCH GOLD FRANCS PER KILOGRAM IS APPROXIMATELY USD 20.00 PER KILOGRAM ON THE BASIS OF USD 42.22 PER OUNCE OF GOLD.

CONDITIONS OF CONTRACT

1. As used in this contract 'carrier' means all air carriers that carry or undertake to carry the goods hereunder or perform any other services incidental to such air carriage, 'Warsaw Convention' means the Convention for the Unification of certain rules relating to International Carriage by Air, signed at Warsaw, 12 October 1929, or that Convention as amended at The Hague, 28 September 1955, which ever may be applicable, and French gold francs means francs consisting of 65 1/2 milligrams of gold with a fineness of nine hundred thousandths.

2. 2.1. Carriage hereunder is subject to the rules relating to liability established by the Warsaw Convention unless such carriage is not 'international carriage' as defined by that Convention.
   2.2. To the extent not in conflict with the foregoing, carriage hereunder and other services performed by each carrier are subject to:
   2.2.1. applicable laws (including national laws implementing the Convention), government regulations, orders and requirements;
   2.2.2. provisions herein set forth, and
   2.2.3. applicable tariffs, rules, conditions of carriage, regulations and timetables (but not the times of departure and arrival therein) of such carrier, which are made part hereof and which may be inspected at any of its offices and at airports from which it operates regular services. In transportation between a place in the United States or Canada and any place outside thereof the applicable tariffs are the tariffs in force in those countries.

3. The first carrier's name may be abbreviated on the face hereof, the full name and its abbreviation being set forth in such carrier's tariffs, conditions of carriage, regulations and timetables. The first carrier's address is the airport of departure shown on the face hereof. The agreed stopping places (which may be altered by carrier in case of necessity) are those places, except the place of departure and the place of destination, set forth on the face hereof or shown in carrier's timetables as scheduled stopping places for the route. Carriage to be performed hereunder by several successive carriers is regarded as a single operation.

4. Except as otherwise provided in carrier's tariffs or conditions of carriage, in carriage to which the Warsaw Convention does not apply carrier's liability shall not exceed USD 20.00 or the equivalent per kilogram of goods lost, damaged or delayed, unless a higher value is declared by the shipper and a supplementary charge paid.

5. If the sum entered on the face of the air waybill as 'Declared Value for Carriage' represents an amount in excess of the applicable limits of liability referred to in the above Notice and in these Conditions and if the shipper has paid any supplementary charge that may be required by the carrier's tariffs, conditions of carriage or regulations, this shall constitute a special declaration of value and in this case carrier's limit of liability shall be the sum so declared. Payment of claims shall be subject to proof of actual damages suffered.

6. In cases of loss, damage or delay of part of the consignment, the weight to be taken into account in determining carrier's limit of liability shall be only the weight of the package or packages concerned.
   Note:
   Notwithstanding any other provision, for foreign air transportation as defined in the U.S. Federal Aviation Act as amended, in case of loss or damage or delay of a shipment or part thereof, the weight to be used in determining the carrier's limit of liability shall be the weight which is used (or a pro rata share in the case of a part shipment loss, damage or delay) to determine the transportation charge for such shipment.

7. Any exclusion or limitation of liability applicable to carrier shall apply to and be for the benefit of carrier's agents, servants and representatives and any person whose aircraft is used by carrier for carriage and its agents, servants and representatives. For purpose of this provision carrier acts herein as agent for all such persons.

8. 8.1. Carrier undertakes to complete the carriage hereunder with reasonable dispatch. Carrier may use alternate carriers or aircraft and may without notice and with due regard to the interests of the shipper use other means of transportation.
   Carrier is authorized by shipper to select the routing and all intermediate stopping places that it deems appropriate or to change or deviate from the routing shown on the face hereof.
   This Sub-paragraph is not applicable to/from USA.

8.2. Carrier undertakes to complete the carriage hereunder with reasonable dispatch. Except within USA where carrier tariffs will apply, carrier may use alternate carriers or aircraft and may without notice and with due regard to the interests of the shipper use other means of transportation. Carrier is authorized by shipper to select the routing and all intermediate stopping places that it deems appropriate or to change or deviate from the routing shown on the face hereof.
   This Sub-paragraph is applicable only to/from USA.

9. Subject to the conditions herein, the carrier shall be liable for the goods during the period they are in its charge or the charge of its agent.

10. 10.1. Except when the carrier has extended credit to the consignee without the written consent of the shipper, the shipper guarantees payment of all charges for carriage due in accordance with carrier's tariffs, conditions of carriage and related regulations, applicable laws (including national laws implementing the Convention), government regulations, orders and requirements.
    10.2. When no part of the consignment is delivered, a claim with respect to such consignment will be entertained even though transportation charges thereon are unpaid.

11. Notice of arrival of goods will be given promptly to the consignee or to the person indicated on the face hereof as the person to be notified. On arrival of the goods at the place of destination, subject to the acceptance of other instructions from the shipper prior to arrival of the goods at the place of destination, delivery will be made to, or in accordance with the instructions of the consignee. If the consignee declines to accept the goods or cannot be communicated with, disposition will be in accordance with instructions of the shipper.

12. 12.1. The person entitled to delivery must make a complaint to the carrier in writing in the case;
    12.1.1. of visible damage to the goods, immediately after discovery of the damage and at the latest within fourteen (14) days from receipt of the goods;
    12.1.2. of other damage to the goods, within fourteen (14) days from the date of receipt of the goods;
    12.1.3. of delay, within twenty-one (21) days of the date the goods are placed at his disposal; and
    12.1.4. of non-delivery of the goods, within one hundred and twenty (120) days from the date of the issue of the air waybill.
    12.2. For the purpose of 12.1. complaint in writing may be made to the carrier whose air waybill was used, or to the first carrier or to the last carrier or to the carrier who performed the transportation during which the loss, damage or delay took place.
    12.3. Any rights to damages against carrier shall be extinguished unless an action is brought within two years from the date of arrival at the destination, or from the date on which the aircraft ought to have arrived, or from the date on which the transportation stopped.

13. The shipper shall comply with all applicable laws and government regulations of any country to, from, through or over which the goods may be carried, including those relating to the packing, carriage or delivery of the goods, and shall furnish such information and attach such documents to this air waybill as may be necessary to comply with such laws and regulations. Carrier is not liable to the shipper for loss or expense due to the shipper's failure to comply with this provision.

14. No agent, servant or representative of carrier has authority to alter, modify or waive any provisions of this contract.

15. If carrier offers insurance and such insurance is requested, and if the appropriate premium is paid and the fact recorded on the face hereof, the goods covered by this air waybill are insured under an open policy for the amount requested as set out on the face hereof (recovery being limited to the actual value of goods lost or damaged provided that such amount does not exceed the insured value). The insurance is subject to the terms, conditions and coverage (from which certain risks are excluded) of the open policy, which is available for inspection at an office of the issuing carrier by the interested party. Claims under such policy must be reported immediately to an office of carrier.

Carrier maintains cargo liability insurance to protect itself against claims for which it is legally liable.

each package, the size of each package, and any markings that may be on the packages. Forms for packing lists are available through commercial stationers or are provided by packing companies who prepare export shipments. Sometimes packing lists are required by the customs laws of foreign countries, but even if they are not, an important use of the packing list is for filing insurance claims if there is damage or casualty to the shipment during transportation and for locating specific freight should Customs decide it wants to examine the cargo. (See Figure 4–8.)

G. Inspection Certificates

In some situations, the buyer may request and the seller may agree to a preshipment inspection; in other cases, preshipment inspection may be required by the buyer's government (see discussion in Chapter 3, Section B.2.j). If there will be preshipment inspection, one of the documents provided as part of the export documentation is the certificate issued by the inspection company. Sometimes the inspection certificate will be furnished directly to the buyer (or the buyer's government) by the inspection company, but other times the seller must provide the inspection certificate to the bank, as for example in a letter of credit transaction specifying that an inspection certificate is required in order to obtain payment. (A sample certificate issued by an inspection company is shown in Figure 4–9.) Some countries require preshipments inspections only when the value exceeds a certain amount; whereas other countries will require it regardless of value. In some Middle Eastern countries the document required is called a "Certificate of Conformity." In that instance it is to confirm that the merchandise meets certain standards and may require testing.

Although the list tends to change frequently, countries requiring preshipment inspection include Angola, Bangladesh, Benin, Burkina Faso, Burundi, Cambodia, Cameroon, Central African Republic, Comoros, Republic of Congo (Brazzaville), Democratic Republic of Congo (Kinshasa), Cote d'Ivoire, Ecuador, Ethiopia, Guinea, India, Indonesia, Iran, Kenya, Kuwait, Liberia, Madagascar, Malawi, Mali, Mauritania, Mexico, Mozambique, Niger, Senegal, Sierra Leone, Togo, and Uzbekistan.

Although not all inclusive, some of the major inspection services with offices worldwide are listed below:

Bureau Veritas	http://www.bureauveritas.com
Intertek, Americas	http://www.intertek.com
SGS	http://www.sgs.com

Figure 4–8. Packing list.

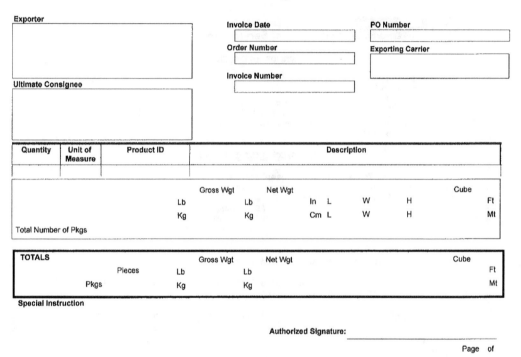

This document created using Shipping Solutions Professional export software, www.shipsolutions.com.

Figure 4–9. Preshipment inspection certificate.

SGS•SGS•SGS•SGS•SGS•SGS•SGS•SGS•SGS•SGS•SGS•SGS•SGS•SGS•SGS•SGS•SGS•SGS•SGS•SGS•SGS•SGS•SGS•SGS•SGS •

SGS Control Services Inc.

CERTIFICATE OF INSPECTION

42 Broadway
New York, N.Y. 10004
Tel. (212) 482-8700
Telex: 426974
     426975
     426976
Cables: Supervise

January 29, 1990

John Doe Co., Inc.
P.O. Box 789
Chicago, IL 60601

REF: 12345/CONTRACT I.K. 678

Inspection, Testweighing and Sampling were carried out at Warehouse 2D, Municipal Docks, Houston, Texas on January 26, 1990 on a shipment of 10,000 bags of Wheat Flour marked

       ABC Flour Mills
       Wheat Flour
       Product of U.S.A.
       100 lbs. net

PACKING: In polypropylene bags in good condition

WEIGHT: Testweighing of 500 bags (or 5%) selected at random, and test-taring of 5 empty bags, indicated:

                    Average per bag 100.5 lbs. gross
                                       0.5 lbs. tare
                                 100.0 lbs. net

On this basis 10,000 bags would weigh
                  1,005,000 lbs. gross
                      5,000 lbs. tare
            1,000,000 lbs. or 453.597 tonnes net

SAMPLING & ANALYSIS: Representative sampling of 500 bags (or 5%) selected at random yielded 10 samples, a composite of which was analyzed by our Houston Laboratory with these results, which meet contract specifications:

              (14% Moisture Basis)
              Protein   11.27
              Ash   0.46%
              Moisture   13.30%

LOADING: Shipment loaded aboard MV "MARY LOU," Lower Hold and Tweendeck No. 1, January 28, 1990 under our supervision.

                                 SGS CONTROL SERVICES INC.

SPECIMEN

Member of the **SGS** Group (Société Générale de Surveillance)

ALL INSPECTIONS ARE CARRIED OUT TO THE BEST OF OUR KNOWLEDGE AND ABILITY
AND OUR RESPONSIBILITY IS LIMITED TO THE EXERCISE OF REASONABLE CARE

•SGS•SGS•SGS•SGS•SGS•SGS•SGS•SGS•SGS•SGS•SGS•SGS•SGS•SGS•SGS•SGS•SGS•SGS•SGS•SGS•SGS•SGS•SGS•SGS•SGS •

Courtesy of SGS Government Programs Inc.

The costs for inspections are covered under the Incoterms®, which states that if the foreign government requires the inspection then the Seller is generally responsible for those costs; but if the requirement is made by the buyer, then the buyer is responsible. However, it is always advisable to be discussing these costs with the buyer to ensure that both parties understand who is responsible for payment.

H. Marine and Air Casualty Insurance Policies and Certificates

Why purchase cargo insurance for international shipments, aren't the carriers responsible for any damage that may occur? The carrier's liability is limited in its terms and conditions. Notably these are all standardized by various international organizations. For example, domestic transportation carriers have a limited of liability at only $0.50 per pound; international air carriers have a limitation of liability at $28.00 per kilogram, and the international ocean carriers have a limit of only $500 per shipping unit and that shipping unit is generally the container. Even with those limits, there are times when the carriers are still not responsible, such as an act of God or other force majeure incident.

As discussed in Chapter 2, Section P, it is extremely important to identify both who is arranging for the transportation insurance (to guard against casualty and loss) and who is going to pay for it. Even when the buyer is responsible for paying for such insurance, the buyer may be expecting the seller to arrange for it and to provide an insurance policy or certificate at the time of shipment as evidence that the shipment is properly covered. Recall that under the Incoterms® (see Chapter 2, Section M), CIF and CIP require the seller to purchase insurance in the name of the buyer. However, the buyer is only responsible to buy the minimum coverage, so a buyer will always want to ensure that it has coverage beyond minimum on its own. The usual practice is to insure for 110 percent of the CIF or invoice value of the goods (in order to cover loss, as well as any incidental surveying, inspection, or other expenses) and to obtain a policy or certificate in negotiable form and covering "all risks." Note that even "all risk" insurance does not cover wars, riots, political insurgencies, etc. So it is important to discuss with your insurance provider exactly what is covered and what is not and obtain any additional riders as needed. Large exporters usually issue their own certificates under their open cargo policy. Others may obtain insurance certificates issued by the freight forwarder under its open cargo policy or individual policies from insurance agents for individual shipments. Letters of credit may require that an insurance policy or certificate be provided by the exporter in order to obtain payment. The exporter may receive the actual policy (see Figure 4–10) or a separate certificate (see Figure 4–11) certifying that the insurance has been issued. A sample form for presentation of loss or damage claims is shown in Figure 4–12. Under the Carriage of Goods by Sea Act, shortages must be notified to the steamship line at the time of delivery and concealed damage within three days after delivery. Any lawsuit against the steamship line for loss or damage must be made within one year of delivery of the goods.

I.   Dock and Warehouse Receipts

Upon completion of the inland transportation to the port of export, the inland carrier may deliver the goods to a warehouse company or to a warehouse operated by the steamship company as arranged by the freight forwarder. A dock receipt (see Figure 4–13) is often prepared by the freight forwarder on the steamship company's form and is signed by the warehouseman or agent of the steamship company upon receipt of the goods at the steamship terminal as evidence of the receipt. The inland carrier then provides a signed copy of the dock receipt to the freight forwarder as evidence that it has completed the delivery.

J.   Consular Invoices

In addition to a commercial invoice, some countries require that a consular invoice be prepared. A consular invoice is usually prepared from the information in the commercial invoice, stating the names of the consignor (the shipper) and the consignee (the party receiving the goods), but it must be signed by a representative of the country of destination stationed at that country's embassy or consulate located in the United States nearest the exporter. One reason for requiring such invoices is that the country of destination may deduct certain charges from the price of the goods in order to determine the value for customs duties. If the commercial invoice does not contain all of the information necessary, the foreign customs service would be unable to complete the duty assessment. The consular invoice (see Figure 4–14) lists the specific items about which that country requires information. The consul charges a fee for this service. The State Department maintains a list of the consular offices located in the United States. See http://www.state.gov/s/cpr/rls/fco/.

Figure 4–10. Marine insurance policy.

MARINE POLICY «PolicyNo»

1. **ASSURED**

   hereinafter referred to as the Company, in consideration of premiums to be paid at rates hereinafter stated, does insure, lost or not lost

   «Assured»
   «Address1»
   «Address2»
   «City», «State» «PostalCode»

   Hereinafter referred to as the Assured. For account of whom it may concern.

2. **LOSS PAYABLE**

   Loss, if any, payable to the Assured or order.

3. **GOODS INSURED:**

   To cover on lawful goods and/or merchandise of every description (under and/or On Deck) but consisting principally of **INSERT COMMODITY DESCRIPTIONS**   , **and other merchandise incidental to the business of the Assured and** consigned and/or shipped by or to the Assured or by or to others for the Assured's account or control or in which the Assured may have an interest, but excluding shipments sold on F.O.B., F.A.S., C.&F. or similar terms whereby the Assured is not obliged to furnish marine insurance and excluding shipments purchased on terms which include insurance to destination; also to cover all shipments for the account of others on which the Assured may receive instructions to insure, such instructions being given in writing prior to sailing of vessel and prior to any known or reported loss or accident.

4. **INSURABLE INTEREST**

   This insurance is to cover all shipments made by or to the Assured or by or to others for the Assured's account or control, or in which the Assured may have an interest, also to cover all shipments for the account of others on which the Assured may receive instructions to insure or deem themselves responsible to insure, prior to sailing of vessel and prior to any known or reported loss or accident. This Policy does not and is not intended to provide any legal liability coverage, except as explicitly agreed, absent a specific endorsement herein to the contrary.

5. **ATTACHMENT:**

   To attach and cover for 100 (one hundred) percent interest on goods and/or merchandise of every description shipped on and after «EffDate» and to remain in force continuously thereafter until cancelled by either party giving the other 30 days written notice; such cancellation, however, not to affect any transit risk on which this insurance has attached prior to the effective date of said cancellation. Notwithstanding the above, coverage provided hereunder on any risks insured on a time basis or insured for coverage at any location shall terminate as of the effective date of the cancellation.

   Policy No. «PolicyNo»   **Page 1 of 17**   **Assured: «Assured»**

Figure 4–10. (*continued*)

6. **CONVEYANCES**
   By:
   a. Metal self-propelled vessels and connecting conveyances;
   b. Aircraft and connecting conveyances;
   c. Mail or express

7. **CRAFT CLAUSE (February 1949)**

   Including transit by craft and/or lighter to and from the vessel. Each craft and/or lighter to be deemed a separate insurance. The Assured are not to be prejudiced by any agreement exempting lightermen from liability.

8. **LIMITS OF LIABILITY**

   In respect of the above stated interest, however, this policy shall not be liable for more than:

   A. $«VesselLimit»   any one vessel or conveyance or in any one place at any one time;
   B. $«OnDeckLimit»   any one vessel subject to an On-Deck bill(s) of lading;
   C. $«AirLimit»   any one aircraft or connecting conveyance;
   D. $«perBarge»   any one barge, except as a connecting conveyance, but not exceeding
   E. $«PerTow»   any one tow;
   F. $«PostalLimit»   any one package by parcel post, mail, Express Courier or similar parcel delivery service;
   G. $«DomesticLimit»   any one land or air conveyance in any one place at any one time Domestic Transit)

   Note: Wherever the words "ship, vessels, seaworthiness or vessel owner" appear in this policy, they are deemed to also include the words "aircraft, airworthiness and aircraft owner."

9. **ACCUMULATION**

   Should there be an accumulation of interest beyond the limits expressed in this policy by reason of any interruption of transit and/or occurrence beyond the control of the Assured, or by reason of any casualty and/or at a transshipping point, and/or on a connecting steamer or conveyances, these Underwriters shall hold covered such excess interest and shall be liable for the full amount at risk, but in no event to exceed twice the applicable policy limit, provided notice be given to Underwriters as soon as known to the Assured.

10. **GEOGRAPHICAL LIMITS**

    At and from ports and or places in the World to ports and or places in the World (but excluding to/from Russia and other C.I.S. countries, former Yugoslavia, Afghanistan, Bolivia, Paraguay, Angola, Nigeria and Iraq) with privilege of transshipment by land and/or water and including domestic shipments that are shipped directly between points within a country and pass through coastal and/or international waters or international airspace. All other domestic shipments are excluded unless specifically endorsed hereon.

11. **VALUATION**

    A. Commercial Goods and/or Merchandise (under invoice): Valued at amount of invoice, including all charges therein, plus any prepaid and/or advanced and/or guaranteed freight, if any, plus 10%

    B. Commercial Goods and/or Merchandise (not under invoice): Valued and insured for the fair market value at place of shipment or arrival, provided such declaration be made prior to shipment. It is further agreed that irrespective of the value insured, claims for repairs shall be payable for the fair market costs of such repairs but in no event for more than the insured value.
    In no event shall claims exceed the value declared prior to shipment and declared for premium purposes.

    Foreign currency to be converted into U.S. dollars at rate of exchange current in New York on date of invoice.

    Policy No. «PolicyNo»   **Page 2 of 17**   **Assured:** «Assured»

132

Figure 4–10. (*continued*)

---

12. FULL VALUE REPORTING

If the total value at risk exceeds the limit of liability provided by this insurance, the Assured shall nevertheless, as soon as known, report the full amount at risk to Underwriters and shall pay full premium thereon, in consideration of which the principle of co-insurance is waived by Underwriters.

Acceptance of such reports and premium shall not alter or increase the limit of liability of Underwriters but Underwriters shall be liable for the amount of covered loss up to but not exceeding the applicable limit of liability.

13. SHORE COVERAGE

Including while on docks, wharves or elsewhere on shore and/or during land transportation, risks of collision, derailment, fire, lightning, sprinkler leakage, wind, hail, flood, earthquake, landslide, volcanic eruption, aircraft, objects falling from aircraft, the rising of navigable waters, or any accident to the conveyance and/or collapse and/or subsidence of docks and/or structures, and to pay loss or damage caused thereby, even though the insurance is otherwise F.P.A.

14. AVERAGE TERMS AND CONDITIONS

A. Except while on deck of ocean vessel subject to an On Deck Bill of Lading, the following average terms and conditions will apply, via steamer and/or aircraft to shipments of <u>NEW GOODS AND/OR MERCHANDISE</u> AS PER CLAUSE 4 OF THIS Policy (UNLESS OTHERWISE AGREED UPON AS PER CLAUSE 14.A.1 BELOW) ARE INSURED:

Against all risks of physical loss or damage from any external cause, excepting those risks excluded by the F.C.& S., Nuclear and S.R. & C.C. warranties of this Policy, subject to:

Deductible Amount of: **Insert Deductible Amt**

1) **OPTIONAL TERMS**

Option is hereby granted the Assured (except while on deck of ocean vessel), when exercised and so declared to these Underwriters prior to sailing of vessel and before any known or reported loss or accident, of insuring approved general merchandise in approved overseas packing subject to one of the following Terms of Average.

<u>F.P.A.</u>: Warranted free from Particular Average unless the vessel or craft be stranded, sunk or burnt, but notwithstanding this warranty Underwriters are to pay any loss or damage to the interest insured which may reasonably be attributed to fire, collision or contact of the vessel and/or conveyance with any external substance (ice included) other than water, or to discharge of cargo at port of distress.

If shipment by aircraft - FPA AIR PERILS: This insurance covers only loss of or damage to the interest insured which may be reasonably attributed to crash of aircraft, fire, lightning or explosion, collision, forced landing, jettison or throwing overboard for the safety of aircraft, crew or passengers.

Note: **Wherever the above F.P.A. terms appear in the Policy, they are deemed to also include the F.P.A. Air Perils as written above,** *Including the risks of theft of or non-delivery of an entire shipping package, jettison, washing or loss overboard.*

2) <u>USED GOODS/MERCHANDISE</u> **is insured:**

Warranted free from Particular Average unless the vessel or craft be stranded, sunk or burnt, but notwithstanding this warranty Underwriters are to pay any loss or damage to the interest insured which may reasonably be attributed to fire, collision or contact of the vessel and/or conveyance with any external substance (ice included) other than water, or to discharge of cargo at port of distress; and also to pay the insured value of any merchandise and/or goods jettisoned and/or washed or lost overboard, and the risks of theft of or non-delivery of an entire shipping package.

Policy No. «PolicyNo»   Page 3 of 17   Assured: «Assured»

Figure 4–10. *(continued)*

B. Goods on Deck Subject to an On-Deck Bill of Lading are insured subject to the following terms and conditions: Warranted free of particular average unless caused by stranding, sinking, burning and/or collision of the vessel; but to pay the insured value of any merchandise and/or goods jettisoned and/or washed overboard, irrespective of percentage. Notwithstanding the foregoing, merchandise and/or goods shipped On Deck under an Under-Deck Bill of Lading, without the knowledge and consent of the shipper, shall be treated as under-deck cargo and insured as per Sub-division A of this clause.

15. IMPROPER PACKING

In no case shall this insurance cover loss, damage or expense caused by the insufficiency or unsuitability of packing or preparation of the subject-matter insured. For the purpose of this clause "packing" shall be deemed to include stowage in a container or liftvan but only when such stowage is carried out prior to attachment of this insurance or by the Assured or their servants.

16. DELAY

Warranted free of claim for loss of market or for loss, damage or deterioration arising from delay, whether caused by a peril insured against or otherwise.

17. GENERAL AVERAGE

General average and salvage charges payable according to United States laws and usage and/or as per foreign statement and/or as per York-Antwerp rules (as prescribed in whole or in part) if in accordance with the contract of affreightment. Payable in full irrespective of insured or contributory values, but in no event for amounts greater than the applicable limit of liability shown elsewhere in this Policy.

18. WAREHOUSE TO WAREHOUSE CLAUSE

This insurance attaches from the time the goods leave the Warehouse and/or Store at the place named in the Policy, certificate or declaration for the commencement of the transit and continues during the ordinary course of transit, including customary transshipment, if any, until the goods are discharged overside from the overseas vessel at the final port. Thereafter the insurance continues whilst the goods are in transit and/or awaiting transit until delivered to final warehouse at the destination named in the Policy, certificate or declaration or until the expiry of 15 days (or 30 days if the destination to which the goods are insured is outside the limits of the port) whichever shall first occur. The time limits referred to above to be reckoned from midnight of the day on which the discharge overside of the goods hereby insured from the overseas vessel is completed. Held covered at a premium to be arranged in the event of transshipment, if any, other than as above and/or in the event of delay in excess of the above time limits arising from circumstances beyond the control of the Assured. It is necessary for the Assured to give prompt notice to Underwriters when they become aware of an event for which they are "held covered" under this Policy and the right to such cover is dependent on compliance with this obligation.

Figure 4–10. (*continued*)

---

19. MARINE EXTENSION CLAUSES

Notwithstanding anything to the contrary in this Policy, it is understood and agreed that the following terms, extension and conditions shall apply to all shipments which become at risk under this Policy.

A. This insurance attaches from the time the goods leave the warehouse at the place named in the Policy, Certificate or Declaration for the commencement of the transit and continues until the goods are delivered to the final warehouse at the destination named in the Policy, Certificate, or Declaration, or substituted destination as provided in Clause C hereunder.

B. This insurance specially to cover the goods during

   1) Deviation, delay, forced discharge, reshipment and transshipment.

   2) any other variation of the adventure arising from the exercise of a liberty granted to the shipowner or charterer under the contract of affreightment.

C. In the event of the exercise of any liberty granted to the shipowner or charterer under the contract of affreightment whereby such contract is terminated at a port or place other than the originally insured destination, the insurance continues until the goods are sold and delivered at such port or place; or, if the goods not be sold but are forwarded to the originally insured destination or to any other destination, this insurance continues until the goods have arrived at final warehouse as provided in Clause A above.

D. If while this insurance is still in force before the expiry of 15 days from midnight of the day on which the discharge overside of the goods hereby insured from overseas vessel at the final port of discharge is complete, the goods are re-sold (not being a sale within the terms of Clause C) and are to be forwarded to a destination other than that covered hereunder while deposited at such port of discharge until again in transit or until the expiry of the aforementioned 15 days whichever shall first occur. If a sale is effected after the expiry of the aforementioned 15 days whilst this insurance is still in force the protection afforded hereunder shall cease as from the time of the sale.

E. Held covered at a premium to be arranged in case of change of voyage or of any omission or error in the description of the interest, vessel or voyage.

F. This insurance shall in no case be deemed to extend to cover loss, damage or expense proximately caused by delay or inherent vice or nature of the subject matter insured.

G. It is a condition of this Insurance that there shall be no interruption or suspension of transit unless due to circumstances beyond the control of the Assured.

   Nothing in the forgoing shall be construed as overruling the F.C. & S. Clause or as extending this insurance to cover any risks of war or consequences of hostilities.

20. SOUTH AMERICAN CLAUSE

It is hereby understood and agreed that the following clause will apply to all shipments to South America.

Notwithstanding anything contained elsewhere herein to the contrary, (particularly the Warehouse to Warehouse and Marine Extension Clauses) the insurance provided hereunder shall continue to cover the goods for sixty (60) days on shipments via the Magdalena River) after completion of discharge from the overseas vessel at port of destination or until the goods are delivered to the final warehouse at destination, whichever may first occur, and shall then terminate.

The time limit referred to above to be reckoned from midnight of the day on which the discharge from the overseas vessel is completed.

Policy No. «PolicyNo»   Page 5 of 17   Assured: «Assured»

Figure 4–10. *(continued)*

21. PARAMOUNT WARRANTIES

THE FOLLOWING WARRANTIES SET FORTH IN CLAUSE 21, SHALL BE PARAMOUNT AND SHALL NOT BE MODIFIED OR SUPERSEDED BY ANY OTHER PROVISION INCLUDED HEREIN OR STAMPED OR ENDORSED HEREON UNLESS SUCH OTHER PROVISION REFERS TO RISKS EXCLUDED BY SUCH WARRANTIES AND EXPRESSLY ASSUMES THE SAID RISKS.

F.C. & S.

Notwithstanding anything herein contained to the contrary, this insurance is warranted free from capture, seizure, arrest, restraint, detainment, confiscation, preemption, requisition or nationalization, and the consequences thereof or any attempt thereat, whether in time or peace or war and whether lawful or otherwise; also warranted free, whether in time of peace or war, from all loss, damage or expense caused by any weapon of war employing atomic or nuclear fission and/or fusion or other reaction or radioactive force or matter or by any mine or torpedo, also warranted free from all consequences of hostilities or warlike operations (whether there by declaration of war or not), but this warranty shall not exclude collision or contact with aircraft, rockets or similar missiles or with any fixed or floating object (other than a mine or torpedo), stranding, heavy weather, fire or explosion unless caused directly (and independently of the nature of the voyage or service which the vessel concerned or, in the case of a collision, any other vessel involved therein, is performing) by a hostile act by or against a belligerent power; and for the purposes of this warranty "power" includes any authority maintaining naval, military or air forces in association with a power.

Further warranted free from the consequences of civil war, revolution, rebellion, insurrection or civil strife arising therefrom, or piracy.

NUCLEAR EXCLUSION

Notwithstanding anything contained to the contrary herein, it is hereby understood and agreed that this Policy shall not apply to any loss, damage or expense due to or arising out of, whether directly or indirectly, nuclear reaction, radiation or radioactive contamination, regardless of how it was caused. However, subject to all provisions of this Policy, if this Policy insures against fire, then direct physical damage to the property insured located within the United States or Puerto Rico by fire directly caused by the above excluded perils, is insured, provided that the nuclear reaction, radiation, or radioactive contamination was not caused, whether directly or indirectly, by any of the perils excluded by the F.C. & S. Warranty of this Policy.

Nothing in this clause shall be construed to cover any loss, damage, liability or expense caused by nuclear reaction, radiation or radioactive contamination arising directly or indirectly from the fire mentioned above.

S.R. & C.C.

Notwithstanding anything herein to the contrary, this insurance is warranted free from loss, damage or expense caused by or resulting from:

A.   Strikes, lockouts, labor disturbances, riots, civil commotions, or the acts of any person or persons taking part in any such occurrences or disorders.

B.   Vandalism, sabotage or malicious act, which shall be deemed also to encompass the act or acts of one or more persons, whether or not agents of a sovereign power, carried out for political, terroristic or ideological purposes and whether any loss, damage or expenses resulting therefrom is accidental or intentional.

DELAY (d) Warranted free of claim or loss of market or for loss, damage or deterioration arising from delay whether caused by a peril insured against or otherwise.

INHERENT VICE(e) Warranted free from claim for loss or damage or expense caused by or resulting from inherent vice or nature of the subject matter insured.

Policy No. «PolicyNo»   Page 6 of 17   Assured: «Assured»

Figure 4–10. (*continued*)

---

22. **BILL OF LADING, ETC., CLAUSE**

The Assured is not to be prejudiced by the presence of the negligence clause and/or latent defect clause in the Bill of Lading and/or charter party. The seaworthiness of the vessel as between the Assured and these Underwriters is hereby admitted and the wrongful act or misconduct of the shipowner or his servants causing a loss is not to defeat the recovery by an innocent Assured if the loss in the absence of such wrongful act of misconduct would have been a loss recoverable under this Policy. With leave to sail with or without pilots and to tow and assist vessels or craft in all situations, and to be towed.

23. **EXPLOSION**

Including the risk of explosion, however or wheresoever occurring during the currency of this insurance unless excluded by the F.C. & S. warranty or the SR & CC. warranty set forth herein or unless proximately caused by inherent vice or nature of the subject matter insured or by the personal negligence or act of the Assured.

24. **BOTH TO BLAME**

Where goods are shipped under a Bill of Lading containing the so called "both to blame collision" clause, these Underwriters agree as to all losses covered by this insurance, to indemnify the Assured for this Policy's proportion of any amount (not exceeding the amount insured) which the Assured may be legally bound to pay to the shipowners under such clause. In the event that such liability is asserted, the Assured agrees to notify these Underwriters who shall have the right at their own cost and expense to defend the Assured against such claim.

25. **INCHMAREE CLAUSE**

This insurance is also specially to cover any loss of or damage to the interest insured hereunder, through the bursting of boilers, breakage of shafts or through any latent defect in the machinery, hull or appurtenances, or from faults or errors in the navigation and/or management of the vessel by the master, mariners, mates, engineers or pilots.

26. **SUE AND LABOR**

In case of any imminent or actual loss or misfortune, it shall be lawful and necessary to and for the Assured, his or their factors, servants and assigns, to sue, labor and travel for, in and about the defense, safeguard and recovery of the said goods and merchandise, or any part thereof, without prejudice to this insurance, to the charges whereof, Underwriters will contribute according to the rate and quantity of the sum hereby insured; nor shall the acts of the Assured or Underwriters, in recovering, saving and preserving the property insured, in case of disaster, be considered a waiver or an acceptance of abandonment.

27. **CONSTRUCTIVE TOTAL LOSS**

No recovery for a constructive total loss shall be had hereunder unless the property insured is reasonably abandoned on account of its actual total loss appearing to be unavoidable, or because it cannot be preserved from actual total loss without an expenditure which would exceed its value when the expenditure had been incurred.

28. **CARRIER CLAUSE**

Warranted that this insurance shall not inure, directly or indirectly, to the benefit of any carrier or bailee.

29. **WAREHOUSING/FORWARDING CHARGES**

Notwithstanding any average warranty contained herein, Underwriters agree to pay any landing, warehousing, forwarding or other expenses and/or particular charges should same be incurred following any instance recoverable hereunder, as well as any partial loss arising from transshipment. Underwriters also agree to pay

Policy No. «PolicyNo»   Page 7 of 17   Assured: «Assured»

Figure 4–10. *(continued)*

the insured value of any package, piece, or unit totally lost in loading, transshipment and/or discharge and to pay for any loss or damage to the interest insured which may be reasonably attributed to discharge of cargo at port of distress.

30. DEVIATION

This insurance shall not be vitiated by an unintentional error in description of vessel, voyage or interest, or by deviation, over carriage, change of voyage, transshipment or any other interruption in the ordinary course of transit from causes beyond the control of the Assured. It is agreed, however, that any such error, deviation or other occurrence mentioned above shall be reported to these Underwriters as soon as known to the Assured and additional premium paid if required.

31. CHANGE OF DESTINATION

In case of voluntary change of destination and/or deviation and/or delay, within the Assured's control, the insured goods are held covered at an additional premium, if any, to be agreed upon; the Assured agreeing to report, as soon as possible, all events to these Underwriters.

32. INSOLVENCY

In no case shall this insurance cover loss, damage or expense arising from insolvency or financial default of the owners, managers, charterers or operators of the vessel where, at the time of loading of the subject matter insured on board the vessel, the Assured is aware, or in the ordinary course of business should be aware, that such insolvency or financial default could prevent the normal prosecution of the voyage.

33. FUMIGATION

In the event that any vessel, conveyance, wharf or warehouse is fumigated by order of properly constituted authority and loss or damage to goods and/or merchandise insured hereunder results therefrom Underwriters hereon agree to indemnify the Assured for such loss or damage and the Assured agrees to subrogate to Underwriters any recourse that the Assured may have for recovery of such loss or damage from others.

34. DUTY

This insurance also covers, subject to Policy terms of average, the risk of partial loss by reason of perils insured against on import duties imposed on goods imported into the United States or Canada insured hereunder, and collect freight (unless guaranteed or payable "vessel lost or not lost") it being understood and agreed however, that when the risk upon the goods continues beyond the time of discharge from the overseas vessel (including lighterage, if any) or, if received into bond, upon the release of said bond, the increased value consequent upon the payment of such duties and/or freight shall attach as additional insurance upon the goods from the time such duty and/or freight is paid or becomes due, to the extent of the amounts actually paid or payable.

Any limit of liability expressed in this Policy shall be applied separately to such increased value.

The Assured warrants that on each shipment insured under this clause, a separate amount shall be reported sufficient to cover said import duty and/or freight, upon which premium shall be payable at an agreed percentage of the merchandise rate.

The Assured agrees in all cases to use reasonable efforts to obtain abatement or refund of duties paid or claimed in respect of goods lost, damaged or destroyed. It is further agreed that the Assured shall, when these Underwriters so elect, surrender the merchandise to the Customs Authorities and recover import duties thereon as provided by law, in which event the claim under the Policy shall be only for total loss of the merchandise so surrendered, and expenses.

This insurance on import duty and/or freight shall terminate at the end of the import movement covered under the Policy (including the Warehouse to Warehouse an/or Marine Extension Clauses), but nothing contained in these clauses shall alter or effect any coverage granted elsewhere in the Policy during the storage or transit subsequent thereto.

Policy No. «PolicyNo»   Page 8 of 17   Assured: «Assured»

Figure 4–10. (*continued*)

35. CONSOLIDATION

Notwithstanding anything contained herein to the contrary, (particularly the Warehouse to Warehouse and Marine Extension Clauses) this insurance is extended to cover the property insured hereunder wherever same is stopped in transit, anywhere in the world, short of final destination, whether prior to loading and/or after discharge from overseas vessel or at any transshipment point for the purpose of consolidation, deconsolidation, packing, repacking, containerization, decontainerization, distribution, redistribution, on or at the premises of freight forwarders, consolidators, truckers, warehousemen, or others anywhere in the world for a period not exceeding thirty (30) days after receipt of the insured merchandise at such premises. Held covered in excess of the above time limit upon approval of Underwriters and at an additional premium if required.

36. DEMURRAGE CHARGES

If the Assured is instructed by Underwriters to hold a container, and the Assured is assessed a late penalty and/or demurrage charge for holding the container past the return date, Underwriters will pay the late penalties and/or demurrage charges. The amount Underwriters will pay shall be the charges assessed from the time Underwriters direct the Assured to hold the container until the time Underwriters inform the Assured that the container can be released.

37. MACHINERY

At the option of the Assured in case of loss or damage to any part of a machine, Underwriters will pay the proportion that the part lost or damaged bears to the insured value; or Underwriters will pay for the cost and expense including labor and forwarding charges of replacing or repairing the lost or damaged part. Loss, if any, sustained by payment of additional duty on replacement parts shipped for damaged machinery shall only be recoverable if duty was insured with the original shipment of machinery.

In no event, however, shall Underwriters be liable for more than the insured value of the complete machine.

38. REPLACEMENT CLAUSE (USED/REFURBISHED MACHINERY)

In the event of a claim for loss of or damage to any part of parts of the interest insured, in consequence of a peril covered by this Policy, the amount recoverable hereunder shall not exceed such proportion of the cost of replacement of the part or parts lost or damaged as the insured value bears to the value of a new machine, plus additional charges for forwarding and refitting the new part or parts if incurred, but excluding duty unless the full duty is included in the amount insured, in which case loss, if any, sustained by payment of additional duty shall also be recoverable.

Provided always that in no case shall the liability of Underwriters exceed the insured value of the complete machine.

Furthermore constructive total loss of the machine reasonably attributable to obsolescence of part or parts is specifically excluded.

39. EXPEDITING EXPENSE CLAUSE

In the event of loss of or damage to the subject-matter insured, Underwriters agree to pay the costs of airfreighting the damaged parts to manufacturers for repair and return, or the airfreighting of replacement parts from suppliers to destination, notwithstanding that the insured goods were not originally dispatched by airfreight.

40. REFUSED OR RETURNED SHIPMENTS

In the event of refusal or inability of the Assured or other consignee to accept delivery of goods or merchandise insured hereunder, this insurance is extended to cover such shipments subject to original insured value and insuring conditions while awaiting shipment or reshipment and/or return or until otherwise disposed. The

Policy No. «PolicyNo»   Page 9 of 17   Assured: «Assured»

Figure 4–10. (*continued*)

Assured agrees to report all such shipments as soon as practicable after they have knowledge of them and to pay premium if required, at rates to be agreed.

41. BRANDS

In case of damage to property bearing a Brand or Trade Mark, the sale of which in any way carries or implies a guarantee of the supplier or Assured, the salvage value of such damaged property shall be determined after removal of all Brands and any Trade Marks. On containers from which the Brand or TradeMark cannot be removed, contents shall be transferred to plain bulk containers. With respect to any merchandise, and/or containers from which it is impracticable to destroy all evidence of the Assured's connection therewith, these Underwriters agree to consult with the Assured with respect to the disposition of said merchandise and/or containers.

42. LABELS

A. In case of damage affecting labels, capsules or wrappers, Underwriters, if liable therefore under the terms of this Policy, shall not be liable for more than an amount sufficient to pay the cost of new labels, capsules or wrappers and the cost of reconditioning the goods, but in no event shall Underwriters be liable for more than the insured value of the damaged merchandise.

B. This Policy is extended to indemnify the Assured for actual expenses incurred in the reconditioning of or the replacing of, at final point of destination, the package of goods and/or merchandise insured under this Policy during transit to such destination provided:

   1) The type of package would normally withstand the transit without damage.
   2) Packing is free from damage at inception of transit risk as evidenced by issuance of a clean Bill of Lading (without a letter of indemnity to the shipper) or otherwise proven by the Assured.
   3) Damage to packing is due to a peril insured against.
   4) Reconditioning of packing or repacking is actually necessary.

In no event, however, shall Underwriters be liable for more than the insured value of the damaged goods.

43. PAIRS AND SETS

In the event of loss of or damage to one or more pieces of a set consisting, when complete for sale or use, of two or more component pieces, the liability of Underwriters shall be to pay the insured value of the total set.

44. DELIBERATE DAMAGE / POLLUTION HAZARD

This Policy covers, but only while the property insured is on board a waterborne conveyance, loss of or damage to property directly caused by governmental authorities acting for the public welfare to prevent or mitigate a pollution hazard or threat thereof, provided that the accident or occurrence creating the situation which required such governmental action would have resulted in a recoverable claim under the Policy (subject to all of its terms, conditions and warranties) if the property insured would have sustained physical loss or damage as a direct result of such accident or occurrence.

The coverage afforded hereunder shall not increase the Limits of Liability provided herein.

45. DELIBERATE DAMAGE BY CUSTOMS SERVICE

This insurance is also specially to cover physical loss of or damage to goods insured arising out of the performance of inspection duties of Customs Services or another duly constituted governmental agency.

46. ADDITIONAL FREIGHT/DUTY

This insurance also covers, subject to Policy terms, the risk of partial loss by reason of perils insured against on the freight payable at port of destination (unless guaranteed or payable "vessel lost or not lost") and/or on duties

Policy No. «PolicyNo»   Page 10 of 17   Assured: «Assured»

Figure 4–10. (*continued*)

imposed on goods insured hereunder, it being understood and agreed, however, that when the risk upon goods continues beyond the time of landing from the overseas vessel, the increased value, consequent upon the payment of such freight and/or duties, shall attach as an additional insurance upon the goods from the time such freight and/or duty is paid or becomes due to the extent of the amounts thereof actually paid or payable.

This clause shall not increase the Limits of Liability provided for elsewhere herein.

The Assured will, in all cases, use reasonable efforts to obtain abatement or refund of duties paid or claimed in respect of goods lost, damaged or destroyed. It is further agreed that the Assured shall, when the Underwriters so elect, surrender the merchandise to the Customs authorities and recover duties thereon as provided by law, in which event the claim under this Policy shall be only for a total loss of the merchandise so surrendered and expenses.

This insurance on freight and/or duty shall terminate at the end of the import movement covered under this Policy, but nothing contained in these clauses shall alter or affect any coverage granted elsewhere in the Policy during the storage or transit subsequent thereto.

47. INCREASED VALUE

With respect to goods and/or merchandise and/or property purchased by the Assured on C.I.F. or other similar terms whereby insurance is provided by the Seller or purchased by the Assured while still afloat on such terms prior to any known report of loss or accident, this Policy is extended to cover increased value, to be valued at the difference between the amount of insurance furnished by the Seller as evidenced by certificates or policies of insurance or otherwise, and valuation provided in this Policy applying to shipments purchased on C.I.F. or similar terms.

This insurance to pay the same percentage of loss on increased value or original Underwriters would pay on cargo subject to the Average Terms and Conditions contained in Clause 15 of this Policy; However, all references to deductibles appearing in this policy shall not be applicable to this insurance. In the event that the merchandise is short delivered or sold unidentifiable in consequences of perils insured against, this insurance is to pay a total loss on the increased value on the part short delivered or sold unidentifiable. Free of General Average and/or Salvage Charges except on the excess of contributory value over the original amount insured if uncollectible under original insurance on cargo.

48. F.O.B./F.A.S. SALES

1) In consideration of premiums to be paid at rates set forth in the Schedule of Rates in this Policy, subject to all its terms and conditions, the insurance is hereby extended to cover shipments originating in the Continental United States and sold by the Assured to others on F.A.S., F.O.B. or similar terms.

2) This Policy shall cover such F.A.S./F.O.B. shipments from the time of leaving store, warehouse or factory at interior point of shipment and continue while in due course of transit to the port of export and while there, until loaded on board overseas vessel or until Assured's interest and responsibility cease in accordance with the terms of sale, whichever shall first occur.

3) It is expressly understood and agreed that this insurance on F.A.S./F.O.B. shipments shall apply only as excess insurance placed by the Assured's suppliers or buyers which may have attached at the time of loss or damage.

49. F.O.B./F.A.S. PURCHASES

Notwithstanding anything to the contrary herein, it is agreed that this Cover's liability to the Assured commences from time the goods leave the suppliers' factory, warehouse, store or mill, notwithstanding the goods and/or interest may have been purchased Free on Board, Free Alongside Ship or Cost and Freight, and the Assured subrogating their right or recourse against suppliers for any loss or damage that may occur prior to delivery at the point designated in the applicable Free on Board, Free Alongside Ship or Cost and Freight terms.

Policy No. «PolicyNo»   **Page 11 of 17**   **Assured: «Assured»**

Figure 4–10. (*continued*)

The Assured agrees to report, the total value of all such shipments and pay premium thereon at rates set forth in the Schedule of Rates in this Cover Note.

50. CONTINGENT INSURANCE

This insurance is also specially to cover goods sold by the Assured on terms which do not obligate them to provide insurance, if there is loss or damage from a peril insured herein, and

A. The Assured cannot collect from the consignee or other party because of a refusal or inability to pay;
B. The Assured has been paid but remains contractually obligated to replace the loss or damaged goods.

Underwriters shall advance to the Assured, as a loan, the amount of loss as provided herein. Such loss to be repayable upon remittance of the purchase price by the buyer or otherwise. Goods insured under this coverage shall be valued at the amount of the Assured's invoice, plus freight and other charges (if not included in the invoice). This insurance is for the sole account of the Assured and in no event is it to inure to the benefit of buyers, consignees or any other party.

It is a condition precedent to this coverage that the Assured shall not divulge the existence of this coverage to any party. Such disclosure shall void coverage provided by this clause.
The Assured shall preserve their rights against the buyer or other parties and, upon receipt of payment from Underwriters, shall subrogate to Underwriters all rights and shall give all assistance, other than pecuniary, in enforcing them.

The Assured agrees to report the total value of all such shipments and pay premium thereon at rates set forth in the Schedule of Rates named in this Policy.

51. DEBRIS REMOVAL

This insurance is extended to cover, in addition to any other amount recoverable under this insurance, extra expenses reasonably incurred by the Assured for the removal and disposal of debris of the subject matter insured, or part thereof, by reason of damage thereto caused by an insured risk, but excluding absolutely:

A. Any expenses incurred in consequence of or to prevent or mitigate pollution or contamination, or any threat or liability therefore

B. The cost of removal of cargo from any vessel or craft.

In no case shall Underwriters be liable under this clause for more than 10% of the insured value under this Policy of the damaged subject-matter removed.

52. ATMOSPHERIC CONDITIONS

In the event of the goods insured hereunder being wetted or exposed to any odor occurring during the period of the insurance provided in this Cover Note, and the quality of the goods is thereby affected, the extra expenses of drying and/or reconditioning will be reimbursed by Underwriters. In the event the goods cannot be reconditioned, the liability of Underwriters shall be to pay the insured value of the affected goods.

53. NOTICE OF LOSS

In case of actual or expected loss of or damage to the goods insured, it shall be reported to the Underwriters or their claim representatives as soon as practicable upon knowledge by the Assured of the actual or expected loss.

54. PAYMENT ON ACCOUNT

Policy No. «PolicyNo»   Page 12 of 17   Assured: «Assured»

Figure 4–10. (*continued*)

Underwriters agree that where claim papers submitted demonstrate that only the quantum of the claim is in question, they will make a "payment on account" equal to 75% of the lower of the amounts claimed and agreed by Underwriters.

55. SUBROGATION

It is agreed that, on payment of any loss, the Assured shall assign and subrogate to Underwriters all their rights against third parties to the extent of such payments and shall permit suit to be brought in their name but at the Underwriters expense. The Assured further agrees to render all reasonable assistance in the prosecution of any suit. Should the sound market value of the damaged or lost goods exceed the amount insured, any recovery obtained will be pro-rated between Underwriters and the Assured as their respective interests bear to the sound market value of the goods. However, except in General Average, Underwriters shall not be subrogated to any rights and/or claims against the Assured's affiliates or subsidiaries.

56. CONTROL OF DAMAGED GOODS

It is agreed that in the event of damage to goods insured under this policy, the Assured shall retain control of all damaged goods. The Assured, however, agrees whenever practicable to recondition and sell such goods after removal of all brands and trademarks, the Company being entitled to the proceeds from such sale.

57. WAIVER AND/OR RELEASE

Privilege is hereby given to the Assured to accept from Carriers' bills of lading, receipts or contracts of transportation containing a release or limitation of liability as to the value of the goods, without prejudice to this insurance.

Further, in the event of loss or damage to property covered hereunder the Assured shall immediately make claim in writing against the carriers, bailees, or others involved.

58. MULTIPLE RECOVERY

No loss shall be paid hereunder if the Assured has collected the same from others

59. OTHER INSURANCE

If at the time of loss or damage there is available to the Assured or any other interested party, any other insurance which would apply in the absence of this Policy (excepting such insurance as may be arranged by the shipper or consignee), the insurance provided for hereunder shall apply only as excess insurance over such other insurance.

60. CONCEALED DAMAGE CLAUSE

Should delay occur in the opening of any package after arrival of goods at the final destination or should the goods be placed in bond or warehouse or any other place of deposit by the Assured or ultimate consignee prior to unpacking; if loss or damage is found when such packages are eventually opened, such loss shall be paid or adjusted by the Underwriters in the same manner as though the packages had been opened immediately upon their arrival, provided that:

a. It is no later than **30 days** after arrival at final destination and which can be reasonably shown to have occurred prior to delivery into such places of deposit.
b. Such loss or damage is recoverable under the terms of the policy.

Packages showing external damage are to be opened immediately upon arrival.

61. UNEXPLAINED SHORTAGES

This insurance is also specially to cover unexplained shortages of goods insured shipped in sealed container(s) whether or not the original seals are intact upon arrival at the final destination, provided that:

Policy No. «PolicyNo»   Page 13 of 17   Assured: «Assured»

Figure 4–10. (*continued*)

A. The coverage for the shipment includes loss caused by theft;
B. The Assured makes every attempt to recover the loss from anyone who may have been responsible for the shortage through involvement in stuffing the container.

It is a condition precedent to this coverage that the Assured shall not divulge the existence of this coverage to any party. Such disclosure shall void coverage provided by this clause.

62. FRAUDULANT BILL OF LADING CLAUSE

This policy covers physical loss or damage to merchandise insured under this Policy occasioned through the acceptance by the Assured and/or their agents or shippers of fraudulent Bills of Lading and/or shipping receipts and/or messenger receipt.

Also loss or damage caused by the utilization of legitimate bills of lading and/or other shipping documents without the authorization and/or consent of the Assured or its agents.

In no event, however, does this Policy cover loss or damage arising from the shipper's fraud or misstatement.

63. ERRORS & OMISSIONS

It is, however, agreed that this insurance shall not be prejudiced by any unintentional delay or inadvertent omission in reporting hereunder or any unintentional error in the description of the interest, vessel or voyage, if prompt notice be given Underwriters in all such cases as soon as said delay and/or omission and/or error becomes known to the Assured and adjustment of premium be made if and as required.

64. MISREPRESENTATION AND FRAUD

This policy shall be void if the Assured has concealed or misrepresented any material fact or circumstance concerning this insurance or the subject thereof or in case of any fraud, attempted fraud or false swearing by the Assured touching any matter relating to this insurance or the subject thereof, whether before or after the loss.

65. LETTERS OF CREDIT

Notwithstanding the conditions of this Policy, it is agreed that Certificates and/or Policies may be issued hereunder to the Assured to comply with the insurance requirements of any letter of credit and/or sales contract concerned, provided the cover required is not wider than that provided by the current Policy Wording. In the event that wider coverage is required, prior agreement of Underwriters is to be obtained at an additional premium to be agreed.

66. CERTIFICATES OF INSURANCE

Underwriters agree to issue "Claims Payable Abroad" and "Claims Payable to London" certificates as required subject to the inclusion of the following clause:

The Clauses referred to herein are those current at the inception of this open cover but should such clauses be revised during the period of this open cover and provided that Underwriters shall have given at least 30 days notice thereof, then the revised Clauses shall apply to risks attaching subsequent to the date of expiry of said notice."

67. AUTHORITY TO ISSUE CERTIFICATES

Authority is hereby granted the Assured to issue Underwriters' certificates hereunder, provided such certificates shall conform to the terms and conditions of this Policy and/or any written instructions that are or may be given by Underwriters and/or Roanoke Trade Insurance, Inc. from time to time. All such certificates issued shall be countersigned by a duly authorized representative of the Assured.

Policy No. «PolicyNo»   Page 14 of 17   Assured: «Assured»

Figure 4–10. (*continued*)

---

68. REPORTING

It is warranted that the Assured by acceptance of this Policy agrees to report all shipments in respect of which insurance is provided hereunder to

for transmission to Underwriters as soon as known to the Assured, or as soon thereafter as may be practicable.

70. INSPECTION OF RECORDS

Underwriters or their duly appointed representative shall be permitted at any time during business hours during the time this Policy is in force, or within a year after its termination, to inspect the records of the Assured as respects goods insured within the terms of this Policy.

71. BROKERS

(a) It is understood that for the purposes of this insurance the Assured's Broker of Record is

(b) It is a condition of this policy that the above brokers, or any substituted brokers, shall be deemed to be exclusively the agents of the Assured and not of this company in any and all matters related to, connected with, or affecting t his insurance. Any notice given or mailed by or on behalf of this Company to the above brokers in connection with or affecting this insurance, or its cancellation, shall be deemed to have been delivered to the Assured.

72. NOTICE OF SUIT

No suit, action or proceeding against this Company for recovery of any claim shall be sustainable unless commenced within one year from the date of the happening of the accident out of which the claim arises, provided that if such limitation is invalid by the laws of the state within which the policy is issued then such suit, action or proceeding shall be barred unless commenced within the shortest limit of time permitted by the laws of such state.

73. CANCELLATION

This Policy shall be subject to 30 days Notice of Cancellation, by either party, giving the other party written notice to that effect, but such cancellation shall not affect any risk on which this insurance has attached prior to the effective date of such notice.

Notwithstanding the foregoing notice period, Underwriters may effect immediate cancellation by giving written notice thereof at any time when premiums have been due and unpaid for a period of sixty (60) days or more.

74. CLASSIFICATION CLAUSE

Rates are for shipments of merchandise as specified herein, made Under Deck without transshipment unless otherwise state specifically. Shipped on:

1) Metal-hull, self-propelled vessels which are not over 20 years of age nor less than 1,000 net registered tons and which are classed A1 American Record or equivalent by a member of the International Association of Classification Societies; or

Policy No. «PolicyNo»   **Page 15 of 17**   **Assured:** «Assured»

Figure 4–10. *(continued)*

---

2) Vessels over 20 years of age which are approved by Underwriters, and which are not less than 1,000 net registered tons and classed as in (1) above, but while operating in their regular trades;

3) but in either case excluding vessels built:

   a) for service on the Great Lakes;
   b) solely for Military or Naval Service; or
   c) for carriage of dry bulk or liquid bulk cargoes, and which are more than 15 years of age, unless specifically approved by Underwriters.

Shipments by vessel which are not described in (1) or (2) above or which are excluded in (3) above are subject to additional rates to be quoted by Underwriters at the time of the reporting of shipment.

IN WITNESS WHEREOF, this Policy shall not be valid unless countersigned by an authorized representative of this Company and Roanoke Trade Insurance, Inc.

Countersigned at Boston, Massachusetts on this date: 4/28/2009

By: _____
    Authorized Representative

By: _____
    Authorized Representative

Policy No. «PolicyNo»   Page 16 of 17   Assured: «Assured»

Figure 4–10. (*continued*)

Dated: «EffDate»

Part of Policy No. «PolicyNo»
of the

American Institute
Strikes, Riots & Civil Commotions (Cargo)
(December 2, 1992)

S.R. & C.C. ENDORSEMENT

This insurance also covers:

1. Physical loss of or damage to the property insured directly caused by strikers, locked-out workmen, or persons taking part in labor disturbances or riots or civil commotions and,

2. Physical loss of or damage to the property insured directly caused by vandalism, sabotage or malicious act, which shall be deemed also to encompass the act or acts of one or more persons, whether or not agents of a sovereign power, carried out for political, terroristic or ideological purposes and whether any loss, damage or expense resulting therefrom is accidental or intentional; PROVIDED that any claim to be recoverable under this sub-section (2) be not excluded by the FC&S Warranty in the Policy to which this endorsement is attached.

While the property insured is at risk under the terms and conditions of this insurance within the United States of America, the Commonwealth of Puerto Rico, the U.S. Virgin Islands and Canada, this insurance is extended to cover physical loss of or damage to the property insured directly caused by acts committed by an agent of any government, party or faction engaged in war, hostilities or other warlike operations, provided such agent is acting secretly and not in connection with any operation of military or naval armed forces in the country where the described property is situated.

Nothing in this clause shall be construed to include or cover any loss, damage, deterioration or expense directly or indirectly arising from, contributed to or caused by any of the following, whether due to a peril insured against or otherwise:

A. Change in temperature or humidity.

B. The absence, storage, or withholding of power, fuel, or labor of any description whatsoever during any strike, lockout, labor disturbance, riot or civil commotion.

C. Loss of market or loss, damage or deterioration arising from delay;

D. Hostilities, warlike operations, civil war, revolution, rebellion or insurrection, or civil strife arising therefrom, except to the limited extent that the acts of certain agents acting secretly have been expressly covered above; or,

E. Any weapon of war employing atomic or nuclear fission and/or fusion or other like reaction or radioactive force or matter.

The Assured agrees to report all shipments attaching under this cover and to pay premiums therefore at the rates established by Underwriters from time to time.

Notwithstanding the Cancellation Clause provided herein, the coverage provided under this clause may be cancelled by either party upon forty-eight hours written or telegraphic notice to the other party, but such cancellation shall not affect any risks which have already attached hereunder.

Policy No. «PolicyNo»   **Page 17 of 17**   **Assured:** «Assured»

Figure 4–11. Marine insurance certificate.

Special Marine Policy

No. ______________

Open Policy No. ______________________ of SERVICE OFFICE: ______________ **ORIGINAL** (ORIGINAL AND DUPLICATE ISSUED ONE OF WHICH BEING ACCOMPLISHED, THE OTHER TO BE NULL AND VOID)

$ ______________________ (PLACE & DATE) ______________________

This Company, in consideration of a premium as agreed, and subject to the Terms and Conditions printed or stamped hereon and/or attached hereto, does insure, lost or not lost ______________________.

For account of whom it may concern; to be shipped by the vessel ______________________, and connecting conveyances.

MARKS AND NUMBERS

From ______________________

To ______________________,

Lawful Goods Consisting Of ______________________, Number of ______________

Valued at **Sum hereby Insured**

Inv. #

B/L #

Loss, if any, payable to **Assured** ______________________ or order.

TERMS AND CONDITIONS - SEE ALSO BACK HEREOF

WAREHOUSE TO WAREHOUSE: This insurance attaches from the time the goods leave the Warehouse and/or Store at the place named in the Policy for the commencement of the transit and continues during the ordinary course of transit, including customary transshipment if any, until the goods are discharged overside from the overseas vessel at the final port. Thereafter the insurance continues whilst the goods are in transit and/or awaiting transit until delivered to final warehouse at the destination named in the Policy or until the expiry of 15 days (or 30 days if the destination to which the goods are insured is outside the limits of the port) whichever shall first occur. The time limits referred to above to be reckoned from midnight of the day on which the discharge overside of the goods hereby insured from the overseas vessel is completed. Held covered at a premium to be arranged in the event of transshipment, if any, other than as above and/or in the event of delay in excess of the above time limits arising from circumstances beyond the control of the Assured. NOTE -- IT IS NECESSARY FOR THE ASSURED TO GIVE PROMPT NOTICE TO THESE ASSURERS WHEN THEY BECOME AWARE OF AN EVENT FOR WHICH THEY ARE "HELD COVERED" UNDER THIS POLICY AND THE RIGHT TO SUCH COVER IS DEPENDENT ON COMPLIANCE WITH THIS OBLIGATION.

SHORE CLAUSE: Where this insurance by its terms covers while on docks, wharves or elsewhere on shore, and/or during land transportation, it shall include the risks of collision, derailment, overturning or other accident to the conveyance, fire, lightning, sprinkler leakage, cyclones, hurricanes, earthquakes, floods (meaning the rising of navigable waters), and/or collapse or subsidence of docks or wharves, even though the insurance be otherwise F.P.A.

BOTH TO BLAME CLAUSE: Where goods are shipped under a Bill of Lading containing the so-called "Both to Blame Collision" Clause, these Assurers agree as to all losses covered by this insurance, to indemnify the Assured for this Policy's proportion of any amount (not exceeding the amount insured) which the Assured may be legally bound to pay to the shipowners under such clause. In the event that such liability is asserted the Assured agrees to notify these Assurers who shall have the right at their own cost and expense to defend the Assured against such claim.

MACHINERY CLAUSE: When the property insured under this Policy includes a machine consisting when complete for sale or use of several parts, then in case of loss or damage covered by this insurance to any part of such machine, these Assurers shall be liable only for the proportion of the insured value of the part lost or damaged, or at the Assured's option, for the cost and expense, including labor and forwarding charges, of replacing and repairing the lost or damaged part; but in no event shall these Assurers be liable for more than the insured value of the complete machine.

LABELS CLAUSE: In case of damage affecting labels, capsules or wrappers, these Assurers, if liable therefor under the terms of this policy, shall not be liable for more than an amount sufficient to pay the cost of new labels, capsules or wrappers, and the cost of reconditioning the goods, but in no event shall these Assurers be liable for more than the insured value of the damaged merchandise.

DELAY CLAUSE: Warranted free of claim for loss of market or for loss, damage or deterioration arising from delay, whether caused by a peril insured against or otherwise, unless expressly assumed in writing hereon.

AMERICAN INSTITUTE CLAUSES: This insurance, in addition to the foregoing, is also subject to the following American Institute Cargo Clauses, current forms:

1. CRAFT, ETC.
2. DEVIATION
3. WAREHOUSE & FORWARDING CHARGES, PACKAGES TOTALLY LOST LOADING, ETC.
4. GENERAL AVERAGE
5. EXPLOSION
6. BILL OF LADING, ETC.
7. INCHMAREE
8. CONSTRUCTIVE TOTAL LOSS
9. CARRIER
10. EXTENDED R.A.C.E.
11. CHEMICAL, BIOLOGICAL, ELECTROMAGNETIC EXCLUSION

PERILS CLAUSE: Touching the adventures and perils which this Company is contented to bear, and takes upon itself, they are of the seas, assailing thieves, jettisons, barratry of the master and mariners, and all other like perils, losses and misfortunes (illicit or contraband trade excepted in all cases), that have or shall come to the hurt, detriment or damage of the said goods and merchandise, or any part thereof.

AVERAGE TERMS: ON DECK AND SUBJECT TO AN "ON DECK" BILL OF LADING -- (which must be so declared by the Assured): Free of Particular Average unless caused by the vessel being stranded, sunk, burnt, on fire or in collision, but including jettison and/or washing overboard irrespective of percentage. EXCEPT WHILE SUBJECT TO AN "ON DECK" BILL OF LADING:

ALL RISK STANDARD WORDING: To cover against all risks of physical loss or damage from any external cause irrespective of percentage, but excluding, nevertheless, the risks of war, strikes, riots, seizure, detention and other risks excluded by the F.C. & S. (Free of Capture & Seizure) Warranty and the S.R. & C.C. (Strikes, Riots, and Civil Commotions) Warranty policy, excepting to the extent that such risks are specifically covered by endorsement.

This Policy is extended to include the provisions of the following clauses as if the current form of each were endorsed hereon:

American Institute Clauses -

F.C. & S. Warranty
Marine Extension Clauses
S.R.&C.C. Endorsement
War Risk Insurance
Nuclear Exclusion

Where appropriate -
South America 60-Day Clause

PARAMOUNT WARRANTIES: THE FOLLOWING WARRANTIES SHALL BE PARAMOUNT AND SHALL NOT BE MODIFIED OR SUPERSEDED BY ANY OTHER PROVISION INCLUDED HEREIN OR STAMPED OR ENDORSED HEREON UNLESS SUCH OTHER PROVISION REFERS SPECIFICALLY TO THE RISKS EXCLUDED BY THESE WARRANTIES AND EXPRESSLY ASSUMES THE SAID RISKS C.& S.(a) NOTWITHSTANDING ANYTHING HEREIN CONTAINED TO THE CONTRARY THIS INSURANCE IS WARRANTED FREE FROM: (a) capture, seizure, arrest, restraint, detainment, confiscation, preemption, requisition or nationalization, and the consequences thereof or any attempt thereat, whether in time of peace or war and whether lawful or otherwise; (b) all loss, damage or expense, whether in time of peace or war, caused by (i) any weapon or war employing atomic or nuclear fission and/or fusion or other reaction or radioactive force or matter or (ii) any mine or torpedo; (c) all consequences of hostilities or warlike operations (whether there be a declaration of war or not), but this warranty shall not exclude collision or contact with aircraft, or with rockets or similar missiles (other than weapons of war) or with any fixed or floating object (other than a mine or torpedo), stranding, heavy weather, fire or explosion unless caused directly (and independently of the nature of the voyage or service which the vessel concerned or, in the case of a collision, any other vessel involved therein, is performing) by a hostile act by or against a belligerent power; and for the purposes of this warranty "power" includes any authority maintaining naval, military or air forces in association with a power; (d) the consequences of civil war, revolution, rebellion, insurrection, or civil strife arising therefrom; or from the consequences of the imposition of martial law, military or usurped power; or piracy. S.R.&C.C. (b) Notwithstanding anything herein contained to the contrary, this insurance is warranted free from loss, damage or expense caused by or resulting from: (1) strikes, lockouts, labor disturbances, riots, civil commotions, or the acts of any person or persons taking part in any such occurrences or disorders, (2) vandalism, sabotage or malicious act, which shall be deemed also to encompass the act or acts of one or more persons, whether or not agents of a sovereign power, carried out for political, terroristic or ideological purposes and whether any loss, damage or expense resulting therefrom is accidental or intentional.

ECONOMIC SANCTIONS AND EMBARGO PROGRAMS OF THE UNITED STATES: This policy excludes loss otherwise payable to an individual, organization, or authority that is the subject of any trade embargo or other trade sanction imposed by the United States Government; or that arises out of any trade in, or shipment of, any goods or merchandise prohibited by such embargo or sanction, whether or not deemed lawful under the laws of another nation.

DRAFT

Figure 4–11. (*continued*)

Insurance Document (or Certificate)

Definition

A document indicating the type and amount of insurance coverage in force on a particular shipment. In documentary credit transactions the insurance document is used to assure the consignee that insurance is provided to cover loss of or damage to cargo while in transit subject to policy terms and conditions.

A completed insurance document includes the following elements:

1. The name of the insurance company
2. Policy number
3. Description of the merchandise insured
4. Points of origin and destination of the shipment. Coverage is indicated by the terms of sale. For example, for goods sold "FOB," coverage commences once the cargo is on board the vessel and continues until the consignee takes possession at either the seaport or in-land port of destination.
5. Conditions of coverage, exclusions, and deductible, if applicable.
6. A signature by the insurance carrier, underwriter or agent for same
7. Indication that the cover is effective at the latest from the date of loading of the goods on board a transport vessel or the taking in charge of the goods by the carrier, as indicated by the transport document (bill of lading, etc.)
8. Statement of the sum insured
9. In a documentary letter of credit, specifies coverage for at least 110 percent of either: (a) the CIF or CIP value of the shipment, if such can be determined from the various documents on their face, otherwise, (b) the amount of the payment, acceptance or negotiation specified in the documentary credit, or (c) the gross amount of the commercial invoice
10. Is presented as the sole original, or if issued in more than one original, the full set of originals

Cautions & Notes

In documentary credit transactions the insurance currency should be consistent with the currency of the documentary credit.

Documentary credit transactions indicating CIF (Cost Insurance Freight) or CIP (Carriage and Insurance Paid) pricing should list an insurance document in the required documentation.

"Cover notes" issued by insurance brokers (as opposed to insurance companies, underwriters, or their agents) are not accepted in letter of credit transactions unless authorized specifically by the credit terms.

In Case of Loss or Shortfall

The consignee should always note on the delivery document any damage or shortfall prior to signing for receipt of the goods. The consignee has the responsibility to make reasonable efforts to minimize loss. This includes steps to prevent further damage to the shipment. Expenses incurred in such efforts are almost universally collectible under the insurance policy. Prompt notice of loss is essential.

The original copy of the insurance certificate is a negotiable document and is required in the filing of a claim.

Copies of documents necessary to support an insurance claim include the insurance policy or certificate, bill of lading, invoice, packing list, and a survey report (usually prepared by a claims agent).

Figure 4–12. Standard form for presentation of loss or damage claim.

Figure 4–13. Dock receipt.

(SPACES IMMEDIATELY BELOW ARE FOR SHIPPERS MEMORANDA--NOT PART OF DOCK RECEIPT)

DELIVERING CARRIER TO STEAMER:	CAR NUMBER—REFERENCE
FORWARDING AGENT—REFERENCES	EXPORT DEC. No.

DOCK RECEIPT
NON-NEGOTIABLE

SHIPPER

SHIP	VOYAGE NO.	FLAG	PIER	PORT OF LOADING
FOR. PORT OF DISCHARGE *(Where goods are to be delivered to consignee or on-carrier)*			For TRANSSHIPMENT TO *(If goods are to be transshipped or forwarded at port of discharge)*	

PARTICULARS FURNISHED BY SHIPPER OF GOODS

MARKS AND NUMBERS	No. of PKGS.	DESCRIPTION OF PACKAGES AND GOODS	MEASURE-MENT	GROSS WEIGHT
		SAMPLE		

DIMENSIONS AND WEIGHTS OF PACKAGES TO BE SHOWN ON REVERSE SIDE

DELIVERED BY:

RECEIVED THE ABOVE DESCRIBED MERCHANDISE FOR SHIPMENT AS INDICATED HEREON, SUBJECT TO ALL CONDITIONS OF THE UNDERSIGNED'S USUAL FORM OF DOCK RECEIPT AND BILL OF LADING. COPIES OF THE UNDERSIGNED'S USUAL FORM OF DOCK RECEIPT AND BILL OF LADING MAY BE OBTAINED FROM THE MASTER OF THE VESSEL, OR THE VESSEL'S AGENT

LIGHTER
TRUCK

ARRIVED— DATE .... TIME ....

UNLOADED— DATE .... TIME ....

CHECKED BY ....

PLACED IN SHIP ON DOCK LOCATION ....

AGENT FOR MASTER

BY ....
RECEIVING CLERK

DATE ....

Form 35-586 • 700 Central Ave., New Providence, N.J. 07974 • (800) 631-3098

151

Figure 4–14. Consular invoice.

FACTURE CONSULAIRE | **CONSULAT DE LA REPUBLIQUE D'HAITI** | **CONSULAR INVOICE**

B. L. No. ————

Marks (Marques) and Country of Origin

Merchandise Shipped on the S. S.: ———— on ————
Marchandises expédiées sur le SS. Nationality - Name (nom) le Date of Sailing
Sailing from the Port of ———— for ————, Haiti
Partant du port de Pour
Name and Address of Shipper ————
Nom et adresse de l'expéditeur
Consigned to order of ———— of ————
Consignées à l'ordre de
Notify ———— of ————, Haiti
Notifier de

Numbers Numéros	Number of pieces Nombre de colis	Nature of Packing Nature de l'emballage	Denomination and Details of Each Article (Quantity, Quality, Measure, Yardage, etc.) in Terms of the Haitian Tariff. Dénomination et détails de chaque article (quantité, qualité, mesure, yardage, etc.) dans les termes du Tarif Haïtien.	Weights in / Poids en Gross / Brut	Weights in / Poids en Net / Net	Values in U.S. Currency Valeur en Monnaie des E.U.

We affirm that this invoice is a correct and faithful expression of the truth,
J'affirme que cette facture est l'expression sincère et fidèle de la vérité,
that it corresponds in every particular with our books, and that neither the
qu'elle est en tout conforme à mes livres, qu'aucune dénomination usuelle,
usual designation, nor the weights, nor the quantity or quality, nor the value
ni le poids, ni la quantité ou la qualité, ni la valeur, ni l'origine des articles
and origin named therein are in any way altered, and are thereof exactly the
qui y sont portés, n'ont été altérés et sont, en conséquence, les mêmes que
same than those appeared on our Export Declaration No.
of (date) submitted to the U. S. Custom House.
ceux accusés sur ma déclaration No.
du soumise à la Douane des Etats-Unis.

———— Date ———— 19 ————

———— For Account of
Name of forwarding agent, broker or commissioner, etc.

Shippers ————
Expediteurs

Per: ————
Signature

NOTE:—In all cases where the merchandise is taxed at net weight, the weight to be taxed of said merchandise will include all interior or immediate packing, including the paste board boxes or objects made of paste board, not subject to a higher tax. (Article 29, Law of July 26, 1926.)

Dans tous les cas où les marchandises sont taxées au poids net, le poids imposable des dites marchandises comprendra tous les emballages antérieurs ou immédiats, y compris les cartons ou objets en carton, non soumis à un droit plus élevé (Article 29, loi du 26 Juillet, 1926.)

ARRANGEMENT OF DOCUMENTS:

3 Consular Invoices and 3 Original Bills of lading clipped or stapled together, the invoice on top.

To each of the remaining Consular invoices a copy of signed B/L must be stapled and the whole set clipped together.

Value of merchandise Valeur des marchandises		
Packing (if not included in the value of the merchandise) Emballage (s'il n'est pas compris dans la valeur des marchandises)		
Inland Freight. Bill of Lading. Wharfage and Trucking Charges Frét et frais du connaissement, embarquement et camionnage.		
Total F. O. B. Value		
Brokerage fees Commission d'achat		
Interest Intérêts		
Export Duties paid at Port of Origin Droits d'exportation acquittés au port d'origine		
Ocean Freight and Bill of Lading Expenses (including embarking and disembarking) Frêt et frais du connaissement, embarquement et débarquement compris		
Insurance Assurance		
Consular fees: / Droits consulaires: *2% of F O B value $		
Stamp on Inv. ($1.20)		
B/L visa ($2.00)		
Stamp on B/L ($1.20)		
Other expenses Autres frais		
Total amount of invoice Montant total de la facture		

CONSULAR INVOICE FEES

*For any merchandise being shipped by boat to Haiti and whose value FOB is inferior to $200.00 — the fee is $3.00 plus B/L visa and Stamps ———— 7.40
Over $200.00 — the fee is 2% on the value FOB plus B/L visa and Stamps
Visa for Certificate of Origin $2.00 plus Stamps $1.20 ———— 3.20
Visa for Commercial Invoice if requested $2.00 plus Stamp $1.20 ———— 3.20

ADDITIONAL FEES:
Visa on Consular Invoice requested after 4 p. m. ———— 2.00*
Visa on Consular Invoice requested on holidays ———— 4.00*

K. Certificates of Origin

Some countries require that goods shipped to the country be accompanied by a certificate of origin designating the place of manufacture or production of the goods. This is signed by the exporter, and, usually, a local chamber of commerce that is used to performing this service (again, for a fee) certifies to the best of its knowledge that the products are products of the country specified by the exporter. The exporter may request the freight forwarder to ascertain and advise it whether a certificate of origin is required, but prior thereto, the exporter should check with the buyer for a list of all documents required to make customs entry in the country of destination.

In some instances, a certificate of origin is required in order to claim preferential duty rates such as the one required under the North American Free Trade Agreement (NAFTA). NAFTA contains product-specific country of origin criteria that must be met to qualify for reduced duty treatment on exports to or imports from Canada or Mexico. More information regarding these certificates of origin may be found in Chapter 11.

Certificates of origin must be distinguished from country of origin marking. Many countries require that the products themselves and the labels on the packages specify the country of origin (see discussion in Chapter 2, Section R). The country of origin certificate may be in addition to or in lieu of that requirement. (A generic sample, to be executed by a local chamber of commerce, is shown in Figure 4–15.)

L. Certificates of Free Sale

Sometimes an importer will request that an exporter provide a certificate of free sale. Loosely speaking, this is a certification that a product being purchased by the importer complies with any U.S. government regulations for marketing the product and may be freely sold within the United States. Sometimes, depending upon the type of product involved, the importer will be able to accept a self-certification by the exporter. Frequently, however, the importer seeks the certificate of free sale because the importer's own government requires it. For example, these requests are common with regard to food, beverages, pharmaceuticals, and medical devices. The foreign government may or may not require the importer to conduct its own testing of the products for safety but may, either as a primary source or as backup for its own testing, seek confirmation that the products are in compliance with the U.S. Food, Drug and Cosmetics Act. The U.S. Food and Drug Administration has procedures for issuing a Certificate for Products for Export certifying that the product is registered with the FDA in the United States and is in compliance with U.S. law. (A sample certificate

Figure 4–15. Certificate of origin.

Certificate of Origin

The undersigned ———————————————————————————————
(Owner or Agent)

for _____
(Name and Address of Shipper)

declares the following listed goods shipped on _____
(Name of Carrier)

on _____ consigned to _____
(Shipment Date)   (Recipient's Name)

_____
(Recipient's Name and Address)
are the products of the United States of America.

Marks & Numbers	No. of Packages, Boxes or Cases	Weight in Kilos		Full Description of Item
		Gross	Net	

State of _____ County of _____

Sworn to me _____

this _____ day of _____, 20____ _____
(Signature of Owner or Agent)

_____

The _____, a recognized Chamber of Commerce Under

the laws of the State of _____, has examined the manufacturer's

invoice or shipper's affidavit concerning the origin of the merchandise and, according to the best

of its knowledge and belief, finds that the products named originated in the United States of North

America.

Secretary _____

is shown in Figure 4–16; an FDA Application Form 3613-e is shown in Figure 4–17; and guidance from the FDA on the information needed to request a certificate of free sale is shown in Figure 4–18.)

M. Delivery Instructions and Delivery Orders

The delivery instructions (see Figure 4–19) form is usually issued by the freight forwarding company to the inland transportation carrier (the trucking or rail company), indicating to the inland carrier which pier or steamship company has been selected for the ocean transportation and giving specific instructions to the inland carrier as to where to deliver the goods at the port of export. This must be distinguished from the delivery order (see Figure 4–20), which is a document used to instruct the customs broker at the foreign port of destination what to do with the goods, in particular, the method of foreign inland transportation to the buyer's place of business.

N. Special Customs Invoices

In addition to the commercial invoice, some countries require a special customs invoice (see Figure 4–21) designed to facilitate clearance of the goods and the assessment of customs duties in that country. Such an invoice lists specific information required under the customs regulations of that country. It is similar in some ways to the consular invoice, except that it is prepared by the exporter and need not be signed or certified by the consulate.

O. Shipper's Declarations for Dangerous Goods

Under the U.S. Hazardous Materials Transportation Act, the International Air Transport Association Dangerous Goods Regulations, and the International Maritime Dangerous Goods Code, exporters are required to provide special declarations or notices to the inland and ocean transportation companies when the goods are hazardous. This includes explosives, radioactive materials, etiological agents, flammable liquids or solids, combustible liquids or solids, poisons, oxidizing or corrosive materials, and compressed gases as well as aerosols, dry ice, batteries, cotton, anti-freeze, cigarette lighters, motor vehicles, diesel fuel, disinfectants, cleaning liquids, fire extinguishers, pesticides, animal or vegetable fabrics or fibers, matches, paints, and many other

Figure 4–16. Certificate of free sale.

DEPARTMENT OF HEALTH & HUMAN SERVICES   Public Health Service

Food and Drug Administration
2098 Gaither Road
Rockville MD 20850

CERTIFICATE FOR PRODUCTS FOR EXPORT

The Food and Drug Administration certifies that the products as described below are subject to its jurisdiction. Products which are legally distributed in accordance with the Federal Food, Drug, and Cosmetic Act within the United States may be exported without restriction.

21 CFR 820 of the Food and Drug Administration regulations requires the manufacturer to follow Good Manufacturing Practices. The plant in the United States where these products are manufactured is subject to periodic inspections by the Food and Drug Administration.

This certificate is not valid unless the Foreign Country Certification Statement is completed by a responsible individual of the exporting firm.

PRODUCTS   **MANUFACTURING PLANT LOCATION**

See Attached List
 (one page)

Marilyn K. Schoenfelder
Acting Branch Chief
Information Processing and
   Office Automation Branch
Division of Program Operations
Office of Compliance

COUNTY OF MONTGOMERY
STATE OF MARYLAND

Subscribed and sworn to before me this 1st day of June . 1994.

MARY JO O'CONNELL
NOTARY PUBLIC   MARYLAND
My Commission Expires October 19, 1997

Figure 4–17. FDA Form 3613e - application.

Form Approved: OMB No. 0910-0498; Expiration Date: 3/31/2015

Department of Health and Human Services Food and Drug Administration Center for Food Safety and Applied Nutrition	**FOOD EXPORT CERTIFICATE APPLICATION**	Date

1. Food Manufacturer Information

Manufacturer name	Doing business as name (*If other than "Manufacturer name" to left, and you wish this name to appear on the export certificate*)

State License/Registration number	Address		
Contact person name			
Contact phone/fax	City	State or Province	ZIP/postal code
Contact email		Country	

2. Exporting Company Information (if applicable)

Export company name

State License/Registration number	Address		
Contact person name	City	State or Province	ZIP/postal code
Contact phone/fax/or email		Country	

3. Shipment Description

Product	Common Name	Manufacturer	Description/Comments

Continue on additional page(s) as needed.

4. Intended Destination of Shipment (Country)

Name of country

5. Send Certificate To ☐ Manufacturer ☐ Distributor ☐ Other (*provide the following information*)

Firm name	Address		
	City	State	ZIP/postal code
Contact person name	Country		

6. Send Certificate Via

Carrier name (*U.S. Mail, FedEx, etc.*)	Account number (*If applicable*)

7. Fees

Fees are $10 per certificate, and will be billed upon receipt of this application.	☐ Copies of certificate: ___ x ___ = Total $ ___ Number Fee/copy

FORM FDA 3613e (3/12)   Page 1 of 2   PSC Publishing Services (301) 443-6740 EF

Figure 4–17. (*continued*)

8. Label(s)	
Attach an original or an electronic copy of any applicable product label(s). A fax copy is acceptable only if it is readable.	

9. Verification

The undersigned verifies that all ingredients are approved for use by FDA or appear on the GRAS list, and each product is intended for human consumption and is available for sale in the U.S. without restriction.

Signature	Name and Title	Date

**Department of Health and Human Services
Food and Drug Administration
Center for Food Safety and Applied Nutrition**

**FOOD EXPORT CERTIFICATE APPLICATION
Instructions**

For Manufacturers/Distributors

1. The Manufacturer/Distributor fills out the application information describing the consignment, manufacturer (note that different processing facilities of the manufacturer may be listed on the table describing the foods), where and how to send the certificate, optional information as needed, and applicant signature, name, and date.

2. The Manufacturer/Distributor submits the application (by mail, fax, email), along with labels as applicable. For contacts, refer to *http://www.fda.gov/Food/InternationalActivities/Exports/ExportCertificates/UCM151486.htm*

For FDA Officials

3. FDA Official reviews the application to be sure all the blanks are filled in properly, verifies manufacturer's license or registration, and investigates inspection data on the listed products.

4. The Official may require an inspection prior to issuance of the export certificate.

5. The Official prints the Certificate on watermarked Department letterhead, assigns a unique registration number and expiration date, signs, dates, seals, and issues the Certificate as indicated.

6. The Official maintains in his records an identical copy of the signed Certificate, marked "Copy" *for a period of at least two years.*

7. In the event that the Manufacturer fails to comply with the law as stated on the Certificate, the Official will reject the application and promptly notify the Manufacturer that the Certificate cannot be issued.

After the Certificate Has Been Issued

8. The Manufacturer/Distributor forwards the Certificate to the foreign Importer and verifies that it is acceptable.

9. If the Certificate is not acceptable, the Exporter notifies the FDA Official that the certificate has not been accepted by the Importer, and the Official will promptly attempt to reconcile the issue with the Importer.

This section applies only to requirements of the Paperwork Reduction Act of 1995.

"DO NOT SEND YOUR COMPLETED FORM TO THE PRA STAFF ADDRESS BELOW."

The burden time for this collection of information is estimated to average 1 hour per response, including the time to review instructions, search existing data sources, gather and maintain the data needed and complete and review the collection of information. Send comments regarding this burden estimate or any other aspect of this information collection, including suggestions for reducing this burden, to:

Department of Health and Human Services
Food and Drug Administration
Office of Chief Information Officer
Paperwork Reduction Act (PRA) Staff
1350 Piccard Drive, Room 400
Rockville, MD 20850

"An agency may not conduct or sponsor, and a person is not required to respond to, a collection of information unless it displays a currently valid OMB control number."

FORM FDA 3613e (3/12)   Page 2 of 2

Figure 4–18. FDA guidelines for Export Certificates.

Guidance for Industry
FDA Export Certificates

> This guidance will represent the Food and Drug Administration's (FDA's) current thinking on this topic. It does not create or confer any rights for or on any person and does not operate to bind FDA or the public. You can use an alternative approach if the approach satisfies the requirements of the applicable statutes and regulations. If you want to discuss an alternative approach, contact the FDA staff responsible for implementing this guidance. If you cannot identify the appropriate FDA staff, call the appropriate telephone number listed on the title page of this guidance.

I. Introduction

This guidance document is intended to provide a general description of FDA Export Certificates to industry and foreign governments. Firms exporting products from the United States are often asked by foreign customers or foreign governments to supply a certification relating to products subject to the Federal Food, Drug, and Cosmetic Act (the Act), 21 U.S.C. §§321-397, and other statutes FDA administers. This guidance supersedes the document issued under this title in August 2002.

FDA's guidance documents, including this guidance, do not establish legally enforceable responsibilities. Instead, guidances describe the Agency's current thinking on a topic and should be viewed only as recommendations, unless specific regulatory or statutory requirements are cited. The use of the word "should" in Agency guidances means that something is suggested or recommended, but not required.

II. What are FDA Export Certificates?

Firms exporting products from the United States are often asked by foreign customers or foreign governments to supply a "certificate" for products regulated by the Food and Drug Administration (FDA). A certificate is a document prepared by FDA containing information about a product's regulatory or marketing status.

III. Why do foreign governments want FDA Export Certificates?

In many cases, foreign governments are seeking official assurance that products exported to their countries can be marketed in the United States or meet specific U.S. regulations, for example current Good Manufacturing Practice (cGMP) regulations. Review of an FDA Export Certificate may be a required part of the process to register or import a product into another country.

(continues)

159

Figure 4–18. *(continued)*

IV. What Types of Export Certificates does FDA issue?

At the current time, FDA issues the following types of Export Certificates, although not all certificate types are issued for every FDA regulated product:

- The "**Certificate of Free Sale**" (Certificate of Export for Seafood) is for food, including dietary supplements, and cosmetic products that may be legally marketed in the United States. (CFSAN)

- The "**Health Certificates for Food/Feed**" currently required primarily by the European Union (EU), are usually consignment-specific and often contain language pertaining to "compliance" of the particular product/consignment with foreign regulations. As a matter of policy, FDA does not issue export certificates that attest to compliance with another country's requirements. Rather, FDA may work with other governments to develop mutually acceptable language for the certificate, e.g., language recognizing "equivalence" rather than "compliance". (Office of Regulatory Affairs-Field Offices)

- The "**Specified Risk Materials of Bovine, Ovine and Caprine Origin Certificate**" is used for the export of gelatin that can be legally marketed in the United States. These certificates address concerns on raw material in regard to transmissible spongiform encephalopathies. (CFSAN)

- The "**Certificate of a Pharmaceutical Product**" conforms to the format established by the World Health Organization (WHO) and is intended for use by the importing country when considering whether to license the product in question for sale in that country. (CBER, CDER, and CVM)

- The "**Non-clinical Research Use Only Certificate**" is for the export of a product, material, or component, for non-clinical research use only, that is not intended for human use and which may be marketed in, and legally exported from, the United States under the Act. These non-clinical research use only materials will be labeled in accordance with 21 CFR 809.10(c)(2) or 21 CFR 312.160, as appropriate, and exported as they are presently being sold or offered for sale in the United States. (CBER and CDRH)

- The "**Certificate to Foreign Government**" is for the export of human drugs and biologics, animal drugs, and devices that can be legally marketed in the United States. (CBER, CDRH, and CVM)

- The "**Certificate of Exportability**" is for the export of human drugs and biologics, animal drugs, and devices that cannot be legally marketed in the United States, but meet the requirements of sections 801(e) or 802 of the Act and may be legally exported. (CBER, CDRH, and CVM)

(continues)

Figure 4–18. *(continued)*

V. Is FDA required to issue Export Certificates?

Section 801(e)(4) of the Act provides that FDA shall, upon request, issue certificates for human drugs and biologics, animal drugs, and devices that either meet the applicable requirements of the Act and may be legally marketed in the United States or may be legally exported under the Act although they may not be legally marketed in the United States. The Act does not require FDA to issue certificates for food, including animal feeds, food and feed additives, and dietary supplements, or cosmetics. However, since foreign governments may require certificates for these types of products, the agency intends to continue to provide this service as resources permit.

VI. Does FDA issue Export Certificates for unapproved products?

The 1996 FDA Export Reform amendments to the Act provided for FDA to issue certificates for exports of certain products even though the products are not allowed to be marketed in the United States. FDA issues Certificates of Exportability for biologics, animal drugs, and devices that may be exported under these provisions of the Act but may not otherwise be marketed, sold, offered for sale, or distributed in the United States. For human drug products, FDA issues a Certificate of a Pharmaceutical Product, containing a special notation that the product is unapproved, instead of a Certificate of Exportability. FDA does not issue Certificates of Exportability for foods, dietary supplements, and cosmetics.

VII. What does FDA mean, when it attests to compliance with current Good Manufacturing Practice (cGMP) regulations in an Export Certificate?

FDA performs inspections for compliance with cGMP regulations for drug, biologic, medical devices, human food and animal feed manufacturers that are registered and listed with the Agency. FDA bases its attestation of compliance with cGMP regulations on the manufacturer's most recent FDA inspection and other available information. Generally, FDA cGMP regulations are intended to assure that the manufacturer can manufacture, process, package, and hold a product to assure that it meets the requirements of the Act as to safety, identity, strength, quality, and purity.

VIII. When does FDA refuse to issue an Export Certificate?

FDA will not issue a Certificate to Foreign Government or a Certificate of a Pharmaceutical Product for products that do not meet the applicable requirements of the Act. Additionally, such certificates will not be issued if FDA has initiated an enforcement action (e.g., a seizure or an injunction). Other examples of circumstances for which certificates will not be issued include:

(continues)

161

Figure 4–18. *(continued)*

- Failure of the manufacturing facility(ies) to operate in compliance with the cGMP regulations (unless the particular exported product is not affected by the specific cGMP deficiencies);

- Manufacturing facility(ies) not registered or listed with FDA; and

- When the product is not exported from the United States.

FDA will not issue Certificates of Exportability for products subject to section 802 of the Act if the manufacturing facility(ies) does not comply with cGMP regulations, unless the particular exported product is not affected by the specific cGMP deficiencies.

FDA also will not issue Certificates of Free Sale and Health Certificates for Food/Feed when products are under FDA regulatory action (e.g., the product is under seizure or the firm is under injunction).

IX. Does FDA charge a fee for Export Certificates?

For human drug, biologic, animal drug, and device export certificates issued under section 801(e)(4) of the Act; the agency may charge a fee of up to $175 if FDA issues a certificate within 20 days of receipt of a complete request for such a certificate. This fee may vary depending on the product type, but it will not exceed $175. FDA has interpreted the 20-day period to mean 20 government working days.

X. What are the legal requirements for exporting unapproved products under sections 801(e) and 802 of the Act?

Sections 801(e) and 802 of the Act contain numerous legal requirements for exporting unapproved products and other products that do not comply with the relevant requirements of the Act for distribution and sale in the United States. For sections 801(e) and 802 of the Act, refer to FD&C Act Chapter VIII: Imports and Exports.

XI. What are FDA's cGMP requirements for drugs, devices and biologics?

FDA's cGMP requirements for drugs are the requirements for the methods to be used in, and the facilities or controls to be used for, the manufacture, processing, packing, or holding of a drug (including a biologic) to assure that such drug meets the requirements of the Act as to safety, and has the identity and strength and meets the quality and purity characteristics that it purports or is represented to possess (21 CFR Parts 210 and 211).

The cGMP requirements for devices are set forth in the quality system regulation (21 CFR Part 820). The requirements govern the methods used in, and the facilities and controls used for, the design, manufacture, packaging, labeling, storage, installation, and servicing of all finished devices intended for human use.

(continues)

Figure 4–18. (*continued*)

Biological products, depending on their intended use, must meet the cGMP requirements for either drugs or devices. Supplementary requirements for biological products are in 21 CFR Parts 600-680.

XII. Where do I get more information?

For further information on Export Certification refer to the Compliance Policy Guide for FDA Staff, Sec. 110.100 Certification for Exports (CPG 7150.01).

For further information on Export Certification processing for specific product areas refer to the following websites:

- For **Biological Products** visit Importing & Exporting (Biologics) to obtain a Certificate of Exportability, Certificate to Foreign Government, Certificate of a Pharmaceutical Product, or a Non-Clinical Research Use Only Certificate.

- For **Medical Devices** visit Exporting Medical Devices to obtain a Certificate of Exportability, Certificate to Foreign Government, or a Non-Clinical Research Use Only Certificate.

- For **Drug Products** visit Certificate of a Pharmaceutical Product Application Instructions to obtain a Certificate of a Pharmaceutical Product.

- For **Veterinary Products** visit Exporting - Animal Feed and Drugs to obtain a Certificate of Exportability, Certificate to Foreign Government, Certificate of Free Sale, or a Certificate of a Pharmaceutical Product.

- For **Cosmetics** visit Cosmetic Exports to obtain a General Certificate or Product Specific Certificate.

- For **Foods** (including **Dietary Supplements**) visit "Enter a Food Export Certificate Application Step-by-Step Instructions" to obtain a Certificate of Free Sale or Certificate of Export.

  o European Union (EU) Export Certificates For Fishery and Aquaculture Products visit "Export Certificates for Fishery/Aquaculture Products and Live/Raw Molluscan Shellfish."

  o Notice: Establishment of lists of exporters of animal-derived commodities to the European Union visit *Federal Register* Volume 75, Number 225, Nov. 23, 2010, pp. 71444-71446.

  o US FDA - EU Seafood Processor Export Certificate Lists visit European Union (EU) Export Certificate List.

- For further information on Information for FDA Regulated Industry visit For Industry on FDA's website.

- For further information on FDA Issued/Supported Export Certificates for Food visit http://www.cfsan.fda.gov/~lrd/certifi3.html.

Figure 4–19. Delivery instructions.

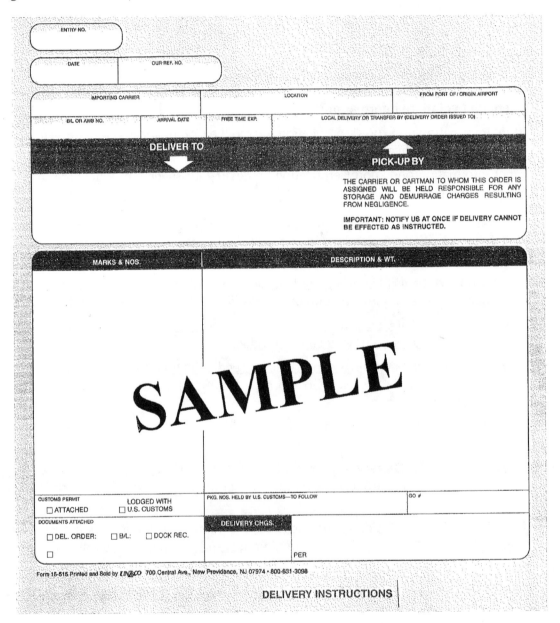

Figure 4–20. Delivery order.

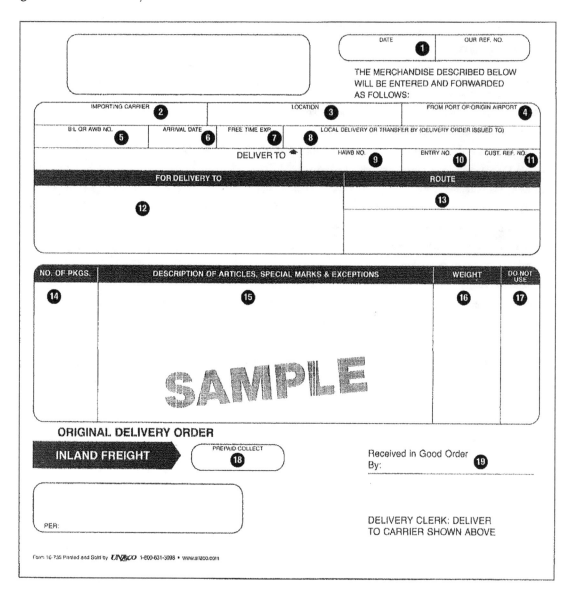

Figure 4–20. *(continued)*

Instructions for completing the
Delivery Order

1. **Date of form preparation**

2. **Enter the name of the importing carrier, shipping line, or air line as applicable.**

3. **Enter the location of the port of entry.**

4. **Enter the shipment city and state or country** of the port of origin or airport name and location.

5. **Enter bill of lading or air waybill number** of the shipment.

6. **Specify the scheduled date of arrival** at the seaport or airport.

7. **Enter estimated expiration date of "free time" period** before storage charges are assessed.

8. **Specify name of local delivery or cartage agent** if applicable.

9. **Enter the house air waybill number** for airfreight shipments.

10. **Enter the Customs Entry Number** if applicable.

11. **Enter the customer reference number** specified by the shipper.

12. **Enter the complete delivery name and address of the consignee** (recipient) of the freight.

13. **Specify the carrier's, forwarder's, or agent's delivery routing.**

14. **Enter the total number of packages** to be delivered.

15. **Enter the description of the freight** to include packaging and contents.

16. **Enter the gross weight of the shipment** (indicate whether pounds or kilograms).

17. **Leave this column blank.**

18. **Specify if the shipment is freight prepaid or collect.**

19. **Consignee signature** to verify delivery.

Figure 4–21. Canadian Customs Coding Form.

1. IMPORTER NAME AND ADDRESS / NOM ET ADRESSE DE L'IMPORTATEUR		NO. - N°	2. TRANSACTION NO. - N° DE TRANSACTION			Help	Aide	Restore - Restaurer

PROTECTED (WHEN COMPLETED) / PROTÉGÉ (UNE FOIS REMPLI)

CANADA CUSTOMS CODING FORM / DOUANES CANADA - FORMULE DE CODAGE

Canada Border Services Agency / Agence des services frontaliers du Canada

3. TYPE	4. OFFICE NO. N° DE BUREAU	5. GST REGISTRATION NO. N° DE TPS	6. PAYMENT CODE CODE DE PAIEMENT	7. MODE OF - DE TRANS.	8. PORT OF UNLADING PORT DE DEBARQ.	9. TOTAL VFD - TOTAL DE LA VD

10. SUB HDR NO. N° DE SOUS-EN-TÊTE	11. VENDOR NAME - NOM DU VENDEUR	NO. - N°	12. COUNTRY OF ORIGIN PAYS D'ORIGINE	13. PLACE OF EXPORT LIEU D'EXPORTATION	14. TARIFF TREATMENT TRAITEMENT TARIFAIRE	15. U.S. PORT OF EXIT BUREAU DE SORTIE DES É.-U.

16. DIRECT SHIPMENT DATE DATE D'EXPÉDITION DIRECTE M D/J	17. CRCY. CODE DEVISE	18. TIME LIMIT - DÉLAI	19. FREIGHT - FRET

20. RELEASE DATE - DATE DE LA MAINLEVÉE

21. LINE LIGNE	22. DESCRIPTION DÉSIGNATION	23. WEIGHT / KGM POIDS / KGM	PREVIOUS TRANSACTION - TRANSACTION ANTÉRIEURE		26. SPECIAL AUTHORITY AUTORISATION SPÉCIALE
			24. NUMBER - NUMÉRO	25. LINE-LIGNE	
27. CLASSIFICATION NO N° DE CLASSEMENT	28. TARIFF CODE TARIFAIRE	29. QUANTITY QUANTITÉ	30. U - M	31. VFD CODE CODE VD	32. SIMA CODE CODE DE LMSI	33. RATE OF CUSTOMS DUTY TAUX DE DROIT DE DOUANE	34. E.T. RATE TAUX T.A.	35. RATE OF GST TAUX DE TPS	36. VALUE FOR CURRENCY CONVERSION CONVERSION VALEUR POUR CHANGE
37. VALUE FOR DUTY VALEUR EN DOUANE	38. CUSTOMS DUTIES DROITS DE DOUANE	39. SIMA ASSESSMENT COTISATION DE LMSI	40. EXCISE TAX TAXE D'ACCISE	41. VALUE FOR TAX VALEUR POUR TAXE	42. GST TPS

21. LINE LIGNE	22. DESCRIPTION DÉSIGNATION	23. WEIGHT / KGM POIDS / KGM	PREVIOUS TRANSACTION - TRANSACTION ANTÉRIEURE		26. SPECIAL AUTHORITY AUTORISATION SPÉCIALE
			24. NUMBER - NUMÉRO	25. LINE-LIGNE	
27. CLASSIFICATION NO N° DE CLASSEMENT	28. TARIFF CODE TARIFAIRE	29. QUANTITY QUANTITÉ	30. U - M	31. VFD CODE CODE VD	32. SIMA CODE CODE DE LMSI	33. RATE OF CUSTOMS DUTY TAUX DE DROIT DE DOUANE	34. E.T. RATE TAUX T.A.	35. RATE OF GST TAUX DE TPS	36. VALUE FOR CURRENCY CONVERSION CONVERSION VALEUR POUR CHANGE
37. VALUE FOR DUTY VALEUR EN DOUANE	38. CUSTOMS DUTIES DROITS DE DOUANE	39. SIMA ASSESSMENT COTISATION DE LMSI	40. EXCISE TAX TAXE D'ACCISE	41. VALUE FOR TAX VALEUR POUR TAXE	42. GST TPS

21. LINE LIGNE	22. DESCRIPTION DÉSIGNATION	23. WEIGHT / KGM POIDS / KGM	PREVIOUS TRANSACTION - TRANSACTION ANTÉRIEURE		26. SPECIAL AUTHORITY AUTORISATION SPÉCIALE
			24. NUMBER - NUMÉRO	25. LINE-LIGNE	
27. CLASSIFICATION NO N° DE CLASSEMENT	28. TARIFF CODE TARIFAIRE	29. QUANTITY QUANTITÉ	30. U - M	31. VFD CODE CODE VD	32. SIMA CODE CODE DE LMSI	33. RATE OF CUSTOMS DUTY TAUX DE DROIT DE DOUANE	34. E.T. RATE TAUX T.A.	35. RATE OF GST TAUX DE TPS	36. VALUE FOR CURRENCY CONVERSION CONVERSION VALEUR POUR CHANGE
37. VALUE FOR DUTY VALEUR EN DOUANE	38. CUSTOMS DUTIES DROITS DE DOUANE	39. SIMA ASSESSMENT COTISATION DE LMSI	40. EXCISE TAX TAXE D'ACCISE	41. VALUE FOR TAX VALEUR POUR TAXE	42. GST TPS

21. LINE LIGNE	22. DESCRIPTION DÉSIGNATION	23. WEIGHT / KGM POIDS / KGM	PREVIOUS TRANSACTION - TRANSACTION ANTÉRIEURE		26. SPECIAL AUTHORITY AUTORISATION SPÉCIALE
			24. NUMBER - NUMÉRO	25. LINE-LIGNE	
27. CLASSIFICATION NO N° DE CLASSEMENT	28. TARIFF CODE TARIFAIRE	29. QUANTITY QUANTITÉ	30. U - M	31. VFD CODE CODE VD	32. SIMA CODE CODE DE LMSI	33. RATE OF CUSTOMS DUTY TAUX DE DROIT DE DOUANE	34. E.T. RATE TAUX T.A.	35. RATE OF GST TAUX DE TPS	36. VALUE FOR CURRENCY CONVERSION CONVERSION VALEUR POUR CHANGE
37. VALUE FOR DUTY VALEUR EN DOUANE	38. CUSTOMS DUTIES DROITS DE DOUANE	39. SIMA ASSESSMENT COTISATION DE LMSI	40. EXCISE TAX TAXE D'ACCISE	41. VALUE FOR TAX VALEUR POUR TAXE	42. GST TPS

21. LINE LIGNE	22. DESCRIPTION DÉSIGNATION	23. WEIGHT / KGM POIDS / KGM	PREVIOUS TRANSACTION - TRANSACTION ANTÉRIEURE		26. SPECIAL AUTHORITY AUTORISATION SPÉCIALE
			24. NUMBER - NUMÉRO	25. LINE-LIGNE	
27. CLASSIFICATION NO N° DE CLASSEMENT	28. TARIFF CODE TARIFAIRE	29. QUANTITY QUANTITÉ	30. U - M	31. VFD CODE CODE VD	32. SIMA CODE CODE DE LMSI	33. RATE OF CUSTOMS DUTY TAUX DE DROIT DE DOUANE	34. E.T. RATE TAUX T.A.	35. RATE OF GST TAUX DE TPS	36. VALUE FOR CURRENCY CONVERSION CONVERSION VALEUR POUR CHANGE
37. VALUE FOR DUTY VALEUR EN DOUANE	38. CUSTOMS DUTIES DROITS DE DOUANE	39. SIMA ASSESSMENT COTISATION DE LMSI	40. EXCISE TAX TAXE D'ACCISE	41. VALUE FOR TAX VALEUR POUR TAXE	42. GST TPS

DECLARATION - DÉCLARATION	43. DEPOSIT - DÉPÔT	47. CUSTOMS DUTIES DROITS DE DOUANE

I / JE

PLEASE PRINT NAME - LETTRES MOULÉES S.V.P.

OF / DE

IMPORTER / AGENT - IMPORTATEUR / AGENT

DECLARE THE PARTICULARS OF THIS DOCUMENT TO BE TRUE, ACCURATE AND COMPLETE / DÉCLARE QUE LES RENSEIGNEMENTS CI-DESSUS SONT VRAIS ET COMPLETS.

DATE   SIGNATURE

44. WAREHOUSE NO. - N° D'ENTREPÔT

45. CARGO CONTROL NO. - N° DE CONTRÔLE DU FRET

46. CARRIER CODE AT IMPORTATION / CODE DE TRANSPORTEUR À L'IMPORTATION

48. SIMA ASSESSMENT COTISATION DE LMSI

49. EXCISE TAX TAXE D'ACCISE

50. GST TPS

51. TOTAL

B3-3 (04)

Canada

products. The shipper must certify on the invoice that the goods are properly classed, described, packaged, marked, and labeled, and are in proper condition for transportation in accordance with the regulations of the Department of Transportation (see Chapter 2, Section L). The hazardous materials regulations are extremely detailed, and an exporter who has any doubt must check to determine whether its product is listed. If it is, the required declarations, invoicing, and labeling must be completed. (A sample declaration is shown in Figure 4–22.) Sometimes the exporter will be required to certify that the shipment is *not* a hazardous material (see Figure 4–23).

P. Precursor and Essential Chemical Exports

Those who export (or import) "precursor" chemicals and "essential" chemicals that can be used to manufacture illegal drugs are required to file Drug Enforcement Administration (DEA) Form 486 (see Figure 4–24). In some cases, this form must be filed fifteen days in advance of exportation (or importation).

Q. Animal, Plant, and Food Export Certificates

The U.S. Department of Agriculture is supportive of companies that want to export livestock, animal products, and plants and plant products. Often, the destination country will have specific requirements in order to permit import to that country, but sometimes the foreign country will accept or require inspections performed and certificates issued in the United States. In general, the U.S. Department of Agriculture offers inspection services and a variety of certificates to enable exporters to satisfy foreign government requirements. One example is an "Export Certificate/ Health Certificate—Animal Products" issued by the Veterinary Services Division (VS Form 17-140; see Figure 4–25) to certify that animals and poultry are free from communicable disease and meet the requirements of the importing country. Another type of certification is a "Federal Phytosanitary Certificate" (PPQ Form 577) to certify that live plants are free from plant pests. An exporter may apply for an export certificate to the Food Safety Inspection Service on Form 9060-6 and a "Meat and Poultry Export Certificate of Wholesomeness" will be issued. See http://www.aphis. usda.gov for more information.

Figure 4–22. Shipper's declaration for dangerous goods.

SHIPPER'S DECLARATION FOR DANGEROUS GOODS

Shipper	Air Waybill No.
	Page of Pages
	Shipper's Reference Number *(optional)*

Consignee	

Two completed and signed copies of this Declaration must be handed to the operator.	**WARNING**

TRANSPORT DETAILS

This shipment is within the limitations prescribed for: *(delete non-applicable)* PASSENGER AND CARGO AIRCRAFT / CARGO AIRCRAFT ONLY	Airport of Departure:	Failure to comply in all respects with the applicable Dangerous Goods Regulations may be in breach of the applicable law, subject to legal penalties.

Airport of Destination:	Shipment type: *(delete non-applicable)* NON-RADIOACTIVE / RADIOACTIVE

NATURE AND QUANTITY OF DANGEROUS GOODS

Dangerous Goods Identification						
UN or ID No.	Proper Shipping Name	Class or Division (Subsidiary Risk)	Packing Group	Quantity and type of packing	Packing Inst.	Authorization

SAMPLE

Additional Handling Information

24 HR. Emergency Contact Telephone_____

I hereby declare that the contents of this consignment are fully and accurately described above by the proper shipping name, and are classified, packaged, marked and labelled/placarded, and are in all respects in proper condition for transport according to applicable international and national governmental regulations. I declare that all of the applicable air transport requirements have been met.	Name and Title of Signatory Place and Date Signature *(see warning above)*

Figure 4–23. Shipper's certification of articles not restricted.

SHIPPER'S CERTIFICATION OF ARTICLES NOT RESTRICTED

WARNING: Failure to comply in all respects with Government and IATA restricted articles regulations may be a violation of the law, subject to fines, imprisonment, or both. This certification shall in no circumstance be signed by an employee of a forwarder, carrier or cargo agent.

NUMBER OF PACKAGES	ARTICLE AND DESCRIPTION Specify each article separately.	NET QUANTITY PER PACKAGE	FLASH POINT (for liquids)	
			°C.	°F.
	SAMPLE			

I hereby certify that the contents of this consignment, in spite of product name or appearance, are not restricted for air transportation by the Air Transport Restricted Articles Tariff No. 6-D, Government Hazardous Material Regulations or IATA Restricted Articles regulations. I acknowledge that I may be liable for damages resulting from any misstatement or omission and I further agree that any air carrier involved in the shipment of this consignment may rely upon this Certification.

Name and full address of shipper	Name and title of person signing
Date	Signature of shipper

FOR CARRIER'S USE ONLY

Air Waybill No.	Airport of Departure	Airport of Destination

THIS CERTIFICATION IS NOT A REQUIREMENT OF U.S. DEPT. OF TRANS.

Form 30-070L Printed and Sold by *UNZCO* (800) 631-3098 • www.unzco.com

Figure 4–24. DEA import/export declaration.

This form should be completed ONLINE and PRINTED on your printer. Complete the first two pages of this form ONLY. The remaining pages will be completed automatically. Refer to the instructions for guidance on the use of the 4 copies of this form.

U.S. Department of Justice	**Import / Export Declaration for List I and List II Chemicals**	Drug Enforcement Administration

SEE REVERSE INSTRUCTIONS FOR PRIVACY ACT	OMB Approval No. 1117-0023

1a. Type of Transaction: ☐ IMPORT ☐ EXPORT ☐ INTERNATIONAL   1b. Type of Submission ☐ ORIGINAL ☐ AMENDED ☐ WITHDRAWAL

1c. **WARNING!** 15-day advance notice required for initial shipment or for company that has lost regular importer or regular customer status. See 21 C.F.R. Part 1313 for further details.
☐ I certify I have met the conditions for the waiver of 15-day advance notice requirement.

DEA Transaction Number

2a. U.S. IMPORTER/ U.S. EXPORTER / U.S. BROKER
(Name, address, telephone, and fax no.)

2b. IF IMPORT, LIST FOREIGN CONSIGNOR; IF EXPORT OR INTERNATIONAL TRANSACTION, LIST FOREIGN TRANSFEREE. (Name, address, telephone, and fax no.)

DEA Registration Number (for List I only): _____

Purchase/Invoice no. _____

Foreign permit no. (if applicable)_____

3. Listed Chemicals to be Imported / Exported / Brokered

3a. Name and Description of chemical appearing on label or container. For drug products, show dosage strength and dosage size.	3b. Name of chemicals as designated by Title 21 C.F.R. 1310.02	3c. Number of containers, size, net weight of each chemical (kg). For drug products, show number of dosage units. Show net total weight per chemical.	3d. DATE OF ACTUAL IMPORT/EXPORT AND ACTUAL QUANTITY (To be completed by person named in (2a).) If same as 3c, write "same as 3c."

4a. ☐ FOREIGN ☐ DOMESTIC
PORT OF EXPORTATION:_____
APPROX. DEPARTURE DATE:

4b. ☐ FOREIGN ☐ DOMESTIC
PORT OF IMPORTATION: _____
APPROX. ARRIVAL DATE:

5. MODE OF TRANSPORTATION, NAME OF VESSEL, OR NAME OF CARRIER:

SIGNATURE OF AUTHORIZED INDIVIDUAL (Print or Type Name below Signature)   DATE:

Print Name:

DEA form - 486 (Previous version obsolete.)
2/29/2016

Copy 1

Figure 4–24. *(continued)*

6. **RETURN DECLARATION FOR EXPORTS AND INTERNATIONAL TRANSACTIONS** (Name & Quantity of List I and List II Chemicals exported to the Transferee or resulting from International Transaction. MUST be returned within 30 days from actual date of export (3d).

SIGNATURE: DATE:

For IMPORTS: List TRANSFEREE(S) UPON INITIAL APPLICATION (Names, address, telephone, and fax no.) Fill in 7 through 9. USE SEPARATE SHEET IF MORE THAN 3 TRANFEREES. **For INTERNATIONAL TRANSACTIONS:** Show foreign supplier in 7a and 7b only.

7a. NAME OF TRANSFEREE OF IMPORT | 7b. ADDRESS OF TRANSFEREE OF IMPORT

7c. Name & Quantity of List I and List II chemical to be Imported for this transferee. (Enter names as shown on labels; numbers and sizes of packages; and strength.) | 7d. Name & Quantity of List I and List II Chemical Actually Imported and Date Imported for this Transferee

7e. **RETURN DECLARATION** (Name & Quantity of List I and List II Chemical Distributed to the Transferee. MUST be returned within 30 days of date of actual import (7d) If amount not completely distributed, send a Return Declaration 30 days from the next distribution.). If the whole order was distributed, may say "all import distributed" and the date.

SIGNATURE: DATE:

8a. NAME OF TRANSFEREE OF IMPORT | 8b. ADDRESS OF TRANSFEREE OF IMPORT

8c. Name & Quantity of List I and List II chemical to be Imported for this transferee. (Enter names as shown on labels; numbers and sizes of packages; and strength.) | 8d. Name & Quantity of List I and List II Chemical Actually Imported and Date Imported for this Transferee.

8e. **RETURN DECLARATION** (Name & Quantity of List I and List II Chemical Distributed to the Transferee. MUST be returned within 30 days from actual date of import (8d) If amount not completely distributed, send a Return Declaration 30 days from the next distribution.). If the whole order was distributed, may say "all import distributed" and the date.

SIGNATURE: DATE:

9a. NAME OF TRANSFEREE OF IMPORT | 9b. ADDRESS OF TRANSFEREE OF IMPORT

9c. Name & Quantity of List I and List II chemical to be Imported for this transferee. (Enter names as shown on labels; numbers and sizes of packages; and strength.) | 9d. Name & Quantity of List I and List II Chemical Actually Imported and Date Imported for this Transferee.

9e. **RETURN DECLARATION** (Name & Quantity of List I and List II Chemical Distributed to the Transferee. MUST be returned within 30 days of date of actual import (9d) If amount not completely distributed, send a Return Declaration 30 days from the next distribution.). If the whole order was distributed, may say "all import distributed" and the date.

SIGNATURE: DATE:

DEA form - 486 (Previous version obsolete.)   Copy 1
2/29/2016

Reset Form   **Print Form**   Complete only the first two pages of form. The remaining pages will be automatically completed.

Figure 4–25. USDA Export Certificate Animal Products.

According to the Paperwork Reduction Act of 1995, an agency may not conduct or sponsor, and a person is not required to respond to, a collection of information unless it displays a valid OMB control number. The valid OMB control number for this information collection is 0579-0256. The time required to complete this information collection is estimated to average .5 hours per response, including the time for reviewing instructions, searching existing data sources, gathering and maintaining the data needed, and completing and reviewing the collection of information.	**OMB Approved** 0579-0256

Port:

UNITED STATES DEPARTMENT OF AGRICULTURE
ANIMAL AND PLANT HEALTH INSPECTION SERVICE

**EXPORT CERTIFICATE FOR
ANIMAL PRODUCTS**

FOR OFFICIAL USE ONLY

Date:

Certificate Number:

This certificate is for veterinary purposes only. It is valid for 30 days after the date of signature (*in the case of transport by ship or rail, the time is prolonged by the time of the voyage*).

This is to certify that rinderpest, foot-and-mouth disease, classical swine fever, swine vesicular disease, African swine fever, and contagious bovine pleuropneumonia do not exist in the United States of America.

ADDITIONAL DECLARATIONS

SIGNATURE OF ENDORSING OFFICIAL:

TYPED NAME:

TITLE OF ENDORSING OFFICIAL:

DESCRIPTION OF THE CONSIGNMENT

NAME AND ADDRESS OF EXPORTER:

NAME AND ADDRESS OF CONSIGNEE:

PRODUCT (*type of product, quantity, unit of measure, and animal product species of origin*):

IDENTIFICATION:

CONVEYANCE:

VS Form 16-4
MAR 2010

Figure 4–25. *(continued)*

According to the Paperwork Reduction Act of 1995, an agency may not conduct or sponsor, and a person is not required to respond to, a collection of information unless it displays a valid OMB control number. The valid OMB control number for this information collection is 0579-0256. The time required to complete this information collection is estimated to average .5 hours per response, including the time for reviewing instructions, searching existing data sources, gathering and maintaining the data needed, and completing and reviewing the collection of information.	**OMB Approved** 0579-0256

UNITED STATES DEPARTMENT OF AGRICULTURE ANIMAL AND PLANT HEALTH INSPECTION SERVICE **EXPORT CERTIFICATE FOR ANIMAL PRODUCTS** CONTINUATION PAGE	Page Number:
	FOR OFFICIAL USE ONLY
	Date:
	Certificate Number:
	Initials of Endorsing Official:

This is a continuation page which must be used in conjunction with VS Form 16-4.

VS Form 16-4A
MAR 2010

R. Drafts for Payment

If payment for the sale is going to be made under a letter of credit or by documentary collection, such as documents against payment ("D/P" or sight draft) or documents against acceptance ("D/A" or time draft), the exporter will draw a draft on the buyer's bank in a letter of credit transaction or the buyer in a documentary collection transaction payable to itself (sometimes it will be payable to the seller's bank on a confirmed letter of credit) in the amount of the sale. This draft will be sent to the seller's bank along with the instructions for collection, or sometimes the seller will send it directly to the buyer's bank (direct collection). If the payment agreement between the seller and the buyer is at sight, the buyer will pay the draft when it is received, or if it is issued under a letter of credit, the buyer's bank will pay the draft when it is received. If the agreement between the seller and the buyer is that the buyer will have some grace period before making payment, the amount of the delay, called the usance, will be written on the draft (time draft), and the buyer will usually be responsible for payment of interest to the seller during the usance period unless the parties agree otherwise. The time period may also be specified as some period after a fixed date, such as ninety days after the bill of lading or commercial invoice date, or payment simply may be due on a fixed date. (Samples of a sight draft and a time draft under a letter of credit are shown in Figures 4–26 and 4–27, respectively.)

S. Letters of Credit

When two companies do not know each other very well, then using a letter of credit is the best way to ensure that both parties live up to their expectations. So when the buyer has agreed to provide a letter of credit as part of the payment terms, the buyer will apply to its local bank in its home country and a letter of credit will be issued. The seller should send instructions to the buyer before the letter of credit is opened, advising the buyer as to the terms and conditions it desires. (A documentation checklist and sample set of instructions are shown in Figures 4–28 and 4-29.) The seller should always specify that the letter of credit must be irrevocable. The bank in the buyer's country is called the issuing bank. The buyer's bank will contact a correspondent bank near the seller in the United States, and the U.S. bank will send a notice or advice to the exporter that the letter of credit has been opened. If the letter of credit is a confirmed letter of credit, the U.S. bank is called the confirming bank; otherwise, it is called the advising bank. The advice will specify the exact documents that the exporter must provide to the bank in order to receive payment. Since the foreign and

Figure 4–26. Sight draft.

US $ _250,000_ _____ DATE _March 1, 1990_ NO. _1_ _____

TENOR _At sight_

PAY TO THE ORDER OF _ABC Export Company_ — Payee must endorse draft on reverse side prior to payment

Two hundred fifty thousand and no/100 _____U.S. Dollars

DRAWN UNDER LETTER OF CREDIT NO. _2738_ _____ DATED _January 31, 1990_

ISSUED BY _The Mitsui Bank, Ltd._

DRAWN ON _XYZ Import Company_

2-3, Toranomon 1-chome   ABC Export Company

Tokyo, Japan   AUTHORIZED SIGNATURE

SOLE BILL OF EXCHANGE

Courtesy of The First National Bank of Chicago.

Figure 4–27. Time draft.

US $ _$250,000_ _____ DATE _March 1, 1990_ NO. _2_ _____

TENOR _90 days after sight_

PAY TO THE ORDER OF _ABC Export Company_ — Payee must endorse draft on reverse side prior to payment

Two hundred fifty thousand and no/100 _____U.S. Dollars

DRAWN UNDER LETTER OF CREDIT NO. _2021_ _____ DATED _January 31, 1990_

ISSUED BY _The Mitsui Bank, Ltd._

DRAWN ON _XYZ Import Company_

2-3, Toranomon 1-chome   ABC Export Company

Tokyo, Japan   AUTHORIZED SIGNATURE

SOLE BILL OF EXCHANGE

Courtesy of The First National Bank of Chicago.

Figure 4–28. Applicant's checklist for letter of credit.

CHECKLIST FOR A COMMERCIAL LETTER OF CREDIT—APPLICANT

The following checklist identifies points that an applicant for a commercial letter of credit should consider when making an agreement with the seller (beneficiary) and completing an application for a letter of credit.

1. Does the beneficiary agree that the letter of credit should be irrevocable?
2. Do you have the complete name and address of the beneficiary, including street address and postal code, if applicable? If the beneficiary is a large company, what is the name of the person to whom correspondence should be addressed?
3. Is the letter of credit to be delivered to the beneficiary by the issuing bank through its correspondent bank, by the issuing bank directly, or by you directly?
4. How is the letter of credit to be delivered to the beneficiary—by air mail or by telex?
5. Do you or the beneficiary wish to designate an advising bank to deliver the letter of credit to the beneficiary, or do you want the issuing bank to choose the advising bank? If you wish to designate the advising bank, do you have its complete name and address?
6. Is the advising bank or another bank going to confirm the letter of credit? Or does the beneficiary wish another bank to act as the confirming bank? Do you have the complete name and address of the confirming bank, if any?
7. What is the total amount of credit, and in what currency is it to be denominated? If you want to approximate the total value of the transaction, is the credit amount preceded by a qualification such as "not exceeding" or "approximately" (meaning 10 percent more or less)?
8. What is the expiration date of the letter of credit?
9. What is the location for presentation of documents?
10. To what bank (nominated bank) is the beneficiary going to present documents?
11. How many days does the beneficiary have after shipment of goods to present documents to the nominated bank?
12. What is the method of payment under the letter of credit—sight draft, time draft, deferred payment?
13. What is the tenor of the draft(s), and what percentage of the invoice value is each draft to cover?
14. Is (are) the draft(s) to be drawn on you or another drawee?
15. How many copies of the commercial invoice should the beneficiary present to the nominated bank?
16. What is the agreed-upon description of the merchandise and/or services to be itemized in the commercial invoice? (Include quantity and unit price, if applicable.)
17. What are the origin and destination of the shipment?
18. What are the terms of shipment (FOB, CFR, CIF, other)?

Figure 4–29. Letter of credit instructions.

Letter of Credit Instructions	copyright Unz & Co 1997

Date: _____ Re: Our Pro Forma Invoice/Sales Contract Number_____ Dated: _____

To (Importer):	From:

Please instruct your bank to issue a letter of credit by teletransmission in accordance with the following terms and conditions and subject to the current revision of the <u>Uniform Customs and Practice for Documentary Credits</u> (1993 Revision) ICC Publication No. 500.

1. The Letter of Credit must be irrevocable.

2. The Credit must be advised to us through:

       ☐ With their confirmation.
       ☐ Without their confirmation.
       (Please check one box)

Name and Address of Advising Bank

3. The credit should expire on the date _____ at the counters of the Advising/Confirming bank

   in (insert place of expiry): _____ .

4. The Beneficiary's name and address must read
   exactly as:

Exact Name and Address of Beneficiary

SAMPLE

5. The credit must be issued in the amount of U.S. Dollars $ _____ ,

   ☐ approximately, or ☐ plus/minus _____ percent (please check one).

6. The credit must be available with the Advising/Confirming Bank by ☐ payment, or ☐ acceptance, or ☐ deferred payment, or ☐ negotiation (please check one).

7. Drafts are to be drawn on _____ , ☐ at sight, or

   ☐ at _____ days sight, or ☐ at _____ days date (please check one). **Note: the draft is to be dated the same date as the date of shipment.**

8. Partial shipments are ☐ allowed, ☐ not allowed (please check one). Transshipments are ☐ allowed, ☐ not allowed (please check one).

9. Shipments to be effected from : _____ , for transportation

   to: _____ , not later than the date: _____ .

10. The following documents are to be required:

    TRANSPORT DOCUMENT(S) (It is very important that you select the appropriate transport document for the mode of shipment being used. Refer to Articles 23 through 30 of UCP 500).

Form 10-026 Printed and Sold By Unz & Co, Inc. 700 Central Ave, New Providence, NJ 07974 (800) 631-3098

U.S. banks are acting as agent and subagent, respectively, for the buyer, the U.S. bank will refuse to pay unless the exact documents specified in the letter of credit are provided. The banks never see the actual shipment or inspect the goods; therefore, they are extremely meticulous about not releasing payment unless the documents required have been provided. The issuing bank and advising bank each have up to seven banking days to review the documents presented before making payment. When the seller receives the advice of the opening of a letter of credit, the seller should review in detail the exact documents required in order to be paid under the letter of credit. Where the documentation does not agree with the Letter of Credit is called a "discrepancy" and requires correction before the bank will agree to make payment. The bank charges additional fees for correcting discrepancies. A list of common discrepancies that may prevent payment is shown in Figure 4–30. A checklist that the seller (beneficiary of the letter of credit) should follow in reviewing the letter of credit and other documents is shown in Figure 4–31. Sometimes, if the seller is a good customer of the advising bank, the bank may be willing to make payment even when there are discrepancies if the seller signs a letter of indemnity (see Figure 4–32). The buyer can also instruct the bank to waive discrepancies. If, for any reason, the seller anticipates that it cannot provide a document exactly as required, it should contact the buyer immediately and have the buyer instruct its bank and the U.S. correspondent bank to amend the letter of credit. If this is not done, even though the seller has shipped the goods, payment will not be made by the bank. It is also important to note the date for presentation of documents and the expiration date of the letter of credit, and if for any reason shipment cannot be made within the time period, the seller should contact the buyer, and the buyer must instruct the banks to amend the letter of credit to extend the presentation and/or expiration date. (Sample advice for an irrevocable letter of credit is shown in Figure 4–33.) Generally letters of credit are issued in the "SWIFT" format, an established format by the Society for Worldwide Interbank Financial Telecommunication. SWIFT is a member-owned cooperative through which the financial world conducts its business operations with speed, certainty, and confidence.

T. Electronic Export Information

Export shipments require the filing of the Electronic Export Information (EEI) through the Automated Export System (AES). The EEI is electronically transmitted through the Internet to the Census Bureau and to U.S. Customs and Border Protection in advance of the shipment.

Figure 4–30. Common discrepancies in letters of credit.

- Documents presented after the expiration date of the letter of credit.

- Documents presented more than twenty-one days after shipment (or other date specified in the letter of credit).

- Missing documents, such as a full set of bills of lading, insurance certificates, and inspection certificates.

- Description of merchandise on the invoice differs from the description in the letter of credit (such as being written in a different language or different wording in the same language).

- Shipment terms and charges (ex-works, CFR, CIF) on the invoice differ from the terms specified in the letter of credit.

- Transshipment when it is not allowed.

- Shipment made after the date specified in the letter of credit.

- On board stamp on bills of lading not dated and signed or initialed by the carrier or his agent.

- Bills of lading improperly consigned, not endorsed, or show damage to goods.

- Documents inconsistent with one another (e.g., weights or packing information not the same on all documents presented).

- Insurance document not as per the credit terms, not in a sufficient amount, not endorsed, or after the shipment date.

- Drafts drawn on wrong person or for wrong amount or not signed or endorsed.

- Invoice not made out in the name of the applicant shown on the letter of credit.

The U.S. Principal Party in Interest (USPPI) is generally the party responsible for filing the EEI through the AES. The USPPI is the party in the United States that receives the primary benefit, financial or otherwise, from the export transaction. Only in a "routed export transaction," such as an Incoterms® ex-works sale, is the buyer or the Foreign Principal Party in Interest (FPPI) responsible for ensuring that the information is filed. To do so, the FPPI must appoint a freight forwarder in the United States to file the EEI on its behalf. With a valid power of attorney, freight forwarders may file the EEI information through the AES on behalf of the USPPI or the FPPI depending on who is responsible. When the transaction is a routed export transaction, the USPPI is still responsible for providing in writing information about the shipment to the FPPI or its agent so that the EEI may be completed fully and accurately (see Figure 4–34). The USPPI must also obtain a written certification from the FPPI that it accepts

Figure 4–31. Checklist for a letter of credit beneficiary.

CHECKLIST FOR A COMMERCIAL LETTER
OF CREDIT BENEFICIARY

The following checklist identifies points that a beneficiary of a commercial letter of credit should consider when receiving the letter of credit and when preparing required documents.

Letters of Credit

1. Are the names and addresses of the buyer and seller spelled correctly?

2. Is the credit irrevocable and issued in accordance with the latest International Chamber of Commerce (ICC) publication of the Uniform Customs and Practice for Documentary Credits (UCP)?

3. Which bank issued the credit? Is this bank satisfactory, or should a U.S. bank add its confirmation?

4. Do the terms of the letter of credit agree with the terms of the contract? Can you meet these terms?

5. Is the shipping schedule, as stipulated in the letter of credit, realistic? If necessary, is partial shipment or transshipment allowed?

6. Is the merchandise described correctly, including unit price, weight, and quantities?

7. Can presentation of documents be made on time? Will documents arrive before the expiration date and any other time limits indicated in the letter of credit?

8. Are the points of shipment and destination as agreed?

9. Are the terms of sale regarding freight charges and insurance as agreed?

10. If necessary, is the credit transferable?

11. Are the payment terms as agreed? If time payment terms are stated, which party is responsible for discount and acceptance charges?

12. Which party is responsible for banking charges?

Drafts

1. Are the drafts drawn by the beneficiary for the amount shown on the commercial invoice and in accordance with the tenor indicated?

2. Are drafts properly identified with the letter of credit?

3. Are the drafts drawn on (addressed to) the proper drawee and signed by authorized parties, with their titles indicated?

4. Are the drafts endorsed in blank if made out "to order" of the beneficiary (drawer)?

(continues)

Figure 4–31. *(continued)*

Commercial Invoices

1. Is the commercial invoice in the name of the beneficiary?

2. Is the commercial invoice addressed to the applicant named in the letter of credit?

3. Did you sign the commercial invoice if required?

4. Was the commercial invoice countersigned by any other party if required in the letter of credit?

5. Does the commercial invoice conform to the letter of credit's terms relative to the following items:

   • Total amount?

   • Unit prices and computations?

   • Description of merchandise and terms (FOB, CFR, CIF, and so on)?

   • Foreign language used for the merchandise description, if used in the letter of credit?

   • Description of packing, if required?

   • Declarations or clauses properly worded?

6. Do the shipping marks on the commercial invoice agree with those appearing on the bill of lading?

7. Do the shipping charges on the commercial invoice agree with those on the bill of lading?

8. If partial shipments are prohibited, is all merchandise shipped? Or, if partial shipments are permitted, is the value of the merchandise invoiced in proportion to the quantity of the shipment when the letter of credit does not specify unit prices?

Consular Invoices (If Required)

1. Does the consular invoice match the commercial invoice and bill of lading?

2. Is the description of merchandise in a foreign language, if it is shown that way in the letter of credit?

3. Is the official form completed in all the indicated places?

4. Are there no alterations, except by a Letter of Correction issued by the consulate?

5. If legalized commercial invoices are required, have the required number of copies been properly legalized?

Marine Bills of Lading (Ocean Shipments)

1. Are bills of lading in negotiable form if required in the letter of credit?

2. Are all originals being presented to the bank or accounted for?

(continues)

Figure 4–31. (*continued*)

---

3. Are all originals properly endorsed when consigned "to the order" of the shipper?

4. Are bills of lading clean (no notation showing defective goods or packaging)?

5. Do bills of lading indicate that merchandise was loaded on board and loaded within the time specified in the letter of credit? If this provision is not part of the text but in the form of a notation, is the notation dated and signed (initialed) by the carrier or its agent?

6. Are the bills of lading made out as prescribed in the letter of credit (in other words, with names and addresses of beneficiary, applicant, notify parties, and flag, if any)?

7. If freight was prepaid, is this payment clearly indicated by either "FREIGHT PREPAID" or "FREIGHT PAID"?

8. If charter party, sailing vessel, on deck, forwarder's, or consolidator's bills of lading is presented, does the credit specifically allow for them?

9. Do marks and numbers, quantities, and the general description of goods agree with the commercial invoice and letter of credit, with no excess merchandise shipped?

10. Does the bill of lading show transshipment if prohibited in the letter of credit?

11. Is the document signed by the carrier or its agent? Are corrections, if any, signed or initialed by the carrier or agent?

Insurance Documents

1. Are you presenting an insurance policy or a certificate? (Acknowledgments or a broker's cover are acceptable only if expressly allowed in the letter of credit.)

2. Is the insured amount sufficient?

3. Is the insurance coverage complete and in conformity with the letter of credit as it relates to:

   • Special risks where required?

   • Coverage of destination and time (in other words, carried through to the proper point and covering the entire period of shipment)?

   • Proper warehouse clauses?

4. Has the insurance document been countersigned where required?

5. Was the insurance document endorsed in blank if payable to the shipper?

6. Are shipping marks identical to those on the commercial invoice and bill of lading?

7. Are all corrections signed or initialed, and are riders or binders attached or cross-referenced?

(*continues*)

Figure 4–31. *(continued)*

Other Shipping Documents—Air Waybills, Inland Bills of Lading, Parcel Post Receipts

1. Do marks and numbers, quantities, and the general description of goods agree with the invoice and letter of credit, with no excess merchandise shipped?
2. Are the documents made out as prescribed by the letter of credit (including names and addresses of beneficiary, applicant, notify parties, flag, flight number, and visa, if any)?
3. If freight or dispatch expenses were to be prepaid, is this clearly indicated?
4. Are the documents dated within the terms specified by the letter of credit?
5. Are the bills of lading signed by the carrier or its agent? Are corrections, if any, initialed by the carrier or agent?

Certificates of Origin, Weight, Inspection, and Analysis

1. Are names and addresses as per the commercial invoice and letter of credit?
2. Is the country of origin, if required, as per the commercial invoice and letter of credit?
3. Have they been issued by the proper party and signed?
4. Do they show a description relative to the commercial invoice and letter of credit?
5. Are they in exact compliance with the letter of credit and dated with a reasonably current date?

Packing and Weight List

1. Does the packing type shown agree with the commercial invoice?
2. Does the quantity, or do the units, match the commercial invoice?
3. Is the exact breakdown of merchandise per individual packages shown, if required?

Have you made a final comparative check of all documents to make sure they are consistent with one another?

Figure 4-32. Letter of indemnity.

(Company letterhead)

ABC Bank
Export Services Department
111 Main St.
Chicago, IL 60606

BLANKET INDEMNITY

Gentlemen:

In consideration of your honoring/negotiating our drawings presented to you under any
and all letters of credit issued in our favor notwithstanding any discrepancies that
might exist therein, we hereby agree to indemnify and hold you harmless, on demand, for
the amount of each such drawing, together with any costs and expenses incurred in
connection therewith, in the event that the documents included in the drawing are refused
by the issuing bank.

responsibility for filing this document. The USPPI should also receive confirmation
from the freight forwarder that the EEI has been filed, such as a copy of the filing. The
EEI must be electronically filed in advance of the export. Once it is transmitted, the
exporter receives an Internal Transaction Number (ITN). The ITN must be provided to
the exporting carrier in advance of the export. The specific time frames differ based on
the mode of transport as follows:

- For vessel exports, the EEI must be filed and the ITN provided to the carrier 24
  hours prior to loading.

- For air exports, including courier shipments, the EEI must be filed and the ITN
  provided to the carrier no later than 2 hours prior to the departure of the aircraft.

- For truck exports, the EEI must be filed and the ITN provided no later than one
  hour prior to the arrival of the exporting truck at the border.

- For rail exports, the EEI must be filed and the ITN provided no later than two
  hours prior to the train's arrival at the border.

To register for filing through the AES system, the terms and conditions state that
that any false or misleading statements transmitted through the AES system (which
is interpreted to include accidentally false statements as well as intentionally false

185

Figure 4–33. Advice of irrevocable letter of credit (confirmed).

ABC BANK

MAR 05, 2009

1000 ABC BANK CENTER
CHICAGO, IL 60606

XYZ EXPORT COMPANY
111 MAIN STREET
SPRINGFIELD, IL 62111

ATTENTION : EXPORT DEPARTMENT

EXPORT IRREVOCABLE LC.

OUR REF :   12345678
LETTER OF CREDIT NO :   IC09/1234
ISSUED BY :   JKL BANK, BEIRUT LEBANON
EXPIRY DATE :   MAY 26, 2009
BY ORDER OF :   BEIRUT BUYING COMPANY
AMOUNT: USD50,000.00

GENTLEMEN:

AT THE REQUEST OF THE JKL BANK, BEIRUT LEBANON, WE ENCLOSE HEREWITH THE ORIGINAL LETTER OF CREDIT OR A COPY THEREOF, AS INDICATED HEREIN. ABC BANK IS SOLELY PROVIDING AN ADVICE AND CONVEYS NO ENGAGEMENT ON OUR PART.

ALL PRESENTATIONS UNDER THIS LETTER OF CREDIT MUST BE IN FULL COMPLIANCE WITH THE TERMS AND CONDITIONS OF THIS CREDIT AND IF YOU CANNOT FULFILL ONE OR MORE OF THEM, PLEASE CONTACT YOUR CUSTOMER IMMEDIATELY TO ARRANGE FOR NECESSARY AMENDMENTS. WHEN PRESENTING YOUR DRAFT(S) AND DOCUMENTS OR WHEN COMMUNICATING WITH US, PLEASE QUOTE OUR REFERENCE NUMBER SHOWN ABOVE.

ORIGINAL CREDIT AND SUBSEQUENT AMENDMENTS, IF ANY, SHOULD ACCOMPANY ALL DRAFT(S) AND DOCUMENTS.

ADDITIONAL INFORMATION:
ABC BANK ADVISING CHARGES USD $75.00
ANY BANK NEGOTIATING DOCUMENTS MUST DEDUCT OUR CHARGES AND REMIT TO ABC BANK AT THE BELOW ADDRESS.

BY RECEIVING AND ACCEPTING PAYMENT UNDER THIS CREDIT, YOU CERTIFY THAT YOU ARE IN COMPLIANCE WITH THE UNITED STATES EXPORT CONTROL REGULATIONS AND OTHER TRADE RELATED LAWS AND REGULATIONS, IF ANY.

ALL PARTIES TO THIS LETTER OF CREDIT ARE ADVISED THAT THE U.S. GOVERNMENT HAS IN PLACE SANCTIONS AGAINST CERTAIN COUNTRIES, RELATED ENTITIES AND INDIVIDUALS UNDER THESE SANCTIONS. ABC BANK IS PROHIBITED FROM ENGAGING TRANSACTIONS THAT VIOLATE ANY OF SUCH SANCTIONS.

IF THE DOCUMENTS PRESENTED DO NOT COMPLY WITH THE TERMS AND CONDITIONS OF THIS LETTER OF CREDIT, A DOCUMENT DISCREPANCY FEE OF $25.00 WILL BE DEDUCTED FROM ANY REMITTANCE MADE UNDER THIS LETTER OF CREDIT.

Figure 4–33. (*continued*)

ABC BANK

BENEFICIARY AS PER THE LC:

XYZ EXPORT COMPANY
111 MAIN ST.
SPRINGFIELD, IL 62111 USA

THIS ADVICE IS SUBJECT TO THE UNIFORM CUSTOMS AND PRACTICE FOR DOCUMENTARY CREDITS CURRENTLY IN FORCE.

ABC BANK'S OBLIGATIONS, IF ANY, UNDER THIS LETTER OF CREDIT SHALL BE GOVERNED BY THE LAWS OF THE STATE OF ILLINOIS.

PLEASE DIRECT INQUIRIES ALONG WITH OUR REFERENCE NUMBER TO:

CUSTOMS SERVICE DEPARTMENT
ABC BANK
1000 ABC BANK CENTER
CHICAGO IL 60606
TEL: 312.111.1000 EXT. 100 (CUSTOMER SERVICE)
FAX: 312.111.1105 EXT. 105 (CUSTOMER SERVICE)
CUSTOMERSERVICE@ABCBANK.COM

WE CONFIRM THIS LETTER OF CREDIT AND THEREBY UNDERTAKE THAT ALL DRAWINGS DRAWN UNDER AND IN COMPLIANCE WITH THE TERMS AND CONDITIONS OF THIS LETTER OF CREDIT WILL BE DULY HONORED BY US ON DELIVERY OF DOCUMENTS AS SPECIFIED IF PRESENTED AT THIS OFFICE ON OR BEFORE THE EXPIRY DATE.

ABC BANK   (AUTHORIZED REPRESENTATIVE)

Figure 4–33. *(continued)*

ABC BANK

REFERENCE NUMBER 12345678

UVR 2222 PSS 4321
CHLCE
.CHMITAB 1233333 400567

0509 40ABCBUS11RXXX11111
0509 40ORSTUS1TTXXX22222
700 00

:27 SEQUENCE OF TOTAL : 1/2

:40B FORM OF DOC CREDIT: IRREVOCABLE WITHOUT OUR CONFIRMATION

:20 OUR REF NUMBER: A00666666

:21 DOC CREDIT NUM: IC009/1234

:31C DATE OF ISSUE: 090305

:40E LC SUBJECT TO: UCP LATEST VERSION

:31D DATE AND PLACE OF EXPIRY: 090430 CHICAGO, ILLINOIS USA

:50 APPLICANT:

BEIRUT BUYING COMPANY
222-A KASLIK STREET
BEIRUT LEBANON

:59 BENEFICIARY:

XYZ EXPORT COMPANY
111 MAIN ST.
SPRINGFIELD, IL 62111 USA

:32B CURRENCY: USD50,000

:39C ADDITIONAL AMTS COVERED: NOT EXCEEDING

:41D AVAILABLE WITH..BY.. THE BANK OF CHICAGO, CHICAGO
BY ACCEPTANCE

:42C DRAFTS AT: DRAFTS AT 120 DAYS FROM B/L DATE

:42D DRAWEE: DRAWN ON BANK OF CHICAGO, CHICAGO

:43P PARTIAL SHIPMENT: NOT ALLOWED

:43T TRANS SHIPMENT: NOT ALLOWED

:44E PORT OF LOADING: ANY US SEAPORT

Figure 4–33. (*continued*)

ABC BANK

:44F: PORT OF DISCHARGE: BEIRUT PORT, LEBANON

:44G LATEST DATE OF SHIPMENT: 090415

:48 PERIOD FOR PRESENTATION: DRAFTS AND DOCUMENTS MUST BE PRESENTED 21 DAYS AFTER SHIPMENT DATE AND WITHIN L/C VALIDITY

:49 CONFIRM INSTRUCTIONS: CONFIRM

:57D "ADV THRU BANK"
ABC BANK
1000 ABC BANK CENTER
CHICAGO, IL 60606 USA

:45B DESCRIPTION OF GOODS: PAPER MAKING MACHINERY
CIF BEIRUT PORT, LEBANON

:46B DOCUMENTS REQUIRED: OUR CORRESPONDENT STATES THE FOLLOWING DOCUMENTS ARE REQUIRED UNDER THEIR CREDIT ISSUED ON JANUARY 3, 2009.

1-BENEFICIARIES' HANDSIGNED AND DATED COMMERCIAL INVOICE IN ONE ORIGINAL AND 2 COPIES, SHOWING NAME OF MANUFACTURER OR EXPORTER OF GOODS, FULL DESCRIPTION OF GOODS AND ITS QUANTITY, NET AND GROSS WEIGHT, UNIT AND TOTAL PRICE, THEIR MARKS AND SERIAL NUMBER AND BEARING BENEFICIARIES' FOLLOWING STATEMENT: 'WE CERTIFY THAT THIS INVOICE IS TRUE AND AUTHENTIC, THAT IT IS THE ONLY ONE ISSUED BY US FOR THE GOODS DESCRIBED HEREIN, THAT IT SHOWS THEIR EXACT VALUE WITHOUT ANY DEDUCTION OR ADVANCE PAYMENT AND THAT THEIR ORIGIN IS FROM THE UNITED STATES OF AMERICA'. ORIGINAL COMMERCIAL INVOICE SHOULD BE CERTIFIED BY THE CHAMBER OF COMMERCE.

2-CERTIFICATE OF ORIGIN IN 1 ORIGINAL AND 2 COPIES ISSUED BY THE CHAMBER OF COMMERCE.

3-FULL SET OF CLEAN 'SHIPPED ON BOARD' MARINE BILLS OF LADING ISSUED TO THE ORDER OF JKL BANK, BEIRUT LEBANON MARKED FREIGHT PREPAID, NOTIFY APPLICANTS.

4-FULL SET OF INSURANCE CERTIFICATE/POLICY ISSUED TO THE ORDER OF JKL BANK, BEIRUT LEBANON, MARKED PREMIUM PAID, INDICATING THEIR PAYING AGENT'S NAME AND ADDRESS IN LEBANON, THE NAME OF THE CARRYING VESSEL AND COVERING GOODS AGAINST THE FOLLOWING RISK: INSTITUTE CARGO CLAUSES (A)1.1.82 FIRE, THEFT IN THE CUSTOMS HOUSE, RIOTS AND CIVIL COMMOTION CLAUSES. TRANSHIPMENT RISKS IF ANY VALID FOR 6- DAYS AFTER DISCHARGE OF GOODS AT FINAL DESTINATION.

5-PACKING LIST IN 3 COPIES.

6-WEIGHT LIST IN 3 COPIES.

7-CERTIFICATE ISSUED AND SIGNED BY THE SHIPPING COMPANY OR ITS AGENT CERTIFYING THE FOLLOWING: WE CERTIFY THAT THE VESSEL CARRYING THE GOODS UNDER SUBJECT CREDIT IS SELF PROPELLED OF STEEL CONSTRUCTION CLASSED WITH A CLASSIFICATION SOCIETY WHICH IS A MEMBER OF THE INTERNATIONAL ASSOCIATION OF CLASSIFICATION SOCIETY (IACS) MENTIONED IN IACS WEBSITE WWW.IACS.ORG.UK. WE ALSO CERTIFY THAT, AT THE TIME OF LOADING, THE CARRYING VESSEL NAMED (TO BE INDICATED) IS ISM CODE CERTIFIED AND HOLDS A VALID INTERNATIONAL SAFETY MANAGEMENT CERTIFICATE, AS WELL AS A VALID ISM CODE DOCUMENT OF COMPLIANCE AS REQUIRED BY THE SOLAS' CONVENTION 1974 AS AMENDED.

:47B ADDITIONAL CONDITIONS:

OUR CORRESPONDENT STATES THE FOLLOWING CONDITIONS ARE REQUIRED UNDER

Figure 4–33. *(continued)*

ABC BANK

THEIR CREDIT ISSUED ON JANUARY 3, 2009.
ALL THE DOCUMENTS TO BE ISSUED IN THE NAME OF THE APPLICANT AS THE BUYER UNLESS OTHERWISE REQUESTED.
TRANSPORT DOCUMENTS SHOWING NAME OF A THIRD PARTY AS SHIPPER ARE NOT ACCEPTABLE.
DOCUMENTS INCLUDING B/L ISSUED OR DATED PRIOR TO THE ISSUANCE OF THE L/C ARE NOT ACCEPTABLE.
PAYMENT UNDER RESERVE IS PROHIBITED.
THIS CREDIT NUMBER, DATE AND OUR BANK'S NAME MUST BE QUOTED ON ALL REQUIRED DOCUMENTS.
A DISCREPANCY FEE FOR USD $25 IS TO BE BORNE BY BENEFICIARIES FOR EACH SET OF DOCUMENTS PRESENTED TO US WITH DISCREPANCIES.
PHOTOCOPIES OF DOCUMENTS PRESENTED FOR NEGOTIATION ARE NOT ACCEPTABLE EVEN IF STAMPED ORIGINAL.
ALL BANKING CHARGES AND COMMISSIONS OUTSIDE LEBANON PLUS REIMBURSING BANK CHARGES ARE ON BENEFICIARIES' ACCOUNT UNQUOTE.
PLEASE NOTE THAT IF THE CREDIT PROVIDES THE OPTION OF HAVING THE PORT ELIGIBILITY CERTIFICATION SUBMITTED BY AN AGENT, PURSUANT TO U.S. DEPARTMENT OF COMMERCE REGULATIONS, WE ARE PROHBITED FROM ACCEPTING, AND WILL NOT ACCEPT, THE AGENT'S CERTIFICATE.

Figure 4–34. Shipper's Letter of Instructions.

© Copyright Unz & Co. 2008

EASI-SLI™ Exporter AES & Shipper Instructions™ (EASI-SLI™)

1. U.S.P.P.I (complete name and addess + Zip)	4. Exporter's Reference No.	5. Date Prepared
	6. AES XTN	7. AES ITN / Filing Exemption
1a. EIN or ID No.		
2. Ultimate Consignee	8. Dangerous Goods ☐ Yes ☐ No	9. Routed Export Transaction ☐ Yes ☐ No
	10. Point/State of Origin	11. Ultimate Destination
2a. Related Party: ☐ Yes ☐ No		
3. Intermediate Consignee	12. Forwarding Agent	
	13. Special Instructions	

Schedule B Description of Commodities

14. D/F or M	15. Schedule B No.	16. Description License No. Exception/Exemption ECCN/ITAR Category	17. Schedule B Quantity	18. Shipping Wt (kg)	19. Value (U.S. $)
		SAMPLE			

20. Shipment Mode	21. Containerized ☐ Yes ☐ No	22. Consolidate ☐ Yes ☐ No	23. Freight Charges: ☐ Prepaid ☐ Collect	24. If unable to deliver: ☐ Abandon ☐ Return ☐ Notify Shipper

25. Inland Carrier	26. Ship Date	27. B/L No.	The U.S.P.P.I. authorizes the Forwarding Agent named above to act as an authorized agent on behalf of the U.S.P.P.I. for export control, Customs & Border Protection, and Census Bureau purposes to transmit export information electronically through the Automated Export System.
28. Exporting Carrier	29. Export Date	30. B/L No.	

31. Shipper requests insurance: ☐ Yes $_____ ☐ No If insurance is requested, shipment is insured to the amount indicated. Recovery is limited to actual loss in acceptance with the carrier's tariff.	32. Duly authorized office r or employee of U.S.P.P.I. Name: Signature	Date: Telephone: Email: DDTC Registration No.

Form No. 15-306 Printed and Sold by *UNZ&CO* 800-631-3098 • www.unzco.com

EXPORTER COPY

statements) will subject the exporter to various civil and criminal penalties, including a $10,000 fine and up to five years' imprisonment. Consequently, the exporter has a real interest in making sure that any agent, such as the freight forwarder, prepares the EEI correctly and that the information being submitted to U.S. Customs and Border Protection is accurate. If the exporter discovers the EEI that it or its freight forwarder has prepared is inaccurate, it should electronically file an amended EEI through the AES system.

There is an exemption from filing an EEI where the value of the shipment is $2,500 or less per Schedule B number. Any shipment that requires an export license (see discussion in Chapter 5) is not exempt even if the value is less than $2,500. EEI is required within U.S. territories as well. See Figures 4-35a and 4-35b.

Specific information is required for completion of the EEI. If the seller is a corporation, it requires its Federal Employer Identification Number issued by the Internal Revenue Service. The EEI also requires that the seller specify whether the transaction is a related-party transaction. This means that the seller has a 10 percent or more stockholding or similar interest in the foreign consignee, or vice versa.

The seller must specify the Schedule B Commodity Number for the product being exported. Schedule B classifications are available on the Census Bureau's web site at

Figure 4-35a. EEI required.

Shipped From	To
United States	Canada (if a license is required)
United States	Foreign Countries
United States	Puerto Rico
United States	U.S. Virgin Islands
Puerto Rico	United States
Puerto Rico	Foreign Countries
Puerto Rico	U.S. Virgin Islands
U.S. Virgin Islands	Foreign Countries
U.S. Foreign Trade Zones	Foreign Countries

Figure 4-35b. EEI not required.

Shipped From	To
United States	Canada (unless an export license is required)
U.S. Virgin Islands	United States
U.S. Virgin Islands	Puerto Rico
United States/Puerto Rico/Virgin Islands	Other U.S. Territories
Other U.S. Territories	United States
Other U.S. Territories	Foreign Countries
Other U.S. Territories	Other U.S. Territories

www.census.gov. Since the adoption of the Harmonized Tariff System (HTS) the HTS number may be used instead of the Schedule B classification number, with only a few exceptions. However, the HTS specifically identifies that certain commodities are still required to use the Schedule B number. See the "Notice to Exporters" section in the General Notes of the HTS available at the U.S. International Trade Commission web site: http://hotdocs.usitc.gov/docs/tata/hts/bychapter/0901n2x.pdf.

The seller must designate whether the product being shipped is "D" (domestic) or "F" (foreign). Domestic products are those grown, produced, or manufactured in the United States or imported and enhanced in value. Foreign products are those that have been imported into the United States and exported in the same condition as when imported.

For the EEI form, the seller must declare the value of the goods. This is defined to mean the selling price, or if not sold, the cost, including the inland freight, insurance, and other charges, to the U.S. port of export. It does not include unconditional discounts and commissions. This value declaration is extremely important, because if it varies from the selling price stated in the commercial invoice, consular invoice, special customs invoice, insurance certificate, or, especially, any forms filed by the buyer with the foreign customs or exchange control authorities, a charge of false statement may arise, subjecting the exporter and/or the foreign buyer to civil or criminal penalties. In addition, the exporter must identify the ultimate consignee type, i.e. direct consumer, government entity, reseller or other/unknown. In addition, there is a field for the license value for merchandise exporting under an export license. The purpose of the license value is to allow for the automatic decrementing of the value against the license.

Finally, the EEI calls for an export license number or exception symbol, and the Export Control Classification Number (ECCN). This information relates to the export licensing system applicable in the United States. A detailed discussion of that system follows in Chapter 5. The important thing to note at this point is that prior to clearance for shipment from the United States, the exporter or its agent must declare, under penalty of perjury, that no export license is required; or that the export can be made under a license exception, and the correct license exception symbol must be inserted in the EEI; or that a license is required and has been obtained, and the license number issued by the U.S. Department of Commerce is stated in the EEI. When an individual license is required, there will be an ECCN that also must be inserted in the EEI. If this information is not put in the form, the shipment will be detained and will not be permitted to clear. Under the revised regulations, the seller will be responsible for making the license determination unless the buyer has expressly agreed in writing to accept such responsibility and has appointed a U.S. agent (such as a freight forwarder) to share such responsibility.

U. Freight Forwarder's Invoices

The freight forwarder will issue a bill to the exporter for its services. Sometimes the forwarder will include certain services in its standard quotation, while other services will be add-ons. It is important to make clear at the outset of the transaction which services will be performed by the exporter, the freight forwarder, and others, such as the bank.

V. Air Cargo Security and C-TPAT

1. *Air Cargo Security*

Recent security threats and airline disasters have increased the demand for greater transparency regarding shippers and cargo. This necessitates advance information about the shipment, the parties, the routing, and the destination. The Transportation Security Administration (TSA) is the agency responsible for screening passengers prior to boarding a plane, but it is also responsible for the Indirect Air Carrier Cargo Security Program (IACCSP), which oversees air freight forwarders and all cargo that is destined for passenger planes.

Air freight forwarders are considered Indirect Air Carriers (IAC) and are required to register for this confidential program. The program requires the development of internal procedures regarding the acceptance of air cargo from "known" shippers and screening all cargo prior to lading. A "known" shipper is one that has an ongoing shipping relationship with the IAC forwarder, and the IAC forwarder has visited the shipper to ensure that it is a legitimate business. Once a shipper has been substantiated as a known shipper, its name is entered into a national databank that only IACs may access. Shipments from any unknown shipper require specific documentation and identification from the driver delivering the cargo to the forwarder as well as screening before it may be shipped on a cargo-only aircraft. Additional measures include restricted access to cargo facilities, ongoing training for staff, and background checks for certain personnel. TSA continuously changes and updates the program, and that information may be disseminated on a need-to-know basis only.

2. *Customs and Trade Partnership Against Terrorism (C-TPAT)*

U.S. Customs and Border Protection have developed an extensive program to combat terrorism through a voluntary program known as the Customs and Trade Partnership Against Terrorism, or C-TPAT. Although the program is voluntary and has primarily been focused at importers, it is expanding to all parties in the supply chain whether import or export.

Chapter 5
Export Controls and Licenses

A. Introduction

The export control laws of the United States had languished for many years without review. In fact, the Export Administration Act of 1976, which established some of the primary export control statues actually expired in 2001 and was never renewed. Every year since then the President declares a state of emergency in order to use the power vested in him under the International Emergency Economic Power Act (IEEPA) to continue to enforce the export control regulations under the Export Administration Act. Although that is one of the primary statutes, export control regulations reside in a multitude of agencies.

In August 2009, President Obama launched an interagency task force to review all of the various export regulations and the report was disturbing. The laws and regulations were complex and overlapping and hindered U.S. manufacturing and technology companies from competing in the global marketplace.

Task Force Agencies

- The Department of Commerce, Bureau of Industry and Security
- The Department of Defense, Defense Technology Security Administration
- The Department of State, Directorate of Defense Trade Controls and Bureau of International Security and Nonproliferation
- The Department of Energy, National Nuclear Security Administration
- The Department of Homeland Security, Immigration and Customs Enforcement and Directorate of Science and Technology

- The Department of Justice, Federal Bureau of Investigation and National Security Division
- Office of Management and Budget
- Office of the Director of National Intelligence
- The Department of the Treasury, Office of Foreign Assets Control

The result was the Export Control Reform Initiative (ECR), whose goal is to fundamentally change the United States export control regulations to refocus on those articles and technology that are essential to our national security, while not impeding U.S. competitiveness in a global marketplace for U.S. manufacturing and technology. In addition, the changes must keep the U.S. in compliance with the various international export control agreements to which the U.S. is a member party, including the Australia Group (for the harmonization of chemical and biological weapons controls); the Missile Technology Control Regime; the Nuclear Suppliers Group; and the Wassenaar Agreement (for the harmonization of conventional arms and dual-use goods and technologies).

The ECR established a three-phase transition with Phases I and II devoted to reconciling definition, licensing, processing and procedures between the agencies. Phase III is to create a single agency responsible for all export controls, a single list of items that are ranked in various tiers according to their sensitivity to the U.S. goals and to create a more transparent system of understanding just what exports are controlled. This goal of a single agency has been quite contentious and most recently the White House has backed off this aspect of the Reform's plans.

While there are many agencies with responsibilities over U.S. exports, there are three that maintain most of the controls: the Bureau of Industry and Security, the Directorate of Defense Trade Controls (DDTC) and The Office of Foreign Assets Control (OFAC). In this chapter we touch on each of these agencies and their responsibilities.

The Bureau of Industry and Security, Department of Commerce (BIS) is the primary agency overseeing all exports out of the United States that are not controlled by another agency. So even everyday articles like clothing, food, appliances, etc. are covered by BIS. An exporter may be shocked to learn, the Export Administration Regulations (EAR) require the exporter to proceed through a twenty-nine-step analysis for each of its products. These can be summed up in four major steps: First, analyzing the scope of the EAR; second, determining the applicability of the Ten General Prohibitions; third, determining the applicability of the various license exceptions; and fourth, complying with the export documentation requirements. The following discussion is divided between the export of products, on the one hand, and the export of technology, software, and technical assistance, on the other. It also distinguishes between the initial export from the United States and re-exports of U.S.-origin products (including foreign origin products that are located in and then exported out of the U.S.) from one foreign country to another. The following discussion is a summary of the EAR. Exporters should seek legal counsel for advice for specific export transactions.

B. Scope of the EAR

The first step in determining whether or not an export license is required is to determine whether the contemplated activity is "subject to" (that is, within the scope of) the EAR. In general, the coverage of the EAR is very broad. Items subject to the EAR include all items in the United States no matter where they originated, including any located in a U.S. foreign trade zone or moving in transit through the United States; all U.S.-origin items wherever located; U.S.-origin parts, components, materials, or other commodities incorporated abroad in foreign-made products (in quantities exceeding de minimis levels); and certain foreign-made direct products of U.S.-origin technology. Items not subject to the EAR include prerecorded phonograph records reproducing the content of printed books, pamphlets, newspapers and periodicals, children's picture and painting books, music books, sheet music, calendars and calendar blocks, paper, maps, charts, atlases, gazetteers, globes and covers, exposed and developed microfilm reproducing the contents of any of the foregoing, exposed and developed motion picture film and soundtrack, and advertising printed matter exclusively related thereto. Step 1 is to determine whether or not the item being exported is subject to the exclusive export control jurisdiction of another government agency. Note that many items that were originally controlled exclusively by the Department of State have transitioned to the EAR. However, if the item is still controlled by another agency, then the item is outside the scope of the EAR and administrative control of the Department of Commerce but will be subject to the regulations and administration of that other government agency. Steps 4 and 5 relate to determining whether or not a product manufactured in a foreign country contains more than the permitted (de minimis) level of U.S.-origin parts, components, or materials. For embargoed countries, the U.S.-origin parts, components, or materials cannot exceed 10 percent of the total value of the foreign-made product; for all other countries, the limit is 25 percent. If an exporter is unsure whether or not its proposed transaction is within the scope of the EAR, it may request an advisory opinion, which would normally be answered within thirty calendar days after receipt. (Steps 2 and 6, pertaining to technology and software exports, and Step 3, pertaining to re-export of U.S.-origin items, are discussed below.)

C. Commerce Control List

The first of the Ten General Prohibitions is concerned with exporting (or re-exporting) controlled items to countries listed on the Country Chart without a license. All products manufactured or sold in the United States are classified somewhere in the Commerce Control List. The Commerce Control List states that it is not all-inclusive, so exporters should carefully review their items in conjunction with the list to identify any similar products. Specific products that are of concern for various reasons are specifically listed by name in great detail using scientific and engineering specifications. At the end of each category or commodity group classification, there is a catch-all, or basket, category, "EAR 99," which applies to all other commodities not specifically named but that fall within that general commodity category.

The general commodity categories are:

0—Nuclear materials, facilities, and equipment and miscellaneous products

1—Materials, chemicals, microorganisms, and toxins

2—Materials processing

3—Electronics

4—Computers

5—Telecommunications and information security

6—Lasers and sensors

7—Navigation and avionics

8—Marine

9—Propulsion systems, space vehicles, and related equipment

Within each of the foregoing categories, controlled items are arranged by group. Each category contains the same five groups. The groups are as follows:

A—Equipment, assemblies, and components

B—Test, inspection, and production equipment

C—Materials

D—Software

E—Technology

The Commerce Department has issued "interpretations" relating to various products, including anti-friction bearings and parts; parts of machinery, equipment, or other items; wire or cable cut to length; telecommunications equipment and systems; numerical control systems; parts, accessories, and equipment exported as scrap; scrap arms, ammunition, and implements of war; military automotive vehicles and parts for such vehicles; aircraft parts, accessories, and components; civil aircraft inertial navigation equipment; "precursor" chemicals; technology and software; and chemical mixtures. An alphabetical index to the Commerce Control List is included in the EAR but, in fact, it is not very helpful in actually finding a product. It is much more useful to conduct a computerized search of the EAR. A further complication is that technology changes constantly, and new products do not fit well into the old classifications.

The descriptions in the Commerce Control List are extremely detailed, containing engineering and scientific language, and it is unlikely that a person in the export sales or traffic department will be able to determine whether his company's products are covered by a particular description without the assistance of company engineers. If it is unclear whether a product falls under one of the classifications, the exporter can request a commodity classification through the Simplified Network Application Process–Revised (SNAP-R) program. Such requests will ordinarily be answered within 30 days after receipt. (See more about the SNAP-R program below in Section H).

Step 7 is the process of reviewing the Commerce Control List and determining whether or not the item being exported falls under a specific classification number and reviewing the "Reasons for Control" specified within the Commerce Control List for that item. Items are controlled for one of the following fourteen reasons:

AT—Anti-Terrorism

CB—Chemical and Biological Weapons

CC—Crime Control

CW—Chemical Weapons Convention

EC—Encryption Items

FC—Firearms Convention

MT—Missile Technology

NS—National Security

NP—Nuclear Nonproliferation

RS—Regional Stability

SS—Short Supply

UN—United Nations

SI—Significant Items

SL—Surreptitious Listening

For each product listed in the Commerce Control List, the reason for control is specified. Some products are subject to multiple reasons for control, and some reasons apply to only some of the products listed within the Export Control Classification Number (ECCN). In order to proceed with the analysis, it is necessary to obtain the Reason for Control and "column" shown for the controlled product within the ECCN for that product.

Certain products are controlled because they are in short supply within the United States and are listed on the Commerce Control List. But for these, unlike other products, the Commerce Control List does not specify the "column," or possible license exceptions. These products include crude oil, petroleum products (which is rather an extensive list), unprocessed western red cedar, and horses exported by sea for slaughter. For such products, the applicable licensing requirements and exceptions are specified under Part 754 of the EAR.

Sample pages from the Commerce Control List for ECCN 2A001, "Anti-friction bearings and bearing systems, as follows, (see List of Items Controlled) and components therefor," are shown in Figure 5–1. If the item being exported is not specifically described on the Commerce Control List, it thereby falls within EAR 99 and no license (abbreviated on the Electronic Export Information as "NLR") will be required for export, but records analyzing and demonstrating that the item falls outside of any of the classifications must be maintained, and proper export documentation must be completed (see Section J below).

With the changes under the Export Control Reform, the licensing of defense articles that are considered of "lesser sensitivity" by the State Department has been transferred to the BIS for licensing purposes. This is one step towards the unification of all of the export agencies into one.

What has happened is the creation of new ECCNs in the Commodity Control List that are considered the "600" series. For example, there is now ECCN:

9A610 Military aircraft and related commodities, other than those enumerated in 9A991.a (see List of Items Controlled); and
9A619 Military gas turbine engines and related commodities (see List of Items Controlled).

Items that fall within these categories are licensed by BIS. No Department registration is required for manufacturers or for exporters and online submission of licensing through Commerce's web site is available. In some instances, defense components which are itemized within these "600" series provisions may be exempt from licensing completely. As will be explained in Section R, the transition has been handled on

Figure 5–1. Sample pages from the Commerce Control List (ECCN 2A001).

CATEGORY 2 - MATERIALS PROCESSING

Note: For quiet running bearings, see the U.S. Munitions List.

A. SYSTEMS, EQUIPMENT AND COMPONENTS

2A001 **Anti-friction bearings and bearing systems, as follows, (see List of Items Controlled) and components therefor.**

License Requirements

Reason for Control: NS, MT, AT

Control(s)	Country Chart
NS applies to entire entry	NS Column 2
MT applies to radial ball bearings having all tolerances specified in accordance with ISO 492 Tolerance Class 2 (or ANSI/ABMA Std 20 Tolerance Class ABEC-9, or other national equivalents) or better and having all the following characteristics: an inner ring bore diameter between 12 and 50 mm; an outer ring outside diameter between 25 and 100 mm; and a width between 10 and 20 mm.	MT Column 1
AT applies to entire entry	AT Column 1

License Exceptions

    LVS: $3000, N/A for MT
    GBS: Yes, for 2A001.a and 2A001.b,
            N/A for MT
    CIV: Yes, for 2A001.a and 2A001.b,
            N/A for MT

List of Items Controlled

Unit: $ value
Related Controls: (1) See also 2A991. (2) Quiet running bearings are subject to the export licensing authority of the Department of State, Directorate of Defense Trade Controls. (See 22 CFR part 121.)
Related Definitions: Annular Bearing Engineers Committee (ABEC).
Items:

Note: 2A001 does not control balls with tolerance specified by the manufacturer in accordance with ISO 3290 as grade 5 or worse.

Note: 2A001 does not control balls with tolerance specified by the manufacturer in accordance with ISO 3290 as grade 5 or worse.

a. Ball bearings and solid roller bearings having all tolerances specified by the manufacturer in accordance with ISO 492 Tolerance Class 4 (or ANSI/ABMA Std 20 Tolerance Class ABEC-7 or RBEC-7, or other national equivalents), or better, and having both rings and rolling elements (ISO 5593) made from monel or beryllium;

Note: 2A001.a does not control tapered roller bearings.

b. Other ball bearings and solid roller bearings having all tolerances specified by the manufacturer in accordance with ISO 492 Tolerance Class 2 (or ANSI/ABMA Std 20 Tolerance Class ABEC-9 or RBEC-9, or other national equivalents), or better;

Note: 2A001.b does not control tapered roller bearings.

c. Active magnetic bearing systems using any of the following:

    c.1. Materials with flux densities of 2.0 T or greater and yield strengths greater than 414 MPa;

    c.2. All-electromagnetic 3D homopolar bias

a U.S. Munitions List category by category basis, so the changes have been happening gradually requiring all parties to pay attention.

D. Export Destinations

If an item is listed in the Commerce Control List, it is prima facie subject to an export license requirement. However, to determine whether or not an export license will actually be required, it is necessary to proceed to determine the country of ultimate destination (Step 8). Products being exported may pass through one or more countries (except certain prohibited countries), but licenses are issued based on the country of ultimate destination—the country that, according to the representation of the purchaser, is the last country of delivery and use.

The Commerce Country Chart is divided into four main groups: Groups A (four subgroups), B, D (four subgroups), and E (two subgroups). These country listings overlap and are different depending upon the Reason for Control (see Figures 5–2 through 5–5).

Using the Reason for Control listed in the Commerce Control List for the product being exported and the column listed there, the exporter can review the Commerce Country Chart by country of destination. Wherever the exporter observes that an "X" is shown for that country in the same Reason for Control and columns specified in the ECCN for that product, an export license will be required (Step 9). For example, under the 2A001 category listed above, if the item being exported is a radial ball bearing having all tolerances specified in Figure 5–1, then it is controlled for Missile Technology and may not be exported to any country listed on the Country Chart (see Figure 5–6) with an "X" under MT column 1 without a license. A license may or may not be granted depending on the consignee and the intended use (see Section E below).

Where the item being exported is not a finished good but is a part or component being exported for incorporation into a product being manufactured abroad, if the part or component being exported is described in an entry on the Commerce Control List and the Country Chart requires a license to the intended export destination, then a license will be required unless the parts or components meet the de minimis 10 percent or 25 percent standards (Step 10).

Where the export is to certain embargoed destinations, it is unlikely that a license will be granted. Presently, the EAR prohibits exports to Cuba, Iran, Syria, and Sudan. All exports to North Korea require a license. The Department of Treasury, Office of Foreign Assets Control, also maintains controls on the foregoing destinations plus to persons or

Figure 5–2. Country group A.

Country Group A

Country	[A:1]	[A:2] Missile Technology Control Regime	[A:3] Australia Group	[A:4] Nuclear Suppliers Group	[A:5]	[A:6]
Albania						X
Argentina		X	X	X	X	
Australia	X	X	X	X	X	
Austria[1]		X	X	X	X	
Belarus				X		
Belgium	X	X	X	X	X	
Brazil		X		X		
Bulgaria		X	X	X	X	
Canada	X	X	X	X	X	
Croatia			X	X	X	
Cyprus			X	X		
Czech Republic		X	X	X	X	
Denmark	X	X	X	X	X	
Estonia			X	X	X	
Finland[1]		X	X	X	X	
France	X	X	X	X	X	
Germany	X	X	X	X	X	
Greece	X	X	X	X	X	
Hong Kong[1]						X
Hungary		X	X	X	X	
Iceland		X	X	X	X	
India		X				X
Ireland[1]		X	X	X	X	
Israel						X
Italy	X	X	X	X	X	
Japan	X	X	X	X	X	
Kazakhstan				X		
Korea, South[1]		X	X	X	X	
Latvia			X	X	X	

Figure 5–2. (*continued*)

Country	[A:1]	[A:2] Missile Technology Control Regime	[A:3] Australia Group	[A:4] Nuclear Suppliers Group	[A:5]	[A:6]
Lithuania			X	X	X	
Luxembourg	X	X	X	X	X	
Malta			X	X		X
Mexico			X	X		
Netherlands	X	X	X	X	X	
New Zealand[1]		X	X	X	X	
Norway	X	X	X	X	X	
Poland		X	X	X	X	
Portugal	X	X	X	X	X	
Romania			X	X	X	
Russia		X		X		
Serbia				X		
Singapore						X
Slovakia			X	X	X	
Slovenia			X	X	X	
South Africa		X		X		X
Spain	X	X	X	X	X	
Sweden[1]		X	X	X	X	
Switzerland[1]		X	X	X	X	
Taiwan						X
Turkey	X	X	X	X	X	
Ukraine		X	X	X		
United Kingdom	X	X	X	X	X	
United States	X	X	X	X		

[1] Cooperating Countries

Figure 5–3. Country group B.

Country Group B
Countries

Afghanistan	El Salvador	Malta	Martin)
Albania	Equatorial Guinea	Marshall Islands	Slovakia
Algeria	Eritrea	Mauritania	Slovenia
Andorra	Estonia	Mauritius	Solomon Islands
Angola	Ethiopia	Mexico	Somalia
Antigua and Barbuda	Fiji	Micronesia, Federated	South Africa
Argentina	Finland	States of	South Sudan,
Aruba	France	Monaco	(Republic of)
Australia	Gabon	Montenegro	Spain
Austria	Gambia, The	Morocco	Sri Lanka
The Bahamas	Germany	Mozambique	Surinam
Bahrain	Ghana	Namibia	Swaziland
Bangladesh	Greece	Nauru	Sweden
Barbados	Grenada	Nepal	Switzerland
Belgium	Guatemala	Netherlands	Taiwan
Belize	Guinea	New Zealand	Tanzania
Benin	Guinea-Bissau	Nicaragua	Thailand
Bhutan	Guyana	Niger	Timor-Leste
Bolivia	Haiti	Nigeria	Togo
Bosnia & Herzegovina	Honduras	Norway	Tonga
Botswana	Hong Kong	Oman	Trinidad & Tobago
Brazil	Hungary	Pakistan	Tunisia
Brunei	Iceland	Palau	Turkey
Bulgaria	India	Panama	Tuvalu
Burkina Faso	Indonesia	Papua New Guinea	Uganda
Burundi	Ireland	Paraguay	United Arab
Cameroon	Israel	Peru	Emirates
Canada	Italy	Philippines	United Kingdom
Cape Verde	Jamaica	Poland	United States
Central African Republic	Japan	Portugal	Uruguay
Chad	Jordan	Qatar	Vanuatu
Chile	Kenya	Romania	Vatican City
Colombia	Kiribati	Rwanda	Venezuela
Comoros	Korea, South	Saint Kitts & Nevis	Western Sahara
Congo (Democratic	Kosovo	Saint Lucia	Yemen
Republic of the)	Kuwait	Saint Vincent and the	Zambia
Congo (Republic of the)	Latvia	Grenadines	Zimbabwe
Costa Rica	Lebanon	Samoa	
Cote d'Ivoire	Lesotho	San Marino	
Croatia	Liberia	Sao Tome & Principe	
Curaçao	Lithuania	Saudi Arabia	
Cyprus	Luxembourg	Senegal	
Czech Republic	Macedonia, The Former	Serbia	
Denmark	Yugoslav Republic of	Seychelles	
Djibouti	Madagascar	Sierra Leone	
Dominica	Malawi	Singapore	
Dominican Republic	Malaysia	Sint Maarten (the Dutch	
Ecuador	Maldives	two-fifths of the	
Egypt	Mali	island of Saint	

Figure 5–4. Country group D.

Country Group D

Country	[D: 1] National Security	[D: 2] Nuclear	[D: 3] Chemical & Biological	[D: 4] Missile Technology	[D:5] U.S. Arms Embargoed Countries[1]
Afghanistan			X		X
Armenia	X		X		
Azerbaijan	X		X		
Bahrain			X	X	
Belarus	X		X		X
Burma	X		X		X
Cambodia	X				
Central African Republic					X
China (PRC)	X		X	X	X
Congo, Democratic Republic of					X
Cote d'Ivoire					X
Cuba		X	X		X
Cyprus					X
Egypt			X	X	
Eritrea					X
Fiji					X
Georgia	X		X		
Haiti					X
Iran		X	X	X	X
Iraq	X	X	X	X	X
Israel		X	X	X	
Jordan			X	X	
Kazakhstan	X		X		
Korea, North	X	X	X	X	X
Kuwait			X	X	
Kyrgyzstan	X		X		
Laos	X				
Lebanon			X	X	X

Figure 5–4. *(continued)*

Country	[D: 1] National Security	[D: 2] Nuclear	[D: 3] Chemical & Biological	[D: 4] Missile Technology	[D:5] U.S. Arms Embargoed Countries[1]
Liberia					X
Libya	X	X	X	X	X
Macau	X		X	X	
Moldova	X		X		
Mongolia	X		X		
Oman			X	X	
Pakistan		X	X	X	
Qatar			X	X	
Russia	X		X		
Saudi Arabia			X	X	
Somalia					X
Sri Lanka					X
Sudan					X
Syria			X	X	X
Taiwan			X		
Tajikistan	X		X		
Turkmenistan	X		X		
Ukraine	X				
United Arab Emirates			X	X	
Uzbekistan	X		X		
Venezuela					X
Vietnam	X		X		X
Yemen			X	X	
Zimbabwe					X

[1] Note to Country Group D:5: Countries subject to U.S. arms embargoes are identified by the State Department through notices published in the *Federal Register*. The list of arms embargoed destinations in this paragraph is drawn from 22 CFR §126.1 and State Department *Federal Register* notices related to arms embargoes (compiled at http://www.pmddtc.state.gov/embargoed_countries/index.html) and will be amended when the State Department publishes subsequent notices. If there are any discrepancies between the list of countries in this paragraph and the countries identified by the State Department as subject to a U.S. arms embargo (in the *Federal Register*), the State Department's list of countries subject to U.S. arms embargoes shall be controlling.

Figure 5–5. Country group E.

Country Group E [1]

Country	[E:1] Terrorist Supporting Countries [2]	[E:2] Unilateral Embargo
Cuba	X	X
Iran	X	
Korea, North	X	
Sudan	X	
Syria	X	

[1] In addition to the controls maintained by the Bureau of Industry and Security pursuant to the EAR, note that the Department of the Treasury administers:

(a) A *comprehensive embargo* against Cuba, Iran, and Sudan; and

(b) An *embargo against certain persons,* e.g., Specially Designated Terrorists (SDT), Foreign Terrorist Organizations (FTO), Specially Designated Global Terrorists (SDGT), and Specially Designated Narcotics Traffickers (SDNT). Please see part 744 of the EAR for controls maintained by the Bureau of Industry and Security on these and other persons.

[2] The President made inapplicable with respect to Iraq provisions of law that apply to countries that have supported terrorism.

entities on the Specially Designated Nationals list who participate in Terrorist Activities, Nuclear Proliferation Activities, and Narcotics Trafficking. The analysis of whether or not the intended export is subject to control under those regulations is Step 14.

Related to the country of destination, BIS established the Transshipment Country Export Control Initiative, whose goal is to strengthen export controls in countries and companies that are transshipment hubs, where legally exported goods are transshipped to prohibited destinations. Currently these areas include Panama, Malta, Cyprus, United Arab Emirates, Singapore, Malaysia, Thailand, Taiwan, and Hong Kong. Most of these areas are working with the U.S. government to strengthen controls for legitimate trade. There are certain countries through which the goods cannot transit on the way to their ultimate destination. These countries include the following: Albania, Armenia, Azerbaijan, Belarus, Bulgaria, Cambodia, Cuba, Estonia, Georgia, Kazakhstan, Kyrgyzstan, Laos, Latvia, Lithuania, Mongolia, North Korea, Russia, Tajikistan, Turkmenistan, Ukraine, Uzbekistan, and Vietnam (Step 8).

Let's review the determination process by using an example. Assume an exporter wants to export ball bearings to France. She will look in the Commerce Control List Index and see that they are listed under ECCN 2A001. Next she will look up 2A001 (see Figure 5-1) and she determines that her particular bearings are mentioned in paragraph (a). So her complete ECCN is 2A001.a. Next the exporter will look at the other information on that page. In reviewing this, the exporter will learn that the reasons for control include "NS" (National Security), "AT" (Anti-Terrorism), and, for certain items within the classification, "MT" (Missile Technology). It also indicates that certain common license exceptions are available; e.g., "LVS" (Low Value Shipment) is available if the value is not over $3,000, but it is not available to those countries designated for MT controls. "GBS" and "CIV" are available, but only for certain items and not to countries designated for MT controls. GBS is a license exception for ball and solid roller bearings that match the requirements under 2A001.a allowing for exports and re-exports to any country listed in Country Group B, except for those articles that fall in the Missile Technology (MT) restrictions (see Figure 5-1). Country Group B includes countries with an "NS" or National Security control designation only in the Country Code list (see Figure 5-3). There is also a license exception Civil End Users (CIV) which, like the GBS designation, allows for exports and re-exports to those countries in Group D:1 (see Figure 5-4) as designated under 2A001.a, except for those that meet the MT restrictions.

Next, the exporter looks up the Country Chart (Figure 5-6) to see what controls are placed on France. We see that France has an "X" marked in the box for NS and for MT, but not for AT. However, if we look to Country Group B, we see that France is listed.

Figure 5-6. Excerpt from Commerce Country Chart.

Commerce Control List Overview and the Country Chart

Supplement No. 1 to Part 738 page 5

Commerce Country Chart

Reason for Control

Countries	Chemical & Biological Weapons			Nuclear Nonproliferation		National Security		Missile Tech	Regional Stability		Firearms Convention	Crime Control			Anti-Terrorism	
	CB 1	CB 2	CB 3	NP 1	NP 2	NS 1	NS 2	MT 1	RS 1	RS 2	FC 1	CC 1	CC 2	CC 3	AT 1	AT 2
Dominican Republic	X	X		X		X	X	X	X	X	X	X		X		
Ecuador	X	X		X		X	X	X	X	X	X	X		X		
Egypt	X	X	X	X		X	X	X	X	X		X		X		
El Salvador	X	X		X		X	X	X	X	X	X	X		X		
Equatorial Guinea	X	X		X		X	X	X	X	X		X		X		
Eritrea[1]	X	X		X		X	X	X	X	X		X		X		
Estonia[3]	X					X		X	X							
Ethiopia	X	X		X		X	X	X	X	X		X		X		
Fiji	X	X		X		X	X	X	X	X		X	X			
Finland[3,4]	X					X		X	X			X		X		
France[3]	X					X		X	X							
Gabon	X	X		X		X	X	X	X	X		X		X		
Gambia, The	X	X		X		X	X	X	X	X		X		X		

Export Administration Regulations

Bureau of Industry and Security

August 7, 2014

Therefore, our exporter can export to France using the license exception "GBS." The exporter must let the forwarder know to indicate "2A001.a" and "GBS." on the Electronic Export Information filing.

As is evident by reviewing this one designation for bearings, it can be an extremely complicated process to determine whether a product is named in the EAR. If it is, then the exporter must determine whether there is an exception available (and there are a number of exceptions, we've only discussed three above) or whether she will need to obtain a license to export.

E. Customers, End Users, and End Uses

The Commerce Department maintains three lists of persons and entities that are either restricted or have specific requirements in order to export to them. The first is the "Denied Persons List." This list identifies persons who have previously violated U.S. export control laws and who are prohibited from engaging in export activities. The second list is the "Unverified List." This list is comprised of parties that the Commerce Department has been unable to verify in prior transactions. In the past, this was a "red flag" to the exporter which it should resolve before exporting, but as of January 21, 2014, the Commerce Department has suspended all license exceptions to parties on the Unverified List and exporters must file an EEI for all exports to these parties even if the products are EAR99 and the EEI would not normally be filed for some reason. The third list is called the "Entity List" and it is a list of parties who, if named in a transaction, will trigger a license requirement.

The Commerce Department's three lists are not the only ones that must be checked. The Department of Treasury maintains a similar list of "Specially Designated Nationalists and Terrorists." It also has a relative new list called the "Foreign Sanction Invaders" list.

The State Department also has its own list, called the "Debarred List," of persons that are prohibited from participating directly or indirectly in the export of any defense article.

It is a violation of the export control laws for a person on such lists to be involved in any export as a purchaser, consignee, freight forwarder, or any other role. Whenever an exporter is engaged in a transaction, it is incumbent upon the exporter to check various lists to ensure that none of the parties to the transaction appear on any list. (Step 12). A complete list of the all the prohibited parties published by the various agencies with control over exports is available at http://export.gov/ecr/eg_main_023148.asp. In addition, there are a number of vendors with software that will scan export documentations against these lists for exporters. These software vendors may integrate with an exporter's primary programs. It is advisable to scan the names of the parties prior to accepting an order and then again prior to exporting as the lists are updated regularly.

Even where an export may be ordinarily made, if the product being exported will be used in certain end-use activities, a license may be required or the license may be unavailable. These include nuclear explosive activities; unsafeguarded nuclear activities; exports of items for nuclear end uses that are permitted for countries in Supplement Number 3 to Part 744; design, development, production, or use of missiles in a country listed in Country Group D:4; and design, development, production, stockpiling, or use of chemical or biological weapons.

Finally, "U.S. persons" are prohibited from engaging in, facilitating, or supporting proliferation activities. This includes the design, development, production, or use of nuclear explosive devices in or by a country listed in Country Group D:2; the design, development, production, or use of missiles in or by a country listed in Country Group D:4; and the design, development, production, stockpiling, or use of chemical and biological weapons in any country listed in Country Group D:3. This includes any action such as financing, employment, transportation, and/or freight forwarding. The definition of "U.S. person" includes any individual who is a citizen of the United States, a permanent resident alien of the United States, or a protected individual; any juridical person organized under the laws of the United States, including foreign branches; and any person in the United States. This prohibition relates to any activities, including products produced entirely abroad without any U.S.-origin parts, components, or technology, and services provided entirely abroad—it need not involve a U.S. export or import. Confirming that the intended transaction does not violate the prohibition on proliferation activities is Step 15.

The Commerce Department expects exporters to know their customer. Step 18 involves deciding whether there are any "red flags" in the transaction. If there are red flags, the exporter is under a duty to inquire further, employees must be instructed how to handle red flags, and the exporter must refrain from the transaction or advise the Department of Commerce, Bureau of Industry and Security and wait for its guidance. The red flags are listed in Figure 5–7.

F. Ten General Prohibitions

Step 19 involves a review of the "Ten General Prohibitions" to confirm whether or not the intended export violates any of the prohibitions. Proceeding with the

Figure 5–7. Red flags.

1. The customer or its address is similar to one of the parties found on the Commerce Department's [BIS's] list of denied persons.

2. The customer or purchasing agent is reluctant to offer information about the end use of the item.

3. The product's capabilities do not fit the buyer's line of business, such as an order for sophisticated computers for a small bakery.

4. The item ordered is incompatible with the technical level of the country to which it is being shipped, such as semiconductor manufacturing equipment being shipped to a country that has no electronics industry.

5. The customer is willing to pay cash for a very expensive item when the terms of sale would normally call for financing.

6. The customer has little or no business background.

7. The customer is unfamiliar with the product's performance characteristics but still wants the product.

8. Routine installation, training, or maintenance services are declined by the customer.

9. Delivery dates are vague, or deliveries are planned for out of the way destinations.

10. A freight forwarding firm is listed as the product's final destination.

11. The shipping route is abnormal for the product and destination.

12. Packaging is inconsistent with the stated method of shipment or destination.

13. When questioned, the buyer is evasive and especially unclear about whether the purchased product is for domestic use, for export, or for re-export.

transaction with knowledge that a violation has occurred or is about to occur is prohibited. This prohibition includes selling, transferring, exporting, re-exporting, financing, ordering, buying, removing, concealing, storing, using, loaning, disposing of, transferring, transporting, forwarding, or otherwise servicing any item subject to the EAR.

The Ten General Prohibitions are as follows:

1. Exporting or re-exporting controlled items to listed countries without a license

2. Re-exporting and exporting from abroad foreign-made items incorporating more than a de minimis amount of controlled U.S. content

3. Re-exporting and exporting from abroad the foreign-produced direct product of U.S. technology and software.

4. Engaging in actions prohibited by Denial Orders

5. Exporting or re-exporting to prohibited end uses or end users

6. Exporting or re-exporting to embargoed destinations

7. Support of proliferation activities

8. Shipping goods through, transiting, or unloading in prohibited countries

9. Violating any order, terms, and conditions of the EAR or any license or exception

10. Proceeding with transactions with knowledge that a violation has occurred or is about to occur

If none of the Ten General Prohibitions will be violated by the intended export transaction, then no license is required (Step 20). The last general prohibition is the catch-all provision. It states that a party may not:

> [S]ell, transfer, export, reexport, finance, order, buy, remove, conceal, store, use, loan, dispose of, transport, forward, or otherwise service, in whole or in part, any item subject to the EAR and exported or to be exported with knowledge that a violation of the Export Administration Regulations, the Export administration Act, or any order, license, License Exception or other authorization issued thereunder has occurred, is about to occur, or is intended to occur in connection with them.

It is exceptionally and intentionally broad to ensure enforcement of the regulations.

G. License Exemptions and Exceptions

If an item is outside of the scope of the EAR, that is, it is not subject to the EAR, then, assuming that it is not subject to licensing by or the requirements of any other agency, it can be exported "No License Required" (NLR). In addition, an item that is subject to the EAR because it is a U.S. export or a certain type of re-export but is not specifically identified on the Commerce Control List (therefore falling into the basket category "EAR 99"), can also be exported NLR provided it is not subject to any of the Ten General Prohibitions. Finally, if the item is listed on the Commerce Control List but there is no "X" in the country box of ultimate destination, it may be exported NLR provided, again, that it does not violate any of the Ten General Prohibitions.

Assuming, however, that the foregoing analysis indicates that a license will be required for export, before applying for a license, the exporter can review the license exceptions designated in the EAR. Although there are numerous license exceptions specified, Step 21 involves reviewing a list of restrictions that apply to all license exceptions contained in Section 740.2 of the EAR. Again, assuming that none of those restrictions apply, the exporter may review each of the available license exceptions and assess whether or not the intended export transaction qualifies for one of the specific exceptions.

One large group of exceptions is based upon the Commerce Control List. As discussed above in regard to the Commerce Control List, identifying a product intended for export on the list will also show various types of license exceptions that may be available under the ECCN. As indicated in our example above, there are common license exceptions: (1) LVS (Low Value Shipments) may be available for small valued shipments, the dollar amount will be listed in the ECCN provision; (2) GBS may be available for shipments to Country Group B with restrictions identified in the ECCN provisions; and CIV may be available for shipments to civil (nonmilitary) end users. Others include: (1) TSR (Technology and Software Restricted) may be available for certain restricted technology and software destined for countries in Group B, and APP (Computers) may be available for certain computers when exported to specific computer tier countries that are listed in Section 740.7. Another exception, TMP (Temporary), encompasses temporary imports, exports, re-exports, and in-country transfers. RPL (Replacement) includes both servicing and the replacement of parts and equipment. Exports to government end users, international organizations, international inspections under the Chemical Weapons Convention, and the International Space Station may qualify for GOV (Government) exception. GFT (Gift) covers gifts and humanitarian donations. TSU (Technology and Software Unrestricted) allows for the exports and re-exports of operation technology and software, sales technology and software, software updates including bug fixes. BAG (Baggage) covers the export of commodities and software that are personal effects, household effects, vehicles, and tools of trade. (They must be owned by the individual and intended for and necessary and appropriate for the use of the individual. Such items must accompany the traveler, or in certain cases may be shipped within three months before or after the individual's departure.) AVS is an exception for the export of foreign registry civilian aircraft temporarily in the United States and of U.S. civilian aircraft temporarily abroad, and equipment and spare parts for permanent use on a vessel or aircraft, and ship and plane stores. APR (Additional Permissive Re-exports) is a license exception for re-exports from Country Group A:1 (see Figure 5-2) destined for cooperating countries provided that: (1) the export is in compliance with the export control regulations of the exporting country and (2) that the reason for control is not NP, CB, MT, SS, or SI reasons. The export must be to either a country in Country Group B *that is not also included* in Country Group D:2, D:3, D:4, Cambodia, or Laos, and the commodity being re-exported is both controlled for national security reasons and not controlled for export to Country Group A:1; or a country in Country Group D:1 other than Cambodia, Laos, or North Korea and the commodity being re-exported is controlled for national security reasons.

In addition, the ENC (Encryption Commodities, Software and Technology) allow for the export and re-export of systems, equipment, commodities and components classified under certain 5A002 provisions and 5B002 provisions or related software and technology under 5D002 or 5E002, There are a couple of license exemptions for Cuba only: (1) AGR (Agricultural Commodities) is for exports of U.S. origin agricultural products, including food and beverages, to Cuba provided that the contract, financing, and export transportation meet certain requirements. However, it should be noted that no U.S.-origin good (or foreign-origin good with greater than 10% U.S.-origin content) may be exported to Cuba from any other country using this exception; and (2) Consumer Communication Devices (CCDs) were added for the export of computers, monitors, printers, modems, and cell phones to Cuba.

Finally license exception STA (Strategic Trade Authorization) allows for the exports, re-exports, and transfers (in-country) to countries where the only applicable reasons for control are: (NS) Nationals Security; (CB) Chemical and Biological weapons; (NP) Nuclear Proliferation; (RS) Regional Stability; (CC) Crime Control; and/or (SI) Significant items to nationals or to countries in Country Group A:5 (see Figure 5-2). There are additional requirements to using this license exception and a number of excluded ECCNs. There is a decision tree on BIS' web site at: http://www.bis.doc.gov/index.php/statool.

It is important when attempting to use one of the license exceptions, that you review the requirements of each in 15 CFR 740; determine whether the item to be exported is named as an exclusion to the license exemption; and retain all supporting documentation to support the basis for concluding the exception is available.

Analyzing whether an export qualifies for an exception comprises Steps 22 and 23. If the exporter believes that an exception applies, it must export in accordance with the terms and conditions of the exception (Steps 17 and 24).

In completing the export documentation, including specifically the Electronic Export Information, designation of NLR license exception is made under penalty of perjury and subjects any false or inaccurate designation to the penalties described in Section O below.

H. License Applications and Procedures

If the transaction is subject to the EAR, the product is on the Commerce Control List, there is an "X" in the Country Chart for the intended destination, and no exception applies, the exporter will have to apply for a license (see Figure 5–8). The first step in applying for a license is determining what documentation is required from the buyer.

1. *Documentation From Buyer*

If the item being exported is controlled for national security reasons (except for 5A002, 5B002, or any items controlled to the People's Republic of China), valued at over $50,000, and destined for one of the following countries, an import or end-user certificate from the buyer's government is required: Argentina, Australia, Austria, Belgium, Bulgaria, Czech Republic, Denmark, Finland, France, Germany, Greece, Hong Kong, Hungary, India, Republic of Ireland, Italy, Japan, Republic of Korea, Liechtenstein, Luxembourg, Netherlands, New Zealand, Norway, Pakistan, Poland, Portugal, Romania, Singapore, Slovakia, Spain, Sweden, Switzerland, Taiwan, Turkey, and United Kingdom. A list of government agencies issuing import certificates is contained in the EAR in 15 CFR 748. For exports destined for the People's Republic of China, an import or end-user certificate is required for all transactions exceeding $50,000 involving items that require a license for any reason.

A sample of the form used for U.S. imports is shown in Figure 5–9. In a number of situations, no support documentation is required from the buyer to apply for an export license. These include exports and re-exports involving ultimate consignees located in any of the following countries: Bahamas, Barbados, Belize, Bermuda, Bolivia, Brazil, Canada, Chile, Colombia, Costa Rica, Dominican Republic, Ecuador, El Salvador, French Guiana, French West Indies, Greenland, Guatemala, Guyana, Haiti, Honduras, Jamaica, Leeward and Windward Islands, Mexico, Miquelon and Saint Pierre Islands, Netherlands Antilles, Nicaragua, Panama, Paraguay, Peru, Surinam, Trinidad and Tobago, Uruguay, and Venezuela. No support documentation is required for license applications where the ultimate consignee or purchaser is a foreign government or foreign government agency except for the People's Republic of China. Likewise, no support documentation is required for items exported for temporary exhibit, demonstration, or testing purposes; the application is filed by or on behalf of a relief agency registered with the Advisory Committee on Voluntary Foreign Aid, U.S. Agency for International Development, for export to a member agency in the foreign government; the license

Figure 5–8. Decision tree for exporters.

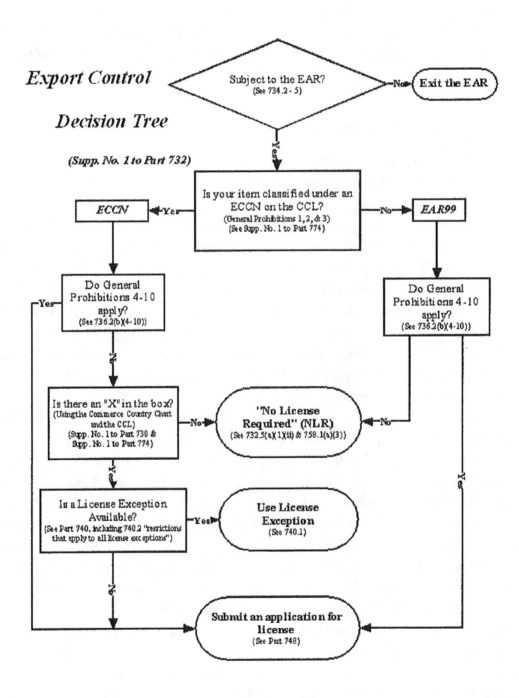

Figure 5–9. Import certificate (U.S.).

FORM BIS-645P/ATF-4522/DPS-53 (REV 8/02)   Form Approved: OMB No. 0694-0017 - Modele approuvé: OMB No. 0694-0017

U.S. DEPARTMENT OF COMMERCE Bureau of Industry and Security U.S. DEPARTMENT OF THE TREASURY Bureau of Alcohol, Tobacco and Firearms U.S. DEPARTMENT OF STATE Office of Munitions Control	INTERNATIONAL IMPORT CERTIFICATE (CERTIFICAT INTERNATIONAL D'IMPORTATION)
NOTE: Read instructions on the reverse side before completing and submitting this form. (Lire les instructions au verso avant de remplir et de presenter la présente formule.)	Certificate Number
1. U.S. Importer/Importateur (Name and address—Nom et adresse)	FOR U.S. GOVERNMENT USE (Réservé pour le Gouvernement des Etats-Unis)
2. Exporter/Exportateur (Name and address—Nom et adresse)	If this form has been approved by the Department of Commerce or the Department of State, it is not valid unless the official seal of the Department of Commerce, or the Department of State, appears in this space. If this form is approved by the Treasury Department, a seal is not required. (Si ce formulaire a été approuvé par le Ministère du Commerce, ou le Ministère des Affaires Etrangères, il n'est pas valide à moins qu'un sceau officiel du Ministère du Commerce ou du Ministère des Affaires Etrangères soit apposé sur le document. Si ce formulaire est approuvé par le Ministère des Finances, un sceau officiel n'est pas nécessaire.

3.	Description of goods (Désignation de la Marchandise)	TSUS Anno. No. (Numéro de la liste)	Quantity (Quantité)	Value (Valeur) (FOB, CIF, etc.)

4. Representation and undertaking of U.S. importer or principal

The undersigned hereby represents that he has undertaken to import into the United States of America under a U.S. Consumption Entry or U.S. Warehouse Entry the commodities in quantities described above, or, if the commodities are not so imported into the United States of America, that he will not divert, transship, or reexport them to another destination except with explicit approval of the Department of Commerce, the Department of State, or the Department of the Treasury, as appropriate. The undersigned also undertakes to notify the appropriate Department immediately of any changes of fact or intention set forth herein. If a delivery verification is required, the undersigned also undertakes to obtain such verification and make disposition of it in accordance with such requirement. **Any false statement willfully made in this declaration is punishable by fine and imprisonment. (See experts from U.S. Code on reverse side.)**

Déclaration et engagement de l'importateur ou du commettant des Etats-Unis

Le soussigné déclare par la présente qu'il a pris l'engagement d'importer aux Etats-Unis d'Amérique, en vertu d'une Déclaration américaine de Mise en Consommation, ou d'une Declaration américaine d'Entrée en entrepôt, la quantité de produits ci-dessus et que, dans le cas ou ces produits ne seraient pas ainsi importés aux Etats-Unis d'Amérique, il ne le détournera, ni les transbordera, ni les réexportera a destination d'un autre lieu, si ce n'est avec l'approbation explicite du Ministère du Commerce, du Ministère des Affaires Etrangères ou du Ministère des Finances, comme il est requis. Le soussigné prend également l'engagement d'aviser le Ministère intéressé des Etats-Unis de tous changements survenus dans les actes ou les intentions énoncés dans la présente déclaration. Si demande est faite d'une confirmation de la livraison le soussigné prend également l'engagement d'obtenir cette confirmation et d'en disposer de la manière prescrite par cette demande. **Toute fausse déclaration faite intentionnellement expose l'auteur aux pénalités prévues par la loi. (Voir Extrait du Code des Etats-Unis au verso.)**

Type or Print (Prière d'écrire a la machine ou en caractères d'imprimerie)	Type or Print (Prière d'écrire a la machine ou en caractères d'imprimerie)
Name of Firm or Corporation (Nom de la Firme ou de la Société)	Name and Title of Authorized Official (Nom et titre de l'agent ou employé autorisé)
Signature of Authorized Official (Signature de l'agent ou employé autorisé)	Date of Signature (Date de la signature)

This document ceases to be valid unless presented to the competent foreign authorities within six months from its date of issue. (Le présent document perd sa validité s'il n'est pas remis aux autorités étrangères compétentes dans un délai de six mois à compter de sa délivrance.)

No import certification may be obtained unless this International Import Certificate has been completed and filed with the appropriate U.S. Government agency (Department of Commerce: 50 U.S.C. app. §2411, E.O. 12214 15 C.FR. §368; Department of the Treasury; 22 U.S.C. §2778, E.O. 11959, 27 C.FR. §47; Department of State: 22 U.S.C. 2778, 2779, E.O. 11958, 22 C.F.R. §123). Information furnished herewith is subject to the provisions of Section 12(c) of the Export Administration Act of 1979, 50 U.S.C. app. 2411(c), and its unauthorized disclosure is prohibited by law.

FOR U.S. GOVERNMENT USE (Réservé au Gouvernement des Etats-Unis)

Certification: This is to certify that the above declaration was made to the U.S. Department of Commerce, State, or Treasury through the undersigned designated official thereof and a copy of this certification is placed in the official files.	Certification : Il est certifié par la présente que la déclaration ci-dessus a été faite au Ministère du Commerce, des Affaires Etrangères, ou des Finances des Etats-Unis par l'intermédiaire du fonctionnaire autorisé soussigné de ce Ministère et qu'une copie de ce certificat a été conservée dans les archives officielles.

Signature_____Date_____

Designated Commerce, State, or Treasury Official (Fonctionnaire competent du Ministère du Commerce, d'Etat, ou du Trésor)   Date

USCOMM DC 89-24414

ORIGINAL COPY

is for the export or re-export of items for temporary exhibit, demonstration, or testing purposes; the license is for items controlled for short supply reasons; the license application is for the export or re-export of software or technology; the license application is submitted for certain encryption items; or the license application is submitted under the Special Comprehensive License procedures (see Section K below).

All other export transactions require a "Statement by Ultimate Consignee and Purchaser." This is a revised form, BIS-711. A sample is shown in Figure 5–10. No Statement by Ultimate Consignee and Purchaser is required where the transaction is valued at $5,000 or less. If the country of ultimate destination is listed in either Country Group D:2, D:3, or D:4, a copy of the Statement must be submitted with the license application. Otherwise, the Statement must be maintained in the records of the applicant for the license.

2. License Application Form

Figure 5–11 shows the online license application form through the Simplified Network Application Program-Revised (SNAP-R) system. First the parties must register for the SNAP-R program. This is a simple online procedure that will provide a Company Identification Number (CIN) within a matter of hours. As mentioned earlier, the SNAP-R program can also be used to obtain an ECCN from BIS. Complete information regarding the commodity must be supplied. All licenses must now be filed electronically through the SNAP-R system by a registered party, either the exporter or an agent for the exporter. The instructions for completion of the form are on the web site at http://www.bis.doc.gov/snapr/snapr_exporter_user_manual.pdf. In addition to the general instructions, specific information must be provided for certain items or types of transactions ("unique license application requirements"). These include the export of chemicals, medicinals, and pharmaceuticals; communications intercepting devices; computers; telecommunications, information security items, and related equipment; gift parcels; goods transiting the United States; goods transiting other countries; nuclear nonproliferation items and end uses; numerical control devices; motion control boards; numerically controlled machine tools; dimensional inspection machines; direct numerical control systems; specially designed assemblies and specially designed software; parts, components, and materials incorporated abroad in foreign-made products; ship stores and plane stores, supplies, and equipment; regional stability controlled items; re-exports; robots; short supply controlled items; technology; temporary exports or re-exports; exports of chemicals controlled for CW reasons by ECCN 1C350 to countries not listed on Supplement No. 2 to Part 745 of the EAR; encryption review

Figure 5–10. Statement by ultimate consignee and purchaser.

FORM **BIS-711** FORM APPROVED UNDER OMB CONTROL NO. 0694-0021, 0694-0093	U.S. DEPARTMENT OF COMMERCE BUREAU OF INDUSTRY AND SECURITY Information furnished herewith is subject to the provisions of Section 12(c) of the Export Administration Act of 1979, as amended, 50 U.S.C. app 2411(c) and its unauthorized disclosure is prohibited by law.	DATE RECEIVED (Leave Blank)

STATEMENT BY ULTIMATE CONSIGNEE AND PURCHASER

1. ULTIMATE CONSIGNEE	CITY	
ADDRESS LINE 1	COUNTRY	
ADDRESS LINE 2	POSTAL CODE	TELEPHONE OR FAX

2. DISPOSITION OR USE OF ITEMS BY ULTIMATE CONSIGNEE NAMED IN BLOCK 1

We certify that the items: *(left mouse click in the appropriate box below)*

A. ☐ Will be used by us (as capital equipment) in the form in which received in a manufacturing process in the country named in Block 1 and will not be reexported or incorporated into an end product.

B. ☐ Will be processed or incorporated by us into the following product (s) _____ to be manufactured in the country named in Block 1 for distribution in _____

C. ☐ Will be resold by us in the form in which received in the country named in Block 1 for use or consumption therein. The specific end-use by my customer will be _____

D. ☐ Will be reexported by us in the form in which received to _____

E. ☐ Other (describe fully) _____

NOTE: If BOX (D) is checked, acceptance of this form by the Bureau of Industry and Security as a supporting document for license applications shall not be construed as an authorization to reexport the items to which the form applies unless specific approval has been obtained from the Bureau of Industry and Security for such export.

3. NATURE OF BUSINESS OF ULTIMATE CONSIGNEE NAMED IN BLOCK 1

A. The nature of our usual business is _____

B. Our business relationship with the U.S. exporter is _____

and we have had this business relationship for _____ year(s).

4. ADDITIONAL INFORMATION

5. ASSISTANCE IN PREPARING STATEMENT

STATEMENT OF ULTIMATE CONSIGNEE AND PURCHASER

We certify that all of the facts contained in this statement are true and correct to the best of our knowledge and we do not know of any additional facts which are inconsistent with the above statement. We shall promptly send a supplemental statement to the U.S. Exporter, disclosing any change of facts or intentions set forth in this statement which occurs after the statement has been prepared and forwarded, except as specifically authorized by the U.S. Export Administration Regulations (15 CFR parts 730-774), or by prior written approval of the Bureau of Industry and Security, we will not reexport, resell, or otherwise dispose of any items approved on a license supported by this statement (1) to any country not approved for export as brought to our attention by means of a bill of lading, commercial invoice, or any other means, or(2) to any person if we know that it will result directly or indirectly, in disposition of the items contrary to the representations made in this statement or contrary to Export Administration Regulations.

6. SIGNATURE OF OFFICIAL OF ULTIMATE CONSIGNEE	7. NAME OF PURCHASER
NAME OF OFFICIAL	SIGNATURE OF PURCHASER
TITLE OF OFFICIAL	NAME OF OFFICIAL
DATE *(mmmm,dd,yyyy)*	TITLE OF OFFICIAL
CERTIFICATION FOR USE OF U.S. EXPORTER - We certify that no corrections, additions, or alterations were made on this form by us after the form was signed by the (ultimate consignee)(purchaser).	DATE *(mmmm,dd,yyyy)*
8. NAME OF EXPORTER	SIGNATURE OF PERSON AUTHORIZED TO CERTIFY FOR EXPORTER
NAME OF PERSON SIGNING THIS DOCUMENT	TITLE OF PERSON SIGNING THIS DOCUMENT	DATE *(mmmm,dd,yyyy)*

We acknowledge that the making of any false statements or concealment of any material fact in connection with this statement may result in imprisonment or fine, or both and denial, in whole or in part, of participation in U.S. exports and reexports.

Public reporting burden for this collection of information is estimated to average 15 minutes per response plus one minute for recordkeeping, including the time for reviewing instruments, searching existing data sources, gathering and maintaining the data needed, and completing and reviewing the collection of information. Send comments regarding this burden estimate or any other aspect of this collection of information, including suggestions for reducing this burden, to the Director of Administration, Room 3889, Bureau of Industry and Security, U.S. Department of Commerce, Washington, DC 20230, and to the Office of Management and Budget Paperwork Reduction Project (0694-0021, 0694-0093), Washington, D.C. 20503. Notwithstanding any other provision of law, no person is obligated to respond to nor shall a person be subject to a penalty for failure to comply with a collection of information subject to the Paperwork Reduction Act unless that collection of information displays a currently valid OMB Control Number.

Figure 5–11. SNAP-R application.

Edit Work Item

SNAP- R

SNAP-R HOME
CREATE WORK ITEM
LIST WORK ITEMS
SEARCH WORK ITEMS
SEARCH DOCUMENTS
VIEW MESSAGES
MANAGE USER PROFILE
HELP
LOGOUT

Export License Application
Reference Number: ABC1111   Status: DRAFT   BIS-748P

Edit Export License Application

Please click **Save Draft** to save your unfinished work. Required fields are marked with an asterisk (*). The numbers ⍰ next to the fields are only for reference to the paper version of this form and do not need to be considered to complete this application.
To delete this Work Item: Delete Work Item

To grant or delete rights to others to view, edit, or submit this Work Item: Manage User Rights ⍰

[Collapse All]

Contact Information*

Reference Number*(AAA9999) ⍰   ABC1111

1. Contact Person (First, Last)* ⍰

2. Telephone Number* (999-999-9999) ⍰

3. Fax Number (999-999-9999) ⍰

Email ⍰

4. Creation Date ⍰   04/18/2009

5. Type Of Application   Export License Application

Save Draft

Document Checklist

6. Documents submitted with application ⍰   7. Documents on file with applicant ⍰

     Export Items (BIS-748P-A) ⍰   ☐ BIS-711

     End Users (BIS-748P-B) ⍰   ☐ Letter of Assurance

☐ BIS-711   ☐ Import/End-User Certificate

☐ Import/End-User Certificate   ☐ Nuclear Certification

☐ Technical Specification   ☐ Other

☐ Letter of Explanation

☐ Foreign Availability

☐ Other

Save Draft

License Information

9. Special Purpose ⍰

10. Resubmission ACN ⍰

11. Replacement License Number ⍰

13. Import Certificate Country ⍰   Please Select

Import Certificate Number

Save Draft

Applicant Information* ⍰

* Required field

14. CIN (Applicant ID)*

Applicant*

Address Line 1*

Address Line 2

City*

Export Controls and Licenses

Figure 5–11. *(continued)*

State/Province* (Required for US address)

Postal Code*

Country*   Please Select

EIN

Save Draft

Other Party Information ⏺

* Required field (only if entering an Other Party). Otherwise leave blank.

15. Other Party ID
    Other Party*
    Address Line 1*
    Address Line 2
    City*
    State/Province* (Required for US address)
    Postal Code*
    Country*
    Telephone or Fax*

Save Draft

Purchaser Information ⏺

* Required field (only if entering a Purchaser). Otherwise leave blank.

16. Purchaser*

    Address Line 1*

    Address Line 2

    City*

    Postal Code

    Country*   Please Select

    Telephone or Fax

Save Draft

Intermediate Consignee Information ⏺

* Required field (only if entering an Intermediate Consignee). Otherwise leave blank.

17. Intermediate Consignee*

    Address Line 1*

    Address Line 2

    City*

    Postal Code

    Country*   Please Select

    Telephone or Fax

Save Draft

Ultimate Consignee Information* ⏺

* Required field

18. Ultimate Consignee*

    Address Line 1*

    Address Line 2

    City*

    Postal Code

    Country*   Please Select

    Telephone or Fax

Save Draft

Figure 5–11. (*continued*)

Edit Work Item

End User Information ⍰

Enter information for a new End User
* Required field (only if entering an End User). Otherwise leave blank.

19. End User*

    Address Line 1*

    Address Line 2

    City*

    Postal Code

    Country*   Please Select

    Telephone or Fax

    [Add End User]

Specific End Use* ⍰

21. Specific End Use*

[Save Draft]

Export Item Information* ⍰

Enter information for a new Export Item

22. a. ECCN*   Please Select

    b. APP(9.9999999)

    c. Product/Model Number

    d. CCATS Number

    e. Quantity*   0

    f. Units   each

    g. Unit Price

    h. Total Price*   0.0

    i. Manufacturer

    j. Technical Description*

[Add Export Item]

Total Application Dollar Value

23. Total Application Dollar Value $0.00

Additional Information ⍰

24. Additional Information

Figure 5–11. (*continued*)

Save Draft

Documents attached to application

To upload a new supporting document or view or delete attached supporting documents: <u>View and Manage Supporting Documents</u> ?

Title | **Author** | **Type**

There are no documents attached.

Please remember to **Save Draft** before leaving this form to avoid losing work

Save Draft | Check For Errors | Preview Work Item to Submit

<u>FOIA</u> | <u>Disclaimer</u> | <u>Privacy Policy Statement</u> | <u>Information Quality</u>
<u>Department of Commerce</u> | <u>Contact Us</u>

https://snapr.bis.doc.gov/snapr/exp/WorkItem/168297?action=Edit%20Work%20Item

4/18/2009

requests; foreign national review requests; aircraft and vessels on temporary sojourn; and in-country transfers.

The specific instructions for such items and transactions are contained in the EAR. Completion of the license application form comprises Steps 25 and 26.

3. Procedures

As indicated earlier, the license application form must be filed electronically through the SNAP-R program. Once it is filed, the registered party will receive email notices that there are messages from BIS on the SNAP-R web site when further action is required or when it is available. If the license application is not complete, it will be returned without action (RWA). If the Department of Commerce intends to deny the license (ITD), it will inform the applicant, specifying the reasons, and permit the applicant to respond before finally denying the license application. In some cases, the Commerce Department can hold the application without action (HWA). If the exporter desires to know the status of a license application, he must use the BIS online system for tracking export license applications (STELA); https://snapr.bis.doc.gov/stela.

Note that licenses are issued to one purchaser although the purchase may have multiple ultimate consignees as long as they are in the same country. So you will need to obtain multiple licenses if you intend to ship to different purchasers or different countries. You may list multiple items on the same license. Licenses were originally two years, but with the transition under the Export Control Reform, BIS issues licenses for four years now. It is important to note the time frame since the exporter may want to anticipate its exports through the length of the license if it is a refillable product. There is no violation for not exporting everything that is listed in a license.

When the license is issued, the registered party prints the license from the SNAP-R web site. The licenses will carry a license number and validation date (a sample is shown in Figure 5–12). The license number must be entered in the Electronic Export Information form filed through the Automated Export System for export clearance. When a license has been issued, the export must be carried out in accordance with the terms and conditions of the license (Step 17). As exports are made against the license, the quantities (and values) are decremented against the license until either the licensed quantity has been used up or the license has expired. A variance in the value is allowed over time because of the change in exchange rates or the increased price of the merchandise over time.

Figure 5–12. Sample export license.

```
EXPORT LICENSE                                  UNITED STATES DEPARTMENT OF COMMERCE
    VALIDATED: MAR 22 2008                      BUREAU OF INDUSTRY AND SECURITY
    EXPIRES:   MAR 31 2010                      P.O. Box 273, Ben Franklin Station
                                                Washington, DC 20044

---------------------------------------------------------------------------------

    THIS LICENSE AUTHORIZES THE LICENSEE TO CARRY OUT THE EXPORT TRANSACTION
    DESCRIBED ON THE LICENSE (INCLUDING ALL ATTACHMENTS).  IT MAY NOT BE
    TRANSFERRED WITHOUT PRIOR WRITTEN APPROVAL OF THE OFFICE OF EXPORT
    LICENSING.  THIS LICENSE HAS BEEN GRANTED IN RELIANCE ON REPRESENTATIONS
    MADE BY THE LICENSEE AND OTHERS IN CONNECTION WITH THE APPLICATION FOR EXPORT
    AND IS EXPRESSLY SUBJECT TO ANY CONDITIONS STATED ON THE LICENSE, AS WELL AS
    ALL APPLICABLE EXPORT CONTROL LAWS, REGULATIONS, RULES, AND ORDERS.  THIS
    LICENSE IS SUBJECT TO REVISION, SUSPENSION, OR REVOCATION WITHOUT PRIOR NOTICE.

    APPLICANT REFERENCE NUMBER:
                                                PURCHASER:




    ULTIMATE CONSIGNEE:                         INTERMEDIATE CONSIGNEE:




    APPROVED END USER(S):




                                    ;A




    COMMODITIES:                                                    TOTAL
        QTY  DESCRIPTION                            ECCN            PRICE
         30                                         1C107
          :
          :
          :
        180                                         1C107
```

Figure 5–12. (*continued*)

EXPORT LICENSE
    VALIDATED: MAR 22 2008
    EXPIRES: MAR 31 2010

UNITED STATES DEPARTMENT OF COMMERCE
BUREAU OF INDUSTRY AND SECURITY
P.O. Box 273, Ben Franklin Station
Washington, DC 20044

---

        8   1C107

                                                    TOTAL:

THE EXPORT ADMINISTRATION REGULATIONS REQUIRE YOU TO TAKE THE FOLLOWING ACTIONS
WHEN EXPORTING UNDER THE AUTHORITY OF THIS LICENSE.

    A. RECORD THE EXPORT COMMODITY CONTROL NUMBER IN THE BLOCK
       PROVIDED ON EACH SHIPPER'S EXPORT DECLARATION (SED).

    B. RECORD YOUR VALIDATED LICENSE NUMBER IN THE BLOCK
       PROVIDED ON EACH SED.

    C. PLACE A DESTINATION CONTROL STATEMENT ON ALL BILLS OF LADING,
       AIRWAY BILLS, AND COMMERCIAL INVOICES.

RIDERS AND CONDITIONS:

    1. STATED END USE ONLY.   NOT FOR USE IN MISSILE, SPACE LAUNCH
       VEHICLES, UNMANNED AIR VEHICLES, RESEARCH, DEVELOPMENT, PRODUCTION
       OR ANY MISSILE RELAT ED END USES.

    2. APPLICANT MUST INFORM CONSIGNEE OF ALL LICENSE CONDITIONS.

    3. NO RESALE, TRANSFER, OR REEXPORT OF THE ITEMS LISTED ON THIS LICENSE
       IS AUTHORIZED WITHOUT PRIOR AUTHORIZATION BY THE U.S. GOVERNMENT.

I. Re-Exports

Items that originated in the United States and were originally exported with or without a license continue to potentially be subject to the EAR. Step 3 requires a person engaging in a re-export transaction to determine whether the re-export can be made without a license, whether a license exception applies, or whether a license must be obtained.

As explained above, if a transaction is subject to the EAR, it is necessary to assess whether or not the transaction is also prohibited by one of the Ten General Prohibitions. General Prohibition #1 includes re-export of controlled items to listed countries; #2 includes re-export from abroad of foreign-made items incorporating more than the de minimis amount of controlled U.S. content (parts and components of re-exports), the de minimis amount is 25 percent for most countries and 10 percent for countries in Group E1 and China for defense articles on the CCL; #3 includes re-exports from abroad of the foreign-produced direct product of U.S. technology and software; #4 includes re-export to prohibited end uses or end users; and #5 includes re-exports to embargoed destinations without a license.

J. Export Documentation and Record-Keeping

In order to complete the exportation, whether a license is required or not, it is necessary for the exporter to complete certain export documentation and maintain certain records. The EAR requires an exporter to complete the Electronic Export Information filing through the Automated Export System declaring the eligibility of the export. The exporter will be required to enter "NLR" when no license is required; the license exception symbol where the export qualifies for a license exception, for example, "GBS"; or the license number where a license has been obtained. The ECCN number or munitions list category number must also be shown in EEI.

In addition to the Electronic Export Information, a destination control statement must be entered on all copies of the bill of lading, the air waybill, and the commercial invoice for an export. All exports that are not controlled by the State Department require a destination control statement on the export documentation. It should read: "These commodities, technology or software were exported from the United States in accordance with the Export Administration Regulations. Diversion contrary to law is prohibited."

An additional document that may be required is a delivery verification (see Figures 5–13 and 5–14). When an export is being made to a country where an import certificate

Figure 5–13. Notification of delivery verification requirement.

Form Approved: OMB No. 0694-0016

FORM BIS-648P *(formerly form BXA-648P)* (REV.4-03)	U.S. DEPARTMENT OF COMMERCE BUREAU OF INDUSTRY AND SECURITY	Date *(mmmm,dd,yyyy)*
	NOTIFICATION OF **DELIVERY VERIFICATION REQUIREMENT**	Export License No.
		Applicant's Reference No.
Information furnished herewith is subject to the provisions of Section 12(c) of the Export Administration Act of 1979. 50 U.S.C app. 2411 (c), and its unauthorized disclosure is prohibited by law. Your failure to complete and return this form along with required delivery verification(s) may subject you to administrative action under the Export Administration Act.		International Import Certificate No.

IMPORTANT NOTICE

LICENSEE: You are required to provide the Bureau of Industry and Security with a document verifying the delivery of each shipment made against the attached license. For your information, Instructions on what you must do about obtaining and submitting delivery verification documents will be found of the last page of this form.

AGENT OR FREIGHT FORWARDER: When this form BIS-648P is attached to a license which has been forwarded by the Bureau of Industry and Security to an agent or freight forwarder of the licensee, it is the responsibility of the agent or freight forwarder to notify the licensee that verification of delivery is required for exports made against the license.

Select item 1, 2, or 3, as applicable, using the letter 'X', and complete the item. The ORIGINAL of this form must be returned to the Bureau of Industry and Security, P.O. Box 273, Washington, DC 20044, as soon as you have received all delivery verification documents for shipments made against the attached license. (See paragraph A3 on the back of the Duplicate Copy.)

1. ☐ The total quantity authorized for export by this license has been exported and all delivery verification documents are attached hereto.

2. ☐ A part of the quantity authorized for export by this license will not be exported. Delivery verification documents covering all commodities exported are attached hereto.

3. ☐ No shipment has been made against this license and none is contemplated.

4. The License:

a. ☐ is returned herewith for cancellation.

b. ☐ was returned to the Bureau of Industry and Security as required by 386.2(d) of the Export Administration Regulations.

Remarks:

Print or type name of Licensee	Print or type name and title of authorized representative
Date signed *(mmmm,dd,yyyy)*	Signature of authorized representative

(See instructions on page 3)

Figure 5–14. Delivery verification certificate.

Form Approved: OMB No. 0694-0016, 0694-0093

FORM BIS-647-P (REV.4/03)	U.S. DEPARTMENT OF COMMERCE Bureau of Industry and Security

DELIVERY VERIFICATION CERTIFICATE

Public reporting burden for this collection of information is estimated to average 15 minutes per response,, including the time for reviewing instructions, searching existing data sources, gathering and maintaining the data needed, and completing and reviewing the collection of information. Send comments regarding this burden estimate or any other aspect of this collection of information, including suggestions for reducing the burden, to the Director of Administration, room-3889, Bureau of Industry and Security, U.S. Department of Commerce, Washington, D.C. 20230; and to the Office of Management and Budget Paperwork Reduction Project (0694-0016, 0694-0093) Washington, DC 20503.

Notwithstanding any other provision of law, no person is required to respond to nor shall a person be subject to a penalty for failure to comply with a collection of information subject to the requirements of the Paperwork Reduction Act unless that collection of information displays a currently valid OMB Control Number.

Instructions- When required to obtain a delivery verification, the U.S. Importer shall submit this form in duplicate, to the Customs Office. U.S. importer is required to complete all items on this form except the portion to be completed by the U.S. Customs Service. The Customs Office will certify a Delivery Verification Certificate only after the import has been delivered to the U.S. importer. The duly certified form shall then be dispatched by the U.S. importer to the foreign exporter or otherwise disposed of in accordance with instructions of the exporting country.

No delivery verification may be obtained unless a completed application form has been received. (50 U.S.C App § 2401 et seq.,15 C.F.R. §748)

EXPORTER *(Name and Address)*

Name

Address

City   State/Country   Zip/ Postal Code

This certification applied to the goods described below, shown on

U.S. Department of Commerce International Import Certificate

No.

ARRIVED *(Name of Port)*	DATE OF ARRIVAL *(mm/dd/yyyy)*

IMPORTER *(Name and Address)*

Name

Address

City   State/Country   Zip/ Postal Code

NAME OF SHIP, AIRCRAFT, OR CARRIER *(Include numbers on bills of lading, airways bills, etc.)*

DESCRIPTION OF GOODS	QUANTITY	VALUE *(FOB, CIR, etc)*

TO BE COMPLETED BY U.S. CUSTOMS SERVICE	REGION NO.

(Custom's Seal) CERTIFICATION-It is hereby certified that the importer has produced evidence that the goods specified above have been delivered and brought under the Export Administration Regulations of the United States.

Signature   Date

ENTRY	☐ WAREHOUSE ☐ CONSUMPTION	NUMBER	DATE

issued by the government of a foreign country is required for application for the export license, the Department of Commerce will on a selective basis require the exporter to obtain a delivery verification. If verification of delivery is required, the requirement will appear as a condition on the face of the license when issued. The list of countries issuing import certificates and delivery verification is contained in Supplement Number 4 to Part 748 of the EAR.

Where an Electronic Export Information was filed incorrectly or the transaction is altered, a corrected Electronic Export Information must be resubmitted.

Exporters are required to maintain the originals of all documents pertaining to export transaction, including license applications, memoranda, notes, correspondence, contracts, invitations to bid, books of account, and financial records. If the exporter complies with certain specific requirements, the exporter may maintain the records electronically. The system must be able to record and reproduce all marks, information, and other characteristics of the original record, including both sides of the paper; the system must preserve the initial image and record all changes, who made them, and when they were made; and this information must be stored in such a manner that none of it may be altered once it is initially recorded. The records must be maintained for a period of five years from the time of the export from the United States, any known re-export, or any other termination of the transaction. The record-keeping requirement extends to records maintained outside the United States if they pertain to any U.S. export transaction or any re-export. Any person subject to the jurisdiction of the United States may be required to produce the records in response to an inquiry from the Department of Commerce. (In some cases, a request for records located abroad may conflict with the laws and regulations of a foreign country.)

K. Special Comprehensive Licenses

It is possible to obtain a Special Comprehensive License (SCL). Ordinary licenses granted by the Bureau of Industry and Security cover only single export transactions. With an SCL, multiple exports and re-exports can be authorized. The SCL authorizes specific exports and re-exports that are otherwise prohibited by General Prohibitions 1, 2, and 3. All items subject to the EAR are eligible for export under an SCL except the following:

1. Items controlled for missile technology reasons that are identified by the letters MT in the applicable Reason for Control paragraph of the Commerce Control List

2. Items controlled by ECCN 1C351, 1C352, 1C353, 1C354, 1C991, 1E001, 2B352, 2E001, 2E002, and 2E301 on the Commerce Control List that can be used in the production of chemical and biological weapons

3. Items controlled by ECCN 1C350, 1C355, 1D390, 2B350, and 2B351 on the Commerce Control List that can be used in the production of chemical weapons, precursors, and chemical warfare agents to destinations listed in Country Group D:3

4. Items controlled for short supply reasons that are identified by the letters SS in the applicable Reason for Control paragraph on the Commerce Control List

5. Items controlled for EI reasons on the Commerce Control List

6. Maritime (civil) nuclear propulsion systems or associated design or production

7. Communications intercepting devices and related software and technology controlled by ECCNs 5A001.f.1, 5A980, 5D001 (for 5A001.f.1 or for 5E001.a (for 5A001.f.1, or for 5D001.a (for 5A001.f.1))), 5D980, 5E001.a (for 5A001.f.1, or for 5D001.a (for 5A001.f.1)) or 5E980 on the CCL

8. Hot section technology for the development, production, or overhaul of commercial aircraft engines controlled under ECCN 9E003.a.1 through a.12.f and related controls

9. Items specifically identified as ineligible by the Bureau of Industry and Security on the SCL

10. Additional items consistent with international commitments

Shipments under an SCL may be made to all countries specified in the SCL except Cuba, Iran, Iraq, North Korea, Sudan, and Syria and other countries that the Bureau of Industry and Security may designate on a case-by-case basis. Servicing items owned or controlled by or under the lease of entities in the foregoing countries is also prohibited.

In order to apply for an SCL, an exporter must apply to BIS and have an internal control program (ICP). BIS will vet the company reviewing the company's past exporting history, knowledge of the EAR, commitment to its ICP. The SCL consignee will also be vetted based on past history, ownership interests, evidence of ongoing business with exporter, assurances that any exports or re-exports are not made contrary to the Export Administration Regulations. Details for the requirements for obtaining a SCL are available in the EAR Section 752.

An SCL, when issued, is valid for four years and may be extended for an additional four years. Certain changes in the export relationship or procedures require prior written approval from the Bureau of Industry and Security, whereas other changes must be reported to the Bureau of Industry and Security within thirty days after their occurrence.

L. Technology, Software, and Technical Assistance Exports

A significant portion of the EAR is concerned with the export of technology, software, and technical assistance. Within each category of the Commerce Control List, there is a "group" that includes software ("D") and technology ("E") pertaining to that category. Such exports would normally take place pursuant to a license agreement between the U.S. licensor and the foreign licensee. However, in fulfillment of a license agreement, tangible documents as well as oral information may be communicated. The definition of "export" includes an actual shipment or transmission of items subject to the EAR out of the United States and, with regard to the export of technology or software, includes any "release" of technology or software subject to the EAR in a foreign country or any release of technology or source code subject to the EAR to a foreign national, in the United States or in another country. The release of technology or software includes visual inspection by foreign nationals of U.S.-origin equipment and facilities, the oral exchange of information in the United States or abroad, or the application to situations abroad of personal knowledge or technical experience acquired in the United States. This is considered a "deemed export." "Technology" is defined as information necessary for the development, production, or use of a product. Information may take the form of "technical data" or "technical assistance." Controlled technology is defined in the General Technology Note (Supplement Number 1 to Part 774). Technical data may include blueprints, plans, diagrams, models, formulas, tables, engineering designs, specifications, manuals, and instructions written or recorded on other media or devices such as disk, tape, or read-only memories. Technical assistance may take the form of instruction, skills training, working knowledge, or consulting services.

Two steps in analyzing the scope of the EAR, Step 2 and Step 6, pertain to technology. Step 2 exempts from control of the EAR publicly available technology and software. This is both for exports and for re-exports. Publicly available technology and software includes that which has already been published or will be published, which includes software generally accessible to the interested public in any form either free or at a price that does not exceed the cost of reproduction and distribution; patents and open, published patent applications; information readily available at libraries open to the public; and/or information released at an "open" conference meeting, seminar, or trade show. The EAR contains questions and answers further developing and clarifying what type of technology and software is publicly available. It also includes information arising from "fundamental" (as opposed to "proprietary") and educational research. Step 6 of the EAR pertains to foreign-made items produced with certain U.S. technology. If the foreign-produced item is described in an entry on the Commerce Control List, and the Country Chart requires a license for a direct export from the United States for national security reasons, or if the destination is Cuba or a country in Group D:1 and the technology or software that was used to create the foreign-produced direct product required a written assurance from the licensee as a supporting document for the license or as a condition to utilizing license exception TSR, a license is required. In addition to the exemption for publicly available technology and software, several exceptions from license requirements are also available. License exception TSR (Technology and Software under Restriction) permits exports and re-exports of technology and software when so specified on the specific entry in the Commerce Control List and the export is to destinations in Country Group B. The exporter must receive written assurances from the consignee prior to export that the technology or software will not be released to a national in Country Group D:1 or E:2 and will not export to those same countries the direct product of the technology if the product is subject to national security controls.

Another license exception, TSU (Technology and Software Unrestricted), permits the export of "operating technology and software" (OTS) and "sales technology" (STS). Operating technology is the minimum technology necessary for the installation, operation, maintenance (checking), and repair of products lawfully exported. It must be in object code and exported to the destination to which the equipment for which it is required has been legally exported. Sales technology is data supporting a prospective or actual quotation, bid, or offer to sell, lease, or otherwise supply any item. It does not include information that discloses the design, production, or manufacture of the item being offered for sale. Software updates that are intended for and are limited to correction of errors are also authorized. Finally, "mass market" software may be exported under this exception. Generally, this is software sold from stock at retail selling points or by mail order and designed for installation by the user without further substantial support by the supplier.

License exception TMP authorizes temporary exports. Within that exception is included exports of "beta test" software (BETA). This pertains only to software that the producer intends to market to the general public, is provided free of charge or at a price that does not exceed the cost of reproduction and distribution, does not require further substantial support from the supplier, and for which the importer provides a certification that it will not be transferred. The software must be returned or destroyed within thirty days after completion of the test.

An Interpretation has been issued by the Bureau of Industry and Security for the purposes of clarifying what technology and software may be exported to Country Group D:1. Under the controls relating to end users and end use, technology pertaining to maritime nuclear propulsion plants may not be exported without a license.

A "deemed export" occurs when a foreign national is exposed to controlled technology in the United States. This can occur by having the foreign national work on technology in a research setting, by exposing the foreign national to the technology by having them accessible through shared computer storage files, by touring a plant facility and seeing the manufacturing process that is using the controlled technology. The principle behind the concept of a deemed export is that once the foreign national has been exposed to the controlled technology, she can take that technology back to her home county by having seen it.

A company must obtain a license for the foreign national work on a project, if the technology would have been licensed to that country. Immigration forms now require a statement as to whether the foreign national will be required to work on products that require export control license or not and that the company will obtain the necessary licenses if required.

An exporting company that has controlled technology must establish a Technology Control Plan to ensure that the technology is safeguarded and only those people who are authorized have access to that technology.

M. Validated End-User Program

The Validated End-User program (VEU) allows for the export, re-export, and transfer to validated end users of any eligible items that are destined to a specific eligible destination without a license. Currently only China and India are eligible under the VEU program. Companies in the country of destination request authorization to become a VEU. The Office of Exporter Services reviews the companies for such things as the entity's exclusive engagement in civil end-use activities, its compliance with U.S. export controls, the ability to comply with the VEU requirements, the entity's agreement to on-site reviews by U.S. government officials, and the entity's relationship with both U.S. and foreign companies. Items that are controlled under the Missile Technology (MT) or Crime Control (CC) reasons are ineligible for authorization under this program. In addition, there are end-use restrictions to the VEU's own facility in the eligible destination. There are certification, record-keeping, reporting, and review requirements. U.S. subsidiaries in these destinations are ideal candidates for the VEU program.

N. Antiboycott Regulations

If you plan to make sales in the Middle East or you receive an order from a customer located there, before proceeding to accept and ship the order, you should be aware of the U.S. antiboycott regulations. Certain countries are members of the Arab League and those countries maintain a boycott against Israel. The Treasury Department updates the list of countries that participate in international boycotts on a quarterly basis. Currently those countries include Kuwait, Lebanon, Libya, Qatar, Saudi Arabia, Syria, United Arab Emirates, and Republic of Yemen. Iraq is not currently on the list, but it remains under review by the Department of Treasury.

U.S. law prohibits any U.S. company from refusing or agreeing to refuse to do business pursuant to an agreement or request from a boycotting country or to discriminate on the basis of race, religion, sex, or national origin. Perhaps more important, the law requires that if a U.S. company receives a request for information about its business relationships with blacklisted companies or boycotted countries, it must promptly report the request to the Bureau of Industry and Security at the U.S. Department of Commerce. Failure to do so can result in penalties including civil penalties of $250,000 per violation, criminal penalties for intentional violations, and denial of export privileges altogether. The forms for reporting requests for single and multiple transactions are shown in Figures 5-15 and 5-16, respectively.

The Internal Revenue Service also has antiboycott regulations under Section 999 of the I.R.S. Code. Section 999 prohibits U.S. taxpayers from participating in or cooperating with an international boycott by reducing certain foreign tax credits and other tax benefits that the U.S. company would be allowed to receive. The regulation requires that companies complete an I.R.S. Form 5713 reporting any operations relating to a boycotting country. See Figure 5-17.

Figure 5–15. Single antiboycott request report.

Form BIS-621P OMB No.0694-0012	U.S. DEPARTMENT OF COMMERCE BUREAU OF INDUSTRY AND SECURITY	THIS SPACE FOR BIS USE
(REV 1-04)		

REPORT OF REQUEST FOR RESTRICTIVE TRADE PRACTICE OR BOYCOTT
SINGLE TRANSACTION

(For reporting requests described in Part 769 of the Export Administration Regulations)

A BATCH____ ____ ____

MONTH/YEAR ____ ____ ____

NOTICE OF RIGHT TO PROTECT CERTAIN INFORMATION FROM DISCLOSURE

The Export Administration Act permits you to protect from public disclosure information regarding the quantity, description, and value of commodities or technical data supplied in item 11 of this report and in any accompanying documents. *If you do not claim this protection, all of the information in your report and accompanying documents will be made available for public inspection and copying.*

You can obtain this protection by certifying, in item 10 of the report, that disclosure of the information referred to above would place a United States company or individual involved in the report at a competitive disadvantage. If you make such a certification in item 10, you may remove information regarding the quantity, description, and value of the commodities or technical data supplied by you from item 11 of the inspection copy of the report form and from the public inspection copies of the accompanying documents.

The withholding of this information will be honored by the Department unless the Secretary determines that disclosure of the information would not place a United States company or individual at a competitive disadvantage or that it would be contrary to the national interest to withhold the information.

RSN __ ____ ____ ____   SUBSET ____ ____

RTP __ ____ ____ ____ ____ ____

CLASS ____   FILING ____   TAG ____ ____

This report required by law (50 U.S.C. App. § 2407 (b) (2) P.L. 96-72; E.O. 12214; 15 C.F.R. Part 769). Failure to report can result both in criminal penalties, including fines or imprisonment, and administrative sanctions.

Instructions: 1. Complete all items that apply. 2. Assemble original report form and accompanying documents as a unit, and submit intact and unaltered. 3. Assemble and submit the duplicate copy of the report form (marked Duplicate (Public Inspection Copy)) and additional copies of accompanying documents (marked with the legend "Public Inspection Copy.") 4. *If you certify, in item 10, that the disclosure of the information specified there would cause competitive disadvantage, edit the "Public Inspection Copy" of the report form relating to item 11.*

Public reporting for this collection of information is estimated to average one hour per request, including the time for reviewing instructions, searching existing data sources, gathering and maintaining the data needed, and completing and reviewing the collection o information. Send comments regarding this burden estimate or any other aspect of this collection of information, including suggestions for reducing the burden, to the Director of Administration, Bureau of Industry and Security, room 3889, U.S. Department of Commerce, Washington, DC 20230, and to the Office of Management and Budget, Paperwork Reduction Project (0694-0012), Washington, DC 20503.

1a. Identify firm submitting this report:	Type an 'x' to specify firm type:	1b. Type an 'x' in any applicable box:
Name:	☐ Exporter	☐ Revision of a previous report (attach two copies of the previously submitted report)
Address:	☐ Bank	
City: State: ZIP:	☐ Forwarder	☐ Resubmission of a deficient report returned by BIS (attach form letter that was returned with deficient report)
Country (if other than USA):	☐ Carrier	
Telephone:	☐ Insurer	☐ Report on behalf of the person identified in item 2.
Firm Identification No. (if known):	☐ Other	☐ Dual report on behalf of self and the person in item 2

2. If you are authorized to report and are reporting on behalf of another U.S. person, identify that person (e.g., domestic subsidiary, controlled Foreign subsidiary, exporter, beneficiary):	3. Identify exporting firm, unless same as Item 1a or 2:
Name:	Name:
Address:	Address:
City: State: ZIP:	City: State: ZIP:
Country (if other than USA):	Country (if other than USA):
Type of firm: *(see list in item 1a)*	Firm Identification No. *(if known):*
Firm Identification No. *(if known):*	

4. (a) Name of boycotting country from which request originated: (b) Name of country directing inclusion of request, if different from (a) above:	5. Name of country or countries against which request is directed:

6. Reporting firm's reference number (e.g., *letter of credit, customer order, invoice*):	7. Date firm received request: *(mm/dd/yyyy)*

8.   Specify type(s) of document conveying this request by typing an 'x' in the appropriate box:

☐ Request to carrier for blacklist certificate *(submit two copies of blacklist certificate or transcript of request)*

☐ Unwritten, not otherwise provided for *(make transcript of request and submit copies)*

☐ Letter of credit

☐ Requisition/purchase order/accepted contract/shipping instruction

☐ Bid invitation/tender/proposal/trade opportunity

☐ Questionnaire *(not related to a particular dollar value transaction)*

☐ Other written (specify) _____

Submit two copies of each document or relevant page in which the request appears

9.   Decision on request: *(select one by typing an 'x' in the appropriate box)*

☐ Have not taken and will not take the action requested.

☐ Have taken or will take the action requested.

☐ Have taken or will take the action requested but in a modified form *(attach detailed explanation)*

☐ Unable to report ultimate decision on the request at this time and will inform the Bureau of Industry and Security of the decision within ten days after decision is made.

Additional information: The firm submitting this report may, if it so desires, state on a separate sheet any additional information relating to the request reported or the response to that request. This statement will constitute a part of the report and will be made available for public inspection and copying, subject to the right to protect certain confidential information from disclosure described in item 10.

10.   Protection of Certain Information from disclosure: (Type an 'x' in the appropriate boxes and sign below)

1. ☐   I (We) certify that disclosure to the public of the information regarding quantity, description, and value of the commodities or technical data contained in:

☐   Item 11 below (if you check this box, be sure to remove the bottom of the Duplicate (Public Inspection Copy) of the report form relating to item 11.)

☐   Attached documents (if you check this box, be sure to edit the "Public Inspection Copy" of the documents submitted to exclude the specified information.) would place a United States person involved at a competitive disadvantage, and I (We) request that it be kept confidential.

2. ☐   I (We) authorize public release of all information contained in the report and in any attached documents. I (We) certify that all statements and information contained in this report are true and correct to the best of my (our) knowledge and belief.

Sign here in ink _____   Type name _____   Date _____

11. Describe the commodities or technical data involved, and specify quantity and value:	Quantity:
Description	Value to nearest whole dollar $

Submit the original and 1 copy to Office of Antiboycott Compliance, BIS, Room 6099C, U.S. Department of Commerce, Washington, D.C. 20230; Retain a copy for your records.

Figure 5–16. Boycott reporting form for multiple requests.

FORM BIS-6051P
(REV 7-03)

U.S. DEPARTMENT OF COMMERCE
BUREAU OF INDUSTRY AND SECURITY

REPORT OF REQUEST FOR RESTRICTIVE TRADE PRACTICE OR BOYCOTT
MULTIPLE TRANSACTIONS (Sheet No. 1)

THIS SPACE FOR BIS USE

A

BATCH _____

MONTH/YEAR _____

(For reporting requests described in 769 of the Export Administration Regulations)

NOTICE OF RIGHT TO PROTECT CERTAIN INFORMATION FROM DISCLOSURE: The Export Administration Act permits you to protect from public disclosure information regarding the quantity, description, and value of the commodities or technical data supplied in item 9 of this report and in any accompanying documents. *If you do not claim this protection, all of the information in your report and in accompanying documents will be made available for public inspection and copying.* You can obtain this protection by certifying, in item 5 of the report, that disclosure of the information regarding the quantity, description and value of the commodities or technical data referred to above would place a United States company or individual involved in the report at a competitive disadvantage. If you make such a certification in item 5, you may remove information regarding the quantity, description, and value of the commodities or technical data supplied by you from item 9 of the public inspection copy of the report form and from the public inspection copies of the accompanying documents. The withholding of this information will be honored by the Department unless the Secretary determines that disclosure of the information would not place a United States company or individual at a competitive disadvantage or that it would be contrary to the national interest to withhold the information.

INSTRUCTIONS: 1. This form may not include a transaction report that is filed late, nor indicate a decision on request other than those coded in item 4 below. 2. This form may be used to report on behalf of another United States person if all transactions apply to the person identified in item 2, but may not be considered as a dual report on behalf of both persons identified in item 1a and item 2. 3. Limit each report to 75 transactions or less. 4. Attach as many continuation sheets as needed. Enter sheet number and name of reporting firm on each continuation sheet (starting with Sheet No. 2). 5. List each transaction across the continuation sheet, completing all items that apply. Use as many lines as necessary but separate transactions with a blank space or line. 6. Assemble original report form and accompanying documents as a unit, and submit intact and unaltered. 7. Assemble and submit the duplicate copy of report form (marked Duplicate (Public Inspection Copy) and additional copies of accompanying documents (marked with the legend "Public Inspection Copy.") 8. *If you certify, in item 5, that the disclosure of the information specified here would cause competitive disadvantage, edit the "Public Inspection Copy" of the documents submitted to exclude the specified information and remove the right hand portion of the Duplicate(Public Inspection Copy) of the continuation sheet(s) relating to Column 9.* MULTIPLE TRANSACTIONS: Public reporting for this collection of information is estimated to average one hour per reported request, including the time for reviewing instructions, searching existing data sources, gathering and maintaining the data needed, and completing and reviewing the collection o information. Send comments regarding this burden estimate or any other aspect of this collection of information, including suggestions for reducing this burden to Office of Administration, Bureau of Industry and Security, H3889, U.S. Department of Commerce, Washington, D.C. 20230, and to the Office of Management and Budget, Paperwork Reduction Project (0694-0012), Washington, D.C. 20503.

This report is required by law (50 U.S.C. App. §2403-1a(b); P.L. 95-52; E.O. 12002; 15 CFR Part 769). Failure to report can result both in criminal penalties, including fines or imprisonment, and administrative sanctions.

1a. Identify firm submitting this report:

Name: _____

Address: _____

City: _____ State: _____ ZIP: _____

Country *(if other than USA):* _____

Telephone: _____

Firm: Identification No. *(If known):* _____

1b. **Specify firm type:**

☐ Exporter ☐ Carrier

☐ Bank ☐ Insurer

☐ Forwarder ☐ Other

2. If you are authorized to report and are reporting on behalf of another U.S. person, identify that person (e.g. domestic subsidiary, controlled foreign subsidiary, exporter, beneficiary):

Name: _____

Address: _____

City: _____ State: _____ ZIP: _____

Country *(if other than USA):* _____

Type of firm: (see list in item 1a) _____

Check any applicable box:

☐ Revision of a previously report (attach two copies of the previously submitted report)

☐ Resubmission of a deficient report returned by BTR (attach form letter that was returned with deficient report)

☐ Report on behalf of the person identified in item 2

3. REQUESTING DOCUMENT CODES *(use to code Column 6 of continuation sheet)*

C Request to carrier for blacklist certificate (submit two copies of blacklist certificate or transcript of request)

U Unwritten, not otherwise provided for (make transcript of request and submit two copies)

L Letter of credit

R Requisition/purchase order/accepted contract/shipping instruction

B Bid invitation/tender/proposal/trade opportunity

Q Questionnaire (not related to a particular dollar value transaction)

9 Other written

Submit two copies of each document or relevant page in which the request appears.

4. DECISION ON REQUEST CODES *(use to code Column 7 of continuation sheet)*

R Have not taken and will not take the action requested

T Have taken or will take the action requested

5. Protection of certain information from disclosure: *(Check appropriate boxes and sign below)*

☐ I (we) certify that disclosure to the public of the information regarding quantity, description, and value of the commodities or technical data contained in:

  ☐ Column 9 of the attached continuation sheets (If you check this box, be sure to remove column 9 from the Duplicate (Public Inspection Copy) of the continuation sheets.

  ☐ Attached documents (If you check this box, be sure to edit the "Public Inspection Copy" of the documents submitted to exclude the specified information.) would place a United States person involved at a competitive disadvantage, and I (we) request that it be kept confidential

☐ I (we) authorize public release of all information contained in the report and in any attached documents.

I (we) certify that all statements and information contained in this report are true and correct to the best of my (our) knowledge and belief. _____ Date _____

Sign here in ink _____ Type or print _____

Submit original and 1 copy to Office of Antiboycott Compliance, BIS, Room 6099C, U.S. Department of Commerce, Washington, D.C. 20230; Retain a copy for your records.

Figure 5–17. IRS Form 5713.

Form **5713**	**International Boycott Report**	OMB No. 1545-0216

Form **5713**
(Rev. December 2010)
Department of the Treasury
Internal Revenue Service

International Boycott Report

For tax year beginning _____ , 20 _____ ,
and ending _____ , 20 _____ .
▶ **Controlled groups, see instructions.**

OMB No. 1545-0216
Attachment Sequence No. 123
Paper filers must file in duplicate (see **When and Where to File** in the instructions)

Name _____

Identifying number _____

Number, street, and room or suite no. If a P.O. box, see instructions.

City or town, state, and ZIP code

Address of service center where your tax return is filed

Type of filer (check one):

☐ Individual   ☐ Partnership   ☐ Corporation   ☐ Trust   ☐ Estate   ☐ Other

1 **Individuals**—Enter adjusted gross income from your tax return (see instructions)

2 **Partnerships and corporations:**

a Partnerships—Enter each partner's name and identifying number.

b Corporations—Enter the name and employer identification number of each member of the controlled group (as defined in section 993(a)(3)). Do not list members included in the consolidated return; instead, attach a copy of Form 851. List all other members of the controlled group not included in the consolidated return.

If you list any corporations below or if you attach Form 851, you must designate a common tax year. Enter on line 4b the name and employer identification number of the corporation whose tax year is designated.

Name	Identifying number

If more space is needed, attach additional sheets and check this box . . . . ▶ ☐

	Code	Description
c Enter principal business activity code and description (see instructions)		
d IC-DISCs—Enter principal product or service code and description (see instructions)		

3 **Partnerships**—Each partnership filing Form 5713 must give the following information:

a Partnership's total assets (see instructions) . . . .

b Partnership's ordinary income (see instructions) . . . .

4 **Corporations**—Each corporation filing Form 5713 must give the following information:

a Type of form filed (Form 1120, 1120-FSC, 1120-IC-DISC, 1120-L, 1120-PC, etc.) . . .

b Common tax year election (see instructions)

(1) Name of corporation ▶ _____

(2) Employer identification number . . . .

(3) Common tax year beginning _____ , 20 _____ , and ending _____ , 20 _____ .

c Corporations filing this form enter:

(1) Total assets (see instructions) . . . .

(2) Taxable income before net operating loss and special deductions (see instructions) . .

5 **Estates or trusts**—Enter total income (Form 1041, page 1) . . . .

6 Enter the total amount (before reduction for boycott participation or cooperation) of the following tax benefits (see instructions):

a Foreign tax credit . . . .

b Deferral of earnings of controlled foreign corporations . . . .

c Deferral of IC-DISC income . . . .

d FSC exempt foreign trade income . . . .

e Foreign trade income qualifying for the extraterritorial income exclusion . . . . .

Please Sign Here

Under penalties of perjury, I declare that I have examined this report, including accompanying schedules and statements, and to the best of my knowledge and belief, it is true, correct, and complete.

▶ _____ Signature   _____ Date   ▶ _____ Title

For Paperwork Reduction Act Notice, see separate instructions.   Cat. No. 12030E   Form **5713** (Rev. 12-2010)

Figure 5–17. (*continued*)

Form 5713 (Rev. 12-2010)   Page **2**

		Yes	No
7a	Are you a U.S. shareholder (as defined in section 951(b)) of any foreign corporation (including a FSC that does not use the administrative pricing rules) that had operations reportable under section 999(a)?		
b	If the answer to question 7a is "Yes," is any foreign corporation a controlled foreign corporation (as defined in section 957(a))?		
c	Do you own any stock of an IC-DISC?		
d	Do you claim any foreign tax credit?		
e	Do you control (within the meaning of section 304(c)) any corporation (other than a corporation included in this report) that has operations reportable under section 999(a)?		
	If "Yes," did that corporation participate in or cooperate with an international boycott at any time during its tax year that ends with or within your tax year?		
f	Are you controlled (within the meaning of section 304(c)) by any person (other than a person included in this report) who has operations reportable under section 999(a)?		
	If "Yes," did that person participate in or cooperate with an international boycott at any time during its tax year that ends with or within your tax year?		
g	Are you treated under section 671 as the owner of a trust that has reportable operations under section 999(a)? .		
h	Are you a partner in a partnership that has reportable operations under section 999(a)?		
i	Are you a foreign sales corporation (FSC) (as defined in section 922(a), as in effect before its repeal)?		
j	Are you excluding extraterritorial income (defined in section 114(e), as in effect before its repeal) from gross income?		

Part I   **Operations in or Related to a Boycotting Country** (see instructions)

		Yes	No
8	**Boycott of Israel**—Did you have any operations in or related to any country (or with the government, a company, or a national of that country) associated in carrying out the boycott of Israel which is on the list maintained by the Secretary of the Treasury under section 999(a)(3)? (See **Boycotting Countries** in the instructions.)		

If "Yes," complete the following table. If more space is needed, attach additional sheets using the exact format and check this box . . . . ▶ ☐

	Name of country (1)	Identifying number of person having operations (2)	Principal business activity		IC-DISCs only—Enter product code (5)
			Code (3)	Description (4)	
a					
b					
c					
d					
e					
f					
g					
h					
i					
j					
k					
l					
m					
n					
o					

Form **5713** (Rev. 12-2010)

Figure 5–17. *(continued)*

Form 5713 (Rev. 12-2010)   Page **3**

				Yes	No
9	**Nonlisted countries boycotting Israel—** Did you have operations in any nonlisted country which you know or have reason to know requires participation in or cooperation with an international boycott directed against Israel?				

If "Yes," complete the following table. If more space is needed, attach additional sheets using the exact format and check this box . . . . ▶ ☐

Name of country (1)	Identifying number of person having operations (2)	Principal business activity		IC-DISCs only—Enter product code (5)
		Code (3)	Description (4)	
a				
b				
c				
d				
e				
f				
g				
h				

				Yes	No
10	**Boycotts other than the boycott of Israel—** Did you have operations in any other country which you know or have reason to know requires participation in or cooperation with an international boycott other than the boycott of Israel?				

If "Yes," complete the following table. If more space is needed, attach additional sheets using the exact format and check this box . . . . ▶ ☐

Name of country (1)	Identifying number of person having operations (2)	Principal business activity		IC-DISCs only—Enter product code (5)
		Code (3)	Description (4)	
a				
b				
c				
d				
e				
f				
g				
h				

		Yes	No
11	Were you requested to participate in or cooperate with an international boycott?		
	If "Yes," attach a copy (in English) of any and all such requests received during your tax year. If the request was in a form other than a written request, attach a separate sheet explaining the nature and form of any and all such requests. (See instructions.)		
12	Did you participate in or cooperate with an international boycott?		
	If "Yes," attach a copy (in English) of any and all boycott clauses agreed to, and attach a general statement of the agreement. If the agreement was in a form other than a written agreement, attach a separate sheet explaining the nature and form of any and all such agreements. (See instructions.)		

Note: *If the answer to either question 11 or 12 is "Yes," you must complete the rest of Form 5713. If you answered "Yes" to question 12, you must complete Schedules A and C or B and C (Form 5713).*

Form **5713** (Rev. 12-2010)

Figure 5–17. *(continued)*

Part II	Requests for and Acts of Participation in or Cooperation With an International Boycott	Requests		Agreements	
		Yes	No	Yes	No

13a Did you receive requests to enter into, or did you enter into, any agreement (see instructions):

 (1) As a condition of doing business directly or indirectly within a country or with the government, a company, or a national of a country to—

  (a) Refrain from doing business with or in a country which is the object of an international boycott or with the government, companies, or nationals of that country?

  (b) Refrain from doing business with any U.S. person engaged in trade in a country which is the object of an international boycott or with the government, companies, or nationals of that country? . . . .

  (c) Refrain from doing business with any company whose ownership or management is made up, in whole or in part, of individuals of a particular nationality, race, or religion, or to remove (or refrain from selecting) corporate directors who are individuals of a particular nationality, race, or religion?

  (d) Refrain from employing individuals of a particular nationality, race, or religion?

 (2) As a condition of the sale of a product to the government, a company, or a national of a country, to refrain from shipping or insuring products on a carrier owned, leased, or operated by a person who does not participate in or cooperate with an international boycott? . . . .

 b Requests and agreements—if the answer to any part of 13a is "Yes," complete the following table. If more space is needed, attach additional sheets using the exact format and check this box . . . . ▶ ☐

Name of country (1)	Identifying number of person receiving the request or having the agreement (2)	Principal business activity		IC-DISCs only— Enter product code (5)	Type of cooperation or participation			
					Number of requests		Number of agreements	
		Code (3)	Description (4)		Total (6)	Code (7)	Total (8)	Code (9)
a								
b								
c								
d								
e								
f								
g								
h								
i								
j								
k								
l								
m								
n								
o								
p								

Form **5713** (Rev. 12-2010)

O. Violations and Penalties

The Export Administration Act expired many years ago and to date has not been renewed; however, the president annually authorizes application of the EAA regulations under the International Emergency Economic Powers Act (IEEPA). Penalties under IEEPA were raised in 2007 to $250,000 per violation or twice the amount of the transaction in question. In addition, export privileges can be denied for up to ten years. Since these are extremely serious penalties, it is important to make every effort not to violate the law, even accidentally. Exports in violation of the law may be seized by the U.S. Customs and Border Protection. If the exporter, its freight forwarder, or any other of the exporter's agents receives such a subpoena or even an informal inquiry from Customs or the Office of Export Enforcement, Bureau of Industry and Security, the exporter should take it very seriously and make sure that it is in compliance with the law before responding.

It is possible to file a voluntary disclosure to the BIS and self-report. An initial disclosure letter may be filed if the exporter determines it may have made some mistakes. The company has 180 days to complete its internal review and submit the final disclosure. While the disclosure will not eliminate the penalties, it is given great weight in the mitigation of any potential penalties. Likewise, having an export compliance program is a significant mitigation factor in the disclosure. An attorney should be consulted prior to filing any prior disclosure to discuss the company's options.

P. Embargoes and Trade Sanctions Programs

The Office of Foreign Assets Control (OFAC) Department of Treasury is responsible for the administrating and enforcing economic and trade sanctions based on U.S. foreign policy. This includes blocking the assets of individuals and companies that are in the United States or coming to the United States. OFAC has established the Specially Designated Nationals (SDN) list of individuals as well as businesses, partnerships, organizations, banks and vessels that are owned or controlled by targeted countries or individuals. The assets are blocked and trade is prohibited with any party on the SDN list. In addition, it has created the Foreign Sanctions Evaders list of foreign individuals and entities determined to have violated, attempted to violate, conspired to violate, facilitated or caused a violation of U.S. sanctions on Syria or Iran. Similarly the assets of these parties are frozen and trade is restricted to any party on the list.

The OFAC sanction are either country-based sanctions, such as the broad embargoes against Cuba, Iran, Sudan, and Syria or they are targeted sanctions against individuals engaged in narcotics trafficking, terrorism, or weapons of mass destruction proliferation. Each program is different and each country has different general licenses (otherwise known as license exceptions) that may be for food, medicine, medical supplies, certain telecommunications, etc. OFAC also issues some specific licenses for exports of other products. OFAC license is in a written letter form at this time and must provide complete details regarding the transaction including payment mechanisms, since only certain payment mechanisms may be allowed.

R. U.S. Munitions and Arms Exports

Under the Arms Export Control Act, exports and imports of defense articles and services without a license are prohibited. Export licenses are issued by the Department of State, Directorate of Defense Trade Controls (DDTC), under the International Traffic in Arms Regulations. Import licenses are issued by the Department of Justice, Bureau of Alcohol, Tobacco and Firearms.

The Export Control Reform charged the State Department with created a positive list of items that require license as opposed a list of all potential items and their components in various categories that were designed or modified for military applications. The result has been the transfer of defense articles of a lesser sensitivity to the Commerce Control List. It has been a gradual process of reviewing the items in the individual categories to create the positive list of controlled items.

As of the publication of this book, approximately one half of the categories have become positive lists, with the balance of the items transferring to the CCL. It is anticipated that all of the revised categories will become effective by 2016-2017. One of the first changes was the addition of a new category XIX for diesel engines, whereas previously they would have been categorized with the type of equipment on which they were used. The U.S. Munitions List is comprised of 20 categories (Figure 5-18).

The next step is to determine if an exporter's products are defense articles and controlled by USML. Articles that "specially designed" as defense articles are controlled. The Export Control Reform changed the definition of "specially designed" and now it is a two-part analysis; a "catch and release" definition. The first part is inclusive and reads as follows:

(a) Except for commodities or software described in paragraph (b) of this section, a commodity or software (see § 121.8(f) of this subchapter) is "specially designed" if it:

(1) As a result of development, has properties peculiarly responsible for

Figure 5–18. U.S. Munitions List.

I.	Firearms
II.	Artillery
III.	Ammunition
IV.	Launch Vehicles, Guided Missiles, Ballistic Missiles, Rockets, Torpedoes, Bombs, and Mines
V.	Explosives and Energetic Materials, Propellants, Incendiary Agents, and Their Constituents
VI.	Surface Vessels of War and Special Naval Equipment
VII.	Ground Vehicles
VIII.	Aircraft and Related Articles
IX.	Military Training Equipment
X.	Personal Protective Equipment
XI.	Military Electronics
XII.	Fire Control/Sensors/Night Vision
XIII.	Materials and Miscellaneous Articles
XIV.	Toxicological Agents
XV.	Spacecraft and Related Articles
XVI.	Nuclear Weapons Related Articles
XVII.	Classified Articles, Technical Data, and Defense Services
XVIII.	Directed Energy Weapons
XIX.	Gas Turbine Engines and Associated Equipment
XX.	Submersible Vessels and Related Articles
XXI.	Articles, Technical Data, and Defense Services Otherwise Not Enumerated

achieving or exceeding the controlled performance levels, characteristics, or functions described in the relevant U.S. Munitions List paragraph;

(2) Is a part (see § 121.8(d) of this subchapter),component (see § 121.8(b) of this subchapter), accessory(see § 121.8(c) of this subchapter), attachment (see §121.8(c)of this subchapter), or software for use in or with a defense article.

The second part "releases" or excludes items that were "caught" in the first part as follows:

(a) A part, component, accessory, attachment, or software is not controlled by a U.S. Munitions List "catch-all" or technical data control paragraph if it:

(1) Is subject to the EAR pursuant to a commodity jurisdiction determination;

(2) Is, regardless of form or fit, a fastener (e.g., screws, bolts, nuts, nut plates, studs, inserts, clips, rivets, pins),washer, spacer, insulator, grommet, bushing, spring, wire, or solder;

(3) Has the same function, performance capabilities, and the same or "equivalent" form and fit as a commodity or software used in or with a commodity that:

(i) Is or was in production (i.e., not in development); and

(ii) Is not enumerated on the U.S. Munitions List

(4) Was or is being developed with knowledge that it is or would be for use in or with both defense articles enumerated on the U.S. Munitions List and also commodities not on the U.S. Munitions List

(5) Was or is being developed as a general purpose commodity or software, i.e., with no knowledge for use in or with a particular commodity (e.g., a F/A–18 or HMMWV) or type of commodity (e.g., an aircraft or machine tool).

While this definition is quite confusing there are several tools on the DDTC web site to assist exporters in making the determination. First there is a Commodity Control List order of review interactive tool at http://www.bis.doc.gov/index.php/export-control-classification-interactive-tool. Second, there is a "specially designed" interactive tool to walk the exporter through the definition above at http://www.bis.doc.gov/index.php/specially-designed-tool. It is also possible to obtain a Commodity Jurisdiction through the DDTC's online request form at http://www.bis.doc.gov/index.php/specially-designed-tool.

Once the exporter knows its products are defense articles, then the next step is registration with the DDTC on Form DS-2032. See http://www.pmddtc.state.gov/registration/crp.html. The Form must be submitted through the electronic DTAS system at https://dtas-online.pmddtc.state.gov/.

Even if the manufacturer is not exporting, if it manufactures any article that is found on the U.S. Munitions List, it must be registered with the DDTC as a Defense

Manufacturer. Defense brokers, parties that arrange for the sourcing of defense articles on behalf of a government entity must also register with the DDTC.

Once registered, an exporter must enroll in the D-Trade electronic licensing system in order to obtain a license for the permanent export, temporary export, or temporary import of U.S. Munitions List items. This requires the user to access to the D-Trade system and purchase software which will allow for individual digital certificates. The application for permanent export of U.S. Munitions List items is filed through D-Trade on a DSP-5 (see Figure 5–19). For some items, specified as "significant military equipment," the applicant must obtain a signed Nontransfer and Use Certificate (DSP-83) from the consignee and end user prior to making application. (See Figure 5–20.) In some cases, as a condition of granting the license, the DDTC may require that the applicant obtain an import certificate signed by the government of the foreign country and/or provide verification of delivery of the item to the foreign country. Different procedures and license forms apply to classified articles and technical data. Additionally, there are separate forms that apply to direct, commercial sales and to sales to the U.S. Department of Defense for resale to foreign countries under the Foreign Military Assistance program. Before appointing any foreign distributors who are authorized to resell the products, the exporter must submit the Distributorship Agreement to the DDTC for approval. Agreements to grant manufacturing licenses or provide technical assistance to any parties outside of the United States, including related parties, must be approved in advance through Technical Assistance Agreements and Manufacturing License Agreements.

Not all countries are eligible for licenses from the DDTC. In fact, there is a list of countries that are prohibited by the U.S. in Section 126.1 of the International Traffic in Arms Regulations. To obtain the most recent information on the specific countries DDTC has provided a link which provides the details on a country basis at https://www.pmddtc.state.gov/embargoed_countries/index.html.

An area of particular sensitivity is the requirement that if the amount of the export sale is $500,000 or more, the license applicant must disclose to the DDTC the names and detailed payment information on any fees or commissions of $1,000 or more paid to any person to promote or secure the sale of a defense article or service to the armed forces of a foreign country. The applicant must also report any political contributions of $1,000 or more to any government employee, political party, or candidate. These requirements are required as part of the Foreign Corrupt Practices Act. (See Chapter 3, Section D for more information.) The applicant must also survey its suppliers, subcontractors, and agents to ascertain whether they have paid or agreed to make any such payments. In addition to the disclosure to the DDTC, such payments may violate foreign law as many foreign jurisdictions have enacted similar anti-bribery provisions.

Figure 5–19. Application/license for permanent export.

Electronic Form Version Number: 2.3

OMB APPROVAL NO. 1405-0003
EXPIRATION DATE: 09-30-2008
*ESTIMATED BURDEN: 1 HOUR

* PAPERWORK REDUCTION ACT STATEMENT: Public reporting burden for this collection of information is estimated to average 1 hour per response, including time required for searching existing data sources, gathering the necessary data, providing the information required, and reviewing the final collection. Send comments on the accuracy of this estimate of the burden and recommendations for reducing it to: Department of State (A/RPS/DIR) Washington, D.C. 20520.

U.S. DEPARTMENT OF STATE

DIRECTORATE OF DEFENSE TRADE CONTROLS

APPLICATION/LICENSE FOR PERMANENT EXPORT OF UNCLASSIFIED DEFENSE ARTICLES AND RELATED UNCLASSIFIED TECHNICAL DATA

*Transaction Number:

Please note that an Asterisk (*) next to a field in the documents designates a mandatory field.

No classified information can be included in this application. Classified information must be sent separately to PM/DDTC in accordance with Defense Security Service guidelines.

Classified information is being sent under separate cover ☐

To select and open a document, highlight a form and select the "Open Document" button. The document that you selected will open.

Required Documents

DSP-5

Included Documents

Optional Documents

126.13 Eligibility Letter
Basic Ordering Agreement
Contract
DSP-83
Firearms and Ammunitions Import Permit
Firearms and Ammunitions Letter of Explanation
Letter of Intent
Other Amplifying Data
Part 130 Report
PM/DDTC Sec 126.8 Prior Approval
Precedent (identical/similar) Cases
Product Brochures
Purchase Order
Supplementary Explanation of Transaction
Technical Data to Support Hardware License
Technical Drawings, Schematics, or Blue Prints
Transaction Exception Request

DSP-5
Revised 02-2006

Figure 5–19. (*continued*)

DSP-5, Page 1 of 4

SEAL		DATE ISSUED	

Signature

License is hereby granted to the applicant for the described commodity to be permanently exported from the United States. This license may be revoked, suspended or amended by the Secretary of State without prior notice whenever the Secretary deems such action advisable.

DATE ISSUED [ ]

LICENSE NO. [ ]   **LICENSE VALID FOR** [ ]
MONTHS FROM ABOVE DATE

UNITED STATES OF AMERICA   DEPARTMENT OF STATE

APPLICATION/LICENSE FOR PERMANENT EXPORT OF UNCLASSIFIED
DEFENSE ARTICLES AND RELATED UNCLASSIFIED TECHNICAL DATA

1. Date Prepared	* 2. PM/DDTC Applicant/ Registrant Code	* 3. Country of Ultimate Destination:	* 4. Probable Port of Exit from U.S.:

NOTE: You may only select 1 country as the ultimate destination if the commodity(ies) being shipped include Hardware type.

5. Applicant's Name, Address, ZIP Code, Telephone Number

*Applicant is: ☐ Government   ☐ Manufacturer   ☐ Exporter
☐ Subsidiary

*Name

*Attention

*Address

*City

*State [ ]   * ZIP Code [ ]

*Telephone # [ ]   Ext. [ ]

6. Name, agency and telephone number of U.S. Government personnel (not PM/DDTC) familiar with the commodity.

Name [ ]

Telephone # [ ]   Ext. [ ]

Agency [ ]

Add

* 7. Name and telephone numbers of applicant contact if U.S. Government needs additional information.

*Name [ ]

*Telephone # [ ]   Ext. [ ]

Add

8. Description of Transaction:

*a. This application represents: ☐ ONLY completely new shipment   ☐ ONLY the unshipped balance under license numbers

b. This application has related license numbers: ☐

c. This application is in reference to an agreement: ☐

*d. Commodity is being financed under: ☐ Foreign Military Sale ☐ Foreign Military Financing ☐ Grant Aid Program ☐ Not Applicable

Line Item #	*9. Quantity	*10. Commodity	* 11. USML Category Number
1	Unit Type		Category [ ] [ ]
			Item is SME and DSP-83 is required ☐
			Is a DSP-83 attached? [ ]
			If SME, and DSP-83 is not attached, state why.
			*12. $ Value
			Unit Price Line Item Total
		Defense Article Type [ ]	[ ] [ ]
	Add ☐	*13. TOTAL VALUE (Sum of All Pages) $ [ ]	

Export Controls and Licenses

Figure 5–19. (*continued*)

DSP-5, Page 2 of 4

14. Name and address of foreign end-user

* Name

*Address

*City

*Country

Add ☐

15. Manufacturer of Commodity

☐ Same as Block 5

*Name

*Address

*City

State   ZIP Code

*Country

Add ☐

16. Name and address of foreign consignee

☐ Same as Block 14

*Name

*Address

*City

*Country

Add ☐

17. Source of Commodity

☐ Same as Block 5   ☐ Same as Block 15

*Name

*Address

*City

State   ZIP Code

*Country

Add ☐

18. Name and address of foreign intermediate consignee

☐ None

* Name

*Address

*City

*Country

*Role

Add ☐

19. Name and address of Seller in United States

☐ Same as Block 5   ☐ Same as Block 15   ☐ Same as Block 17

* Name

*Address

*City

*State   *ZIP Code

Add ☐

* 20. Specific purpose for which the material is required, including specific Program/End Item.

Select at least one:

☐ Off-Shore   ☐ Request for Prior Approval (22 CFR 126.8)

☐ Brokering (22 CFR 129) ☐ Other (Please Provide Details)

21. Name and address of consignor and/or freight forwarder in United States

☐ Same as Block 5

* Name

*Address

*City

*State   *ZIP Code

Add ☐

253

Figure 5–19. *(continued)*

DSP-5

22. Applicant's statement

I [   ]

an empowered official (ITAR 120.25) or an official of a foreign government entity in the U.S., hereby apply for a license to complete the transaction described above; warrant the truth of all statements made herein; and acknowledge, understand and will comply with the provisions of Title 22 CFR, 120-130, and any conditions and limitations imposed.

I am authorized by the applicant to certify the following in compliance with 22 CFR 126.13:

(1)   Neither applicant, its chief executive officer, president, vice presidents, other senior officers or officials (e.g., comptroller, treasurer, general counsel) nor any member of its board of directors is:

　　　(a) the subject of an indictment for or has been convicted of violating any of the U.S. criminal statutes enumerated in 22 CFR120.27 since the effective date of the Arms Export Control Act, Public Law 94-329, 90 Stat. 729 (June 30, 1976); or

　　　(b) ineligible to contract with, or to receive a license or other approval to import defense articles or defense services from, or to receive an export license or other approval from any agency of the U.S. Government;

(2)   To the best of the applicant's knowledge, no party to the export as defined in 22 CFR 126.7 (e) has been convicted of violating any of the U.S. criminal statutes enumerated in 22 CFR 120.27 since the effective date of the Arms Export Control Act, Public Law 94-329, 90 Stat. 729 (June 30, 1976); or is ineligible to contract with, or to receive a license or other approval to import defense articles or defense services from, or to receive an export lisence or other approval from any agency of the U.S. Government.

*22 CFR 126.13 Certification (Select one)

☐ I am authorized by the applicant to certify that the applicant and all the parties to the transaction can meet in full the conditions of 22 CFR 126.13 as listed above.

☐ I am authorized by the applicant to certify to 22 CFR 126.13. The applicant or one of the parties of the transaction cannot meet one or more of the conditions of 22 CFR 126.13 as listed above. A request for an exception to policy is attached.

☐ I am not authorized by the applicant to certify the conditions of 22 CFR 126.13 as listed above. The applicant and all the parties to the transaction can meet in full the conditions of 22 CFR 126.13 as listed above. Please see the attached letter for such certification.

☐ I am not authorized by the applicant to certify the conditions of 22 CFR 126.13 as listed above. The applicant or one of the parties of the transaction cannot meet one or more of the conditions of 22 CFR 126.13 as listed above. A letter of such certification and request for an exception to policy is attached.

*Compliance with 22 CFR 130 (Select one)

☐ This transaction does not meet the requirements of 22 CFR 130.2

☐ This transaction meets the requirements of 22 CFR 130.2. The applicant or its vendors have not paid, nor offered, nor agreed to pay, in respect of any sale for which a license or approval is requested, political contributions, fees or commissions in amounts as specified in 22 CFR 130.9(a).

☐ The applicant or its vendors have paid, or offered, or agreed to pay, in respect of any sale for which a license or approval is requested, political contributions, fees or commissions in amounts as specified in 22 CFR 130.9(a). Information required under 22 CFR 130.10 is attached.

☐ I am not authorized by the applicant to certify the conditions of 22 CFR 130.9(a). Please see the attached for such certification.

*Signature

[Signature]

23. License to be to: (Enter name, address and phone number)

[This block is inactive on electronic form.]

☐ Same as Block 5　　　☐ Hold for Pickup

Name	
Address	
City	
State	ZIP Code
Telephone #	

Export Controls and Licenses

Figure 5–19. *(continued)*

CONDITIONS OF ISSUANCE

1. This license is issued under the conditions cited in 22 CFR 120 - 130, including the provisos as applicable, that:

    A. It shall not be construed as implying U.S. Government approval or commitment to authorize future exports of any article (equipment or technical data) on the Munitions List, or a U.S. Government commitment with regard to any proposed manufacturing license or technical assistance agreements which may result from an authorized export.

    B. If a license is issued for technical data only, it does not authorize the export of any hardware; if a license is issued for hardware only, it does not authorize the export of any technical data, unless specifically covered by an exemption.

    The issuance of this license does not release the licensee from complying with other requirements of U.S. law and regulations.

2. The prior written approval of the Department of State must be obtained before U.S. Munitions List articles exported from the U.S. under license or other approval may be resold, diverted, transferred, transshipped, reshipped, reexported to, or used in any country, or by any end-user, other than that described on the license or other approval as the country of ultimate destination or the ultimate end-user.

RETURN OF LICENSE

This license must be returned to PM/DDTC, SA-1, 12th Floor, Directorate of Defense Trade Controls, Bureau of Political-Military Affairs, U.S. Department of State, Washington, DC 20522-0112 when: (1) the total value authorized has been shipped; (2) the applicant states that there will be no further shipments; (3) the date of expiration is reached; or (4) when requested by the Directorate of Defense Trade Controls.

ENDORSEMENT

Indicate below which ITEM on the face of the license is BEING EXPORTED and maintain a CONTINUING BALANCE of the remaining value:

SHIPMENT DATE	QUANTITY	COMMODITY (Include classification)	SHIPMENT VALUE	SED NO.	INITIALS	PORT OF EXIT/ENTRY
TOTAL AUTHORIZED VALUE:						
REMAINING BALANCE:						

NOTE: Continuation of additional shipments must be authenticated by use of continuation sheets in the U.S.Customs handbook.

255

Figure 5–20. Nontransfer and Use Certificate.

U.S. Department of State **UNITED STATES OF AMERICA** **NONTRANSFER AND USE CERTIFICATE**	1. This certificate is submitted in connection with export application no. _____	OMB No. 1406 0021 EXPIRATION DATE: 09-30-2008 *ESTIMATED BURDEN: 1 Hour (Instruction Page)

2. Name of United States applicant	3. Name of foreign end-user	4. Country of ultimate destination

5. Articles/data
We certify that we have placed an order with the person named in item 2 for the following articles/data in the quantity and value shown below:

QUANTITY	ARTICLES/DATA DESCRIPTION	VALUE (U.S. $)

6. Certification of foreign consignee
We certify that we are importing the articles/data listed in item 5 for delivery to the end-user in item 3. Except as specifically authorized by prior written approval of the U.S. Department of State, we will not re-export, resell, or otherwise dispose of any of those articles/data (1) outside the country in item 4 above, or (2) to any person, including the end-user, if there is reason to believe that it will result, directly or indirectly, in disposition of the articles/data contrary to the representations made in this certificate by any party. We further certify that all of the facts contained in this certificate are true and correct to the best of our knowledge and belief and we do not know of any additional facts that are inconsistent with this certificate. We will promptly send a supplemental certificate to the U.S. applicant in item 2 disclosing any change of facts or intentions set forth in this statement.

Sign here in ink _____
Signature of Official, Foreign Consignee

Date Signed *(mm-dd-yyyy)*

Type or print _____
Name and Title of Signer

Seal

7. Certification of foreign end-user
We certify that we are the end-user of the articles/data in item 5. Except as specifically authorized by prior written approval of the U.S. Department of State, we will not re-export, resell, or otherwise dispose of any of those articles/data (1) outside the country in item 4 above, or (2) to any other person. If the end-user is a foreign government, we certify that we will observe the assurances contained in item 8. We further certify that all of the facts contained in this certificate are true and correct to the best of our knowledge and belief and we do not know of any additional facts that are inconsistent with this certificate.

Sign here in ink _____
Signature of Official, End-User

Date Signed *(mm-dd-yyyy)*

Type or print _____
Name and Title of Signer

Seal

8. Certification of foreign government
We certify that we will not authorize the re-export, resales or other disposition of the articles/data authorized in item 5 outside the country in item 4 without prior written approval of the U.S. Government. If the articles/data are for use by our "armed forces" (i.e., army, navy, marine, air force, coast guard, national guard, national police, and any military unit or military personnel organized under or assigned to an international organization), we certify that we will use the authorized articles/data only: (a) for the purposes specified in the Mutual Defense Assistance Agreement, if any, between the U.S. Government and this government; (b) for the purposes specified in any bilateral or regional defense treaty to which the U.S. Government and this government are both parties, if subparagraph (a) is inapplicable; or (c) for internal security, individual self-defense, and/or civic action, if subparagraphs (a) and (b) are inapplicable.

Sign here in ink _____
Signature of Government Official

Date Signed *(mm-dd-yyyy)*

Type or print _____
Name and Title of Signer

Seal

9. We certify that no corrections, additions or alterations were made on this form by us after it was signed by the foreign consignee, foreign end-user or foreign government.

Sign here in ink _____
Signature of Applicant

Date Signed *(mm-dd-yyyy)*

Type or print _____
Name and Title of Signer

Seal

DSP-83
10-2005

Page 1 of 1

Figure 5–20. (*continued*)

INSTRUCTIONS FOR DSP-83

The U.S. Department of State requires that this completed form DSP-83 be included as a part of an application for authorization to export significant military equipment and classified equipment or data (22 CFR §§123.10(a), 124.10 and 125.7.) Failure to submit will result in the application being returned without action. The form DSP-83 must be completed by the appropriate foreign persons (e.g., consignee, end-user, government) and forwarded to the U.S. Department of State through the U.S. person making the application.

1. *Item 1.* The U.S. Department of State will enter the application number when the form DSP-83 is submitted with the application. The U.S. applicant must provide the application number when form DSP-83 is submitted separately from the application.

2. *Item 2.* Show the name of the U.S. person submitting the application to the U.S. Department of State.

3. *Item 3.* Show the foreign person that will receive the articles/data for end-use. A bank, freight forwarding agent, or other intermediary is not acceptable as an end-user.

4. *Item 4.* Show the country in which the articles/data will ultimately receive end-use.

5. *Item 5.* Show precise quantities of the articles/data. List each article/data clearly, giving type, model number, make and (if known) U.S. military designation or national stock number. When components and spare parts are involved, fully identify the minor component, major component and end item in which they will be used (e.g., turbine blades for C-34 jet engine for F24B aircraft). Give a separate value for each major component. Values must represent only the selling price and not include supplementary costs such as packing and freight.

6. *Item 6.* To be completed by the foreign person who has entered into the export transaction with the applicant to purchase the articles/data for delivery to the end-user. This item shall be completed only if the foreign consignee is not the same as the foreign end-user.

7. *Item 7.* To be completed by the foreign person, in the country of ultimate designation, who will make final use of the articles/data.

8. *Item 8.* When requested by the U.S. Department of State, this item is to be completed by an official of the country of ultimate destination having the authority to so commit the government of that country.

9. *Item 9.* Certification of U.S. applicant.

*Public reporting burden for this collection is estimated to average 1 hour per response, including time required for searching existing data sources, gathering the necessary data, providing the information required, and reviewing the final collection. Send comments on the accuracy of this estimate of the burden and recommendations for reducing it to: U.S. Department of State (A/RPS/DIR) Washington, DC 20520.

DSP-83
10-2005

Instruction Page 1 of 1

The DDTC's policy is that persons engaged in the export of defense articles and services should maintain an export procedures manual containing DDTC-specified policies and procedures to reduce the risk of violations. The DDTC also has a voluntary disclosure program which will mitigate potential fines. Once a voluntary disclosure is filed, the exporter has 180 days to "perfect" the disclosure, so that the final disclosure gives details on all violations including commodities, all parties involved, dates, whether licenses would have been allowed, what steps the exporter has taken to ensure future compliance, etc. It is wise to consult with an attorney before filing the disclosure.

Persons who violate the Arms Export Control Act are subject to the civil and criminal penalties and can be debarred from exporting for a period of up to three years.

S. Enforcement

With the implementation of the Export Control Reform Act, the President created the Export Enforcement Coordination Center (E2C2). This group is charged with coordinating and enhancing criminal, administrative, and related export enforcement activities. It is a multi-agency center with representation from eight U.S. governmental departments and fifteen federal agencies. Its goal is to create a whole-government approach with an eye to eliminating the duplication of efforts while ensuring that there is communication between intelligence efforts, law enforcement and all of the various export licensing agencies.

Part III

Importing: Procedures and Documentation

Chapter 6

Importing: Preliminary Considerations

Before beginning to import, and on each importation, the importer/buyer should consider a number of preliminary matters that will make a great deal of difference in smooth and efficient importing.

A. Products

Before actually importing, or whenever the importer is considering importing a new item, the characteristics of that item should be reviewed. Is the product being imported as a raw material or component to be used in the manufacturing process? Is it a finished product that is going to be resold in the form imported or with some slight or significant modification? Is it a replacement or spare part? Is the item sold singly or as a part of a set or system? Does the product need to be modified, such as in size, weight, or color, to be suitable for the U.S. market? Often the appropriate methods of manufacturing and marketing, the appropriate purchase and import documentation, the appropriate procedures for importation, and the treatment under U.S. law, including U.S. customs law, will depend upon these considerations (for example, whether or not the product may be imported duty-free or what the correct classification and duty will be).

In addition to the general procedures and documents, some products are subject to special import restrictions, permits, licenses, standards, and/or procedures. These include foods, drugs, cosmetics, alcoholic beverages, tea, medical devices, certain energy-using commercial and industrial equipment, civil aircraft and parts, educational and scientific apparatus, children's products including toys and books, products containing phthalates, wood products, ethyl alcohol, master records and matrices. There are a number of products that are prohibited from importation, such as white or yellow phosphorous matches; certain fireworks; "cultural property"; switchblades; lottery tickets; most endangered species; African elephant ivory and articles; counterfeit articles; treasonable or obscene material; and products of child and forced labor.

The Bureau of International Labor Affairs, a division of the Department of Labor, keeps a list of products which it has reason to believe are produced with child or forced labor. See http://www.dol.gov/ilab/reports/child-labor/list-of-goods/. The list is meant as a guideline for importers to conduct additional research of their supplier and to verify that their imported products are not made using child or forced labor. If Customs has reason to believe, either on its own or having received information from outside Customs that it believes has validity, it will open an investigation of the imported merchandise and require the ports to withhold release of the goods. Customs will schedule publication in the Federal Register notice that the goods will not be admitted. The importer must provide proof as the admissibility of the merchandise within three months. This means that the importer must provide evidence that the articles were *not* mined, produced or manufactured with child or forced labor and obtain a signed Certificate or Origin by the foreign seller or owner of the article. As most importers know, foreign sellers may be willing to sign documents that are not accurate, so it behooves an importer to obtain third-party verification as to the accuracy of the statements made on the Certificate of Origin. If by the end of the three months, the importer has not been able to prove the allegations, the merchandise will be considered prohibited and the Federal Register notice will be published. The merchandise may be exported customs will seize the merchandise. Probably the worst consequence of importing goods subject to child or forced labor is the negative publicity that may arise since the media scans the Federal Registers for information of this nature.

B. Volume

What is the expected volume of imports of the product? Will this be an isolated purchase of a small quantity or an ongoing series of transactions amounting to substantial quantities? Small quantities may be imported under purchase orders and purchase order acceptance documentation. Large quantities may require more formal international purchase agreements; more formal methods of payment; special shipping, packing, and handling procedures; an appointment as the U.S. sales agent and/or distributor from the foreign exporter; or commitments to perform after-sales service. (See the discussion in Chapter 7, Section B.)

C. Country Sourcing

One of the principal preliminary considerations will be to identify those countries that have the products that the importer is seeking to purchase. If the importer seeks to import a raw material or natural resource, the importer may be limited to purchasing from those countries where such products are grown or mined. If the importer is looking for a manufactured product, it is likely that the number of countries where such products are available for sale will be much greater; however, identifying the low-cost countries based upon proximity to raw materials, labor costs of manufacturing, current exchange rates with the United States, or transportation costs may require considerable study and analysis. This information is not always easy to obtain. Since the U.S. government is more interested in promoting exports, it does not regularly collect such information and make it available to U.S. companies wishing to import. Importers will probably have to contact foreign governments directly (or through their U.S. embassies and consulates), foreign chambers of commerce, and foreign trade associations. Sometimes, foreign banks operating in the United States, U.S. accounting firms or law firms that have offices in the foreign country, or U.S. banks with offices in the foreign country can be helpful in supplying information. The United Nations publishes its *International Trade Statistics Yearbook* showing what countries are selling and exporting all types of products. In identifying the potential country, the importer should ascertain whether the products of that country are eligible for duty-free or reduced duty treatment under the any of the numerous free trade agreements, including those with Australia, Bahrain, Chile, Morocco, Oman, and Singapore or other program that are designed to encourage the growth of underdeveloped countries, such as the Generalized System of Preferences, the African Growth and Opportunity Act or others. Under the U.S. Foreign Assets Control Regulations, importation from Cuba, Iran, North Korea, Sudan, and Syria is prohibited without a license or approval from the Department of the Treasury (with a general policy of denial), and imports from such countries will be immediately seized by U.S. Customs and Border Protection.

Rough diamonds may be imported into or exported from the United States only from or to countries participating in the Kimberly Process Certification Scheme. It should also be noted that importers are prohibited from making or receiving any funds, goods, or services from parties that are identified in the Specially Designated Nationals List who are sponsors of terrorism, narcotics drug trafficking, or the proliferation of weapons of mass destruction (see Chapter 5, Section E).

D. Identification of Suppliers

Once the countries with the products available for supply have been identified, of course, the importer still needs to identify a specific supplier. This will be just as important as identifying which countries can provide the products at the lowest cost. An unreliable supplier or one that has poor product quality control will certainly result in disaster for the importer. The importer should spend a significant amount of time in evaluating the potential supplier if there are going to be ongoing purchase transactions. The importer should ascertain the business reputation and performance of the potential supplier. If possible, the importer should inspect the plant and manufacturing facilities of the supplier. The importer should determine whether there are other customers within its own country who might be able to confirm the quality and supply reliability of the potential supplier. Related thereto, if the importer will be acting as the distributor or sales agent for the foreign manufacturer, the importer needs to ascertain whether the supplier has already appointed (on either an exclusive or a nonexclusive basis) other U.S. distributors or sales agents. The importer should also determine if a supplier is acting as an agent for the manufacturer or if the supplier will be acting as the buying agent for the buyer. If the latter, the buyer should enter into a separate agency agreement and pay all commissions separately, since the importer need not pay customs duties on buying commissions but must do so on commissions paid to the seller's agent.

Once potential suppliers have been identified, if an ongoing relationship is contemplated, a personal visit to evaluate the supplier is essential. One efficient way that the author has used is to arrange a schedule of interviews at its foreign law office so that the U.S. importer can meet with numerous potential suppliers in that country in the course of a two- or three-day period. Based on such meetings, one or more suppliers can be selected and the capabilities of those suppliers can be clearly understood. In evaluating potential suppliers, it is important to obtain a credit report. International credit reports are available from Dun & Bradstreet, www.dnb.com/us; Graydon America, www.graydon-group.com; Teikoku Data Bank America, Inc. [Japan], www.teikoku.com; Owens Online, www.owens.com; and local offices of the U.S. Department of Commerce (International Company Profiles).

E. Compliance with Foreign Law

Prior to importing from a foreign country or even agreeing to purchase from a supplier in a foreign country, a U.S. importer should be aware of any foreign laws that might affect the purchase. Information about foreign law can often be obtained from the supplier from whom the importer intends to purchase. However, if the supplier is incorrect in the information that it gives to the importer, the importer may have to pay dearly for having relied solely upon the advice of the supplier. Incorrect information about foreign law may result in the prohibition of importation of the supplier's product, or it may mean that the importer cannot resell the product as profitably as expected. Unfortunately, suppliers often overlook those things that may be of the greatest concern to the importer. As a result, it may be necessary for the U.S. importer to confirm its supplier's advice with third parties, including attorneys, banks, or government agencies, to feel confident that it properly understands the foreign law.

1. *Foreign Export Controls*

A number of countries, particularly those that are politically allied with the United States, enforce a system of export controls on dual-use items. The Coordinating Committee for Multilateral Export Controls was originally formed five years after the end of World War II. When COCOM ceased to function in 1994, it was superseded by the "Wassenaar Arrangement on Export Controls for Conventional Arms and Dual-Use Goods and Technologies." See http://www.wassenaar.org/introduction/index.html. The name was based on high level meetings that occurred in Wassenaar, Netherlands in 1995. The controls established under the Wassenaar Agreement are the basis for the United States' export controls and those of the forty-one member countries to the Agreement. In order to export certain dual-use products from those countries, even to the United States, certain procedures of the foreign country must be followed. The first step is for the importer to ascertain whether or not the product is a controlled commodity under the foreign country's laws. If it is, the U.S. importer will be required to furnish a document to the foreign supplier to enable the foreign supplier to obtain a license from its own government to export the product to the United States. The importer will have to identify the documents required either through the potential supplier or directly from the foreign government agency, but in most cases an import certificate (see Chapter 5, Figure 5–9) will be required. The U.S. importer must have this document signed by the U.S. Department of Commerce, and it must be forwarded to the foreign supplier to enable it to apply for and obtain the necessary foreign government license for exporting the product. See https://www.bis.doc.gov/index.php/forms-documents/doc_view/1-bis-645p-international-import-certificate. In addition, there may be other documents that the supplier must provide to its own government in order to obtain an export license. When an export license will be required, the importer should clearly ascertain the time period required in order to adequately plan its import schedule. The importer should also take certain steps in its purchase and sale documentation with the supplier to adequately obligate the supplier to obtain the necessary export licenses. (See discussion in Chapter 7, Section B.2.k.)

2. Exchange Control Licenses

Many countries of the world control their foreign exchange. Consequently, before an exporter can export valuable products produced or manufactured in its own country to a U.S. importer, the exporter's government will insist that the exporter have adequate assurance of payment by the U.S. importer. The foreign exporter will need a license in order to convert U.S. dollars received from the U.S. importer into its local currency to obtain payment. This is important for the importer to confirm in order to make sure that the products are not detained prior to export because the necessary exchange control license has not been obtained. Of significant importance to the importer is the requirement by the exporter's country that payment must be made by certain means, such as confirmed irrevocable letter of credit. In order to protect their companies against nonpayment, some governments impose strict payment requirements on foreign trade contracts. If the importer is unable or unwilling to pay by letter of credit, importation from that country may be practically impossible.

3. Export Quotas

Generally, the importing country establishes quotas for imported products. These are discussed in Section F.6 below. However, the U.S. government, through its negotiating representatives such as the U.S. Trade Representative's office, often requires the foreign government to agree to impose export quotas on products destined for the United States. These are sometimes designated Voluntary Restraint Agreements (VRA), and foreign government "visas" are required. (This "visa" should not be confused with the visa required by the immigration laws of foreign countries in order to travel there.)

Ordinarily, the foreign supplier should be aware of any export quotas or export visa requirements, but if the foreign supplier has been selling only domestically in the past, the supplier may not be familiar with those requirements. The U.S. importer should double-check on the existence of any foreign government quotas or visas prior to entering into purchase transactions that cannot be fulfilled. Sometimes these export visas or export rights are auctioned in the foreign country, and a potential exporter must participate in the government auction at the correct time in order to get an allocation for the coming year. Where export quotas or VRAs have been established, competition for such export visas is usually intense, and an importer will be unable to enter into spot transactions on short notice for the purchase of the products from suppliers who have not obtained the necessary government visas.

The United States does not have any VRAs or any commodities requiring import visas at this time; however, it is always possible that they may be reinstituted depending on political and economic factors. The International Trade Administration does monitor numerous commodities to see potential impact on U.S. industries.

F.   U.S. Customs Considerations

Various aspects of the U.S. Customs and Border Protection laws as they affect potential importers will be discussed in greater detail throughout subsequent chapters; however, there are a number of items that should be part of the importer's preliminary planning.

U.S. Customs and Border Protection is organized into a number of different "offices," but from an importer's perspective there are two distinct divisions that will impact its imports. The Tactical Operations side includes the enforcement division, contraband enforcement, cargo clearance and control, agricultural inspections, and passenger clearances. The Trade Operations side includes the revenue group for collections of duties, the entry group for administrative processing, the Import Specialists and in some locations Drawback specialists. When a customs broker submits electronically information regarding the shipment from the moment of the Importer Security Filing occurs before the goods are exported from the foreign country, decisions are being made electronically as to whether to inspect the shipment at the time of arrival, review the documentation or allow the shipment to bypass any human review. If the submissions are flagged, then the inspection team will require the merchandise to be stopped until its review. If documentation is to be reviewed, the customs broker will be notified to forward the documentation to the import specialists. Recently Customs reorganization has been to create the Centers of Excellence and Expertise (CEEs). The CEEs are populated with specialists in certain fields, such as textiles and apparel, machinery, electronics, retail merchandising, etc. The purpose was to minimize variances in the manner in which clearances were handled by the ports and to create experts in the products. In addition, there are offices in Washington, D.C. that oversee the processes and have the ultimate say over the import transactions. Because of these layers of authority and because the party with ultimate responsibility is the importer, it is critical to understand the import process.

1. Utilization of Customs Brokers

A customs broker is a party licensed by U.S. Customs to transact customs business on behalf of others. To become a customs broker in the United States, there is an examination that is held twice a year on the Customs regulations. The passage rate is extremely low. Once the broker passes the exam, then they must undergo a review for "fitness." This basically means that Customs checks into the individual's background for criminal activity and their responsibilities with the handling of money as customs brokers will handle customs duties and fees on behalf of their customers. A customs brokerage business must have at least one licensed customs broker responsible for overseeing the customs transactions of that business. Where there are multiple locations, the broker must have a licensed individual in each of those locations, although with the ability to do Remote Entry Filings in another port, this has become easier to handle without the added licenses. Customs brokers are required to maintain a surety bond for the transaction they handle on behalf of their customers (see more in Part 2 below) and they generally carry errors and omissions insurance, although that is not a requirement of Customs. The National Customs Brokers and Freight Forwarders Association provides guidance and creates standardized documentation such as a Power of Attorney Form and Terms and Conditions of Service that are structured to limit their liability. Most brokers use these documents with relatively few modifications.

Whether or not an importer should utilize a customs broker primarily depends upon the amount of imports the importer will have, and the number and expertise of its own personnel. If the importer has sufficient personnel with sufficient expertise, these people can be trained to handle the importing procedures and documentation themselves. Even large importers, however, often use the services of a customs broker. The most difficult problem may be the selection of a customs broker. There are many customs brokers with varying levels of expertise and various levels of financial stability. More important, some customs brokers are more familiar with certain types of products. Today, it is becoming increasingly important that the customs broker have an automated electronic interface with U.S. Customs and Border Protection and the ability to process documentation electronically. Customs is currently in the process of switching over from the proprietary "Automated Broker Interface" system to an Internet-based system called the Automated Commercial Environment, which will make it easier to self-file a number of documents. Interviews with a number of potential brokers and a frank discussion of the products and quantities that the importer intends to import, the source countries, and the brokers' capabilities are worthwhile. A visit to the brokers' premises may be even more helpful.

This concern and effort is more than merely academic. The broker acts as the agent for the importer, and, therefore, even though the importer may pay a fee to the broker, expecting to obtain the broker's expertise, if the broker makes a mistake or an error, U.S. Customs and Border Protection will attribute the responsibility for it to the importer, the principal. For example, if the broker fails to pay customs duties to Customs that were paid to the broker by the importer, the importer may be required to pay twice. In performing its services, the broker will require a power of attorney from the importer. (A sample power of attorney acceptable to U.S. Customs and Border Protection is shown in Figure 6–1.) Although the brokers will generally use the power of attorney suggested by the National Association, the importer should review the power of attorney and make appropriate modifications. In addition, the importer should review the terms and conditions at the beginning of the relationship. The broker should at least agree to indemnify and hold the importer harmless from any penalties, costs, or damages due to the broker's negligence or errors. Another form that is essential to the importer in order to provide guidance to the broker as to the specifics of each transaction is an importer's letter of instruction (see Figure 6–2). Remember that the importer is ultimately responsible to Customs for what is declared by the broker, so the importer needs to learn the details of its transactions and tell the broker what to do to ensure compliance.

In the event that a broker is intransigent and refuses to perform its services as required by law, an importer can request that license revocation proceedings be initiated by U.S. Customs and Border Protection.

2. *Importation Bonds*

In order to import merchandise into the United States, it is necessary for the importer to obtain a bond from a surety company. This is to guarantee that all customs duties, customs penalties, and other charges assessed by Customs will be properly paid, even if the importer goes bankrupt. There are essentially two types of bonds: the single transaction bond and the continuous bond. Single transaction bonds cover individual importations and may be for as much as three times the value of the importer merchandise depending upon the type of goods and whether there may be other government agencies involved in the import or whether there are antidumping of countervailing duties involved. The single transaction bond is practical only for an importer who is engaged in very few importations. Continuous bonds are issued to cover all of the importations of an importer for a particular time period, usually one year. The amount is usually equal to 10 percent of the total customs duties paid for the previous year or reasonably estimated for the current year, but not less than $50,000 of imported value. Obviously, before a surety company will provide the importation bond, it will be necessary for the importer to make application, undergo a credit investigation, and

Figure 6–1. Power of attorney for customs broker.

Figure 6–2. Importer's letter of instruction.

INSTRUCTIONS TO CUSTOMS BROKER

Dear customs broker:

Please arrange for Customs clearance of the following merchandise. Please note that failure to follow the instructions below will result in an incorrect entry. Please forward a copy of the CF7501 for our review prior to submission to Customs:

SHIPPING DETAILS:

Air waybill/Ocean bill of lading: _____

Scheduled Arrival Date: _____

Carrier: _____

In-Bond Carrier: _____

Exporting Country: _____

CUSTOMS DETAILS:

HTS Numbers: _____

Descriptions: _____

Values: _____

Origin of goods: _____

Manufacturer/Shipper: _____

Other Government Agency requirements: _____

Payment of duties:_____

DELIVERY INFORMATION:

Deliver to: _____

_____

Carrier:_____

Other Instructions:_____

Please contact _____ at _____ or email _____ if you have **any** additional questions prior to taking action on our behalf.

show financial stability. Customs brokers have their own customs bonds, and will sometimes handle imports for importers under the coverage of their bond, although this is the exception more than the rule and they will charge for that service. An application to file a continuous bond and the bond must be filed with the Revenue Division of U.S. Customs and Border Protection in Indianapolis, IN. (A sample customs bond is shown in Figure 6–3.) It should be noted that couriers clear merchandise under their own bonds to ensure the expedited service, but that does not clear the importer from the responsibility for the accuracy of those clearances if they ordered the merchandise that was shipped.

3. *Importer's Liability and Reasonable Care*

The company that intends to import should fully comprehend that liability for all U.S. customs duties, penalties, and charges is the responsibility of the importer. U.S. Customs and Border Protection generally will not have jurisdiction (or it will be too much trouble for it to obtain jurisdiction) over the foreign supplier to collect or assess any customs penalties. Most importers understand that they are obligated to pay import duties, but may not realize that Customs treats importers in the same manner as the IRS treats corporate taxpayers, it is the responsibility of the importer to understand the laws and regulations and to ensure that all information provided to Customs is true and accurate. If certain events occur, such as the imposition of antidumping duties, or if false documents, even documents furnished by the foreign supplier (such as commercial invoices), are filed with U.S. Customs and Border Protection in connection with the importation, whether intentionally or accidentally, the importer's liability can dramatically escalate, including the imposition of substantial criminal fines and civil penalties amounting to the full domestic value of—not just the customs duties on—the merchandise. This liability can extend backward up to five years from the date of violation or, in the case of fraud, five years from the date of discovery of the violation by U.S. Customs and Border Protection. Under the Customs Modernization Act, the importer is required to use "reasonable care" in determining the value, classification, and admissibility of imported merchandise. We will discuss each of these issues in depth in Chapters 9 and 10. A sample of a reasonable care checklist is shown in Appendix D. See http://www.cbp.gov/document/publications/reasonable-care.

In order to avoid some of these risks, the buyer may decide to insist that the exporter act as the importer of record. This can be done if the exporter establishes a branch office or subsidiary company in the United States, or if the exporter obtains a bond from a surety company incorporated in the United States and the exporter appoints a

Figure 6–3. Customs bond.

DEPARTMENT OF HOMELAND SECURITY U.S. Customs and Border Protection **CUSTOMS BOND** 19 CFR Part 113		

OMB No. 1651-0050 Exp. 12-31-2010

| CBP USE ONLY | BOND NUMBER 1 (Assigned by CBP) |
| | FILE REFERENCE |

In order to secure payment of any duty, tax or charge and compliance with law or regulation as a result of activity covered by any condition referenced below, we, the below named principal(s) and surety(ies), bind ourselves to the United States in the amount or amounts, as set forth below.

Execution Date

SECTION I—Select Single Transaction OR Continuous Bond (not both) and fill in the applicable blank spaces.

☐ SINGLE TRANSACTION BOND — Identification of transaction secured by this bond (e.g., entry no., seizure no., etc.) — Date of transaction — Port code

☐ CONTINUOUS BOND — Effective date — This bond remains in force for one year beginning with the effective date and for each succeeding annual period, or until terminated. This bond constitutes a separate bond for each period in the amounts listed below for liabilities that accrue in each period. The intention to terminate this bond must be conveyed within the period and manner prescribed in the Customs Regulations.

SECTION II— This bond includes the following agreements. 2 (Check one box only, except that, 1a may be checked independently or with 1, and 3a may be checked independently or with 3. Line out all other parts of this section that are not used.

Activity Code	Activity Name and Customs Regulations in which conditions codified	Limit of Liability	Activity Code	Activity Name and Customs Regulations in which conditions codified	Limit of Liability
☐ 1	Importer or broker . . . 113.62		☐ 5	Public Gauger. . . 113.67	
☐ 1a	Drawback Payments Refunds . . . 113.65		☐ 6	Wool & Fur Products Labeling Acts Importation (Single Entry Only) . . . 113.68	
☐ 2	Custodian of bonded merchandise. . . 113.63 (includes bonded carriers, freight forwarders, cartmen and lightermen, all classes of warehouse, container station operators)		☐ 7	Bill of Lading (Single Entry Only) . . . 113.69	
☐ 3	International Carrier. . . 113.64		☐ 8	Detention of Copyrighted Material (Single Entry Only). . . 113.70	
☐ 3a	Instruments of International Traffic . . . 113.66		☐ 9	Neutrality (Single Entry Only) . . . 113.71	
☐ 4	Foreign Trade Zone Operator. . . 113.73		☐ 10	Court Costs for Condemned Goods (Single Entry Only) . . . 113.72	

SECTION III— List below all tradenames or unincorporated divisions that will be permitted to obligate this bond in the principal's name including their CBP identification Number(s). 3 (If more space is needed, use Section III (Continuation) on back of form.)

Importer Number	Importer Name	Importer Number	Importer Name

Total number of importer names listed in Section III:

Principal and surety agree that any charge against the bond under any of the listed names is as though it was made by the principal(s).

Principal and surety agree that they are bound to the same extent as if they executed a separate bond covering each set of conditions incorporated by reference to the Customs Regulations into this bond.

If the surety fails to appoint an agent under Title 6, United States Code, Section 7, surety consents to service on the Clerk of any United States District Court or the U.S. Court of International Trade, where suit is brought on this bond. That clerk is to send notice of the service to the surety at:

Mailing Address Requested by the Surety

PRINCIPAL 4	Name and Address	Importer No. 3 / SIGNATURE 5	SEAL
PRINCIPAL 4	Name and Address	Importer No. 3 / SIGNATURE 5	SEAL
SURETY 4, 6	Name and Address 6	Surety No. 7 / SIGNATURE 5	SEAL
SURETY 4, 6	Name and Address 6	Surety No. 7 / SIGNATURE 5	SEAL
SURETY AGENTS	Name 8	Identification No. 9	Name 8 — Identification No. 9

PART 1 - CBP, PART 2 - SURETY, PART 3 - PRINCIPAL

CBP Form 301 (05/98)

273

Figure 6–3. (*continued*)

Note: Turn carbons over before writing on back of form.

SECTION III (Continuation)			
Importer Number	Importer Name	Importer Number	Importer Name

SIGNED, SEALED, and DELIVERED in the PRESENCE OF:

WITNESSES

Two witnesses are required to authenticate the signature of any person who signs as an individual or partner; however a witness may authenticate the signatures of both such non-corporate principals and sureties. No witness is needed to authenticate the signature of a corporate official or agent who signs for the corporation.

Name and Address of Witness for the Principal	Name and Address of Witness for the Surety
SIGNATURE:	SIGNATURE:
Name and Address of Witness for the Principal	Name and Address of Witness for the Surety
SIGNATURE:	SIGNATURE:

EXPLANATIONS AND FOOTNOTES

1 The CBP Bond Number is a control number assigned by CBP to the bond contract when the bond is approved by an authorized CBP official.

2 For all bond coverage available and the language of the bond conditions refer to Part 113, subpart G, Customs Regulations.

3 The Importer Number is the CBP identification number filed pursuant to section 24.5, Customs Regulations. When the Internal Revenue Service employer identification number is used the two-digit suffix code must be shown.

4 If the principal or surety is a corporation, the name of the State in which incorporated must be shown.

5 See witness requirement above.

6 Surety Name, if a corporation, shall be the company's name as it is spelled in the Surety Companies Annual List published in the Federal Register by the Department of the Treasury (Treasury Department Circular 570).

7 Surety Number is the three digit identification code assigned by CBP to a surety company at the time the surety company initially gives notice to CBP that the company will be writing CBP bonds.

8 Surety Agent is the individual granted a Corporate Surety Power of Attorney, CBP 5297, by the surety company executing the bond.

9 Agent Identification No. shall be the individual's Social Security number as shown on the Corporate Surety Power of Attorney, CBP 5297, filed by the surety granting such power of attorney.

Paperwork Reduction Act Notice: The Paperwork Reduction Act says we must tell you why we are collecting this information, how we will use it, and whether you have to give it to us. We ask for this information to carry out U.S. Customs and Border Protection laws and regulations of the United States. We need it to ensure that persons transacting business with CBP have the proper bond coverage to secure their transactions as required by law and regulation. Your response is required to enter into any transaction in which a bond is a prerequisite under the Tariff Act of 1930, as amended. The estimated average burden associated with this collection of information is 15 minutes per respondent or recordkeeper depending on individual circumstances. Comments concerning the accuracy of this burden estimate and suggestions for reducing this burden should be directed to U.S. Customs and Border Protection, Information Services Branch, Washington, DC 20229, and to the Office of Management and Budget, Paperwork Reduction Project (1651-0050), Washington, DC 20503.

Privacy Act Statement: The following notice is given pursuant to section 7(b) of the Privacy Act of 1974 (5 U.S.C. 552a). Furnishing the information of this form, including the Social Security Number, is mandatory. The primary use of the Social Security Number is to verify, in the CBP Automated System, at the time an agent submits a CBP bond for approval that the individual was granted a Corporate Surety Power of Attorney by the surety company. Section 7 of Act of July 30, 1947, chapter 390, 61 Stat. 646, authorizes the collection of this information.

CBP Form 301 (05/98)(Back)

person in the United States in the state of the port of entry who is authorized to accept service of process in the event of any court action commenced against the exporter. The broker can also act as the importer of record but, because of the potential liability, it will normally seek to relieve itself from this responsibility by asking the importer to sign a Declaration of Consignee, Customs Form 3347A (see Figure 6–4).

4. *Application for Importer's Number*

As a general rule, U.S. Customs and Border Protection will use the importer's Federal Employer Identification Number (FEIN) to track the company's imports or, in the case of an individual importer, her social security number. However, companies without an FEIN that have not previously engaged in importing must file an application for an importer's number with U.S. Customs and Border Protection. (When the importer's name or address changes, it should file an amendment to its application.) A sample application is shown in Figure 6–5. Thereafter, Customs will notify the applicant of its assigned importer's number. This number must be used on many documents that the importer or its broker will file with U.S. Customs and Border Protection on future importations. If the importer is a non-resident company, it will need to file for a Customs Assigned Serial Number and as noted above, have a surety bond and agent for service of process.

5. *Ports of Entry*

The importer should determine what the appropriate ports of entry in the United States should be. If goods are traveling by air or by ship, it will be easy enough to determine their place of arrival. However, where the goods are unloaded is not necessarily the place where customs entry will be made. Goods can be unloaded on the East or West Coast and be transported in-bond to an inland port of entry for the filing of entry documents and release from Customs custody. Because of the congestion that may occur at certain ocean ports, efficient importing may sometimes mandate the use of inland ports. In most instances the negotiated ocean freight rates will dictate where the port of entry is. If an importer is booking transportation from the foreign port of lading through to his location, then the steamship line is responsible for the intermodal transport of the ocean carriage as well as the inland portion of the move. Ocean carriers do this in order to position their empty containers inland for loading them again to be exported. In addition, there are situations where different U.S. Customs offices will treat importations differently. This port shopping is not illegal; however, if an importer has sought a determination of a classification and proper duty for a prospective import at one port, under

Figure 6–4. Owner's declaration.

DEPARTMENT OF HOMELAND SECURITY
U.S. Customs and Border Protection

OMB No. 1651-0093
Exp. 03-31-2012

DECLARATION OF OWNER
FOR MERCHANDISE OBTAINED (OTHERWISE THAN) IN PURSUANCE OF A PURCHASE OR AGREEMENT TO PURCHASE
19 CFR 24.11(a)(1), 141.20

This declaration must be presented at the port of entry within 90 days after the date of entry in order to comply with Section 485(d), of the Tariff Act of 1930. **LINE OUT EACH PHRASE SHOWN IN ITALICS NOT APPLICABLE TO THIS DECLARATION.**

1. NAME OF OWNER	2. ADDRESS OF OWNER (STREET, CITY, STATE, ZIP CODE)	3. SUPERSEDING BOND SURETY CODE

4. PORT OF ENTRY	5. PORT CODE	6. IMPORTER NUMBER OF AUTHORIZED AGENT (SHOW HYPHENS)	7. VESSEL/CARRIER ARRIVED FROM

8. IMPORTER NUMBER OF OWNER (SHOW HYPHENS)	9. ENTRY NUMBER	10. DATE OF ENTRY	11. DATE OF ARRIVAL

I, the undersigned, representing the above named owner in the capacity indicated herein, declare that they are the actual owners for CBP purposes of the merchandise covered by the entry identified in Blocks 9 and 10 above, and that they will pay all additional and increased duties thereon pursuant to Section 485(d), of the Tariff Act of 1930, and that such entry exhibits a full and complete account of all the merchandise imported by them in the vessel identified in the entry and obtained by them (otherwise than) in pursuance of a purchase, or an agreement to purchase, except as listed in columns 20-26 below.

I also declare to the best of my knowledge and belief that all statements appearing in the entry and in the invoice or invoices and other documents presented therewith and in accordance with which the entry was made, are true and correct in every respect; that the entry and invoices set forth the true prices, values, quantities, and all information as required by the law and the regulations made in pursuance thereof; that the invoices and other documents are in the same state as when received; that I have not received and do not know of any other invoice, paper, letter, document, or information showing a different currency, price, value, quantity, or description of the said merchandise; and that if any time hereafter I discover any information showing a different state of facts, I will immediately make the same known to the Port Director of CBP at the port of entry.

I further declare, if the merchandise was entered by means of a seller's or shipper's invoice, that no CBP invoice for any of the merchandise covered by the said seller's or shipper's invoice can be produced due to causes beyond my control, and that if entered by means of a statement of the value or the price paid in the form of an invoice it is because neither seller's, shipper's, nor CBP invoice can be produced at this time.

12. EXCEPTIONS (IF ANY)	13. NOMINAL CONSIGNEE OR AUTHORIZED AGENT FILED BY:

14. I REQUEST THAT:
☐ BILLS, REFUNDS, AND NOTICES OF LIQUIDATION   ☐ BILLS ONLY
☐ CHECKS FOR REFUNDS ONLY   ☐ NOTICES OF LIQUIDATION ONLY
BE ADDRESSED TO ME IN CARE OF THE AUTHORIZED AGENT WHOSE IMPORTER NUMBER IS SHOWN ABOVE.

15. SIGNATURE OF PRINCIPAL MEMBER OF FIRM **X**	16. DATE	17. ADDRESS OF PRINCIPAL MEMBER OF FIRM (STREET, CITY, STATE, ZIP CODE)
18. TITLE		

19. EXECUTE THIS PORTION <u>ONLY IF OWNER DOES NOT HAVE AN IMPORT NUMBER</u> (I.E., HAS NOT FILED CBP FORM **5106**)

IRS EMPLOYER NUMBER OF FIRM OWNER SUFFIX	NAME
OR IF NO EMPLOYER NUMBER: SSN OF INDIVIDUAL OWNER	ADDRESS (STREET, CITY, STATE, ZIP CODE)
OR IF NEITHER OF THE ABOVE NUMBERS: CUSTOMS SERIAL NUMBER	**NOTE:** IF OWNER HAS NO IRS OR SOCIAL SECURITY NUMBER OR A CBP SERIAL NUMBER HAS NOT BEEN PREVIOUSLY ASSIGNED, FILE AN ADDITIONAL COPY OF THIS FORM. THE COPY WILL BE RETURNED TO OWNER WITH A CBP SERIAL NUMBER ASSIGNED. SUCH NUMBER SHALL BE USED BY OWNER IN ALL FUTURE CBP TRANSACTIONS REQUIRING THE IMPORTER NUMBER.

20. NUMBER OF PACKAGES	21. SELLER OR SHIPPER	22. PLACE AND DATE OF INVOICE	23. AMOUNT PAID OR TO BE PAID IN FOREIGN CURRENCY	24. RATE OF EXCHANGE	25. ENTERED VALUE (FOREIGN CURRENCY)	26. ENTERED VALUE (U.S. DOLLARS)

CBP Form 3347 02/14)

Figure 6–4. *(continued)*

Privacy Act Notice: The following information is provided as required by the Privacy Act of 1974 (P.L. 93-579):

1. The disclosure of the social security number on CBP Form 3347 is mandatory.
2. The regulatory authority for requesting the social security number on CBP Form 3347 is 19 CFR 24.5(a).
3. When the importer of record has declared at the time of entry that they are not the actual owner of the merchandise, the social security number shown on CBP Form 3347 will identify the actual owner and establish liability for any increased duties and taxes.

CBP Form 3347 (02/14)

Figure 6–5. Application for importer's number and instructions.

Approved OMB NO. 1651-0064
Exp. 03-31-2014

See back of form for Paperwork Reduction Act Notice.

DEPARTMENT OF HOMELAND SECURITY
U.S. Customs and Border Protection

IMPORTER ID INPUT RECORD
19 CFR 24.5

1. TYPE OF ACTION *(Mark all applicable)*

☐ Notification of importer's number
☐ Change of name*
☐ Change of address*
☐ Check here if you also want your address updated in the Fines, Penalties, and Forfeitures Office

*NOTE--If a continuous bond is on file, a rider must accompany this change document.

2. IMPORTER NUMBER *(Fill in one format).--*

2A. I.R.S. Number

2B. Social Security Number

2C. ☐ Check here if requesting a CBP-assigned number and indicate reason(s). *(Check all that apply.)* ☐ I have no IRS No. ☐ I have no Social Security No. ☐ I have not applied for either number. ☐ I am not a U.S. resident

2D. CBP-Assigned Number

3. Importer Name

4. DIV/AKA/DBA ☐ DIV ☐ AKA ☐ DBA

5. DIV/AKA/DBA Name

6. Type

☐ Corporation ☐ Partnership ☐ Sole Proprietorship ☐ Individual ☐ U.S. Government ☐ State/Local Governments ☐ Foreign Governments

7. Importer Mailing Address (2 32-character lines maximum)

8. City

9. State Code

10. ZIP

11. Country ISO Code *(Non-U.S. Only)*

12. Importer Physical Location Address (2 32-character lines maximum, see instructions)

13. City

14. State Code

15. ZIP

16. Country ISO Code *(Non-U.S. Only)*

17a. Has importer ever been assigned a CBP Importer Number using the same name as in Block 3? ☐ No ☐ Yes *(List number(s) and/or name(s) in Block 17c.)*

17b. Has importer ever been assigned a CBP Importer Number using a name different from that in Block 3? ☐ No ☐ Yes *(List number(s) and/or name(s) in Block 17c.)*

17c. If "Yes" to 17a and/or 17b, list number(s) and/or name(s)

I CERTIFY: That the information presented herein is correct; that if my Social Security Number is used it is because I have no IRS Employer Number, that if my CBP assigned number is used it is because I have neither a Social Security Number nor an IRS Employer Number, that if none of these numbers is used, it is because I have none, and my signature constitutes a request for assignment of a number by CBP.

18. Printed or Typed Name and Title

19. Telephone No. Including Area Code

20. Signature

X

21. Date

22. Broker Use Only

Figure 6–5. *(continued)*

PAPERWORK REDUCTION ACT STATEMENT: An agency may not conduct or sponsor an information collection and a person is not required to respond to this information unless it displays a current valid OMB control number and an expiration date. The control number for this collection is 1651-0064. The estimated average time to complete this application is 15 minutes. If you have any comments regarding the burden estimate you can write to U.S. Customs and Border Protection, Office of Regulations and Rulings, 799 9th Street, NW., Washington DC 20229.

PRIVACY ACT STATEMENT: Pursuant to the requirements of Public Law 93-579 (Privacy Act of 1974, notice is hereby given that 19 CFR 24.5 authorizes the disclosure of Social Security numbers (SSN) on the CBP Form 5106. The principal purpose for disclosure of the Social Security number is to assure maintenance of records that have a high degree of usefulness in regulatory investigations or proceedings. The information collected may be provided to those officers and employees of the CBP and any constituent unit of the Department of the Homeland Security who have a need for the records in the performance of their duties. The records may be referred to any department or agency of the federal government upon the request of the head of such department or agency. The authority to collect the SSN is 31 CFR 103.25. The SSN will be used to identify the individuals conducting business with the CBP.

BLOCK 1 - TYPE OF ACTION
Notification of Importer's Number - Check this box if you are a first time importer, using an importer number for the first time, or if you have not engaged in CBP business within the last year.

Change of Name - Check this box if this importer number is on file but there is a change in the name on file.

Change of Address - Check this box if this importer number is on file but there is a change in the address on file.

BLOCK 2 - IMPORTER

2A   -IRS Number - *Complete this block if you are assigned an Internal Revenue Service employer identification number.*

2B   -Social Security Number - *Complete this block if no Internal Revenue Service employer identification number has been assigned. The Social Security number should belong to the principal or owner of the company or the individual who represents the importer of record.*

2C   -Requesting a CBP Assigned Number - *Complete this block if no Internal Revenue Service employer identification number has been assigned, or no Social Security number has been assigned. If this box is checked, all corresponding boxes in 2C must also be marked. PLEASE NOTE. A CBP Assigned Number is for CBP use **only** and does not replace a Social Security number or Internal Revenue Service employer identification number. In general, a CBP Assigned Number will only be issued to foreign businesses or individuals, provided no IRS or Social Security number exists for the applicant. If Block 2C is completed, this form must be submitted in duplicate. CBP will issue an Assigned Number and return a copy of the completed form with the Assigned Number to the requester. This identification number will be used for all future CBP transactions when an importer number is required. If an Internal Revenue Service employer identification number and/or a Social Security number are obtained after an importer number has been assigned by CBP; the importer will continue to use the assigned number unless otherwise instructed.*

2D   -CBP Assigned Number - *Complete this block if you are assigned a CBP Assigned Number but there is an Action change (Block 1).*

BLOCK 3 - IMPORTER NAME
If the name is an individual, input the last name first, first name, and middle initial. Business names should be input first name first.

BLOCK 4 - DIV/AKA/DBA
Complete this block if an importer is a division of another company (DIV), is also known under another name (AKA), or conducts business under another name (DBA).

BLOCK 5 - DIV/AKA/DBA NAME
Complete this block only if Block 4 is used.

BLOCK 6 - TYPE OF COMPANY
Check applicable box. *Please Note:* Place an "X" after U.S. Gov't **only** for a U.S. federal government department, agency, bureau or office. All federal agencies are assigned I.R.S. numbers which should be used for any CBP transactions by that agency.

BLOCK 7 - IMPORTER MAILING ADDRESS
This block must always be completed. It may or may not be the importer's business address. Insert a post office box number, or a street number representing the first line of the importer's mailing address (up to 32 characters). For a U.S. or Canadian mailing address, additional mailing address information may be inserted (up to 32 characters). If a P.O. box number is given for the mailing address, a second address (physical location) must be provided in Block 12.

BLOCK 8 - CITY
Insert the city name of the importees mailing address.

BLOCK 9 - STATE
For a U.S. mailing address, insert a valid 2-position alphabetic U.S. state postal code (see list below). For a Canadian mailing address, insert a 2-character alphabetic code representing the province of the importer's mailing address (see list below).

BLOCK 10 - ZIP CODE
For a U.S. mailing address, insert a 5 or 9 digit numeric ZIP code as established by the U.S. Postal Service. For a Canadian mailing address, insert a Canadian postal routing code. For a Mexican mailing address, leave blank. For all other foreign mailing addresses, a postal routing code may be inserted.

BLOCK 11 -COUNTRY ISO CODE
For a U.S. mailing address, leave blank. For any foreign mailing address, including Canada and Mexico, insert a 2 character alphabetic International Standards Organization (ISO) code representing the country. Please Note: Valid ISO codes may be found in Annex B of the Harmonized Tariff Schedule of the United States; Customs Directive 099 5610-002, "Standard Guidelines for the Input of Names and Addresses into ACS Files"; or CBP Form 7501 Instructions".

BLOCK 12 - SECOND IMPORTER ADDRESS
If the importer's place of business is the same as the mailing address, leave blank. If different from the mailing address, insert the importer's business address in this space. A second address representing the importer's place of business is to be provided if the mailing address is a post office box or drawer.

BLOCK 13 - CITY
Insert the city name for the importer's business address.

BLOCK 14 - STATE
For a U.S. address, insert a 2 character alphabetic U.S. state postal code (see list below). For a Canadian address, insert a 2 character alphabetic code representing the province of the importer's business address (see list below).

BLOCK 15 - ZIP CODE
For a U.S. business address, insert a 5 or 9 digit numeric ZIP code as established by the U.S. Postal Service. For a Canadian address, insert a Canadian postal routing code. For a Mexican address, leave blank. For all other foreign addresses, postal routing code may be inserted.

BLOCK 16 - COUNTRY ISO CODE
For a U.S. address, leave blank. For any foreign address, including Canada and Mexico, insert a 2 character alphabetic ISO code representing the country.

BLOCK 17 - PREVIOUSLY ASSIGNED CUSTOMS IMPORTER NUMBER
Indicate whether or not importer has previously been assigned a CBP Importer Number under the same name or a different name. If "Yes" to either question, list name(s) and/or number(s) in Block 17c.

OFFICIAL UNITED STATES POSTAL SERVICE TWO-LETTER STATE AND POSSESSION ABBREVIATIONS

AL	Alabama	MT	Montana
AK	Alaska	NE	Nebraska
AZ	Arizona	NV	Nevada
AR	Arkansas	NH	New Hampshire
AS	American Samoa	NJ	New Jersey
CA	California	NM	New Mexico
CO	Colorado	NY	New York
CT	Connecticut	NC	North Carolina
DE	Delaware	ND	North Dakota
DC	Distric of Columbia	MP	Northern Mariana Islands
FM	Federated States of Micronesia	OH	Ohio
FL	Florida	OK	Oklahoma
GA	Georgia	OR	Oregon
GU	Guam	PW	Palau
HI	Hawaii	PA	Pennsylvania
ID	Idaho	PR	Puerto Rico
IL	Illinios	RI	Rhode Island
IN	Indiana	SC	South Carolina
IA	Iowa	SD	South Dakota
KS	Kansas	TN	Tennessee
KY	Kentucky	TX	Texas
LA	Louisiana	UT	Utah
ME	Maine	VT	Vermont
MH	Marshall Islands	VA	Virginia
MD	Maryland	VI	Virgin Islands
MA	Massachusetts	WA	Washington
MI	Michigan	WV	West Virginia
MN	Minnesota	WI	Wisconsin
MS	Mississippi	WY	Wyoming
MO	Missouri		

OFFICIAL TWO-LETTER CANADIAN PROVINCE CODES

AB	Alberta	NS	Nova Scotia
BC	British Columbia	ON	Ontario
MB	Manitoba	PE	Prince Edward Island
NB	New Brunswick	QC	Quebec
NL	Newfoundland (Incl. Labrador)	SK	Saskatchewan
NT	Northwest Territories	YT	Yukon Territory

CBP Form 5106 (05/13)

new Customs regulations, the importer must disclose its inquiry and answer to any other port where it may enter merchandise. Customs is working hard to eliminate potential port shopping by creating Centers for Excellence and Expertise (CEEs). The CEEs are comprised of import specialists dedicated to handling certain types of commodities, and while they may be located throughout different ports, their goal is to ensure that the commodities are handled the same and that one importer will not be receiving multiple requests for information from multiple ports of entry. This will eliminate port shopping and ensure consistency across the United States. Finally, in some cases, such as the importation of goods subject to U.S. Department of Agriculture or Fish and Wildlife requirements, entry is permitted only at certain designated ports of entry.

6. Import Quotas

Through legislation, enacted as often as yearly, the U.S. Congress imposes quotas on different types of imported merchandise. Quotas may be worldwide or related to specific countries. Some quotas are absolute; that is, once a specific quantity has been entered into the United States, no further imports are permitted.

Most quotas are tariff-rate quotas, meaning that a certain quantity of the merchandise is entered at one duty rate, and once that quantity has been exceeded, for the United States as a whole, not for the specific importer, the tariff duty rate increases. Thus, the importer can continue to import, but it will have to pay a much higher tariff duty. Additionally, there are specific tariff-rate quotas for products under the jurisdiction of the U.S. Department of Agriculture, which require the importer to have an import license. With a license, the importer may import at a lower duty rate; without a license, the importer may still import the product, but it must pay a higher duty rate.

Examples of the Department of Agriculture quotas are certain butters, sour creams, dried milks or creams, butter substitutes, blue-molded cheese, cheddar cheese (except Canadian cheddar), American-type cheese, Edam and Gouda cheeses, Italian-type cheeses, Swiss or Emmentaler cheese, and cheese substitutes.

Under the NAFTA agreement, there are also specific tariff-rate quotas for products imported from Mexico, including certain dried milks and creams, condensed and evaporated milks and creams, cheese, tomatoes, onions and shallots, eggplants, chili peppers, watermelons, peanuts, sugars derived from sugarcane or sugar beets, orange juice, cotton, and brooms. Imports of some products from both Canada and Mexico are subject to tariff-rate quotas, such as certain cotton, man-made fiber, or wool apparel and cotton or man-made fiber fabrics and yarns. Other Free Trade Agreements also may have specific tariff-rate quotas depending on the country and the products that may pose potential harm to US origin products.

Following the Uruguay Round negotiations of the General Agreement on Tariffs and Trade (GATT), specific tariff-rate quotas on certain products were also implemented.

These quotas include beef, milk and cream, dried milk and cream, dairy products, condensed or evaporated milk and cream, dried whey, Canadian cheddar cheese, peanuts, sugar (including sugarcane), certain articles containing sugar, blended syrups, cocoa powder, chocolate, chocolate crumb, infant formula, mixes and dough, peanut butter and paste, mixed condiments and seasonings, ice cream, animal feed, cotton, card strips made from cotton, and fibers of cotton.

Finally, so as not to harm U.S. farm production, there are tariff-rate preferences for certain vegetables and fresh produce when entered during the peak growing season in the United States. Importers of produce during peak season will be assessed a lower duty rate. However, in the off season, the tariff classification and associated duty rate are higher.

Before agreeing to purchase products for importation and in planning the cost of the product, the importer must ascertain in advance whether any absolute or tariff-rate quotas exist on the merchandise as it will significantly impact the bottom line. For example, if an importer expects to pay the lower rate of duty for most of the time and then finds out that the quota is full and he has to pay the higher rate of duty.

7. *Antidumping, Countervailing, and Other Special Duties*

Before entering into an agreement to purchase products for importation, the importer should specifically confirm whether those products are subject to an antidumping or countervailing duty order of the U.S. Department of Commerce in conjunction with the International Trade Commission and administered by U.S. Customs and Border Protection through the import entry summary process. When goods are subject to one of these orders, the amount of customs duties (which are payable by the importer) can be much greater than on ordinary importations. While in recent years manufactured items have been subject to a relatively low rate of normal duty (in the range of 3 to 5 percent), cases under these laws exist where duties of as much as 300 percent of the value of the goods have been assessed. Furthermore, U.S. Customs regulations prohibit the reimbursement of the duties to the U.S. importer by the foreign supplier. Where goods are subject to an antidumping or countervailing duty order, the importer will be required to sign a certificate for U.S. Customs and Border Protection under penalty of perjury that it has not entered into any agreement for reimbursement of such duties by the supplier or anyone else. When an importer is negotiating the price for purchase from the foreign supplier, it is important for the importer to ascertain the price at which the foreign supplier is selling in its own country and for export to third countries. This will help the importer determine whether there is a risk that an antidumping investigation can be initiated in the future on the imports of the product being purchased.

Furthermore, if the importer determines that the goods are already subject to an antidumping order, it can take certain steps, such as insisting that the exporter act as the importer of record or substantially transforming the merchandise in a third country, to reduce or eliminate the dumping risks. This is one of those areas that may cause a potential elimination of all profit and even cost the importer more, if he is unaware that there may be antidumping duties assessed on the imported good. The importer should have an attorney research their product against the scope of the antidumping order and prior scope rulings to see if there is an exception in place or if they wish to file for an exception. If an importer files for an exception the petitioners in the anti-dumping case will have the ability to present their arguments as to why the product should be included within if the scope before a final determination is made. This area of the Customs laws is extremely involved and requires care if an importer's product may become subject to antidumping duties. There are a number of ways to lower the antidumping or countervailing duty rate, but they may require cooperation with a company's foreign suppliers to provide detailed information regarding manufacturing pricing. If an importer wants to investigate these options they should look to those specialized attorneys only.

8.   *Classification*

Before importing and during the time that the importer is trying to calculate the potential duties payable on the imported product, it will be necessary for the importer to ascertain the correct customs classification for the product. Under the Customs Modernization Act, an importer must use "reasonable care" in classifying the product. As of January 1, 1989, the United States became a party to the Harmonized Tariff System (HTS), a new commodity classification system that has been adopted in one hundred and thirty-five countries. This is an attempt to standardize among those countries a common classification system for all merchandise. The HTS classification system is extensive. A copy of the table of contents of the HTS, the General Rules of Interpretation used to classify merchandise, the symbols for special tariff reduction programs, and a sample page relating to women's coats are included in Appendix E. All merchandise is classified in some provision of this tariff system, including a catch-all provision for items not elsewhere specified. Only by identifying the appropriate classification in the HTS can the importer ascertain the duty that will be payable on the imported product. Sometimes, in order to attempt to classify the merchandise, the importer will have to obtain information from the exporter—for example, which material constitutes the chief value when the goods are classified by component material. This issue is discussed in detail in Chapter 9.

9.   *Valuation*

When the importer imports merchandise, it is generally required to state a value for the merchandise on the documents filed with U.S. Customs and Border Protection, and the seller will be required to furnish the buyer with a commercial invoice evidencing the sales price. Under the Customs Modernization Act, an importer must use "reasonable care" in determining the value of the merchandise. Even when the item is duty-free, for U.S. import balance of payments statistical purposes, the Department of Commerce, through U.S. Customs and Border Protection, wants to know the value of the merchandise. Where the goods are dutiable at an ad valorem duty, that is, a percentage of the value, obviously it makes a great deal of difference whether the value is $100 or $100,000. In general, the value will be the price of the merchandise paid or payable by the importer/buyer to the exporter/seller. This is known as the transaction value. The transaction value has a number of items that must be added if not already included in the price. In addition, there are some items that may be subtracted from the price if included. A detailed discussion of value is in Chapter 10. One area of concern occurs when the buyer and the seller are related parties. The assumption is that the relationship influenced the price and so Customs requires that the importer provide evidence that the price is that of an arms-length price or uses other methods of determining valuations, such as the transaction value of identical or similar merchandise, the deductive value, or the computed value. When Customs determines that one of these alternative valuation methods is required, the importer can often be surprised by a retroactive increase in customs duties that can substantially and adversely affect the importer.

Where the purchase is in a foreign currency, Customs requires the price to be converted to U.S. dollars for valuation of the merchandise on the date of export, even though the date of payment will probably be different. Customs uses quarterly exchange rates based on the average of the exchange rates for that particular country during the first three business days of the quarter. Should the daily exchange rate vary by 5 percent from the quarterly rate, Customs will switch to the daily rate based on the date of export. See additional information of valuation in Chapter 10.

10. Duty-Free and Reduced Duty Programs

Before importing, the importer should ascertain whether or not the product is eligible for one of the special duty-free or reduced duty programs that Congress has allowed.

The largest program is known as the Generalized System of Preferences (GSP). This program was designed to encourage the economic development of less-developed countries by permitting the importation of those countries' products duty-free. The HTS contains a list of the approximately 101 countries eligible for this program. (See Chapter 11.) The fact that a product will be imported from one of the GSP beneficiary countries, however, does not guarantee duty-free treatment. Some specific products even from eligible countries have been excluded, and it is necessary for the importer to identify whether the particular product is on the exclusion list. In addition, at least 35 percent of the final appraised value must be added in that country. The importer must claim the duty-free status by putting an "A" in the Entry Summary and, if requested by Customs, obtaining evidence from the supplier that the goods meet the criteria. This program has frequently expired and required Congressional renewal. Meanwhile importers must pay the duties but declare that the goods are eligible for free duty treatment. When Congress renews the program, Customs automatically issues refunds on those entries. However, the retroactive refunds are not guaranteed and Congress has been more aggressive about not applying retroactive application in the future.

For imports from the twenty-four countries located in the Caribbean Basin, a similar duty-free program is available. Similar programs are available for imports from Israel under the Israel Free Trade Agreement; imports from Jordan under the Jordan Free Trade Agreement; and imports under the African Growth and Opportunity Act. Some of the programs allow 15 percent U.S.-origin content to be calculated into the 35 percent origin criteria for preferential duty purposes.

Under the North American Free Trade Agreement, implemented on January 1, 1994, products of Canadian and Mexican origin can be imported duty-free to the United States if various requirements are met. Usually, this means that the product must be of Canadian or Mexican origin under one of six eligibility rules and the exporter must provide the importer with a certificate of origin (see Figure 11-1). Many items were granted duty-free status immediately, but other items had their duties reduced over a fifteen-year phase-out period. All eligible items are now duty-free. Thus, if the importer can comply with the requirements, the duty will be less than on ordinary imports from Canada or Mexico.

Recently the United States has entered into numerous free trade agreements that very similar to the NAFTA with phases in reductions of duties and origin requirements.

See more information regarding the country of origin and the associated free trade benefits in Chapter 11.

11. Column 2 Imports

The HTS presently classifies imports according to their source. Products coming from nations that are members of the General Agreement on Tariffs and Trade (GATT) are entitled to be imported at the lowest duty rates ("Normal Tariff Rate [NTR]"— generally 0 to 10 percent). Products from Cuba and North Korea are assessed duties at much higher rates, in the range of 20 to 110 percent. However, importations from certain countries—Cuba, Iran, North Korea, Sudan, and Syria—are prohibited without a license from the Office of Foreign Assets Control, Department of Treasury.

12. Deferred Duty Programs (Bonded Warehousing and Foreign Trade Zones)

An importer may wish to plan its importations in a manner that defers the payment of duties. Two possible programs exist for this purpose. The first is bonded warehouse importations. Importers can apply for and obtain authorization from U.S. Customs and Border Protection to establish a bonded warehouse on their own premises, or they can utilize the services of a public warehouse that has received similar Customs authorization. When such authorization has been received, goods can be imported and placed in such warehouses, to be withdrawn for use or consumption at a later date (up to five years) with a warehouse entry. In the meantime, no customs duties are payable. When the goods are withdrawn for consumption, the goods will be dutiable at the value at the time of withdrawal rather than the time of entry into the warehouse. A bond must be secured to prevent loss of duties in case the merchandise is accidentally or intentionally released into U.S. commerce. The importer can manipulate, mark, relabel, repackage, and perform a number of other operations (except manufacturing) on the merchandise. (See Figure 6-6.) A warehouse entry and a withdrawal form are filed with Customs by the importer's customs broker using the regular Entry Summary form and changing the designated code. (See Chapter 8, Section L.) Where the importer wants to designate a portion its own warehouse as a bonded facility, it must make application to do so and there are specific requirements which must be met to comply, including secured locked space, limited access, record-keeping requirements, etc.

Merchandise may not be withdrawn from the warehouse until the duties have been paid and Customs will perform audits and may issue penalties for failure to comply with the requirements.

Figure 6–6. Bonded warehouse manipulation form.

DEPARTMENT OF HOMELAND SECURITY
U.S. Customs and Border Protection

APPLICATION AND APPROVAL
TO MANIPULATE, EXAMINE, SAMPLE OR TRANSFER GOODS
19 CFR 19.8, 19.11, 158.43

Form Approved
OMB No. 1651-0006
Exp. 02-28-2015

1. GOODS CONSIGNED TO *(Name)*	2. GOODS EXPORTED FROM	3. PORT/PORT CODE AND DATE OF APPLICATION
4. LOCATION OF GOODS	5. CARRIER OR SHIP *(Name)*	6. BILL OF LADING OR CBP 7512 NO.
7. IS AREA BONDED? ☐ YES ☐ NO	8. ENTRY INFORMATION ☐ Warehouse ☐ Consumption	Number: _____ Date:

PERMISSION IS REQUESTED TO: (Describe the complete operation to be performed under CBP supervision on the goods listed below):

		FOR CBP USE ONLY
9. MARKS AND NUMBERS	10. DESCRIPTION	11. MANIPULATED VALUE

12. SIGNATURE OF APPLICANT

APPROVED

13. DATE	14. SIGNATURE AND TITLE OF APPROVING CBP OFFICER

See Page 2 of form for Paperwork Reduction Act Notice. Customs and Border Protection Officers Report on Reverse

CBP Form 3499 (10/95)

Figure 6–6. *(continued)*

CUSTOMS AND BORDER PROTECTION OFFICER'S REPORT

		Date:

MANIPULATION COMPLETED AS REQUESTED: When goods are repacked the CBP (warehouse) officer will report hereon the marks and numbers of packages repacked and the marks and numbers of packages and the weights or guage of same after repacking.

(CBP Officer and Title)

PAPERWORK REDUCTION ACT STATEMENT: An agency may not conduct or sponsor an information collection and a person is not required to respond to this information unless it displays a current valid OMB control number and an expiration date. The control number for this collection is 1651-0006. The estimated average time to complete this application is 6 minutes. If you have any comments regarding the burden estimate you can write to U.S. Customs and Border Protection, Office of Regulations and Rulings, 799 9th Street, NW., Washington DC 20229.

CBP Form 3499 (10/95)

The second program for the deferral of duties is the use of a foreign trade zone. Foreign trade zones are operations authorized by the U.S. Foreign Trade Zones Board and are operated on a charge basis for importers using them. In authorized locations, importers may place imported merchandise for manipulation, and, more importantly, actual manufacturing operations can occur there. (Further manufacturing is not permitted in bonded warehouse operations.) The merchandise can then be entered for consumption in the United States or exported. While the merchandise is in the foreign trade zone (there is no time limit), no duty is payable, and if the merchandise is exported, no U.S. duties will be paid at all. A number of importers have established very foreign trade zone operations on their own premises, called subzones, and customs duties are reduced by importing components and raw materials and finishing them into final products in the subzone. The final product is then entered into the United States at the classification and duty rate applicable to the final product, which is often lower than that for the raw materials and components. The importer may also export from the zone without the payment of duties at all. Another advantage for the use of a foreign trade zone is the weekly entry summary. An importer may withdraw numerous products from the zone for entry into the commerce of the United States and file one entry for the week. This consolidates the payments of the Merchandise Processing Fee and takes advantage of paying the maximum amount of $485 once instead of paying an amount that may be higher than that with each withdrawal. There are applications to a Foreign Trade Zone board in the area and a number of requirements for implementation that must be filed with the Foreign Trade Zone board in addition to the Customs requirements. Other agency requirements, such as Food and Drug requirements, are not waived at the time of importation for entry into foreign trade zones. Again there are specialists in Foreign Trade Zone applications and administration, so it is important to work with knowledgeable experts in the field.

The establishment of bonded warehousing and foreign trade zone operations requires significant lead time and record-keeping, and the importer should take this into account in its preimportation planning. (Samples of applications to Customs in order to admit merchandise to a foreign trade zone and to perform activities there are shown in Figures 6-7 and 6-8.)

Customs regulations specify that certain types of products must be marked in certain ways, such as die-stamping, cast-in-the-mold lettering, or etching, during the manufacturing process. The importer should check the country of origin regulations prior to purchasing products to ascertain whether or not it must advise the supplier or seller of any special marking methods prior to the manufacture of the products. Sometimes off-the-shelf inventory manufactured in a foreign country cannot be modified

Figure 6–7. Application for Foreign Trade Zone Admission.

CENSUS USE ONLY	DEPARTMENT OF HOMELAND SECURITY U.S. Customs and Border Protection **APPLICATION FOR FOREIGN-TRADE ZONE ADMISSION AND/OR STATUS DESIGNATION** 19 CFR 146.22, 146.32, 146.35-146.37, 146.39-146.41, 146.44, 146.53, 146.66	Approved OMB No. 1651-0029 Exp. 06/30/2015

1. ZONE NO. AND LOCATION *(Address)*

2. PORT CODE

3. IMPORTING VESSEL (& FLAG)/OTHER CARRIER	4. EXPORT DATE	5. IMPORT DATE	6. ZONE ADMISSION NO.
7. U.S. PORT OF UNLADING	8. FOREIGN PORT OF LADING	9. BILL OF LADING/AWB NO.	10. INWARD M'FEST NO.
11. INBOND CARRIER	12. I.T. NO. AND DATE	13. I.T. FROM *(Port)*	

14. STATISTICAL INFORMATION FURNISHED DIRECTLY TO BUREAU OF CENSUS BY APPLICANT? ☐ YES ☐ NO

15. NO. OF PACKAGES AND COUNTRY OF ORIGIN CODE	16. DESCRIPTION OF MERCHANDISE	17. HTSUS NO.	18. QUANTITY (HTSUS)	19. GROSS WEIGHT	20. SEPARATE VALUE & AGGR CHGS.

21. HARBOR MAINTENANCE FEE (19 CFR 24.24) ▶

22. I hereby apply for admission of the above merchandise into the Foreign-Trade Zone. I declare to the best of my knowledge and belief that the above merchandise is not prohibited entry in the Foreign-Trade Zone within the meaning of section 3 of the Foreign-Trade Zones Act of 1934, as amended, and section 146.31, Customs Regulations.

23. I hereby apply for the status designation indicated:
☐ NONPRIVILEGED FOREIGN (19 CFR 146.42) ☐ PRIVILEGED FOREIGN (19 CFR 146.41) ☐ ZONE RESTRICTED (19 CFR 146.44) ☐ DOMESTIC (19 CFR 146.43)

24. APPLICANT FIRM NAME	25. BY *(Signature)*	26. TITLE	27. DATE

F.T.Z. AGREES TO RECEIVE MERCHANDISE INTO THE ZONE ▶	28. FOR THE F.T.Z. OPERATOR *(Signature)*	29. TITLE	30. DATE

PERMIT	Permission is hereby granted to transfer the above merchandise into the Zone.	31. PORT DIRECTOR OF CBP: BY *(Signature)*	32. TITLE	33. DATE
PERMIT	The above merchandise has been granted the requested status.	34. PORT DIRECTOR OF CBP: BY *(Signature)*	35. TITLE	36. DATE

PERMIT TO TRANSFER	37. The goods described herein are authorized to be transferred: ☐ without exception ☐ except as noted below
	38. CBP OFFICER AT STATION *(Signature)*	39. TITLE	40. STATION	41. DATE
	42. RECEIVED FOR TRANSFER TO ZONE *(Driver's Signature)*	43. CARTMAN	44. CHL NO.	45. DATE

FTZ OPERATOR'S REPORT OF MERCHANDISE RECEIVED AT ZONE	46. To the Port Director of CBP: The above merchandise was received at the Zone on the date shown except as noted below:
	47. FOR THE FTZ OPERATOR *(Signature)*	48. TITLE	49. DATE

(See page 2 for Paperwork Reduction Act Notice.)   *Previous Editions are Obsolete*   CBP Form 214 (11/09)

Figure 6–7. (*continued*)

Paperwork Reduction Act Statement: An agency may not conduct or sponsor an information collection and a person is not required to respond to this information unless it displays a current valid OMB control number and an expiration date. The control number for this collection is 1651-0029. The estimated average time to complete this application is 15 minutes. If you have any comments regarding the burden estimate you can write to U.S. Customs and Border Protection, Office of Regulations and Rulings, 799 9th Street, NW., Washington DC 20229.

CBP Form 214 (11/09)

Figure 6–8. Application for Foreign Trade Zone Activity Permit.

Approved through OMB No. 1651-0029 Exp. 01-31-2010

DEPARTMENT OF HOMELAND SECURITY U.S.Customs and Border Protection **APPLICATION FOR FOREIGN-TRADE ZONE ACTIVITY PERMIT** 19 CFR 146.52, 146.66	1. ZONE NO. AND LOCATION *(Address)*

2. ZONE ADMISSION NO.	3. APPLICATION DATE -

4. TYPE OF ACTIVITY FOR WHICH PERMIT REQUESTED

☐ Manipulate ☐ Manufacture ☐ Exhibit ☐ Destroy ☐ Temporary Removal

5. FULL DESCRIPTION OF THE ACTIVITY *(Include designation of the exact place in zone where the operation is to be performed and, in the case of a proposed manipulation or manufacture, a statement as to whether merchandise with one zone status is to be packed, commingled, or combined with merchandise having different zone status. If additional space required, attach separate sheet. If first application for manufacturing of this kind, state whether Foreign-Trade Zones board has occurred in proposed operation.)*

6. ZONE LOT NO. OR UNIQUE IDENTIFIER	7. MARKS AND NUMBERS	8. DESCRIPTION OF MERCHANDISE	9. QUANTITY	10. WEIGHTS, MEASURES	11. ZONE STATUS

If any merchandise is to be manipulated in any way or manufactured, I agree to maintain the records provided for in sections 146.21(a), 146.23, and 146.52(d) of the Customs Regulations and to make them available to CBP officers for inspection.

12. APPLICANT FIRM NAME	13. BY *(Signature)*	14. TITLE
APPROVED BY FOREIGN-TRADE ZONE OPERATOR ➤	15. BY *(Signature)*	16. TITLE

PERMIT

The application made above is hereby approved and permission is granted to manipulate, manufacture, exhibit, destroy, or temporarily removed, as requested, on condition that the applicable regulations are complied with and the records required to be maintained will be available for inspection.

17. PORT DIRECTOR OF CBP: By *(Signature)*	18. TITLE	19. DATE

FTZ OPERATOR'S

20. TO THE PORT DIRECTOR OF CBP:

I certify that the goods described herein have been disposed of as directed except as noted below.

21. FOR THE FTZ OPERATOR: *(Signature)*	22. TITLE	23. DATE

CBP Form 216 (01/01)

Figure 6–9. Application for Exportation of Articles Under Special Bond.

after manufacture to comply with the U.S. country of origin marking requirements. Merchandise that is not properly marked may be seized by U.S. Customs and Border Protection. In some cases, the products can be marked after such seizure, but only upon payment of a marking penalty of 10 percent, which increases the cost of importing the products. More seriously, sometimes Customs will release the merchandise to the importer, and the importer may resell it. Then, Customs may issue a notice of redelivery of the products (see Figure 6–10). If the importer is unable to redeliver the products, a substantial customs penalty may be payable. The marking must remain on the product (including after any repacking) until it reaches the ultimate purchaser, which is usually the retail customer. Recently, penalties for any intentional removal of markings were raised to a $100,000 fine and/or imprisonment for one year. See Chapter 11 for more information on country of origin requirements.

13. Record-Keeping Requirements

Under the U.S. Customs regulations, importers are required to keep copies of all documents relating to their importations for a period of five years. In the event of any question, Customs has the right to inspect such records (on reasonable advance notice) to ascertain that the importer has complied with U.S. customs laws. Prior to engaging in importing, the importer should establish record retention policies and procedures; this will ensure that the relevant records are kept for the appropriate period of time. (See the fuller discussion of this issue in Chapter 1, Section E.) There are penalties of $10,000 per document for failing to have a Customs document if requested by Customs and the penalties can go up to $100,000 for will omission of a required document. In this era, most documentation is never submitted to Customs, but this does not relieve the importer from keeping them if requested by Customs.

14. Customs Rulings

Where the importer has questions about the proper application of the customs laws, it may be necessary for the importer to seek a ruling from U.S. Customs and Border Protection. Without such rulings, the importer may take the risk that it is violating customs laws. For example, rulings may be requested relating to the proper classification of merchandise, the proper valuation of merchandise, whether merchandise qualifies for a duty-free or deferred duty treatment, or the proper country of origin marking. As a general rule, classification rulings are issued within approximately 30 days, but more complicated rulings may take from several months to one year. In the event of a

Figure 6–10. Notice of redelivery.

1. FROM	DEPARTMENT OF THE TREASURY

DEPARTMENT OF THE TREASURY
UNITED STATES CUSTOMS SERVICE

NOTICE TO MARK
AND/OR
NOTICE TO REDELIVER

19 CFR 134.51, 134.52, 141.113

2. NAME OF CONTACT PERSON

3. TELEPHONE NO.

SECTION I (To Be Completed By Customs)

4. TO *(Importer of Record Name and Address):*

ENTRY DATA

5. PORT OF ENTRY

6. ENTRY NO.

7. DATE OF ENTRY

8. BROKER OR IMPORTER FILE NO.

The merchandise described below is in violation of statutes(s)/regulation(s) as indicated, and cannot be entered into the commerce of the U.S. until brought into conformity as noted below in Section II. If it is not brought into conformity, redelivered, exported, or destroyed under Customs supervision within 30 days from the date of this Notice or the time specified by another Government agency having jurisdiction over the importation, **liquidated damages and/or criminal/civil penalties shall apply.**

9. STATUTE(S)/REGULATION(S) VIOLATED

☐ 19 U.S.C. 1304 (Section 304, Tariff Act of 1930) (Country of Origin Marking Violation)   ☐ Other, Namely:

10. DESCRIPTION OF MERCHANDISE	11. QUANTITY	12. IDENTIFYING MARKS AND NUMBERS	13. SHIPPER/MANUFACTURER

SECTION II (To Be Completed By Customs)

14. ACTION REQUIRED OF IMPORTER

☐ Merchandise must be brought into compliance as specified below or returned to Customs custody within 30 days of this Notice or other time specified.

☐ Marking or other corrective action must be done under Customs supervision.

☐ Customs supervision of marking or other corrective action not required. After all merchandise has been brought into conformity with cited statute(s)/regulation(s), complete the certification below and return copy to Customs ☐ with ☐ without a sample. **WARNING: All merchandise must be retained until you are notified by Customs that corrective action is acceptable.**

☐ Merchandise must be redelivered to Customs within 30 days from date of this notice or other time specified.

15. REMARKS/INSTRUCTIONS/OTHER ACTION REQUIRED OF IMPORTER

16. SIGNATURE OF CUSTOMS OFFICER

17. DATE

SECTION III — IMPORTER CERTIFICATION *(To Be Completed By Importer/Authorized Agent)*
IMPORTER:— APPROPRIATE ITEMS MUST BE COMPLETED, SIGNED, AND DATED BEFORE ACCEPTANCE BY CUSTOMS.

☐ Merchandise to be ☐ exported. ☐ destroyed under Customs supervision in lieu of marking or other required corrective measures.

I certify that all merchandise has been marked to indicate the country of origin as required by 19 U.S.C. 1304, or otherwise brought into compliance with cited statute(s) or regulation(s). Sample ☐ is ☐ is not submitted herein. Merchandise and original containers being held intact and available for Customs inspection at: *(Indicate Place and Phone No.)*

PLACE   DATE   TIME

I (We) guarantee the payment of all expenses incident to the above action.

SIGNATURE OF IMPORTER OR AUTHORIZED AGENT	TITLE	TELEPHONE	DATE
X			

SECTION IV (To Be Completed By Customs)

☐ Merchandise excepted from marking under

☐ Merchandise has been legally marked or otherwise brought into conformity with cited statute(s)/regulation(s):   ☐ under Customs supervision   ☐ certification accepted.

☐ Merchandise was ☐ exported ☐ destroyed under Customs supervision. ☐ Other, namely:

SIGNATURE OF CUSTOMS OFFICER   DATE

PART 1 - IMPORTER - RETURN TO CUSTOMS   **Customs Form 4647 (121592)**

Figure 6–10. (*continued*)

CUSTOMS FORM 4647 INFORMATION AND INSTRUCTIONS

This form is notification that the imported merchandise is not in conformity with statutory or regulatory requirements and must be marked, labeled, or otherwise brought into conformity with the applicable requirements within 30 days of this notice. The form also serves as a redelivery notice and requires redelivery to Customs custody within the specified time.

The following instructions are provided to assist importers in fulfilling the statutory and regulatory obligations.

SECTIONS I AND II: COMPLETED BY THE CUSTOMS SERVICE.

SECTION III: COMPLETED BY THE IMPORTER OF RECORD OR AUTHORIZED AGENT.

1. Retain control of all merchandise described on the Customs Form 4647. The merchandise must be held intact; it cannot be moved or distributed until authorized by the Customs Service.

2. Marking and/or additional instructions are provided in SECTION II.

3. Upon completion of marking, complete the appropriate item(s). **SIGNATURE MUST BE THAT OF THE IMPORTER OR AUTHORIZED AGENT.**

4. Identify the location where the merchandise will be available for Customs verification and provide a contact telephone number.

5. Upon completion of SECTION III, submit the "Return to Customs" copy of the form with a sample, if requested, to the office specified in SECTION I of this form. NOTE: Appropriate items must be completed, signed, and dated before acceptance by Customs.

SECTION IV: COMPLETED BY THE CUSTOMS SERVICE.

Upon return of the Customs Form 4647, Customs will review the form to ensure that SECTION III has been completed, signed, and dated by the IMPORTER OF RECORD OR AUTHORIZED AGENT, and take one of the following actions:

1. A Customs officer will visit your premises to verify your certification of marking and to notify you whether or not it is acceptable.

2. Notify you (in writing) that (a) the marking or corrective action is acceptable and the merchandise is officially released by Customs; or (b) the marking or corrective action is not acceptable and that the merchandise must be redelivered to Customs custody within the prescribed time.

If you have any questions or find that the marking procedure or other corrective action requires more than 30 days, contact the office indicated in SECTION I.

Customs Form 4647 (121592)(Back)

substantial volume of planned importations and significant ambiguity regarding the appropriate method of compliance, a ruling may be advisable, and enough lead time to obtain the ruling must be allowed. Certain rulings can be filed electronically with CBP. See https://apps.cbp.gov/erulings/index.asp.

G. Import Packing and Labeling

Prior to the exportation of the purchased products, the importer should ascertain the type of packaging and labeling that the exporter will use. Different packaging is often required to withstand the rigors of international transportation and to ensure that the importer is going to receive the products in an undamaged condition. Generally, container transportation will protect best against damage and pilferage. Certain types of containers may be needed, such as ventilated, refrigerated, flat, open top, or high-cube. If the merchandise is a hazardous material, it cannot be transported unless it complies with the International Maritime Dangerous Goods Code or the International Air Transportation Association Dangerous Goods regulations depending on the mode of transport. In addition, the U.S. Department of Transportation has harmonized the U.S. hazardous materials regulations with the international standards. (Hazardous material is discussed in Chapter 2, Section L.) The packing, labeling, and invoicing requirements for such hazardous materials must be communicated to the seller before shipment. Under the Carriage of Goods by Sea Act, steamship lines are not responsible for damage to cargo that is insufficiently packed. Even with insurance, the importer should make an effort to prevent losses due to improper packing by contractually obligating the supplier to ensure that the goods are packed in a manner to ensure the safety of the article through traditional shipping measures. Identification marks on the packages should be put in the packing list. The buyer should keep in mind that upon arrival, the goods will have to be examined by U.S. Customs and Border Protection. The Buyer should require a detailed packing list, so that if there is a Customs examination it will be easy to determine which boxes contain which items to reduce the costs of the examination by the Container Exam Station operators. As of July 5, 2006, all wood packaging material (WPM), including pallets, crates, boxes, and pieces of wood used to support or brace cargo, must meet the import requirements and be free of timber pests before entering or transiting the United States. WPM must be heat treated or fumigated with methyl bromide and must be marked with an approved international logo according to the *International Standards for Phytosanitary Measures: Guidelines for Regulating Wood Packaging Material in International Trade* (ISPM 15). U.S. Customs and Border Protection will refuse import to any WPM without the appropriate logo. It cannot be brought into compliance after arrival in the United States. It must be exported. Importers of plant and wood products must declare country of harvest beginning in 2009. (See Figure 6–11.)

Similarly, in order to sell or transport some merchandise after its arrival in the United States, it must be labeled in a certain way. Through its own investigation or through consultation with third parties, the importer should determine if any special labeling is required and should notify the exporter of this prior to exportation of the merchandise. For example, the Consumer Product Safety Act; the regulations of the Bureau of Alcohol, Tobacco and Firearms; the Energy Policy Conservation Act; the Food, Drugs, and Cosmetics Act; the Wool Products Labeling Act; the Textile Fiber Products Identification Act; the Hazardous Substances Act; and the Fur Product Labeling Act are some U.S. laws that impose requirements relating to the proper labeling of imported products. Shipments that are not properly labeled may be refused entry. (See Chapter 8, Section P for more information.)

H. U.S. Commercial Considerations

There are several commercial considerations that the importer must take into account.

1. *Prevailing Market Price*

In planning its import purchases, the importer must pay attention to the prevailing market price. Obviously, if raw materials or components can be purchased in the United States at a lower price than they can be purchased abroad, depending upon the source country, importation will not be economically feasible. In purchasing for resale, if the purchase price is not sufficiently low to permit an adequate markup when the product is resold at the prevailing U.S. market price, the importation will not be economic. If the product is resold in the U.S. market below the prevailing market price, competitors may charge that the sales are predatory pricing (sales below fully allocated costs) or dumping (sales below the price at which the same products are sold to customers in the country of origin).

2. *Buy American Policies*

In planning import transactions, the importer should determine if there are any Buy American policies applicable to the resale of the products. In particular, sales to the U.S. federal or state governments or their agencies, there may be certain preferences given to U.S. manufactured products. Sometimes there is a maximum foreign

Figure 6–11. Lacey Act Certification.

According to the Paperwork reduction Act of 1995, an agency may not conduct or sponsor, and a person is not required to respond to, a collection of information unless it displays a valid OMB control number. The valid OMB control number for this information collection is 0579-0349. The time required to complete this information collection is estimated to average 0.5 hours per response, including the time for reviewing instructions, searching existing data sources, gathering and maintaining the data needed, and completing and reviewing the collection of information.

OMB APPROVED
0579-0349
Exp. Date:

Plant and Plant Product Declaration Form

Section 3: Lacey Act Amendment (16 U.S.C. 3372)

APHIS

U.S. DEPARTMENT OF AGRICULTURE
ANIMAL AND PLANT HEALTH INSPECTION SERVICE

SECTION 1 - Shipment Information

1. ESTIMATED DATE OF ARRIVAL: (MM/DD/YYYY)

2. ENTRY NUMBER:

3. CONTAINER NUMBER: ☐ See Attachment

4. BILL OF LADING:

5. MID:

6. IMPORTER NAME:

7. IMPORTER ADDRESS:

8. CONSIGNEE NAME:

9. CONSIGNEE ADDRESS:

10. DESCRIPTION OF MERCHANDISE:

SECTION 2 - Compliance with Lacey Act Requirements (16 U.S.C. 3372(f))

For each article or component of an article, provide the following:

11. HTSUS NUMBER: (no dashes/symbols)	12. ENTERED VALUE:	13. ARTICLE/ COMPONENT OF ARTICLE	14. PLANT SCIENTIFIC NAME: Genus / Species	15. COUNTRY OF HARVEST:	16. QUANTITY OF PLANT MATERIAL:	17. UNIT:	18. PERCENT RECYCLED:
0 0 0 0 0 0 0 0							
0 0 0 0 0 0 0 0							
0 0 0 0 0 0 0 0							
0 0 0 0 0 0 0 0							
0 0 0 0 0 0 0 0							

I certify under penalty of perjury that, to the best of my knowledge and belief, the information furnished is true and correct:

Prepaer's Phone Number and Area Code

Signature

Type or Print Name

Date

Knowingly making a false statement in this Declaration for Importation may subject the declarant to criminal penalties in accordance with 16 U.S.C. 3373(d).

Version 08-15-2011-0856
PPQ FORM 505
AUGUST 2011

Page 1

Figure 6–11. (*continued*)

Version 08-15-2011-0856

1. **Estimated Date of Arrival:** Enter the date (MM/DD/YYYY) that the product is expected to enter the United States of America.

2. **Entry Number:** Enter the U. S. Customs entry number assigned to this shipment. (Format: xxx-xxxxxxx-x)

3. **Container Number:** Enter the number of the shipping container in which the product is being shipped - available from your shipping company. If you have more than container number in your shipment, check the "see attachment" box, and list all of the containers on a separate sheet. Attach the container list to the PPQ 505. If there is no container number, please leave this section blank.

4. **Bill of Lading:** Enter the Bill of Lading (BOL) number assigned to this shipment - available from the shipping company. If there is no Bill of Lading number, please leave this section blank.

5. **MID:** Manufacturer Identification Code - available from the manufacturer or customs broker (19 CFR Appendix to Part 102).

6. **Importer Name:** Enter the name of the import company or individual for the product.

7. **Importer Address:** Enter the address of the import company or individual in #6.

8. **Consignee Name:** Name of the individual or company who ordered and will ultimately receive the shipment.

9. **Consignee Address:** Enter the address of the individual or company in #8.

10. **Description of the Merchandise:** Enter the name of the plant or plant product, and its use (example: wooden spoons for kitchenware). If the use is unknown, enter only the name of the product(example: lumber). If the product is protected under CITES also input CITES permit number here. If product was manufactured prior to the Lacey Act Amendment also input "Manufactured Prior to May 22, 2008".

11. **HTSUS Number:** Enter the Harmonized Tariff Code for the merchandise described in #10 - available at http://www.usitc.gov/tata/hts/.

12. **Entered Value (in U.S. Dollars):** Write the entered value of the imported merchandise described in #10 in U.S. Dollars.

13. **Article/Component of Article:** Enter a brief description of each article, or component of an article, that is manufactured from plants or plant parts. (Example: A decorative item including a wood frame and 100 % recycled paperboard - enter the frame as a line item, and record the percent recycled material in the paperboard in section #18.)

14. **Plant Scientific Name:** For each article/component in #13 enter the scientific name (example: See next page). If the species of plant used to produce the product varies, and the species used to produce the product is unknown, enter each species that may have been used to produce the product. If product was manufactured prior to the Amendment and you cannot determine species, enter "Special" for Genus and "PreAmendment" for Species. The Scientific Name is NOT the trade/common name of the plant.

Page 1

299

Figure 6–11. *(continued)*

Version 08-15-2011-0856

15. **Country of Harvest:** Enter the country where the plant was harvested (example: See below). If the country of harvest varies, and is unknown, enter all countries from which the plant material in the product may have been harvested. This is NOT the country of manufacture/origin.

16. **Quantity of Material:** How much plant material is in the shipment (example: See below).

17. **Unit:** This is the Unit of Measure of the Plant Material. Use the drop down box on the form to enter the units for #17. (example: See below).

 kg - kilograms
 m - meter
 m² - square meters
 m³ - cubic meters

18. **% Recycled Material:** If the product is paper or paperboard, enter the percentage of recycled material it contains (0 - 100%). If the percentage of recycled material varies, enter the average percentage of recycled material used in the product (example: If the percentage of recycled material used is between 25% and 45%, enter 35%).

11. HTSUS Number	12. Entered Value	13. Article/Component of Article	14. Plant Scientific Name		15. Country of Harvest	16. Quantity of Plant Material	17. Unit	18. Percent Recycled
			Genus	Species				
9401692010	1354	Bentwood Seats Made of Oak	Quercus	lineata	Indonesia	500	kg	0
4407950000	8442	European ash lumber (2" x 4")	Fraxinus	excelsior	Switzerland	52	M3	0

Submission of Paper Declaration: Importers should have a copy of the form available for Customs and Border Protection (CBP) to review at the port of entry. After CBP clears the shipment, the importer must mail the original form to the USDA at the following address:

 The Lacey Act
 c/o U.S. Department of Agriculture
 Box 10
 4700 River Road
 Riverdale, MD 20737

Note: You may use Form PPQ 505B should more space be required. Make as many copies as necessary.
 Failure to include any and all of the required information will result in the rejection of your declaration.

SPECIAL NOTE: IF YOU HAVE FILED A LACEY ACT DECLARATION ELECTRONICALLY THROUGH THE CUSTOMS SYSTEM, THERE IS NO NEED TO FILE A PAPER DECLARATION.

Page 2

content limitation or there are price preferences. If the importer expects to make such sales, it may be necessary to determine if the cost savings of the foreign product is sufficient to overcome the potential sales differential under Buy American policies. The proliferation of the various free trade agreements with bilateral provisions for nondiscrimination in government procurement contracts has made the use of foreign-origin materials from those countries acceptable, if the contract meets certain criteria. It is important to clarify the origin of the merchandise under the Buy American Act or the Trade Agreements Act to be certain before entering into a government contract. See more information about these requirements in Chapter 11.

3. U.S. Industry Standards

Merchandise manufactured abroad may not comply with standards adopted by U.S. trade associations or enacted into law, such as local building codes. Prior to agreeing to purchase foreign products, the importer should check any applicable U.S. industry standards to make sure that the products will comply. The importer may need to advise the manufacturer of the appropriate specifications so that the products can be manufactured to meet U.S. industry standards.

I. Terms of Purchase

Although there are ordinarily many terms and conditions that the buyer will include in its import purchase agreements, the terms of purchase upon which seller and buyer must agree is that relating to passage of title, risk of loss, price, and payment. Although a buyer can purchase on different terms of sale from different sellers in accordance with whatever terms are expressed in each seller's quotation or purchase order acceptance, it is ordinarily much better for the buyer to think about and formulate policies relating to its terms of purchase in advance of placing its order. There are a number of considerations, the first of which relates to the use of abbreviations.

In order to standardize the understanding of the seller and buyer relating to their obligations in international purchase agreements, various nomenclatures have been developed that use abbreviations such as *ex-factory, FOB plant, CIF,* and *landed.* While these shorthand abbreviations can be useful, they can also be sources of confusion.

The International Chamber of Commerce developed the "Incoterms®," which were revised in 2010 (see Chapter 2, Figures 2–2 and 2–3). Even though it is assumed that sellers and buyers know the responsibilities and obligations that flow from utilizing specific terms such as *FCA plant,* the parties in fact may not always understand all of their responsibilities in the same way, and disputes and problems may arise. For example, even though on an FCA seller's plant sale, the buyer is responsible for obtaining and paying for ocean insurance, often the buyer will want the seller to obtain such insurance, which the buyer will reimburse the seller for paying. Although from a practical standpoint on imports, the buyer may want insurance obtained through a U.S. insurance provider and determine the level of insurance as a foreign seller may only obtain minimum coverage. Or, even though the buyer may be responsible for paying freight, the buyer may expect the seller to arrange for shipment "freight collect." Finally, under the new Incoterms®, certain traditional terms such as "DAF," "DEQ," "DES" and "DDU," have been abolished and certain new terms such as "DAT" and "DAP" have been created. In the author's experience, even if the parties choose to use an abbreviation to specify the way in which risk will pass, the author strongly recommends that the "who does what" be stated in detail in the purchase agreement to avoid the possibility of a misunderstanding.

It is also important for the buyer to realize that the price term does not dictate where the transfer of title takes place, only where the risk of loss occurs. For example, under an Incoterm® of CFR or CIF, the seller will be quoting a price to the buyer that includes the seller's cost of shipping the merchandise to the destination, but, in actuality, risk of loss will pass to the buyer when the merchandise is loaded on the ship at the time of export. Similarly, in a sales quotation, CIF means only that the price quoted by the seller will include all expenses to the point of destination—it does not mean that payment will be made upon arrival. Payment may be made earlier or later, depending upon the agreement of the parties. Buyers should be sure that their import purchase documentation distinguishes between price terms, title and risk of loss terms, and payment terms. See more on the Incoterms® in Chapter 2, Section M.

Under the new Convention on Contracts for the International Sale of Goods (discussed in Chapter 7, Section B.2.l), if the parties do not agree upon a place for transfer of title and delivery in their sale agreement, title and delivery will transfer when the merchandise is delivered to the first transportation carrier, and payment by the buyer will be due at that time.

In most international transactions, the buyer will be responsible for importing the products to its own country, clearing customs, and paying any applicable customs duties. This is because the importer is liable for all customs duties, even antidumping duties. However, if the seller agrees to sell landed, duty paid, or delivered to the buyer's place of business (so-called "free domicile" or "free house" delivery), the seller will be responsible for such customs duties. Ordinarily, the seller cannot act as the importer of record in the United States unless it obtains a bond from a U.S. surety company and appoints an agent in the United States for all claims for customs duties. Generally, a seller would not want to sell delivered, duty paid, but sometimes the buyer's bargaining leverage is such or competition is such that the seller cannot get the business unless it is willing to do so. Similarly, if the buyer is wary of paying dumping duties, she may insist that the seller act as the importer of record. Another situation is when the buyer is purchasing from a related seller, such as a parent company. In such a case, the parent company may want to sell landed, duty paid and assume such expenses. In most other countries foreign sellers cannot act as the importer for Customs purposes.

In general, if the seller sells ex-factory, it will have the least responsibilities and risks. The buyer will then be responsible for arranging and paying for inland transportation to the port of export, ocean transportation, and U.S. importation. In some cases, an ex-factory purchase can result in the buyer's being able to avoid U.S. customs duties on the inland freight from the seller's factory to the port of export. In such cases, the buyer will have the responsibility for complying with all foreign export laws, such as obtaining export control licenses, export visas, and exchange control licenses; arranging insurance; and complying with foreign laws. In order to ensure that the seller has the responsibility to complete all of these requirements of foreign law, ordinarily the buyer should not buy ex-factory, but FOB port of export, CIF, or landed. If the buyer buys landed, it should discuss with the seller and make sure that the seller understands its responsibilities during the formation of the purchase agreement. If the seller is unable to affect import, the fact that the buyer is not legally responsible will be of little consolation and will lead to lawsuits, nondelivery, and loss of future supply.

Even though purchasing on a landed, delivered duty-paid basis may be attractive to the buyer, there are many reasons why the buyer may need or want to purchase on other terms. For example, the seller may be inexperienced in arranging international shipments, the buyer's competitors may be willing to purchase ex-factory, the buyer may be buying from an affiliated company, or the buyer may have warehouse-to-warehouse marine insurance under a blanket policy and, therefore, by agreeing to pay the insurance costs, can save the seller some money. Sometimes the buyer is in a better position to obtain lower ocean transportation or insurance rates. For all of these reasons, a thorough discussion of the terms and conditions of purchase between the seller and the buyer, rather than simply following a set policy, may be advantageous.

J. Consignments

In addition to purchase transactions, where title to the merchandise transfers to the U.S. buyer in the foreign country or sometime up to delivery in the United States in accordance with the terms of purchase between the parties, in consignment transactions the exporter/seller maintains ownership of the goods and the consignee in the United States takes possession of the goods. The consignee then offers the goods for sale, and when a customer purchases the goods, title transfers from the exporter/seller to the importer/buyer and to the customer simultaneously. Such transactions have various procedural and documentary considerations. As the owner, the exporter/seller will be responsible for all transportation costs, insurance, filing of export declaration, and obtaining foreign export control license. While U.S. Customs regulations may permit the consignee to affect customs clearance, legally the goods are owned by the exporter/seller, and the exporter/seller will be liable for the U.S. customs duties. Additional taxes may be assessed, such as personal property taxes assessed on the goods while they are awaiting sale and income taxes, because title will pass to the importer/buyer at the buyer's place of business in the United States. In addition, to avoid the inability to take possession of the goods in case of bankruptcy of the importer/buyer or other claims by the importer's creditors, special arrangements under the buyer's law, such as public notices or security interests, may be required. Because the export/import transaction is not a sale at the time of entry, transaction value cannot be used—U.S. Customs and Border Protection will assess customs duties based upon an alternative valuation method.

K. Leases

In import transactions that are leases, no purchase documentation should be used, although a commercial "invoice" declaring the names of the parties, the commodity, the quantity, and the value for Customs purposes must be provided at the time of importation. The ability of the exporter/lessor to retain title and ownership, repossess the goods at the end of the lease, and obtain income tax benefits depends upon using lease documentation rather than sales agreements. Similar to the consignment situation, the exporter/seller is legally responsible for all exporting and importing obligations, although those obligations can be delegated to the importer in the lease agreement. For U.S. customs valuation purposes, a lease is not a sale; therefore, transaction value will not be used, and the customs duties payable will depend upon an alternative valuation method. See more on value methodologies in Chapter 10.

L. Marine and Air Casualty Insurance

If the supplier sells ex-works or port of export, the importer will be responsible for the ocean (marine) or air insurance covering the shipment from either the seller's door or the port of export, respectively. The importer should make arrangements for the insurance or make sure that it is properly obtained prior to exportation. Without such insurance, the carriers have limited their liability to the extent that even if the carrier can be proven liable, responsibility is limited to $500 per "package" on ocean shipments and $28 per kilogram on air shipments unless a higher value is disclosed in advance and a higher transportation charge paid to cover those added insurance costs. The importer's letter of credit or payment instructions should require insurance unless the importer already has its own or, under the terms of purchase, the importer has agreed to be responsible for the insurance. Even when the importer believes that the terms of sale are clear, the importer should coordinate with the exporter to avoid a situation in which both the importer and exporter obtain such insurance and the importer is billed twice, or neither party obtains the insurance. Under the CIF and CIP terms of sale, the risk of loss transfers to the buyer/importer at the port of export, but the seller is to purchase insurance in the name of the buyer. It can be minimum coverage purchased in the country of export. Importers may want to purchase their own insurance and bypass the use of those terms in favor of CFR. See more on Incoterms® in Chapter 2. Importers can obtain single shipment insurance or use open cargo policies covering all of their imports during a specific time period. "Warehouse-to-warehouse" and "all risk" rather than "named peril" coverage is best. Even "all risk" coverage does not include war risk or "strike, riot, and civil commotion" coverage, and the buyer must specifically request the added coverage from the insurance company if the buyer desires it. (A sample marine insurance policy and certificate are shown in Figures 4–10 and 4–11, respectively.) For additional information, see Chapter 2, Section P, and Chapter 4, Section H.

M. Method of Transportation; Booking Transportation

When the importer is responsible for the transportation of the merchandise from the foreign country to the United States, the importer will have to make a decision concerning the mode of transportation and arrange for shipment. Transportation may be made by air or by ship. Transportation can be arranged directly with air carriers or steamship companies or through freight forwarders and NVOCCs (see Chapter 4, Section E for more information). Air transportation is obviously much quicker, but is more expensive. Large shipments cannot be shipped by air. In obtaining quotations from various carriers, it is important to record and confirm any such quotations to avoid future increases and discrepancies. When checking with transportation carriers, the name of the person making the quotation, the date, the rate, and the appropriate tariff classification number used by the carrier should be recorded. (Additional information is contained in Chapter 2, Section Q.) Unless the company has a substantial quantity of cargo, it is best to work with a freight forwarding company or NVOCC to obtain more favorable rates or to discuss whether it is advisable to co-load with other companies in the same container to reduce the transportation costs.

N. Import Financing

Some foreign governments offer financing assistance to U.S. importers who are purchasing merchandise from exporters in their countries. Some state government agencies even offer financing to purchase imported components if the finished products will be exported. If the importer intends to utilize any import financing program, the program should be investigated sufficiently in advance of commencing imports. The necessary applications and documentation must be filed and approvals obtained prior to importation of the merchandise.

O. Patent, Trademark, and Copyright Registrations and Infringements

In purchasing foreign products for importation to the United States, the importer should satisfy itself that the products will not infringe the patent, trademark, and/or copyright registration (sometimes called intellectual or industrial property rights) of another person. If the trademark or copyright has been registered with U.S. Customs and Border Protection, entry of the merchandise may be prohibited and the merchandise seized. U.S. Customs has made the enforcement of U.S. trademarks and copyrights as one of its trade enforcement priorities. This means that it is seizing fraudulent imported or in-transit goods in the United States. Once the goods are seized the copyright or trademark owner has the right to determine what should be done with the goods. They might allow the goods to be exported, but more likely they will request removal of the trademark or destruction of the goods. Under the Anti-Counterfeiting Consumer Protection Act of 1996, importing or trading in counterfeit goods is punishable by a fine of up to $1 million.

Even though the foreign manufacturer may have a patent, trademark, or copyright in its own country, unless such patent, trademark, or copyright has been registered in the United States, importation of the product may infringe a valid right of another person. That person may be a U.S. manufacturer or a foreign company that has registered its rights in the United States. Under the new Convention on Contracts for the International Sale of Goods (discussed in Chapter 7, Section B.2.l) and contrary to U.S. law, there is no implied warranty that a foreign-manufactured product will not infringe on U.S. intellectual property rights as long as the foreign seller was not aware of an infringement. The importer should initiate a patent, trademark, or copyright search to make sure that the patent, trademark, or copyright has not been registered in the United States, and in its purchase documentation, the importer should receive warranties and representations from its supplier that it will indemnify and hold the importer harmless from any such infringement actions. Obviously, if the supplier is a small company without much financial strength or has no offices in the United States and is not subject to the jurisdiction of the U.S. courts, the complaining party may proceed only against the importer in an infringement action. The importer will be unable to obtain indemnification from the supplier unless the supplier has consented to jurisdiction in the United States in the purchase agreement or the importer files another lawsuit against the supplier in the foreign country.

If the foreign supplier has not registered its patents, trademarks, or copyrights in the United States, the importer may wish to do so. To avoid disputes, generally the importer should do so only with the authorization of the foreign supplier. If the supplier is manufacturing the product with the importer's brand or trademark in a private branding arrangement, the importer should register such trademark and the supplier should disclaim all rights therein.

A related area concerns gray market imports. Even though the importer may have obtained an exclusive purchase right, distributorship, or sales agency in the United States, products manufactured by the supplier may be diverted from other customers in the manufacturer's home country or third countries for sale in the United States. Such situations will occur only where the price at which the manufacturer sells in its home market or to third countries is below the prevailing market price in the United States, and, therefore, third persons can make a profit by buying at the lower price and reselling in the United States. However, this may arise as a result of exchange rate fluctuations rather than intentional disregard of the importer's exclusive rights. Under current U.S. Customs regulations, trademarks and copyrights can be registered with U.S. Customs and Border Protection, and products that are counterfeit will be seized. Genuine products manufactured by the original manufacturer or its authorized licensee (gray market goods) will also be seized unless they were manufactured by a foreign affiliated company of the U.S. trademark or copyright owner. An exception to this is where the foreign goods are manufactured differently for a foreign market, such as a different formula under what is known as the "Lever Brothers" rule based on a court case.

P. Confidentiality and Non-Disclosure Agreements

If the importer will be furnishing any samples to the exporter, for example, when the foreign manufacturer is manufacturing products in accordance with specifications of the importer in a contract manufacturing arrangement, or when the importer will be providing other confidential or proprietary information regarding its business or products, the importer should require the manufacturer/exporter to sign a confidentiality and non-disclosure agreement in advance of disclosure of any proprietary information. In some countries where laws against counterfeiting are weak, this contractual agreement may be the importer's only protection against unauthorized copying or unfair competition by the manufacturer/exporter or dishonest third parties.

Q. Payment

An importer may be required to pay for merchandise it purchases by cash in advance or a letter of credit, unless the exchange control regulations of the government of the buyer do not require it or the buyer has sufficient bargaining leverage to purchase on more liberal terms. The buyer's methods of payment are discussed in Chapter 7, Section B.2.e. If a letter of credit is required, the seller will often provide instructions to the importer (see Chapter 4, Figure 4–29), and the importer will have to make an application in the nature of a credit application to a bank that offers letter of credit services. An applicant's checklist for a commercial letter of credit is shown in Figure 4-28. A sample of an advice of letter of credit as it will be issued to the seller is shown in Chapter 4, Figure 4–33. A sample credit notification sent by the importer's bank to a correspondent bank in the seller's country (who will advise the seller that the letter of credit has been opened) is shown in Figure 6–10. For payment by documentary collection, a sample of the seller's instructions to the bank is shown in Chapter 4, Figure 4–29. Sample sight or time drafts that the seller will present to the correspondent bank under a letter of credit to obtain payment when the goods are shipped are shown in Figures 4–26 and 4–27, respectively.

A buyer using a letter of credit should realize that the bank does not verify the quantity, the quality, or even the existence of the goods. The bank will make payment as long as the seller presents documents that appear on their face to be in compliance with the terms of the letter of credit. For this reason, a buyer may wish to arrange for a preshipment inspection by an inspection service.

R. Translation

The importer must also give consideration to the necessity of translating into English any foreign language documents, such as advertising materials, instruction manuals, warranties, and labeling. The importer may be able to get the seller to agree to perform such translations and bear the cost. These translations may be necessary to achieve sales and adequately protect the importer's rights. For example, if a patent application is incorrectly translated, the patent owner may lose its rights. The location of a competent translator and completion of the translation may require significant lead time and, depending on the volume of material, may involve significant expense. U.S. Customs and Border Protection requires that all documentation it requires must be in English.

S. Foreign Branch Operations, Subsidiaries, Joint Ventures, and Licensing

Sometimes the importer will be importing from its or its parent company's existing branch or subsidiary company in a foreign country. Or, rather than purchasing from an independent manufacturer or distributor, the importer may decide to establish such a branch operation or subsidiary company. If personnel are available to staff the foreign branch or company, this may increase the importer's sourcing capability and may smooth export and import operations. Similarly, the importer may form a joint venture with a foreign company to manufacture or export the importer's desired product to the United States and perhaps other countries. Where the laws prohibit the establishment of branches, subsidiaries, or satisfactory joint ventures, the importer may need to license to or contract with a foreign company to manufacture the product for sale to the importer. All of these methods of doing business will require some modifications to the purchase and other export and import documentation and procedures. For example, purchases from affiliated entities often raise income tax issues of transfer pricing and the related issue of proper customs valuation. License royalties may in certain circumstances be dutiable, and licensed technology may require export control approvals.

T. Electronic Commerce

The development of the Internet and email and the proliferation of web sites have created a revolution in electronic commerce. Because of the essentially worldwide availability of the Internet and access to web sites, new issues for cross-border importing and exporting have arisen. This has opened a new channel of direct marketing using electronic catalogs and has created conflict with the seller's traditional foreign distribution channels, such as distributors and sales agents. Sellers are more interested in marketing internationally and are forced to cope with the logistical issues that arise from purchase orders from abroad. Some of the more important issues that must be considered and managed include the following:

- *Validity and enforceability of electronic sales contracts.* This concern has required the consideration and development of legal terms of sale on the web site that are modified and appropriate for foreign as well as domestic customers. It has also forced the use of "click-wrap" agreements to record the purchaser's agreement to the sales terms and authentication procedures to confirm that the person purporting to place the order is actually that person. For low-price items, sellers may be willing to accept the risk of lack of enforceability of the sales contract, but for expensive items or ongoing business, this is not feasible. Many sellers have required their distributors and customers who are making ongoing purchases to sign hard-copy "umbrella" agreements at the outset of the relationship before undertaking electronic sales. This is a less satisfactory solution for onetime purchasers.

- *Delivery and logistics.* At least with direct sales to consumers, and for consumer goods, the customer wants and expects the convenience of direct delivery to his door. These "delivered duty paid" terms of sale are almost a necessity for this type of business. Customers also want prompt delivery, which is difficult to achieve if there is no stock of inventory in the buyer's country. For smaller products, delivery by international courier services such as UPS, Federal Express, and DHL has become more practical. In such cases, the transportation carrier is also able to act as the customs broker in the United States, paying customs duties and value-added taxes and billing them back to the seller. For large capital goods, however, such as in B2B transactions, the issues of containerized or other packing, transportation booking, export licenses or permits, U.S. customs clearance, and lack of skilled in-house personnel, thereby requiring the use of a freight forwarder, have limited the expansion of Internet sales. Challenges continue to exist relating to establishing in-country inventory for immediate delivery without the expenses of establishing branch offices or subsidiary companies.

- *Price.* Since many customers want to have delivery to their door, when they see a price quotation on a web site, they expect to see an "all-in" (delivered duty paid) price. The difficulty of maintaining up-to-date quotations online, including freight charges, insurance, duties, quotas, and value-added taxes for multiple countries, has forced many sellers to hire software companies that offer such services.

- *Payment.* For low-price consumer goods, payment by credit card has enabled sellers to increase Internet sales. However, since credit card purchases do not guarantee payment to the seller (the buyer can instruct the credit card company not to pay the seller in certain circumstances, such as a dispute over quality), the seller is always at risk when payment is by credit card. That fact, together with the virtual impossibility of pursuing a collection lawsuit against the buyer overseas due to prohibitive costs, has limited the expansion of Internet sales. For expensive purchases or ongoing accounts, the seller may need the security of a letter of credit or documents against payment. On the other side, buyers dislike having to pay for purchases in advance without inspection of the goods. Where the seller has done business in the past on open account, or is willing to do so in the future, Internet sales can be practical.

- *Taxation.* Although one of the great spurs to the growth of electronic commerce in the past has been the ability to avoid certain taxes in certain countries, such as sales, value-added, corporate franchise, or personal property taxes, there is an increasing demand by governments to recover those tax revenues that are being lost. It is likely that some forms of taxation will increase and that sellers and buyers may have to comply with U.S. and foreign tax claims.

- *Information security.* Although there has been significant progress in maintaining the confidentiality of information transmitted over the Internet, the sophistication of "hackers" has also increased. For information from credit card numbers to purchase order numbers and customer lists, confidentiality, particularly from competitors and fraud artists, is crucial. The most secure current technologies using "key" systems are cumbersome, especially for small orders and onetime sales. Furthermore, exporting such software may require an export license.

Despite the foregoing difficulties, the outlook is good that more creative ways of dealing with these problems will evolve and that Internet sales will continue to expand.

Chapter 7
Importing: Purchase Documentation

The single most important document in importing is the purchase agreement. Just as in exporting, most of the problems that occur in importing can be eliminated or greatly reduced by using a suitable purchase agreement. Far too often companies will seek products suppliers over the Internet with little background research on the company and then purchase without even knowing if the foreign seller has terms and conditions; then when something happens to the shipment there is a dispute over the purchase order requirements or the responsibilities of the parties. Generally, different types of documentation are used for isolated purchase transactions as opposed to ongoing purchase transactions. The various types of documentation, including the important provisions in international purchase agreements, import distribution agreements, and import sales agent agreements, will be discussed. (In order to understand how the seller views the transaction, you may wish to read Chapter 3.)

A. Isolated Purchase Transactions

For the purposes of discussion in this chapter, isolated purchase transactions are defined as situations where, for example, the importer purchases infrequently or purchases are made on a trial basis in anticipation of establishing an ongoing purchase relationship, or when the exporter is unwilling to grant any credit to the importer until a satisfactory history of payment has been established. Purchase agreements for such transactions should be in writing, and the seller and buyer may use a variety of common, preprinted forms. The author is not suggesting that the use of the preprinted forms is the wisest choice, but the reality of what happens in the real world. The importer/buyer should check carefully to try to eliminate as much as possible any conflicting provisions between the seller/exporter's forms and the forms used by the buyer and that the agreement reflects the intent of the buyer.

1. Importance of Written Agreements

In some industries (for example, the commodities industry), it is common to conduct purchases and sales orally through telephone orders and acceptances. Sometimes oral agreements occur in international purchasing when the buyer gives an order at a trade show, by telephone, or in a meeting. Under the new Convention on Contracts for the International Sale of Goods (discussed in Section B.2.l), a sales agreement may be formed or modified orally. It is highly advisable to formalize the purchase and sale agreement in a written document even for domestic purchases, and there are many additional reasons why import purchases should be memorialized in a written agreement. Under the Uniform Commercial Code applicable in the United States, an agreement to purchase, and therefore to require delivery, is enforceable by the buyer only if the agreement is in writing and if the purchase exceeds $500 in value. While there are some exceptions to this law, and sometimes even informal notes will be sufficient to create an enforceable purchase agreement, by far the safest practice is to formalize the purchase agreement in a written document.

In addition to legal issues, an old Chinese proverb states: "The lightest ink is better than the brightest memory." This is one way of saying that disputes in international purchase transactions often arise because the parties did not record their agreement or failed to discuss an issue and reach agreement. A written purchase agreement acts as both a checklist to remind the buyer and seller of what they should discuss and agree upon and as a written record of their agreement. All modifications of the agreement should also be in writing.

2. Email or Internet Orders

While an email order and acceptance can satisfy the legal requirements as written evidence of an agreement, such communications commonly contain only the specification of the quantity, sometimes an offering price, and possibly a shipment date. There are many other terms and conditions of purchase that should be inserted in a good purchase agreement, and a simple order by the buyer in response to such email offers to sell will fall far short of adequately protecting the buyer in the event of problems in the transaction. Consequently, acceptances of offers to sell by email should specifically and expressly state that the purchase incorporates the buyer's other standard terms and conditions of purchase. Those additional terms and conditions of purchase should be included in the buyer's earliest email response to the seller, so that there can be no argument that the seller was not aware of such terms and conditions of purchase before proceeding with the transaction.

Internet orders generally have the foreign buyers standard terms and conditions automatically attaching to the order, by means of a note in the small print that the buyer accepts the sellers terms and conditions or by requiring the buyer to affirmatively accept those terms and conditions through checking a box during the course of the order process. If the buyer is a small or limited quantity purchaser, it will have limited ability to amend those terms and conditions, but the buyer should review them and print them out or save them for future reference in case of a dispute. The foreign seller may modify those terms and conditions at will and so the next order may not have the same terms and conditions as the last one. If the buyer wants a substantial quantity of the seller's products, then negotiating the terms and conditions and establishing a written purchase agreement to formalize the intent of the parties is the better way to go.

3.   *The Formation of Purchase Agreements*

The purchase agreement is a formal contract governed by law. In general, a purchase agreement is formed by agreement between the seller and the buyer and is the passing of title and ownership to goods for a price. An agreement is a mutual manifestation of assent to the same terms. Agreements are ordinarily reached by a process of offer and acceptance. This process of offer and acceptance can proceed by the seller and the buyer preparing a purchase agreement contained in a single document that is signed by both parties, by the exchange of documents such as purchase orders and purchase order acceptances, or by conduct, such as when the buyer offers to purchase and the seller ships the goods.

From the view of clarity and reducing risks, preparation of a purchase agreement contained in a single document is best. Both parties negotiate the agreement by exchanges of letters or emails or in person. Before proceeding with the performance of any part of the transaction, both parties reach agreement and sign the same purchase agreement. This gives both the seller and the buyer the best opportunity to understand the terms and conditions under which the other intends to transact business, and to negotiate and resolve any differences or conflicts. This type of purchase agreement is often used if the size of the transaction is large, if the seller is concerned about payment or the buyer is concerned about manufacture and shipment, or if there are particular risks involved, such as government regulations or exchange controls, or differences in culture, language, or business customs that might create misunderstandings.

Quite often, however, the process of formation of the purchase agreement is an exchange of documents that the seller and buyer have independently prepared, and that, in the aggregate, constitute the purchase agreement. These documents may contain differences and conflicts. Figure 3–1 in Chapter 3 shows the chronology of this exchange and common documents used in many purchase transactions. Although not all documents will be used in every purchase transaction, these documents are in common use.

Several questions arise when a purchase transaction is formed by such an exchange of documents. The first relates to the time of formation of the purchase agreement. For example, a seller or buyer may send certain preliminary inquiries or information, such as a price list, without intending to actually offer to sell or place an order, but may find that the other party's understanding (or the applicable law) has created a binding purchase agreement prior to the first party's intention to do so. This can arise because under some countries' laws, an offer to sell or buy is accepted when the acceptance is dispatched, rather than when it is received. It can also arise because silence can be considered as acceptance if the parties are merchants.

The second issue that arises relates to the governing law. Contracts are often governed by the law of the country in which the contract is negotiated and performed or in which the offer to sell or buy was accepted. Since an international agreement may be partly negotiated and partly performed in both countries and since there may be a question as to whether the buyer accepted the offer to sell or the seller accepted the offer to purchase, situations can arise in which the purchase agreement is governed by the law of the seller's country. Since foreign law may be quite different from U.S. law, the buyer's rights and responsibilities may differ greatly from what he anticipated. Customary local ways of doing business, called trade usages, may unknowingly become a part of the purchase agreement under the sales laws of some countries. Sellers and buyers sometimes try to resolve this problem by including a governing law term in their documents, but again, these may conflict.

A final method of formation of a purchase agreement involves conduct. A simple example is where a buyer sends a purchase order, and the seller, without communicating, simply ships the goods, or where the seller offers to sell the goods and the buyer simply sends payment. In such cases, the conduct in accepting the offer will include all of the terms and conditions of the offer. If the buyer is not satisfied with the seller's terms and conditions of sale, she should send some communication to negotiate those terms before simply sending an order or making payment.

4. Common Forms for the Formation of Purchase Agreements

There are a number of forms that are customarily used in the formation of purchase agreements. In order to save time (and discourage changes by the other party), both buyers and sellers often purchase preprinted forms from commercial stationers or develop and preprint their own forms. Not all of these documents are used by the seller or the buyer in all purchase transactions. For example, a seller may submit a quotation to a potential buyer without receiving any request for quotation, or the first communication the seller receives may be a purchase order from the buyer. However, it is important to be familiar with the various forms.

a. Price Lists. Sometimes a seller will send a price list to a prospective buyer as its first communication. Ordinarily, a buyer should not consider such lists as offers to sell that entitle the buyer to accept. The buyer should ordinarily communicate with the seller (specifying that he is not making an order), asking for a quotation and confirming that the terms of the price list are still current.

b. Requests for Quotations and Offers to Purchase. Sometimes the first document involved in the formation of a purchase agreement is a request from the buyer to the seller for a quotation (RFQ) (see Figure 3–2). Ordinarily, such a request—whether it is informal, in an email, letter, or formal, in a printed form—will ask for a price quotation from the seller for a specific quantity and often a shipping date. When requesting a quotation, the buyer should be particularly careful to specify that its request is not an offer to purchase and that such an offer will be made only by the buyer's subsequent purchase order. Another method is to expressly state that the buyer's request is subject to or incorporates all of the buyer's standard terms and conditions of purchase. The most cautious approach is for the buyer to print all of its terms and conditions of purchase in its request for quotation. In that way, there is absolutely no argument that the seller was not aware of all the terms and conditions on which the buyer is willing to purchase, and if the seller has any objection thereto, it should so state in its quotation to the buyer. The buyer should request that the seller's quotation be in writing.

c. Quotations. In response to a request for a quotation, the seller ordinarily prepares and forwards a quotation or a pro forma invoice. In making quotations, the seller may use a printed form that may contain all of its terms and conditions of sale on the front or back thereof (see Figures 3–4 and 3–8). If this is the first communication from the seller to the buyer, the buyer should be careful to ascertain whether the quotation contains other terms and conditions of sale in addition to the price, quantity, and shipment date. This may be expressly stated in fine print boilerplate provisions on the front or back or by reference to the seller's terms and conditions of sale being incorporated by reference. If the seller refers to terms and conditions that are not expressly stated in the quotation, the best course is for the buyer to ask the seller to provide a copy of such terms and conditions of sale prior to sending any order. If such terms and conditions are stated, the buyer should carefully review them to determine if there are any discrepancies between the buyer's standard terms and conditions of purchase or if there are any terms and conditions that are objectionable to the buyer. If there are objectionable terms, it is far better to negotiate and resolve these items before placing any order. The quotation may expressly state that the offer is firm or irrevocable for a certain period of time, and it may also state that it is not an offer to sell and that the seller is not agreeing to sell until it has received a purchase order from the buyer and has issued an acceptance of the order. If the quotation does not state that it is firm for a certain period of time, the buyer may wish to immediately inquire if this is so; otherwise, the seller is generally free to withdraw its quotation anytime before acceptance, which could mean even after the buyer has sent a purchase order, especially if the seller has reserved the right not to sell until it accepts the buyer's purchase order.

d. Purchase Orders. The next document that may occur in a purchase transaction is a purchase order (PO) issued by the buyer. Again, the purchase order may be informal, such as in an email, letter, or it may be on a printed form. This is the most important document for the buyer because it should contain all of the additional terms and conditions that the buyer wants to be a part of the purchase agreement when the purchase order is accepted by the seller. (See samples in Figures 3–5 and 3–6.) Before issuing a purchase order in response to a quotation, the buyer should carefully calculate its costs. The buyer should determine whether the quotation is ex-factory, FOB port, CIF, or delivered, since all expenses of transportation from the point quoted will be expenses of the buyer, including U.S. customs duties. (See more about Incoterms® in Chapter 2.) If the buyer intends to resell the product in its imported form, it should determine whether the quoted price plus additional expenses of importation will still permit the buyer to sell at the prevailing U.S. market price with a reasonable profit or, if the product will be used as a raw material or component, that its delivered cost will be lower than that from U.S. suppliers (compare Figure 3–3). If the price is unacceptable, the buyer should make a counteroffer at a lower price before sending a purchase order. Even though the buyer may expect that no purchase agreement will be formed until she has sent a purchase order, if the seller has previously sent a quotation to the buyer, the terms and conditions stated in the seller's quotation may govern the purchase agreement. Of course, the terms and conditions contained in the seller's quotation or purchase order acceptance are always written to be most favorable to the seller. An important way in which the buyer can try to guard against such a result is for the buyer to specify in its purchase order that its purchase order is an offer to purchase only on the terms and conditions stated therein and that any acceptance with different terms and conditions will be void unless expressly accepted by the buyer in writing. The purchase order should also limit acceptance to a certain time period so that the offer to purchase is not open indefinitely. Finally, the purchase order should specify that any acceptance and purchase agreement will be governed by the law of the buyer's state and the United States, excluding the Convention on Contracts for the International Sale of Goods, to avoid a purchase order acceptance being issued in the foreign country and the formation of a purchase agreement governed by foreign law.

e. Purchase Order Acknowledgments, Acceptances, and Sales Confirmations. When a purchase order is received, some sellers prepare a purchase order acknowledgment, purchase order acceptance, or sales confirmation form (see sample in Figure 3–7). A purchase order acknowledgment may state that the seller has received the purchase order from the buyer and is in the process of evaluating it, such as checking on the credit of the buyer or determining the availability of raw materials for manufacture, but that the seller has not yet accepted the purchase order and will issue a purchase order acceptance at a later date. In other cases, the language of the purchase order acknowledgment is also clearly an acceptance of the order, and no further communication is issued. Sales confirmations usually perform the same role as purchase order acceptances. The seller will normally include its detailed terms and conditions of sale in its purchase order acknowledgment or purchase order acceptance. If this is the first time that the buyer has seen such terms and conditions of sale (that is, if they were not included in the seller's earlier quotation), even if the buyer has stated in its purchase order that it is offering to purchase only on its own terms and conditions, the buyer should confirm that there is no conflict and that the seller has not purported to accept the purchase order only on its own terms and conditions. If a conflict exists, the buyer should immediately negotiate and resolve the conflict; otherwise, the seller may proceed with manufacture and shipment, and the buyer may be bound by the seller's terms and conditions. If the seller's quotation and purchase order acceptance do not contain detailed terms and conditions of sale, the buyer can feel reasonably comfortable that its terms or conditions will control.

f. Commercial Invoices. Later, when manufacture is complete and the product is ready for shipment, ordinarily the seller will prepare a commercial invoice, which is the formal statement for payment to be sent directly to the buyer or submitted through banking channels for payment by the buyer. Such invoices may also contain the detailed terms or conditions of sale on the front or back of the form (see sample in Figure 3–9). However, if this is the first time that the seller has brought such terms to the attention of the buyer, and the buyer has previously advised the seller of its detailed terms and conditions of purchase in its request for quotation or purchase order, the buyer should immediately object if the seller's terms and conditions are in conflict.

  g. Conflicting Provisions in Seller and Buyer Sales Documentation. It is common in international trade for sellers and buyers to use preprinted forms that are designed to reduce the amount of negotiation and discussion required for each sales agreement. Undoubtedly, such forms have been drafted by attorneys for each side and contain terms and conditions of purchase or terms and conditions of sale that are favorable to the buyer and the seller, respectively. Consequently, it is not unusual for sellers and buyers who are intent on entering into a sales transaction to routinely issue such documentation with little or no thought being given to the consistency of those provisions. Afterward, if the sales transaction breaks down and either the buyer or the seller consults its attorney regarding its legal rights and obligations, the rights of the parties may be very unclear. In the worst case, the buyer may find that a purchase agreement has been validly formed on all of the terms and conditions of the seller's quotation or purchase order acceptance and is governed by the law of the seller's country. In order to reduce or eliminate this problem, often the buyer's attorney drafts requests for quotations and purchase orders with language that states that, notwithstanding any terms or conditions that might be contained in the seller's quotation or purchase order acceptance, the buyer agrees to make the purchase only on its own terms or conditions. While this can be of some help, sometimes the seller's quotation and purchase order acceptance also contain such language, and consequently, the buyer's terms and conditions may not win out. In fact, the only way to be comfortable regarding the terms or conditions of sale that will govern a purchase agreement is to actually review the terms or conditions contained in the seller's forms and compare them with the terms and conditions that the buyer desires to utilize. Where specific conflicts exist or where the seller's terms or conditions of purchase differ from the buyer's terms or conditions of purchase, the buyer should expressly bring that to the attention of the seller, the differences should be negotiated to the satisfaction of the buyer, and appropriate changes should be made in the form of a rider to the purchase agreement or a letter to clarify the agreement reached between the parties (which should be signed by both parties).

  In some isolated sales transactions where the quantities are small, the buyer may simply choose to forgo this effort and accept the risk that the transaction will be controlled by the seller's terms and conditions of sale. However, the buyer should establish some dollar limit over which a review is to be made and should not continue a practice that might be appropriate for small purchases but would be very dangerous for large purchases.

h. Side Agreements. Occasionally, the seller may suggest that the seller and buyer enter into a side or letter agreement. In some cases, the suggestion may be innocent enough, for example, where the parties wish to clarify how they will interpret or carry out a particular provision of the purchase agreement. Even then, however, it is better practice to incorporate all of the agreements of the parties in a single document. Unfortunately, more often the seller's proposal of a side agreement is designed to evade the seller's foreign exchange control, tax, or antitrust laws. Buyers should be wary of entering into such agreements unless they fully understand the consequences. Such agreements may be unenforceable, the buyer may not be able to get delivery of the goods for which it paid, and/or the buyer may be prosecuted as a co-conspirator for violating such laws.

B. Ongoing Purchase Transactions

When an importer begins to purchase on a regular basis, or when the importer desires to make regular purchases from a particular supplier, the buyer and the seller should enter into a more comprehensive agreement to govern their relationship. Often these types of agreements are a result of the buyer's being willing to commit to regular purchases, and, therefore, to purchase a larger quantity of the goods, in return for obtaining a lower price. Or, they may result from the buyer's desire to tie up, that is, to obtain more assurance from the seller to commit to supply the buyer's requirements, or from the seller's desire to plan its production. The three major types of agreements used in ongoing sales transactions are (1) international purchase agreements, that is, supply agreements where the seller sells directly to the buyer, who either incorporates the seller's product as a component into a product that the buyer manufactures or consumes the product itself and does not resell the product; (2) distributor agreements, where the buyer buys the product from a foreign seller and resells the product in the United States or for export, usually in the same form but sometimes with modifications; and (3) sales agent or sales representative agreements, where a U.S. person is appointed to solicit orders from potential customers in the United States for a foreign seller. In the last case, the sale is not made to the sales agent, but is made directly to the U.S. customer, with payment of a commission or other compensation to the sales agent.

In any of the three foregoing agreements, there is a correlation between the documentation used in isolated purchase transactions and the documentation used in ongoing purchase transactions. Furthermore, there are a number of important provisions in international purchase, distributor, and sales agent agreements that are not relevant to domestic purchases but should be included in such agreements.

1. Correlation with Documentation for Isolated Purchase Transactions

As discussed in Section A.4, it is common for sellers and buyers to use forms such as requests for quotation, purchase orders, purchase order acknowledgments, purchase order acceptances, sales confirmations, and invoices during the course of buying and selling products. When an ongoing purchase relationship with a particular seller is being established, it is usual to enter into an umbrella or blanket agreement that is intended to govern the relationship between the parties over a longer period of time, for example, one year, five years, or longer. Sometimes the parties will enter into a trial purchase agreement that will last for a short period of time, such as one year, before deciding to enter into a longer-term agreement. In any event, the international purchase (supply) agreement, the distributor agreement, and the sales agent (representative) agreement define the rights and obligations of the parties over a fairly long period of time and commit the buyer and the seller to doing business with each other so that both sides can make production, marketing, and advertising plans and expenditures. Special price discounts in return for commitments to purchase specific quantities are common in such agreements. Such agreements may contain a commitment to purchase a specific quantity over the life of the agreement and may designate a specific price or a formula by which the price will be adjusted over the life of the agreement. To this extent, these agreements serve as an umbrella over the parties' relationship, with certain specific acts to be accomplished as agreed to by the parties. For example, it is usually necessary during the term of such agreements for the buyer to advise the seller as to the specific quantity it wishes to order at that time, to be applied against the buyer's overall purchase commitment.

If the price of the product is likely to fluctuate, no price may be specified in the umbrella agreement. Instead, the price may be changed from time to time by the seller depending upon the seller's price at the time the buyer submits an order, perhaps with a special discount from such price because the buyer has committed to buy a substantial quantity over the life of the agreement. In such cases, depending upon whether or not a specific price has been set in the umbrella agreement, the buyer will send a request for quotation and the seller will provide a quotation, or a purchase order will be sent describing the specific quantity that the buyer wishes to order at that time, a suggested shipment date, and the price. The seller will still use a purchase order acknowledgment and/or a purchase order acceptance form to agree to ship the specific quantity on the specific shipment date at the specific price. The seller will continue to provide a commercial invoice against which the buyer must make payment.

In summary, when the seller and the buyer wish to enter into a longer-term agreement, they will define their overall relationship in an umbrella agreement, but the usual documentation utilized in isolated purchase transactions will also be utilized to order specific quantities and to confirm prices and shipment dates. Sometimes conflicts can arise between the terms and conditions in the umbrella agreement and those in the specific documentation. Usually the parties provide that, in such cases, the umbrella agreement will control, but this can also lead to problems in situations where the parties wish to vary the terms of their umbrella agreement for a specific transaction.

2. *Important Provisions in International Purchase Agreements*

There are numerous terms and conditions in an international purchase agreement that require special consideration different from the usual terms and conditions in a domestic purchase agreement. A sample international purchase agreement is included as Appendix F.

a. Purchasing and Selling Entities. One consideration that may arise in an international purchase agreement is the identity of the purchasing and selling entities. In some cases, the buyer may want to organize a separate company to handle all importations. One reason for this is to insulate the U.S. company's assets against claims related to the imported article, such as product liability claims. If the U.S. company will be reselling the products, it may wish to conduct such business in a separate subsidiary company that conducts the importing and resale operations. (Ordinarily, unless the parent corporation is in the chain of ownership and takes title to the products, it would not be liable for product liability claims.) Generally, however, a U.S. company will not be able to protect its assets against unforeseen U.S. Customs liability by organizing a subsidiary to act as the importer. That usually will make no difference, as the importer will be required to post a bond to guarantee payment of all customs duties and penalties. If the importing company has limited assets, the bonding company will not issue the bond unless the parent company guarantees the debts of the subsidiary/importer.

If the seller and the buyers are related entities, such as a subsidiary and parent corporation, the U.S. Customs treatment may be different, for example, in the valuation of the merchandise or assessment of antidumping duties. Some transactions may be structured to involve the use of a trading company on the exporting side, the importing side, or both. Depending upon whether the trading company takes title or is appointed as the agent (of either the buyer or the seller), or whether the trading company is related to the seller or the buyer, the customs value may be different. For example, commissions paid to the seller's agent are ordinarily subject to customs duties in the United States, but commissions paid to the buyer's agent are not.

b. *Quantity.* The quantity term is even more important than the price. Under U.S. law, if the parties have agreed on the quantity, the purchase agreement is enforceable even if the parties have not agreed on the price—a current, or market, price will be implied. When no quantity has been agreed upon, however, the purchase agreement will not be enforceable.

One reason for forming a formal purchase agreement is for the buyer to obtain a lower price by committing to purchase a large quantity, usually over a year or more. The seller may be willing to grant a lower price in return for the ability to plan ahead, schedule production and inventory, develop economies of scale, and reduce shipping and administrative costs. The buyer should be aware that price discounts based on quantity may violate U.S. price discrimination laws unless the amount of the discount can be directly related to the cost savings of the seller for that particular quantity.

Quantity agreements can be for a specific quantity or a target quantity. Generally, if the commitment is a target only, failure to actually purchase such an amount will not justify the seller in claiming damages or terminating the agreement (although sometimes the buyer may agree to a retroactive price increase). Failure to purchase a minimum purchase quantity, however, will justify termination and a claim for breach. Sometimes the buyer may wish to buy the seller's entire output or the seller may seek a commitment that the buyer will purchase all of its requirements for the merchandise from the seller. Usually, such agreements are lawful, but in certain circumstances they can violate the U.S. antitrust laws, such as when the seller is the only supplier or represents a large amount of the supply, or the buyer is the only buyer or represents a large segment of the market.

c. *Pricing.* There are a number of considerations in formulating the buyer's pricing policy for international purchase agreements. A delivered price calculation sheet will identify all additional costs of importing to make sure that the price of resale results in a net profit that is acceptable to the buyer. The buyer also has to be aware of several constraints in formulating its pricing policy.

The first constraint relates to dumping. The United States has laws prohibiting dumping. This generally means that the price at which products are sold for export to the United States cannot be lower than the price at which such products are sold for domestic consumption in the country from which they are exported. However, the mere fact that sales to the United States are made at lower prices does not automatically mean that a dumping investigation will be initiated or that a dumping finding will occur. Under the laws of the United States, no dumping will occur if the price to the United States is above the current U.S. market price, even if the seller's price to the United States is lower than its sale price in its own country.

Additionally, there are U.S. legal constraints on the extent to which a price quoted for import can vary from buyer to buyer. The antitrust laws in the United States (in particular, the price discrimination provisions of the Robinson-Pitman Act) apply when two or more sales to two or more buyers are being made in the United States. If the seller is selling to two or more buyers in the United States at different prices, such sales may violate the price discrimination provisions of U.S. law. The buyer who is paying the higher price may sue the foreign seller. Moreover, if the buyer purchasing at the lower price induced the price discrimination, the buyer would also violate U.S. law. In order to gain some assurance that it is getting the best price, sometimes a buyer will obtain a covenant from the seller in the purchase agreement that the seller agrees to grant the buyer the best price that it grants to any other purchaser during the term of the agreement. Such covenants may be helpful, but the buyer must have the right to inspect the sales records of the seller to confirm that it is getting the best price.

If the price is below the seller's total cost of production, there is a risk that such purchases will be attacked as predatory pricing in violation of U.S. antitrust laws. The accounting calculation of cost is always a subject of dispute, particularly where the seller may feel that the costs of foreign advertising or other costs should not be allocated to export sales. However, in general, any sales below total, fully allocated costs are at risk. Obviously, it will be the importer's competitors who will object to, and sue to stop, such sales.

Another very important pricing area relates to rebates, discounts, allowances, and price escalation clauses. Sometimes the buyer will ask for and the seller will be willing to grant some form of rebate, discount, or allowance under certain circumstances, such as the purchase of large quantities of merchandise. Such price concessions generally do not, in and of themselves, violate U.S. or foreign law, but if such payments are not disclosed to the proper government authorities, both the U.S. importer and the foreign seller may violate various U.S. and foreign laws and may be charged with conspiracy to violate or aiding and abetting the other's violation of those laws. For example, the U.S. importer must file customs entry documents on each shipment and must declare the price at which the goods are being purchased. If, in fact, this price is false (because the exporter has agreed to grant some rebate, discount, or allowance or, in fact, does so), the U.S. importer will violate U.S. law and be subject to civil and criminal penalties.

Similarly, when the seller exports the goods to the United States, the seller will be required to state a value for export purposes in its country. If the seller sends the buyer two invoices for different amounts, or if the seller asks the buyer to pay any part of the purchase price outside of the seller's country (for example, by deposit in a bank account in the United States, Switzerland, or some other country), there is considerable risk that the intended action of the seller will violate the seller's foreign exchange control, tax, and/or customs laws. If the buyer cooperates by making any such payment, or is aware of the scheme, the buyer can also be charged with conspiracy to violate those foreign laws and can risk fines, arrest, and imprisonment in that country. Similarly, retroactive price increases (for example, due to currency fluctuations) or price increases under escalation clauses may cause a change in the final price, which may have to be reported to foreign exchange authorities or to U.S. Customs. Before agreeing to accept any price rebate, discount, or allowance; to use a price escalation clause; to implement a retroactive price increase; or to make any payment to the seller in any place except the seller's own country by check or wire transfer (not cash), the buyer should satisfy itself that its actions will not result in the violation of any U.S. or foreign law.

If the purchase is from an affiliated company, such as a foreign parent or subsidiary, additional pricing considerations arise. Because the buyer and the seller are related, pricing can be artificially manipulated. For example, a U.S. importer whose U.S. profits are taxable at a rate of 35 percent may, when purchasing from an affiliated seller in a country that has a higher tax rate, attempt to minimize taxes in the foreign country by purchasing from its foreign affiliate at a low price. Thus, when the foreign affiliate sells the product, its profit will be small and its taxes reduced. When the purchase is from a country where the tax rate is lower than that in the United States, the considerations are reversed and the transfer price is set at a high rate, in which case the U.S. profits will be low. These strategies are well known to the tax authorities in foreign countries and to the Internal Revenue Service in the United States. Consequently, purchases from affiliated companies are always susceptible to attack by the tax authorities. In general, the tax authorities in both countries require that the buyer purchase from its affiliated seller at an arm's-length price, as if it were purchasing from an unaffiliated seller. Often, preserving evidence that the seller was selling to its unaffiliated customers at the same price as its affiliated customers will be very important in defending a tax audit. When the U.S. buyer is purchasing from a country with a higher tax rate, the U.S. Customs authorities will also be suspicious that the transfer price is undervalued, and, therefore, customs duties may be underpaid. Under U.S. tax regulations, the U.S. importer cannot claim any income tax deduction for cost of goods greater than the value declared for U.S. Customs purposes.

Another consideration in the pricing of goods for import concerns parallel imports or gray market goods. If buyers in one country are able to purchase at a lower price than that in the United States, an economic incentive will exist for customers in the lower-price country to divert such goods to the United States in hopes of making a profit. Obviously, the seller's distributor in the United States will complain about such unauthorized imports and loss of sales. The U.S. Supreme Court has held that genuine goods, that is, those that are made by the same manufacturer and are not mere copies or imitations, can be imported into the United States under the U.S. Customs laws. An importer who experiences such gray market goods may have other legal remedies available to stop or prevent such imports, but the best remedy is to make sure that the seller is not selling at lower prices in other markets. Unfortunately, maintaining pricing parity is not always easy because of floating exchange rates, not only between the United States and other countries, but also among those other countries.

Finally, the import price as shown in the seller's invoice and as declared to the U.S. Customs for duty purposes affects the "cost of goods" for U.S. income tax purposes, as specified in section 1059A of the Internal Revenue Code.

d. Currency Fluctuations. An issue related to that of pricing is the currency fluctuations that occur between the countries of the seller and the buyer. If the U.S. importer purchases only in U.S. dollars, the fluctuations of the foreign currency will not affect the final U.S. dollar amount that the importer makes as payment. However, if the seller is a much larger company than the buyer and has more negotiating and bargaining leverage, or if the buyer is anxious to make the purchase, it may be necessary to agree to a purchase agreement denominated in foreign currency, such as the Japanese yen or the euro. In such cases, if the foreign currency strengthens between the time of the price agreement and the time of payment, the U.S. importer will have to pay more U.S. dollars than it had anticipated when it agreed to the price and calculated the expected cost. In such cases, the importer is assuming the foreign exchange fluctuation risk. Sometimes, when the term of the agreement is long, or when major currency fluctuations are anticipated, neither the seller nor the buyer is comfortable in entirely assuming such risk. Consequently, they may agree to some sharing of the risk, such as a 50/50 price adjustment due to any exchange fluctuations that occur during the life of the agreement, or some other formula that attempts to protect both sides against such fluctuations. If the two parties have agreed to a currency exchange formula and documented that formula in writing prior to import, U.S. Customs and Border Protection will accept that methodology for calculating the value for duty purposes instead of using the standard quarterly exchange rate.

e. Payment Methods. In a domestic sales transaction, the buyer may be used to purchasing on open account, receiving credit, or paying cash on delivery. In international purchases, it is more customary to utilize certain methods of payment that are designed to give the overseas seller a greater level of protection. The idea is that if the buyer fails to pay, it is much more difficult for a seller to come to the United States, institute a lawsuit, attempt to attach the buyer's assets, or otherwise obtain payment. When a seller is dealing with a buyer who is essentially unknown to it, with whom it has no prior payment experience, or who is small, the seller often requires that the buyer pay cash in advance or obtain a documentary letter of credit from a bank in the buyer's country. The seller may also require that the letter of credit be confirmed by a bank in the seller's country to guarantee payment by the buyer's bank. The seller may still sell on terms with payment to be made at the time of arrival, or the seller may give the buyer some longer period of time (for example, from 30 days to 180 days) to make payment, but the letter of credit acts as an umbrella obligation of the bank guaranteeing such payment, and the buyer does not pay the seller directly, but through the bank that issues the letter of credit. In some cases, however, the buyer will be unable to obtain a letter of credit, for example, because the buyer's bank does not feel comfortable with the buyer's financial solvency. Furthermore, the issuance of letters of credit involves the payment of bank fees, which are normally paid by the buyer, and the buyer usually does not wish to incur such expenses in addition to the cost of purchasing the goods. Another disadvantage to the buyer is that it will be unable to inspect the goods before its bank is obliged to make payment. In such cases, particularly if the seller is anxious to make the sale, or if other sellers are willing to offer more liberal payment terms, the buyer may be able to force the seller to give up a letter of credit and agree to make the sale on some other, more liberal, method of payment.

The best method of purchase for the buyer is on open account, where the seller makes the sale and the shipment by forwarding the bill of lading and a commercial invoice directly to the buyer for payment. Because the bill of lading is sent directly to the buyer, once it leaves the possession of the seller, the seller will be unable to control what happens to the goods, and the buyer will be able to obtain the goods whether or not payment is made. This also gives the buyer an opportunity to inspect the goods prior to making payment. When a seller agrees to sell on open account, the seller may request that the buyer open a standby letter of credit or grant a security interest under U.S. law to protect the seller's right to payment in case the buyer goes bankrupt or otherwise fails to pay at the agreed time (see subsection g, below).

The next best method of payment for the buyer is to utilize a time draft, commonly known as a document against acceptance or D/A transaction. The bill of lading and time draft (that is, a document like a check in the amount of the sale drawn by the seller on the buyer—rather than a bank—and payable to the seller) are forwarded through banking channels, but the buyer agrees to make payment within a certain number of days (for example, 30 to 180) after it receives and accepts the draft. Normally, this permits the buyer to obtain possession of the goods and may give the buyer enough time to resell them before its obligation to pay comes due. However, documents against acceptance transactions are a significantly greater risk for the seller because, if the buyer does not pay at the promised time, the seller's only recourse is to file a lawsuit—the goods have already been released to the buyer. Where the buyer is financially strong, however, sometimes such acceptances can be discounted by the seller, permitting the seller to get immediate payment but giving the buyer additional time to pay. This discounting may be done with recourse or without recourse, depending upon the size of the discount the seller is willing to accept. The seller may decide to waive the interest charge for the delay in payment in order to make the sale.

The next best method of payment for the buyer is by sight draft documentary collection, commonly known as documents against payment or D/P transactions. In this case, the seller uses the services of a bank to effect collection, but neither the buyer's bank nor the seller's bank guarantees payment by the buyer. The seller will ship the goods, and the bill of lading and a draft will be forwarded to the seller's bank. The seller's bank will forward such documents to a correspondent bank in the United States (sometimes the seller or its freight forwarder sends the documents directly to the buyer's bank—this is known as direct collection), and the U.S. bank will collect payment from the buyer prior to the time that the goods arrive. If payment is not made by the buyer, the U.S. bank does not release the bill of lading to the buyer, and the buyer will be unable to take possession of the goods or clear U.S. Customs. Although it can still be a significant problem for the seller if the buyer does not make payment and the shipment has already arrived in the United States, the seller should still be able to control the goods upon arrival, for example, by asking the bank to place them in a warehouse or by requesting that they be shipped to a third country or back to the seller at the seller's expense. Direct collections are often used for air shipments to avoid delays through the seller's bank, and also because air waybills are nonnegotiable.

Sometimes a buyer will begin purchasing from a particular seller under letters of credit, and as the seller becomes more familiar with the buyer (the buyer honors its obligations, increases its purchases, or enters into an ongoing purchase relationship agreement), the seller will be willing to liberalize its payment terms.

In addition, in international transactions, the buyer may be required to use alternative payment methods, such as wire transfers via banking channels, since payment by check will often involve an inordinate length of time if the check is first sent to the seller in the foreign country and then sent back to the United States to be collected from the buyer's bank. Direct wire transfer from bank account to bank account is a highly efficient and useful way to deal with international payments. However, the buyer should resist making a wire transfer until after the goods have arrived and have been inspected, or at least until after the goods are shipped under a non-negotiable (straight) bill of lading. Other methods of payment, such as cash payments made by employees traveling from the buyer to the seller or vice versa, or payments made in third countries, all carry the risk of violating the seller's foreign exchange control and/ or tax laws and should be agreed to only after detailed investigation of the possible risks. A chart comparing these various methods of payment is shown in Figure 3–10.

Finally, an additional method of payment that sellers sometimes use is the factoring of export accounts receivable. This may represent an opportunity for a foreign seller to obtain its money immediately on open account sales in return for accepting a lesser amount, or some discount from the sales price. Such factoring arrangements usually involve a disadvantage for the buyer, however, because the buyer may be obligated to pay the factor when the obligation is due even though the buyer may have a dispute, such as a claim for defective goods, with the seller. To guard against that problem, the buyer should try to make sure that the purchase agreement provides that the seller cannot assign its accounts receivable without the buyer's consent.

f. Import Financing. The substantive aspects of import financing were discussed in Chapter 6, Section N. If import financing is going to be utilized, it should be discussed in the international purchase agreement. The seller will thus be clearly aware that the buyer intends to use such financing. The documentation that the seller is required to provide in order for the buyer to obtain such financing should be specified in the agreement, and the buyer's obligation to purchase should be excused if such import financing is not granted.

g. Security Interest. As discussed in subsection e, above, on payment methods, if the buyer intends to purchase on open account or on documents against acceptance, the seller may request a security interest to protect its rights to payment. Under U.S. law, unless the seller has registered its lien or security interest with a government agency, if the buyer goes into bankruptcy or falls into financial difficulties, the seller will be unable to repossess the merchandise it sold, even if the merchandise is still in the possession of the buyer. Also, the seller may be unable to obtain priority over other creditors, and after such creditors are paid, nothing may remain for the seller. Although granting a security interest does reduce the buyer's flexibility in negotiating with creditors in the event that the buyer falls into financial difficulties, in practice, the buyer will have a difficult time objecting to granting such a security interest. However, the buyer should not accept responsibility for preparing or filing such a security interest or notifying other creditors, since, if it does so improperly, the seller may sue the buyer for negligence. If a security interest is granted by the buyer and the buyer does experience financial difficulties, it should make sure that it makes payments in accordance with the priority of the security interests or the directors of the company may become personally liable. Sometimes, the buyer's bank or other creditor will have been granted a security interest in the assets of the buyer. In order for a seller to take priority over the previous creditors, it may try to impose upon the buyer an obligation to obtain subordination agreements from the buyer's other creditors. Generally, the buyer should resist this and insist that the seller obtain such agreements itself.

h. *Passage of Title, Delivery, and Risk of Loss.* Ownership is transferred from the seller to the buyer by the passage of title. Under the Convention on Contracts for the International Sale of Goods (discussed in subsection l), unless otherwise agreed, title and risk of loss will pass to the buyer when the seller delivers the merchandise to the first transportation carrier. The buyer's payment will be due at that time. Under U.S. law, title passes at the time and place agreed to by the parties to the international purchase agreement. It can pass at the seller's plant, at the port of export, upon arrival in the United States after clearance of Customs, upon arrival at the buyer's place of business, or at any other place, time, or manner agreed to by the parties. Usually the risk of loss for any subsequent casualty or damage to the products will pass to the buyer at the same time as the title passes. However, it is possible to specify in the purchase agreement that it will pass at a different time.

i. *Warranties and Product Defects.* From the buyer's point of view, one of the most important provisions in the international purchase agreement is the one that specifies the warranty terms. Under the law of the United States and the Convention on Contracts for the International Sale of Goods (discussed in subsection l), unless the seller limits its warranty expressly in writing in the international purchase agreement, the seller will be responsible and liable for all foreseeable consequential damages that result to the buyer from defective products. Consequently, it is common for the seller to try to eliminate all or most warranties. The purchase agreement should specify exactly what warranty the seller is giving for the products, whether the products are being sold "as is" with no warranty, whether there is a limited warranty such as repair or replacement, whether there is a dollar limit on the warranty, whether there is a time period within which the warranty claim must be made, and/or whether there is any limitation on consequential damages. In the United States, as a matter of public policy, the law prohibits certain types of warranty disclaimers or exclusions. For example, imported products have to comply with the Magnuson-Moss Warranty Act. Consequently, in reviewing the warranty limitation, the buyer may need to consult with an attorney to make sure that the warranty will be effective. If the sales agreement is formed by a mere exchange of preprinted forms, the buyer may find that the seller's terms or conditions control the sale and that no warranty exists. Therefore, the buyer should carefully read the seller's communications, and if the warranty is too limited, the buyer must negotiate a warranty acceptable to both sides before going ahead with the purchase.

j. Preshipment Inspections. Even if the buyer has not paid in advance, if the products arrive in the United States and are defective, the buyer may be faced with substantial losses or the necessity of re-exporting the merchandise to the seller. Consequently, the buyer should generally insist upon preshipment inspection in the international purchase agreement. In an international purchase agreement, if the buyer can get the seller to agree that the buyer is entitled to purchase at the lowest price at which it sells to any of its other customers, the inspection company may be able to review more than the quality of the goods. For example, the inspection company may require the seller to produce documentation relating to sales of the same product to other customers to ascertain the prices at which such sales were made. If the buyer getting the preshipment inspection determines that the price it is paying is higher than the prices the seller had charged other customers, the buyer can refuse to go forward with the transaction or renegotiate the price.

The buyer should realize, however, that asking for a preshipment inspection will usually delay the shipment anywhere from twenty to forty days and that it will have to pay for such inspection unless it can get the seller to agree to share the costs.

In some instances the foreign government may require a preshipment inspection. In those instances, the party responsible under the Incoterms® for the foreign export requirements should pay for the costs of the inspection. Under most of the Incoterms®, this will be the seller.

k. Export Licenses. The importance of an export license has been touched upon in Chapter 6, Section E.1. In an international purchase agreement, the buyer should require the seller to warrant that no export license is required, or the exporter should state that an export license is required and should promise to obtain the license in a timely manner. If the seller fails to obtain the license, the buyer could claim damages. The buyer should be aware that, if the seller is required to obtain an export license, the buyer will usually be required to provide an International Import Certificate issued by the U.S. Department of Commerce. The seller will be unable to apply for its export license until it obtains the certificate, and the buyer should obtain it and send it to the seller as soon as possible to avoid delays in obtaining the export license. (Under the Incoterms®, the buyer is responsible for obtaining the export license on ex-works sales.)

l. Governing Law. In any international purchase agreement, whether the agreement is formed by a written agreement between the parties or whether it is an oral agreement, the rights and obligations of the parties will be governed either by the law of the country of the seller or by the law of the country of the buyer. The laws of most countries permit the seller and the buyer to specifically agree on which law will apply, and that choice will be binding upon both parties whether or not a lawsuit is brought in either the buyer's or the seller's country. Of course, whenever the subject is raised, the seller will prefer the agreement to be governed by the laws of the seller's country, and the buyer will prefer it to be governed by the laws of the buyer's country. If the bargaining leverage of the parties is approximately equal, it is fair to say that it is more customary for the buyer to agree that the seller's law will govern the agreement. However, if the buyer has more bargaining leverage, the buyer may be able to prevail. Before agreeing to have the foreign seller's law govern the agreement, however, the buyer should check on what differences exist between the foreign law and U.S. law, so that the buyer can fully appreciate the risks it is assuming by agreeing to the application of foreign law. The buyer can also determine whether or not the risk is serious enough to negotiate a specific solution to that particular problem with the seller. Frequently, however, the parties do not raise, negotiate, or expressly agree upon the governing law. This may occur as a result of an exchange of preprinted forms wherein the buyer and the seller each have specified that their own law governs, which results in a clear conflict between these two provisions. It may also occur when the parties have not discussed the governing law, as in a situation where an oral agreement or sale has occurred, or when the facsimile, email, or other purchase or sale documentation does not contain any express specification of the governing law. In such cases, if a dispute arises between the parties, it will be extremely difficult to determine with any confidence which law governs the purchase agreement. Often the buyer believes that the law of the country where the offer is accepted will govern. However, the laws of the two countries may be in conflict on this point, and it may be unclear whether this means an offer to sell or an offer to buy, and whether or not the acceptance must be received by the offeror before the formation of the purchase agreement.

An additional development relating to this issue is the Convention on Contracts for the International Sale of Goods (the Convention). On January 1, 1988, this multinational treaty went into effect among the countries that have signed it, including the United States. For a current listing see: http://www.uncitral.org/uncitral/about/origin_history. html. The Convention is a detailed listing of over one hundred articles dealing with the rights and responsibilities of the buyer and the seller in international purchase agreements. It is similar in some respects to Article 2 of the U.S. Uniform Commercial Code. Nevertheless, there are many concepts, such as fundamental breach, avoidance, impediment, and nonconformity that are not identical to U.S. law.

The Convention permits buyers and sellers located in countries that are parties to the Convention to exclude the application of the Convention (by expressly referring to it) and to choose the law of either the seller or the buyer to apply to the international purchase agreement. However, for companies located in any of the countries that are parties to the Convention (including U.S. companies), if the seller and buyer cannot or do not agree on which law will apply, the provisions of the Convention will automatically apply.

In summary, the buyer should include provisions on governing law in its international purchase agreement, and if the seller disagrees, the buyer should negotiate this provision. The buyer should also determine what differences exist between the Convention and U.S. law in case the parties cannot agree and the Convention thereby becomes applicable.

m. Dispute Resolution. One method of resolving disputes that may arise between the parties is litigation in the courts. For a U.S. importer, the most likely dispute to arise relates to defective goods. In such cases, the importer may be limited to going to the courts of the seller's country in order to institute litigation and seek a judgment to obtain assets of the seller. Even if the parties have agreed that U.S. law will govern the purchase agreement, there is a risk that a foreign court may misapply U.S. law, disregard U.S. law, or otherwise favor and protect the seller located in its own country. Furthermore, there can be significant delays in legal proceedings (from two to five years), court and legal expenses can be high, and the outcome may be questionable. In order to reduce such risks, the importer can specify in the international purchase agreement that all disputes must be resolved in the courts of the importer's country, and that the seller consents to jurisdiction there and to the commencement of any such lawsuit by the simple forwarding of any form of written notice by the importer to the seller. Of course, sellers may resist such provisions, and whether the buyer will be able to finally obtain this agreement will depend upon the negotiating and bargaining strength of the parties.

Another form of dispute resolution that is common in international purchase agreements is arbitration. In many foreign countries, sellers take a less adversarial approach to the resolution of contractual disputes, and they feel more comfortable with a less formal proceeding, such as arbitration. While arbitration can be included in an international purchase agreement, an importer should thoroughly understand the advantages and disadvantages of agreeing to resolve disputes by arbitration. First, arbitration is unlikely to save much in expenses and quite often may not involve a significantly shorter time period to resolve the dispute. In fact, from the point of view of expense, in some cases, if the seller refuses to go forward with the arbitration, the buyer will have to advance the seller's portion of the arbitration fees to the arbitration tribunal, or the arbitrators will not proceed with the dispute. Furthermore, in litigation, of course, the judges or juries involved are paid at the public expense, whereas in arbitration, the parties must pay the expenses of the arbitrators, which can be very substantial, especially if there are three arbitrators.

Second, the administering authority must be selected. The International Chamber of Commerce is commonly designated as the administering authority in arbitration clauses, but the fees that it charges are very high. The American Arbitration Association also handles international disputes, but the foreign seller may be unwilling to agree to arbitration by a U.S. administering authority. Other administering authorities, such as the Inter-American Commercial Arbitration Commission, the London Court of International Arbitration, the Stockholm Chamber of Commerce Arbitration Institute, the British Columbia International Arbitration Centre, or an arbitration authority in the seller's country, may be acceptable.

Third, the number of arbitrators should be specified. Since the parties will be paying for them, the author recommends that one arbitrator be utilized to resolve disputes of a smaller amount (a specified dollar figure) and those three arbitrators be utilized for larger disputes.

Fourth, the place of arbitration must be specified. Again, the seller and the buyer will have a natural conflict on this point, so some third country or intermediate location is probably most likely to be mutually agreeable. Another variation that has developed, although its legal validity has been questioned, is an agreement that if the seller commences the arbitration, arbitration will be conducted in the buyer's country, and if the buyer commences the arbitration, the arbitration will be conducted in the seller's country. This has the effect of discouraging either party from commencing arbitration and forcing the parties to reach amicable solutions to their disputes.

Finally, the buyer should ascertain beforehand whether an arbitral award would be enforced in the courts of the seller's country. Some sixty countries have become parties to a multinational treaty known as the New York Convention, which commits them to enforcing the arbitral awards of member countries. Without this assurance, the entire dispute may have to be relitigated in the seller's country.

n. Termination. Protection against termination of an international purchase agreement or distributor or sales agent agreement may prove to be difficult for the U.S. buyer. No federal law specifically protects U.S. buyers, distributors, or sales agents against unfair terminations, although some states have enacted protective legislation. Although the U.S. buyer may have invested a great deal of time in purchasing products or building up a market for the resale of such products, the seller may terminate the agreement on short notice or without payment of compensation. In general, the buyer may be able to claim damages if the termination is the result of conspiracy, such as the agreement of two or more suppliers not to sell to the buyer (concerted refusal to deal); if the termination is by a seller with monopoly power (such as a 60 percent or greater market share); or if the termination is for an anticompetitive, rather than a business, reason (such as a refusal of the buyer to adhere to the seller's suggested resale prices). The buyer should try to get some protection by entering into an ongoing purchase agreement (rather than simply dealing on a purchase-order-by-purchase-order basis) and inserting a provision that there be a long lead time prior to termination or that the seller will pay the buyer some termination compensation for goodwill created by the buyer's market development. (If the purchaser is selling the goods under its own trademark, the seller will not be able to appoint another distributor to sell under the same brand name unless the seller is willing to buy the trademark from the buyer.) Of course, the buyer should always specify in the purchase agreement that it will have no obligation to continue to purchase from the seller if there is a change in control, bankruptcy, insolvency, or breach of the agreement by the seller.

C. Import Distributor and Sales Agent Agreements

In addition to the foregoing provisions, which arise in all international purchase agreements, there are other specific provisions that arise in import distributor agreements and sales agent agreements.

1. *Distinction Between Distributor and Sales Agent*

A distributor is a company that buys products from a seller, takes title thereto, and assumes the risk of resale. A distributor will purchase at a specific price and will be compensated by reselling the product at a higher price. Under the antitrust laws of the United States, the seller cannot restrict or require a distributor to resell the product at any specific price, although it may be able to restrict the customers to whom or the territories in which the buyer resells.

A sales agent does not purchase from the seller. The sales agent or representative locates customers and solicits offers to purchase the product from the potential buyers. In order to avoid tax liability for the seller in the United States, the sales agent normally will not have any authority to accept offers to purchase from potential customers. Instead, the offers from the customer are forwarded to the seller for final acceptance, and shipment and billing is direct between the seller and the customer. Furthermore, since the sales agent normally does not take title, it will ordinarily not act as importer of record and will not assume liabilities for customs duties or penalties. For such services, the sales agent is paid a commission or some other type of compensation. Because no sale occurs between the seller and the sales agent, the seller can specify the price at which it will sell to customers, and the sales agent can be restricted to quoting only that price to a potential customer. Likewise, the sales agent can be restricted as to its territory or the types of customers from which it has been given the right to solicit orders. Sometimes the sales agent will guarantee payment by the customers or perform other services, such as after-sales service or invoicing of the customers.

A chart summarizing these differences is shown in Figure 3–12. Another chart analyzing the financial comparison of acting as a distributor or a sales agent is shown in Figure 3–13.

2. *Import Distributor Agreements*

As previously indicated, when a distributor agreement is utilized, such agreement will act as an umbrella agreement, and specific orders for specific quantities, shipment dates, and possibly prices will be stated in purchase orders, purchase order acceptances, and similar documentation discussed in relation to isolated purchase transactions. A checklist for negotiation issues for a distributor agreement is shown in Figure 3–14.

The important provisions in an import distributor agreement include the following:

a. Territory and Exclusivity. The distributor will normally want to be the exclusive distributor in a territory, whereas the seller would generally prefer to make a nonexclusive appointment so that if the distributor fails to perform, it can appoint other distributors. Also, the seller may simply wish from the outset to appoint a number of distributors in the United States to adequately serve the market. A possible compromise is that the appointment will be exclusive unless certain minimum purchase obligations are not met, in which case the seller has the right to convert the agreement to a nonexclusive agreement.

Usually the entire United States or the part of the United States that is granted to the distributor is specified. The distributor may be required to agree not to solicit sales from outside the territory. The distributor may be prohibited from establishing any warehouse or sales outlet outside of the territory.

b. Pricing. As indicated, normally it is illegal for the seller to specify the price at which the U.S. distributor can resell the merchandise. Of course, ordinarily the distributor would not mark up the product too much, gouging end users and resulting in less sales and market penetration for the products. In addition, because of the gray market problem, the price at which the buyer resells should not be set too high, thereby attracting diversions from other countries. Gray markets can occur as a result of exchange rate fluctuations, where one of the seller's other distributors in another country is able to obtain a product at a lower price in its own currency than is available in the United States.

Currency fluctuations must be monitored, and the right to price reductions is normally necessary to make sure that the buyer is participating fairly in the profits that are being created along the chain of distribution. For example, if a French seller sells a product for $1 at a time when the French exchange rate is 5 euros to $1, the seller will be receiving $1 (or 5 euros) when it's cost of production may be 4 euros, or a 1 euro profit. However, if the euro weakens to 10 euros to $1, and the seller still sells the product for $1, now it will receive 10 euros and its profit will increase. Sometimes the seller will continue to ask for price increases from the buyer even though the seller has had a very favorable exchange rate movement. Normally it is in the buyer's interest to have the seller reduce the price whenever the foreign currency weakens (or the dollar strengthens). When the seller does decrease its price to the U.S. distributor, however, normally the seller will also want the U.S. distributor to reduce its price on resale to the end users so that more sales will be made, volume will increase, and the seller can increase its market share.

c. Minimum Purchase Quantities. In most long-term purchase agreements or distributor agreements, the seller will ask for a commitment for purchase of a significant quantity. The buyer should request some price discount for such a commitment. Ordinarily, it is in the buyer's interest to commit only to a target amount or to use its best efforts to make sales. In such cases, if the buyer fails to make the target, there is no breach of the agreement and the seller cannot sue the buyer for damages. If the buyer commits to purchase fixed quantities or dollar amounts, however, and fails to perform, the seller may be able to sue for damages and terminate the distributor agreement.

d. Handling Competing Products. Normally a seller will want a provision wherein the distributor agrees not to handle competing products. If the distributor is already handling any competing products (either manufacturing them or purchasing them from alternative sources), the distributor may not want to agree to this provision, and there is no legal requirement that it do so. In fact, in certain situations, such as where other competing sellers do not have adequate outlets for their products, a violation of the U.S. antitrust laws can result if the buyer is required not to handle competing products. However, the seller will normally be unwilling to give the distributor an exclusive appointment in the territory unless the distributor agrees not to handle competing products.

e. Appointment of Subdistributors. Whether or not the distributor has the right to appoint subdistributors should be expressly stated in the distributor agreement. If this right is not discussed, the distributor may not have the right under U.S. law to appoint subdistributors. This can cause various problems for the distributor. Not only will the distributor possibly be unable to meet its purchase commitments to the seller, which could result in termination of the distributor agreement, but the distributor may lose chances to multiply its sales. In appointing subdistributors, the distributor needs to control the resale territories (but not the prices) to maximize distribution and sales potential. If the right to appoint subdistributors is granted, the distributor should try to avoid responsibility for their activities in the distribution agreement, such as sales outside their territories; otherwise, the distributor may find that its master distribution agreement with the seller is being terminated due to breaches by the independent subdistributors.

f. Use of Trade Names, Trademarks, and Copyrights. As discussed in Chapter 6, Section O, control of intellectual property rights is quite important. Sometimes U.S. distributors can protect their market position by registering their intellectual property rights, such as trademarks, in the United States. This is a particular disadvantage for the foreign seller, because if the seller wishes to terminate the distributor and to appoint a new distributor, the past distributor may own the intellectual property rights to distribute the products in the United States. Until the distributor consents to the assignment of the intellectual property rights to the seller or the new distributor, any sales by the seller into the United States or by the new distributor will be an infringement of the intellectual property rights owned by the former distributor. This puts the former distributor in a very strong bargaining position to negotiate a substantial termination compensation payment. The distributor may do this in a private branding arrangement where the seller, if it is a manufacturer, puts the distributor's own trademark or brand on the product. In the international purchase agreement, the distributor could specify that it has the exclusive rights to that name or brand, and the distributor should register the name with the U.S. Patent and Trademark Office. Upon termination of the distributorship agreement, the seller could not sell the products under that name or appoint another distributor to do so (but the seller could sell identical products under another brand name).

g. Warranties and Product Liability. In addition to the considerations discussed in Section B.2.i, the importer should require the seller to maintain product liability insurance in its own name and to name the importer as an additional insured in amounts deemed satisfactory by the importer. Product liability claims are not as common overseas as they are in the United States, and foreign sellers may not have product liability insurance. Furthermore, the customer will find it easier to sue the importer in the United States. The overseas seller may have no office in the United States, and the importer may be unable to sue the seller in the United States for warranty claims by the importer's customers. The seller should use a U.S. insurance company or a foreign insurance company that is doing business in the United States and is subject to the jurisdiction of the United States. Before modifying or adding to any of the seller's warranties, the buyer should obtain the seller's consent. If the distributor agrees to perform warranty or after-sales service for the seller, it should make sure that it clearly understands its responsibilities and the terms for reimbursement for warranty labor it performs.

3. Import Sales Agent Agreements

Like distributor agreements, sales agent agreements often contain many of the same provisions that are included in an international purchase agreement, but there are certain provisions peculiar to the sales agent agreement that must be considered. A checklist for negotiation issues for a sales agent agreement is shown in Figure 3–15.

a. Commissions. The sales agent is compensated for its efforts by payment of a commission by the seller. The sales agent is appointed to solicit orders, and when such orders are accepted by the seller, the agent is paid a commission. The U.S. sales agent should try to have its commission due upon solicitation or acceptance of the order instead of when the customer actually makes payment to the seller. The sales agent is not normally guaranteeing payment by the customers or making credit decisions, so it should not have to wait for its commission—its work is done when it brings a customer to the seller. Generally, the seller should not bill the agent for the price of the product (less commission) because such practice could result in characterizing the relationship as a distributorship rather than a sales agency.

b. *Pricing.* Because there is no sale between the seller and the sales agent, the seller can lawfully require the sales agent to quote only prices that the seller has authorized. For sellers who wish to establish uniform pricing on a worldwide basis, eliminate gray markets, and control markups, use of the sales agent appointment can be highly beneficial. However, the trade-off is that the seller will ordinarily assume the credit risk and will have to satisfy itself with regard to the ability of the customer to pay. This sometimes presents difficulties in obtaining sufficient information, although the sales agent can be given the responsibility of gathering such information and forwarding it to the seller prior to acceptance of any orders. In addition, some sales agents are willing to be appointed as *del credere* agents, wherein the sales agent guarantees the payment by any customer from whom it solicits an order. Obviously, a sales agent should require higher commissions for guaranteeing payment.

c. *Shipment.* Shipment is not made to the sales agent; it is made directly to the customer from whom the sales agent solicited the order. Generally there will be problems associated with trying to maintain an inventory at the agent's place of business in the United States. If the seller maintains an inventory in its own name or through an agent, the seller can become taxable on its own sales profits to customers in the United States. If the customer cannot wait for shipment from the foreign country, or if it is important to maintain an inventory in the United States, the appropriate way to do so while using sales agents must be investigated with a knowledgeable attorney.

Chapter 8
Import Process and Documentation

In addition to the purchase agreement, there are numerous other documents that the importer will commonly encounter in the process of importing merchandise. U.S. Customs and Border Protection treats the importer like the Internal Revenue Service treats the taxpayer. It expects that the importer has knowledge of the customs laws and regulations and the information provided to Customs regarding its import transactions are true and accurate. While U.S Customs may review the documentation or call for an inspection of the merchandise, the majority of transactions are reviewed by computer programs looking for discrepancies, which then will result in questions for clarification or review of the transaction. As a result auditing has become a primary enforcement tool for Customs, just as with the IRS and the documentation that the importer must keep become critical to maintain. Since some of these documents may be prepared by the customs broker or others, the importer may not see such documents or realize that they have been prepared. Nevertheless, because the importer is responsible for the actions of its agent, the customs broker, it is imperative that the importer understand what documents are being prepared and filed on each importation. Furthermore, since the documents filed by the customs broker may be based on information provided by the importer, if the importer does not understand the documents or provides incorrect information, the customs broker will disclaim any responsibility therefor. Additionally, U.S. Customs expects that an importer will audit the information filed by the customs broker on its behalf in exercising reasonable care over its import transactions.

An overview of the U.S. Customs import process, which will be described in more detail in this chapter, is shown in Figure 8–1.

Figure 8–1. Import process.

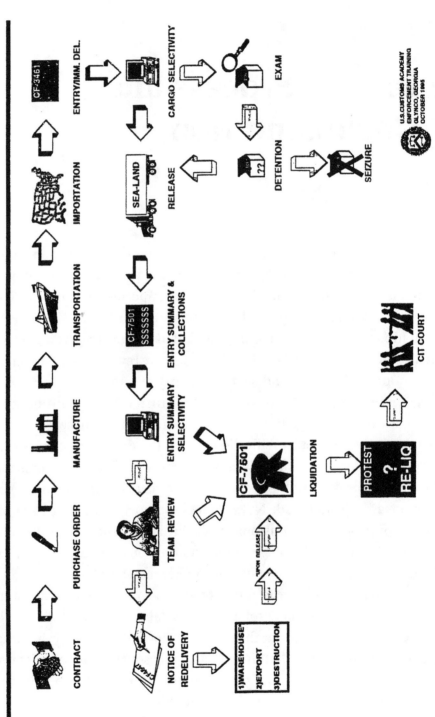

A. Importer Security Filing and the 10+2 Program

Increased security since September 11, 2001, has resulted in a number of new measures to collect data on shipments arriving in the United States prior to their departure from the country of exportation. Among these measures is the Importer Security Filing, which was implemented on January 26, 2009, with full compliance required by January 26, 2010. The program requires ten data elements to be transmitted by the importer prior to export. The time frames in which to transmit differ according to the type of transportation. These include:

1. Manufacturer* —consistent with Customs Entry/Immediate Delivery form
2. Seller
3. Buyer
4. Ship to party (if not the buyer)
5. Container stuffing location
6. Consolidator
7. Importer of record
8. Consignee
9. Country of origin*
10. Harmonized Tariff Number*

*Manufacturer, country of origin, and Harmonized Tariff Number must be at the line item level.

The remaining two elements must be supplied by the carrier: (1) the vessel stow plan and (2) container status messages. The information is to be reported at the lowest bill of lading level. The importer may file this information directly with CBP or use an agent with a valid power of attorney. This advance reporting allows for Customs to review what is going to be arriving and make determinations well in advance as to whether there should be an inspection, another government agency involved, or to allow the goods to be released.

B. Bills of Lading

The bill of lading or loading is issued by the transportation carrier, either the airline or the steamship company. It evidences receipt of the merchandise for transportation to the destination specified in the bill. In the case of ocean shipments, the original bill of lading will have been obtained by the exporter and will be forwarded by air courier service through banking channels (or directly to the buyer on open account purchases) for arrival in advance of the shipment. Customs requires that the party making entry of the goods into the United States (the importer of record) must present a copy of the air waybill, ocean bill of lading, or truck manifest with the other customs entry documents in order to establish that the party filing for release has the right to make entry of the goods and to match the entry documents to the transportation information filed directly by the carrier in order to crosscheck the imports against the import clearances. Where the transportation is under a negotiable bill of lading, the importer will also have to present the properly endorsed bill of lading to the transportation carrier in order to obtain release of the goods from the carrier. On import transactions, the Uniform Commercial Code requires that the bill of lading be negotiable unless the parties agree to a non-negotiable bill of lading in their purchase agreement. Where a negotiable bill of lading has been lost or the importer cannot present it, the steamship line may permit the importer to obtain the merchandise if it signs a "letter of indemnity" and the importer is determined to be a good credit risk. Sample ocean and air bills of lading are shown in Figures 4–6 and 4–7. Additional information on bills of lading is contained in Chapter 4, Section D.

C. Commercial Invoices

At the same time that the exporter forwards the bill of lading, it will include a commercial invoice (which must be in the English language) itemizing the merchandise sold and the amount due for payment. There must be one invoice for each separate shipment. Under U.S. Customs regulations, these commercial invoices must contain very specific items of information, such as quantities, description, and purchase price, country of origin, assists, transportation charges, commissions, installation service, and financing charges. For numerous classes of products, the commercial invoice must contain certain additional information. Prior to exportation, the importer should identify what specialized information is required by the U.S. Customs regulations and communicate that to the exporter. A summary of the required contents is shown in Figure 4–4. U.S. Customs and Border Protection has the authority and has indicated that it will detain and refuse to release shipments where the invoice does not contain all of the necessary information. (A sample invoice is shown in Figure 3–9.) Showing the package numbers and quantities on the commercial invoice facilitates Customs examination of the merchandise. Putting the commercial invoice number on all of the shipping documents helps to tie the documents together. The importer should understand that the invoice amount and the declared value have consequences for the "cost of goods" calculation for U.S. income tax purposes under section 1059A of the Internal Revenue Code.

D. Pro Forma Invoices

When the importer receives a shipment and no commercial invoice is available, it can prepare its own invoice, known as a pro forma invoice, and submit it to Customs for entry of the merchandise, provided it supplies a bond for its production. (A sample pro forma invoice is shown in Figure 8–2.) This is merely the representation by the buyer as to the price that it paid or that is payable for purchase of the goods. The commercial invoice signed by the exporter must be furnished to Customs within fifty days or the bond will be forfeited.

E. Packing Lists

The buyer may request or the seller may include a packing list with the merchandise. While of less importance if there is only one or two commodities, this document is critical should Customs decide to conduct an intensive examination as it will facilitate finding the specific products that Customs wants to review. In the event that there is any shortage, damage, or defects, the packing list is also important for making insurance claims. When the buyer is responsible for obtaining such insurance, the buyer/importer should require the seller to send a packing list (see Figure 4–8).

F. Inspection Certificates

If the buyer requires a preshipment inspection in its purchase agreement, the inspection certificate should be furnished by the third-party company that performed the inspection prior to exportation. This need not be filed with U.S. Customs and Border Protection, but in the event of any discrepancy between the merchandise upon arrival and the inspection certificate, the importer should notify the inspection service (and the courier and the insurance company) immediately.

Figure 8–2. Pro forma invoice.

ProForma Invoice

Exporter

Date

PO Number

Order Number

Terms

Ultimate Consignee

Commercial Invoice Number

ProForm Invoice Number

Ultimate Consignee Phone

Customer Account Number

Exporting Carrier

Loading Pier/Terminal

Intermediate Consignee

Origination State

Country of Destination

Exporter Contact Name

Exporter Contact Phone

Quantity	Product ID	Description	Schedule B Code	Unit Price	Total Price

Ex-Works Value	
Inland Freight Fees	
Handling Fees	
Consular Fees	
Ocean/Air Fees	
Insurance Fees	
Other Charges	

Total:

USD

Title:

Authorized Signature:

Page of

This document created using Shipping Solutions Professional export software, www.shipsolutions.com.

G. Drafts for Payment

Where the seller/exporter has made shipment under a letter of credit opened by the buyer/importer, or under an agreement with a bank for documentary collection, the buyer's bank will pay the amount owed on sight drafts to the seller's bank immediately and will present any time drafts to the buyer/importer for acceptance. (Samples are shown in Figures 4–29 and 4–30, respectively.)

H. Arrival Notices

The transportation carrier (steamship company or airline) will send an arrival notice to the customs broker or to the importer (the consignee or notify party in the bill of lading) upon arrival of the merchandise in the port. The party who is notified will be in accordance with the instructions that the transportation carrier received from the seller/exporter or the seller's freight forwarder in the foreign country, which is usually based on the instructions of the buyer to the seller. After receiving an arrival notice, the importer or its customs broker will ordinarily have five days within which to supply the necessary documents to U.S. Customs and Border Protection to make entry and obtain release and delivery of the merchandise.

I. Pickup and Delivery Orders

If the foreign exporter has agreed to deliver the merchandise to the buyer/ importer's premises, the foreign exporter or, more usually, its freight forwarder will issue a delivery order to the freight forwarder in the United States upon arrival of the goods in the United States to effect the inland transportation between the U.S. port of arrival and the buyer's premises. Or, if the title has passed to the buyer prior to or upon arrival, the importer will instruct the customs broker to make entry with U.S. Customs and Border Protection. Once entry has been made, the customs broker will instruct the trucking company to pick up the merchandise from the international transportation carrier and deliver it to the importer. Customs brokers may also make arrangements to deliver the merchandise for the importer. They usually have relationships with local carriers and can provide that service.

J. Automated Commercial Environment (ACE)

U.S. Customs and Border Protection has spent many years developing the Automated Commercial Environment (ACE) System to replace its aged Automated Broker Interface system. The goal is to expedite trade facilitation, while still maintaining a strong and secure border. ACE is an Internet-based system and in its final stages of development. It will become the sole mandatory method of electronically filing information with U.S. Customs and other federal agencies involved within the next few years. It has also provided added benefits to those companies that have already migrated to the ACE system through the use of individual ACE Secure Portals including:

- Periodic monthly statements, allowing for the payment of duties once a month in place of payment with each entry summary filed
- Reduced processing time at the border
- The ability to review shipment status through the ACE Portal
- Capabilities to produce over 100 reports based on the data filed

For the most recent updates as to the status of the ACE program, see: http://www.cbp.gov/trade/ace/features.

K. Entry/Immediate Delivery

Traditionally, when an importer imports merchandise, it must prepare the necessary customs entry documents and present them to U.S. Customs and Border Protection along with payment of estimated duties before release of the goods to the importer can be authorized by U.S. Customs and Border Protection. However, as a general practice, most importers have provided a customs surety bond, as discussed in Chapter 6, Section F.2, and so (if the importer is not in default on the payment of its customs bills) the importer can apply for immediate release of the goods by filing an Entry/Immediate Delivery form (Customs Form 3461). (See sample in Figure 8–3.) Customs brokers or importers who have been accepted under the Automated Broker Interface (ABI) or more recently under the Automated Commercial Environment (ACE) may file this form electronically. If entry is made using this form, the importer is required to file an Entry Summary form (CF-7501), with the additional information required by that form and payment of estimated duties, within ten days thereafter or Customs will make a liquidated damages assessment, a form of customs penalty. If an importer is using the ACE system, the entry

Figure 8–3. Entry/Immediate Delivery form.

DEPARTMENT OF HOMELAND SECURITY U.S.
Customs and Border Protection

OMB No. 1651-0024
Exp. 04-30-2015

ENTRY/IMMEDIATE DELIVERY
19 CFR 142.3, 142.16, 142.22, 142.24

1. ARRIVAL DATE	2. ELECTED ENTRY DATE	3. ENTRY TYPE CODE/NAME	4. ENTRY NUMBER
5. PORT	6. SINGLE TRANS. BOND	7. BROKER/IMPORTER FILE NUMBER	
	8. CONSIGNEE NUMBER		9. IMPORTER NUMBER
10. ULTIMATE CONSIGNEE NAME		11. IMPORTER OF RECORD NAME	
12. CARRIER CODE	13. VOYAGE/FLIGHT/TRIP	14. LOCATION OF GOODS-CODE(S)/NAME(S)	
15. VESSEL CODE/NAME			
16. U.S. PORT OF UNLADING	17. MANIFEST NUMBER	18. G.O. NUMBER	19. TOTAL VALUE
20. DESCRIPTION OF MERCHANDISE			

21. IT/BL/AWB CODE	22. IT/BL/AWB NO.	23. MANIFEST QUANTITY	24. H.S. NUMBER	25. COUNTRY OF ORIGIN	26. MANUFACTURER NO.

27. CERTIFICATION

I hereby make application for entry/immediate delivery. I certify that the above information is accurate, the bond is sufficient, valid, and current, and that all requirements of 19 CFR Part 142 have been met.

SIGNATURE OF APPLICANT

PHONE NO. | DATE

29. BROKER OR OTHER GOVT. AGENCY USE

28. CBP USE ONLY

☐ OTHER AGENCY ACTION REQUIRED, NAMELY:

☐ CBP EXAMINATION REQUIRED.

☐ ENTRY REJECTED, BECAUSE:

DELIVERY AUTHORIZED: | SIGNATURE | DATE

Paperwork Reduction Act Statement: An agency may not conduct or sponsor an information collection and a person is not required to respond to this information unless it displays a current valid OMB control number and an expiration date. The control number for this collection is 1651-0024. The estimated average time to complete this application is 15 minutes. If you have any comments regarding the burden estimate you can write to U.S. Customs and Border Protection, Office of Regulations and Rulings, 799 9th Street, NW., Washington DC 20229.

CBP Form 3461 (10/09)

summary form just be filed within ten days after the release of the merchandise, but the duties may be paid monthly. The entry summary form can be filed within five days prior to the arrival of the merchandise if shipped by ocean or as soon as the wheels are up in the exporting country on air shipments. When the Entry/Immediate Delivery form has been submitted electronically, it is processed electronically and audited against pre-determined criteria based on the past import records of the importer, the exporter, the Manufacturer Identification Code (MID), the classification, and the country of origin to determine whether the merchandise should be examined or not. The computer determines which shipments should undergo a physical examination, which should have their documentation reviewed, and which may bypass an examination entirely and be released "paperless." Local Customs authorities have the ability to alter the instructions from the computer audit, but they are required to provide an explanation for any deviation and as a result do not tend to override any decisions made by the automated review.

L. Entry Summary

The Entry Summary is the main document used to enter goods into the United States. Either the Entry/Immediate Delivery form or the Entry Summary must be filed with U.S. Customs and Border Protection within five working days after arrival of the shipment at the port of entry (or the port of destination for in-bond shipments). Where no Entry/Immediate Delivery form was filed before the filing of the Entry Summary, the Entry Summary is referred to as a "live entry." Certain commodities require a live entry to be submitted, with all duties and fees paid prior to the release of merchandise, for example, food products that are under a quantitative quota subject to immediate filing on the date of opening. Importers who are on the ACE system may pay the duties on a monthly basis using the Automated Clearing House wire transfer process. The entry may specify that the merchandise is for consumption or is for storage in a warehouse, to be withdrawn for consumption at a later date. If no entry is made, the merchandise will be transferred to a "general order" warehouse. If no entry is made within six months (immediately for perishable goods); the merchandise will be sold.

Several items on the Entry Summary are worthy of note. (An Entry Summary and Continuation Sheet are shown in Figure 8–4.) Box 21 of the Entry Summary requires the importer to show the manufacturer's/shipper's identification code. This is a special code that must be constructed from the name and address of the manufacturer/shipper. Column 32 of the Entry Summary requires the importer to state the entered value. CHGS stands for charges, and means items such as foreign inland freight, ocean

Figure 8–4. Entry Summary and Continuation Sheet.

Form Approved OMB No. 1651-0022
EXP. 08-31-2014

DEPARTMENT OF HOMELAND SECURITY U.S. Customs and Border Protection **ENTRY SUMMARY**		1. Filer Code/Entry No.	2. Entry Type	3. Summary Date
		4. Surety No.	5. Bond Type	6. Port Code	7. Entry Date

8. Importing Carrier	9. Mode of Transport	10. Country of Origin	11. Import Date
12. B/L or AWB No.	13. Manufacturer ID	14. Exporting Country	15. Export Date
16. I.T. No.	17. I.T. Date	18. Missing Docs	19. Foreign Port of Lading	20. U.S. Port of Unlading
21. Location of Goods/G.O. No.	22. Consignee No.	23. Importer No.	24. Reference No.

25. Ultimate Consignee Name and Address	26. Importer of Record Name and Address
City State Zip	City State Zip

27. Line No.	28. Description of Merchandise			32. A. Entered Value B. CHGS C. Relationship	33. A. HTSUS Rate B. ADA/CVD Rate C. IRC Rate D. Visa No.	34. Duty and I.R. Tax
	29. A. HTSUS No. B. ADA/CVD No.	30. A. Grossweight B. Manifest Qty.	31. Net Quantity in HTSUS Units			Dollars Cents

Other Fee Summary for Block 39	35. Total Entered Value $	**CBP USE ONLY**		**TOTALS**
		A. LIQ CODE	B. Ascertained Duty	37. Duty
	Total Other Fees $	REASON CODE	C. Ascertained Tax	38. Tax

36. DECLARATION OF IMPORTER OF RECORD (OWNER OR PURCHASER) OR AUTHORIZED AGENT	D. Ascertained Other	39. Other
I declare that I am the ☐ Importer of record and that the actual owner, purchaser, or consignee for CBP purposes is as shown above, **OR** ☐ owner	E. Ascertained Total	40. Total

or purchaser or agent thereof. I further declare that the merchandise ☐ was obtained pursuant to a purchase or agreement to purchase and that the prices set forth in the invoices are true. **OR** ☐ was not obtained pursuant to a purchase or agreement to purchase and the statements in the invoices as to value or price are true to the best of my knowledge and belief. I also declare that the statements in the documents herein filed fully disclose to the best of my knowledge and belief the true prices, values, quantities, rebates, drawbacks, fees, commissions, and royalties and are true and correct, and that all goods or services provided to the seller of the merchandise either free or at reduced cost are fully disclosed. I will immediately furnish to the appropriate CBP officer any information showing a different statement of facts.

41. DECLARANT NAME TITLE	SIGNATURE DATE
42. Broker/Filer Information (Name, address, phone number)	43. Broker/Importer File No.

Paperwork Reduction Act Notice CBP Form 7501 (06/09)

Figure 8–4. *(continued)*

OMB No. 1651-0022
EXP. 08-31-2014

DEPARTMENT OF HOMELAND SECURITY   **ENTRY SUMMARY CONTINUATION SHEET**
U.S. Customs and Border Protection

1. Filer Code/Entry No.

27. Line No.	28. Description of Merchandise			32.	33.	34. Duty and I.R. Tax
	29. A. HTSUS No. B. ADA/CVD No.	30. A. Grossweight B. Manifest Qty.	31. Net Quantity in HTSUS Units	A. Entered Value B. CHGS C. Relationship	A. HTSUS Rate B. ADA/CVD Rate C. IRC Rate D. Visa No.	Dollars Cents

CBP Form 7501 (06/09)

Figure 8–4. *(continued)*

OMB No. 1651-0022
EXP. 08-31-2014

DEPARTMENT OF HOMELAND SECURITY **ENTRY SUMMARY CONTINUATION SHEET**
U.S. Customs and Border Protection

1. Filer Code/Entry No.

27. Line No.	28. Description of Merchandise			32.	33.	34.
	29. A. HTSUS No. B. ADA/CVD No.	30. A. Grossweight B. Manifest Qty.	31. Net Quantity in HTSUS Units	A. Entered Value B. CHGS C. Relationship	A. HTSUS Rate B. ADA/CVD Rate C. IRC Rate D. Visa No.	Duty and I.R. Tax — Dollars / Cents

CBP Form 7501 (06/09)

Figure 8–4. *(continued)*

DEPARTMENT OF HOMELAND SECURITY
U.S. Customs and Border Protection

ENTRY SUMMARY CONTINUATION SHEET

OMB No. 1651-0022
EXP. 08-31-2014

1. Filer Code/Entry No.

27. Line No.	28. Description of Merchandise			32.	33.	34. Duty and I.R. Tax	
	29. A. HTSUS No. B. ADA/CVD No.	30. A. Grossweight B. Manifest Qty.	31. Net Quantity in HTSUS Units	A. Entered Value B. CHGS C. Relationship	A. HTSUS Rate B. ADA/CVD Rate C. IRC Rate D. Visa No.	Dollars	Cents

CBP Form 7501 (06/09)

Figure 8–4. (*continued*)

DEPARTMENT OF HOMELAND SECURITY
U.S. Customs and Border Protection

ENTRY SUMMARY CONTINUATION SHEET

OMB No. 1651-0022
EXP. 08-31-2014

1. Filer Code/Entry No.

27. Line No.	28. Description of Merchandise			32.	33.	34.
	29. A. HTSUS No. B. ADA/CVD No.	30. A. Grossweight B. Manifest Qty.	31. Net Quantity in HTSUS Units	A. Entered Value B. CHGS C. Relationship	A. HTSUS Rate B. ADA/CVD Rate C. IRC Rate D. Visa No.	Duty and I.R. Tax Dollars Cents

CBP Form 7501 (06/09)

transportation, and ocean insurance, which are not dutiable. The "relationship" line is asking whether or not the seller and buyer are affiliated companies. It is important to ensure that the proper relationship is indicated, as this will affect the entered value.

In addition to the customs duties, the importer is required to calculate the merchandise processing fee (currently 0.3464 percent) and the harbor maintenance fee (currently 0.125 percent) for shipments using a U.S. harbor and make payment at the times of entry. There is a cap of $485 per entry on merchandise processing fees, but no cap on harbor maintenance fees. Other fees may be required depending on the commodity, such as excise taxes on alcohol, perfume, and certain fishing and archery sporting goods; cotton fees on the import of cotton or products containing cotton; pork check-off fees for imports of pork products; etc.

At the bottom of the form, the signer is required to declare that the statements in the Entry Summary fully disclose the true prices, values, quantities, rebates, drawbacks, fees, commissions, and royalties on the purchase, and that all goods or services provided to the seller of the merchandise either free or at reduced costs have been fully disclosed. The signer represents that it will immediately furnish to the appropriate U.S. Customs officer any information showing facts different from those stated in the Entry Summary. This is extremely important, because incorrect and therefore false statements on the Entry Summary can be the basis for both criminal and civil penalties assessed by U.S. Customs and Border Protection against the importer. Such errors need not be intentional, and even accidental errors can be the basis for penalties.

M. Other Entries

In place of the Entry Summary used for consumption, warehouse, and temporary import entries, transportation and exportation entries, immediate transportation entries, and entries for admission to a foreign trade zone are listed on their own forms. (Samples are shown in Figure 8–5 and back in Chapter 6, Figure 6-7. The Application for a Foreign Trade Zone Activity Permit was shown in Figure 6-8.) Transportation and exportation entries are used when the importer knows at the time of import that the product will be exported and the merchandise is merely being transported temporarily through the United States. No manipulation or modification of the merchandise is permitted during the time that it is in the United States, and the merchandise technically remains in Customs' custody. No customs duties are payable, but the importer must have a customs bond to guarantee payment of the customs duties in case the shipment is accidentally diverted into the United States. In addition, the carriers must be

Figure 8–5. Transportation Entry.

OMB No. 1651-0003 Exp. 02/28/2014

TRANSPORTATION ENTRY AND MANIFEST OF GOODS SUBJECT TO CBP INSPECTION AND PERMIT

U.S. Customs and Border Protection

19 CFR 10.60, 10.61, 123.41, 123.42

_____ Entry No. _____

Port _____

Date _____

Entry No. _____

Class of Entry _____

(I.T.) (T.E.) (WD.1E) (Drawback, etc.)

PORT CODE NO. _____ FIRST U.S. PORT OF UNLADING _____

PORT OF _____ DATE _____

Entered or imported by _____ Importer/IRS # _____ to be shipped

in bond via _____ consigned to

(C.H.L number)　　　　(Vessel or carrier)　　　　(Car number and initial)　　　　(Pier or station)

CBP Port Director _____ Final foreign destination _____

(For exportations only)

Consignee _____

(At CBP port of exit or destination)

Foreign port of lading _____ B/L No. _____ Date of sailing _____

(Above information to be furnished only when merchandise is imported by vessel)

Imported on the _____ Flag _____ on _____ via _____

(Name of vessel or carrier and motive power)　　　　　　　　(Date imported)　　　　(Last foreign port)

Exported from _____ on _____ Goods now at _____

(Country)　　　　(Date)　　　　　　　　(Name of warehouse, station, pier, etc.)

Marks and Numbers of Packages	Description and Quantity of Merchandise Number and Kind of Packages (Describe fully as per shipping papers)	Gross Weight in Pounds	Value (Dollars only)	Rate	Duty

G.O. No. _____　　☐ Check if withdrawn for Vessel supplies (19 U.S.C. 1309)

CERTIFICATE OF LADING FOR TRANSPORTATION IN BOND AND/OR LADING FOR EXPORTATION FOR

_____
(Port)

WITH THE EXCEPTIONS NOTED ABOVE, THE WITHIN-DESCRIBED GOODS WERE:

Delivered to the Carrier named above, for delivery to the CBP Port Director at destination sealed with CBP seals Nos. _____ or the packages (were) (were not) labeled, or corded and sealed.

Laden on the--

_____
(Vessel, vehicle, or aircraft)

which cleared for--

_____

on _____
(Date)

as verified by export records.

_____
(Inspector)

_____
(Inspector)

_____
(Date)

_____
(Date)

I truly declare that the statements contained herein are true and correct to the best of my knowledge and belief.

Entered or withdrawn by _____

_____

_____

_____

_____

To the Inspector: The above-described goods shall be disposed of

_____
For the Port Director

Received from the Port Director of the above CBP location the merchandise described in this manifest for transportation and delivery into the custody of the CBP officers at the port named above, all packages in apparent good order except as noted hereon.

_____

_____
Attorney or Agent of Carrier

CBP Form 7512 (02/12)

Figure 8–5. (*continued*)

INSTRUCTIONS

Consult CBP officer or Part 18, Customs Regulations, for the appropriate number of copies required for entry, withdrawal, or manifest purposes.

For the purpose of transfer under the cartage or lighterage provisions of a proper bond to the place of shipment from the port of entry, extra copies bearing a stamp, or notation as to their intended use may be required for local administration.

As the form is the same whether used as an entry or withdrawal or manifest, all copies may be prepared at the same time by carbon process, unless more than one vessel or vehicle is used, in which case a separate manifest must be prepared for each such vessel or vehicle.

Whenever this form is used as an entry or withdrawal, care should be taken that the kind of entry is plainly shown in the block in the upper right-hand corner of the face of the entry.

This form may be printed by private parties provided that the supply printed conforms to the official form in size, wording arrangement, and quality and color of paper.

RECORD OF CARTAGE OR LIGHTERAGE
Delivered to Cartman or Lighterman in apparent good condition except as noted on this form

Conveyance	Quantity	Date	Delivered	Received	Received	
			(Inspector)	(Cartman or Lighterman)	(Date)	(Inspector)
			(Inspector)	(Cartman or Lighterman)	(Date)	(Inspector)
			(Inspector)	(Cartman or Lighterman)	(Date)	(Inspector)
Total						

(Warehouse proprietor)

CERTIFICATES OF TRANSFER. (If required)

I certify that within-described goods were transferred by reason of _____

to _____

on _____ , at _____

and sealed with _____ or seals

Nos. _____ , and that

goods were in same apparent condition as noted on

original lading except _____

_____

_____
Inspector, Conductor, or Master

I certify that within-described goods were transferred by reason of _____

to _____

on _____ , at _____

and sealed with _____ or seals

Nos. _____ , and that

goods were in same apparent condition as noted on

original lading except _____

_____

_____
Inspector, Conductor, or Master

INSPECTED

at _____

on _____
(Date)

and seals found _____

_____

_____

_____

_____

_____
Inspector.

If transfer occurs within city limits of a CBP port or station, CBP officers must be notified to supervise transfer.

INSPECTOR'S REPORT OF DISCHARGE AT DESTINATION

Port _____ Station _____ , _____
(Date)

TO THE PORT DIRECTOR: Delivering line _____ Car No. _____ Initial _____

Arrived _____ Condition of car _____ , of seals _____ , of packages _____
(Date)

Date of Delivery to Importer, or Gen. Order	Packages	No. and Kind of Entry or General Order	Bonded Truck or Lighter No.	Conditions, Etc.

I certify above report is correct. _____ , Inspector.

CBP Form 7512 (02/12)(Back)

bonded carriers, having their own Customs surety bonds to ensure that the merchandise remains intact through the course of the transportation through the United State Immediate transit entries are used to move merchandise from the port of arrival to an inland port of entry nearer to the buyer where the customs entries and formalities are completed and the merchandise is released to the importer. In most instances in-transit entries allow for steamship lines to move carriers through intermodal carriers, like trains and trucks, to an inland port for customs clearance at the inland port. Although importers may also request individual shipments be moved inland if the bill of lading is only routed to an outer port of entry. Again, the carriers must have their own surety bonds and the merchandise must be registered at the first port and with the final destination port to close out the inland portion of the move.

There are also ways to postpone filing the entry through the use of temporary import bonds and bonded warehouses. When merchandise is intended to be in the United States on temporarily, the importer can file a temporary import entry that is covered by surety bond. The merchandise must be exported within the terms of the temporary import bond under Customs supervision. Entry is made on the same entry summary form, just designated as a temporary import.

Finally, when merchandise is to be stored in a public or private customs-bonded warehouse for future consumption, entry is made on the regular Entry/Immediate Delivery or Entry Summary, marked with the type code for warehouse entries, in which case no estimated duties need be paid until the merchandise is later withdrawn for consumption. Depending on the type of warehouse, merchandise in a bonded facility may be manipulated, but only under Customs supervision. The importer must file an Application and Approval to Manipulate, Examine, Sample or Transfer Goods, CBP 3499. (Look back at Figure 6-6.)

N. Reconciliation

Sometimes, the importer may not have the final information necessary to complete and file an Entry Summary at the time of importation. In some cases, such situations may be routine, for example, when the importer is using the constructed value method of calculation or importing under Harmonized Tariff classification 9802 and the costs of manufacture or processing are based on standard costs subject to revision at the end of the accounting period. It can also arise when regional value content calculations are necessary for NAFTA eligibility. Customs has developed a program, first offered in 1998 as a prototype, but now extended indefinitely, for filing the usual Entry Summary at the time of entry with the "best information available," but "flagging" individual entries or all entries during a specified period. The result is that the importer is allowed twenty-one months (twelve months for NAFTA and other U.S. Free Trade Agreement claims) to file a "reconciliation" containing the final information. This process is available for missing information relating to the correct value of the imported merchandise (including value under 9802), classification, and NAFTA and CAFTA-DR eligibility. In order to participate in the program, it is necessary to file an application with U.S. Customs and Border Protection and to provide a rider to the importer's customs bond to cover the open import entries. Once accepted, reconciliation may be filed either with entry-by-entry adjustments or with an aggregate calculation for all the entries covered by the reconciliation (aggregate adjustment is not allowed when the reconciler claims a refund, and refunds may not be netted against duties owed). Failure to file the reconciliation "entry" in a timely fashion will result in penalties.

O. GSP, AGOA—Special Programs

There are many special duty programs available to importers provided the imported goods meet the qualifying criteria. Where the importer is claiming duty-free importation of the merchandise under the terms of the Generalized System of Preferences (GSP) program and the tariff classification is eligible, it is necessary for the importer to indicate its intention by using the letter "A" next to the tariff number on the Entry Summary (or A+ or A* depending on the country). The importer should advise the customs broker that the imported goods qualify under GSP, and the broker will make the proper indication. It is important that the importer issue clear instructions to the broker that it should NOT claim preferential duty treatments unless the importer is confident that the merchandise qualifies. Under audit, the exporter must provide evidence to Customs that the merchandise meets the 35 percent origin criteria. In the past a "GSP Declaration" was all that was needed to comply, but recently those documents have been called into question, and so further substantiating documentation will be required. If the auditor is unable to confirm that the imported goods qualify, then the importer will owe past duties plus interest. In addition, the importer could be subject to penalties for making a false statement on the Entry Summary; therefore, it is always advisable that the importer and the exporter are clear on the requirements and that the exporter can and will provide the necessary evidence to support the claim. The GSP program has expired a number of items over the years and the importer is required to pay the duties until Congress renews the program. In the past, Congress has renewed with an automatic retroactive applicability. Customs then issues refunds to all importers that have the GSP indicator on the entry summaries filed. However, there is no guarantee that if Congress does renew the program, there will be a retroactive application of benefits, so importers should pay careful attention to the current status of the program. See more in Chapter 11.

The same is true with the other preferential duty programs. Any importer wishing to claim the benefits of the Caribbean Basin Economic Recovery Act, the U.S.–Israel Free Trade Agreement, or the African Growth and Opportunity Act must be able prove similar requirements: 35 percent of the finished goods must originate in the eligible country, and the goods must be shipped directly from the eligible country to the United States. Unlike the GSP program, under these agreements, 15 percent of the 35 percent may come from U.S.-origin components. However, similar to GSP, the importer will also be required to obtain similar evidence from the exporter, even if the exporter provides it directly to U.S. Customs and Border Protection in order to maintain the confidentiality of the information. It is strongly recommended that an importer obtain guarantees from its manufacturer that it will produce any necessary supporting documentation directly to U.S. Customs and Border Protection if requested before making a claim of preferential duty under one of these programs.

P. NAFTA/Other FTA Certificates of Origin

Under the North American Free Trade Agreement, articles from Canada and Mexico may be imported duty-free or at a reduced rate of duty. In order to qualify for the tariff concession, however, the articles must be a product of Canada or Mexico under one of six eligibility rules. The exact method of determining eligibility is specific to each type of merchandise involved and must be checked in the headnotes of the Harmonized Tariff Schedules. The importer must obtain a certificate from the Canadian or Mexican exporter certifying the country of origin. (A sample of the certificate is shown in Figure 11-1.)

Each new FTA has similar requirements in that there are rules of origin based on the tariff number of the final imported good, some of which may require specific regional value content; evidence of origin is required and the basis for such origin claim must follow certain standards. Some of the FTAs have certificate of origin forms, while others use general certificates of origin to substantiate the origin of goods eligible for preferential duties. (See Figures 11-2, 11-3, and 11-4.) More on origin under the FTAs may be found in Chapter 11.

Q. Specialized Products Import Entry Forms

Food, drug, cosmetic, and medical device imports are monitored by the Food and Drug Administration (FDA) through U.S. Customs and Border Protection. For shipments subject to the FDA, the customs broker must file information about the shipment through the OASIS (Operational and Administrative System for Import Support) system at the same time it is filing the Customs Form 3461 (Entry/Immediate Delivery). The FDA inspector will then determine whether the product is being imported in compliance with U.S. law. It should also be noted that the FDA requires that all owners or operators in charge of domestic or foreign facilities that manufacturer, process, pack, or hold food for human or animal consumption in the United States be registered with the FDA prior to export. Importers of certain radiation-producing electronic products such as televisions, monitors, microwave ovens, x-ray equipment, laser products, ultrasound equipment, sunlamps, CD-ROM players, and cellular and cordless telephones are required to file FDA Form 2877 (see Figure 8–6), and importers of certain radio-frequency devices such as radios, tape recorders, stereos, televisions, and citizen's band radios are required to file FCC Form 740. Importers of plants are required to file U.S. Department of Agriculture Form 368, Notice of Arrival (see Figure 8–7). A number of agricultural products require import permits, including plants and timber logs, and some products require import licenses, such as dairy products. In addition, the USDA enforces the International Standards for Phytosanitary Measures No. 15 (ISPM-15) and requires export certifications for all wood packaging materials (WPM) to reduce the risk of introducing quarantined pests, such as the Asian long-horned beetle, into the United States. All WPM must be heat-treated or fumigated with methyl bromide and marked with the International Plant Protection Convention Logo.

Originally introduced in 1900, the Lacey Act was enacted to protect wildlife, fish, and plants. A 2008 amendment brought increased focus on illegal logging by banning the import, transport, sale, receipt, acquisition, or purchase of illegally obtained plants from a foreign country or a U.S. state. These include plants that are (1) stolen; (2) taken from officially protected areas, such as parks and reserves; (3) taken without or contrary to required authorization; (4) taken without payment of the applicable taxes, royalties, or fees; or (5) shipped in violation of governing export or transshipment laws, such as log export bans. In addition, the amendment makes it unlawful to falsely identify or label any plant or plant product. The amendment requires that importation of any product containing any form of plant species must—electronically—file a certification, the Plant Protection and Quarantine Form 505, as to the country of harvest by the scientific name of the species. There is a phased-in compliance program beginning in March of 2009. See Appendix L for more information on the form and the requirements.

Figure 8–6. FDA Form 2877.

DEPARTMENT OF HEALTH AND HUMAN SERVICES FOOD AND DRUG ADMINISTRATION **DECLARATION FOR IMPORTED ELECTRONIC PRODUCTS SUBJECT TO RADIATION CONTROL STANDARDS**	*Form Approved OMB No. 0910-0025* *Expiration Date: October 31, 2013* **INSTRUCTIONS** 1. If submitting entries electronically through ACS/ABI, hold FDA-2877 in entry file. Do not submit to FDA unless requested. 2. If submitting paper entry documents, submit the following to FDA: a. 2 copies of Customs Entry Form (e.g. CF 3461, CF 3461 Alt, CF 7501, etc.) b. 1 copy of FDA 2877 c. Commercial Invoice(s) in English.

U.S. CUSTOMS PORT OF ENTRY	ENTRY NUMBER	DATE OF ENTRY

NAME & ADDRESS OF MANUFACTURING SITE; COUNTRY OF ORIGIN	NAME & ADDRESS OF IMPORTER & ULTIMATE CONSIGNEE *(if not importer)*

PRODUCT DESCRIPTION	QUANTITY *(Items/Containers)*	MODEL NUMBER(S) & BRAND NAME(S)

DECLARATION: I / WE DECLARE THAT THE PRODUCTS IDENTIFIED ABOVE: *(Mark X applicable statements, fill in blanks, & sign)*

☐ **A. ARE NOT SUBJECT TO RADIATION PERFORMANCE STANDARDS BECAUSE THEY:**

☐ 1. Were manufactured prior to the effective date of any applicable standard; Date of Manufacture _____ .

☐ 2. Are excluded by the applicability clause or definition in the standard or by FDA written guidance.

Specify reason for exclusion _____

☐ 3. Are personal household goods of an individual entering the U.S. or being returned to a U.S. resident. (Limit: 3 of each product type).

☐ 4. Are property of a party residing outside the U.S. and will be returned to the owner after repair or servicing.

☐ 5. Are components or subassemblies to be used in manufacturing or as replacement parts (NOT APPLICABLE to diagnostic x-ray parts).

☐ 6. Are prototypes intended for on going product development by the importing firm, are labeled "FOR TEST/EVALUATION ONLY," and will be exported, destroyed, or held for future testing (i.e., not distributed). (Quantities Limited - see reverse.)

☐ 7. Are being reprocessed in accordance with P.L. 104-134 or other FDA guidance, are labeled "FOR EXPORT ONLY," and will not be sold, distributed, or transferred without FDA approval.

☐ **B. COMPLY WITH THE PERFORMANCE STANDARDS** WHICH ARE APPLICABLE AT DATE OF MANUFACTURE AND THAT A CERTIFICATION LABEL OR TAG TO THIS EFFECT IS AFFIXED TO EACH PRODUCT. COMPLIANCE DOCUMENTED IN:

☐ 1. Last annual report or Product/Initial report

_____   _____
ACCESSION NUMBER of Report   Name of MANUFACTURER OF RECORD *(Filed report with FDA/CDRH)*

☐ 2. Unknown manufacturer or report number; State reason: _____

☐ **C. DO NOT COMPLY WITH PERFORMANCE STANDARDS;** ARE BEING HELD UNDER A TEMPORARY IMPORT BOND; WILL NOT BE INTRODUCED INTO COMMERCE; WILL BE USED UNDER A RADIATION PROTECTION PLAN; AND WILL BE DESTROYED OR EXPORTED UNDER U.S. CUSTOMS SUPERVISION WHEN THE FOLLOWING MISSION IS COMPLETE:

☐ 1. Research, Investigations/Studies, or Training (attach Form FDA 766)

☐ 2. Trade Show/Demonstration; List dates & use restrictions _____ .

☐ **D. DO NOT COMPLY WITH PERFORMANCE STANDARDS;** ARE HELD AND WILL REMAIN UNDER BOND; AND WILL NOT BE INTRODUCED INTO COMMERCE UNTIL NOTIFICATION IS RECEIVED FROM FDA THAT PRODUCTS HAVE BEEN BROUGHT INTO COMPLIANCE IN ACCORDANCE WITH AN FDA APPROVED PETITION. *(See Form FDA 766.)*

☐ 1. Approved Petition is attached.   ☐ 2. Petition Request is attached.   ☐ 3. Request will be submitted within 60 days.

WARNING: Any person who knowingly makes a false declaration may be fined not more than $10,000 or imprisoned not more than 5 years or both, pursuant to Title 18 U.S.C. 1001. Any person importing a non-compliant electronic product may also be subject to civil penalties of $1000 per violation, up to a maximum $300,000 for related violations pursuant to Title 21 U.S.C. 360pp.	SIGNATURE OF IMPORTER OF RECORD NAME AND TITLE OF RESPONSIBLE PERSON

Public reporting burden for this collection of information is estimated to average 0.2 hour per response, including the time for reviewing instructions, searching existing data sources, gathering and maintaining the data needed, and completing and reviewing the collection of information. Send comments regarding this burden estimate or any other aspect of this collection of information, including suggestions for reducing this burden to:

Department of Health and Human Services
Food and Drug Administration
Office of Chief Information Officer
1350 Piccard Drive, Room 400
Rockville, MD 20850

An agency may not conduct or sponsor, and a person is not required to respond to, a collection of information unless it displays a currently valid OMB control number.

FORM FDA 2877 (1/11)   PREVIOUS EDITION IS OBSOLETE.   PSC Publishing Services (301) 443-6740   PAGE 1 OF 2 PAGES   EF

Figure 8–6. (*continued*)

INSTRUCTIONS TO IMPORTERS/BROKERS OF ELECTRONIC PRODUCTS

PURPOSE: The Form FDA 2877 must be completed for electronic products subject to Radiation Control Standards (21 CFR 1010 and 1020-1050) prior to entry into the United States. The local Food and Drug Administration (FDA) district office will review the declaration and notify the importer/agent if the products may be released into U.S. commerce or if they must be held under bond until exported, destroyed, or reconditioned. Until the shipment is released, it may be subject to redelivery for FDA examination.

PAPER OR ELECTRONIC SUBMISSION: Paper entries may be made by submitting the signed original FDA 2877 along with U.S. Customs forms to the local FDA district office; if electronic products are given a MAY PROCEED, a signed copy of CF 3461 will be returned, or if not given a MAY PROCEED, a FDA Notice of Action will be issued. For electronic entries, follow U.S. Customs Service ACS/ABI format and procedures, supported by a signed copy of this form or similar letter. Multiple entries of the same product and model families that are filed electronically may be supported by one form dated not more than 12 months previously.

DECLARATION: Select A, B, C, or D and then select the appropriate number; fill in requested information and sign. For electronic entries, AofC (affirmation of compliance) = RA#, RB#, RC#, or RD# (e.g., Radiation Declaration A5 = RA5). **Transmit model number using AofC code MDL and transmit brand name using FDA line level brand name field. If RA3 or RA6 is selected, you must transmit quantity (number of units) using the Quantity and Unit of Measure Pairs at the FDA line level.**

DECLARATION A: Importers should be prepared to demonstrate compliance to or non-applicability of FDA standards, regulations, or guidance. Components or sub-assemblies must be non-functioning. Products being reprocessed must be exported by the importer, without intermediate transfer of ownership. For RA3 the quantity limit is 3 and for RA6 the limit = 50 units TV products, microwave ovens, and Class 1 laser products limit = 200 units CD-ROM and DVD (digital versatile disc) laser products; see May 14, 1997, notice to industry issued by the Center for Devices and Radiological Health (CDRH).

DECLARATION B: If declaration RB1 is selected, provide the FDA Establishment Identifier (FEI) of the manufacturer who filed the radiation product/abbreviated report to FDA, CDRH, Rockville, Maryland. To transmit the accession number of that report use AofC code ACC. If the manufacturer cannot be determined or located, the importer must be able to provide evidence showing a certification (certifi.) label on each product and state reason: returned to orig exporter or certifi. label evidence. The new AofC codes (RB1, RB2) for this declaration will not be activated until a process is made available to determine the FEI of the responsible firm. Continue to use RAB in electronic transmission until the FEI query is available and industry is notified of its availability.

DECLARATION C: Noncompliant products may be imported only for research, investigations/studies, demonstration or training. They should be used only by trained personnel and under controlled conditions to avoid unnecessary radiation exposure. Product(s) will be detained by the local FDA district office. Since product(s) for which "C" Declarations are made will be under Temporary Import Bond (TIB) or equivalent, ultimate disposition is limited to export or destruction under U.S. Customs supervision when the purpose has been achieved or the length of time stated has expired. For purposes other than demonstration, the Form FDA 766, outlining protections, must be approved by FDA prior to use. The importer/broker must include with the FDA 766:

1. A full description of the subject electronic product(s).
2. The purpose for which the product(s) is being imported.
3. How the product(s) will be used.
4. Where the product(s) will be located.
5. The approximate length of time and dates the product(s) will be in this country.

For product(s) being used for trade shows/demonstrations, list the dates and use restrictions (Form FDA 766 is not required). A sign stating that the product does not comply with FDA performance standards must be displayed and viewable at all times during the use of product(s). All medical products, cabinet x-ray, or Class IIIb and IV lasers may NOT operate (turn on product(s)) at trade shows.

DECLARATION D: Noncompliant products must be brought into compliance with standards under FDA supervision and following a plan approved by FDA. The plan, documented on the Form FDA 766, must address technical requirements, labeling, and reporting. Some plans may need approval by both the CDRH and the local FDA district office. Use of this declaration is limited to occasional shipments; ongoing reconditioning is considered manufacturing that is handled through other means. Product(s) will be detained by the local FDA district office. An FDA 766 must be filed indicating the procedure intended to bring the product into compliance. This procedure will include a satisfactory corrective action plan and/or a product report. The FDA 766 must include all of the information requested under Declaration C. The approximate length of time will be for the amount of time needed to bring product(s) into compliance. Declaration D is also made for failure to provide reports, failure to certify, etc.

If an importer/broker intends to import equipment into the United States for purposes of research, investigation, studies, demonstrations, or training but also wishes to retain the option of bringing the product into compliance with the performance standard, check Declarations C and D on the FDA 2877 and insert the word "or " between the Affirmations. Note: The U.S. Customs Service will treat this entry as a "D" Declaration for purposes of duty. Such requests must be made on the FDA 766; include Items 1, 2, and 3 under Declaration C, a statement of the need to use the option "C" or "D" Declaration, a statement of how the product(s) will be brought into compliance and the approximate length of time necessary to evaluate or demonstrate the product(s) and the time necessary to bring the product(s) into compliance (both actions must be accomplished within the period of time granted by FDA). For electronic entries select Declaration RD3.

Ultimately, product(s) must be brought into compliance with the applicable standard in accordance with a corrective action plan which has been approved by the FDA. If the product(s) are not brought into compliance within the allotted time frame of the approved application and an extension is not requested of, or granted by, the FDA, the local FDA district office shall refuse entry on the shipment and require the product(s) to be either exported or destroyed under U.S. Customs supervision.

If additional guidance is needed, please contact your local FDA district office or consult the following FDA web pages: www.fda.gov/, www.fda.gov/ora/hier/ora_field_names.txt, and http://www.fda.gov/ora/compliance_ref/rpm/.

[Ref: 21 U.S.C. 360mm, 21 CFR 1005, 19 CFR 12.90-12.91.]   FDA: CP 7382.007/.007A

FORM FDA 2877 (1/11)   PREVIOUS EDITION IS OBSOLETE.   PAGE 2 OF 2 PAGES

Figure 8–7. U.S. Department of Agriculture Form 368, Notice of Arrival.

Figure 8–7. (*continued*)

Instructions for completing PPQ Form 368
Notice of Arrival to import plants or plant products

Please TYPE or PRINT legibly.

1. Name of Carrier: List the name of carrier by identifying the airline with the flight number, ship name with the voyage number, truck and container number used to transport the agricultural product.

2. Date of Arrival: List the date on which the carrier arrives at the port on entry.

3. Name of Permittee/Consignee: List the name and street address of the person responsible for the importation. The applicant must be a United States resident. List the organization or company name, if applicable. A physical address of the facility or business is required. You may include a post office box address **in addition** to the street address for mailing purposes. List your daytime telephone number, including the Area Code. List your facsimile number, including the Area Code. List your email address if applicable.

4. Port of Arrival: List the port on which the carrier arrives.

5. Permit No.: List the USDA-APHIS-PPQ permit if the commodity requires a permit as a condition of entry.

6. Port of Departure: List the name of the port where the carrier originated in the country of origin.

7. Customs Entry No.: List the Customs and Border Protection entry number associated with this shipment.

8. Consignor/Shipper: List the name and street address of the person responsible for the shipping. List the organization or company name, if applicable. A physical address of the facility or business is required. You may include a post office box address **in addition** to the street address for mailing purposes. List your daytime telephone number, including the country code, facsimile number, including the Area Code. List the email address, if applicable.

9. Present Location: List the physical location where the commodity is to be inspected.

10. Country and Locality Where Grown: List Country, Province, State and Location where the commodities where grown.

11. Name of Previous U.S. Port: List If the commodity transited in any country prior to arrival to U.S. port.

12. I.T. No. (In transit shipment only): list the in-bond IT number this shipment is moving under.

13. Description of Product: List the following information in the space provided: Marks, Bill of Lading No., and/or Container No.; Quantity and Net Weight; and the Commodity arriving under this notice of arrival.

14. Signature of Importer or Broker: The person that is responsible for the accuracy of the responses submitted on this form.

15. Full Business Address of Importer or Broker: List the full business address and telephone number of the person whose signatory appears in Block 14.

16. Date Signed: List the date the form is completed and signed, using this format: dd/mm/yyyy.

If attachments are necessary, type or print "PPQ Form 368" along with the Company Name and address of the Importer or Broker, at the top of each page.

Send the completed original signed form to the CBP Agriculture office or PPQ port office where the shipment is arriving and making official entry. In the case of IT shipments, send the form to the port of arrival and port of entry.

For assistance with filling out this form, contact:
USDA-APHIS-PPQ-QPAS-Agriculture Quarantine Inspection
4700 River Road, Unit # 60
Riverdale, MD 20737
Phone number (301) 734-8295; ask for a staff officer.

When importing (or exporting) fish or wildlife, U.S. Fish and Wildlife Service Form 3-177 must be filed (see Figure 8–8). The United States supports the Convention on International Trade of Endangered Species (CITES) to protect endangered species. There are more than 170 countries that are parties to the CITES. In compliance with the CITES, imports of certain species are prohibited and others require import permits (see Figure 8–9). More information is available at www.fws.gov. Note that not all U.S. ports of entry have Fish and Wildlife offices, so imports may be cleared only at the ports of Anchorage, AK; Atlanta, GA; Baltimore, MD; Boston, MA; Chicago, IL; Dallas, TX; Honolulu, HI; Houston, TX; Los Angeles, CA; Louisville, KY; Memphis, TN; Miami, FL; New Orleans, LA; New York, NY; Newark, NJ; Portland, OR; San Francisco, CA; or Seattle, WA.

Importers of "precursor" and "essential" chemicals that can be used to manufacture illegal drugs are required to file DEA Form 486 (sometimes fifteen days in advance) (see Chapter 4, Section P and Figure 4–24).

The Consumer Products Safety Commission has recently taken a very active role in regulating imports of children's and consumer products. New certifications regarding the lead levels in children's toys and other articles require the importer to provide a certificate (based on test analysis) that the imported goods do not contain over 100 ppm. CPSC also has prohibited the sale of certain children's products containing phthalates. Currently CPSC is requesting that importers provide general certificates of compliance (see Figure 8–10) that imported consumer goods meet the CPSC standards currently in place under the Federal Hazardous Substances Act, the Poison Prevention Packaging Act, the Flammable Fabrics Act, the Refrigerator Safety Act, or the Consumer Products Safety Act. More information is available at www.cpsc.gov.

R. Examination and Detention

After a customs entry is electronically filed (Entry/Immediate Delivery or Entry Summary, along with any other specialized forms), the computer audits the information against historical data and makes a determination as to whether Customs will examine the merchandise. If Customs elects not to examine the merchandise and is otherwise satisfied from the entry documents that the goods are entitled to entry, it will release the goods by stamping the Entry/Immediate Delivery or Entry Summary form, perforating the form, or issuing an electronic "paperless" release. This releases the merchandise and authorizes the transportation carrier to surrender possession of the goods to the importer and is effective when the importer presents the release to the transportation carrier.

Figure 8–8. U.S. Fish and Wildlife Service Declaration for Importation and Exportation, Form 3-177.

Figure 8–9. U.S. Fish and Wildlife Permit Application, Form 3-200-3.

Department of the Interior
U.S. Fish and Wildlife Service

Federal Fish and Wildlife Permit Application Form

OMB Control No. 1018-0092
Expires: 12/31/2016

Return to:

U.S. Fish and Wildlife Service
Office of Law Enforcement

Send to the appropriate Issuing Office listed on
Page 4 for the State you listed in Block B.1.c.

Type of Activity: Import/Export License

☐ New - $100.00
☐ Requesting Renewal of Permit #LE-_____ - $100.00
☐ Requesting Change/Amendment of Permit #LE-_____ $50.00

Complete all sections of this application.
See attached instruction pages for information on how to make your application complete and help avoid unnecessary delays.

A.	All applicants MUST complete		
1. Name of Business (as shown on Company's invoice and other shipping documents)			

2. Federal Tax Identification No. or Social Security No.	3. Date of Birth (mm/dd/yyyy)	4. Description of Business	

5.a. Principal Officer Last Name	5.b. Principal Officer First Name	5.c. Principal Officer Middle Name	5.d. Suffix

6. Principal Officer Title	7. Primary Contact Name

8.a. Business Telephone Number	8.b. Alternate Telephone Number	8.c. Business Fax Number	8.d. Business E-mail Address

B.	All applicants MUST complete				
1a. Address (No P.O. Boxes, Retail Postal or Mail Service Center) (as shown on Company's invoice and other shipping documents) Normally where you will receive all official notices sent from the Service.					
1.b. City	1.c. State	1d. Zip code/Postal Code	1.e. County/Province	1.f. Country (If not US)* *See Page 2: Question 1	
2a. Mailing Address (include ONLY if different than above and this is where you want to receive all official notices from the Service) Include name of contact person.					
2.b. City	2.c. State	2d. Zip code/Postal Code	2.e. County/Province	2.f. Country (If not US)* *See Page 2: Question 1	

C.	All applicants MUST complete
1.	Attach check or money order payable to the U.S. FISH AND WILDLIFE SERVICE in the amount listed above. Application fees are non-refundable.
2.	Do you currently have or have you ever had any Federal Fish and Wildlife permits? Yes ☐ If yes, list the number of the most current permit you have held: _____ No ☐
3.	Certification: I hereby certify that I have read and am familiar with the regulations contained in *Title 50, Part 13 of the Code of Federal Regulations* and the other *applicable parts in subchapter B of Chapter I of Title 50*, and I certify that the information submitted in this application for a permit is complete and accurate to the best of my knowledge and belief. I understand that any false statement herein may subject me to the criminal penalties of 18 U.S.C. 1001.
	_____ Signature (in blue ink) of applicant/person responsible for permit (No photocopied or stamped signatures) Date of signature (mm/dd/yyyy)

Please continue to next page

3-200-3 Revised December 2013

Page 1 of 6

Figure 8–9. (*continued*)

IMPORT/EXPORT LICENSE APPLICATION CONTINUATION SHEET

SECTION D: ALL APPLICANTS MUST COMPLETE

NOTE: An Import/Export License is required ONLY if you commercially import (bring into the U.S. from another country) or export (send out from the U.S. to another country). No Import/Export License is required if your business ships exclusively within the U.S. (or its Territories).

1.   **U.S. address** (not a P.O. Box, Retail Postal or Mail Service Center) **for foreign applicant.** (50 CFR 13.12 requires this information for issuance). This is the mailing address where you will receive all official notices sent from the Service. Question 7 must also be completed. **NOTE: No Import/Export License will be issued without this information.**

_____

_____

_____

2.   **Name, street address** (not a P.O. Box, Retail Postal or Mail Service Center), **telephone, fax number, and email address** of additional partners and principal officers of the entity applying for this license. If the applicant is the sole owner, indicate "same as Page 1."

_____

_____

_____

3.   **Street address** (not a P.O. Box, Retail Postal or Mail Service Center), **telephone,** and **fax number** of the location(s) where business records concerning imports or exports of wildlife will be kept. If the location(s) is the same as on the first page, indicate "same as Page 1". 50 CFR 13.46 describes the required records that are to be maintained five (5) years from date of expiration of the license.

_____

_____

_____

4.   **Street address** (not a P.O. Box, Retail Postal or Mail Service Center), **telephone,** and **fax number** of the location(s) wildlife inventories will be kept. If the location(s) is the same as on the first page, indicate "same as Page 1".

_____

_____

_____

5.   **General description** of the wildlife or wildlife products to be imported/exported. (Choose all that apply)

   a. ☐ Live   ☐ Dead
      ☐ Products (Describe: sport hunted trophies, jewelry, footwear, carvings, etc.)_____

      _____

      ☐ Other (Describe)_____

   b. ☐ Fish   ☐ Coral   ☐ Reptiles   ☐ Amphibians
      ☐ Mammals   ☐ Birds   ☐ Insects/Arachnids   ☐ Other_____

   c. ☐ Venomous

Please continue to next page

Figure 8–9. (*continued*)

6.   Location of the U.S. Fish and Wildlife Service Port of Entry you wish to import/export your goods through (check all that apply):

☐ Anchorage, Alaska	☐ Honolulu, Hawaii	☐ New Orleans, Louisiana
☐ Atlanta, Georgia	☐ Houston, Texas	☐ New York, NY
☐ Baltimore, Maryland	☐ Los Angeles, California	☐ Newark, NJ
☐ Boston, Massachusetts	☐ Louisville, Kentucky	☐ Portland, Oregon
☐ Chicago, Illinois	☐ Memphis, Tennessee	☐ San Francisco, California
☐ Dallas/Ft. Worth, Texas	☐ Miami, Florida	☐ Seattle, Washington

Locations listed below may require an additional Designated Port Exception Permit (Form 3-200-2)

☐ Blaine, Washington	☐ Dunseith, North Dakota	☐ Port Huron, Michigan
☐ Brownsville, Texas	☐ El Paso, Texas	☐ San Diego, California
☐ Champlain, New York	☐ Laredo, Texas	☐ Sweetgrass, Montana
☐ Denver, Colorado	☐ Minneapolis, Minnesota	☐ Tampa, Florida
☐ Detroit, Michigan	☐ Nogales, Arizona	☐ Guaynabo, Puerto Rico
☐ Dulles, Virginia	☐ Pembina, North Dakota	☐ Tamuning, Guam
☐ Other _____		

7.   **Applicants residing or located outside the United States.** The **name, physical address** (no P.O. Box, Retail Postal or Mail Service Center address) and **telephone and fax numbers** of your agent that is located in the United States who will maintain your records for five (5) years from the expiration of the permit. If the location is the same as Question 1, then indicate "same as Question 1". (50 CFR 13.12 and 13.46 requires this information for issuance). **NOTE: No Import/Export License will be issued without this information.**

_____

_____

_____

_____

Certification of U.S. Agent:

I hereby agree to be U.S. Agent for _____.

(Print name of Business listed in Block A on Page 1 of this application)

Acting in the capacity of U.S. Agent includes maintaining complete and accurate records of any taking, possession, transportation, sale, purchase, barter, exportation or importation of wildlife for the above mentioned Business for a period of five (5) years from the date of the expiration of this Import/Export License. Such records shall be kept current and shall include names and addresses of persons with whom any wildlife has been purchased, sold, bartered, or otherwise transferred, and the date of such transaction, and other information as may be required or appropriate. Such records shall be legibly written or reproducible in English. The name, address and telephone number listed above in #7 is complete and accurate and is not a retail postal or mail service center.

_____

Printed Name of Responsible Person from #7 Above

_____

Signature   **Date**

NOTE: You must notify the U.S. Fish and Wildlife Service immediately of any change in U.S. Agent

Please continue to next page

3-200-3 Revised December 2013

Figure 8–9. *(continued)*

Office of Law Enforcement Regional Permit Offices

Region 1: Guam, Hawaii, Idaho, Oregon, & Washington	Region 2: Arizona, New Mexico, Oklahoma, & Texas
U.S. Fish & Wildlife Service Office of Law Enforcement 911 NE 11th Ave. Portland, OR 97232 Tel: (503) 231-6899 Fax: (503) 231-2193 Email: permitsR1LE@fws.gov	U.S. Fish & Wildlife Service Office of Law Enforcement 2545 W. Frye Road Suite 8 Chandler, AZ 85224-6273 Tel: (480) 967-2007 Fax: (480) 966-9766 Email: permitsR2LE@fws.gov
Region 3: Illinois, Indiana, Iowa, Michigan, Minnesota, Missouri, Ohio, & Wisconsin U.S. Fish & Wildlife Service Office of Law Enforcement 5600 American Blvd, West, Suite 990 Bloomington, MN 55437-1458 Tel: (612) 713-5356 Fax: (612) 713-5283 Email: permitsR3LE@fws.gov	**Region 4: Alabama, Arkansas, Florida, Georgia, Kentucky, Louisiana, Mississippi, North Carolina, South Carolina, Puerto Rico, & Tennessee** U.S. Fish & Wildlife Service Office of Law Enforcement 1875 Century Blvd, Suite 380 Atlanta, GA 30345 Tel: (404) 679-7195 Fax: (404) 679-7065 Email: permitsR4LE@fws.gov
Region 5: Connecticut, District of Columbia, Delaware, Maine, Maryland, Massachusetts, New Hampshire, New Jersey, New York, Pennsylvania, Rhode Island, Vermont, Virginia, & West Virginia U.S. Fish & Wildlife Service Office of Law Enforcement 70 E. Sunrise Hwy, Suite 419 Valley Stream, NY 11580 Tel: (516) 825-3950 Fax: (516) 825-3597 Email: permitsR5LE@fws.gov	**Region 6: Colorado, Kansas, Montana, Nebraska, North Dakota, South Dakota, Utah, & Wyoming** U.S. Fish & Wildlife Service Office of Law Enforcement P.O. Box 492098 Attn: Wildlife Inspector (DIA) Denver, CO 80249 Tel: (303) 342-7430 Fax: (303) 342-7433 Email: permitsR6LE@fws.gov
Region 7: Alaska U.S. Fish & Wildlife Service Office of Law Enforcement P.O. Box 190045 Anchorage, AK 99519-0045 Tel: (907) 786-3311 Fax: (907) 786-3313 Email: permitsR7LE@fws.gov	**Region 8: California and Nevada** U.S. Fish & Wildlife Service Office of Law Enforcement 2800 Cottage Way, W-2928 Sacramento, CA 95825 Tel: (916) 414-6660 Fax: (916) 414-6715 Email: permitsR8LE@fws.gov

Please continue to next page

Figure 8–9. (*continued*)

PERMIT APPLICATION FORM INSTRUCTIONS

The following instructions pertain to the form 3-200-3 that must be completed as an application for a U.S. Fish and Wildlife Service permit. The General Permit Procedures in 50 CFR 13 address the permitting process.

GENERAL INSTRUCTIONS:
- Complete all blocks/lines/questions in Sections A through D.
- **An incomplete application may cause delays in processing or may be returned to the applicant. Be sure you are filling in the appropriate application form for the proposed activity.**
- Print clearly or type in the information. Illegible applications may cause delays.
- Sign the application in <u>blue</u> ink. Faxes or copies of the original signature will not be accepted.
- Mail the original application to the appropriate address on the attached address list. The application is to be submitted to the issuing office address in the Region your company is located.
- **Keep a copy of your completed application.**
- **Please plan ahead. Allow at least 60 days for your application to be processed. (50 CFR 13.11)**
- Applications are processed in the order they are received.

COMPLETE SECTION A:
- Enter the complete name of the business who will be the Licensee if an Import/Export License is issued. If no company name exists, then use the Name (Last, First, Middle) of the owner of the business. Enter personal information that identifies the applicant.
- If you are applying on behalf of a client, the personal information must pertain to the client, and a document evidencing power of attorney must be included with the application.
- Give a brief description of the type of business in which the applicant is engaged (Taxidermy, Jewelry, Apparel, etc.).
- **Doing business as (dba):** dba's are not accepted. The name on the Import/Export License must match the invoice and other shipping documents that accompany the shipment to or from the United States.
- **Principal Officer** is the person in charge of the listed business. The principal officer is the person responsible for the application and any permitted activities. Often the principal officer is a Director or President. **Primary Contact** is the person at the business who will be available to answer questions about the application or permitted activities. Often this is the preparer of the application.

COMPLETE SECTION B:
- Mailing address: This is the address where you will receive all official notices sent from the Service (ONLY if different than address listed in Block 1.a.).

COMPLETE SECTION C:
Application processing fee:
- An application processing fee is required at the time of application. **The fee does not guarantee the issuance of a permit. Fees will not be refunded for applications that are approved, abandoned, or denied.** We may return fees for withdrawn applications if no significant processing has occurred.

Federal Fish and Wildlife permits:
- List the number(s) of your most current Service permit or the number of the most recent permit if none are currently valid.

CERTIFICATION:
- **The individual identified in Section A or person with a valid power of attorney (documentation must be included in the application) must sign and date the application <u>in blue ink</u>.** This signature binds the applicant to the statement of certification. This means that you certify that you have read and understand the regulations that apply to the permit. You also certify that everything included in the application is true to the best of your knowledge. Be sure to read the statement and re-read the application and your answers before signing the application.

COMPLETE SECTION D:
- Question 1. **Foreign Applicant ONLY:** Enter the complete U.S. address. This is the address where you will receive all official notices sent from the Service. 50 CFR 13.12 requires this information for issuance.
- Question 7. **Foreign Applicant ONLY:** Enter the complete name, physical address, telephone and fax numbers of your agent located in the United States where your records (as defined in 50 CFR 13.46) will be maintained for five (5) years from the date of expiration of the license. This can be a customshouse broker, relative, etc. It cannot be a retail postal or mail service center. 50 CFR 13.12 requires this information for issuance.

Please continue to next page

3-200-3 Revised December 2013

Figure 8–9. *(continued)*

APPLICATION FOR A FEDERAL FISH AND WILDLIFE PERMIT
Paperwork Reduction Act, Privacy Act, and Freedom of Information Act – Notices

In accordance with the Paperwork Reduction Act of 1995 (44 U.S.C. 3501, *et seq.*) and the Privacy Act of 1974 (5 U.S.C. 552a), please be advised:

1. The gathering of information on fish and wildlife is authorized by:
   (Authorizing statutes can be found at: http://www.gpoaccess.gov/cfr/index.html and http://www.fws.gov/permits/ltr/ltr.shtml.)
   a. Bald and Golden Eagle Protection Act (16 U.S.C. 668), 50 CFR 22;
   b. Endangered Species Act of 1973 (16 U.S.C. 1531-1544), 50CFR 17;
   c. Migratory Bird Treaty Act (16 U.S.C. 703-712), 50 CFR 21;
   d. Marine Mammal Protection Act of 1972 (16 U.S.C. 1361, *et. seq.*), 50 CFR 18;
   e. Wild Bird Conservation Act (16 U.S.C. 4901-4916), 50 CFR 15;
   f. Lacey Act: Injurious Wildlife (18 U.S.C. 42), 50 CFR 16;
   g. Convention on International Trade in Endangered Species of Wild Fauna and Flora (TIAS 8249), http://www.cites.org/ , 50 CFR 23;
   h. General Provisions, 50 CFR 10;
   i. General Permit Procedures, 50 CFR 13; and
   j. Wildlife Provisions (Import/export/transport), 50 CFR 14.

2. Information requested in this form is purely voluntary. However, submission of requested information is required in order to process applications for permits authorized under the above laws. Failure to provide all requested information may be sufficient cause for the U.S. Fish and Wildlife Service to deny the request. Response is not required unless a currently valid Office of Management and Budget (OMB) control number is displayed on the form.

3. Certain applications for permits authorized under the Endangered Species Act of 1973 (16 U.S.C. 1539) and the Marine Mammal Protection Act of 1972 (16 U.S.C. 1374) will be published in the **Federal Register** as required by the two laws.

4. Disclosures outside the Department of the Interior may be made without the consent of an individual under the routine uses listed below, if the disclosure is compatible with the purposes for which the record was collected. (Ref. 68 FR 52611, September 4, 2003)

   a. Routine disclosure to subject matter experts, and Federal, tribal, State, local, and foreign agencies, for the purpose of obtaining advice relevant to making a decision on an application for a permit or when necessary to accomplish a FWS function related to this system of records.
   b. Routine disclosure to the public as a result of publishing **Federal Register** notices announcing the receipt of permit applications for public comment or notice of the decision on a permit application.
   c. Routine disclosure to Federal, tribal, State, local, or foreign wildlife and plant agencies for the exchange of information on permits granted or denied to assure compliance with all applicable permitting requirements.
   d. Routine disclosure to Captive-bred Wildlife registrants under the Endangered Species Act for the exchange of authorized species, and to share information on the captive breeding of these species.
   e. Routine disclosure to Federal, tribal, State, and local authorities who need to know who is permitted to receive and rehabilitate sick, orphaned, and injured birds under the Migratory Bird Treaty Act and the Bald and Golden Eagle Protection Act; federally permitted rehabilitators; individuals seeking a permitted rehabilitator with whom to place a bird in need of care; and licensed veterinarians who receive, treat, or diagnose sick, orphaned, and injured birds.
   f. Routine disclosure to the Department of Justice, or a court, adjudicative, or other administrative body or to a party in litigation before a court or adjudicative or administrative body, under certain circumstances.
   g. Routine disclosure to the appropriate Federal, tribal, State, local, or foreign governmental agency responsible for investigating, prosecuting, enforcing, or implementing statutes, rules, or licenses, when we become aware of a violation or potential violation of such statutes, rules, or licenses, or when we need to monitor activities associated with a permit or regulated use.
   h. Routine disclosure to a congressional office in response to an inquiry to the office by the individual to whom the record pertains.
   i. Routine disclosure to the Government Accountability Office or Congress when the information is required for the evaluation of the permit programs.
   j. Routine disclosure to provide addresses obtained from the Internal Revenue Service to debt collection agencies for purposes of locating a debtor to collect or compromise a Federal claim against the debtor or to consumer reporting agencies to prepare a commercial credit report for use by the FWS.

5. For individuals, personal information such as home address and telephone number, financial data, and personal identifiers (social security number, birth date, etc.) will be removed prior to any release of the application.

6. The public reporting burden on the applicant for information collection varies depending on the activity for which a permit is requested. The relevant burden for an Import/Export license application is 1.25 hours. This burden estimate includes time for reviewing instructions, gathering and maintaining data and completing and reviewing the form. You may direct comments regarding the burden estimate or any other aspect of the form to the Service Information Clearance Officer, U.S. Fish and Wildlife Service, MS 2042-PDM, 4401 North Fairfax Drive, Arlington, VA 22203 (mail); or INFOCOL@fws.gov (email). Please include "1018-0092" in the subject line of your comments.

Freedom of Information Act – Notice

For organizations, businesses, or individuals operating as a business (i.e., permittees not covered by the Privacy Act), we request that you identify any information that should be considered privileged and confidential business information to allow the Service to meet its responsibilities under FOIA. Confidential business information must be clearly marked "Business Confidential" at the top of the letter or page and each succeeding page and must be accompanied by a non-confidential summary of the confidential information. The non-confidential summary and remaining documents may be made available to the public under FOIA [43 CFR 2.13(c)(4), 43 CFR 2.15(d)(1)(i)].

Figure 8–10. General certificate of compliance.

---

1. Elements Required in a GCC

1. Identification of the product covered by this certificate: *Describe the product(s) covered by this certification in enough detail to match the certificate to each product it covers and no others.*

2. Citation to each consumer product safety regulation to which this product is being certified: *The certificate must identify separately each consumer product safety rule administered by the Commission that is applicable to the product.*

3. Identification of the U.S. importer or domestic manufacturer certifying compliance of the product: *Provide the name, full mailing address, and telephone number of the importer or U.S. domestic manufacturer certifying the product.*

4. Contact information for the individual maintaining records of test results: *Provide the name, full mailing address, email address, and telephone number of the person maintaining test records in support of the certification.*

5. Date and place where this product was manufactured: *For the date(s) when the product was manufactured, provide at least the month and year. For the place of manufacture provide at least the city (or administrative region) and country where the product was manufactured or finally assembled. If the same manufacturer operates more than one location in the same city, provide the street address of the factory.*

6. Provide the date(s) and place when the product was tested for compliance with the consumer product safety rule(s) cited above: *Provide the location(s) of the testing and the date(s) of the test(s) or test report(s) on which certification is being based.*

7. Identification of any third party laboratory on whose testing the certificate depends: *Generally, this section should be labeled "N/A" for a GCC because third party laboratory testing is not a requirement for non-children's products. (It is only a requirement for children's products and must be included in a CPC.) However, if a certifier voluntarily uses test results from a third party laboratory as the basis for issuing its GCC, the law requires that the certifier must then provide the name, full mailing address, and telephone number of the third party laboratory.*

> A GCC may be used only for general use, or non-children's products. Children's products require a "children's product certificate," or CPC.

2. General Certificate of Conformity - Sample #1
(Available at www.chinos1.net/5aaTy)

1. Identification of the product covered by this certificate: *Men's chino pants model CH-123 (Sizes 28-36)*

Figure 8–10. *(continued)*

---

2. Citation to each CPSC product safety regulation to which this product is being certified: *16 CFR Part 1610, Standard for the Flammability of Clothing Textiles.*

> In this example, the standard for flammability of clothing textiles is the only applicable requirement.

3. Identification of the U.S. importer or domestic manufacturer certifying compliance of the product:

Chino Pants Importers
123 Fabric Way
Smithfield, IL 12345
(538) 763-0980

4. Contact information for the individual maintaining records of test results:

Bob Smith, Compliance Manager
Chino Pants Importers
123 Fabric Way
Smithfield, IL 12345
(538) 763-0987, bsmith@chinos1.net

5. Date and place where this product was manufactured: *September 2011, Svay Rieng Province, Cambodia*

6. Date and place where this product was tested for compliance with the regulation(s) cited above: *N/A. Exempted from testing per 16 CFR § 1610(1)(d)*

> In this example, the pants are exempt from testing because they are made from 100% plain surface cotton with a fabric weight of 2.6 ounces or more per square yard. See 16 CFR §§ 1610.1(c) and 1610.1(d) for other exceptions and exemptions.

7. Identification of an third party laboratory on whose testing the certificate depends: *N/A*

> In this example, the pants are not required to be tested due to the exemption cited above. Even if testing were required, the use of an accredited, third party laboratory accepted by the CPSC is not a requirement for non-children's products. You do not need to include this section in such an example, or you can label this section "N/A."

If Customs elects to examine the merchandise, it has a period of five days following presentation for examination to determine whether to detain the merchandise. If it determines to detain the merchandise, it must give a notice to the importer within an additional five days specifying the reason for the detention, the anticipated length of the detention, and additional information being requested. If Customs determines that the merchandise is not eligible for entry, it may pursue the procedures for seizure and forfeiture of the merchandise. If Customs takes no action within thirty days after presentation of the merchandise for examination, the importer may file a protest and seek expedited review in the appropriate court (usually the Court of International Trade).

S. Liquidation Notices

After entry has been made, U.S. Customs and Border Protection will process the entry documentation and liquidate the entry. Liquidation is when the Customs review is complete. When the importer makes the original entry, it is required to declare (state its opinion of) the correct classification, value, and duties payable and to tender those duties. After Customs has reviewed the classification, value, and duties payable, if it agrees with the importer's entry, liquidation will occur with no change. Currently, entries are scheduled on an automatic liquidation cycle of 314 days after entry. Sometimes, when information is needed by Customs to verify the classification or value (or when the importer requests for good cause), liquidation may be suspended up to a maximum of four years from the date of entry. The official notice of liquidation, known as the Bulletin Notice, is published in the port where entry was made at the Customs office. The official notice is the only one binding upon Customs. Paper courtesy no-change notices have been discontinued for those importers who file electronically and now the notifications are electronic as well. Only if there is a change in the liquidation will the importer receive notification in the way of an increased duty bill or a refund notice and there will be a Notice of Action issued prior to either of those events. See Section W below.

It is important to keep track of when an entry liquidates because if the importer disputes the information that is filed in the entry, then it has the ability to file a Protest against the liquidation within 180 days of the date of liquidation. More on this is in Section X below.

T. Notices of Redelivery

Where merchandise has been released to the importer and Customs comes to believe that the merchandise has been entered in violation of the laws of the United States—for example, the goods have not been properly marked with the foreign country of origin—Customs may issue a notice of redelivery to the importer (CF-4647 was shown in Chapter 6, Figure 6-10). The form will specify the law that has been violated and will order the redelivery of the merchandise to Customs' custody within a thirty-day period. If no redelivery is made, the customs bond covering the entry of the merchandise will be declared forfeited and the importer will become liable for liquidated damages. For the purpose of determining the country of origin on textiles and apparel, Customs has up to 180 days to issue the notice of redelivery after release of the merchandise. It is important for the importer to realize that Customs has this 30-day redelivery time frame, as most importers are completely unaware of this requirement. In this day of "just in time" delivery, importers do not maintain imported goods on its shelves for 30 days pending a request for redelivery. One of the provisions of the Customs surety bond, which allows for release of the merchandise under the Entry/Entry Summary provisions is that the importer will redeliver upon demand. If the importer cannot redeliver then, Customs will issue a penalty to the importer. Redelivery is not demanded very often and only upon a reasonable belief by Customs that the imported goods are in violation of the Customs law in some manner, so importers take the risk of delivering prior to the expiration of 30-day waiting period.

U. Post Entry Amendment

After the entry summary has been filed and duties paid, if the importer determines that an error has been made, the importer may file a Post Entry Amendment (PEA) (see Figure 8–11) to amend the information that is incorrect. This may be done prior to liquidation. All of the details regarding the changes must be identified in the PEA. If Customs agrees with the information provided on the PEA, it will liquidate the entry as suggested. If Customs disagrees with the information on the PEA, it will liquidate as entered and the importer will be required to file a protest. The PEA is an easy way to correct clerical errors and even more significant classification or value disputes; however, it should be noted that the PEA does not have the same legal validity as a Protest and so a Protest must be filed if Customs does not amend the entry in accordance with the request under the PEA.

Figure 8–11. Post Entry Amendment.

POST ENTRY AMENDMENT
(CORRECTION TO AN ENTRY SUMMARY)

FILER [   ] DATE [   ] LIQUIDATION DATE[1] [   ]
[1]IF AVAILABLE.

ENTRY NUMBER [   ] PORT [   ]

IMPORTER NUMBER [   ] REASON CODE [   ]

IMPORTER NAME [   ]

NARRATIVE DESCRIPTION

[   ]

CORRECTED DUTY AMOUNT: TOTAL ASCERTAINED AMOUNT SHOWN ON CORRECTED 7501

DUTY [ ]	[ ]	PAYMENT
HMF [ ]	[ ]	REFUND
MPF [ ]	[ ]	BILL
TAX [ ]	[ ]	NON-REVENUE[2]
ADD [ ]		
CVD [ ]		
TOTAL [ ]		

[2]STATISTICAL INFORMATION ERRORS THAT MEET OR EXCEED CENSUS BUREAU REPORTING LEVELS. REFERENCE FEDERAL REGISTER NOTICE DATED NOVEMBER 28, 2000.

TOTAL PAID, REFUND OR BILL AMOUNT

[   ]

FILER POINT OF CONTACT NAME/PHONE

[   ]

CUSTOMS & BORDER PROTECTION ONLY

INTEREST [   ] TOTAL LIQUIDATION AMOUNT [   ]

381

Figure 8–11. (*continued*)

REASON CODES

11- VALUATION
12- CLASSIFICATION
13- QUANTITY
14- ANTI-DUMPING DUTY
15-COUNTERVAILING DUTY
16- SPECIAL TRADE PROGRAMS
17- INTEREST ONLY
18- NON-REVENUE
19- OTHER

AMOUNTS ON THE WORKSHEET SHOULD BE THE CORRECTED DUTY
AMOUNT - NOT THE DIFFERENCE

WORKSHEET SHOULD HAVE THE SAME ASCERTAINED AMOUNTS AS THE
CORRECTED CBP FORM 7501

V. Requests for Information

Sometimes, after the importer has made entry of merchandise, Customs will decide that it needs additional information in order to determine whether or not it agrees with the classification, value, and duties payable declared by the importer at the time of entry. Ordinarily, in such cases, Customs will send the importer a Request for Information (see Figure 8–12). A common request by Customs is for more information relating to the relationship between the seller and the buyer (Field 12A). The reason for the question is to determine whether the valuation between related parties reflects an arms-length transaction. See more on this in Chapter 10. Other standard items requested include brochures or catalogs describing the merchandise in order to determine if the classification is correct, or information about the dutiable and nondutiable charges or assists and royalties to determine if the total value has been properly declared under the Customs value laws. Customs may request any information that it believes is necessary in order to confirm that the merchandise is being entered in accordance with the customs laws of the United States. These requests are being sent electronically through the ACE system these days.

W. Notices of Action

When Customs determines that it disagrees with the way in which the importer originally entered the merchandise, either prior to sending a Request for Information or after receiving a response to a Request for Information, it will send a Notice of Action to the importer (see Figure 8–13). A Notice of Action may indicate that Customs proposes to take certain action and may invite the importer to give its reasons as to why that action should not be taken within twenty days, or the notice may specify that Customs has already taken that action. Often, the action taken is an advance in value, where Customs has determined that the value declared by the importer at the time of entry was too low, and therefore, additional customs duties are being assessed. Other actions, such as reclassification of the merchandise, can also be taken. If Customs receives no response from the importer, the entry will be liquidated in accordance with Customs' notice. This means that additional customs duties will be payable, and a bill for such duties will be sent to the importer.

Figure 8–12. Request for Information.

DEPARTMENT OF HOMELAND SECURITY U.S. Customs and Border Protection **REQUEST FOR INFORMATION** 19 CFR 151.11	OMB No. 1651-0023 Exp. 03-31-2014
	1. Date of Request
	2. Date of Entry and Importation

3. Manufacturer/Seller/Shipper	4. Carrier	5. Entry No.

5a. Invoice Description of Merchandise	5b. Invoice No.	6. HTSUS Item No.

7. Country of Origin/Exportation	8. CBP Broker and Reference or File No.

9. TO:	10. FROM:

Production of Documents and/or Information Required by Law: If you have provided the information requested on this form to U.S. Customs and Border Protection at other ports, please indicate the port of entry to which it was supplied, and furnish a copy of your reply to this office, if possible.	➤	11a. Port	11b. Date Information Furnished

General Information and Instructions on Reverse

12. Please Answer Indicated Question(s)	13. Please Furnish Indicated Item(s)
☐ A. Are you related (see reverse) in any way to the seller of this merchandise? If you are related, please describe the relationship, and explain how this relationship affects the price paid or payable for the merchandise.	☐ A. Copy of contract (or purchase order and seller's confirmation thereof) covering this transaction, and any revisions thereto.
	☐ B. Descriptive or illustrative literature or information explaining what the merchandise is, where and how it is used, and exactly how it operates.
	☐ C. Breakdown of components, materials, or ingredients by weight and the actual cost of the components at the time of assembly into the finished article.
☐ B. Identify and give details of any additional costs/ expenses incurred in this transaction, such as: ☐ (1) packing ☐ (2) commissions ☐ (3) proceeds that accrue to the seller ☐ (4) assists ☐ (5) royalties and/or license fees	☐ D. Submit samples: Article number and description _____ _____ from container _____ mark(s)and number _____ Samples consumed in analysis, and other samples whose return is not specifically requested, will not normally be returned. ☐ E. See item 14 below.

14. CBP Officer Message

15. Reply Message (Use additional sheets if more space is needed.)

16. CERTIFICATION	It is required that an appropriate corporate/company official execute this certificate and/or endorse all correspondence in response to the information requested. (**NOTE**: NOT REQUIRED IF FOREIGN FIRM COMPLETES THIS FORM.)		
I hereby certify that the information furnished herewith or upon this form in response to this inquiry is true and correct, and that any samples provided were taken from the shipment covered by this entry. ➤	16a. Name and Title/Position of Signer (Owner, Importer, or Corporate/Company Official)	l6b. Signature	
		16c. Telephone No.	16d. Date

17. CBP Officer	18. Team Designation	19. Telephone No.

CBP Form 28 (03/11)

Figure 8–12. (continued)

GENERAL INFORMATION AND INSTRUCTIONS

1. The requested information is necessary for proper classification and/or appraisement of your merchandise and/or for insuring import compliance of such merchandise. Your reply is required in accordance with section 509(a), Tariff Action of 1930, as amended (19 U.S.C. 1509).

2. All information, documents, and samples requested must relate to the shipment of merchandise described on the front of this form.

3. Please answer all indicated questions to the best of your knowledge.

4. All information submitted will be treated confidentially.

5. If a reply cannot be made within 30 days from the date of this request or if you wish to discuss any of the questions designated for your reply, please contact the CBP officer whose name appears on the front of this form.

6. Return a copy of this form with your reply.

DEFINITIONS OF KEY WORDS IN BLOCK 12

Question A: RELATED - The persons specified below shall be treated as persons who are related:

    (A) Members of the same family, including brothers and sisters (whether by whole or half blood), spouse, ancestors, and lineal descendants.

    (B) Any officer or director of an organization and such organization.

    (C) An officer or director of an organization and an officer or director of another organization, if each such individual is also an officer or director in the other organization.

    (D) Partners.

    (E) Employer and employee.

    (F) Any person directly or indirectly owning, controlling, or holding with power to vote, 5 percent or more of the outstanding voting stock or shares of any organization and such organization.

    (G) Two or more persons directly or indirectly controlling, controlled by or under common control with, any person.

PRICE PAID OR PAYABLE - This term is defined as the total payment (whether direct or indirect and exclusive of any costs, charges, or expenses incurred for transportation, insurance, and other C.I.F. charges) made, or to be made, for imported merchandise by the buyer to, or for the benefit of, the seller.

Question B: ASSISTS - The term "assist" means any of the following if supplied directly or indirectly, and free of charge or at reduced cost, by the buyer of the imported merchandise for use in connection with the production or the sale for export to the United States of the merchandise:

    (1) Materials, components, parts, and similar items incorporated in the imported merchandise.

    (2) Tools, dies, molds, and similar items used in the production of the imported merchandise.

    (3) Merchandise consumed in the production of the imported merchandise.

    (4) Engineering, development, artwork, design work, and plans and sketches that are undertaken elsewhere than in the United States and are necessary for the production of the imported merchandise.

PROCEEDS THAT ACCRUE TO THE SELLER - This term is defined as the amount of any subsequent resale, disposal, or use of the imported merchandise that accrues, directly or indirectly, to the seller.

ROYALTIES AND/OR LICENSE FEES - This term relates to those amounts that the buyer is required to pay, directly or indirectly, as a condition of the sale of the imported merchandised for exportation to the United States.

PAPERWORK REDUCTION ACT STATEMENT - An agency may not conduct or sponsor an information collection and a person is not required to respond to this information unless it displays a current valid OMB control number and an expiration date. The control number for this collection is 1651-0023. The estimated average time to complete this application is 2 hours. If you have any comments regarding the burden estimate you can write to U.S. Customs and Border Protection, Office of Regulations and Rulings, 799 9th Street, NW., Washington DC 20229.

CBP Form 28 (03/11)(Back)

Figure 8–13. Notice of Action.

DEPARTMENT OF THE TREASURY UNITED STATES CUSTOMS SERVICE 19 CFR 152.2	NOTICE OF ACTION *This is NOT a Notice of Liquidation*		1. DATE OF THIS NOTICE
2. CARRIER	3. DATE OF IMPORTATION	4. DATE OF ENTRY	5. ENTRY NO.
6. MFR/SELLER/SHIPPER	7. COUNTRY	8. CUSTOMS BROKER AND FILE NO.	

9. DESCRIPTION OF MERCHANDISE

10. TO ▶	11. FROM

12. THE FOLLOWING ACTION, WHICH WILL RESULT IN AN INCREASE IN DUTIES,—

☐ IS **PROPOSED**   IF YOU DISAGREE WITH THIS PROPOSED ACTION, PLEASE FURNISH YOUR REASONS IN WRITING TO THIS OFFICE WITHIN 20 DAYS FROM THE DATE OF THIS NOTICE. AFTER 20 DAYS THE ENTRY WILL BE LIQUIDATED AS PROPOSED.

☐ HAS BEEN **TAKEN**   THE ENTRY IS IN THE LIQUIDATION PROCESS AND IS NOT AVAILABLE FOR REVIEW IN THIS OFFICE.

TYPE OF ACTION

A. ☐ RATE ADVANCE

B. ☐ VALUE ADVANCE

C. ☐ EXCESS   ☐ WEIGHT   ☐ QUANTITY

D. ☐ OTHER *(See below)*

13. EXPLANATION *(Refer to Action letter designations above)*

14. CUSTOMS OFFICER *(Print or Type)*	15. TEAM DESIGNATION	16. TELEPHONE

Customs Form 29 (031795)

ORIGINAL (WHITE) - IMPORTER

X. Protests

Where the entry is liquidated with an increase in duty, a change in classification, or when merchandise is excluded from entry, the importer may protest such action by filing Customs Form 19. (A sample protest and instructions form is shown in Figure 8–14.) This form must be filed within 180 days of the notice of liquidation or date of exclusion. Consequently, if the importer does not track the date of liquidation, it will miss the protest deadline and lose its right to protest. For this reason, it is important for the importer to establish a procedure whereby the status of entries is checked from time to time.

Similarly, sometimes liquidation will be suspended. In general, entries will be automatically liquidated 314 days from the date of entry. If an entry is not liquidated, the importer should investigate why it is being suspended to avoid a future liquidation with a duty increase long after the time of importation. A protest gives the importer an additional opportunity to present its reasons why the entry should be liquidated as originally entered with no increase in duties. Customs must grant or deny a protest within two years of filing (thirty days for excluded merchandise). In order to obtain a decision more quickly, a request for accelerated disposition may be filed, which Customs must act upon within an additional thirty days. In certain circumstances, an importer may request that its protest be reviewed by Customs Headquarters as an Application for Further Review.

Y. Record-Keeping

The importer is required to keep all records relating to its imports for five years from the date of import. This includes, not only the commercial invoice and bills of lading, but the Customs entry and entry summary forms (which must be obtained from the customs broker) as well as supporting documents that may not be filed with Customs. These include supporting documents for claiming free trade benefits, the payment to the seller, to confirm that goods are of U.S. origin, to show the value of repairs abroad, etc. Customs has issued the (a)(1)(A) list to provide the importer the list of all elements which must be maintained for proper record-keeping. See additional information at: http://www.cbp.gov/trade/trade-community/outreach-programs/entry-summary/recordkeeping.

Figure 8–14. Sample protest form and instructions.

DEPARTMENT OF HOMELAND SECURITY
U.S. Customs and Border Protection

PROTEST

Pursuant to Sections 514 & 514(a), Tariff Act of 1930 as amended, 19 CFR Part 174 et. seq.

Approved OMB No. 1851-0017
Exp. 03/31/2016

1. PROTEST NO. *(Supplied by CBP)*

NOTE: If your protest is denied, in whole or in part, and you wish to CONTEST the denial, you may do so by bringing a civil action in the U.S. Court of International Trade within 180 days after the date of mailing of Notice of Denial. You may obtain further information concerning the institution of an action by writing the Clerk of U.S. Court of International Trade, One Federal Plaza, New York NY 10007 (212-264-2800).

2. DATE RECEIVED *(CBP Use Only)*

SECTION I - IMPORTER AND ENTRY IDENTIFICATION

3. PORT

4. IMPORTER NO.

5. ENTRY DETAILS

PORT CODE | FILER CODE | ENTRY NO. | CHECK DIGIT | DATE OF ENTRY | DATE OF LIQUIDATION

6. NAME AND ADDRESS OF IMPORTER OR OTHER PROTESTING PARTY

7. Is Accelerated Disposition being requested (19 CFR 174.22)?
☐ Yes ☐ No

SECTION II - DETAILED REASONS FOR PROTEST

8. With respect to each category of merchandise, set forth, separately, (1) each decision protested, (2) the claim of the protesting party, and (3) the factual material and legal arguments which are believed to support the protest. All such material and arguments should be specific. General statements of conclusions are not sufficient.

(Attach Additional Sheets if necessary.)

SECTION III - REQUEST FOR DISPOSITION IN ACCORDANCE WITH ACTION ON PREVIOUSLY FILED PROTEST

Protesting party may request disposition in accordance with the action taken on a previously filed protest that is the subject of a pending application for further review and is alleged to involve the same merchandise and the same issues. (See 19 CFR 174.13(a)(7).) To request such disposition, enter in Blocks 9 and 9 the protest number and date of receipt of such previously filed protest.

9. PROTEST NO. OF PREVIOUSLY FILED PROTEST

10. DATE OF RECEIPT

SECTION IV - SIGNATURE AND MAILING INSTRUCTIONS

11. NAME AND ADDRESS OF PERSON TO WHOM ANY NOTICE OF APPROVAL OR DENIAL SHOULD BE SENT

12. NAME, ADDRESS, AND CBP IDENTIFICATION NUMBER TO WHICH REFUND SHOULD BE SENT

13. IF FILING AS ATTORNEY OR AGENT, TYPE OR PRINT YOUR NAME, ADDRESS AND IMPORTER NUMBER, IF ANY

14. SIGNATURE X   DATE

(Optional) **SECTION V - APPLICATION FOR FURTHER REVIEW** *(Fill in Item 1 above if this is a separate Application for Further Review.)*

15. MARK BOX CORRESPONDING TO YOUR ANSWER TO EACH OF THE FOLLOWING QUESTIONS

YES NO

☐ ☐ (A) Have you made prior request of a port director for a further review of the same claim with respect to the same substantially similar merchandise?

☐ ☐ (B) Have you received a final adverse decision from the U.S. Court of International Trade on the same claim with respect to the same category of merchandise or do you have action involving such a claim pending before the U.S. Court of International Trade?

☐ ☐ (C) Have you previously received an adverse administrative decision from the Commissioner of CBP or his designee or have you presently pending an application for an administrative decision on the same claim with respect to the same category of merchandise?

16. JUSTIFICATION FOR FURTHER REVIEW UNDER THE CRITERIA IN 19 CFR 174.24 AND 174.25 (Include Applicable Rulings)

(Attach Additional Sheets If Necessary.)

SECTION VI - DECISION (CBP USE ONLY)

17. APPLICATION FOR FURTHER REVIEW EXPLANATION: ☐ Approved* ☐ Denied for the reason checked: ☐ Untimely filed ☐ Does not meet criteria ☐ Other, namely

*When further review only is approved the decision on the protest is suspended, pending issuance of a protest review decision.

18. PROTEST EXPLANATION: ☐ Approved ☐ Rejected as non-protestable ☐ Denied in full for the reason checked: ☐ Denied in part for the reason checked: ☐ Untimely filed ☐ See attached protest review decision ☐ Other, namely

19. TITLE OF CBP OFFICER

20. SIGNATURE AND DATE

Previous Editions are Obsolete   CBP Form 19 (05/10)

Figure 8–14. (*continued*)

INSTRUCTIONS

PLEASE REFER TO: Part 174, Customs Regulations
Definitions*

"Liquidation" means the final computation or ascertainment of the duties or drawback accruing on an entry.

"Protest" means the seeking of review of a decision of an appropriate CBP officer. Such a review may be conducted by CBP officers who participated directly in the underlying decision.

"Further Review" means a request for review of the protest to be performed by a CBP officer who did not participate directly in the protested decision, or by the Commissioner, or his designee as provided in the CBP Regulations. This request will only be acted upon in the event that the protest would have been denied at the initial level of review. If you are filing for further review, you must answer each question in Item 15 on CBP Form 19 and provide justification for further review in Item 16.

What matters may be protested?

1. The appraised value of merchandise;
2. The classification and rate and amount of duties chargeable;
3. All charges within the jurisdiction of the U.S. Department of Homeland Security;
4. Exclusion of merchandise from entry or delivery, or demand for redelivery;
5. The liquidation or reliquidation of an entry;
6. The refusal to pay a claim for drawback; and

Who may file a protest or application for further review?

1. The importer or consignee shown on the entry papers, or their sureties;
2. Any person paying any charge or exaction;
3. Any person seeking entry or delivery, or upon whom a demand for redelivery has been made;
4. Any person filing a claim for drawback; or
5. Any authorized agent of any of the persons described above.

Where to file protest:

With the port director whose decision is protested (at the port where entry was made).

When to file a protest:

Within 180 days after either: 1) the date of notice of liquidation or reliquidation; or 2) the date of the decision, involving neither a liquidation nor reliquidation, as to which the protest is made (e.g., the date of an exaction, the date of written notice excluding merchandise from entry or delivery or demand for redelivery); or 3) a surety may file within 180 days after the date of mailing of notice of demand for payment against its bond.

Contents of protest:

1. Name and address of the protestant;
2. The importer number of the protestant;
3. The number and date(s) of the entry(s);
4. The date of liquidation of the entry (or the date of a decision);
5. A specific description of the merchandise;
6. The nature of and justification for the objection set forth distinctly and specifically with respect to each category, claim, decision, or refusal;
7. The date of receipt and protest number of any protest previously filed that is the subject of a pending application for further review; and
8. If another party has not filed a timely protest, the surety's protest shall certify that the protest is not being filed collusively to extend another authorized person's time to protest.
9. Whether accelerated disposition is being requested.

NOTE: Under Item 5, Entry Details, "Check Digit" information is optional; however, CBP would appreciate receiving the information if you can provide it. All attachments to a protest (other than samples or similar exhibits) must be filed in triplicate.

CBP Form 19 (05/10)

Figure 8–14. (*continued*)

CONTINUATION SHEET

SECTION II - DETAILED REASONS FOR PROTEST (Continuation)

8. With respect to each category of merchandise, set forth, separately, (1) each decision protested, (2) the claim of the protesting party, and (3) the factual material and legal arguments which are believed to support the protest. All such material and arguments should be specific. General statements of conclusions are not sufficient.

(Optional) **SECTION V - APPLICATION FOR FURTHER REVIEW (Continuation)**

16. JUSTIFICATION FOR FURTHER REVIEW UNDER THE CRITERIA IN 19 CFR 174.24 AND 174.25

CBP Form 19 (05/10)

Z. Administrative Summons

If Customs suspects that a violation of the customs laws has occurred, it may issue a summons to an importer or to third-party record-keepers, such as customs brokers, accountants, and attorneys, requesting them to produce documents or to give testimony relating to the importations. When a summons is being issued to a third-party record-keeper, Customs sends a copy of the notice to the importer of record. If the recipient does not comply with the summons, U.S. Customs and Border Protection can seek an order from the U.S. district court compelling the importer to produce the documents or provide the testimony requested. Upon receipt of a summons and before providing any documents or answering any questions from a Customs agent, the importer should consult with its attorney.

AA. Search Warrants

When Customs believes that a criminal or intentional violation of the customs laws has occurred, it may apply to the appropriate U.S. district court for a search warrant to inspect the premises or seize records of an importer. A sample affidavit, which must be filed with the court, and a search warrant are shown in Figures 8–15 and 8–16, respectively. When Customs agents approach an importer with a search warrant, the importer should realize that the case is a criminal case and that individuals as well as the company may be subject to fines or imprisonment. The importer should not discuss the case with the Customs agent without consulting its attorney. As for some basic instructions, the importer should make notes as to any documentation or other items that Customs seizes so that it can obtain the documentation or samples back. Get the names of the agents and ask for contact information. Cooperate fully, but do not answer any questions without an attorney present. This list is not all-inclusive, follow the guidance of the attorney.

BB. Grand Jury Subpoenas

When Customs investigates a criminal violation of the customs laws, the U.S. attorney may convene a grand jury. The grand jury may subpoena persons employed by the importer or other persons to testify before the grand jury. Obviously, these are extremely serious proceedings, and before any person testifies before a grand jury, he should be advised by legal counsel.

Figure 8–15. Sample affidavit for search warrant.

Form A. O. 106

United States District Court

FOR THE

UNITED STATES OF AMERICA

vs.

Commissioner's Docket No.

Case No.

AFFIDAVIT FOR
SEARCH WARRANT

BEFORE

Name of Commissioner   Address of Commissioner

The undersigned being duly sworn deposes and says:

That he (has reason to believe) that (on the person of)
(is positive)[1]   (on the premises known as)

in the   District of

there is now being concealed certain property, namely

here describe property

which are

here give alleged grounds for search and seizure

And that the facts tending to establish the foregoing grounds for issuance of a Search Warrant
are as follows:

_____
Signature of Affiant.

_____
Official Title, if any.

Sworn to before me, and subscribed in my presence,   , 19

_____
United States Commissioner.

[1] The Federal Rules of Criminal Procedure provide: "The warrant shall direct that it be served in the daytime, but if the affidavit are positive
that the property is on the person or in the place to be searched, the warrant may direct that it be served at any time." (Rule 41C)

Figure 8–16. Sample search warrant.

Form A. O. 93 (Revised June 1964)   **Search Warrant**

United States District Court
FOR THE

UNITED STATES OF AMERICA

vs.

Commissioner's Docket No.

Case No.

SEARCH WARRANT

To

Affidavit having been made before me by

that he { has reason to believe / is positive[1] } that { on the person of / on the premises known as }

in the   District of

there is now being concealed certain property, namely

here describe property

which are

here give alleged grounds for search and seizure

and as I am satisfied that there is probable cause to believe that the property so described is being concealed on the { person / premises } above described and that the foregoing grounds for application for issuance of the search warrant exist.

You are hereby commanded to search forthwith the { person / place } named for the property specified, serving this warrant and making the search { in the daytime / at any time in the day or night[1] } and if the property be found there to seize it, leaving a copy of this warrant and a receipt for the property taken, and prepare a written inventory of the property seized and return this warrant and bring the property before me within ten days of this date, as required by law.

Dated this   day of   , 19

U. S. Commissioner.

[1] The Federal Rules of Criminal Procedure provide: "The warrant shall direct that it be served in the daytime, but if the affidavits are positive that the property is on the person or in the place to be searched, the warrant may direct that it be served at any time." (Rule 41C)

Figure 8–16. *(continued)*

[*reverse*]

RETURN

I received the attached search warrant   , 19   , and have executed it as

follows:

On   , 19   at   o'clock   M, I searched { the person / the premises } described

in the warrant and

I left a copy of the warrant with ....

name of person searched or owner or "at the place of search"

together with a receipt for the items seized.

The following is an inventory of property taken pursuant to the warrant:

This inventory was made in the presence of

and

I swear that this Inventory is a true and detailed account of all the property taken by me on the

warrant.

_____

Subscribed and sworn to and returned before me this   day of   , 19

_____

U. S. Commissioner.

394

CC. Seizure Notices

When Customs believes that goods have been imported into the United States in violation of the customs laws, it may issue a seizure notice and information for claimants. Once a seizure notice has been issued, the importer must proceed by means of the procedures specified in the Customs regulations to try and repossess the merchandise. Sometimes, in order to avoid additional assessments of customs penalties or the expenses of further proceedings, the importer may agree or consent to abandon the merchandise that has been seized. (However, the importer should not be pressured into abandoning the merchandise by threats that Customs will pursue further penalties against the importer unless it abandons the merchandise.) No particular form is required to file a petition for remission or mitigation or to obtain release of the seized merchandise. If the merchandise is not allowed entry into U.S. commerce, there may be options for the importer to arrange for export. If the seizure relates to violation of a trademark or copyright, then the owner of that trademark or violation has the right to determine how the merchandise is handled. It may be a matter of proving the importer has the right to import the goods, or the owner may allow the infringing mark to be removed. However, if the intellectual property owner does allow the imported goods to be imported (or even in the case of transshipments through the U.S., to continue on to the country of destination), then the merchandise must be destroyed under Customs supervision and the importer will be required to pay a penalty.

DD. Prepenalty Notices

When Customs determines that a civil violation of the customs laws has occurred, it issues a prepenalty notice. See Figure 8-17. The prepenalty notice states the customs law or regulation that has been violated and the Customs claim for liquidated damages, for example, because merchandise was released to the importer under an Entry/Immediate Delivery and the importer failed to file the Entry Summary and other necessary customs entry documents within the allotted time period (Figure 8-18). The importer will normally be given thirty days to present reasons explaining why the penalty should not be issued.

EE. Penalty Notices

After U.S. Customs and Border Protection receives and rejects the importer's explanation as to why the penalty notice should not be issued or if the importer files no

Figure 8–17. Prepenalty notice.

U.S. Customs Service

610 S. Canal Street
Chicago, IL 60607-4523

ENF 4-02 PD:P
Port Case

Gentlemen:

This is to inform you that pursuant to Title 19, Code of Federal Regulations, Section 162, notice is hereby given that the United States Customs Service is contemplating assessing a penalty against you in the amount of $_____. This amount represents the maximum penalty for (culpability) for your introduction of merchandise into the United States in violation of Title 19, United States Code, Section 1592.

Prior to the issuance of a notice of penalty, you have the right to make an oral and written presentation as to why the claim for monetary penalty should not be issued in the amount proposed. The written presentation must be made within thirty (30) business days from the date of the mailing of the pre-penalty notice as provided for in sections 162.77/78 of the Customs Regulations. Should you wish to make an oral presentation, please contact _____ of my staff at the above telephone number to arrange a mutually convenient time and date for the presentation. Please be advised that we prefer the oral presentation be arranged after submission of the written response. The penalty notice will be issued automatically should you fail to respond to the pre-penalty notice within the effective period.

Exhibit A contains relevant information concerning the penalty action, i.e. specific details of the violation. Exhibit B represents the consumption entries involved in the penalty action.

If we do not hear from you within the time frame stipulated above the matter will be referred to the Court of International Trade for the institution of judicial proceedings.

Sincerely,

T R A D I T I O N

★

S E R V I C E

★

H O N O R

Fines, Penalties & Forfeitures Officer

Figure 8–17. *(continued)*

EXHIBIT A

1. **Description of Merchandise:**

2. **Shipper/Manufacturer:**

3. **Broker:**

4. **Consignee:**

5. **Details of Entry Introduction:**

6. **Loss of Revenue:**

7. **Law(s) Violated:**

8. **Facts Establishing Violation:**

9. **Culpability**

10. **Penalty Amount:**

Figure 8–18. Notice of Penalty or Liquidated Damages Demand.

DEPARTMENT OF THE TREASURY
UNITED STATES CUSTOMS SERVICE

NOTICE OF PENALTY OR LIQUIDATED DAMAGES INCURRED

AND DEMAND FOR PAYMENT

19 USC 1618, 19 USC 1623

Case Number

Port Name and Code

Investigation File No.

TO:

DEMAND IS HEREBY MADE FOR PAYMENT OF $ _____ , representing ☐ Penalties or ☐ Liquidated Damages
assessed against you for violation or law or regulation, or breach of bond, as set forth below:

LAW OR REGULATION VIOLATED	BOND BREACHED

DESCRIPTION OF BOND (if any)	Form Number	Amount $	Date

Name and Address of Principal on Bond

Name and Address of Surety on Bond	Surety Identification No.

If you feel there are extenuating circumstances, you have the right to object to the above action. Your petition should explain why you should not be penalized for the cited violation.   Write the petition as a letter or in legal form; submit in   (duplicate) (triplicate), addressed to the Commissioner of Customs, and forward to the FP&F Officer at

Unless the amount herein demanded is paid or a petition for relief is filed with the FP&F Officer within the indicated time limit, further action will be taken in connection with your bond or the matter will be referred to the United States Attorney.	TIME LIMIT FOR PAYMENT OR FILING PETITION FOR RELIEF (Days from the date of this Notice) ➡
Signature	Title	Date
By		

Customs Form 5955A (08/00)

explanation, Customs will issue a penalty notice. See Figure 8-19. The importer again has the right to file a petition for remission or mitigation within the time period specified on the penalty notice. Customs at the port and in the Office of Regulations and Rulings at Headquarters will review the petition and make a decision as to whether it will issue the penalty. If it is issued and the importer fails to pay, collection will be referred to the U.S. Department of Justice Civil Division, for the filing of a civil collection action in the Court of International Trade.

FF.   Customs Audits

U.S. Customs and Border Protection has always had the authority to conduct audits in which it reviews an importer's records to determine compliance with the customs laws, but such audits have assumed a new significance following enactment of the Customs Modernization Act. The Act enables importers to file customs entries electronically. Since additional documents that were traditionally attached to the customs entries, such as hard copies of the exporter's commercial invoice and bills of lading, are not available to the Customs officers at the time of electronic filing, post-importation audits become much more critical in Customs' ability to ensure compliance and detect fraud.

Under the Customs Modernization Act, Customs is required to follow certain procedures in conducting audits. It must give the importer an estimate of the duration of the audit, explain the purpose of the audit at the entry conference, explain the preliminary results of the audit at the closing conference, and, subject to certain exceptions, provide a copy of the final audit report to the importer within 120 days of the closing conference.

Customs has issued certain documents to the trade community to inform them of the compliance issues that Customs will review, called "Focused Assessments." Appendix I contains sample Internal Control and Electronic Data Processing Questionnaires. Reviewing these documents will assist an importer in establishing proper importing procedures and compliance.

Customs will notify an importer first by phone that it intends to conduct an audit. It will send out a questionnaire and ask for copies of the importers compliance manuals and internal customs procedures. It will also schedule an entrance conference. The questionnaire will also ask about the corporate structure, relationships with other legal entities, how the company determines the values declared to Customs, how it determines its classifications, what its record-keeping policies are, copies of the company's general ledger and chart of accounts, etc. Customs will also provide a number

Figure 8–19. Notice of penalty.

U.S. Customs Service
610 S. Canal Street
Chicago, IL 60607-4523

FILE: ENF-4-02 PD:P
CASE NO:

Dear   :

    Consideration has been given to the prepenalty response submitted in the above referenced case number. The letter was submitted in response to a prepenalty notice issued to   on   , informing them that U. S. Customs was contemplating issuing a penalty for (level of culpability).   The claim arose due to (facts of violation).

    Based upon information in your prepenalty response, it has been determined that the facts indicate a finding that the violation occurred as a result of (culpability) on the part of _____.   Exhibit A contains relevant information concerning the penalty action, i.e., specific details of the violation. Exhibit B represents the entries involved in this penalty action.

    Pursuant to Section 171.12 of the Customs Regulations, your client has the right to submit a petition.   The petition must be submitted within 30 days from the date of this letter. If payment or a petition is not submitted within the effective period, the matter will be referred to the Court of International Trade for the institution of judicial proceedings. If you have any questions in this matter, please contact _____ of my staff at the above listed telephone number.

                    Sincerely,

                    Fines, Penalties & Forfeitures Officer

TRADITION
Enclosures
★

SERVICE

★

HONOR

of sample entry numbers that it will request to review at the entrance conference. Customs will also want to interview certain key people with the importer who are responsible for Customs compliance, for the financial records, and for tracking company inventory.

At the entrance conference, Customs will want to see the importer's commitment to compliance and so the importer will want to have an officer of the company available to meet with Customs for at least part of the meeting. Customs will walk through the entries it has requested for review to see if it identifies any errors. It will also ask for information about certain accounts that may indicate the company is providing tooling or assists that are not declared in the import entry.

Based on the information obtained at the entrance conference, the auditors will request additional sample files in the areas of classification, value and basis of appraisement. Then based on the history of the client, it may ask for additional files related to the use of free trade agreements, U.S. goods returned, repaired or processed shipments, or other types of entries. The number of entries will be based on the information provided at the entrance conference, the volume of imports, and other criteria. The importer will be given a specific number of days to provide this documentation. Based on its review of the entries, Customs may assess additional duties based on reclassification or determining a change in the proper valuation. In addition, interest will be owed and Customs may assess penalties.

GG. Penalties

Customs has the authority to issue penalties under a number of different provisions in the law, but the primary penalty that affects importers is making a false statement in documents submitted to customs. A violation of the commercial fraud provision occurs when the importer attempts to introduce or introduces merchandise into the United States by means of any document or electronic transmission of data or information whether written or oral that is material and false, or by any omission that is material and false. Materiality is determined by whether the statement of the omission may affect:

1. Determination of the classification, appraisement, or admissibility of merchandise (e.g., whether merchandise is prohibited or restricted)

2. Determination of an importer's liability for duty (including marking, antidumping, and/or countervailing duty)

3. Collection and reporting of accurate trade statistics

4. Determination as to the source, origin, or quality of merchandise

5. Determination of whether an unfair trade practice has been committed under the antidumping or countervailing duty laws or a similar statute

6. Determination of whether an unfair act has been committed involving patent, trademark, or copyright infringement

7. Determination of whether any other unfair trade practice has been committed in violation of federal law

There are three degrees of culpability under the provision:

1. Negligence – an importer will be found to be negligent if it fails to exercise reasonable care and competence of a person in the same circumstances in ascertaining the correct information and providing it to the Customs authorities.

2. Gross Negligence – an importer is deemed to be grossly negligent if it acts with actual knowledge of or wanton disregard for the relevant facts and with indifference to or disregard for the offender's obligations under the statute.

3. Fraud – an importer is deemed to have committed fraud if the material false statement, omission, or act in connection with the transaction was committed (or omitted) knowingly, i.e., was done voluntarily and intentionally, as established by clear and convincing evidence.

The penalties associated with each of the degrees of culpability begin at 0.5 percent - 2 percent of duties or 0.5 percent - 20 percent of the entered value where no duties are assessed for simple negligence; 2.5 percent - 4 percent of the duties or 20 to 40 percent of the entered value where no duties are assessed for gross negligence; and as high as 100 percent of the domestic value of the merchandise for fraud. So in many instances, the penalties may be higher for those commodities that are duty-free than those that are dutiable.

HH. Prior Disclosure

An importer who has become aware that it has accidentally violated the customs laws or who determines that one of its employees intentionally violated the customs laws can utilize a procedure called "prior disclosure," which permits an importer to voluntarily tender the customs duties that were avoided and reduce the penalties it would otherwise have to pay if the Customs authorities discovered the violation themselves. If the importer is notified of an audit it behooves the importer to conduct an internal assessment of its own transactions before the auditors arrive and then file a prior disclosure to prevent the assessment of penalties.

In order to file a valid prior disclosure, there can be no current Customs investigation. An audit is not an investigation. The disclosure must provide complete information detailing the nature of the error, the entries affected by the error, the ports of entry, and the merchandise affected. If the prior disclosure is filed in conjunction with an audit, overpayments and underpayments may be offset. This is the only time when the importer may offset the duties owed by overpayments. There is limited length of time in which to "perfect" the prior disclosure, by filing the corrected data and pay the duties plus interest. A prior disclosure should cover the full five-year statute of limitations.

II.   Court of International Trade

If the importer's protest is denied, the importer may appeal the decision of U.S. Customs and Border Protection to the Court of International Trade. It must file its "summons" and Information Statement with the Court of International Trade within 180 days following the denial of the protest (see Figures 8–32 and 8–33). All additional duties must also be paid. Within thirty days thereafter, the importer must file its complaint with the court. In the meantime, U.S. Customs and Border Protection will transmit all of the documents relating to the case to the Court of International Trade. Electronic filing of documentation is required at the Court of International Trade today through the Case Management/Electronic Case Filing system. The Court of International Trade is a specialized court for dealing with trade issues and the importer should hire attorneys that are licensed and have experienced in this court.

JJ.   Appeals

Following the decision of the Court of International Trade, the importer may appeal to the U.S. Court of Appeals for the Federal Circuit in Washington, D.C. No special form is used to docket an appeal on a customs matter. The Notice of Appeal form must be filed within thirty days following the decision of the Court of International Trade. If the decision of the Court of Appeals is adverse to the importer, the importer may seek review by the U.S. Supreme Court via a petition for certiorari, but such petitions are not granted frequently.

KK. Offers of Compromise

If Customs has assessed a penalty, the importer may make an offer of compromise addressed to the Secretary of the Treasury in Washington, D.C. While there is no guarantee that such an offer will be accepted, this is one avenue to resolve a customs penalty without the necessity of court proceedings or admission of guilt. Normally, such an offer would not be made until some later stage in the administrative process, for example, after denial of a protest, request for reliquidation, or the initiation of court proceedings.

LL. ITC and Commerce Questionnaires

Another type of document that importers may see in the course of importation is a questionnaire sent to the importer by the International Trade Commission (ITC). The ITC has an investigatory or adjudicatory role under a number of different trade laws relating to the importation of merchandise. Sections 201 and 406 of the Trade Act of 1974 permit the ITC, with presidential approval, to assess additional customs duties or impose quotas when importation of merchandise has increased substantially and is injuring U.S. producers. Under Section 301 of the Trade Act of 1974, the ITC can impose similar sanctions when a foreign government is unjustifiably or unreasonably burdening U.S. export commerce. Under the antidumping and countervailing duty laws, the ITC seeks to determine the quantity of imports, prices, and whether U.S. manufacturers have been injured by imported products. Under Section 337 of the Tariff Act, the ITC may impose restrictions on the import of merchandise if it determines that there have been unfair practices in the import trade, such as patent infringement. Under Section 332, the ITC may conduct general investigations simply to determine the quantity of imports, and changes in import trends, and to advise Congress on appropriate legislation to regulate international trade. In all of these investigations, the ITC normally issues lengthy (sometimes fifty- or sixty-page) questionnaires to importers. Under these laws, the importers are required to respond to the questionnaires; however, the ITC will normally grant an extension of time if the importer needs it.

The Department of Commerce conducts national security investigations under Section 232 of the Trade Act of 1974 to determine whether U.S. national security is being endangered by overdependence on foreign products.

Part IV
Global Customs Considerations

Chapter 9

Determining the Proper Classification of a Product

The lack of uniformity in the classification of products moving across borders created concern as global trade increased. In 1952 the Customs Cooperation Council was formed in Brussels, Belgium, to develop a system that could be used for this purpose, but it wasn't until the 1970s that the Harmonized System of Classification and Coding—developed under the Council, now called the World Customs Organization (WCO)—began to garner acceptance. On January 1, 1988, most members of the World Trade Organization adopted the Harmonized Tariff System (HTS). On January 1, 1989, the United States replaced its Tariff Schedule of the United States with a new Harmonized Tariff Schedule of the United States (HTSUSA). Currently, more than 200 countries use the Harmonized Tariff System, and the first six digits of the tariff number are supposed to be the same in each member country. Each country's tariff number can have up to ten digits, but many have less. While the goal is uniformity, interpretation is up to the importing country and thus, even at the six-digit level, there are conflicting determinations.

Every five years, the Harmonized Tariff Schedule is modified to keep it up-to-date regarding new industries and technologies. Member countries can petition the WCO for changes. The last update was done in 2012 and the next is scheduled to be in 2017.

Understanding the proper tariff classification is important for business because it is the legal responsibility of a company to know the correct classification of its products. Not only does the tariff number determine the proper duties and taxes applicable to the product, but it can provide the landed cost for determining profits. If the classification is not correct, it can result in delays in clearance, examinations, requests for additional information, and even fines and penalties. In addition, proper classification allows the importer to take advantage of certain trade benefits based on the classification and the origin of the imported good or the condition of the product at the time of import.

A The Organization of the Tariff Schedules

The Harmonized Tariff Schedule is made up of 21 sections and 97 chapters. Chapter 77 is reserved for future use (http://www.usitc.gov/tata/hts/bychapter/index.htm). Each section has notes to be used for interpreting the items contained within it. For example, there is only one universal note under Section IV:

SECTION IV

PREPARED FOODSTUFFS; BEVERAGES, SPIRITS AND VINEGAR;

TOBACCO AND MANUFACTURED TOBACCO SUBSTITUTES

Note

1. In this section the term "pellets" means products which have been agglomerated either directly by compression or by the addition of a binder in a proportion not exceeding 3 percent by weight.

Other countries may have additional notes for each section in their tariff schedules. For example, the United States has a number of other notes under Section IV, as follows:

Additional U.S. Notes

1. In this section the term "canned" means preserved in airtight containers by heat processing to destroy or inactivate micro-organisms and enzymes that otherwise could cause spoilage.

2. For the purposes of this section, unless the context otherwise requires—

    (a) the term "percent by dry weight" means the sugar content as a percentage of the total solids in the product;

    (b) the term "capable of being further processed or mixed with similar or other ingredients" means that the imported product is in such condition or container as to be subject to any additional preparation, treatment or manufacture or to be blended or combined with any additional ingredient, including water or any other liquid, other than processing or mixing with other ingredients performed by the ultimate consumer prior to consumption of the product;

    (c) the term "prepared for marketing to the ultimate consumer in the identical form and package in which imported" means that the product is imported in packaging of such sizes and labeling as to be readily identifiable as being intended for retail sale to the ultimate consumer without any alteration in the form of the product or its packaging; and

(d) the term "ultimate consumer" does not include institutions such as hospitals, prisons and military establishments or food service establishments such as restaurants, hotels, bars or bakeries.

Likewise, each chapter has notes that are to be used in understanding what products should be classified within the chapter. The notes also direct the user to other chapters for classifications purposes. For example:

CHAPTER 23

RESIDUES AND WASTE FROM THE FOOD INDUSTRIES;

PREPARED ANIMAL FEED

IV

Note

1. Heading 2309 includes products of a kind used in animal feeding, not elsewhere specified or included, obtained by processing vegetable or animal materials to such an extent that they have lost the essential characteristics of the original material, other than vegetable waste, vegetable residues and byproducts of such processing.

Subheading Note

1. For the purposes of subheading 2306.41, the expression "low erucic acid rape or colza seeds" means seeds as defined in subheading note 1 to chapter 12.

Each country may have additional chapter notes clarifying its classification process.

The first two digits of the Harmonized Tariff Number represent the chapter, the next two digits define the heading, and the six total digits constitute the subheading. Thus, the tariff subheading of 3923.50 can be read as follows:

Chapter 39 – Plastic and Articles Thereof

Heading 3923 - Articles for the conveyance or packing of goods, of plastics; stoppers, lids, caps and other closures, of plastics

Subheading 3923.50 - Stoppers, lids, caps and other closures

Anything after the first six digits is called the tariff item and is specific to the importing country. The tariff numbers of the United States have ten digits.

B. The General Rules of Interpretation

With the development of the Harmonized Tariff Schedule, the WCO also created some basic rules of interpretation, known at the General Rules of Interpretation (GRIs). (See Figure 9–1.) There are six GRIs that are universal to all countries. Beyond that, each country can add its own. The United States has four additional U.S. GRIs. The GRIs are meant to be hierarchal. If the first rule is applicable, then the analysis is done. If the first rule is not applicable, then you must review the second and so on until you arrive at the rule that is applicable. Analysis should be done at the tariff heading level.

GRI 1 reads as follows:

Classification of goods in the tariff schedule shall be governed by the following principles:

1. The table of contents, alphabetical index, and titles of sections, chapters and sub-chapters are provided for ease of reference only; for legal purposes, classification shall be determined according to the terms of the headings and any relative section or chapter notes and, provided such headings or notes do not otherwise require, according to the following provisions:

The first rule identifies which sections of the Harmonized Tariff Schedule have legal authority and which do not. While the language does not specifically state so, this rule means that based on the use of the sections, chapters, notes, and headings, if classification is specifically identified, then the analysis is done. This is the *eo nomine* provision. In our earlier example of a tariff number, if the imported product is a plastic lid for a bowl, then the classification of 3923.50 as "stoppers, lids, caps and other closures" of plastic for the conveyance of goods specifically identifies the product in question. Therefore, we do not have to review any of the other GRIs in order to classify our plastic lids.

GRI 2 reads as follows:

2. (a) Any reference in a heading to an article shall be taken to include a reference to that article incomplete or unfinished, provided that, as entered; the incomplete or unfinished article has the essential character of the complete or finished article. It shall also include a reference to that article complete or finished (or falling to be classified as complete or finished by virtue of this rule), entered unassembled or disassembled.

(b) Any reference in a heading to a material or substance shall be taken to include a reference to mixtures or combinations of that material or substance with other materials or substances. Any reference to goods of a given material or substance shall be taken to include a reference to goods consisting wholly or partly of such material or substance. The classification of goods consisting of more than one material or substance shall be according to the principles of rule 3.

Figure 9–1. General Rules of Interpretation.

GENERAL RULES OF INTERPRETATION

Classification of goods in the tariff schedule shall be governed by the following principles:

1. The table of contents, alphabetical index, and titles of sections, chapters and sub-chapters are provided for ease of reference only; for legal purposes, classification shall be determined according to the terms of the headings and any relative section or chapter notes and, provided such headings or notes do not otherwise require, according to the following provisions:

2. (a) Any reference in a heading to an article shall be taken to include a reference to that article incomplete or unfinished, provided that, as entered, the incomplete or unfinished article has the essential character of the complete or finished article. It shall also include a reference to that article complete or finished (or falling to be classified as complete or finished by virtue of this rule), entered unassembled or disassembled.

   (b) Any reference in a heading to a material or substance shall be taken to include a reference to mixtures or combinations of that material or substance with other materials or substances. Any reference to goods of a given material or substance shall be taken to include a reference to goods consisting wholly or partly of such material or substance. The classification of goods consisting of more than one material or substance shall be according to the principles of rule 3.

3. When, by application of rule 2(b) or for any other reason, goods are, *prima facie*, classifiable under two or more headings, classification shall be effected as follows:

   (a) The heading which provides the most specific description shall be preferred to headings providing a more general description. However, when two or more headings each refer to part only of the materials or substances contained in mixed or composite goods or to part only of the items in a set put up for retail sale, those headings are to be regarded as equally specific in relation to those goods, even if one of them gives a more complete or precise description of the goods.

   (b) Mixtures, composite goods consisting of different materials or made up of different components, and goods put up in sets for retail sale, which cannot be classified by reference to 3(a), shall be classified as if they consisted of the material or component which gives them their essential character, insofar as this criterion is applicable.

   (c) When goods cannot be classified by reference to 3(a) or 3(b), they shall be classified under the heading which occurs last in numerical order among those which equally merit consideration.

4. Goods which cannot be classified in accordance with the above rules shall be classified under the heading appropriate to the goods to which they are most akin.

(continues)

Figure 9–1. (*continued*)

---

5. In addition to the foregoing provisions, the following rules shall apply in respect of the goods referred to therein:

   (a) Camera cases, musical instrument cases, gun cases, drawing instrument cases, necklace cases and similar containers, specially shaped or fitted to contain a specific article or set of articles, suitable for long-term use and entered with the articles for which they are intended, shall be classified with such articles when of a kind normally sold therewith. This rule does not, however, apply to containers which give the whole its essential character;

   (b) Subject to the provisions of rule 5(a) above, packing materials and packing containers entered with the goods therein shall be classified with the goods if they are of a kind normally used for packing such goods. However, this provision is not binding when such packing materials or packing containers are clearly suitable for repetitive use.

6. For legal purposes, the classification of goods in the subheadings of a heading shall be determined according to the terms of those subheadings and any related subheading notes and, *mutatis mutandis*, to the above rules, on the understanding that only subheadings at the same level are comparable. For the purposes of this rule, the relative section, chapter and subchapter notes also apply, unless the context otherwise requires.

ADDITIONAL U.S. RULES OF INTERPRETATION

1. In the absence of special language or context which otherwise requires—

   (a) a tariff classification controlled by use (other than actual use) is to be determined in accordance with the use in the United States at, or immediately prior to, the date of importation, of goods of that class or kind to which the imported goods belong, and the controlling use is the principal use;

   (b) a tariff classification controlled by the actual use to which the imported goods are put in the United States is satisfied only if such use is intended at the time of importation, the goods are so used and proof thereof is furnished within 3 years after the date the goods are entered;

   (c) a provision for parts of an article covers products solely or principally used as a part of such articles but a provision for "parts" or "parts and accessories" shall not prevail over a specific provision for such part or accessory; and

   (d) the principles of section XI regarding mixtures of two or more textile materials shall apply to the classification of goods in any provision in which a textile material is named.

GRI 2(a) allows for the import of incomplete or unfinished goods or unassembled or disassembled goods to be classified as if the imported product was complete, finished, or assembled. For example, if the imported product was an unassembled or disassembled bicycle, it should be classified as if it were a finished bicycle. If the bicycle was imported without the seat but the rest of the parts were imported, then the essential character of the bicycle is still there, and so the proper classification is that of a bicycle. However, if the imported bicycle is missing the gears, seat, chain, and handlebars, the question becomes whether the essential character of the imported parts is still a bicycle. At what point is the essential character of the bicycle lost and it is just a variety of imported parts? This is an important analysis and may require a determination by the customs service of the importing country—in other words, a binding ruling. If the ruling is that it is not essentially a bicycle anymore, then there will be a separate classification for each of the remaining parts: the wheels, frame, pedals, sprockets, etc.

GRI 2(b) explains what to do when a classification does not fall within GRI 1 or GRI 2(a). GRI2(b) states that if there is a reference in a heading to any material or substances, then that reference should also include mixtures or combinations of those materials or substances with other materials or substances—for example, milk with vitamins or corn flakes with raisins. In this manner, then, the items could be classified in more than one heading, and so you must look to GRI 3 to determine how to classify the product.

Most items are classified in the tariff by using GRI 3. In fact, there are three different rules for classification contained within GRI 3:

3. When, by application of rule 2(b) or for any other reason, goods are, *prima facie*, classifiable under two or more headings, classification shall be effected as follows:

    (a) The heading which provides the most specific description shall be preferred to headings providing a more general description. However, when two or more headings each refer to part only of the materials or substances contained in mixed or composite goods or to part only of the items in a set put up for retail sale, those headings are to be regarded as equally specific in relation to those goods, even if one of them gives a more complete or precise description of the goods.

    (b) Mixtures, composite goods consisting of different materials or made up of different components, and goods put up in sets for retail sale, which cannot be classified by reference to 3(a), shall be classified as if they consisted of the material or component which gives them their essential character, insofar as this criterion is applicable.

    (c) When goods cannot be classified by reference to 3(a) or 3(b), they shall be classified under the heading which occurs last in numerical order among those which equally merit consideration.

The first sentence of GRI 3(a) states that the classifier should always use the most specific description over a more general one. For example, say the imported good is an automotive muffler. There is a classification for miscellaneous automotive parts under subheading 8708.99, but there is also a specific classification for automotive mufflers under subheading 8708.92. According to GRI 3(a), it is the specific classification that is always preferred over the more general classification. Note that the second sentence of GRI 3(a) states that when there are two or more headings that each refer to only a part of the materials or a part of a composite good, then you must consider both of the headings equally, even if one gives a more precise description.

GRI 3(b) covers two different scenarios. The first is when you have mixtures or composites of goods that are made up of different materials or components. In this case, the rule states that you classify the product under the material or component that gives the finished good its essential character. For example, if the imported product is a travel mug with an inner lining that is made of stainless steel and an outer casing that is made of plastic, along with a plastic lid and a rubber base, how should the product be classified? It is not specifically provided for in the tariff. There are plastic articles under Chapter 39, rubber articles under Chapter 40, and stainless steel articles under Chapter 73, but we must determine which component gives the travel mug its essential character in order to decide the classification. There is no one way to analyze what gives a product its essential character. It can be based on the component that is more expensive; which component weighs the most; the quality of one of the components over the others; the quantity of one of the components; how one component relates to the finished good; or how the product is marketed to the consumer and what makes the consumer want to purchase that particular good. The customs service in each country may consider the example of the travel mug differently. Perhaps the customs service considers the essential characteristic to be the insulating character of the plastic casing, or the stainless steel lining that is not only the most expensive part but also may act as a beverage holder even without the plastic casing. The U.S. Customs and Border Protection actually reviewed such a product and decided that because the stainless steel lining could be used as a cup without the plastic casing, it is the stainless steel that provides the essential character. Thus, U.S. Customs classified the travel mug under subheading 7323.93 as "household articles of stainless steel." Other customs services may view it differently.

The second part of GRI 3(b) references various components that are put together as a retail set and allows the importer to classify the set by the one item that gives the set its essential character. In this part of the rule of origin, the imported good may be a school writing pack comprising three pencils, a pencil sharpener, and a writing pad of paper, all contained in a plastic zippered pouch. To be a retail kit, the articles must be classified in two or more separate headings; be put together to meet a particular need or to carry out a specific activity; and be packaged for retail sale without repackaging. In this example, the pencils would be classified under heading 9609, the pencil sharpener would be classified under heading 8214, the writing pad would be 4817, and the plastic pouch would be 4202. The items are classified in more than two headings; they are put together to perform a specific activity and are packaged for retail sale. Therefore, the school writing pack meets the requirements of GRI 3(b) and can be classified in accordance with the one item that gives the kit its essential character. It could be the pencils, the writing pad, or the plastic pouch. U.S. Customs determined it was the plastic pouch based on the fact that the pouch is used to transport the items within it and to keep them together and safe. Another customs service might disagree. However, if you have components that just happen to be packaged together without having a particular purpose or a specific activity, then the items may not be considered a retail set, even if packaged together for retail sale. In that case, there would be multiple classifications for the articles in the kit.

GRI 3(c) reads as follows:

> When goods cannot be classified by reference to 3(a) or 3(b), they shall be classified under the heading which occurs last in numerical order among those which equally merit consideration.

This provision basically states that if the essential character cannot be determined for a composite good, a mixture, or a retail set, then classification should fall to the item that is last in numerical order. By using our writing pack as an example, if the customs service could not determine which item gave the pack its essential character, then classification would fall to heading 9609 for the pencils, since that is the heading that falls last in numerical order.

GRI 4 reads as follows:

> 4. Goods which cannot be classified in accordance with the above rules shall be classified under the heading appropriate to the goods to which they are most akin.

This rule is to cover those products that may be developed and for which there is no classification currently—for example, wine coolers.

GRI 5 deals with packaging and cases of the imported products. GRI 5(a) is:

> 5. In addition to the foregoing provisions, the following rules shall apply in respect of the goods referred to therein:

(a) Camera cases, musical instrument cases, gun cases, drawing instrument cases, necklace cases and similar containers, specially shaped or fitted to contain a specific article or set of articles, suitable for long-term use and entered with the articles for which they are intended, shall be classified with such articles when of a kind normally sold therewith. This rule does not, however, apply to containers which give the whole its essential character;

Under this provision, a violin case is classified with the violin if the violin and case are imported at the same time. There are three requirements to qualify for this provision: (1) the case must be specific to the articles it contains; (2) the case must generally be sold with the articles ; and (3) the case must be suitable for long-term use. However, if the item is an inexpensive perfume in a crystal bottle, then the bottle would likely be considered the essential character of this "retail set," and so classification would be based on the crystal bottle and not the perfume.

GRI 5(b) covers traditional packing materials and states:

(b) Subject to the provisions of rule 5(a) above, packing materials and packing containers entered with the goods therein shall be classified with the goods if they are of a kind normally used for packing such goods. However, this provision is not binding when such packing materials or packing containers are clearly suitable for repetitive use.

This provision covers typical cardboard packing boxes, Bubble Wrap, Styrofoam peanuts, wrappings, blister packs, etc. The packaging is designed to be discarded after use. It can be for both retail purposes and shipping purposes. However, if the packaging is reusable, then it must be classified separately at the time of entry—for example, reusable drums, plastic crates, wooden pallets, and containers. In the United States and other countries, there is a provision that covers these "Instruments of International Traffic" (IITs). When using these packaging items in the United States, the importer must provide notification, determine a methodology for tracking them, and obtain a surety bond to cover the items; then, they may cross borders repeatedly without paying duty.

Finally, GRI 6 states:

6. For legal purposes, the classification of goods in the subheadings of a heading shall be determined according to the terms of those subheadings and any related subheading notes and, *mutatis mutandis*, to the above rules, on the understanding that only subheadings at the same level are comparable. For the purposes of this rule, the relative section, chapter and subchapter notes also apply, unless the context otherwise requires.

This rule states that in classifying products, the analysis should be determined at the heading level, and once the heading has been determined, the process should be repeated in the same hierarchy at the subheading level.

Each country, then, may have its own General Rules of Interpretation following these six GRIs. The United States has four additional U.S. GRIs as follows:

1. In the absence of special language or context which otherwise requires—

    (a) a tariff classification controlled by use (other than actual use) is to be determined in accordance with the use in the United States at, or immediately prior to, the date of importation, of goods of that class or kind to which the imported goods belong, and the controlling use is the principal use;

    (b) a tariff classification controlled by the actual use to which the imported goods are put in the United States is satisfied only if such use is intended at the time of importation, the goods are so used and proof thereof is furnished within 3 years after the date the goods are entered;

    (c) a provision for parts of an article covers products solely or principally used as a part of such articles but a provision for "parts" or "parts and accessories" shall not prevail over a specific provision for such part or accessory; and

    (d) the principles of section XI regarding mixtures of two or more textile materials shall apply to the classification of goods in any provision in which a textile material is named.

Rule 1(a) simply means that if an item is described in the tariff heading as "for use in" but it could be used in multiple applications, then its intended use at the time of import governs the classification. Rule 1(b) is a special provision that allows duty-free entry for certain products provided they are actually used in the manner designated within three years. There are only a few provisions in the tariff that call for actual use; they can be found in Chapter 98 of the HTSUS. To qualify, the importer must be able to provide evidence acceptable to U.S. Customs that the goods were actually used in the manner indicated at the end of the three-year time period or pay back duties plus interest. Rule 1(c) is similar to GRI 3(a). It just clarifies that while there may be a "parts" or "parts and accessories" provision for a product, a specific classification for that item always trumps the "parts" provision. Rule 1(d) states that wherever textiles are described in the tariff, it is the weight of the textile components that give it the essential character. For example, 60 percent cotton/40 percent polyester would be classified under cotton.

In addition to the General Rules of Interpretation, the WCO also developed the Explanatory Notes. These notes explain what was in the mind of the drafters at the time the Harmonized Tariff System was originally developed, and they are updated as the

Harmonized Tariff Schedule is updated. The Explanatory Notes are not legally binding, but they are considered persuasive authority for use in interpreting various tariff provisions when classifying products. They are not publicly available for free, but it is extremely useful to have them.

A copy of the Harmonized Tariff Schedule of the United States is available online at http://www.usitc.gov/tata/hts/bychapter/index.htm. The WCO version of the Harmonized Tariff Schedule is available at http://ec.europa.eu/taxation_customs/customs/customs_duties/tariff_aspects/harmonised_system/index_en.htm. The Explanatory Notes are available at http://www.wcoomd.org/en/faq/harmonized_system_faq.aspx#q15.

Once an importer has reviewed the GRIs and done the analysis for determining the classification, it might want to review other rulings that are publicly available. While publicly available rulings are binding only on the party that requested them and may not give a full description of the product or the facts surrounding the determination, they may be useful in confirming a classification. An importer may also want to apply for a binding ruling on its products with the customs service of the importing country. All information about the product must be disclosed to the customs authorities in order for the ruling to be accurate. If there is proprietary information, then a request for confidentiality can be made, and that information can be bracketed for purposes of publication. Not all countries publish rulings, but the United States and the European Union both do. U.S. rulings can be found at http://rulings.cbp.gov/, and EU rulings can be found at http://ec.europa.eu/taxation_customs/customs/customs_duties/tariff_aspects/classification_goods/index_en.htm. Both web sites have searchable databases. It should be noted that a binding ruling from one country may not have any authority over another country.

C. Duty Rates

Once the tariff number is determined, then it is possible to calculate the duties and taxes and to see whether a specific product is eligible for a free trade agreement (FTA). There are three types of duties assessed on products: (1) ad valorem, (2) specific, and (3) compound. An ad valorem duty rate is a percentage, such as 5 percent of the entered value. See Figure 9–2 for an example of the HTSUSA. As the figure shows, prunes, for example, other than those soaked in brine and dried, are dutiable at 14 percent of the entered value. A specific duty rate is based on a dollar amount based on the number of pieces or the rate—for example, 2.5¢ per kilogram, or 35¢ each. As

Figure 9–2. HTSUSA example.

Harmonized Tariff Schedule of the United States (2014) (Rev. 1)
Annotated for Statistical Reporting Purposes

II
8-15

Heading/ Subheading	Stat. Suf-fix	Article Description	Unit of Quantity	Rates of Duty		
				1		2
				General	Special	
0813		Fruit, dried, other than that of headings 0801 to 0806; mixtures of nuts or dried fruits of this chapter:				
0813.10.00	00	Apricots...............................	kg.......	1.8¢/kg	Free (A*,AU,BH, CA,CL,CO,E,IL, JO,KR,MA,MX, OM,P,PA,PE,SG)	4.4¢/kg
0813.20		Prunes:				
0813.20.10	00	Soaked in brine and dried................	kg.......	2¢/kg	Free (A+,AU,BH, CA,CL,CO,D,E, IL,JO,KR,MA, MX,OM,P,PA,PE, SG)	4.4¢/kg
0813.20.20	00	Other...............................	kg.......	14%	Free (A+,AU,BH, CA,CO,D,E,IL, JO,MX,OM,P,PA, PE,SG) 1.4% (MA) 2.3% (CL) 5.6% (KR)	35%
0813.30.00	00	Apples..............................	kg.......	0.74¢/kg	Free (A,AU,BH,CA, CL,CO,E,IL,JO, KR,MA,MX,OM,P, PA,PE,SG)	4.4¢/kg
0813.40		Other fruit:				
0813.40.10	00	Papayas............................	kg.......	1.8%	Free (A,AU,BH,CA, CL,CO,E,IL,JO, KR,MA,MX,OM,P, PA,PE,SG)	35%
		Berries:				
0813.40.15	00	Barberries..........................	kg.......	3.5¢/kg	Free (A+,AU,BH, CA,CL,CO,D,E, IL,JO,KR,MA, MX,OM,P,PA,PE, SG)	5.5¢/kg
0813.40.20		Other..............................	....	1.4¢/kg	Free (A,AU,BH,CA, CL,CO,E,IL,JO, KR,MA,MX,OM,P, PA,PE,SG)	5.5¢/kg
	10	Wild blueberries....................	kg			
	20	Cultivated blueberries................	kg			
	60	Other............................	kg			
0813.40.30	00	Cherries............................	kg.......	10.6¢/kg	Free (A+,AU,BH, CA,CL,CO,D,E, IL,JO,MA,MX, OM,P,PA,PE,SG) 4.2¢/kg (KR)	13.2¢/kg
0813.40.40	00	Peaches............................	kg.......	1.4¢/kg	Free (A+,AU,BH, CA,CL,CO,D,E, IL,JO,KR,MA, MX,OM,P,PA,PE, SG)	4.4¢/kg
0813.40.80	00	Tamarinds...........................	kg.......	6.8%	Free (A,AU,BH, CA,CL,CO,E,IL, JO,MA,MX,OM, P,PA,PE,SG) 2.7% (KR)	35%
0813.40.90	00	Other...............................	kg.......	2.5%	Free (A+,AU,BH, CA,CL,CO,D,E, IL,JO,KR,MA, MX,OM,P,PA,PE, SG)	35%

Figure 9–2 indicates, dried apricots are dutiable at 1.8¢/kg. A compound duty rate is a combination of the two, for example, 2 percent of the entered value and 35¢ each.

The tariff schedule also advises whether the tariff number is eligible for reduced duty or duty-free status based on a free trade agreement. For example, in the United States, if there is an "IL" in the second column of the Rates of Duty, under "Special," it means that the commodity is eligible for duty-free treatment from Israel under the U.S.–Israel Free Trade Agreement. (See Figure 9–2.) The various FTAs are designated by the letters indicated in that column. Figure 9–3 presents a key to identify the letter symbols with the trade agreement.

The Generalized System of Preferences (GSP) has three symbols—the A, the A*, and the A+—which each mean different things. (See Figure 9–4 for a list of the countries eligible under the GSP program and for a list of the Least-Developed Developing Nations.) The A symbol is for all the countries on the list of GSP countries in Figure 9-4 only if they meet the 35 percent origin criteria and undergo direct shipment. The A+ symbol means that the goods are eligible for duty-free treatment from only a Least-Developed Developing Nation (http://www.usitc.gov/publications/docs/tata/hts/bychapter/1401gn.pdf#page=11. Page 11/854). The A* symbol means that not all countries are still eligible for duty-free treatment. There is another list (http://www.usitc.gov/publications/docs/tata/hts/bychapter/1401gn.pdf#page=15. Page 15/854) that identifies by tariff number which countries are no longer eligible, for example, HTS 0302.45.11—Ecuador; HTS 2525.2.20—Turkey; and HTS 4412.94.41—Brazil, Ecuador, and Indonesia.

Determining the proper classification and duty rate is a critical aspect of an importer's landed cost, so getting it correct the first time is extremely important. Importers should consult with a knowledgeable customs consultant or a customs attorney or file for a binding ruling from Customs. Evidence as to how the classification was determined should be kept as part of the importer's record-keeping obligations. In a customs audit, if Customs disagrees with the classification, penalties can be mitigated if the importer consulted with an expert and has evidence to prove how the determination was made.

Figure 9–3. Key to special tariff treatment symbols.

Programs under which special tariff treatment may be provided, and the corresponding symbols for such programs as they are indicated in the "Special" subcolumn, are as follows:

Generalized System of Preferences . . . . A, A* or A+

United States-Australia Free Trade Agreement . . . . AU

Automotive Products Trade Act . . . . B

United States-Bahrain Free Trade Agreement Implementation Act . . . . BH

Agreement on Trade in Civil Aircraft C

North American Free Trade Agreement:

      Goods of Canada, under the terms of

      general note 12 to this schedule . . . . CA

      Goods of Mexico, under the terms of

      general note 12 to this schedule . . . . MX

United States-Chile Free Trade Agreement CL

African Growth and Opportunity Act . . . . D

Caribbean Basin Economic Recovery Act . . . . E or E*

United States-Israel Free Trade Area IL

United States-Jordan Free Trade Area Implementation Act . . . . JO

Agreement on Trade in Pharmaceutical Products . . . . K

Dominican Republic-Central America-United States

      Free Trade Agreement Implementation Act . . . . P or P+

Uruguay Round Concessions on Intermediate

      Chemicals for Dyes L

United States-Caribbean Basin Trade Partnership Act . . . . R

United States-Morocco Free Trade Agreement Implementation Act . . . . MA

United States-Singapore Free Trade Agreement . . . . SG

United States-Oman Free Trade Agreement Implementation Act . . . . OM

United States-Peru Trade Promotion Agreement Implementation Act . . . . PE

United States-Korea Free Trade Agreement Implementation Act . . . . KR

United States-Colombia Trade Promotion Agreement Implementation Act . . . . CO

United States-Panama Trade Promotion Agreement Implementation Act . . . . . . PA

Figure 9–4. GSP countries.

Products of Countries Designated Beneficiary Developing Countries for Purposes of the Generalized System of Preferences (GSP).

(a) The following countries, territories and associations of countries eligible for treatment as one country (pursuant to section 507(2) of the Trade Act of 1974 (19 U.S.C. 2467(2)) are designated beneficiary developing countries for the purposes of the Generalized System of Preferences, provided for in Title V of the Trade Act of 1974, as amended (19 U.S.C. 2461 et seq.):

Independent Countries

Afghanistan	Eritrea	Maldives
Albania	Ethiopia	Mali
Algeria	Fiji	Mauritania
Angola	Gabon	Mauritius
Armenia	Gambia, The	Moldova
Azerbaijan	Georgia	Mongolia
Belize	Ghana	Montenegro
Benin	Grenada	Mozambique
Bhutan	Guinea	Namibia
Bolivia	Guinea-Bissau	Nepal
Bosnia and Hercegovina	Guyana	Niger
Botswana	Haiti	Nigeria
Brazil	India	Pakistan
Burkina Faso	Indonesia	Papua New Guinea
Burundi	Iraq	Paraguay
Cambodia	Jamaica	Philippines
Cameroon	Jordan	Russia
Cape Verde	Kazakhstan	Rwanda
Central African Republic	Kenya	Saint Lucia
Chad	Kiribati	Saint Vincent and the
Comoros	Kosovo	Grenadines
Congo (Brazzaville)	Kyrgyzstan	Samoa
Congo (Kinshasa)	Lebanon	Sao Tomé and Principe
Côte d'Ivoire	Lesotho	Senegal
Djibouti	Liberia	Serbia
Dominica	Macedonia, Republic of	Seychelles
Ecuador	Madagascar	Sierra Leone
Egypt	Malawi	Solomon Islands

(continues)

Figure 9–4. (*continued*)

Somalia
South Africa
South Sudan
Sri Lanka
Suriname
Swaziland
Tanzania
Thailand
Timor-Leste

Togo
Tonga
Tunisia
Turkey
Tuvalu
Uganda
Ukraine
Uruguay
Uzbekistan

Vanuatu
Venezuela
Yemen, Republic of
Zambia
Zimbabwe

Non-Independent Countries and Territories

Anguilla
British Indian Ocean Territory
Christmas Island (Australia)
Cocos (Keeling) Islands
Cook Islands
Falkland Islands (Islas Malvinas)
Heard Island and McDonald Islands
Montserrat
Niue
Norfolk Island
Pitcairn Islands
Saint Helena
Tokelau
Virgin Islands, British
Wallis and Futuna
West Bank and Gaza Strip
Western Sahara

Associations of Countries (treated as one country), Member Countries of the Cartagena Agreement (Andean Group) Consisting Of:

Bolivia
Ecuador
Venezuela

Member Countries of the West African Economic and Monetary Union (WAEMU) Consisting Of:

Benin
Burkina Faso
Côte d'Ivoire
Guinea-Bissau
Mali
Niger
Senegal
Togo

Member Countries of the Association of South East Asian Nations (ASEAN) Currently Qualifying:

Cambodia
Indonesia
Philippines
Thailand

Member Countries of the Southern Africa Development Community (SADC) Currently Qualifying:

Botswana
Mauritius
Tanzania

(*continues*)

Figure 9–4. (*continued*)

Member Countries of the South Asian Association for Regional Cooperation (SAARC) Currently Qualifying:
Afghanistan
Bangladesh
Bhutan
India
Maldives
Nepal

Pakistan
Sri Lanka

Member Countries of the Caribbean Common Market (CARICOM) Currently Qualifying:

Belize
Dominica
Grenada

Guyana
Jamaica
Montserrat
St. Kitts and Nevis
Saint Lucia
Saint Vincent and the
   Grenadines

Least-Developed Beneficiary Developing Countries

Afghanistan
Angola
Benin
Bhutan
Burkina Faso
Burundi
Cambodia
Central African
Republic
Chad
Comoros
Congo (Kinshasa)
Djibouti
Ethiopia Gambia, The
Guinea

Guinea-Bissau
Haiti
Kiribati
Lesotho
Liberia
Madagascar
Malawi
Mali
Mauritania
Mozambique
Nepal
Niger
Rwanda
Samoa
Sao Tomé and Principe

Senegal
Sierra Leone
Solomon Islands, The
Somalia
South Sudan
Tanzania
Timor-Leste
Togo
Tuvalu
Uganda
Vanuatu
Yemen, Republic of
Zambia

Chapter 10

Determining the Proper Value to Declare

Standardization of the value for customs duty purposes began shortly after World War II with the General Agreement on Tariffs and Trade (GATT) Section VII. It stated that the value to be declared for assessing customs duties should be based on the actual value of the imported merchandise and not the value of similar merchandise originating in the country of import or on arbitrary or fictitious values. However, there was great discretion as to what "actual value" meant among countries party to the GATT, and other methods of valuation were allowed to be "grandfathered" in even if they had no similarity to the new definition. Although most countries used the Brussels Definition of Value, which was defined in 1950 by the predecessor to the Customs Cooperation Council and went into effect in July 1953, and which states that Customs value should be the "normal market price," which is "the price that a good would fetch in an open market between a buyer and seller independent of each other." However, there was still dissatisfaction with using the "normal value" because it did not take into account price changes or discounts, and companies that were able to gain a competitive advantage in pricing still paid duties at the same rate as those that did not. The United States did not use the normal market valuation process.

In 1974, during the Tokyo Round negotiations for the GATT countries, the Tokyo Round valuation method was developed and a new concept known as the "transaction value" was created. The transaction value was to be a fair and neutral means of determining value that took into account the commercial realities of conducting business on a global level. In 1994, during the Uruguay Round negotiations, the World Trade Organization Implementation of the GATT Valuation Code took the place of the Tokyo Round valuation method, and it is in use by the World Trade Organization members today.

Under this agreement, there are six different methodologies to be used in determining the proper valuation. They are basically hierarchal in nature, with the exception of the fourth and fifth methods, which can be switched at the request of the importer.

A. Transaction Value

Most imports use the transaction value methodology. It is based on the price paid by the purchaser, which is very simple. There *must* be a sale! This methodology allows for discounts, rebates, or prices based on a formula—whatever has been negotiated between the buyer and the seller. You pay duty on the price that is paid or will be paid (if not paid at the time of import), such as when there may be thirty-day payment terms. There are some conditions to using this value. There must be some evidence of a sale, such as a purchase order, contracts, invoices, or payments. So if the goods are not sold—for example, if they are shipped on consignment, shipped on loan, or transferred between two companies—there is no sale and transaction value cannot be used. In addition to evidence of a sale, there cannot be any restrictions on the disposition or the use of the imported merchandise, other than the following:

1. There are no restrictions imposed by the laws of the importing country.

2. There are no geographic restrictions for the resale of the goods, such as the reseller having a specific territory in which it can sell.

3. The restrictions do not substantially affect the value.

4. The transaction value may not be subject to a condition or a consideration for which no value can be determined.

5. The buyer and the seller cannot be related, unless they can show that the sale is a valid arms-length transaction.

If none of these restrictions exist, then transaction value is the proper methodology. However, there are certain additions and deductions that also must be taken into consideration.

1. Additions to the Transaction Value

Certain additions must be made to the transaction value if not already included, whether they are made directly or indirectly:

1. *Packing costs.* The packing costs suitable for the merchandise to travel in international transportation must be included if not already included in the price from the buyer.

2. *Assists.* Any "assists" provided by the buyer to the seller are dutiable. An assist is something that is provided to the seller either free or at a reduced cost, such that the seller does not have to incur the expense. It could be molds or tooling, raw materials, items consumed in the processing, etc. Because the seller does not have to purchase these items, the value that the buyer pays is reduced. The value of the assist is the cost of acquisition or of manufacture by the buyer plus the cost of transportation to the seller. If the assist is a mold or tooling that has been previously used, it may be depreciated in accordance with Generally Accepted Accounting Principles and the value declared at that depreciated value, but it must still include the cost of transportation to the seller's or manufacturer's facilities. Note that assists can be declared against one import or can be apportioned across the production in accordance with the rules of the importing country.

3. *Royalty payments or licensing fees.* Royalties and licensing fees paid for patents in order to manufacture the imported merchandise are usually dutiable. Royalties paid for trademarks or copyrights may or may not be dutiable. The analysis used to determine whether they are dutiable is based on (a) whether the buyer was required to pay them as a condition of sale of the merchandise for exportation to the United States, and (b) to whom and under what circumstances they were paid. Payments made to third parties by the buyer for the right to distribute goods are generally not dutiable.

4. *Selling commissions, but not buying commissions.* Selling commissions are generally paid by the seller to its agents in order to garner more sales in the foreign country. As a rule, these costs will be incorporated into the seller's price to the buyer. Buying commissions are paid by the buyer to an agent to help solicit manufacturers, help in translations, place orders, check quality control, etc. The buyer must be able to place orders directly with the seller and must be in control of the transactions at all times. Buying commissions are not dutiable.

5. *Subsequent proceeds paid to the seller based on the resale of the imported merchandise.* This occurs when the buyer does not pay the full price for an item because it guarantees that it will remit back to the seller a payment for every resale in the country of exportation. For example, the buyer purchases articles at $10 each, guaranteeing that the seller will get $2 back for each resale

made. The seller artificially lowers its price to the buyer because of this future payment. The future payment is considered dutiable, so arrangements must be made to ensure that Customs receives duties on these future payments.

6. *Designs, blueprints, and technical specifications undertaken outside the importing country.* These items are similar to assists in that the buyer is providing work to the seller free of charge; however, when it comes to designs, blueprints, or technical specifications, they are dutiable only if they are incurred outside the buyer's country. If the designs or other similar items are made by the buyer in its country, they are not dutiable. For example, if the buyer is in the United States but the engineering costs are incurred in Germany and the manufacture is in China, the German engineering costs are dutiable as a cost that was not incurred by the seller.

7. *Where the method is based on a CIF value, the cost of transportation and insurance to the port.* In most countries, the proper valuation for customs purposes includes all costs to the port of import, so it includes international transportation and insurance. If those costs are not included, then they must be added. In the United States, U.S. Customs requires the importer to declare the FOB port of export value, so only the charges to get the shipment loaded on board the international carrier are considered dutiable. All international transportation and insurance costs are not dutiable.

2. *Deductions from the Transaction Value*

Similarly, certain deductions may also be taken from the transaction value if they are included:

1. *Transportation occurring after importation.* All transportation, customs brokerage clearance fees, etc., are not dutiable if they occur after the importation in the country of destination, and so they may be deducted if they are included in the price to the buyer, such as in a DDP (delivered duty paid) transaction.

2. *Costs of assembly, erection, maintenance, and technical assistance undertaken after importation.* Similarly, any costs that are incurred following the importation may be deducted.

3. *In the United States, the cost of international freight and insurance based on the FOB port of export valuation.* These costs may be deducted although it must be the actual cost and there must be evidence supporting the value deducted, such as a rated bill of lading or transportation bill.

3. Related Parties

As mentioned above, normally transaction value does not apply to related parties because it is assumed that the relationship between the parties will affect the pricing between the two. Parties are "related" if any of the following situations are present:

1. They are officers or directors of one another's businesses.
2. They are legally recognized business partners.
3. They are employer and employee.
4. Any person directly or indirectly owns, controls, or holds 5 percent or more of the outstanding voting stock or shares of both of the companies.
5. One of them directly or indirectly controls the other.
6. Both of them are directly or indirectly controlled by a third person.
7. They are members of the same family.

The 5 percent common ownership is a very low threshold and so many companies are considered related under the WCO Valuation Code. Related parties can use transaction value methodology if they can prove that the relationship did not affect the price. They can do this in one of two ways: (1) by the test method, whereby the related parties show that the value between the two parties closely approximates that of sales to unrelated parties; or (2) by the circumstances of sale method, whereby the parties show that the price established is consistent with normal pricing practices in the industry, the price is typical of those that the seller makes to unrelated parties, and it is to ensure recovery of all costs plus a profit that is the equivalent of the seller's overall profit for sales of merchandise of the same kind or class during a specified period of time. If the parties can show that the sale is arms-length, then it is possible to still use the transaction value as the proper methodology.

B. Transaction Value of Identical Merchandise

If the transaction value cannot be used, then the second methodology is the transaction value of identical merchandise. This is based on the seller's sale to other unrelated parties at or about the same time as the merchandise in question. Identical merchandise may have minor differences, such as color, but they must have the same physical characteristics, quality, and reputation as the imported goods. If there is a history of identical sales, then this is the proper methodology.

C. Transaction Value of Similar Goods

If there are no instances of sale of identical goods, then sales or transactions of similar goods may be used. Similar goods must be produced in the same country and by the same producer. They must closely resemble the imported goods in terms of component materials and functionality as well as in terms of quality and reputation. Key is that the similar goods should be commercially interchangeable with the imported goods.

D. Deductive Value

If none of the above methodologies can be used, then either the deductive value method or the computed value method may be used. These two methods may be switched in order at the option of the importer. The deductive valuation method begins with the resale of the product in the imported country to an unrelated purchaser in the greatest aggregate quantity at or around the time of import. Determining the greatest aggregate quantity requires that all sales at a given price be taken together, and the sum of all the units of goods sold at that price is compared to the sum of all the units of goods sold at any other price. The greatest number of units sold at one price represents the greatest aggregate quantity. From that value, all of the costs that are incurred in the importing country may be deducted to take the value back to the cost at either the CIF port of import value (for most countries) or the FOB port of export value (for the United States). These deductions may include the import duties and brokerage fees, any transportation costs in the imported country, and the value of any further modification, assembly, or other processes undertaken in the imported country. It should be noted that the same additions identified in the transaction value section above must be included and the same deductions may be taken.

E. Computed Value

If none of the above methods of valuation can be used, then the value must be calculated based on the computed value. Computed value is a bottoms-up calculation. It begins with the costs of materials and production. This includes raw materials, subassemblies, assemblies, and goods used during production. It must include all manufacturing costs including labor and overtime as well as administrative overhead and general expenses (such as utilities) that are directly related to the production of the imported product. Finally, it must include a profit that is typical of the profit margins of other manufacturers of the same product in the same country of manufacture. Likewise, the same additions in the transaction value section above should also be included in the computed value.

F. Fall-Back Methodology

If none of the above methodologies are appropriate, an alternative methodology may be approved by the customs service in the importing country. This method allows for flexibility by using a method that is in accordance with the principles of the WCO valuation but does not fall into any of the above methodologies. For example, this may occur if there is a modification of one of the above acceptable methodologies or if there is a contractual agreement between the parties that will cover the computed value components.

1. *Unacceptable Methods*

The WCO Valuation Code has specific methodologies that are unacceptable for use under the fall-back method. They include:

- The selling price of similar goods manufactured in the country of importation
- When the customs service accepts the higher of two alternative values, the lowest of the two alternatives should be used
- The price of the goods in the domestic market of the country of export
- The cost of production of goods that are not identical or similar
- The price of the goods exported to a third country
- A minimum customs value (unless a developing country takes a reservation to the valuation rules upon joining the WTO, which is allowed for up to five years)
- An arbitrary or fictitious value

Determining the proper valuation is critical for all importers to understand in order to know their landed costs.

G. First-Sale Transactions

Unique to the United States and the European Union is the concept of "first sale" in determining the proper valuation for customs purposes. Although the European Union may be eliminating first sale, the United States is firmly entrenched in allowing transactions to be valued based on an earlier sale in the import transaction.

When an importer purchases from overseas, in most instances, it may not be buying from a factory. Although the importer may believe it is purchasing directly from the factory, there is generally a "middleman" that actually purchases the goods from the factory or factories and then resells them to the importer. In fact, there may be several layers of middlemen in the transaction. When that happens, there is an opportunity for the importer to use the factory-to-middleman price, or the "first sale," in order to take advantage of obtaining a lower duty payment. If the importer cannot use the price of the first sale, then at least it can use the price of an earlier sale if it is a multitiered transaction. However, there has to be evidence that these are bona fide sales between all of the parties and a clear indication that the goods were destined for the United States, and there must be a direct shipment from the factory to the United States, without entering the commerce of any other country along the way. While the first-sale concept was originally very controversial, it has been upheld by the United States Court of International Trade and the Court of Appeals for the Federal Circuit. The most famous example was the case of *Nissho Iwai American Corp.* v. *United States.* (See Figure 10–1 for a diagram of the parties involved.) In that case, the New York Metropolitan Transit Authority (NYC MTA) ordered buses from Nissho Iwai American Corporation (NIAC), which consigned the sale to its parent, Nissho Iwai Corporation (NIC) in Japan. NIC purchased the buses from the factory, Kawasaki Heavy Industries (KHI). The buses were shipped directly from KHI to the NYC MTA, and NIAC acted as the importer of record on the transactions and paid all duty. NIAC wanted to pay duty on the price from KHI to NIC instead of from NIC to the NYC MTA, and the courts agreed. The buses were marked with New York Transit Authority markings, and there were two sales, so NIAC was able to reduce its duty payments to U.S. Customs by eliminating the value of NIC's overhead and profits and calculating the duty from that lower value. One of the big obstacles in first-sale transactions is having the middleman's profits disclosed to the importer, but that can be bypassed by certain guarantees to keep that information confidential to only specific individuals within the Customs group and by guaranteeing to the middleman that the goal is not to reduce its profit but to reduce duty payments and forge long-term partnerships with middlemen. While this is a limited description of a complex

Figure 10–1. First-sale example in the case of *Nissho Iwai American Corp.* v. *United States*.

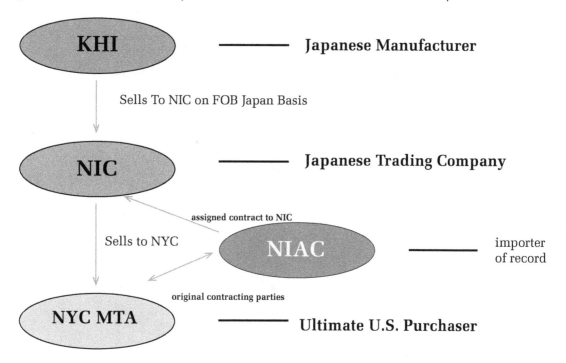

operation, if a company is paying high duties based either on a high duty rate or on the basis of a large number of orders, then it is worthwhile to consult with an expert in first-sale transactions.

Chapter 11

Determining the Proper Country of Origin

In an ever-growing global economy, determining a single country of origin is an extremely difficult task, but it is necessary for all imported goods and in many cases for exported goods. We strongly suggest consulting legal counsel before making any determinations about origin as an incorrect determination can result in penalties and fines. While this chapter is essentially U.S.-centric, the bilateral and multilateral free trade agreements negotiated among other countries follow the same rules, and so a review of U.S. rules will provide an understanding of the general methodologies used.

The United States has multiple rules to determine the country of origin of any finished good. For example, consider steel from China that is manufactured into steel blanks of specific dimensions in Thailand. Those blanks are then shipped to Mexico for further manufacture, including cutting, notching, and bending into specific sizes of steel panels. The manufactured panels are then shipped into the United States, where they are insulated, fitted with electrical components, and assembled into modular steel panels. What is the country of origin? The answer is . . . it depends, and it depends based on the reason you want to know! Do you want to determine the duty rate? Do you want to determine the origin marking on the item? Is it because you want to sell the item to the government? Is it because you want to claim that the panels are "Made in the USA"? Why is it so important to determine a single country of origin?

It would be nice if there was one simple rule to establish the origin of a product for all purposes and that would be applicable worldwide; unfortunately, there is not. In fact, there are many, often contradictory, rules to ascertain the origin of a product, even if the product is being sold in a single market. There may be preferential duty rates available if the product originates in a country where the United States has a free trade agreement[1] or other preferential duty program and the product meets the proper rule for that purpose. The U.S. Customs and Border Protection also regulates country of origin marking laws, which were created to provide U.S. consumers with information on the origin of the product so that they make informed decisions with regard to whether to buy a product from the origination country or not. In addition, there are laws against importing from embargoed countries; laws regarding what is considered a U.S. origin product; and laws that determine the eligibility of merchandise for U.S. government procurement. Also, depending on the type of product, various government agencies have their own rules of origin and marking, which must be followed; consider, for example, the Federal Communications Commission (FCC), the Environmental Protection Agency (EPA), and the Food and Drug Administration (FDA), to name a few. Each of these laws has different requirements making origin determination a quagmire of conflicting rules and regulations.

In addition, each of these laws comes with its own penalty for violations. For example, Customs issues monetary penalties for declaring the wrong country of origin for preferential duty purposes on entries into the United States. Importers are responsible for the accuracy of the declarations. There are marking penalties for declaring an incorrect origin to the consumer, and government contracts may be revoked—all of which make this issue extremely important.

A. Preferential Duty Laws

One of the major reasons for determining the country of origin is to determine the proper duty rate. All countries with the exception of Cuba and North Korea[2] are subject to the normal trade relations (NTR) duty rate, which can be found in the "General" Column 1 under "Rates of Duty" of the Harmonized Tariff Schedule of the United States. (See Figure 9–2.) This is known as the most favored nation (MFN) duty rate in other countries. Cuba and North Korea are still subject to the duty rates shown in Column 2 of the HTSUSA, imposed during the Depression in the 1930s. However, imports from both countries are prohibited. There is also a "Special" Column rate that applies to the reduced duty rates for countries involved in the various preferential duty programs or free trade agreements with the United States. The various trade benefits are identified by codes, either the two-letter code for the country of export or a letter signifying another agreement. (See Figure 9–3.) To determine if a Special rate applies, the importer must know the tariff item of the merchandise it wants to import and then review the list of codes to determine eligibility. Once it determines if there are any preferential duty programs, it must confirm that the imported product will meet the rules of that program.

1. *Substantial Transformation*

Substantial transformation is the basic principle throughout the world for determining the country of origin for purposes of preferential duties when a finished good has been processed in more than one country. This principle states that the country of origin is the last country in which a substantial transformation of the materials or components into the finished product occurs. While this may sound relatively simple, exactly when a substantial transformation has occurred is the subject of numerous U.S. Customs rulings and court cases. In 1908, the U.S. Supreme Court explained substantial transformation by stating that the original components or materials must have lost their identity and "a new and different article" must emerge, "having a distinctive name, character, or use." Note, however, that a substantial transformation does not occur when there is only minor processing, such as dilution with water, cleaning, application of a preservative coating, trimming, filing or cutting off small amounts of excess materials, testing, or packing. This basic tenet for determining origin is still used for determining the origin for duty purposes. All countries are assessed duty rates under Column 1, the normal trade relations rate (except Cuba and North Korea, as mentioned above). However, many countries may be able to take advantage of the reduced or duty-free rates identified under the "Special" column if they meet the criteria listed below for the special programs.

2. *The 35 Percent Agreements*

The United States has implemented a number of a trade programs that allow certain countries' products to be imported into the United States duty-free or at a reduced duty as long as two conditions are met: First, the products must be shipped directly from the designated country to the United States; second, at least 35 percent of the appraised value of the imported products must originate in that designated country. There are certain deviations allowed for U.S. components under several of these trade agreements, but 35 percent is the minimum content allowed. We will discuss the basics of these agreements below. Each of these agreements is designated in the HTSUSA under the "Special" column by either a letter or the two-letter abbreviation for the specific country listed next to specific tariff numbers that are eligible for the reduction in duties. Not all of the agreements are discussed below, but those covered are the most popular.

a. GSP: Generalized System of Preferences

The Generalized System of Preferences (GSP) is a program established in the 1970s to promote the economic growth of developing countries by providing non-reciprocal duty-free benefits to imports from certain Beneficiary Designated Countries (BDCs) and Least-Developed Beneficiary Designated Countries (LDBDCs). This program is also recognized by the European Union. In the United States, the program is administered by the Office of the U.S. Trade Representative. Each year, countries are reviewed to determine their continued eligibility or to determine whether a specific BDC's exports have exceeded the competitive quantity limit, in which case that tariff number is removed from eligibility for that BDC. Over the years as some of the BDCs have developed, they have been removed from the list of beneficiary countries.

To determine if a country is eligible, look at the list of countries designated as BDCs and LDBDCs in General Note 4 of the Harmonized Tariff Schedule of the United States. To determine if a product is eligible, look at the specific tariff number for the finished import good and under the duty rate "Column 1, Special" (see Figure 9–2) for the letter and symbol A, A*, or A+. The A means that all BDCs and LDBDCs listed in General Note 4 are eligible for duty-free treatment. (See Figure 9–4.) The A* means that most of those countries are eligible, but certain countries have been removed because the exports from them have exceeded the competitive limits; those countries are also identified under General Note 4 by the tariff number in question. (See Figure 9-4.) The A+ means that only imports from the LDBDCs are eligible for duty-free treatment. (See Figure 9-4.) Many products, such as textiles and apparel, footwear, agriculture, and other trade-sensitive products, are not eligible under the GSP program.

There are two criteria for qualifying a product as eligible for GSP treatment: (1) the product must be directly shipped from the qualifying BDC, and (2) the sum of (a) the cost or value of the materials produced in the BDC plus (b) the direct costs of processing operations performed in the BDC must be not less than 35 percent of the appraised value of the merchandise as imported into the United States. Any component that originates in a third country must undergo a substantial transformation from the original product into a component in the BDC or LDBDC, and then that component must undergo a second substantial transformation in the BDC or LDBDC in order qualify the foreign value as part of the 35 percent calculation. For example, steel coil sheets that are manufactured in China (which is not a BDC) are imported into Thailand (which is a BDC), where they are cut and formed into a tube (this is a single transformation). Those steel tubes are then further processed in Thailand by placing the tubes into a die and filling it with liquid where the pressure of the liquid forms the tube into the shape of the die, resulting in a suspension pipe (this is the second transformation). Based on the double substantial transformation, the value of the steel that originated in China may now be included in the determination of the 35 percent valuation.

It should be noted that U.S. Customs has the authority to audit claims for the preferential duty, and the importer is responsible for ensuring that the manufacturer will provide documentation to prove the good meets the 35 percent origin requirement. Record-keeping information should include the purchase order, invoice, bill of lading or air waybill, production records, payroll information, factory information, and a GSP declaration. In addition, all records must be maintained for five years after the GSP claim has been made. U.S. Customs has a created an audit document regarding best practices for GSP claims.[3] For manufacturers that are unrelated to the importer, this document can be difficult to obtain as a manufacturer does not want to share the details how about how it arrives at its valuation to its customer. Thus, it is important to ensure that the importer puts the manufacturer on notice through a contract of its obligation to provide documentary evidence directly to Customs or through a third party such as an attorney who would maintain the confidentiality of that information. If Customs is not satisfied with the information provided to prove eligibility, the importer will be required to pay all back duties plus interest and may also be required to pay a penalty.

Unfortunately, renewal of the GSP program is subject to Congress's approval, and it has expired a number of times over the years. Upon expiration, all importers have to pay duties. Thus far, Congress has renewed the program and allowed for a refund of the duties paid plus interest during the interim expiration period. That retroactive application of duty-free status is not guaranteed, however, and in the future, Congress either may not renew the program or may not be willing to allow for refunds of the duties paid in the interim.

b.   CBERA: Caribbean Basin Economic Recovery Act

The Caribbean Basin Economic Recovery Act (CBERA) is listed in the Harmonized Tariff Schedule of the United States under General Note 7. CBERA includes the following countries: Antigua and Barbuda, Aruba, Bahamas, Barbados, Belize, Dominica, Grenada, Guyana, Haiti, Jamaica, Montserrat, Netherlands Antilles, St. Kitts and Nevis, Saint Lucia, Saint Vincent and the Grenadines, Trinidad and Tobago, and the British Virgin Islands. Note that many of these countries are also eligible under the GSP provisions. The two basic eligibility criteria are the same: (1) direct import from the CBERA beneficiary country, and (2) the sum of (a) the cost or value of the materials produced in the BDC plus (b) the direct costs of processing operations performed in the BDC is not less than 35 percent of the appraised value of the merchandise as imported into the United States. In calculating the 35 percent, the term "beneficiary country" includes the Commonwealth of Puerto Rico, the U.S. Virgin Islands, and any other beneficiary country. In addition, if the cost or value of materials produced in the customs territory of the United States (other than the Commonwealth of Puerto Rico) is included in the finished merchandise, an amount not to exceed 15 percent of the appraised value may be applied toward determining the 35 percent referred to in (2) above. So 15 percent of the 35 percent may be comprised of U.S. origin components and direct costs of processing.

Articles that are eligible for the CBERA are designated in the tariff schedule by an E or E*. As with the GSP designations, an E means that goods imported from any CBERA beneficiary country are eligible for duty-free treatment if they qualify. Tariff numbers designated with an E* mean that some countries have exceeded the competitive limits and have been removed.

As mentioned above, an importer making a claim that goods are eligible is subject to audit by U.S. Customs and must be able to have the manufacturer provide evidence of eligibility by providing the appropriate documentation directly to U.S. Customs or through a third party, such as an attorney, to protect the confidentiality of the information. As in the GSP, if U.S. Customs is not satisfied that the imported goods meet the criteria, then the importer is responsible for the unpaid duties plus interest and potentially a penalty.

c. AGOA: African Growth and Opportunity Act

The African Growth and Opportunity Act (AGOA) of 2000 was established to promote increased trade and economic cooperation between the United States and eligible sub-Saharan African countries. It may be found in Note 16 of the Harmonized Tariff Schedule of the United States. The beneficiary countries are Angola, Benin, Botswana, Burkina Faso, Burundi, Cameroon, Cape Verde, Chad, Comoros, Republic of Congo, Democratic Republic of Congo, Côte d'Ivoire, Djibouti, Ethiopia, Gabon, The Gambia, Ghana, Guinea, Kenya, Lesotho, Liberia, Malawi, Mali, Mauritania, Mauritius, Mozambique, Namibia, Niger, Nigeria, Rwanda, Sao Tome and Principe, Senegal, Seychelles, Sierra Leone, South Africa, South Sudan, Swaziland, Tanzania, Togo, Uganda, and Zambia. These countries are all identified in the GSP program, but the AGOA program allows for imports of articles such as textiles and apparel and agricultural products from many of the countries. The basics of the AGOA program are the same as those of the other 35 percent origin programs identified above. The finished merchandise must be imported directly from the beneficiary country, and the cost or value of the materials produced in one or more designated beneficiary sub-Saharan African countries, plus the direct costs of the processing operations performed in the designated beneficiary sub-Saharan African country or any two or more designated beneficiary sub-Saharan African countries that are members of the same association of countries (and may be treated as one country), is not less than 35 percent of the appraised value of such article at the time it is entered. As with the other agreements, the cost or value of any materials in the customs territory of the United States may be included up to 15 percent of the appraised value and may be included in the total 35 percent appraisement value.

d. United States–Israel Free Trade Agreement

The United States–Israel Free Trade Agreement was enacted in April 1985 and is listed in General Note 8 of the Harmonized Tariff Schedule of the United States. This FTA allows for duty-free entry of goods if they originate and ship directly from Israel (or directly from the West Bank, the Gaza Strip, or a qualifying industrial zone) and the sum of (a) the cost or value of the materials produced in Israel (and including the costs or value of materials produced in the West Bank, the Gaza Strip, or a qualifying industrial zone) plus (b) the direct costs of processing operations performed in Israel (and including the direct costs of processing in the West Bank, the Gaza Strip, or a qualifying industrial zone) is not less than 35 percent of the appraised value of the merchandise as imported into the United States. If the cost or value of materials produced in the customs territory of the United States is included with respect to an article to which this note applies, an amount not more than 15 percent of the appraised value of the article that is attributable to such U.S. cost or value may be applied toward determining the 35 percent required. Identification of merchandise qualifying under the U.S.–Israel FTA is by the designation "IL" next to the tariff number in the Harmonized Tariff Schedule of the United States. (See Figure 9–2.) The record-keeping requirements and the obligation to provide production records to U.S. Customs to substantiate the duty-free claim is the same as with the other agreements listed above. Likewise, failure to provide the required evidence will result in the assessment of back duties and interest as well as a potential penalty.

3. The Free Trade Agreement Tariff-Shift or Tariff-Shift Plus Regional Value Content Rules

a. North American Free Trade Agreement (NAFTA)

The implementation of the North American Free Trade Agreement (NAFTA) covering the United States, Canada, and Mexico, began the new era of determining origin based on specific rules of origin when there are components or raw materials originating from outside of the three member countries. NAFTA has a number of different preference criteria:

A. The good is "wholly obtained or produced entirely" in the territory of one or more of the NAFTA countries.

B. The good is produced entirely in the territory of one or more of the NAFTA countries and satisfies the specific rule of origin that applies to its tariff classification. The rule may include a tariff classification change, regional value content requirement, or a combination thereof.

C. The good is produced entirely in the territory of one or more of the NAFTA countries exclusively from originating materials.

D. The good is produced in the territory of one or more of the NAFTA countries but does not meet the applicable rule of origin because certain non-originating materials do not undergo the required change in tariff classification. The good nonetheless meets the regional value content requirement specified in Article 401(d) of the NAFTA agreement. This criterion is limited to the following two circumstances: (1) The good was imported into the territory of a NAFTA country in an unassembled or disassembled form but was classified as an assembled good, pursuant to General Rule of Interpretation 2(a) of the Harmonized Tariff Schedule, or (2) the good incorporated one or more non-originating materials, provided for as parts under the Harmonized Tariff Schedule, which could not undergo a change in tariff classification because the heading provided for both the good and its parts and was not further subdivided into subheadings, or the subheading provided for both the good and its parts and was not further subdivided. *(Note: This criterion does not apply to Chapters 61 through 63 of the Harmonized Tariff Schedule.)*

E. Certain automatic data processing goods and their parts that do not originate in the territory are considered originating upon importation into the territory of a NAFTA country from the territory of another NAFTA country when the most favored nation tariff rate of the good conforms to the rate established in Annex 308.1 of the NAFTA agreement and is common to all NAFTA countries.

F. The good is an originating agricultural good under Preference Criterion A, B, or C and is not subject to a quantitative restriction in the importing NAFTA country because it is a "qualifying good" as defined in Annex 703.2, Section A or B. A good listed in Appendix 703.2B.7 is also exempt from quantitative restrictions and is eligible for NAFTA preferential tariff treatment if it meets the definition of "qualifying good" in Section A of Annex 703.2. *(Note: This criterion does not apply to goods that wholly originate in Canada or the United States and are imported into either country. Also, note that a tariff rate quota is not a quantitative restriction.)*

1) Preference Criterion A

Preference Criterion A is the most basic of provisions. It is essentially for natural resources—items that are grown, harvested, fished, or mined in one of the three member countries. Examples are vegetables, fish, meat, fruit, and wood articles with minimal processing. There are very few products that are actually able to use Preference Criterion A. In fact, legend has it that Customs auditors refer to Preference Criterion A as the "audit me" criterion because most manufactured products do not qualify under this provision.

2) Preference Criterion B

Preference Criterion B is the most common method to qualify goods as eligible for preferential duty treatment. It is based on knowing the Harmonized Tariff Number of the finished imported goods and the Harmonized Tariff Number of the materials and components in the bill of materials as well as the origin of each. For each material or component that originates in a country other than Mexico, Canada, or the United States, there must be a shift in the tariff number of the non-member originating raw material or component to a different tariff number for the finished good, a tariff-shift change, according to the rules of origin that are listed in the Agreement (and in the General Note 12 of the Harmonized Tariff Schedule of the United States). Note the following example from the HTSUSA:

> What is the NAFTA status upon importation into the United States of chewing gum processed in Mexico from sugar cane grown in the Dominican Republic?
>
> Classifications:
>
> Cane sugar 1701.11
>
> Chewing gum ....1704.10.
>
> Rule of Origin for 1704:
>
> A change to heading 1704 from any other heading.

In this example, the sugar cane from the Dominican Republic is classified under HTS subheading 1701.11, and so it makes the tariff shift in accordance with the NAFTA rule for the finished chewing gum since 1701 is the heading of the sugar and 1704 is the heading of the gum. Therefore, the gum qualifies as eligible for NAFTA duty-free treatment.

3) *De Minimis*

Next is the de minimis rule. If the material or component does not make the tariff shift and it is de minimis in value, or less than 7 percent of the transaction value of the good (See Chapter 10, Section A), then it can be ignored. If multiple items do not make the tariff shift, the total value of those items cannot exceed that 7 percent. Let us take the chewing gum example above. Say that in addition to the cane sugar there are sugar confectionary sprinkles from France added to the gum, which are classified under 1704.90. Then, the sprinkles would not make the tariff shift. However, if the value of sprinkles was less than 7 percent of the total value of the gum, then because their value was de minimis, the gum would still qualify as NAFTA originating even with the French sprinkles.

4) *Regional Value Content*

Regional value content (RVC) must also be considered. In some instances, the rule of origin requires that there be a certain amount of regional value content added in addition to a tariff shift. The percentages are either 60 percent of total value of the imported product when transaction value is used (see Chapter 10, Section A) or 50 percent when net cost is used. Net cost is used when there is no sale, when transaction value cannot be used, when the parties are related, or for certain automotive products and footwear. The following explains how to compute transaction value and net cost:

1. *Transaction value method*. The regional value content of a good may be calculated on the basis of the following transaction value method:

$$RVC = \frac{TV - VNM}{TV} \times 100$$

where RVC is the regional value content, expressed as a percentage; TV is the transaction value of the good adjusted to a FOB basis; and VNM is the value of non-originating materials used by the producer in the production of the good.

2. *Net cost method.* The regional value content of a good may be calculated on the basis of the following net cost method:

$$RVC = \frac{NC - VNM}{NC} \times 100$$

where RVC is the regional value content, expressed as a percentage; NC is the net cost of the good; and VNM is the value of non-originating materials used by the producer in the production of the good.

Net cost is generally the sum of all costs to the producer without the marketing costs, after-sales service costs, royalties, and shipping and packing costs that are then allocated to the imported product. *Note: There are specific calculations for certain automotive products.* See the following:

Will padlocks made in Mexico qualify for NAFTA benefits if made from the following?

U.S. clasps	$0.12
German parts	$0.38
Mexican labor	$0.50
TOTAL	$1.00

Classifications:

Padlocks	8301.10 to 8301.40
Clasps and frames	8301.50
Other Parts	8301.60

<u>Rules of Origin</u>

8301.10-8301.50

A change to subheadings 8301.10 through 8301.50 from any other chapter; or a change to 8301.10 through 8301.50 from subheading 8301.60, if there is a regional value content of not less than:

(a) 60% when TV method is used or

(b) 50% when NC method is used.

In the example above, the German parts alone do not make the tariff shift because they are in the same chapter as the padlocks, but there is a second rule that allows parts under 8301.60 if there is a regional value content of 50 percent or 60 percent, depending on the methodology used for the value. Let's assume that transaction value may be used. So the calculation is $1.00 - $0.38 = $0.62 divided by $1.00 = $0.62 x 100 = 62 percent. So the RVC is 62 percent, and it exceeds the requirement needed. Therefore, even though there are German parts, the finished padlocks, which are manufactured in Mexico, qualify under NAFTA for preferential duties. Note that we do not have to conduct the analysis for the U.S. clasps, as they are from one of the three member countries.

5) *Preference Criterion C*

Preference Criterion C is used when all of the components/materials originate in the United States, Mexico, or Canada. Since there are no other foreign components or materials, there is no need to analyze the individual rules of origin. If there is even a de minimis amount of foreign materials or goods, then Preference Criterion B is used. If we use the same example above for the padlocks and the German parts are instead from Canada, we do not have to conduct the regional value content analysis, because all parts and labor occurs in one of the three member countries.

6) *Preference Criterion D*

Preference Criterion D applies when the components/materials do not meet the tariff shift rules, but the regional value content does meet the percentage content. This criterion applies in only two circumstances: (1) The good is imported in an unassembled or disassembled state and because of classification is based on General Rule of Interpretation 2(a) by the essential character; and (2) the imported good is a "part" of a finished good and the heading for the finished good calls for the inclusion of "parts" in the same classification and there is no further subheading breakdown for parts. An example would be for fishing baits and lures. The parts are to be classified with the articles and there is no separate provision for parts. This criterion is not applicable for items in Chapters 61 through 63 of the Harmonized Tariff Schedule, covering textiles.

7) *Preference Criterion E*

Preference Criterion E is for certain computers and components itemized in Annex 803.1 of the NAFTA agreement that are automatically granted NAFTA eligibility when they are imported and duty is paid into one of the three NAFTA countries. Thus, if they are imported into the United States and duty is paid, they will be eligible for NAFTA preferential duties when those same computers or components are exported to Mexico or Canada. While this is a particularly unique provision, it is great for those in the IT industry. See http://www.sice.oas.org/trade/nafta/chap-034.asp for a list of products that qualify.

8) Preference Criterion F

Preference Criterion F is only for agricultural products destined for export to Mexico, excluding dairy, poultry, and eggs.

9) Accumulation/Cumulation

Accumulation allows a producer to treat the costs of any producer in any NAFTA country that provided material for the good as if they were its costs. The same principle applies under cumulation according to the WTO for determining origin in other free trade agreements between countries. The accumulated/cumulated costs include not only the cost of those materials but any labor and other production-related expenses incurred in producing the finished good by another producer. So if a producer/exporter sources raw materials from another producer in the same or another country within the NAFTA agreement, the total costs for labor and materials can be added together in order to arrive at the 50 percent or 60 percent requirements.

10) Fungibility

Fungibility applies where goods or materials are interchangeable for commercial purposes and their properties are essentially identical. Then, according to the Article 406 of the NAFTA agreement, if the fungible goods are handled together and commingled such that it is impossible to determine which are originating and which are not, their origin may be decided based upon any of the inventory methods recognized in the Generally Accepted Accounting Principles. Physical separation of the goods is not necessary.

11) Certificates of Origin

In order to qualify for NAFTA preferential benefits, a NAFTA certificate of origin is required to be completed by the exporter. (See Figure 11–1.) It is always the exporter's certificate of origin that must be used for making the claim of NAFTA preferential treatment. If the exporter is not the manufacturer, then the exporter must obtain either a NAFTA certification or other written statement from the producer that the finished good qualifies for NAFTA preferential duties. The certificate should be completed in the language required by the importing country. The certificate of origin can be for an individual shipment or for all shipments within a twelve-month period of time, but the underlying facts of the shipment and the NAFTA eligibility must remain the same. Any changes to the NAFTA eligibility of the good require the exporter to issue a new NAFTA certificate of origin within thirty days of the change. In order to make

Figure 11–1. NAFTA certificate of origin.

DEPARTMENT OF HOMELAND SECURITY
U.S. Customs and Border Protection

OMB No. 1651-0098
Exp. 08-31-2014

**NORTH AMERICAN FREE TRADE AGREEMENT
CERTIFICATE OF ORIGIN**

19 CFR 181.11, 181.22

1. EXPORTER NAME AND ADDRESS	2. BLANKET PERIOD
	FROM
	TO
TAX IDENTIFICATION NUMBER:	
3. PRODUCER NAME AND ADDRESS	4. IMPORTER NAME AND ADDRESS
TAX IDENTIFICATION NUMBER:	TAX IDENTIFICATION NUMBER:

5. DESCRIPTION OF GOOD(S)	6. HS TARIFF CLASSIFICATION NUMBER	7. PREFERENCE CRITERION	8. PRODUCER	9. NET COST	10. COUNTRY OF ORIGIN

I CERTIFY THAT:

• THE INFORMATION ON THIS DOCUMENT IS TRUE AND ACCURATE AND I ASSUME THE RESPONSIBILITY FOR PROVING SUCH REPRESENTATIONS. I UNDERSTAND THAT I AM LIABLE FOR ANY FALSE STATEMENTS OR MATERIAL OMISSIONS MADE ON OR IN CONNECTION WITH THIS DOCUMENT;

• I AGREE TO MAINTAIN AND PRESENT UPON REQUEST, DOCUMENTATION NECESSARY TO SUPPORT THIS CERTIFICATE, AND TO INFORM, IN WRITING, ALL PERSONS TO WHOM THE CERTIFICATE WAS GIVEN OF ANY CHANGES THAT COULD AFFECT THE ACCURACY OR VALIDITY OF THIS CERTIFICATE;

• THE GOODS ORIGINATED IN THE TERRITORY OF ONE OR MORE OF THE PARTIES, AND COMPLY WITH THE ORIGIN REQUIREMENTS SPECIFIED FOR THOSE GOODS IN THE NORTH AMERICAN FREE TRADE AGREEMENT AND UNLESS SPECIFICALLY EXEMPTED IN ARTICLE 411 OR ANNEX 401, THERE HAS BEEN NO FURTHER PRODUCTION OR ANY OTHER OPERATION OUTSIDE THE TERRITORIES OF THE PARTIES; AND

• THIS CERTIFICATE CONSISTS OF _____ PAGES, INCLUDING ALL ATTACHMENTS.

11.	11a. AUTHORIZED SIGNATURE	11b. COMPANY	
	11c. NAME	11d. TITLE	
	11e. DATE	11f. TELEPHONE NUMBERS ▶ (Voice)	(Facsimile)

CBP Form 434 (04/11)

448

Figure 11–1. (*continued*)

PAPERWORK REDUCTION ACT STATEMENT: An agency may not conduct or sponsor an information collection and a person is not required to respond to this information unless it displays a current valid OMB control number and an expiration date. The control number for this collection is 1651-0098. The estimated average time to complete this application is 15 minutes. If you have any comments regarding the burden estimate you can write to U.S. Customs and Border Protection, Office of Regulations and Rulings, 799 9th Street, NW., Washington DC 20229.

NORTH AMERICAN FREE TRADE AGREEMENT CERTIFICATE OF ORIGIN INSTRUCTIONS

For purposes of obtaining preferential tariff treatment, this document must be completed legibly and in full by the exporter and be in the possession of the importer at the time the declaration is made. This document may also be completed voluntarily by the producer for use by the exporter. Please print or type:

FIELD 1: State the full legal name, address (including country) and legal tax identification number of the exporter. Legal taxation number is: in Canada, employer number or importer/exporter number assigned by Revenue Canada; in Mexico, federal taxpayer's registry number (RFC); and in the United States, employer's identification number or Social Security Number.

FIELD 2: Complete field if the Certificate covers multiple shipments of identical goods as described in Field #5 that are imported into a NAFTA country for a specified period of up to one year (the blanket period). "FROM" is the date upon which Certificate becomes applicable to the good covered by the blanket Certificate (it may be prior to the date of signing this Certificate). "TO" is the date upon which the blanket period expires. The importation of a good for which preferential treatment is claimed based on this Certificate must occur between these dates.

FIELD 3: State the full legal name, address (including country) and legal tax identification number, as defined in Field #1, of the producer. If more than one producer's good is included on the Certificate, attach a list of additional producers, including the legal name, address (including country) and legal tax identification number, cross-referenced to the good described in Field #5. If you wish this information to be confidential, it is acceptable to state "Available to CBP upon request". If the producer and the exporter are the same, complete field with "SAME". If the producer is unknown, it is acceptable to state "UNKNOWN".

FIELD 4: State the full legal name, address (including country) and legal tax identification number, as defined in Field #1, of the importer. If the importer is not known, state "UNKNOWN"; if multiple importers, state "VARIOUS".

FIELD 5: Provide a full description of each good. The description should be sufficient to relate it to the invoice description and to the Harmonized System (H.S.) description of the good. If the Certificate covers a single shipment of a good, include the invoice number as shown on the commercial invoice. If not known, indicate another unique reference number, such as the shipping order number.

FIELD 6: For each good described in Field #5, identify the H.S. tariff classification to six digits. If the good is subject to a specific rule of origin in Annex 401 that requires eight digits, identify to eight digits, using the H.S. tariff classification of the country into whose territory the good is imported.

FIELD 7: For each good described in Field #5, state which criterion (A through F) is applicable. The rules of origin are contained in Chapter Four and Annex 401. Additional rules are described in Annex 703.2 (certain agricultural goods), Annex 300-B, Appendix 6 (certain textile goods) and Annex 308.1 (certain automatic data processing goods and their parts). **NOTE: In order to be entitled to preferential tariff treatment, each good must meet at least one of the criteria below.**

Preference Criteria

A The good is "wholly obtained or produced entirely" in the territory of one or more of the NAFTA countries as referenced in Article 415. **Note: The purchase of a good in the territory does not necessarily render it "wholly obtained or produced".** If the good is an agricultural good, see also criterion F and Annex 703.2. *(Reference: Article 401(a) and 415)*

B The good is produced entirely in the territory of one or more of the NAFTA countries and satisfies the specific rule of origin, set out in Annex 401, that applies to its tariff classification. The rule may include a tariff classification change, regional value-content requirement, or a combination thereof. The good must also satisfy all other applicable requirements of Chapter Four. If the good is an agricultural good, see also criterion F and Annex 703.2. *(Reference: Article 401(b))*

C The good is produced entirely in the territory of one or more of the NAFTA countries exclusively from originating materials. Under this criterion, one or more of the materials may not fall within the definition of "wholly produced or obtained", as set out in article 415. All materials used in the production of the good must qualify as "originating" by meeting the rules of Article 401(a) through (d). If the good is an agricultural good, see also criterion F and Annex 703.2. *Reference: Article 401(c).*

D Goods are produced in the territory of one or more of the NAFTA countries but do not meet the applicable rule of origin, set out in Annex 401, because certain non-originating materials do not undergo the required change in tariff classification. The goods do nonetheless meet the regional value-content requirement specified in Article 401(d). This criterion is limited to the following two circumstances:

1. The good was imported into the territory of a NAFTA country in an unassembled or disassembled form but was classified as an assembled good, pursuant to H.S. General Rule of Interpretation 2(a), or

2. The good incorporated one or more non-originating materials, provided for as parts under the H.S., which could not undergo a change in tariff classification because the heading provided for both the good and its parts and was not further subdivided into subheadings, or the subheading provided for both the good and its parts and was not further subdivided.

NOTE: This criterion does not apply to Chapters 61 through 63 of H.S. (Reference: Article 401(d))

E Certain automatic data processing goods and their parts, specified in Annex 308.1, that do not originate in the territory are considered originating upon importation into the territory of a NAFTA country from the territory of another NAFTA country when the most-favored-nation tariff rate of the good conforms to the rate established in Annex 308.1 and is common to all NAFTA countries. *(Reference: Annex 308.1)*

F The good is an originating agricultural good under preference criterion A, B, or C above and is not subject to a quantitative restriction in the importing NAFTA country because it is a "qualifying good" as defined in Annex 703.2, Section A or B (please specify). A good listed in Appendix 703.2B.7 is also exempt from quantitative restrictions and is eligible for NAFTA preferential tariff treatment if it meets the definition of "qualifying good" in Section A of Annex 703.2. **NOTE 1: This criterion does not apply to goods that wholly originate in Canada or the United States and are imported into either country. NOTE 2: A tariff rate quota is not a quantitative restriction.**

FIELD 8: For each good described in Field #5, state "YES" if you are the producer of the good. If you are not the producer of the good, state "NO" followed by (1), (2), or (3), depending on whether this certificate was based upon: (1) your knowledge of whether the good qualifies as an originating good; (2) your reliance on the producer's written representation (other than a Certificate of Origin) that the good qualifies as an originating good; or (3) a completed and signed Certificate for the good, voluntarily provided to the exporter by the producer.

FIELD 9: For each good described in field #5, where the good is subject to a regional value content (RVC) requirement, indicate "NC" if the RVC is calculated according to the net cost method; otherwise, indicate "NO". If the RVC is calculated over a period of time, further identify the beginning and ending dates (MM/DD/YYYY) of that period. *(Reference: Article 402.1, 402.5).*

FIELD 10: Identify the name of the country ("MX" or "US" for agricultural and textile goods exported to Canada; "US" or "CA" for all goods exported to Mexico; or "CA" or "MX" for all goods exported to the United States) to which the preferential rate of CBP duty applies, as set out in Annex 302.2, in accordance with the Marking Rules or in each party's schedule of tariff elimination.

For all other originating goods exported to Canada, indicate appropriately "MX" or "US" if the goods originate in that NAFTA country, within the meaning of the NAFTA Rules of Origin Regulations, and any subsequent processing in the other NAFTA country does not increase the transaction value of the goods by more than seven percent; otherwise indicate "JNT" for joint production. *(Reference: Annex 302.2)*

FIELD 11: This field must be completed, signed, and dated by the exporter. When the Certificate is completed by the producer for use by the exporter, it must be completed, signed, and dated by the producer. The date must be the date the Certificate was completed and signed.

CBP Form 434 (04/11)

the NAFTA claim at the time of import, the importer or its agent must have a copy of the NAFTA certificate of origin. If the goods qualify but the certificate of origin is not available, then the importer should not make the claim. It has up to one year from the date of import in which to file a petition and obtain a refund of duties on the imported goods. Note that it is an obligation of the producer to obtain underlying certification for all of its raw materials, components, and subassemblies. Even if the goods are acquired in the country of manufacture, that does not mean those goods are originating. Each vendor to the producer must also conduct its own due diligence to ensure that the declaration provided to the exporter is correct. It should be noted that there are separate rules of origin for textiles and apparel under NAFTA and an importer should consult with legal counsel or a textile and apparel expert to review the origin options.

b. The Other Free Trade Agreements

The principles of NAFTA are carried over into all of the other free trade agreements that the United States has entered into and other FTAs negotiated between other countries. The essence of origin still comes down to whether a good is "wholly obtained or produced entirely" in the territory of one of the member countries—in other words, the natural resources provision. It also depends on whether the "foreign" origin components (meaning those that are not originating in one of the parties to the agreement) undergo the requisite tariff shift or tariff shift plus regional value content rule of origin set out for the finished product. There may be additional preference criteria, so it is important to check the specific agreements.

Although the basic premise for determining origin is the same, the rules in the different FTAs are not always the same. For example, the spice saffron is classified under HTS subheading 0910.20. The rule of origin under NAFTA is "A change to subheading 0910.20 from any other chapter," while for the U.S.–Singapore FTA, the rule is "A change to headings 0902 through 0910 from any other chapter." Meanwhile, the rule of origin for the U.S.–Korea FTA is:

a. A change to crushed, ground or powdered spices of subheadings 0910.20 through 0910.99 from spices that are not crushed, ground, or powdered of subheadings 0910.20 through 0910.99, or from any other subheading; or

b. A change to mixtures of spices or any good of subheadings 0910.20 through 0910.99 other than crushed, ground or powdered spices from any other subheading.

So it is always important to make sure that the correct rule of origin is used in determining whether a product is eligible or not.

Another difference between NAFTA and the other FTAs is that they may or may not require a specific certificate of origin format. A generic certificate of origin may be used instead. (See Figures 11–2, 11–3, and 11–4 for sample certificates of origin.)

The third difference has to do with the de minimis value. It is 10 percent under the other FTAs that the United States has negotiated, and other foreign FTAs may have a different de minimis percentage as well.

Finally, the regional value content in the other FTAs that the United States has negotiated is based on a "build-up methodology" or a "build-down methodology." For the build-down method, you begin with the "adjusted value" and subtract the value of the non-originating materials, divide by the adjusted value, and multiply by 100 to get the RVC percentage. For the build-up method, you begin with the value of the materials and divide by the adjusted value, then multiply by 100 to get the RVC percentage. In general, the "value of the material" that is produced is the value of all expenses incurred in the production of the material, including general expenses and an amount for profit equal to the profit added in the normal course of trade. The value of materials should be adjusted as follows:

<u>Adjusted value</u>

For originating materials, the following expenses should be added to the value of the originating materials:

- The costs of freight, insurance, packaging and other costs incurred in transporting the goods within or between the territories of the parties to the location of the producer.

- Duties, taxes, brokerage fees on the material paid into the territories of the parties.

- The costs of waste or spoilage resulting from the use of the materials in production, less the value of renewable scrap or byproducts.

For non-originating materials the following expenses may be deducted from the value of the non-originating materials:

- The costs of freight, insurance, packaging and other costs incurred in transporting the goods within or between the territories of the parties to the location of the producer.

- Duties, taxes, brokerage fees on the material paid into the territories of the parties.

- The costs of waste or spoilage resulting from the use of the materials in production, less the value of renewable scrap or byproducts.

Figure 11–2. Generic certificate of origin.

CERTIFICATE OF ORIGIN
FOR GENERAL USE

The undersigned _____
(Owner or Agent, or Co.)

for_____ declares
(Name and Address of Shipper)

that the following mentioned goods shipped on _____
(Name of Ship)

on the date _____ consigned to _____

_____ are the product of the United States of America.

MARKS AND NUMBERS	NO. OF PKGS. BOXES OR CASES	WEIGHT IN KILOS		DESCRIPTION
		GROSS	NET	

STATE OF
COUNTY OF

Sworn to before me
this _____ day of _____ 20 _____ _____
(Signature of Owner or Agent)

The _____
a recognized Chamber of Commerce under the laws of the State of _____, has examined the
manufacturer's invoice or shipper's affidavit concerning the origin of the merchandise and, according to the best of its knowledge and belief,
finds that the products named originated in the United States of America.

Secretary_____

FORM X101 REV. 01/00

APPERSON PRINT MANAGEMENT SERVICES
(800) 438-0182

Reset Form

Figure 11–3. Certificate of origin for the U.S.–Chile Free Trade Agreement.

UNITED STATES - CHILE FREE TRADE AGREEMENT
TRATADO DE LIBRE COMERCIO CHILE - ESTADOS UNIDOS
CERTIFICATE OF ORIGIN

Field 1: Exporter Name and Address	Field 2: Blanket Period for Multiple Entries
	From:
	To:
Tax Identification Number:	

Field 3: Producer Name and Address	Field 4: Importer Name and Address
Tax Identification Number:	Tax Identification Number

Field 5: Description of Good(s)	Field 6: HS Tariff Classification Number	Field 7: Preference Criterion	Field 8: Producer	Field 9: Regional Value Content	Field 10: Country of Origin

Field 11: Certification of Origin

I CERTIFY THAT:
- THE INFORMATION ON THIS DOCUMENT IS TRUE AND ACCURATE AND I ASSUME THE RESPONSIBILITY FOR PROVIDING SUCH REPRESENTATIONS. I UNDERSTAND THAT I AM LIABLE FOR ANY FALSE STATEMENTS OR MATERIAL OMISSIONS MADE ON OR IN CONNECTION WITH THIS DOCUMENT.
- I AGREE TO MAINTAIN AND PRESENT UPON REQUEST, DOCUMENTATION NECESSARY TO SUPPORT THIS CERTIFICATE, AND TO INFORM, IN WRITING, ALL PERSONS TO WHOM THE CERTIFICATE WAS GIVEN OF ANY CHANGES THAT COULD AFFECT THE ACCURACY OR VALIDITY OF THIS CERTIFICATE.
- THE GOODS ORIGINATED IN THE TERRITORY OF THE PARTIES, AND COMPLY WITH THE ORIGIN REQUIREMENTS SPECIFIED FOR THOSE GOODS IN THE UNITED STATES-CHILE FREE TRADE AGREEMENT, AND UNLESS SPECIFICALLY EXEMPTED IN ARTICLE 4.11, THERE HAS BEEN NO FURTHER PRODUCTION OR ANY OTHER OPERATION OUTSIDE THE TERRITORIES OF THE PARTIES.

Authorized Signature	Company Name
Name (Print or Type)	Title
Date (MM/DD/YY)	Telephone / Fax

Field 12: Remarks

Figure 11–4. Certificate of origin for the Central America–Dominican Republic–United States Free Trade Agreement.

Central America-Dominican Republic-United States Free Trade Agreement	Tratado de Libre Comercio entre Centroamérica, República Dominicana y los Estados Unidos Page 1 of 1
1. Exporter's name, address and tax identification number: Nombre, dirección y número de registro fiscal del exportador: Tax Identification Number:	**2. Blanket Period:** Periodo que cubre: From | D | M | Y-A To | D | M | Y-A De A
3. Producer's name, address and tax identification number: Nombre, dirección y número de registro fiscal del productor: Tax Identification Number:	**4. Importer's name, address and tax identification number:** Nombre, dirección y número de registro fiscal del importador: Tax Identification Number:

5. Description of Good(s) - Descripción de la(s) mercancia(s)	6. HS Tariff Classification Clasificación arancelaria	7. Preferential tariff treatment criteria Criterio para trato arancelario preferencial	8. Other criteria Otros criterious	9. Producer Productor

10. Remarks:
    Observaciones:

11. Under oath I certify that:

- The information on this document is true and accurate and I assume the responsibility for proving such representations. I understand that I am liable for any false statements or material omissions made on or in connection with this document.

- I agree to maintain, and present upon request, documentation necessary to support this certification, and to inform, in writing, all persons to whom the certification was given of any changes that would affect the accuracy or validity of this Certification.

- The goods originated in the territory of one or more of the Parties, and comply with the origin requirements specified for those goods in the Central America - Dominican Republic - United States Free Trade Agreement, and that there has been no further processing or any other operation outside the territories of the Parties, other than unloading, reloading, or any other operation necessary to preserve the goods in good condition or to transport the good to the territory of a Party.

Declaro bajo juramento que:

- La información contenida en este documento es verdadera y exacta y me hago responsable de comprobar lo aquí certificado. Estoy consciente que soy responsable por cualquier declaración falsa u omisión material hecha en o relacionada con el presente documento.

- Me comprometo a conservar y presentar, en caso de ser requerido, los documentos necesarios que respalden el contenido de la presente certificación, así como a notificar por escrito a todas las personas a quienes se ha entregado la presente certificación, de cualquier cambio que pudiera afectar la exactitud o validez del mismo.

- Las mercancías son originarias del territorio de una o más Partes y cumplen con todos los requisitos de origen que les son aplicables conforme al Tratado de Libre Comercio entre Centroamérica, República Dominicana y Estados Unidos, y que no han sido objeto de procesamiento ulterior o de cualquier otra operacion fuera de los territorios de las Partes, excepto la descarga, recarga o cualquier otra operación necesaria para mantener la mercancía en buena condición o para transportarla a terrirtorio de una Parte.

This Certification consists of [1] pages, including all attachments.
Esta Certificacion se compone, de   hojas incluyendo todos sus anexos.

Authorized Signature - Firma autorizada	Company - Empresa
Name - Nombre	Title - Cargo
Date - Fecha | D | M | Y-A Telephone Teléfono	Fax

- The cost of processing incurred in the territory in the production of the non-originating material in the territories; and

- The cost of originating materials used in the product of the non-originating material in the territory of the parties.

As you can see, the calculations for the RVC are different for the other U.S. FTAs and may be different for the other non-U.S. FTAs.

B. Country of Origin Marking Laws

Country of origin marking is not required by most countries as they generally rely on consumer regulations to address issues; there does seem to be a requirement in most countries for labeling food and beverages. Some countries, like Canada, Australia, and Mexico, require only retail goods to be marked with the country of origin. The European Union has made several attempts at instituting a country of origin marking program, but it has not moved forward with it. As a general principle, the requirements of most countries are simply that there cannot be any false statements, so whatever is declared should be true and accurate. The basic premise of substantial transformation as discussed in Section A(1) above applies. It is, therefore, important that exporters should determine the specific requirements prior to exportation of their products as the products may be restricted without the proper labeling.

U.S. Customs established the first country of origin marking rule in 1890 and has developed extensive marking regulations since then. The requirement, according to the Tariff Act of 1930, is that "every article of foreign origin imported into the United States must be marked in a conspicuous place as legibly, indelibly, and permanently as the nature of the article (or container) will permit . . . to indicate to an ultimate purchaser in the United States the English name of the country of origin at the time of importation into the Customs territory of the United States." There are multiple exceptions to the rules. Some of the most common are that the articles are incapable of being marked (e.g. feathers); the articles cannot be marked without injury to them; it is economically unfeasible to mark them prior to import; the importer is going to use the articles for its own purposes without reselling them; and the articles are going to be further processed in the United States for a reason other than concealing the origin. However, if articles are exempted from marking, the container must be marked. In addition, if a container is reusable, then it must also be marked with the country of origin, which may result in their being two origins listed on the container. For example, a barrel of oil could be marked "Oil Made in Saudi Arabia; Barrel Made in China." If the container is disposable—such as bags, boxes, and cans—then the marking should be about the contents. There is also the J-list, exemptions for articles that are incapable of being marked, such as works of art, burlap, buttons, eggs, feathers, cut flowers, newsprint, and rope. However, for these articles, the outermost container that reaches the consumer should be marked with the country of origin. There are also articles that are going to be repacked after arrival in the United States. Say, for example, that the goods are shipped in bulk and are going to be repackaged into blister packs for the retail market. These articles may enter the United States with only the cartons marked as to the country of origin. However, there must be a "repacking" certificate prepared for U.S. Customs that states to the repacker that the goods will be marked with the country of origin in accordance with the law. (See Figure 11–5.)

In some instances, U.S. Customs has determined how an article must be marked. For example, Customs has stated that some articles must be marked by cast-in-the-mold lettering, by etching (acid or electrolytic), by engraving, or by metal plates that are securely attached to the article. Examples of these types of articles are knives, forks, cleavers, clippers, scissors, dental instruments, and pliers. Watches, clocks, and timing apparatuses also have specific origin markings.

If the article has a U.S. address on it, the country of origin marking must be in close proximity to that address and in the same font and size, so that the consumer is not confused into believing that the product is of U.S. origin simply because of the U.S. address.

If an article is imported without the proper marking, there can be a marking penalty of 10 percent of the value of the good assessed by U.S. Customs. In addition, the good has to be marked properly before Customs will release it into the commerce of the United States.

1. *Country of Origin for Marking Purposes*

While it would seem logical that the country of origin for preferential duties would be the same as that for country of origin marking, that is not always the case, particularly in the United States. If a product is not wholly grown or produced in one country, the general principle is that the country of origin for marking purposes is going to be the country where the last substantial transformation takes place. See Section I(A) above. However, there are plenty of exceptions to this rule.

Figure 11–5. Repacking certificate.

(Port of entry) I, _____ of _____, certify that if the article(s) covered by this entry (entry no.(s) __ dated __), is (are) repacked in retail container(s) (e.g., blister packs), while still in my possession, the new container(s) will not conceal or obscure the country of origin marking appearing on the article(s), or else the new container(s), unless excepted, shall be marked in a conspicuous place as legibly, indelibly, and permanently as the nature of the container(s) will permit, in such manner as to indicate the country of origin of the article(s) to the ultimate purchaser(s) in accordance with the requirements of 19 U.S.C. 1304 and 19 CFR Part 134. I further certify that if the article(s) is (are) intended to be sold or transferred by me to a subsequent purchaser or repacker, I will notify such purchaser or transferee, in writing, at the time of sale or transfer, of the marking requirements. Date _____ / Importer _____

---

2. *NAFTA Country of Origin Marking Rules*

In the United States, there are separate country of origin marking rules for NAFTA products. These rules are also based on a tariff shift principle, but there are no regional value content requirements. The rules can be found in 19 CFR Part 102. For example, take the catchall classification for other plastic articles not provided elsewhere under 3926.90. The rule of origin for preferential duty purposes is as follows:

> A change to subheading 3926.90 from any other heading, except from appliances for ostomy use of subheading 3006.91.
>
> In addition, the regional value content must be not less than:
>
>   1. 60 percent where the transaction value method is used, or
>   2. 50 percent where the net cost method is used.

However, the NAFTA rule of origin for marking purposes reads:

> A change to heading 3922 through 3926 from any other subheading, including another heading within that group, except for a change to heading 3926 from articles of apparel and clothing accessories, other articles of plastics, or articles of other materials of headings 3901 to 3914 of heading 9619

Because the NAFTA rule of origin doesn't require a regional value content, it is possible for the raw materials or components to make the requisite tariff shift and the merchandise could be considered Mexican or Canadian for the marking rules, but the finished good would not be eligible for preferential duty treatment.

3. *Other Free Trade Agreement Marking Rules*

Only NAFTA has a specific set of rules for marking. The other free trade agreements that the United States has entered into follow the general substantial transformation marking rules discussed above.

As in the preferential duty provisions, textiles and apparel have their own country of origin marking rules, in addition to Federal Trade Commission rules regarding content and handling instructions that are too detailed to go into here. An importer should contact legal counsel or a textile and apparel consultant before importing to ensure that the marking is correct.

C. Federal Trade Commission Rules on "Made in the USA" Marking

The Federal Trade Commission (FTC) controls the requirements for marking a product "Made in the USA." In fact, with very few exceptions (automobiles, textiles, and wool and fur products), there is no law that requires articles to be marked "Made in the USA." Generally, companies want to mark their products to be of U.S. origin because they want consumers to purchase those products based on their U.S. origin, which is considered a marketing cachet. So the FTC has established a standard to ensure that consumers are not fooled into thinking a product is of U.S. origin when it is not. If a product is said to be "Made in the USA" without any qualifying statement, then the product must be "all or virtually all" made in the United States. Basically, the essence of the standard is that all of the significant parts and all of the manufacturing or processing must be of U.S. origin. The finished good should contain "no or negligible foreign content." There is no specific percentage as to what is considered negligible, and the FTC does not give out rulings on this. Many companies have adopted minimal percentages of foreign content as an internal guideline. The FTC also reviews advertising materials, labels, and other promotional materials including marketing through the Internet or through emails to ensure that there are no marks or references that might be confusing, such as an American flag or reference to a U.S. address or headquarters that might trick the consumer into believing the products are of U.S. origin. Phrases such as "true American quality" or a reference to a company being "born in the USA" might imply that the products are of U.S. origin when they are manufactured elsewhere. Companies that use "American" in their name should be particularly careful with markings so as to be clear when the products do not meet this very tough standard. It should be noted that "manufactured," "produced," "created," or other similar terms should not be used unless they meet the standard as well.

However, the FTC has stated that businesses may use a qualified "Made in the USA" statement, such as "Made in the USA with Chinese components" or "Manufactured in the USA with foreign components." It is not necessary to state the origin of the components, just to alert the consumer that while the product is made or manufactured in the United States, there are foreign components. A company may also state something along the lines of "75 percent U.S. content" or "Assembled in the USA with foreign components." Needless to say, whatever statements are made, they must be truthful and the company must be able to substantiate them. Most enforcement cases come from competitors that contact the FTC through its commercial fraud hotline. See the FTC's web site for more information at http://business.ftc.gov/advertising-and-marketing/made-usa.

D. Government Procurement

Providing goods to government agencies, bureaus, commissions, and armed forces is an extremely lucrative business, and most companies would love to be able to bid on such contracts. However, governments are fiercely loyal to homegrown businesses and endeavor to source domestically whenever possible. Free trade agreements between countries have generally included government procurement provisions that allow the member countries equal access to government contracts as domestic manufacturers when contracts exceed certain financial levels. In addition, there is the World Trade Organization Agreement on Government Procurement, which as of this writing has forty-three signatories (including the United States) and twenty-eight observers, most of which are in the process of ascension to the agreement.

1. The Buy American Act

As in most countries, the U.S. government has a relatively broad restriction on government purchases for use in the United States, requiring those goods to meet the criteria of the Buy American Act. The Buy American Act applies to the acquisition of foreign supplies and construction materials for contracts performed only *inside* the United States. The Buy American Act requires that goods must meet one of two definitions:

1. An unmanufactured end product mined or produced in the United States; or
2. An end product that is manufactured in the United States if:

    i. The cost of its components mined, produced, or manufactured in the United States exceeds 50 percent of the cost of all its components. Components of foreign origin of the same class or kind as those that the agency determines are not mined, produced, or manufactured in sufficient and reasonably available commercial quantities of a satisfactory quality are treated as domestic. Scrap generated, collected, and prepared for processing in the United States is considered domestic; or

    ii. The end product is a COTS (commercial off-the-shelf) item.

The same rules apply for supply contracts or construction contracts in the United States.

There are some exceptions to the Buy American Act requirements: (a) public interest; (b) nonavailability; (c) unreasonable cost; (d) resale for commissary use; and (e) information technology that is a commercial item. The public interest exception is very rare and applies only when the U.S. government issues a blanket exemption to a foreign country under a specific agreement. As for nonavailability, if the articles, materials, or supplies are not available in sufficient quantities or of a satisfactory quality, then the Buy American Act does not apply. There is currently a list of products for which a nonavailability determination has been made. The list contains items such as anise, bananas, cashew nuts, chrome ore or chromite, industrial or abrasive diamonds, crude rubber or latex, and tungsten. The list does not mean that there is no domestic source for them but that the domestic sources can meet only 50 percent or less of the demand. However, if a contracting officer learns that there is sufficient supply, then this exception does not apply. It is also possible to obtain a determination of nonavailability by submitting a written request with supporting documentation to provide evidence that the products are not available from domestic sources. Unreasonable cost is the primary method used for obtaining a waiver of the Buy American Act. The contracting officer must review all bids received from both domestic and foreign suppliers. If the foreign supplier is the lowest bid, then the contracting officer must add either 12 percent or 6 percent to the price of that bid and compare it to the lowest domestic bid; 12 percent is added if the lowest domestic bid is from a small business concern, and 6 percent is added if the lowest domestic bid is from a large business concern, as defined by the Small Business Administration. If the foreign bid is still lower than the lowest domestic bid, then the contracting officer may go with the foreign offer. Acquisitions for resale in commissaries are exempt, and information technology that is a commercial item is also exempt. These provisions are self-explanatory.

The contract will include a specific clause requiring the bidder to attest that the products supplied to the government are in compliance with the Buy American Act.

Commercial off-the-shelf (COTS) goods are a unique exception to the Buy American Act. These are items of supply or construction that are customarily used by the general public or non-governmental entities in the general marketplace. Such an item may have minor modifications, but those modifications do not alter the essential character of physical characteristics of the item. This category does not include bulk items such as agricultural or petroleum products. There is a waiver of the component test above for COTS items. Thus, there is no requirement for at least 50 percent of the cost to be U.S. origin, only that the COTS item *must* be manufactured in the United States. The raw materials and components can be sourced from anywhere.

Although review of the contracts is possible, enforcement generally originates when a competitor questions the authenticity of the claims by the winning bidder. If the bidder needs to subcontract out portions of the project, then each subcontractor will have to supply the general contractor (bidder) with evidence as to compliance with the Buy American Act as well. Also, the certification alone will be insufficient without each contractor and subcontractor maintaining the records to prove eligibility. As to remedies for noncompliance, the contracting officer may require the contractor to remove at its own expense all products that do not comply and replace them with compliant products. In addition, the contracting officer must include the contractor into the database kept on all suppliers that will restrict the possibility of bidding in the future. If performance failures are prolonged or repeated, the contractor can be suspended or debarred completely from bidding on future projects.

2. The Trade Agreements Act and the WTO Agreement on Government Procurement

The previously mentioned WTO Agreement on Government Procurement (GPA) is a plurilateral treaty administered by the Committee on Government Procurement made up of the WTO member parties. Because government acquisition generally represents a large portion of the gross domestic product of any country, there has been great interest in the opportunities available for supplying goods to foreign governments. As a result, the WTO GPA went into effect in 1996. See the WTO web site for more information: http://www.wto.org/english/tratop_e/gproc_e/gp_gpa_e.htm.

In addition to the WTO GPA, there are bilateral and multilateral agreements currently in place and in negotiation that may also have contain equilateral government procurement provisions. The United States has entered into numerous FTAs over the years, which all have government procurement provisions allowing foreign countries access to U.S. government procurement contracts, as well as granting U.S. companies equal access to foreign government procurement contracts. The Trade Agreements Act establishes the policy for these trading partners. The Trade Agreements Act applies to supplies, services, and construction contracts both inside and outside the United States. It does not apply to acquisitions that are set aside for small businesses; the acquisitions of arms, ammunitions, and war materials; and purchases for U.S. national security or national defense purposes. It does not apply to end products that are for resale; it also does not apply to acquisitions made from Federal Prison Industries, or from nonprofit agencies employing people who are blind or severely disabled. In general, the Trade Agreements Act is applicable to contracts that exceed a certain threshold level. In those instances, the contracting officer must accept bids from domestic sources and trading partners alike without the addition of any extra percentages to the foreign bids.

The value of the acquisition determines whether the Trade Agreements Act applies; the U.S. Trade Representative has been granted the authority to determine the dollar thresholds. The thresholds are subject to review every two years. The contracting officer is the party that determines whether the contract is above the threshold or not. It is the total acquisition cost that is analyzed against the threshold levels. Like the Buy American Act, there is a Trade Agreements Act clause that requires certification by the prime contract, and therefore any subcontractors should also provide similar certifications and maintain records to support those certifications to the prime contractor. The 2014–2015 rates are shown in Figure 11–6. For acquisitions that are covered by the WTO GPA, the least developed countries' end products, services, or construction materials must be treated as eligible products.

Origin for the Trade Agreements Act is based on the substantial transformation test, which is defined in the act as the "transforming of an article into a new and different article of commerce, with a name, character or use distinct from the original article." Thus, the country of the last substantial transformation is the country of origin for determining eligibility under the Trade Agreements Act. This determination can actually be a very complex one, and so the act authorizes the U.S. Customs and Border Protection to issue advisory opinions or final determinations, which are judicially binding. A company wishing to confirm the origin may request a ruling by providing a list of all materials with their origins, all processes undertaken and in which countries, the complexity of the processes, the degree of expertise required for each task, the number of man-hours, etc. Once Customs makes a determination, it is published in the Federal Register for a notice and comment period. Remedies are the same as those identified under the Buy American Act above.

Figure 11–6. 2014–2015 Trade Agreements Act thresholds.

Trade Agreement	Supply Contract (equal to or exceeding)	Service Contract (equal to or exceeding)	Construction Contract (equal to or exceeding)
WTO GPA	**$204,000**	**$204,000**	**$7,864,000**
FTAs			
Australia FTA Bahrain FTA	79,507	79,507	7,864,000
CAFTA-DR	204,000	204,000	10,335,931
(Costa Rica, Dominican Republic, El Salvador, Guatemala, Honduras, and Nicaragua)	79,507	79,507	7,864,000
Chile FTA	79,507	79,507	7,864,000
Colombia FTA	79,507	79,507	7,864,000
Korea FTA	100,000	100,000	7,864,000
Morocco FTA	204,000	204,000	7,864,000
NAFTA			
—Canada	25,000	79,507	10,335,931
—Mexico	79,507	79,507	10,335,931
Oman FTA	204,000	204,000	10,335,931
Panama	204,000	204,000	7,864,000
Peru FTA	204,000	204,000	7,864,000
Singapore FTA	79,507	79,507	7,864,000
Israeli Trade Act	50,000	—	—

3.   Other Buy American–Type Requirements

There are a number of other agencies that have Buy American–type provisions with different requirements. Each federal agency can set its own criteria, although generally they follow the two main agreements discussed above. In addition, state laws may also institute Buy American–type requirements into their contracts.

a.   Buy America

Buy America (note the distinction from the Buy American Act in the lack of the letter *n* for "America") is a Department of Transportation program that is designed to ensure that transportation infrastructure projects use American-made products. Thus, any state or federal agency requesting money from the Department of Transportation for transportation purposes must fulfill the requirements of the Buy America program. According to the Department of Transportation, "the Secretary of Transportation shall not obligate any funds unless all iron, steel and manufactured products used in such project are produced in the United States." The program includes the Federal Aviation Administration, the Federal Highway Administration, the Federal Railroad Administration, the National Railroad Passenger Corporation (Amtrak), and the Federal Transit Administration. Although each of these agencies has slightly different requirements under the program, the essence is the same. They each require that all steel and iron manufacturing processes must take place in the United States, except metallurgical processes involving the refinement of steel. These requirements apply to all construction materials made of those materials and used in infrastructure projects including transit and maintenance facilities, rail lines, and bridges. In order for a manufactured product to be considered a U.S. product, it must be manufactured in the United States and all components of the product must be of U.S. origin (which means they must be manufactured in the United States); however, subcomponents may of any origin. This is a very high standard to fulfill. These requirements do not apply to rolling stock (such as buses, train control, communication, and traction power equipment). For rolling stock, if the cost of components produced in the United States is more than 60 percent of the cost of all components and final assembly takes place in the United States, then the goods meet the requirements of the Buy America program. There is also certification required by the supplier attesting to the compliance of the products to the Buy America requirements. There are also waivers available: public interest, nonavailability, and price-differential.

b.   The Berry Amendment

The Berry Amendment applies to the Department of Defense and restricts funding for procurement to domestically produced food, clothing, fabrics, and certain finished goods made of textile materials. Specifically, the products must have been grown, re-processed, reused, or produced in the United States for the following items:

- Clothing and the materials and components thereof, other than sensors, electronics, or other items added to, and not normally associated with, clothing and the materials and components thereof. Clothing includes items such as outerwear, headwear, underwear, nightwear, footwear, hosiery, handwear, belts, badges, and insignia.
- Tents and the structural components of tents, including tarpaulins and covers.
- Cotton and other natural fiber products.
- Woven silk or woven silk blends.
- Spun silk yarn for cartridge cloth.
- Synthetic fabric or coated synthetic fabric, including all textile fibers and yarns that are for use in such fabrics.
- Canvas products.
- Wool (whether in the form of fiber or yarn or contained in fabrics, materials or manufactured articles).
- Any item of individual equipment (Federal Supply Class 8465) manufactured from or containing such fibers, yarns, fabrics, or materials that are manufactured in the United States.

There are exceptions to the Berry Amendment, including prime contracts, which are the main contracts between the government and the Department of Defense, that are below the Simplified Acquisition Threshold, which is currently at a maximum of $150,000. The Simplified Acquisition Threshold is for small value contracts in order to simplify the government acquisition process. There are exceptions for domestic nonavailability; emergency acquisitions for activities and personnel outside the United States; acquisitions to support combat operations; acquisitions for commissary resale; and acquisitions by vessels in foreign waters. Applications can be filed for nonavailability waivers.

Other agencies may have other Buy American–type requirements, both at the federal and state level. Generally, the bidder will know that such requirements exist because the bid requires a certification attesting that the bidder will comply with the regulations. It is up to the party bidding to confirm that there are any specific origin requirements.

Notes

1. The United States is signatory to free trade agreements with several countries, including Australia, Bahrain, Canada, Chile, Colombia, Costa Rica, the Dominican Republic, El Salvador, Guatemala, Honduras, Israel, Jordan, Mexico, Morocco, Nicaragua, Oman, Panama, Peru, Singapore, and South Korea.

2. Imports from Cuba and North Korea are currently prohibited without a license from the Office of Foreign Assets Control, Department of the Treasury, and there is a general policy of denial. However, if the imports were allowed, they would be subject to the high duty rates listed in Column 2 under "Rates of Duty" of the Harmonized Tariff Schedule of the United States. (See Figure 9–2.)

3. http://www.cbp.gov/linkhandler/cgov/trade/trade_programs/audits/focused_assessment/fap_documents/exh4f.ctt/exh4f.pdf

   http://www.cbp.gov/sites/default/files/documents/FA%20Document.pdf

Part V
Specialized Exporting and Importing

Chapter 12

Specialized Exporting and Importing

The transactions described in this part of the book are distinguished by the fact that they involve a combination of both exporting and importing. Several such transactions are described in this chapter.

A. Drawback

Drawback is a program administered by the U.S. Customs and Border Protection that permits a refund of 99 percent of the U.S. customs duties paid on merchandise that has been imported into the United States and is thereafter exported. (Certain duties, such as antidumping duties, are not eligible for drawback.) Several types of drawback programs exist. As with any of these programs, it is necessary to work with experts in the field to ensure that all the requirements are met in order to obtain the refunds.

1. *Unused Drawback*

The first type of drawback is for goods that have not been used while they are in the United States. Perhaps they were imported with the intent to sell them in the United States, but instead a buyer was found in another country. Or perhaps the merchandise is going to be destroyed; it was imported and duty was paid, but the merchandise was unfit for any purpose. If the goods have not been used, the exporter can file a onetime drawback claim within three years of the date of import through its customs broker. This is considered a direct identification drawback program. The goods that were imported are the exact same goods as those that are exported or destroyed; therefore, the exporter must be able to maintain the proper documentation to trace the goods from the import to the export or destruction. At least two days prior to export (seven days if the exporter intends to destroy the merchandise under the supervision of Customs), the exporter must file a Notice of Intent to Export, Destroy, or Return Merchandise for Purposes of Drawback, with U.S. Customs. (See Figure 12–1.) This gives Customs the option to examine the merchandise prior to export or to witness the destruction. If Customs decides not to examine the goods or witness the destruction, it will notify the broker to go ahead with the export or destruction. If Customs decides to examine the goods, they have to be moved to a Customs Exam Station prior to export or to a place of destruction where Customs can be present. If Customs does not receive the Notice of Intent prior to either action, the drawback claim will be denied. Drawback claims (see Figure 12–2) may be filed within three years after the date of export or destruction.

There is also an option to file for a substitution unused drawback claim. This means that the exporter can substitute domestic goods that are commercially interchangeable with the imported merchandise and still obtain the refund of duties. It is the exporter's obligation to prove that the goods are commercially interchangeable and to maintain the proper records to support the claim. As the determination of whether something is commercially interchangeable is not always clear-cut, the exporter can obtain a ruling from Customs to determine if the goods are commercially interchangeable. The drawback claimant may not be the importer of the goods. Perhaps the importer sold the goods to another party in the United States and that party sold them overseas. A Delivery Certificate to show the transfer of the goods from the importer to the exporter is required to track the shipment. (See Figure 12–3). It should be noted that under NAFTA, there are limitations on the types of drawback allowed on exports to Canada and Mexico.

2. *Rejected Merchandise Drawback*

This type of drawback is very similar to the unused drawback program. In this instance, a U.S. importer has received goods that did not conform to the sample or specifications or were shipped without the consent of the consignee. The exporter must provide evidence that the merchandise was defective at the time of importation or did not conform according to its order and is either being rejected for export back to the supplier or destroyed. The same Notice of Intent to Export or Destroy (Figure 12–1) is required to be filed five days prior to the export or destruction. Customs will notify the broker or exporter within two days after receipt as to whether it will examine the merchandise or waive the exam. The drawback claim (see Figure 12–2) must be filed within three years of the date of export or destruction.

Figure 12–1. Notice of Intent to Export form.

Figure 12–2. Drawback Entry form.

Figure 12–2. (continued)

Section III - Manufactured Articles

35. Quantity & Description of Merchandise Used	36. Date(s) of Manufacture or Production	37. Description of Articles Manufactured or Produced	38. Quantity and Unit of Measure	39. Factory Location

Section IV - Information on Exported or Destroyed Merchandise

PERIOD COVERED _____ TO _____

40. Exhibits to be attached for the following:

☐ Relative Value ☐ Petroleum ☐ Domestic Tax Paid Alcohol ☐ Piece Goods ☐ Waste Calculation ☐ Recycled ☐ Harbor Maintenance Fee ☐ Merchandise Processing Fee ☐ Other Taxes/Fees

41. Date (MM/DD/YYYY)	42. Action Code	43. Unique Indentifier No.	44. Name of Exporter/Destroyer	45. Description of Articles (Include Part/Style/Serial Numbers)	46. Quantity and Unit of Measure	47. Export Destination	48. HTSUS No.

Section V - Declarations

☐ Same condition to NAFTA countries - The undersigned herein certifies that the merchandise herein described is in the same condition as when it was imported under above import entry(ies) and further certifies that this merchandise was not subjected to any process of manufacturer or other operation except the following allowable operations:

☐ The undersigned hereby certifies that the merchandise herein described is unused in the United States and further certifies that this merchandise was not subjected to any process of manufacture or other operation except the following allowable operations:

☐ The undersigned hereby certifies that the merchandise herein described is commercially interchangeable with the designated imported merchandise and further certifies that the substituted merchandise is unused in the United States and that the substituted merchandise was in our possession prior to exportation or destruction.

☐ Merchandise does not conform to sample or specifications. ☐ Merchandise was defective at time of importation. ☐ Merchandise was shipped without consent of the consignee.

☐ The undersigned hereby certifies that the merchandise herein described is the same kind and quality as defined in 19 U.S.C. 1313(p)(3)(B), with the designated imported merchandise or the article manufactured or produced under 1313(a) or (b), as appropriate.

☐ The article(s) described above were manufactured or produced and disposed of as stated herein in accordance with the drawback ruling on file with CBP and in compliance with applicable laws and regulations.

The undersigned acknowledges statutory requirements that all records supporting the information on this document are to be retained by the issuing party for a period of three years from the date of payment of the drawback claim. The undersigned is fully aware of the sanctions provided in 18 U.S.C. 1001 and 18 U.S.C. 550 and 19 U.S.C. 1593a.

I declare that according to the best of my knowledge and belief, all of the statements in this document are correct and that the exported article is not to be relanded in the United States or any of its possessions without paying duty.

☐ Member of Firm with Power of Attorney ☐ Officer of Corporation ☐ Broker with Power of Attorney

Printed Name and Title _____   Signature and Date _____

CBP Form 7551 (07/08)

Figure 12–3. Delivery Certificate form.

OMB 1651-0075 Exp. 10/31/2011

DEPARTMENT OF HOMELAND SECURITY
U.S. Customs and Border Protection

DELIVERY CERTIFICATE FOR PURPOSES OF DRAWBACK
19 CFR 191

☐ Certificate of Delivery
☐ Certificate of Manufacture and Delivery

| 1. CM&D No. | 2. Port Code | 3. DBK Ruling No. |
| 4. Type Code | 5. ID No. of Transferor |

PAPERWORK REDUCTION ACT NOTICE: This request is in accordance with the Paperwork Reduction Act. We ask for the information in order to carry out U.S. Department of Homeland Security laws and regulations, to determine the eligibility for refund of taxes on domestic alcohol (if applicable), and to determine the proper amount of drawback. Your response is required to obtain or retain a benefit. The estimated average burden associated with this collection of information is 33 minutes per respondent depending on individual circumstances. Comments concerning the accuracy of this burden estimate and suggestions for reducing this burden should be directed to U.S. Customs and Border Protection, Asset Management, Washington, DC 20229, and to the Office of Management and Budget, Paperwork Reduction Project. (1651-0075) Washington, DC 20503.

RECEIVED DATE

6. FROM TRANSFEROR:
Company Name and Complete Address

7. TO TRANSFEREE:
Company Name and Complete Address

IMPORTED DUTY PAID, DESIGNATED MERCHANDISE OR DRAWBACK PRODUCT

8. Use	9. Import Entry or CM&D Number	10. Port Code	11. Import Date (MM/DD/YYYY)	12. CD	13. (If using 1313(b)) A. Date(s) Received	B. Date(s) Used	14. Date Delivered	15. HTSUS No.	16. Description of Merchandise (Include Part/Style/Serial Numbers)	17. Quantity & Unit of Measure	18. Entered Value Per Unit	19. 100% Duty

20. Total

PREPARER

Phone Number _____ Ext. _____

FAX Number _____

21. Contact Name and Address

CBP Form 7552 (07/08)

Figure 12–3. *(continued)*

22. Quantity & Description of Merchandise Used	23. Date(s) of Manufacture (MM/DD/YYYY)	24. Description of Articles Manufactured or Produced (Include Part/Style/Serial Numbers)	25. Quantity & Unit of Measure	26. Date Delivered

27. Duty Available on Manufacture Articles (Total of Duties in Block 20)	28. Drawback Available Per Unit of Measure on Manufactured Article		29. Factory Location	

30. Exhibits to be attached for the following:
☐ Relative Value   ☐ Petroleum   ☐ Domestic Tax Paid Alcohol   ☐ Piece Goods   ☐ Waste Calculation   ☐ Recycled   ☐ Harbor Maintenance Fee   ☐ Merchandise Processing Fee   ☐ Other Taxes/Fees

31. STATUS - Import Entries listed on this form are subject to (If CD, identify on this form; if CM&D, identify on coding sheet):
☐ Reconciliation   ☐ 19 USC 1514, Protest   ☐ 19 USC 1520 (c)(1)   ☐ 19 USC 1520 (d)

DECLARATIONS

☐ The merchandise transferred on this CD is the imported merchandise.

☐ The merchandise transferred on this CD is pursuant to 19 U.S.C. 1313(j)(2) and will not be designated for any other Drawback purposes.

☐ The article(s) described above were manufactured or produced and delivered as stated herein in accordance with the Drawback ruling on file with CBP and in compliance with applicable laws and regulations.

☐ This Certificate of Delivery is a subsequent transfer and the merchandise is the same as received.

> **The undersigned acknowledges statutory requirements that all records supporting the information on this document are to be retained by the issuing party for a period of three years from the date of payment of the related drawback entry.**
>
> **Assignment of Rights is transferred when this form is prepared as a CD or CM&D.**
>
> **I declare that according to the best of my knowledge and belief, all of the statements in this document are correct and I am fully aware of the sanctions provided in18 U.S.C.1001 and 18 U.S.C. 550 and 19 U.S.C. 1593a.**

☐ Member of Firm with Power of Attorney   ☐ Officer of Corporation   ☐ Broker with Power of Attorney

Signature and Date

Printed Name and Title

CBP Form 7552 (07/08)

3. Manufacturing Drawback

Under a manufacturing drawback, merchandise may be imported by a manufacturer and used as a raw material, component, or subassembly in manufacturing a finished product in the United States that is then exported. There are two types of manufacturing drawback: direct identification and substitution. Direct identification requires that the manufacturer be able to trace the imported material from importation through each step of the manufacturing process to the end product through its documentation to prove that the imported material is in a specific exported end product. In order to encourage U.S. manufacturers to use U.S.-origin raw materials and components, Congress also provided for substitution drawback. In this type of drawback, the U.S. manufacturer imports a foreign-origin raw material or component and may decide to substitute a U.S.-origin raw material or component of the *same kind and quality* in the manufacturing process. Under this substitution process, the manufacturer can still claim a refund of duties on the imported raw materials or components even though they may not have been used for the exported finished goods. In order to file manufacturing drawback claims, the claimant must first apply for a drawback ruling from Customs. There are two types of rulings: general and specific. General drawback rulings are available in the Customs regulations for common manufacturing processes. The claimant files a notice with Customs that it intends to operate under the guidelines of that general ruling. Specific drawback rulings are required when there is any variation to the general rules.

Anytime within three years after exportation, the exporter can file its Drawback Entry (Figure 12–2), along with evidence of exportation, which is a claim for the refund. For a manufacturing drawback claim, the merchandise for which a refund is being sought must have been imported within five years prior to the filing of the claim. (For substitution manufacturing drawback, the exported merchandise also must have been produced within three years from the time the manufacturer received the imported merchandise.)

Where the manufacturer is the exporter of the imported articles, the manufacturer files the Drawback Entry. However, where the exporter is not the manufacturer, the exporter must obtain Delivery Certificates (Figure 12–3) from the importer and each intermediate transferee and file them along with the Drawback Entry. It should be noted that the exporter is the one that is entitled to the refund of the duties, not the importer (unless the exporter has expressly assigned its right to the importer). Congress assumes that the exporter paid the customs duties as part of the price when it purchased the merchandise from the importer.

If an exporter anticipates numerous transactions in the same manner, the company may want to apply for a waiver of the prior notice, which means that the exporter does not have to notify Customs in advance of exporting, as well as apply for accelerated payment, which means that Customs pays the refund prior to reviewing the drawback claim. Customs will then verify the claim and if the records do not support it, will demand the refunded money back with interest and penalties. The manufacturer must apply for and enter into a specific drawback ruling with Customs.

B. Foreign Processing and Assembly Operations

In some circumstances, U.S. companies may wish to export U.S.-origin products to foreign countries for further manufacture, processing, or assembly, and then re-import the resulting products into the United States. Ordinarily, when the products are imported to the United States, they would be subject to U.S. customs duties on the full value of the product, notwithstanding the fact that part of the value was originally U.S.-origin products exported to that country. There are three exceptions to the general rule.

First, when goods that were originally the product of the United States (i.e., not imported) are exported, and then re-imported without having been advanced in value or improved in condition by any process of manufacture or other means while abroad, and the U.S. importer certifies that no drawback was claimed when the goods were exported, then the goods can be imported into the United States without payment of duty (under classification 9801.00.10 of the Harmonized Tariff Schedule). (A sample Foreign Shipper's Declaration and Importer's Endorsement form is shown in Figure 12–4.)

Second, when the exporter exported merchandise for alteration, repair, use abroad, replacement, or processing, when the goods are imported thereafter (under classification 9802.00.40 or 9802.00.50 of the HTS), they will not be subject to U.S. Customs duties except that duties will be assessed on the cost or value of the alterations, repairs, or processing. (A sample declaration is shown in Figure 12–5.)

Finally, an exporter that intends to export U.S.-origin commodities, assemble them abroad, and import the finished product may qualify for reduced duty under classification 9802.00.80 of the HTS. This provision, previously known as classification 807 of the Harmonized Tariff Schedule of the United States, permits only assembly operations; manufacturing operations are prohibited. Since this is a point of importance, these assembly operation programs should be discussed with and approved by Customs in advance. Sometimes Customs rulings are necessary. If the operation qualifies as an assembly operation, the imported finished article is dutiable on the full value of the article reduced by the value of the U.S.-origin parts or components. The person or

Figure 12–4. Sample Foreign Shipper's Declaration and Importer's Endorsement form.

FOREIGN SHIPPER'S DECLARATION AND IMPORTER'S ENDORSEMENT
(U.S. Goods Returned - HS 9801.00.10)

I, _____, declare that to the best of my knowledge and belief the articles herein specified were exported from the United States, from the port of _____ on or about _____, 19__, and that they are returned without having been advanced in value or improved in condition by any process of manufacture or other means.

Marks	Number	Quantity	Description	Value, in U.S. coin

_____   _____
(Date)   (Address)

_____   _____
(Signature)   (Capacity)

I, _____, declare that the above declaration by the foreign shipper is true and correct to the best of my knowledge and belief, that the articles were manufactured by _____ _____ (name of manufacturer) located in _____ (city and state), that the articles were not manufactured or produced in the United States under subheading 9813.00.05, HTSUS, and that the articles were exported from the United States without benefit of drawback.

_____   _____
(Date)   (Address)

_____   _____
(Signature)   (Capacity)

Figure 12–5. Sample Foreign Repairer's Declaration and Importer's Endorsement form.

FOREIGN REPAIRER'S DECLARATION AND IMPORTER'S ENDORSEMENT
(Repairs and Alterations - HS 9802.00.40 and 9802.00.50)

I, _____, declare that the articles herein specified are the articles which, in the condition in which they were exported from the United States, were received by me (us) on _____, 19____, from _____ (name and address of owner or exporter in the United States); that they were received by me (us) for the sole purpose of being repaired or altered; that only the repairs or alterations described below were performed by me (us); that the full cost or (when no charge is made) value of such repairs or alterations are correctly stated below; and that no substitution whatever has been made to replace any of the articles originally received by me (us) from the owner or exporter thereof mentioned above.

Marks and numbers	Description of articles and of repairs or alterations	Full cost or (when no charge is made) value of repairs or alterations (see subchapter II, chapter 98, HTSUS)	Total value of articles after repairs or alterations

_____   _____
(Date)   (Address)

_____   _____
(Signature)   (Capacity)

I, _____, declare that the (above) (attached) declaration by the person who performed the repairs or alterations abroad is true and correct to the best of my knowledge and belief; that the articles were not manufactured or produced in the United States under subheading 9813.00.05 HTSUS; that such articles were exported from the United States for repairs or alterations and without benefit of drawback from _____ (port) on _____, 19___; and that the articles entered in their repaired or altered condition are the same articles that were exported on the above date and that are identified in the (above) (attached) declaration.

_____   _____
(Date)   (Address)

_____   _____
(Signature)   (Capacity)

entity performing the assembly operations must file a Foreign Assembler's Declaration, and any unreported change in the operation or a false declaration can lead to serious customs penalties. (A sample Foreign Assembler's Declaration is shown in Figure 12–6.) Customs must be notified of any variation in the assembly operation of more than 5 percent of the total cost or value. Where cost data is estimated or standard costs are being used at the time of entry, that must be stated on the entry; liquidation of the entry must be suspended, and actual cost data must be submitted as soon as accounting procedures permit. This is submitted via the "reconciliation" procedure (see Chapter 8, Section M). This type of reduced duty treatment is not available on foreign-origin components imported into the United States and then exported for assembly, unless the foreign components were subjected to additional processing in the United States, resulting in a substantial transformation into a new and different article of commerce, and the imported components were not imported under a temporary importation bond. Foreign-origin components can be used in the assembly process; however, no reduction of U.S. duties is allowed for their value. Articles assembled abroad are considered to be a product of the country of assembly for country of origin marking requirements.

When U.S.-origin commodities are exported to foreign countries and further processed, if the country of processing is a beneficiary country under the Generalized System of Preferences (or the Caribbean Basin Economic Recovery Act) and at least 35 percent of the value is added in the foreign country, the foreign country becomes the new country of origin, and importation of the articles to the United States may be made duty-free.

Due to the low labor rates in Mexico and the close proximity to the U.S. market, many U.S. and foreign companies have established assembly or processing operations under Mexican law. Mexican law provides for the equivalent of temporary importations under bond that permit the U.S.-origin raw materials or components to be brought into Mexico, assembled or further processed, and then exported to the United States without payment of Mexican customs duties. In order to establish a successful so-called IMMEX operation, it is necessary to comply with both Mexican and U.S. Customs requirements. Otherwise, the full value of the articles can be dutiable both in Mexico and in the United States. In years past, U.S. components that were sent to Mexico for further processing came under the *maquila* and PITEX programs. In 2006, in its efforts to introduce efficiency, the Mexican government combined the two by publishing the "Decree on the Promotion of the Manufacturing and In-Bond Assembly Industry and Export Services" (IMMEX).

Companies wishing to use the services of an IMMEX should discuss the full ramifications under both Mexican and U.S. regulations before beginning operations.

Figure 12–6. Sample Foreign Assembler's Declaration form.

FOREIGN ASSEMBLER'S DECLARATION

    I, _____, declare that to the best
of my knowledge and belief the _____ were
assembled in whole or in part from fabricated components listed and
described below, which are products in the United States:

Marks of identifica- tion, numbers	Description of component	Quality	Unit value at time and place of export from United States	Port and date of export from United States	Name and address of manufacturer

Date   Signature

Address   Capacity

U.S. IMPORTER'S ENDORSEMENT

    I declare that to the best of my knowledge and belief the
(above), (attached) declaration, and any other information
submitted herewith, or otherwise supplied or referred to, is
correct in every respect and there has been compliance with all
pertinent legal notes to the Harmonized Tariff Schedule of the
United States (19 U.S.C. 1202).

Date   Signature

Address   Capacity

C. Barter and Countertrade Transactions

Currently in international trade, an exporter may be asked to accept payment in merchandise rather than cash (barter). Moreover, in other situations, such as compensation arrangements or switch transactions, both export and import transactions may be involved. Such transactions give rise to unique documentation and procedural problems. First, the U.S. company having a role in such a transaction should not try to use its standard-form sales or purchase documents. These transactions require special terms and conditions to protect the participant and documents should be specifically tailored to the transaction. Second, even though no money will change hands, the parties should value the merchandise or services that will be exchanged. This will be necessary for tax, customs, and foreign exchange control purposes. The U.S. Customs and Border Protection recommends that the parties seek an advance ruling. In most countries, attempts to engage in barter transactions for the purpose of avoiding these laws will subject the participants to prosecution for evasion. Correlatively, the participant should satisfy itself that all necessary government notifications and forms are filed, just as if it were a cash transaction, and that all values stated are accurate, consistent, and supportable.

Appendix A
Incoterms Diagram

Appendix A

UPDATE - 2010 Incoterms®

	ExW	FCA-Sellers	FCA-Port of Export	CPT-Port of Arrival	CPT-Place of Delivery	CIP-Port of Arrival	CIP-Place of Delivery	DAT	DAP-Port of Arrival	DAP-Place of Delivery	DDP	FAS	FOB	CFR	CIF
					OMNIMODAL TRANSPORTATION								MARINE TRANSPORTATION ONLY		
Packing for export	S	S	S	S	S	S	S	S	S	S	S	S	S	S	S
Loading into Inland Carrier	B	S	S	S	S	S	S	S	S	S	S	S	S	S	S
Export requirements	B	S	S	S	S	S	S	S	S	S	S	S	S	S	S
Pre-Shipment Inspection when mandated by Exporting Country	B	S				S	S	S	S	S	S	S	S	S	S
Pre-Carriage (Inland Exporting Country)	B	B	S	S	S	S	S	S	S	S	S	S	S	S	S
Insurance	N/A	N/A	N/A	N/A	N/A	S for B	S for B	N/A	N/A	N/A	N/A	N/A	N/A	N/A	S for B
Pre-shipment inspection (when mandatory by Contract, but not by country of export)	B	B	B	B	B	B	B	B	B	B	B	B	B	B	B
Loading onto International Carrier	B	B	B	S	S	S	S	S	S	S	S	B	B	S	S
Carriage (International)	B	B	B	S	S	S	S	S	S	S	S	B	B	S	S
Unloading from international Carrier	B	B	B	S	S	S	S	S	S	S	S	B	B	S	S
Port charges	B	B	B	S	S	S	S	S	S	S	S	B	B	S	S
Import license	B	B	B	B	B	B	B	B	B	B	S	B	B	B	B
Import Clearance	B	B	B	B	B	B	B	B	B	B	S	B	B	B	B
Post Carriage (Foreign Delivery)	B	B	B	B	S	B	S	B	B	S	S	B	B	B	B
Unloading at Destination	B	B	B	B	B	B	B	B	B	B	B	B	B	B	B

	ExW	FCA-Sellers	FCA-Port of Export	CPT-Port of Arrival	CPT-Place of Delivery	CIP-Port of Arrival	CIP-Place of Delivery	DAT	DAP-Port of Arrival	DAP-Place of Delivery	DDP	FAS	FOB	CFR	CIF
Seller pays freight to:	At S's door	At S's door	At port of export unloaded	At named destination	At named Destination	At named destination	At named Destination	At port of arrival	At port of arrival	At place of delivery	At Place of delivery	At port of export unloaded	At port of export loaded	At named destination.	At named destination
Risk of loss transfers from S to B	At S's door	At S's door	At port of export unloaded	At port of export loaded	At port of export loaded	At port of export loaded	At port of export loaded	At port of arrival	At port of arrival	At place of delivery	At Place of delivery	At port of export unloaded	At port of export loaded	At port of export loaded	At port of export loaded

1

484

Appendix B

International Sales Agreement (Export)

GENERAL CONTRACTS   **Form 4.16**

FORM

AGREEMENT made January 4, 1982, between Panoramic Export Company, Inc., a New York corporation having its principal place of business at 71 West 42d Street, New York, New York (the ''Seller''), and Miguel Vellos, of 31 Avenida de Cortez, Lima, Peru (the ''Purchaser'').

1. *Sale.* The Seller shall cause to be manufactured, and shall sell and deliver to the Purchaser certain machinery and equipment (the ''goods''), to be manufactured specially for the Purchaser by Rollo Manufacturing Company (the ''Manufacturer''), at the Manufacturer's plant in Detroit, Michigan, according to the specifications appearing in Exhibit A annexed.

2. *Price.* The purchase price shall be $1,857.60 F.O.B. mill, freight prepaid to New Orleans, Louisiana, payable in currency of the United States of America. The term ''F.O.B. mill'' means delivery free on board cars at the Manufacturer's works.

3. *Payment.* The terms are net cash on presentation of invoice and inland bill of lading to bankers approved by the Seller, with whom credit in favor of the Seller for the full amount of the purchase price is to be established forthwith. This credit shall be confirmed to the Seller by the bankers, and shall remain in full force until this contract shall have been completely performed. Delay by the Purchaser in establishing this credit shall extend the time for the performance of this contract by the Seller to such extent as may be necessary to enable it to make delivery in the exercise of reasonable diligence after such credit has been established; or, at the Seller's option, such delay may be treated by the Seller as a wrongful termination of this contract on the part of the Purchaser.

4. *Delivery.* The Seller shall notify the Purchaser when the goods are ready for shipment. Thereupon the Purchaser shall furnish shipping instructions to the Seller, stating the date of shipment, the carrier, and the routing. The

(Rel.57–11/82 Pub.240)   4–1089

Form 4.16   S<small>ALE OF</small> G<small>OODS</small>

Purchaser shall be entitled to select any routing officially authorized and published by the transportation companies, provided that the Seller may change the routing if inability to secure cars promptly, or other reasons, would involve delay in forwarding the goods over the route selected by the Purchaser. The Seller shall not be required to ship the goods until it has received shipping instructions from the Purchaser. If the Purchaser fails to furnish shipping instructions promptly, so as to enable the Seller to perform this contract in accordance with its terms, the Seller may, at its option, and in addition to all other rights it may possess, cancel such portion of this contract as may remain unexecuted, or make shipment in accordance with any routing of its own selection.

5. *Freight charges.* Any prepayment by the Seller of freight charges shall be for the account of the Purchaser, and shall be included in the amount of the invoice and repaid by the Purchaser on presentation thereof, and shall not affect the obligations of the Seller with respect to delivery. Insofar as the purchase price includes freight charges, such price is based upon the lowest official freight rate in effect at the date of this contract. Any difference between such rate and the rate actually paid, when the goods are shipped from the Manufacturer's plant, shall be for the Purchaser's account, and shall be reflected in the invoice, whether such difference results from a change in rate or a change in route.

6. *Insurance.* In no case does the purchase price, even though inclusive of freight, cover the cost of any insurance; but if the route selected involves movement of the goods by water, or by rail and water, for which the freight rate does not include insurance, the Seller shall effect marine insurance for the account of the Purchaser, and the Purchaser shall repay to the Seller the cost of such insurance.

7. *Partial delivery.* The Seller may ship any portion of the goods as soon as completed at the Manufacturer's plant, upon compliance with the terms of paragraph 4; and payment for any portion of the goods as shipped shall become

due in accordance with the terms of payment stated in paragraph 3.

8. *Contingencies.* The Seller shall not be liable for any delay in manufacture or delivery due to fires, strikes, labor disputes, war, civil commotion, delays in transportation, shortages of labor or material, or other causes beyond the control of the Seller. The existence of such causes of delay shall justify the suspension of manufacture, and shall extend the time of performance on the part of the Seller to the extent necessary to enable it to make delivery in the exercise of reasonable diligence after the causes of delay have been removed. However, that in the event of the existence of any such causes of delay, the Purchaser may cancel the purchase of such portion of the goods as may have been subjected to such delay, provided such portion of the goods has not been manufactured nor is in process of manufacture at the time the Purchaser's notice of cancellation arrives at the Manufacturer's plant.

9. *Warranty.* The Seller guarantees that the goods will generate or utilize electrical energy to their rated capacities without undue heating, and will do their work in a successful manner, provided that they are kept in proper condition and operated under normal conditions, and that their operation is properly supervised. THE WARRANTIES SPECIFIED IN THIS CONTRACT ARE IN LIEU OF ANY AND ALL OTHER WARRANTIES, EXPRESS OR IMPLIED, INCLUDING ANY WARRANTY OF MERCHANTABILITY OR FITNESS FOR A PARTICULAR PURPOSE.

10. *Inspection.* The Purchaser may inspect the goods at the Manufacturer's plant, and such inspection and acceptance shall be final. Reasonable facilities shall be afforded to inspectors representing the Purchaser to make the inspection, and to apply, before shipment from the Manufacturer's plant, tests in accordance with the specifications contained in paragraph 1. If the Purchaser fails to inspect

Form 4.16   SALE OF GOODS

the goods, the failure shall be deemed an acceptance of the goods, and any acceptance shall be deemed a waiver of any right to revoke acceptance at some future date with respect to any defect that a proper inspection would have revealed.

11. *Claims.* The Seller shall not be liable for any claims unless they are made promptly after receipt of the goods and due opportunity has been given for investigation by the Seller's representatives. Goods shall not be returned except with the Seller's permission.

12. *Country of importation.* The Purchaser represents that the goods are purchased for the purpose of exportation to Peru, and the Purchaser covenants that the goods will be shipped to that destination, and shall furnish, if required by the Seller, a landing certificate duly executed by the customs authorities at the port of importation, certifying that the goods have been landed and entered at that port.

13. *Duties.* All drawbacks of duties paid on materials entering into the manufacture of the goods shall accrue to the Seller, and the Purchaser shall furnish the Seller with all documents necessary to obtain payment of such drawbacks, and to cooperate with the Seller in obtaining such payment.

14. *Cancellation by purchaser.* The Purchaser may cancel this contract, as to any goods not manufactured or in process of manufacture at the time the Purchaser's notice of cancellation arrives at the Manufacturer's plant, in any of the following events:

(a) if the country of importation becomes involved in civil or foreign war, insurrection, or riot, or is invaded by armed forces; or if, as a result of war, treaty, or otherwise, it is added to or becomes a part of the domain of any other sovereignty; or

(b) if a countervailing duty is declared or imposed on the goods by the country of importation; or

4-1092   (Rel.57-11/82 Pub.240)

489

GENERAL CONTRACTS   **Form 4.16**

(c) if by reason of an embargo the goods cannot be exported from the United States; or

(d) if the Purchaser is unable to obtain an export shipping license for the purpose of exporting the goods to Peru.

15. *Benefit.* This agreement shall be binding upon and shall inure to the benefit of the parties, their legal representatives, successors, and assigns, provided that the Purchaser shall not assign this contract without the prior written consent of the Seller.

16. *Construction.* This contract shall be construed under the laws of New York.

In witness whereof the parties have executed this contract.

Corporate Seal   Panoramic Export Company,
Attest: Inc. by . . . .
                                        President

. . . . (L.S.)
        Secretary   Miguel Vellos

(Rel.75–5/87 Pub.240)

Appendix C

Department of Defense – Compliance Program Guidelines

> Bureau of Political Military Affairs
> Directorate of Defense Trade Controls
> Office of Defense Trade Controls
>   Compliance

Compliance Program Guidelines

Comprehensive operational compliance programs include manuals that articulate the processes to be followed in implementing the company program. Important elements of effective manuals and programs include:

Organization Structure

- Organizational charts.
- Description (and flow charts, if appropriate) of company's defense trade functions.
- Description of any management and control structures for implementing and tracking compliance with U.S. export controls (including names, titles, and principal responsibilities of key officers).

Corporate Commitment and Policy

- Directive by senior company management to comply with Arms Export Control Act (AECA) and the International Traffic in Arms Regulations (ITAR).
- Knowledge and understanding of when and how the AECA and ITAR affect the company with ITAR controlled items/technical data.
- Knowledge of corporate internal controls that have been established and implemented to ensure compliance with the AECA and ITAR.

  Examples of detail:
    o Citation of basic authorities (AECA, ITAR).
    o Identification of authorized U.S. Government control body (Directorate of Defense Trade Controls ("DDTC")).
    o Corporate policy to comply fully with all applicable U.S. export control laws and regulations.

1

- o Compliance as a matter for top management attention that needs adequate resources.
- o Identification, duties, and authority of key persons (senior executives, empowered officials) for day-to-day export/import operations and compliance oversight.
- o Corporate Export Administration organization chart.
- o Operating Division Export Administration flow chart.

Identification, Receipt and Tracking of ITAR Controlled Items/Technical Data

- Methodology used, specifically tailored to corporate structure, organization, and functions, to identify and account for ITAR controlled items/technical data the company handles (trace processing steps of ITAR controlled transactions from the time the company manufactures/receives the item to the time an item is shipped from the company – or in the case of a defense service, when provided).

  Examples of questions to be addressed:
  - o Are appropriate employees familiar with the AECA and ITAR and related requirements, including handling export approvals with certain provisos and limitations?
  - o Are company employees notified of changes in U.S. export control restrictions, and are they provided accurate, reliable interpretation of U.S. export control restrictions?
  - o What U.S. origin defense articles are manufactured/received by the firm and from whom? How identified and "tagged"?
  - o What U.S. origin technical data related to defense articles are produced/received by the firm and from whom? How identified and tagged"?
  - o What items are manufactured by the firm using U.S. origin technical data? How identified and "tagged"?
  - o What items or articles are manufactured by the firm that incorporates U.S. origin defense articles (components)? How identified and "tagged"?
  - o What kind of recordkeeping system does the company maintain that would allow for control of, and for retrieval of information on, U.S. origin technical data and/or defense articles exported to the company?

Re-Exports/Retransfers

2

- Procedures utilized to (a) obtain written State Department approval prior to the retransfer to a party not included in a State Department authorization of an item/technical data transferred or exported originally to the company, and (b) track the re-export or re-transfer (including placing parties on notice that the proposed transfers involve US origin products and labeling such products appropriately).

    o Procedure when an ITAR controlled item/technical data is transferred by the company to a foreign national employed at the company.
    o Procedure when an ITAR controlled item/technical data is transferred by the company to a foreign person within the U.S.
    o Procedure when ITAR controlled technical data or defense articles are transferred from the company to a foreign person outside of the U.S.
    o Procedure when an ITAR controlled item/technical data is to be used or transferred for an end-use not included in the State Department authorization.

Restricted/Prohibited Exports and Transfers

- Procedure for screening customers, carriers, and countries.
- Screening procedure for high-risk transactions to combat illegal exports/retransfers.
- Procedures to investigate any evidence of diversion or unauthorized use of U.S. origin products.

Recordkeeping

- Description of record systems concerning U.S. origin products.
- Procedures for maintaining records relating to U.S. origin products for five years from the expiration of the State Department license or other approval.
- Regular internal review of files to ensure proper practices and procedures by persons reporting to top management.

Internal Monitoring

- Perform audits periodically to ensure integrity of compliance program.
- Emphasis on validation of full export compliance, including adherence to license and other approval conditions.
- Measurement of effectiveness of day-to-day operations.

3

- Adopt procedure for highlighting any compliance areas that needs more attention.
- Report known or suspected violations to Corporate export administration office.
- Effective liaison and coordination with Ombudsman.*

  Examples of detail:
  - Specific description of procedures (examination of organizational structure, reporting relationships, and individuals assigned to export/import controls process.
  - Random document review and tracing of processes.
  - Review of internal recordkeeping, communications, document transfer, maintenance and retention.
  - Conclusion and report of violations to Corporate Export Administrator.
  - Coordination with Ombudsman.

Training

- Explanation of company training program on U. S. export control laws and regulations.
- Process to ensure education, training, and provision of guidance to all employees involved on exports (including those in departments such as Traffic, Marketing, Contracts, Security, Legal, Public Relations, Engineering, Executive Office).

Violations and Penalties

- Procedures for notification of potential violations, including use of voluntary disclosure and Ombudsman to report any violation of the company's internal control program or U.S. export controls.
- Emphasis on importance of compliance (to avoid jeopardizing Corporate business and severe sanctions against the Corporation and responsible individuals).
- Description of AECA/ITAR penalties.
- Written statements and procedures to foster employee discipline (e.g., keying certain types of advancement to compliance understanding and implementation, and establishment of internal disciplinary measures).

4

Appendix D

Informed Compliance: Reasonable Care

What Every Member of the
Trade Community Should Know About:
Reasonable Care
(A Checklist for Compliance)

AN INFORMED COMPLIANCE PUBLICATION

FEBRUARY 2004

U.S. CUSTOMS and BORDER PROTECTION

NOTICE:

This publication is intended to provide guidance and information to the trade community. It reflects the position on or interpretation of the applicable laws or regulations by U.S. Customs and Border Protection (CBP) as of the date of publication, which is shown on the front cover. It does not in any way replace or supersede those laws or regulations. Only the latest official version of the laws or regulations is authoritative.

Publication History

First Published January 1998
Revised February 2004

PRINTING NOTE:

This publication was designed for electronic distribution via the CBP website (http://www.cbp.gov) and is being distributed in a variety of formats. It was originally set up in Microsoft Word97®. Pagination and margins in downloaded versions may vary depending upon which word processor or printer you use. If you wish to maintain the original settings, you may wish to download the .pdf version, which can then be printed using the freely available Adobe Acrobat Reader®.

Appendix D

PREFACE

On December 8, 1993, Title VI of the North American Free Trade Agreement Implementation Act (Pub. L. 103-182, 107 Stat. 2057), also known as the Customs Modernization or "Mod" Act, became effective. These provisions amended many sections of the Tariff Act of 1930 and related laws.

Two new concepts that emerge from the Mod Act are "*informed compliance*" and "*shared responsibility*," which are premised on the idea that in order to maximize voluntary compliance with laws and regulations of U.S. Customs and Border Protection, the trade community needs to be clearly and completely informed of its legal obligations. Accordingly, the Mod Act imposes a greater obligation on CBP to provide the public with improved information concerning the trade community's rights and responsibilities under customs regulations and related laws. In addition, both the trade and U.S. Customs and Border Protection share responsibility for carrying out these requirements. For example, under Section 484 of the Tariff Act, as amended (19 U.S.C. 1484), the importer of record is responsible for using reasonable care to enter, classify and determine the value of imported merchandise and to provide any other information necessary to enable U.S. Customs and Border Protection to properly assess duties, collect accurate statistics, and determine whether other applicable legal requirements, if any, have been met. CBP is then responsible for fixing the final classification and value of the merchandise. An importer of record's failure to exercise reasonable care could delay release of the merchandise and, in some cases, could result in the imposition of penalties.

The Office of Regulations and Rulings (ORR) has been given a major role in meeting the informed compliance responsibilities of U.S. Customs and Border Protection. In order to provide information to the public, CBP has issued a series of informed compliance publications, and videos, on new or revised requirements, regulations or procedures, and a variety of classification and valuation issues.

This publication, prepared by the International Trade Compliance Division, ORR, is a Reasonable Care checklist. "Reasonable Care (A Checklist for Compliance)" is part of a series of informed compliance publications advising the public of Customs regulations and procedures. We sincerely hope that this material, together with seminars and increased access to rulings of U.S. Customs and Border Protection, will help the trade community to improve voluntary compliance with customs laws and to understand the relevant administrative processes.

The material in this publication is provided for general information purposes only. Because many complicated factors can be involved in customs issues, an importer may wish to obtain a ruling under Regulations of U.S. Customs and Border Protection, 19 C.F.R. Part 177, or to obtain advice from an expert who specializes in customs matters, for example, a licensed customs broker, attorney or consultant.

Comments and suggestions are welcomed and should be addressed to the Assistant Commissioner at the Office of Regulations and Rulings, U.S. Customs and Border Protection, 1300 Pennsylvania Avenue, NW, (Mint Annex), Washington, D.C. 20229.

Michael T. Schmitz,
Assistant Commissioner
Office of Regulations and Rulings

Appendix D

REASONABLE CARE CHECKLIST

INTRODUCTION

One of the most significant effects of the Customs Modernization Act is the establishment of the clear requirement that parties exercise reasonable care in importing into the United States. Section 484 of the Tariff Act, as amended, requires an importer of record using reasonable care to make entry by filing such information as is necessary to enable U.S. Customs and Border Protection to determine whether the merchandise may be released from Customs custody, and using reasonable care, complete the entry by filing with U.S. Customs and Border Protection the declared value, classification and rate of duty and such other documentation or information as is necessary to enable U.S. Customs and Border Protection to properly assess duties, collect accurate statistics, and determine whether any other applicable requirement of law is met. Despite the seemingly simple connotation of the term reasonable care, this explicit responsibility defies easy explanation. The facts and circumstances surrounding every import transaction differ--from the experience of the importer to the nature of the imported articles. Consequently, neither U.S. Customs and Border Protection nor the importing community can develop a foolproof reasonable care checklist which would cover every import transaction. On the other hand, in keeping with the Modernization Act's theme of informed compliance, U.S. Customs and Border Protection would like to take this opportunity to recommend that the importing community examine the list of questions below. In U.S. Customs and Border Protection's view, the list of questions may prompt or suggest a program, framework or methodology which importers may find useful in avoiding compliance problems and meeting reasonable care responsibilities.

Obviously, the questions below cannot be exhaustive or encyclopedic - ordinarily, every import transaction is different. For the same reason, it cannot be overemphasized that although the following information is provided to promote enhanced compliance with the Customs laws and regulations, it has no legal, binding or precedential effect on U.S. Customs and Border Protection or the importing community. In this regard, U.S. Customs and Border Protection notes that the checklist is not an attempt to create a presumption of negligence, but rather, an attempt to educate, inform and provide guidance to the importing community. Consequently, U.S. Customs and Border Protection believes that the following information may be helpful to the importing community and hopes that this document will facilitate and encourage importers to develop their own unique compliance measurement plans, reliable procedures and reasonable care programs.

As a convenience to the public, the checklist also includes the text of a checklist previously published in the Federal Register for use in certain textile and apparel importations. The full document was published in 62 FR 48340 (September 15, 1997).

As a final reminder, it should be noted that to further assist the importing community, U.S. Customs and Border Protection issues rulings and informed compliance publications on a variety of technical subjects and processes. It is strongly recommended that importers always make sure that they are using the latest versions of these publications.

ASKING AND ANSWERING THE FOLLOWING QUESTIONS MAY BE HELPFUL IN ASSISTING IMPORTERS IN THE EXERCISE OF REASONABLE CARE:

GENERAL QUESTIONS FOR ALL TRANSACTIONS:

1. If you have not retained an expert to assist you in complying with Customs requirements, do you have access to the Customs Regulations (Title 19 of the Code of Federal Regulations), the Harmonized Tariff Schedule of the United States, and the GPO publication Customs Bulletin and Decisions? Do you have access to the Customs Internet Website, Customs Bulletin Board or other research service to permit you to establish reliable procedures and facilitate compliance with Customs laws and regulations?

2. Has a responsible and knowledgeable individual within your organization reviewed the Customs documentation prepared by you or your expert to ensure that it is full, complete and accurate? If that documentation was prepared outside your own organization, do you have a reliable system in place to insure that you receive copies of the information as submitted to U.S. Customs and Border Protection; that it is reviewed for accuracy; and that U.S. Customs and Border Protection is timely apprised of any needed corrections?

3. If you use an expert to assist you in complying with Customs requirements, have you discussed your importations in advance with that person and have you provided that person with full, complete and accurate information about the import transactions?

4. Are identical transactions or merchandise handled differently at different ports or U.S. Customs and Border Protection offices within the same port? If so, have you brought this to the attention of the appropriate U.S. Customs and Border Protection officials?

QUESTIONS ARRANGED BY TOPIC:

Merchandise Description & Tariff Classification

Basic Question: Do you know or have you established a reliable procedure or program to ensure that you know what you ordered, where it was made and what it is made of?

1. Have you provided or established reliable procedures to ensure you provide a complete and accurate description of your merchandise to U.S. Customs and Border Protection in accordance with 19 U.S.C. 1481? (Also, see 19 CFR 141.87 and 19 CFR 141.89 for special merchandise description requirements.)

2. Have you provided or established reliable procedures to ensure you provide a correct tariff classification of your merchandise to U.S. Customs and Border Protection in accordance with 19 U.S.C. 1484?

3. Have you obtained a Customs "ruling" regarding the description of the merchandise or its tariff classification (See 19 CFR Part 177), and if so, have you established reliable procedures to ensure that you have followed the ruling and brought it to U.S. Customs and Border Protection's attention?

4. Where merchandise description or tariff classification information is not immediately available, have you established a reliable procedure for providing that information, and is the procedure being followed?

5. Have you participated in a Customs pre-classification of your merchandise relating to proper merchandise description and classification?

6. Have you consulted the tariff schedules, Customs informed compliance publications, court cases and/or Customs rulings to assist you in describing and classifying the merchandise?

7. Have you consulted with a Customs "expert" (e.g., lawyer, Customs broker, accountant, or Customs consultant) to assist in the description and/or classification of the merchandise?

8. If you are claiming a conditionally free or special tariff classification/provision for your merchandise (e.g., GSP, HTS Item 9802, NAFTA, etc.), How have you verified that the merchandise qualifies for such status? Have you obtained or developed reliable procedures to obtain any required or necessary documentation to support the claim? If making a NAFTA preference claim, do you already have a NAFTA certificate of origin in your possession?

9. Is the nature of your merchandise such that a laboratory analysis or other specialized procedure is suggested to assist in proper description and classification?

10. Have you developed a reliable program or procedure to maintain and produce any required Customs entry documentation and supporting information?

Valuation

Basic Questions: Do you know or have you established reliable procedures to know the price actually paid or payable for your merchandise? Do you know the terms of sale; whether there will be rebates, tie-ins, indirect costs, additional payments; whether assists were provided, commissions or royalties paid? Are amounts actual or estimated? Are you and the supplier related parties?

1. Have you provided or established reliable procedures to provide U.S. Customs and Border Protection with a proper declared value for your merchandise in accordance with 19 U.S.C. 1484 and 19 U.S.C. 1401a?

2. Have you obtained a Customs "ruling" regarding the valuation of the merchandise (See 19 CFR Part 177), and if so, have you established reliable procedures to ensure that you have followed the ruling and brought it to U.S. Customs and Border Protection attention?

3. Have you consulted the Customs valuation laws and regulations, Customs Valuation Encyclopedia, Customs informed compliance publications, court cases and Customs rulings to assist you in valuing merchandise?

4. Have you consulted with a Customs "expert" (e.g., lawyer, accountant, Customs broker, Customs consultant) to assist in the valuation of the merchandise?

5. If you purchased the merchandise from a "related" seller, have you established procedures to ensure that you have reported that fact upon entry and taken measures or established reliable procedures to ensure that value reported to U.S. Customs and Border Protection meets one of the "related party" tests?

6. Have you taken measures or established reliable procedures to ensure that all of the legally required costs or payments associated with the imported merchandise have been reported to U.S. Customs and Border Protection (e.g., assists, all commissions, indirect payments or rebates, royalties, etc.)?

7. If you are declaring a value based on a transaction in which you were/are not the buyer, have you substantiated that the transaction is a bona fide sale at arm's length and that the merchandise was clearly destined to the United States at the time of sale?

8. If you are claiming a conditionally free or special tariff classification/provision for your merchandise (e.g., GSP, HTS Item 9802, NAFTA, etc.), have you established a reliable system or program to ensure that you reported the required value information and obtained any required or necessary documentation to support the claim?

9. Have you established a reliable program or procedure to produce any required entry documentation and supporting information?

Country of Origin/Marking/Quota

Basic Question: Have you taken reliable measures to ascertain the correct country of origin for the imported merchandise?

1. Have you established reliable procedures to ensure that you report the correct country of origin on Customs entry documents?

2. Have you established reliable procedures to verify or ensure that the merchandise is properly marked upon entry with the correct country of origin (if required) in accordance with 19 U.S.C. 1304 and any other applicable special marking requirement (watches, gold, textile labeling, etc)?

3. Have you obtained a Customs "ruling" regarding the proper marking and country of origin of the merchandise (See 19 CFR Part 177), and if so, have you established reliable procedures to

ensure that you followed the ruling and brought it to U.S. Customs and Border Protection's attention?

4. Have you consulted with a Customs "expert" (e.g., lawyer, accountant, Customs broker, Customs consultant) regarding the correct country of origin/proper marking of your merchandise?

5. Have you taken reliable and adequate measures to communicate Customs country of origin marking requirements to your foreign supplier prior to importation of your merchandise?

6. If you are claiming a change in the origin of the merchandise or claiming that the goods are of U.S. origin, have you taken required measures to substantiate your claim (e.g. Do you have U.S. milling certificates or manufacturer's affidavits attesting to the production in the U.S.)?

7. If you are importing textiles or apparel, have you developed reliable procedures to ensure that you have ascertained the correct country of origin in accordance with 19 U.S.C. 3592 (Section 334, Pub. Law 103-465) and assured yourself that no illegal transshipment or false or fraudulent practices were involved?

8. Do you know how your goods are made from raw materials to finished goods, by whom and where?

9. Have you checked with U.S. Customs and Border Protection and developed a reliable procedure or system to ensure that the quota category is correct?

10. Have you checked or developed reliable procedures to check the <u>Status Report on Current Import Quotas (Restraint Levels)</u> issued by U.S. Customs and Border Protection to determine if your goods are subject to a quota category which has part categories?

11. Have you taken reliable measures to ensure that you have obtained the correct visas for your goods if they are subject to visa categories?

12. In the case of textile articles, have you prepared or developed a reliable program to prepare the proper country declaration for each entry, i.e., a single country declaration (if wholly obtained/produced) or a multi-country declaration (if raw materials from one country were produced into goods in a second)?

13. Have you established a reliable maintenance program or procedure to ensure you can produce any required entry documentation and supporting information, including any required certificates of origin?

Intellectual Property Rights

Basic Question: Have you determined or established a reliable procedure to permit you to determine whether your merchandise or its packaging bear or use any trademarks or copyrighted matter or are patented and, if so, that you have a legal right to import those items into, and/or use those items in, the U.S.?

1. If you are importing goods or packaging bearing a trademark registered in the U.S., have you checked or established a reliable procedure to ensure that it is genuine and not restricted from importation under the gray-market or parallel import requirements of U.S. law (see 19 CFR 133.21), or that you have permission from the trademark holder to import such merchandise?

2. If you are importing goods or packaging which consist of, or contain registered copyrighted material, have you checked or established a reliable procedure to ensure that it is authorized and genuine? If you are importing sound recordings of live performances, were the recordings authorized?

3. Have you checked or developed a reliable procedure to see if your merchandise is subject to an International Trade Commission or court ordered exclusion order?

4. Have you established a reliable procedure to ensure that you maintain and can produce any required entry documentation and supporting information?

Miscellaneous Questions

1. Have you taken measures or developed reliable procedures to ensure that your merchandise complies with other agency requirements (e.g., FDA, EPA/DOT, CPSC, FTC, Agriculture, etc.) prior to or upon entry, including the procurement of any necessary licenses or permits?

2. Have you taken measures or developed reliable procedures to check to see if your goods are subject to a Commerce Department dumping or countervailing duty investigation or determination, and if so, have you complied or developed reliable procedures to ensure compliance with Customs reporting requirements upon entry (e.g., 19 CFR 141.61)?

3. Is your merchandise subject to quota/visa requirements, and if so, have you provided or developed a reliable procedure to provide a correct visa for the goods upon entry?

4. Have you taken reliable measures to ensure and verify that you are filing the correct type of Customs entry (e.g., TIB, T&E, consumption entry, mail entry, etc.), as well as ensure that you have the right to make entry under the Customs Regulations?

Additional Questions for Textile and Apparel Importers

Note: Section 333 of the Uruguay Round Implementation Act (19 U.S.C. 1592a) authorizes the Secretary of the Treasury to publish a list of foreign producers, manufacturers, suppliers, sellers, exporters, or other foreign persons who have been found to have violated 19 U.S.C. 1592 by using certain false, fraudulent or counterfeit documentation, labeling, or prohibited transshipment practices in connection with textiles and apparel products. Section 1592a also requires any importer of record entering, introducing, or attempting to introduce into the commerce of the United States textile or apparel products that were either directly or indirectly produced, manufactured, supplied, sold, exported, or transported by such named person to show, to the satisfaction of the Secretary, that such importer has exercised reasonable care to ensure that the textile or apparel products are accompanied by documentation, packaging, and labeling that are accurate as to its origin. Under section 1592a, reliance solely upon information regarding the imported product from a person named on the list does not constitute the exercise of reasonable care. Textile and apparel importers who have some commercial relationship with one or more of the listed parties must exercise a degree of reasonable care in ensuring that the documentation covering the imported merchandise, as well as its packaging and labeling, is accurate as to the country of origin of the merchandise. This degree of reasonable care must rely on more than information supplied by the named party.

In meeting the reasonable care standard when importing textile or apparel products and when dealing with a party named on the list published pursuant to section 592A an importer should consider the following questions in attempting to ensure that the documentation, packaging, and labeling is accurate as to the country of origin of the imported merchandise. The list of questions is not exhaustive but is illustrative.

1.   Has the importer had a prior relationship with the named party?

2.   Has the importer had any detentions and/or seizures of textile or apparel products that were directly or indirectly produced, supplied, or transported by the named party?

3.   Has the importer visited the company's premises and ascertained that the company has the capacity to produce the merchandise?

4.   Where a claim of an origin conferring process is made in accordance with 19 CFR 102.21, has the importer ascertained that the named party actually performed the required process?

5.   Is the named party operating from the same country as is represented by that party on the documentation, packaging or labeling?

6.   Have quotas for the imported merchandise closed or are they nearing closing from the main producer countries for this commodity?

7.   What is the history of this country regarding this commodity?

8.   Have you asked questions of your supplier regarding the origin of the product?

9.   Where the importation is accompanied by a visa, permit, or license, has the importer verified with the supplier or manufacturer that the visa, permit, and/or license is both valid and accurate as to its origin? Has the importer scrutinized the visa, permit or license as to any irregularities that would call its authenticity into question?

ADDITIONAL INFORMATION

The Internet

The home page of U.S. Customs and Border Protection on the Internet's World Wide Web, provides the trade community with current, relevant information regarding CBP operations and items of special interest. The site posts information -- which includes proposed regulations, news releases, publications and notices, etc. -- that can be searched, read on-line, printed or downloaded to your personal computer. The web site was established as a trade-friendly mechanism to assist the importing and exporting community. The web site also links to the home pages of many other agencies whose importing or exporting regulations that U.S. Customs and Border Protection helps to enforce. The web site also contains a wealth of information of interest to a broader public than the trade community. For instance, on June 20, 2001, CBP launched the "Know Before You Go" publication and traveler awareness campaign designed to help educate international travelers.

The web address of U.S. Customs and Border Protection is http://www.cbp.gov

Customs Regulations

The current edition of *Customs Regulations of the United States* is a loose-leaf, subscription publication available from the Superintendent of Documents, U.S. Government Printing Office, Washington, DC 20402; telephone (202) 512-1800. A bound, 2003 edition of Title 19, *Code of Federal Regulations*, which incorporates all changes to the Regulations as of April 1, 2003, is also available for sale from the same address. All proposed and final regulations are published in the *Federal Register*, which is published daily by the Office of the Federal Register, National Archives and Records Administration, and distributed by the Superintendent of Documents. Information about on-line access to the *Federal Register* may be obtained by calling (202) 512-1530 between 7 a.m. and 5 p.m. Eastern time. These notices are also published in the weekly *Customs Bulletin* described below.

Customs Bulletin

The *Customs Bulletin and Decisions ("Customs Bulletin")* is a weekly publication that contains decisions, rulings, regulatory proposals, notices and other information of interest to the trade community. It also contains decisions issued by the U.S. Court of International Trade, as well as customs-related decisions of the U.S. Court of Appeals for the Federal Circuit. Each year, the Government Printing Office publishes bound volumes of the *Customs Bulletin*. Subscriptions may be purchased from the Superintendent of Documents at the address and phone number listed above.

Importing Into the United States

This publication provides an overview of the importing process and contains general information about import requirements. The February 2002 edition of *Importing Into the United States* contains much new and revised material brought about pursuant to the Customs Modernization Act ("Mod Act"). The Mod Act has fundamentally altered the relationship between importers and U.S. Customs and Border Protection by shifting to the importer the legal responsibility for declaring the value, classification, and rate of duty applicable to entered merchandise.

The February 2002 edition contains a section entitled "Informed Compliance." A key component of informed compliance is the shared responsibility between U.S. Customs and Border Protection and the import community, wherein CBP communicates its requirements to the importer, and the importer, in turn, uses reasonable care to assure that CBP is provided accurate and timely data pertaining to his or her importation.

Single copies may be obtained from local offices of U.S. Customs and Border Protection, or from the Office of Public Affairs, U.S. Customs and Border Protection, 1300 Pennsylvania Avenue NW, Washington, DC 20229. An on-line version is available at the CBP web site. *Importing Into the United States* is also available for sale, in single copies or bulk orders, from the Superintendent of Documents by calling (202) 512-1800, or by mail from the Superintendent of Documents, Government Printing Office, P.O. Box 371954, Pittsburgh, PA 15250-7054.

Informed Compliance Publications

U.S. Customs and Border Protection has prepared a number of Informed Compliance publications in the "*What Every Member of the Trade Community Should Know About:...*" series. Check the Internet web site http://www.cbp.gov for current publications.

Appendix D

Value Publications

Customs Valuation under the Trade Agreements Act of 1979 is a 96-page book containing a detailed narrative description of the customs valuation system, the customs valuation title of the Trade Agreements Act (§402 of the Tariff Act of 1930, as amended by the Trade Agreements Act of 1979 (19 U.S.C. §1401a)), the Statement of Administrative Action which was sent to the U.S. Congress in conjunction with the TAA, regulations (19 C.F.R. §§152.000-152.108) implementing the valuation system (a few sections of the regulations have been amended subsequent to the publication of the book) and questions and answers concerning the valuation system. A copy may be obtained from U.S. Customs and Border Protection, Office of Regulations and Rulings, Value Branch, 1300 Pennsylvania Avenue, NW, (Mint Annex), Washington, D.C. 20229.

Customs Valuation Encyclopedia (with updates) is comprised of relevant statutory provisions, CBP Regulations implementing the statute, portions of the Customs Valuation Code, judicial precedent, and administrative rulings involving application of valuation law. A copy may be purchased for a nominal charge from the Superintendent of Documents, Government Printing Office, P.O. Box 371954, Pittsburgh, PA 15250-7054. This publication is also available on the Internet web site of U.S. Customs and Border Protection.

> The information provided in this publication is for general information purposes only. Recognizing that many complicated factors may be involved in customs issues, an importer may wish to obtain a ruling under CBP Regulations, 19 C.F.R. Part 177, or obtain advice from an expert (such as a licensed Customs Broker, attorney or consultant) who specializes in customs matters. Reliance solely on the general information in this pamphlet may not be considered reasonable care.

Additional information may also be obtained from U.S. Customs and Border Protection ports of entry. Please consult your telephone directory for an office near you. The listing will be found under U.S. Government, Department of Homeland Security.

Reasonable Care
February 2004

"Your Comments are Important"

The Small Business and Regulatory Enforcement Ombudsman and 10 regional Fairness Boards were established to receive comments from small businesses about Federal agency enforcement activities and rate each agency's responsiveness to small business. If you wish to comment on the enforcement actions of U.S. Customs and Border Protection, call 1-888-REG-FAIR (1-888-734-3247).

REPORT SMUGGLING 1-800-BE-ALERT OR 1-800-NO-DROGA

Visit our Internet web site: http://www.cbp.gov

Appendix E

USITC Harmonized Tariff Schedule Contents

Appendix E

• HOME

Search www.usitc.gov [Go]

USITC Home > Tata > Hts > Bychapter > By Chapter of HTS :2014-01-01 - Basic, Official Harmonized Tariff Schedule of the United States Annotated

:: By Chapter, Harmonized Tariff Schedule of the United States

Contact Us & FAQs

Acting Director:
David G Michels
202.205.2592

• HTS Help
• Frequently Asked Questions

Tariff Assistance

Search the current Harmonized Tariff
Schedule...

Search hts.usitc.gov   [Go] (See
Disclaimer)

View...
Current HTS by Chapter
HTS Archive
Recent Changes to HTS [PDF]

Need Help?
Frequently Asked Questions
Ask Us a Tariff Question
HTS E-Learning Module

Research Tools

• HTS Archive
• U.S. Classification
  Rulings (Customs and Border
  Protection)
• Non-Tariff Duty Information
• DataWeb
• Tariff Database

Other External Links

• Foreign Tariff Information
• Export.gov
• Schedule B for Classification of
  Exports (Census Bureau)
• USTR
• Customs & Border Protection
• Related Government Links

OPEN GOV
WHITEHOUSE.GOV/OPEN

This edition of the HTS takes effect January 1, 2014

This page contains the chapter-by-chapter listing of the Harmonized Tariff Schedule and general notes. The links below correspond to the various sections in the Table of Contents for the Harmonized Tariff Schedule. Clicking on a link will load the corresponding Adobe .pdf file

(Note: Section notes, if any, are attached to the first chapter of each section. "Page down" to view chapter after selecting.)

Cover

Change Record (The record of legal and statistical changes in this edition of the Harmonized Tariff Schedule)

Preface

General Notes: General Rules of Interpretation; General Statistical Notes

Notice to Exporters

Section I: Live Animals; Animal Products

	Section Notes
Chapter 1	Live animals
Chapter 2	Meat and edible meat offal
Chapter 3	Fish and crustaceans, molluscs and other aquatic invertebrates
Chapter 4	Dairy produce; birds eggs; natural honey; edible products of animal origin, not elsewhere specified or included
Chapter 5	Products of animal origin, not elsewhere specified or included

Section II: Vegetable Products

	Section Notes
Chapter 6	Live trees and other plants; bulbs, roots and the like; cut flowers and ornamental foliage
Chapter 7	Edible vegetables and certain roots and tubers
Chapter 8	Edible fruit and nuts; peel of citrus fruit or melons
Chapter 9	Coffee, tea, maté and spices
Chapter 10	Cereals
Chapter 11	Products of the milling industry; malt; starches; inulin; wheat gluten
Chapter 12	Oil seeds and oleaginous fruits; miscellaneous grains, seeds and fruits; industrial or medicinal plants; straw and fodder
Chapter 13	Lac; gums, resins and other vegetable saps and extracts
Chapter 14	Vegetable plaiting materials; vegetable products not elsewhere specified or included

Section III: Animal or Vegetable Fats and Oils and Their Cleavage Products; Prepared Edible Fats; Animal or Vegetable Waxes

Chapter 15	Animal or vegetable fats and oils and their cleavage products prepared edible fats; animal or vegetable waxes

Section IV: Prepared Foodstuffs; Beverages, Spirits, and Vinegar; Tobacco and Manufactured Tobacco Substitutes

USITC Harmonized Tariff Schedule Contents

Appendix E

Section X: Pulp of Wood or of Other Fibrous Cellulosic Material; Waste and Scrap of Paper or Paperboard; Paper and Paperboard and Articles Thereof

Section Notes

Chapter 47	Pulp of wood or of other fibrous cellulosic material; waste and scrap of paper or paperboard
Chapter 48	Paper and paperboard; articles of paper pulp, of paper or of paperboard
Chapter 49	Printed books, newspapers, pictures and other products of the printing industry; manuscripts, typescripts and plans

Section XI: Textile and Textile Articles

Section Notes

Chapter 50	Silk
Chapter 51	Wool, fine or coarse animal hair; horsehair yarn and woven fabric
Chapter 52	Cotton
Chapter 53	Other vegetable textile fibers; paper yarn and woven fabric of paper yarn
Chapter 54	Man-made filaments
Chapter 55	Man-made staple fibers
Chapter 56	Wadding, felt and nonwovens; special yarns, twine, cordage, ropes and cables and articles thereof
Chapter 57	Carpets and other textile floor coverings
Chapter 58	Special woven fabrics; tufted textile fabrics; lace, tapestries; trimmings; embroidery
Chapter 59	Impregnated, coated, covered or laminated textile fabrics; textile articles of a kind suitable for industrial use
Chapter 60	Knitted or crocheted fabrics
Chapter 61	Articles of apparel and clothing accessories, knitted or crocheted
Chapter 62	Articles of apparel and clothing accessories, not knitted or crocheted
Chapter 63	Other made up textile articles; sets; worn clothing and worn textile articles; rags

Section XII: Footwear, Headgear, Umbrellas, Sun Umbrellas, Walking Sticks, Seatsticks, Whips, Riding-Crops and Parts Thereof; Prepared Feathers and Articles Made Therewith; Artificial Flowers; Articles of Human Hair

Chapter 64	Footwear, gaiters and the like; parts of such articles
Chapter 65	Headgear and parts thereof
Chapter 66	Umbrellas, sun umbrellas, walking sticks, seatsticks, whips, riding-crops and parts thereof
Chapter 67	Prepared feathers and down and articles made of feathers or of down; artificial flowers; articles of human hair

Section XIII: Articles of Stone, Plaster, Cement, Asbestos, Mica or Similar Materials; Ceramic Products; Glass and Glassware

Chapter 68	Articles of stone, plaster, cement, asbestos, mica or similar materials
Chapter 69	Ceramic products
Chapter 70	Glass and glassware

Section XIV: Natural or Cultured Pearls, Precious or Semiprecious Stones, Precious Metals, Metals Clad With Precious Metal, and Articles Thereof; Imitation Jewelry; Coin

Chapter 71	Natural or cultured pearls, precious or semi-precious stones, precious metals, metals clad with precious metal and articles thereof; imitation jewelry; coin

Section XV: Base Metals and Articles of Base Metal

Section Notes

Chapter 72	Iron and steel
Chapter 73	Articles of iron or steel

Appendix E

Section XXII: Special Classification Provisions; Temporary Legislation; Temporary Modifications Proclaimedpursuant to Trade Agreements Legislation; Additional Import Restrictions Proclaimed Pursuant to Section 22 of the Agricultural Adjustment Act, As Amended

Appendix F

International Purchase Agreement (Import)

GENERAL CONTRACTS **Form 4.17**

FORM

AGREEMENT made December 6, 1981, between Renoir Industrielles et Cie., of Paris, France, a corporation organized under the laws of France (the "Seller"), and H. A. Pannay, Inc., of 142 Trimble Avenue, St. Louis, Missouri, U.S.A., a Missouri corporation (the "Buyer").

1. *Sale.* The Seller shall sell to the Buyer 100,000 long tons of No. 1 heavy steel melting scrap up to a length of 1.50 meters, not over 40 centimeters in width, and not less than five millimeters in thickness.

2. *Price.* The purchase price is $27.18 per long ton, F.A.S. Vessel Cherbourg. The price is free alongside the vessel designated by the Buyer (the "Buyer's vessel"), at Cherbourg, the port of shipment. Payment for all merchandise shall be made in currency of the United States of America.

3. *Delivery.* The Seller shall deliver the scrap, in the kind and quantity specified in paragraph 1, alongside the Buyer's vessel, within reach of its loading tackle, at the port of shipment. The scrap shall be delivered by the Seller at a minimum rate of 14,000 long tons every 30 days. If this minimum rate of delivery is not maintained by the Seller during any 30-day period, the total quantity stated in paragraph 1 shall be reduced by an amount equal to the difference between the amount actually delivered and the minimum rate of delivery for such 30-day period.

4. *Notice.* The Seller shall give notice to the Buyer by cable of the quantity of scrap available for loading, the price

(*Text continued on page 4–1097*)

thereof, and the date on which the Seller is ready to commence loading for transportation to the port of shipment. Thereafter, the Buyer shall give adequate notice to the Seller by cable of the date on which it is ready to commence loading upon the Buyer's vessel. The notice shall contain the name, sailing date, loading berth, and date of delivery alongside the Buyer's vessel. Upon the receipt of such notice from the Buyer, the Seller shall prepare and commence loading the scrap for transportation to the port of shipment in sufficient quantities for the Buyer to load at the rate of 700 tons per working day; provided that the Seller shall not be required to have the scrap prepared or loaded for transportation to the port of shipment until after receipt of the letter of credit provided for in paragraph 12, and receipt of notice in writing from the bank, referred to in paragraph 12, that the Buyer has made the deposit of earnest money provided for in paragraph 11.

5. *Insurance.* The Buyer shall obtain and pay for all marine insurance for its own account, provided that all marine insurance obtained by the Buyer shall include, for the protection of the Seller, standard warehouse to warehouse coverage.

6. *Demurrage.* The Seller shall be liable for demurrage charges in excess of one day incurred by the Buyer by reason of the Seller's default. The Buyer shall be liable for demurrage or storage charges in excess of one day incurred by the Seller by reason of the Buyer's failure to load or to have his vessel ready for loading on any stipulated date.

7. *Invoices.* The Seller shall issue provisional invoices and final invoices for every shipment of scrap. The weights as established at the time and place of loading upon the Buyer's vessel shall be used in determining the amounts of the provisional invoices. The Buyer shall forward to the Seller certified weight certificates issued at the time and place of loading upon rail or barge, at the point of importation, for shipment to the Buyer's destination, and the weights as established at such time and place shall be final

(Rel.57–11/82 Pub.240)   4–1097

Form 4.17   Sale of Goods

in determining the total amounts of the final invoices; provided, that if a shipment is lost after loading upon the Buyer's vessel, the weights as established at the time and place of loading upon the Buyer's vessel shall be final in determining the total amounts of the final invoices.

8. *Inspection.* The Buyer shall have the right to inspect the scrap at the yards of the Seller, or at the place of loading upon the Buyer's vessel. All rejected scrap shall be replaced by scrap meeting the description and specifications stated in paragraph 1. The Buyer, or its agent, shall execute a certificate of inspection and acceptance, at its own cost. Failure of the Buyer to inspect shall constitute a waiver of the right of inspection, and shall be deemed acceptance of the scrap as delivered for loading.

9. *Title.* Title to the scrap shall pass to the Buyer upon delivery alongside the Buyer's vessel, provided the Buyer has established the letter of credit and made the deposit of the earnest money provided for in paragraphs 11 and 12.

10. *Covenant against reexportation.* The Buyer covenants that the scrap will be shipped to and delivered in the United States of America, and that the Buyer will not ship the scrap to, or deliver it in, any other country, and will not reexport the scrap after it is delivered in the United States of America.

11. *Earnest money.* Within ten days after the execution of this agreement, the Buyer shall deposit, at the bank at which the Buyer establishes the letter of credit provided for in paragraph 12, the sum of $40,000, in the form of bank cashier's or certified checks payable to the order of the Seller, for disposition in accordance with the terms of this paragraph. Upon full performance of the conditions of this agreement by the Buyer, the earnest money shall be refunded either by direct payment to the Buyer or by application toward the payment for the last shipment. If the Buyer fails to perform all the conditions of this agreement, the earnest money shall be delivered to the Seller as liqui-

4-1098   (Rel.57-11/82 Pub.240)

524

GENERAL CONTRACTS **Form 4.17**

dated damages, and not as a penalty, and this agreement shall thereafter become null and void.

12. *Letter of credit.* Within ten days after receipt of the notice from the Seller provided for in paragraph 4, stating the quantity of scrap available for loading and the price thereof, the Buyer shall establish with a bank in New York, New York, a confirmed, revolving, irrevocable letter of credit in favor of the Seller in the amount stated in the notice, for the term of six months, to cover the first shipment. The amount of the letter of credit shall be replenished, and the term thereof extended, to cover any additional shipments, upon receipt of notice from the Seller stating the quantity of additional scrap available for loading and the price thereof. The letter of credit shall provide that partial shipments against the letter of credit shall be permitted, and shall also provide that payment therefrom shall be made in the amount of 90% of the provisional invoice upon presentation of the following documents: (a) provisional commercial invoice; (b) consular invoice, if required; (c) clean dock or ship's receipt, or received-for-shipment ocean bill of lading, or other transportation receipt; (d) certified weight certificate; (e) Buyer's certificate of inspection and acceptance, but if the Buyer has waived his right of inspection under paragraph 8 the Seller shall so state in the invoices.

13. *Adjustment of payment.* Any difference between the amount of the final invoices, determined as provided in paragraph 7, and the amount paid on the provisional invoices shall be paid against the letter of credit upon presentation of the final invoices.

14. *Cancellation.* In the event that delivery in whole or in part, for a period not exceeding 30 days, shall be prevented by causes beyond the control of the Seller, including but not limited to acts of God, labor troubles, failure of essential means of transportation, or changes in policy with respect to exports or otherwise by the French government, this agreement shall be extended for an additional period equal

(Rel.57–11/82 Pub.240) 4–1099

Form 4.17 SALE OF GOODS

to the period of delay. In the event, however, that such non-delivery continues after such extended period, the Buyer or the Seller shall have the right to cancel this agreement to the extent of such nondelivery by written notice, and in such case there shall be no obligation or liability on the part of either party with respect to such undelivered scrap; provided that any such notice from the Buyer shall not apply with respect to any scrap which the Seller has prepared or loaded for transportation to the port of shipment prior to the receipt by the Seller of such notice.

15. *Assignment.* The Buyer shall not assign its rights nor delegate the performance of its duties under this contract without the prior written consent of the Seller.

16. *Export license.* This agreement shall be subject to the issue of an export license to the Buyer by the appropriate agency of the French government.

17. *Modifications.* All modifications of this agreement shall be in writing signed by both parties.

18. *Benefit.* This agreement shall be binding upon and shall inure to the benefit of the parties, their successors, and assigns, subject, however, to the limitation of paragraph 15.

In witness whereof the parties have executed this agreement.

Corporate Seal   Renoir Industrielles et Cie.
Attest: by ....
....   President
        Secretary
Corporate Seal   H. A. Pannay, Inc.
Attest: by ....
....   President
        Secretary

Appendix G

ACE Program and Standard Reports

AUTOMATED COMMERCIAL ENVIRONMENT

GETTING STARTED WITH ENTRY PROCESSING IN ACE

Importers and Brokers can easily get started accessing the benefits provided by U.S. Customs and Border Protection's (CBP) trade processing system, the Automated Commercial Environment (ACE).

ACE SECURE DATA PORTAL

AUTOMATED BROKER INTERFACE (ABI*)

- ↘ Run more than 125 customizable ACE Reports
- ↘ Query Antidumping/ Countervailing Duty (AD/ CVD) Case information
- ↘ Convert to monthly, interest-free payment of duties and fees

- ↘ File streamlined entry data via Cargo Release/ Simplified Entry Pilot
- ↘ File up to 99% of entry summaries in ACE
- ↘ Transmit Census Warning Overrides and electronic corrections

TO LEARN MORE ABOUT GETTING STARTED WITH ACE

VISIT CBP.GOV/ACE ONLINE:

✔ ACE Secure Data Portal
  • Setting up an ACE Portal Account

✔ ACE Web-based Training (WBT)

✔ Filing transactions in ACE via ABI
  • Introduction and Getting Started
  • ACS to ACE Transition Topics

CALL OR E-MAIL:

✔ Your CBP Client Representative or the Client Representative Outreach Line at 571.468.5500
✔ Your ABI software provider

* All ACE Cargo Release and Entry Summary Transactions MUST be filed via ABI.

www.cbp.gov/ace
3/4/2014

ACE Portal Reports
Dictionary: Importers

U.S. Customs and Border Protection (CBP)
Office of Information Technology
June 2009

ACE Portal Reports Dictionary: Importers

Executive Summary

The ACE Portal Reports Dictionary is a reference guide designed to enhance the understanding of reports for ACE users, to assist in identifying the report that best fulfills a particular business need, and to encourage the overall use of the reporting tool. The dictionary defines each report and their corresponding data attributes (objects) making it easier for ACE users to identify specific reports that meet their data requirements.

This version of the ACE Portal Reports Dictionary contains a detailed description of the most frequently-accessed reports. It also provides the exact location of each report in the ACE reporting tool, the categorical classification of each report, the standard report filters/prompts, and a description of each data attribute contained in the report.

Please note that this version of the dictionary only includes the ACE portal reports most frequently-accessed by importers. Additional versions of the dictionary are available for other stakeholder groups including: CBP Personnel, Brokers, Carriers, Sureties and Participating Government Agencies (PGAs).

The Foundation Business Outcomes team welcomes any questions, feedback or recommendations regarding the ACE Portal Reports Dictionary. Please direct all inquiries to:

FoundationBusinessOutcomes@cbp.dhs.gov

ACE Portal Reports Dictionary: Importers

Account Management Reports

Subcategory: Account Profile

     This report can be used to verify that CBP has accurate and updated company information related to your ACE account.

Subcategory: Aggregate Reports>Cargo Entry

     This report identifies discrepant cargo entries by consignee and can be used to determine future compliance strategies.

     This report identifies discrepant cargo entries by date and consignee. This information can be used to determine future compliance strategies.

     This report identifies discrepant cargo entries by country of origin (COO) code and can be used to determine future sourcing strategies.

     This report identifies discrepant cargo entries by entry type code and can be used for future compliance improvement.

     This report identifies discrepant cargo entries by filer and can be used by importers to work with their brokers to improve compliance.

     This report identifies discrepant cargo entries by their associated Harmonized Tariff Schedule (HTS) number. This report assists importers in identifying those HTS numbers that are frequently non-compliant.

     This report identifies discrepant cargo entries by their associated Importer of Record (IR) number. This report assists importers with multiple IR numbers in identifying those that need improved compliance.

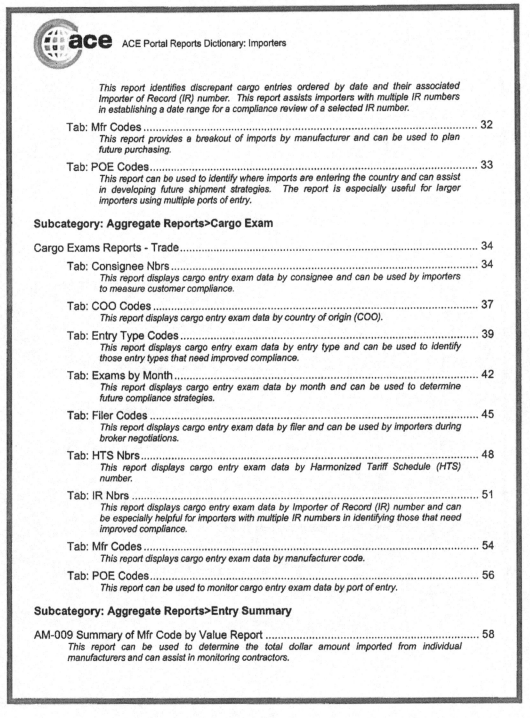

ace   ACE Portal Reports Dictionary: Importers

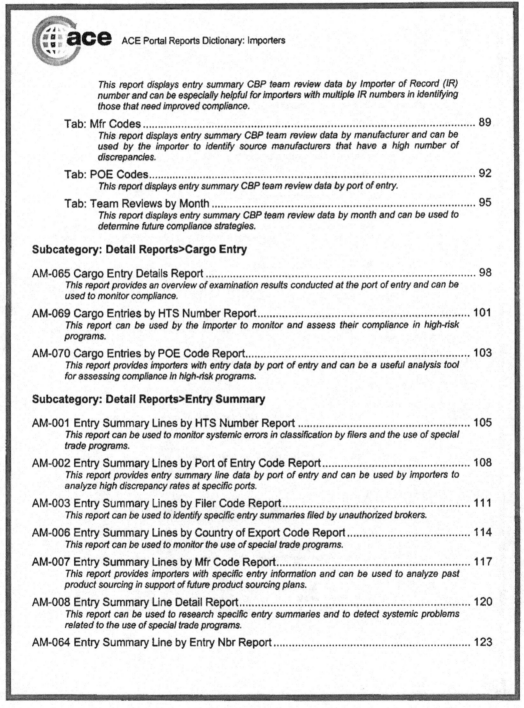

ACE Portal Reports Dictionary: Importers

This report displays entry summary CBP team review data by Importer of Record (IR) number and can be especially helpful for importers with multiple IR numbers in identifying those that need improved compliance.

This report displays entry summary CBP team review data by manufacturer and can be used by the importer to identify source manufacturers that have a high number of discrepancies.

This report displays entry summary CBP team review data by port of entry.

This report displays entry summary CBP team review data by month and can be used to determine future compliance strategies.

Subcategory: Detail Reports>Cargo Entry

This report provides an overview of examination results conducted at the port of entry and can be used to monitor compliance.

This report can be used by the importer to monitor and assess their compliance in high-risk programs.

This report provides importers with entry data by port of entry and can be a useful analysis tool for assessing compliance in high-risk programs.

Subcategory: Detail Reports>Entry Summary

This report can be used to monitor systemic errors in classification by filers and the use of special trade programs.

This report provides entry summary line data by port of entry and can be used by importers to analyze high discrepancy rates at specific ports.

This report can be used to identify specific entry summaries filed by unauthorized brokers.

This report can be used to monitor the use of special trade programs.

This report provides importers with specific entry information and can be used to analyze past product sourcing in support of future product sourcing plans.

This report can be used to research specific entry summaries and to detect systemic problems related to the use of special trade programs.

ace ACE Portal Reports Dictionary: Importers

ace ACE Portal Reports Dictionary: Importers

Additional Report Data Objects

Appendix H
Guidance on Internet Purchases

Appendix H

 Official website of the Department of Homeland Security

 U.S. Customs and Border Protection

Internet Purchases

Your Responsibility and Liability

The Internet has made it easy to find and purchase items from almost anywhere in the world. However, many people are discovering that getting a foreign-bought item successfully delivered to the United States is much more complicated.

When goods move from any foreign country to the United States, they are being IMPORTED. There are specific rules and regulations that govern the act of importing - and they can be extremely complex and confusing - and costly.

That artisan cheese from Italy may be a snap to find and buy on the Internet, but U.S. Customs and Border Protection could seize your purchase because certain regulations prohibit the importation of dairy products from particular countries without a permit.

Your great auction purchase of gorgeous linen products? Depending upon the country of origin, quota restrictions could hold them up in CBP for a long time. And storage charges in such cases can be expensive.

In other words, "Buyer, Beware." When you buy goods from foreign sources, you become the importer. And it is the importer - in this case, **YOU** - who is responsible for assuring that the goods comply with a variety of both state and federal government import regulations. Importing goods that are unsafe, that fail to meet health code requirements, or that violate quota restrictions could end up costing you quite a bit of money in fines and penalties. At the very least, such goods would be detained, and possibly destroyed, by CBP.

Knowing what is admissible is just part of the story. The other part is knowing how to import. Depending upon what you are importing and its value, the procedures can be very complicated.

It does not matter whether you bought the item from an established business or from an individual selling item in an on-line auction. If merchandise, used or new, is imported into the United States, it must clear CBP and may be subject to the payment of duty as well as to whatever rules and regulations govern the importation of that particular product into the United States.

Checklist

Keep the following questions in mind before you buy something from a foreign source. The answers will have far-reaching CBP implications (explained below) that could influence your decision to buy.

- Can the goods be legally imported? Are there restrictions on, or special forms required, for your purchase's importation?
- Are you buying the item(s) for your personal use or for commercial purposes?

Guidance on Internet Purchases

- Will you be responsible for shipping costs? If so, you should discuss with the seller how your purchase will be shipped. The choices are freight, courier service or international postal service. If you're not careful, transportation and handling costs could far outweigh the cost of your purchase. Sometimes, the seemingly cheaper methods can be more expensive in the long run because they are more susceptible to theft, misdeliveries and logistical problems.
- You should discuss with the seller what the exact delivery arrangements will be. If the seller does not make arrangements for postal or door-to-door delivery, you will either need to hire a customs broker to clear your goods and forward them on to you, or go the port of entry and clear them yourself.
- Can you trust the seller to provide accurate information about the item being shipped in the Customs section of the shipping documents? Giving misleading or inaccurate information about the nature of the item and its value is illegal. And it is the importer - **YOU** - who could face legal action and fines for this violation!

The following is a brief primer on the various factors that can impact the clearance of your goods through CBP.

U.S. Customs and Border Protection Declarations

All paperwork for sending packages internationally has a section for providing CBP information. A U.S. Customs and Border Protection Declaration is a form obtainable at most foreign post offices. This declaration form should include a full and accurate description of the merchandise, and should be securely attached to the outside of your shipment. Declaration forms vary from country to country, and they don't all ask for the information required by the U.S. Customs and Border Protection. You should ask the seller to provide the following information, whether or not it is asked for on the paperwork.

- **Seller's name and address. Description of the item(s) in English (a legal requirement).** For example, antique silver teapot, silk kimono, 18-karat gold rope necklace. It is very important that this information be detailed and accurate. What is described here will determine the classification number and duty rate that Customs assigns the item when it arrives in the United States. If this information is inaccurate, you could end up paying the wrong duty rate for what you purchased. If it is inaccurate enough to seem deliberately misleading -- keep in mind that CBP does randomly inspect packages -- your goods could be seized and you may be assessed a fine.
- **Quantity of each type of item being shipped.** For example, two watches (14-karat gold, 17 jewel), one leather purse.
- **Purchase price in U.S. dollars.** Provide both the unit price, and if more than one unit was purchased, the total value for all like items. Fudging or miscalculating the price paid for goods is a bad idea. Many sellers offer to misrepresent costs in an effort to save the purchaser from having to pay duty, but this is illegal. Others sellers are wary of package

Appendix H

handlers and do not want them to know how valuable something may be, which could result in its theft. The most common legal precaution against theft is to insure the package when sending it. You should discuss insurance options with your seller, keeping in mind that misrepresenting the value of an item on the Customs declaration is illegal.

- **Weight** of the item(s).
- **Country of origin** of the product itself. Be aware that this is not necessarily the country where the item was purchased.

Note: It is important to know that foreign shipments that are not accompanied by a U.S. Customs and Border Protection declaration form and an invoice may be subject to seizure, forfeiture or return to sender.

Postal Service, Couriers and Freight

There are three ways goods can be sent to you from abroad. In order to avoid costly problems, you and the seller of your goods should agree on which will be used the international postal service, a courier service, or freight carriers.

1. **International Postal Service:** Merchandise shipped through the international postal service is forwarded upon its arrival in the United States to one of U.S. Customs and Border Protection International Mail Branches for clearance. If the item is less than $2,000 in value and is not subject to a quota or is not a restricted or prohibited item, a CBP official will usually prepare the paperwork for importing it, assess the proper duty, and release it for delivery. This procedure is generally referred to as a mail entry. Packages whose declared value is under $200 ($100 if being sent as a gift to someone other than the purchaser) will generally be cleared without any additional paperwork prepared by CBP. However, CBP always reserves the right to require a formal entry for any importation and generally exercises this option if there is something unusual about the importation, or if important documents such as an invoice or bill of sale do not accompany the item.

If any duty is owed, CBP will charge a processing fee for clearing your package. Duty and the processing fee are usually paid at your local post office, where your package is forwarded.

Hint: To speed a package through CBP examination at a port's International Mail Branch, the seller should affix a completed CN 22 or CN 23 (U.S. Customs and Border Protection Declaration Form) to the outside of the package. This form may be obtained at local post offices worldwide.

Plus: Pretty economical.

Pitfalls: If the item's value is more than $2,000, it may be held at the mail facility until you can arrange for a formal entry. This may require either hiring a customs broker to clear your goods or you may file the paperwork yourself.

Guidance on Internet Purchases

Lost packages are hard to find. Since most packages sent through the mail do not have tracking numbers unless they are insured or you've paid to have a tracking number, it can be impossible to trace a "lost" package. If a package is lost a "tracer" should be initiated by the sender of the package.

2. **Courier Shipping:** Goods shipped by courier, express, or other commercial service usually are expedited through CBP by a customs broker hired by that commercial service and then delivered seamlessly to your door. Customs brokers are not CBP employees. There are a number of different charges associated with these services, including shipping and handling, the fees charged by the service for clearing the merchandise through CBP, as well as any Customs duty and processing fees that may be owed on your importation.

Pluses: Get seamless delivery. All you have to do is sign for the package when it arrives. In most cases delivery is quick and reliable. When there's a problem, there is a tracking number that can help resolve the matter.

Pitfalls: Many people have found the various charges and fees levied to be higher then they expected, and sometimes exceed the cost of their purchase(s).

Buyers often have the misunderstanding that when the purchase price includes shipping and handling, all the costs associated with clearing the package through CBP are covered by the seller. They don't realize that brokers fees and CBP duties may be an additional charge that the buyer is responsible for.

3. **Freight Shipping:** Merchandise shipped by freight can arrive in the United States at an air, sea or land port. If your goods are being shipped by freight, you should ask the seller to instruct the freight company to forward them to your doorstep, which may entail the shipper's use of a customs broker to clear your goods. Alternatively, ask that the goods be forwarded to a port of entry near where you live so that you can clear or "enter" them yourself (advisable only if the shipment is under $2000 in value. See Formal Entry below.)

Pluses: Can be economical, particularly, if you're prepared to handle the logistics of clearing the goods through Customs yourself. Also, the best way to handle large bulky purchases.

Pitfall: If the freight company has not been instructed to forward your goods, they could end up sitting on the dock at the port where they first entered the country.

Heads-Up

U.S. Customs and Border Protection does not inform importers of the arrival of cargo or freight. When cargo or freight arrives at a U.S. port of entry, it is the responsibility of the shipper or a designated agent to inform the importer of its arrival. However, proper notification does not always happen, particularly, if the shipper has incomplete contact information for you, the importer. Therefore, it is important to find out the scheduled arrival date of your import and follow-up.

If you are not notified that your goods have arrived and you or your broker have not presented the proper paperwork to CBP within 15 days of your goods' arrival, your goods will be transferred to a

Appendix H

warehouse, and you will be liable for storage charges. If you have not claimed your goods within six months of their arrival in the USA, they could be sold at auction. (See the Checklist under item #3.)

Importing Process Paying Duty: The importer is ultimately responsible for paying any duty owed on an import. Determining duty can be very complicated, and while shipping services will often give an estimate for what the duty rate on an item might be, only CBP can make a final determination about what is owed. You should not be misled into thinking your purchase price includes duty because the seller cannot say with absolute certainty what the duty will be. As a rule, a purchase price that includes shipping and handling does not include duty or any costs associated with clearing the goods through CBP. First time importers are often surprised by bills they receive for duty, U.S. Customs and Border Protection merchandise processing fee, and something referred to as "customs fees," which are actually charges for the services of the broker who cleared your goods through CBP.

How you pay duty depends on how your goods were shipped. If your goods were shipped through the International Postal Service, you will need to pay the mail carrier and/or go to your local post office to pay any duty and processing fees owed when your package arrives at that post office. If your goods were sent by a courier service, that service will either bill you for the duty they paid on your behalf or require payment on delivery.

If your goods were sent by freight, there are two possible scenarios for paying duty.

If no arrangements were made to forward the goods to your door, you will need to either clear them through CBP yourself, in which case you will pay duty directly to CBP at the port where your goods arrived. Alternatively, you will need to arrange for a broker to clear your goods. If you hire a broker, they will bill you for their services and any duty they paid on your behalf.

If arrangements were made to forward your goods to you, you will be billed for any duty owed, and for the services of the broker who cleared them through CBP.

Reminder: U.S. Customs and Border Protection holds the importer - YOU - liable for the payment of duty not the seller.

- **Personal vs. Commercial Use:** Many import regulations only apply to goods imported for commercial - business or resale - purposes. For instance, most goods imported for personal use are not subject to quota. The one exception to this is made-to-measure suits from Hong Kong, which are subject to quota restrictions regardless of the use they are imported for. On the other hand, import restrictions that are based on health, safety and protecting endangered species apply across the board.

Note: U.S. Customs and Border Protection is authorized to make judgment calls about what qualifies as personal use. Several suits that are identical or a number of very similar handbags will have a hard time passing the credibility test as items for personal use.

For Commercial Purposes: Goods imported for commercial purposes must comply with a variety of special requirements, such as marking of country of origin, which vary depending upon the particular commodity. Please see our publication, "Importing Into the United States," for more detailed information. Be particularly aware that an invoice should always accompany commercial shipments.

Guidance on Internet Purchases

- **Informal Entries:** If the value of your purchase(s) is less than $2500 and your goods are being shipped by mail or freight, they may, in most cases, be imported as an informal entry. However, there are exceptions to this. For instance, if the importation is determined to be for commercial purposes, the value limit for filing an informal entry for many textile items is either $250 or $0 - depending on whether or not the item is subject to Quota (see below). Clearing goods through CBP as an informal entry is less arduous a process than clearing them by filing a formal entry. Essentially, when goods are cleared as an informal entry, CBP will prepare the paperwork, including determining the classification number and duty rate for your merchandise.

The duty rate for many items typically bought in an on-line auction is zero, however, CBP may charge a small processing fee for mail imports that do require the payment of duty.

If your goods are sent by a courier or express service, their brokers will usually handle the paperwork, and bill you for their services. If your goods are being shipped by freight, and you want to clear them through CBP yourself, be sure the shipping company has instructions to deliver them to a port near you. Otherwise, you will need to arrange for someone else to clear the goods for you when they arrive. Your alternative is to ask the seller to make arrangements to have your goods forwarded to your door, in which case you should expect to pay for the services of the customs broker who coordinates this when your goods arrive in the U.S.A.

- **Formal Entries:** If your goods are valued at more than $2500, or for commercial textile shipments (clothes/materials) regardless of value, you will be required to file a formal entry, which can require extensive paperwork and the filing of a U.S. Customs and Border Protection bond. As mentioned above and for various reasons, CBP may require a formal entry for any importation. CBP, however, rarely exercises this right unless there is a particular concern about the circumstances surrounding an importation.

Because filing a formal entry can be complicated, the U.S. Customs and Border Protection recommends importers consider hiring a customs broker to complete the transaction. Lists of brokers can be found on the port pages of CBP web site.

One of the most difficult things about filing formal entries is accurately identifying the correct classification number of the item being imported. The Harmonized Tariff Schedule of the United States (HTSUS) lists classification numbers for every conceivable item under the Sun. The HTSUS is the size of an unabridged dictionary, and specialists train for months to learn how to correctly classify goods.

The classification number of an item determines many requirements pertaining to that item's importation such as its duty rate, eligibility for special import programs like the Generalized System of Preferences (GSP) or the North American Free Trade Agreement (NAFTA), and whether or not the item is subject to quota restrictions.

Appendix H

Failure to correctly classify an item can result in fines and/or delays in delivery. You may write to U.S. Customs and Border Protection for a binding ruling, and/or contact an import specialist at your local port for help to identify the proper classification number for your imported item.

- **Quota:** Many kinds of goods imported for commercial use may be subject to a quota limit. It is the classification number of the article as identified in the Harmonized Tariff Schedule of the United States and the country of origin that determine whether or not an item is subject to quota requirements.

In some cases, the quota is absolute, meaning that once the quota is filled - because the quota has reached its limit for that particular period of time - no additional quantities of that item may be imported until the next open period. Such merchandise must be warehoused or exported. Other quotas are tariff-related, which means that a certain quantity of goods may enter at a low rate of duty, but once that threshold is reached - during a specified period of time - a higher duty rate will be assessed for any additional quantities of that particular imported good. Unlimited quantities of some merchandise subject to tariff-rate quota may, however, enter at over the quota rates.

If you are importing goods for commercial use or resale, it's a good idea to contact your local port of entry for more specific information.

Fill levels for quotas are currently posted on the CBP Electronic Bulletin Board in the file called Quota Threshold Status. Fill levels for textile items can be found in the Quota section of Importing/Exporting.

The Quota program is generally applied only to commercial importations. While the importation of many goods imported under "personal use" quantities are not affected by quota restrictions, there is one exception; made-to-measure suits made in Hong Kong, which are restricted for both personal and commercial use.

- **Prohibited Merchandise:** Purchasers should also be aware that some products might be considered contraband and cannot be brought into the United States under any circumstances. This includes the obvious, such as narcotics and child pornography, as well as less obvious items such as tainted food products, and other items, a list of which can be found in "Importing Into the United States." Such merchandise can be seized by CBP, and attempts to import it may subject the importer to civil or even criminal sanctions. If you have any question at all about your purchase, you should contact your closest CBP port and get an opinion before you complete the transaction.
- **Restricted Merchandise:** Many items cannot be imported into the United States unless the importer has the proper permit or license from the appropriate regulatory authority. Some of the most common restricted items include food, plant and dairy products; alcohol and tobacco products; birds, fish or animals and products thereof; goods from embargoed countries, firearms and ammunition, cultural artifacts from certain countries, and copyrighted materials.

Guidance on Internet Purchases

The entry of prescription medicines is restricted and subject to the approval of the U.S. Food and Drug Administration (FDA). Depending on the FDA review of the medicine, it may be released to the addressee or seized. There are, however, provisions allowing passengers to hand carry prescription drugs into the United States if they enter through a land border with Canada or Mexico.

- **Electronic Transmission Information:** Materials downloaded from the Internet are not subject to duty. This applies to any goods or merchandise that are electronically transmitted to the purchaser, such as CDs, books, or posters. However, the unauthorized downloading of copyrighted items could subject you to prosecution. Downloading child pornography is also a crime. U.S. Customs and Border Protection has the authority to investigate and prosecute persons involved in this and other illegal activities.

Exporting

If you are sending goods to someone outside the United States, you should be aware that most countries have similar regulations governing the importation of goods into their territory. If you are selling goods on a "Payment on Delivery" basis, you might want to contact the Customs authority of the country where the goods are being shipped to make sure they can legally be imported into that country. In addition, some commodities sold for export are subject to enforcement requirements of U.S. Customs and Border Protection and other U.S. government agencies. In particular, cars and goods with potential military applications, including some electronics and software, must be cleared through CBP before they are exported. And if you export goods worth more than $2,500, you will have to follow formal export procedures.

Tags: Trade

Appendix I

Regulatory Audit Questionnaires

Appendix I

U. S. Customs and Border Protection
Office of Strategic Trade
Regulatory Audit Division

Internal Control Questionnaire for Focused Assessments

Introduction

In March 2003, the U.S. Customs Service became part of U.S. Customs and Border Protection, which will continue to be referenced as Customs in this document.

The purpose of the Internal Control Questionnaire for Focused Assessments (FAs) is to obtain information about the company's organizational structure and internal controls related to Customs transactions. The questionnaire is designed to give the audit team a general understanding of the company's import operations and internal control structure as well as to inform the audit candidates of the areas on which the assessment may focus. As each company's operations are unique, this questionnaire may have been modified to fit the circumstances of each audit candidate.

Review Scope

When the importer responds to the questionnaire completely and comprehensively, the Pre-Assessment Survey (PAS) team can plan its approach to the Focused Assessment. The results of the questionnaire, interviews with company officials and Customs personnel, survey of company procedures, and limited testing will be used to determine the effectiveness of the company's internal control system. A PAS of the company's importing operations and internal controls will be used to determine whether more extensive testing is necessary. Any additional testing will be done in the Assessment Compliance Testing (ACT) phase of the Focused Assessment.

Answering the questionnaire affords the company the opportunity to evaluate its own internal controls and operations pertaining to Customs activities. The company will also be more prepared for the Focused Assessment.

I. **General**

    A. Provide the name, title, and telephone number of the official(s) preparing information for this questionnaire.

    B. Provide the name, title, and telephone number of the person who will be the contact for Customs during the Focused Assessment.

II. **Control Environment**

    A. <u>Organizational Structure, Policy and Procedures, Assignment of Responsibilities</u>
       1. Provide a copy of the company's organizational chart and related department descriptions. Include the detail to show the location of the Import Department identified and any structure descriptions that are relevant.

1

October 2003

2. Identify the key individuals in each office responsible for Customs compliance (may be included on the organization chart).
3. Provide the names and addresses of any related foreign and/or domestic companies, such as the company's parent, sister, subsidiaries, or joint ventures.
4. If the company has operating policies and procedures manuals for Customs operations, provide a copy of the manuals (preferably in electronic format).
5. If the policies and procedures have the support and approval of management, identify the individuals who approve the procedures.

B. Employee Awareness Training
1. What specialized Customs training is required for key personnel working in the Import Department? If available, provide copies of training logs or other records supporting training.
2. What Customs experience have key personnel involved in Customs-related activities had?
3. Who in other departments is responsible for reporting Customs-related activities to the Import Department?
4. What training is provided to personnel in other departments responsible for reporting Customs-related activities to the Import Department?
5. How does the company obtain current information on Customs requirements?
6. Does the company use the U.S. Customs and Border Protection Web site?
7. Does the company request and disseminate binding rulings?

III.　Risk Assessment

A. How does the company identify, analyze, and manage risks related to Customs activities?

B. What risks related to Customs activities has the company identified, and what control mechanisms has it implemented?

IV.　Control Procedures

A. Using source records for support, provide a description and/or flowchart of the company's activities, including general ledger account numbers for recording the acquisition of foreign merchandise in the following areas:
- Purchase of foreign merchandise
- Receipt of foreign merchandise
- Recording in inventory
- Payments made to foreign vendor
- Distribution to customers (e.g., drop shipments)
- Export of merchandise (e.g., assists, Chapter 98)

B. For each aspect of value listed below, respond to the following. Where procedures are documented, reference the applicable sections.
1. What internal control procedures are used to assure accurate reporting to Customs?
2. Who is the person assigned responsibility for accurate reporting?
3. What records are maintained?
   ❏ Basis of Appraisement (19 CFR 152.101)

2

October 2003

Appendix I

- ❑ Price Actually Paid or Payable
- ❑ Packing
- ❑ Selling Commissions
- ❑ Assists (e.g., Materials/Component Parts, Tools, Dies, Molds, Merchandise Consumed, Engineering, Development, Art Work, Design Work, Plans)
- ❑ Royalties and License Fees
- ❑ Proceeds of Subsequent Resale
- ❑ Transportation Costs (e.g., International Freight, Foreign inland Freight, Transportation Rebates, Insurance)
- ❑ Retroactive Price Adjustments
- ❑ Price Increases
- ❑ Rebates
- ❑ Allowances
- ❑ Indirect Payments
- ❑ Payment of Seller's Debt by Buyer (e.g., quota)
- ❑ Price Reductions to Buyer to Settle debts (e.g., Reductions for Defective Merchandise)
- ❑ Purchases on Consignment
- ❑ Quota/Visa
- ❑ Currency Exchange Adjustments

C. For each of the following Customs-related activities, respond to the following. Where procedures are documented, reference the applicable sections.
   1. What internal control procedures are used to assure accurate reporting to Customs?
   2. Who is the person assigned responsibility for accurate reporting?
   3. What records are maintained?
   - ❑ Classification
   - ❑ Quantity
   - ❑ Reconciliation
   - ❑ Trade Agreements
     - (1) Generalized System of Preferences (GSP)
     - (2) Caribbean Basin Economic Recovery Act (also known as Caribbean Basin Initiative(and Special Access Provision (SAP)
     - (3) Israel Free Trade
     - (4) Insular Possessions
     - (5) Andean Trade Preference
     - (6) Trade Development Act of 2000
       - i. African Growth and Opportunity Act (AGOA)
       - ii. Caribbean Basin Trade Partnership Act (CBTPA)
   - ❑ Special Duty Provisions
     - (1) 9801.00.10
     - (2) 9802.00.40
     - (3) 9802.00.50
     - (4) 9802.00.60
     - (5) 9802.00.80
     - (6) 9802.00.90
   - ❑ Antidumping/Countervailing Duties

3

V.   Information and Communication

    A. Describe the procedures for the Import Department to disseminate relevant Customs information to other departments.

    B. Describe the procedures for other departments to communicate with the Import Department on matters affecting imported merchandise.

    C. Describe the procedures for the Import Department to participate in major planning processes involving importation activities.

VI.   Monitoring

    A. What methods of oversight and monitoring does the Import Department management use to ensure compliance with Customs requirements?

    B. Provide information and/or reports on the review and evaluation of compliance with Customs requirements by other internal and external entities (e.g., internal audit department, financial statement auditors).

    C. What level of management are these self-reviews reported to for action?

VII.   Miscellaneous

    A. Identify the account numbers in which costs for imported merchandise are recorded.

4

October 2003

U.S. Customs and Border Protection
Office of Strategic Trade
Regulatory Audit Division

Electronic Data Processing (EDP) Questionnaire
for Focused Assessments

In March 2003, the U.S. Customs Service became part of the U.S. Customs and Border Protection, which will continue to be referenced as Customs in this document.

An important factor in conducting Focused Assessments (FAs) in a timely manner may include obtaining electronic data files needed to facilitate comparisons between the company's data and Customs data, sampling, and transactional testing. Generally, two or more data universes are identified. The first universe consists of a fiscal year's imports. The sampling unit may be entry line items unless a more efficient sampling unit, such as invoice line items or the equivalent, is available from the company. Other universes of financial transactions are used to test for possible unreported dutiable expenses. These universes and sampling items will be determined after the team has an understanding of your system and Customs procedures.

Typically, files useful for the FA program may include, but not be limited to: Customs entry log, purchase orders, vendor master, general ledger (GL), invoice line detail, chart of accounts, foreign purchases journal, AP (Payment History File) or GL expense file for imported merchandise, accounts payable with GL reference, cash disbursements, wire transfers, letters of credit, and inventory records.

Please return a hard copy and a *disk copy* of the completed questionnaire to

U.S. Customs and Border Protection

Regulatory Audit Division

Attention:

[address]

Email:

Phone:

Fax:

1

October 2003

Regulatory Audit Questionnaires

1. List the files, or an equivalent of the same information, that are maintained on each of your computer systems, and describe how each system communicates or links with other systems. For each system, identify the contact person responsible for maintaining that system or information. Identify which information is maintained manually. The following format may be used:

Record	System	Link to Other System	Contact Person	Title	Division

Customs entry (CF 7501)
Special duty provision
Payment history
Accounts Payable
Purchase order
Invoice line detail
Inventory and receiving
Shipping, freight, insurance, and bill of lading
Vendor codes and addresses
Finished product specifications
Country of origin certification
Imported product
Cost data
Letters of credit
Wire transfers
Cash disbursement

2. Provide flowcharts and/or narrative description of the data flow between systems

3. Are your computer systems IBM Compatible? Yes/No

4. What types of electronic media do you use to transport data? [C-Tape, E-Tape, CD-ROM, Zip Cartridge

5. Specify the capacity for your electronic media

6. List data center location(s).

7. Specify the EDP Department contact person and phone number.

2

October 2003

Appendix J

Export/Import-Related
Web Sites

Appendix J

EXPORT/IMPORT WEB SITES

EXPORTS	
Bureau of Industry and Security	www.bis.doc.gov
-Export Enforcement	
-Licensing	
-Antiboycott Compliance	
-Embargoed Exports	
-Denied Persons List	
-Ag/Med Licensing to Cuba/Syria	
Office of Foreign Assets Control	www.treas.gov/ofac.
-Embargoed Countries	
-Specially Designated Nationals/Terrorist Lists	
Census Bureau	www.census.gov.
-Electronic Export Information	
-Schedule B Numbers	
-Trade Data Statistics	
Automated Export System	www.aesdirect.gov
Defense Trade Controls	www.pmddtc.state.gov.
-United States Munitions List goods	
-Prohibited Destinations	
U.S. Customs Export Enforcement (EXODUS)	www.cbp.gov

IMPORTS	
U.S. Customs and Border Protection	www.cbp.gov
-Informed Compliance Publications	
-Regulations	
-Rulings	
-Traveler Information	
-Drawback	
-Customs Forms	
-Customs Publications	
-Reconciliation	
-C-TPAT	
-ACE	
Office of Foreign Assets Control	www.treas.gov./ofac
-Embargoed imports	
International Trade Administration	www.ita.doc.gov
-Antidumping/Countervailing Duties	
International Trade Commission	www.usitc.gov
-Harmonized Tariff Schedule	
-Antidumping/Countervailing Duties	

OTHER GOVERNMENT AGENCIES	
Consumer Products Safety Administration	www.cpsc.gov

EXPORT/IMPORT WEB SITES

-CPSIA and Certificates of Conformity	
Department of Agriculture	www.usda.gov
-Animal and Plant Health Inspection Service	www.aphis.usda.gov
-Plant Protection and Quarantine	
-Lacey Act	
Department of Commerce	www.doc.gov
Department of Transportation	www.dot.gov
Environmental Protection Agency	www.epa.gov
Federal Maritime Commission	www.fmc.gov
Federal Trade Commission	www.ftc.gov
-Made in America Standards	
Fish and Wildlife Service	www.fws.gov
Food and Drug Administration	www.fda.gov
Foreign Agricultural Service	www.fas.usda.gov
Hazardous Materials	www.hazmat.dot.gov
Office of the United States Trade Representative	www.ustr.gov

OTHER GOVERNMENT RESOURCES	
Agricultural Exporter Assistance	www.fas.usda.gov.
Code of Federal Regulations	http://www.gpoaccess.gov/cfr/index.html.
Congressional Information	http://www.gpoaccess.gov/crecord/index.html.
Federal Register	http://www.gpoaccess.gov/fr/index.html.
NAFTA Facts	http://www.export.gov/fta/nafta/doc_fta_nafta.asp.
National Trade Data Bank and STAT USA	http://www.stat-usa.gov/
Public Laws	http://www.gpoaccess.gov/plaws/index.html.
Small Business Association	http://www.sba.gov/
U.S. Business Advisor	http://www.business.gov/
U.S. Export Assistance Centers	http://www.export.gov/eac/index.asp.

FINANCIAL	
Asian Development Bank	http://www.adb.org/

Appendix J

EXPORT/IMPORT WEB SITES

Export-Import Bank of the United States	http://www.exim.gov/
Inter-American Development Bank	http://www.iadb.org/
International Monetary Fund	http://www.imf.org.
Overseas Private Investment Corporation	http://www.opic.gov/
World Bank	http://www.worldbank.org/

TRADE ASSOCIATIONS	
American Association of Exporters and Importers	http://www.aaei.org/
American Association of Port Authorities	http://www.aapa-ports.org/
Federation of International Trade Associations	http://www.fita.org/
International Chamber of Commerce	http://www.iccwbo.org/
Joint Industry Group	http://www.jig.org
National Association of Foreign Trade Zone Operators	http://www.naftz.org/
International Compliance Professionals Association	http://www.icpainc.org/
National Council on International Trade Development	http://www.ncitd.org/
National Customs Brokers and Forwarders Assocation of America	http://www.ncbfaa.org/
National Industrial Transportation League	http://www.nitl.org/
National Foreign Trade Council	http://www.nftc.org/
Organization of Women in International Trade	http://owit.org
World Chambers of Commerce	http://www.worldchambers.com/
World Trade Centers Association	http://world.wtca.org/portal/site/wtcaonline

FOREIGN CUSTOMS SERVICES AND TARIFFS	
Argentina	http://www.afip.gov.ar/Aduana/
Australia	http://www.customs.gov.au.
Brazil	http://www.receita.fazenda.gov.br/

Export/Import-Related Web Sites

EXPORT/IMPORT WEB SITES

Canada	http://www.cbsa-asfc.gc.ca/menu-eng.html
Chile	http://www.aduana.cl/prontus_aduana_eng
China	http://english.customs.gov.cn/publish/portal191/
Colombia	http://www.dian.gov.co/
European Union Customs	http://ec.europa.eu/taxation_customs/index_en.htm
France	http://www.douane.gouv.fr/
Germany	http://www.zoll.de/english_version/index.html
Hong Kong	http://www.customs.gov.hk/
Hungary	http://vam.gov.hu/welcomeEn.do
India	http://www.customs.gov.in/cae1-english.htm
Indonesia	http://www.beacukai.go.id/
Ireland	http://www.revenue.ie/en/index.html
Israel	http://ozar.mof.gov.il/customs/eng/mainpage.htm
Japan	http://www.customs.go.jp/english/index.htm
Jordan	http://www.customs.gov.jo/English/about_jordan.shtm
Korea	http://english.customs.go.kr/
Latin American Trade Council	http://www.latco.org/tools.htm
Malaysia	http://www.customs.gov.my/
Mexico	http://www.aduanas.sat.gob.mx/aduana_mexico/2008/home.asp
Netherlands	http://www.douane.nl/organisatie/en/customs/
New Zealand	http://www.customs.govt.nz
Peru	http://www.aduanet.gob.pe/aduanas/version_ingles/aduanetingles.htm
Russia	http://www.customs.ru/en/
Saudi Arabia	http://www.customs.gov.sa/CustomsNew/default_E.aspx
Singapore	http://www.customs.gov.sg/topNav/hom/
Sweden	http://www.tullverket.se/en/
Taiwan	http://eweb.customs.gov.tw/mp.asp?mp=21

EXPORT/IMPORT WEB SITES

Thailand	http://www.customs.go.th/Customs-Eng/indexEng.jsp
United Kingdom	http://www.hmrc.gov.uk/index.htm
World Customs Organization	http://www.wcoomd.org/home.htm
World Trade Organization	www.wto.org

MISCELLANEOUS TRADE/LEGAL INFORMATION	
American National Standards Institute	www.ansi.org
Carnets	www.uscib.org
CIA's World Fact Book	https://www.cia.gov/library/publications/the-world-factbook/
Currency Converter	http://www.xe.com/ucc/
Federal Reserve Board Foreign Exchange Rates	http://www.federalreserve.gov/Releases/H10/Hist/
Foreign Trade Statistics	http://www.census.gov/foreign-trade/statistics/index.html
Incoterms	http://www.iccwbo.org/incoterms/id3045/index.html
International Organization for Standardization	http://www.iso.org/iso/home.htm
International Trademark Association	http://www.inta.org/
Office of International Trade and Ecomonic Analysis	http://www.ita.doc.gov/td/industry/otea/
United Nations	www.un.org

MARKETING	
Commerce Business Daily	http://cbdnet.gpo.gov/
Office of Technology and Electronic Commerce	http://web.ita.doc.gov/ITI/itiHome.nsf/(HotNews)/HotNews
Export.Gov	http://www.export.gov
Online Exporter Services	http://www.buyusa.gov
Trade Opportunities	http://www.commerce.gov/TradeOpportunities/index.htm
U.S. Agency for International Development	http://www.usaid.gov

Glossary of International Trade Terms

Absolute Quota: A fixed limit on the quantity of goods that can be imported into a country during the quota period, usually one year.

Acceptance: A drawee's signed agreement to pay a draft as presented. It must be written on the draft and may consist of the drawee's signature alone. In documentary collections where the exporter (seller) draws a draft on the purchaser, the purchaser does not become legally liable to make payment until he receives the draft and accepts it. Then, at the maturity date of the draft, the drawee should pay. However, if the drawee fails to pay, there is no bank guarantee of payment even if the presentation of the draft was made to the purchaser through banking channels.

Acceptor, Accepter: A drawee who has accepted a draft.

ACE: Automated Commercial Environment—U.S. Customs and Border Protection's new Internet-based commercial trade processing system.

Adjustment Assistance: Financial, training, and re-employment technical assistance to workers and technical assistance to firms and industries to help them cope with difficulties arising from increased import competition. The objective of the assistance is usually to help an industry to become more competitive in the same line of production, or to move into other economic activities. The aid to workers can take the form of training (to qualify the affected individuals for employment in new or expanding industries), relocation allowances (to help them move from areas characterized by high unemployment to areas where employment may be available), or unemployment compensation (while they are searching for new jobs).

Ad Valorem Tariff: A tariff calculated as a percentage of the value of goods; for example, "15 percent ad valorem" means 15 percent of the value. Usually, but not always, the value is the sales price between the exporter (seller) and the importer (buyer).

Advising Bank: A bank located in the exporter's (seller's) country notifying the exporter that the purchaser has opened a letter of credit in favor of the exporter through another (issuing) bank.

Affreightment, Contract of: An agreement by a steamship line to provide cargo space on a vessel at a specified time and for a specified price for an exporter or importer. See "Booking Cargo."

Agent: In a general sense, a person who acts on behalf of another person. This may include selling agents and buying agents. Sales agents are sometimes called sales representatives or manufacturer's representatives. Their role is to perform services for their principal, such as obtaining orders, and they are usually paid a commission for their services.

Air Waybill: A bill of lading for air transportation. Air waybills specify the terms under which the air carrier is agreeing to transport the goods and contain limitations of liability. They are not negotiable.

All Risk Clause: An insurance provision that all loss or damage to goods is insured except that caused by inherent vice (self-caused). This clause affords one of the broadest obtainable protections; however, it excludes war risks and strikes, riots, and civil commotion unless added by special endorsement for an additional premium.

Antidumping Duties: See "Dumping."

Applicant: The person at whose request or for whose account a letter of credit is issued—for example, the purchaser in a sale transaction opening a letter of credit with the purchaser's bank to pay the exporter (seller).

Appraisement: The process of determination by a Customs official of the dutiable value of imported merchandise. This is usually the price paid by the importer for the goods unless Customs believes that the price does not reflect a reasonable value, in which case Customs calculates its own value for the assessment of duties using the methods specified in the customs law.

Arbitrage: The business of making profits by buying and selling currencies that differ in value due to fluctuating exchange rates in world currency markets. Sometimes used to describe the existence of a difference in value from one currency to another and the decision to buy or sell in a particular currency because of the belief that a particular currency is stronger or will strengthen in the future.

Arms Export Control Act: A U.S. law regulating the export (and in some cases import) of defense articles and services listed on the U.S. Munitions List. The International Traffic in Arms Regulations (ITAR) are issued under the law. It is administered by the Department of State, Office of Defense Trade Controls.

Arrival Draft: A modified sight draft that does not require payment until after arrival of the goods at the port of destination. Similar to cash on delivery.

Arrival Notice: A notification by the steamship line, railroad, or over-the-road trucker. It informs the consignee of the arrival of the goods and usually indicates the pickup location and the allowed free time before storage charges begin.

ASEAN: A free trade area established by the Association of Southeast Asian Nations.

Assist: The situation in which an importer, directly or indirectly, is furnishing to a foreign manufacturer raw materials, tools, dies, molds, manufacturing equipment, certain types of research and development know-how or design work, or other things without receiving payment for such items (or receiving payment for less than their full value) in order that the importer can purchase a product manufactured by the foreign manufacturer at a lower price. An assist must be disclosed to the importing country's customs administration and customs duties paid as an addition to the purchase price for the goods.

Assured: The beneficiary of an insurance policy, for example, covering damage or casualty to cargo or goods during transport.

ATA Carnet: An international customs document that may be used in lieu of national customs entry documents and as security for import duties and taxes to cover the temporary admission and transit of goods.

At Sight: A draft drawn by a seller (exporter) for payment for the goods. It must be paid at the time the draft is presented to the buyer (importer) by the seller's agent, such as a freight forwarder or a bank.

Audit: A procedure whereby the customs authorities visit the premises of an importer or exporter and inspect documents and records and interview personnel to determine if importations and/or exportations are being conducted in accordance with applicable law and regulations.

Authority to Pay: Advice from a buyer, addressed through the buyer's bank to the seller, by way of the correspondent of the buyer's bank in the seller's country, authorizing the correspondent bank to pay the seller's drafts for a stipulated amount. The seller has no recourse against cancellation or modification of the Authority to Pay before the drafts are presented, but, once the *drafts drawn on the correspondent bank* are paid by it, the seller is no longer liable as drawer. An Authority to Pay is usually not confirmed by the seller's bank. It is not as safe for a seller as a letter of credit because it is not a promise or guarantee of payment by a bank.

Authority to Purchase: A document similar to an Authority to Pay but differing in that under an Authority to Purchase, the *drafts are drawn directly on the buyer* rather than on the seller's bank. They are purchased by the correspondent bank with or without recourse against the drawer. The Authority to Pay is usually not confirmed by the seller's bank.

Automated Commercial System: The electronic data transmission system used by U.S. Customs and Border Protection, customs brokers, and importers to complete import transactions. It contains various modules such as the Automated Broker Interface, the Automated Manifest System, the Cargo Selectivity System, and the Entry Summary System.

Average: See "General Average" and "Particular Average."

Average Adjuster: When a steamship line transporting goods encounters a condition covered by a general average or a particular average, an independent average adjuster will determine the contribution that each owner of goods being transported on the steamship will have to pay to make the steamship line and the other owners of goods whole.

BAF (Bunker Adjustment Factor): A charge added by ocean carriers to compensate for fluctuating fuel costs.

Bank Draft: A check, drawn by a bank on another bank, customarily used where it is necessary for the customer to provide funds that are payable at a bank in some distant location.

Banker's Acceptance: A time draft where a bank is drawee and acceptor.

Barter: The direct exchange of goods for other goods, without the use of money as a medium of exchange and without the involvement of a third party. For customs purposes, the values still need to be determined and proper duties paid if the exchange involves an importation. See "Countertrade."

Beneficiary: (1) Under a letter of credit, the person who is entitled to receive payment, usually the seller (exporter) of the goods. (2) Under an insurance policy, the assured, or the person who is to receive payment in case of loss of or damage to the goods.

Bill of Exchange: An unconditional order in writing addressed by one person to another, signed by the person issuing it and requiring the addressee to pay a certain sum of money to the order of a specified party at a fixed or determinable future time. In export transactions, it is drawn by the seller (exporter) on the purchaser (importer) or bank specified in a letter of credit or specified by the purchaser. See "Draft."

Bill of Lading (B/L): A document issued by a carrier (railroad, steamship line, or trucking company) that serves as a receipt for the goods to be delivered to a designated person or to her order. The bill of lading describes the conditions under which the goods are accepted by the carrier and details the nature and quantity of the goods, the name of the vessel (if shipped by sea), identifying marks and numbers, destination, etc. The person sending the goods is the "shipper" or "consignor," the company or agent transporting the goods is the "carrier," and the person for whom the goods are destined is the "consignee." Bills of lading may be negotiable or non-negotiable. If they are negotiable, that is, payable to the shipper's order and properly endorsed, title to the goods passes upon delivery of the bill of lading.

Blank Endorsement: The signature, usually on the reverse of a draft (bill of exchange), bill of lading, or insurance certificate, without any qualification, which then becomes payable or consigned to the person to whom the document is delivered.

Bond: A guaranty issued by an insurance or surety company in favor of an importer's government to ensure payment of customs duties in case the importer fails to pay, for example, due to bankruptcy.

Bonded Warehouse: A warehouse in which goods subject to excise taxes or customs duties are temporarily stored without the taxes or duties being assessed. A bond or security is given for the payment of all taxes and duties that may eventually become due. Operations in the warehouse may include assembly, manipulation, or storage, but usually not manufacturing.

Booking Cargo: The reservation of space on a specified vessel for a scheduled sailing, by or on behalf of a shipper. Technically, it may be effected in two ways, either (1) by signing a contract of affreightment, a procedure that applies only to bulk commodities, raw materials, or a large movement of special cargo, such as the transfer of a whole manufacturing plant, or to particular types of goods requiring special stowage, like unboxed cars or trucks; or (2) by informal request (verbal) for general cargo.

Booking Number: A number assigned to a cargo booking by the steamship line, used as an identifying reference on bills and correspondence.

Boycott: A refusal to deal commercially or otherwise with a person, firm, or country.

Buying Commission: A commission paid by a purchaser to an agent or person under the purchaser's control who identifies suppliers, assists with shipments, and provides other services for the purchaser. Under the GATT Valuation Code, amounts separately paid for such services are not dutiable as part of the purchase price of the goods.

Buy National Policy: A price preference, usually by a government purchaser, for purchasing goods produced in the same country as the purchaser's or an absolute prohibition against purchasing foreign goods.

Cabotage: Shipping, navigation, and trading along the coast of a country. In the United States, these services include traffic between any parts of the continental United States, or between Hawaii, Alaska, and Puerto Rico, and are reserved to U.S. flag ships.

CAF (Currency Adjustment Factor): A charge added by ocean carriers to offset currency exchange fluctuations.

CAFTA-DR: The Dominican Republic–Central America–United States Free Trade Agreement allows for preferential duty rates for goods imported that meet the rules of origin from member countries. Member countries include the Dominican Republic, El Salvador, Guatemala, Nicaragua, and Honduras.

Carnet: See "ATA Carnet."

Cash Against Documents (C.A.D.): A method of payment for goods in which documents transferring title—for example, a negotiable bill of lading and a draft—are transferred to the buyer upon payment of cash to an intermediary acting for the seller (usually a bank or freight forwarder).

Cash in Advance (C.I.A.): A method of payment for goods in which the buyer pays the seller in advance of the shipment of the goods. A C.I.A. is usually employed when the goods are built to order, such as specialized machinery.

Cash With Order (C.W.O.): A method of payment for goods in which cash is paid at the time of the order.

Casualty Loss: Damage to goods incurred during transportation, loading, or unloading.

CE Mark: A mark required on certain products imported to the European Community certifying that the product has been tested by an authorized certification agency and meets applicable standards, usually of safety.

Certificate of Conformity: The Consumer Product Safety Commission requires the importer to file a Certificate of Conformity to attest that imported or domestic goods are in compliance with the CPSC laws and regulations.

Certificate of Inspection: A document issued by an inspection company or other person independent of the seller and buyer that has inspected the goods for quality and/or value. It may be required for payment under the terms of the sales agreement or a letter of credit.

Certificate of Insurance: A document containing certain terms of a full-length insurance policy. A one-page document, it is evidence that there is insurance coverage for a shipment. Beneficiaries of open cargo or blanket insurance policies are authorized to issue their own certificates of insurance.

Certificate of Origin: A document in which the exporter certifies the place of origin (manufacture) of the merchandise being exported. Sometimes these certificates must be legalized by the consul of the country of destination, but more often they may be legalized by a commercial organization, such as a chamber of commerce, in the country of manufacture. Such information is needed primarily to comply with tariff laws, which may extend more favorable treatment to products of certain countries. More recently, certain types of certificates of origin, for example, NAFTA Certificates of Origin, require significant analysis of the origin of the raw materials used in production of the product to determine the country of origin.

Certificate of Weight and Measurement: A certificate issued by a company or person independent of the seller and buyer certifying the quantity and dimensions of goods. In some cases, the buyer or buyer's government will allow the seller to make a self-certification.

Charter Party: The contract between the owner of a vessel and a shipper to lease the vessel or a part thereof to transport, usually bulk, goods.

Clean Bill of Lading: One in which the goods are described as having been received in "apparent good order and condition" and without damage. May be required for payment under the sales agreement or letter of credit. See "Foul Bill of Lading."

Collecting Bank: A bank requested by an exporter (seller) to obtain payment from the purchaser. Ordinarily the exporter (seller) will draw a draft on the purchaser and deliver it to the collecting bank with a negotiable bill of lading. The bank will transmit it overseas to its correspondent bank (which is also a collecting bank in the chain). If the draft drawn is a sight draft, the bank will deliver the negotiable bill of lading to the purchaser in return for payment. If it is a time draft, the bank will release the bill of lading, thereby permitting the purchaser to obtain the goods, upon acceptance of the draft by the purchaser. At the time of maturity of the draft, the purchaser will make payment and the collecting banks will remit the proceeds to the exporter (seller). See "Uniform Rules for Collections."

Combined Transport Bill of Lading: See "Through Bill of Lading."

Commercial Invoice: A document prepared by the exporter (seller) describing the goods being sold, the sales price for the goods, and other charges being billed to the purchaser. Because a commercial invoice is commonly required in order to enable the purchaser to clear the goods through customs, it is necessary to include all information required by the purchaser's country. This may include legalization of the commercial invoice by the purchaser's country's embassy or consulate in the exporter's country, certification by a chamber of commerce in the exporter's country, or particular statements, certifications, or information in the invoice.

Commingling: A condition in which goods subject to different rates of customs duty are packed together. This may result in all goods being assessed the highest duty rate applicable to any of the items.

Commission Agent: See "Agent."

Common Carrier: A transportation carrier such as a steamship line, trucking company, or railroad that accepts shipments from the public. Private carriers are those that are under contract for or owned by particular shippers. Common carriers are usually subject to government regulation, including the filing of tariffs (transportation rates) in some countries so that shippers all pay a uniform charge. Laws in some countries permit exceptions to this so that large-volume shippers may obtain discounts in certain circumstances.

Common Market: An agreement between two or more countries to permit importation or exportation of goods between those countries without the payment of customs duties and to permit freedom of travel and employment and freedom of investment. Goods imported from outside the common market will be subject to a common duty rate.

Compound Duty: A tax imposed on imported merchandise based on a percentage of value and also on the net weight or quantity.

Conference Tariff: Two or more steamship lines that have agreed to set the same price for transporting goods in the same ocean lane that they serve. Generally, such agreements are valid if they are properly registered with the government authorities of the countries served.

Confirming Bank: A bank in the exporter's (seller's) country that also adds its own guarantee of payment to a letter of credit issued by the purchaser's bank in the purchaser's country.

Consignment: (1) The shipment or delivery of goods to a person without making a sale. Under consignment arrangements, the consignee will usually have an agreement that when the consignee is able to sell the goods to a purchaser, the consignee will simultaneously purchase the goods from the consignor and make payment. (2) In some international trade documentation—for example, bills of lading—a transportation carrier may not know whether the transportation that it is effecting is pursuant to a sale or not; therefore, the person to whom the goods are to be delivered is referred to as the consignee, and the delivery transaction is loosely referred to as a consignment.

Consular Invoice: A document required by some foreign countries showing information as to the consignor, consignee, value, and description of the shipment. It is usually sold or legalized by the embassy or consulate of the purchaser's country located in the seller's country.

Consulate: An office of a foreign government in the exporter's (seller's) country. The main office is usually the embassy, located in the capital city of the exporter's country, and other offices in different cities in the exporter's country are consulates.

Contract of Affreightment: See "Affreightment, Contract of."

Convention on Contracts for the International Sale of Goods: An international treaty describing the obligations and rights of sellers and buyers in international sales. The Convention automatically applies to international sales where the seller and the buyer are located in countries that are parties to the Convention unless the buyer and the seller have agreed specifically in their sales documentation to exclude applicability of the Convention. The United States and many other countries are parties to the Convention.

Countertrade: A reciprocal trading arrangement. Countertrade transactions include:

A. *Counterpurchase transactions,* which obligate the seller to purchase from the buyer goods and services unrelated to the goods and services sold (usually within a one- to five-year period).

B. *Reverse countertrade contracts,* which require the importer to export goods equivalent in value to a specified percentage of the value of the imported goods—an obligation that can be sold to an exporter in a third country.

C. *Buyback transactions,* which obligate the seller of plant, machinery, or technology to buy from the importer a portion of the resultant production during a five- to twenty-five-year period.

D. *Clearing agreements* between two countries that agree to purchase specific amounts of each other's products over a specified period of time, using a designated "clearing currency" in the transactions.

E. *Switch transactions,* which permit the sale of unpaid balances in a clearing account to a third party, usually at a discount, that may be used for producing goods in the country holding the balance.

F. *Swap transactions,* through which products from different locations are traded to save transportation costs (for example, Soviet oil may be "swapped" for oil from a Latin American producer, so that the Soviet oil is shipped to a country in South Asia, while the Latin American oil is shipped to Cuba).

G. *Barter transactions,* through which two parties directly exchange goods deemed to be of approximately equivalent value without any exchange of money taking place.

Countervailing Duty: Considered a form of unfair competition under the GATT Subsidies Code, an additional duty imposed by the importer's government in order to offset export grants, bounties, or subsidies paid to foreign exporters or manufacturers in certain countries by the governments of those countries for the purpose of promoting export.

CPSIA: Consumer Products Safety Improvement Act, which requires both importers and domestic manufacturers to certify that their products comply with all U.S. consumer products regulations.

C-TPAT: Customs and Trade Partnership Against Terrorism. A voluntary program whereby importers, brokers, carriers, warehouses, consolidators, and exporters enact security measures to protect cargo and containers from the introduction of contraband or terrorist devices.

Customs Broker: A person or firm licensed by an importer's government and engaged in entering and clearing goods through customs. The responsibilities of a broker include preparing the entry form and filing it, advising the importer on duties to be paid, advancing duties and other costs, and arranging for delivery to the importer.

Customs Classification: The particular category in a tariff nomenclature (usually the Harmonized Tariff System) in which a product is classified for tariff purposes, or the procedure for determining the appropriate tariff category in a country's nomenclature used for the classification, coding, and description of internationally traded goods. Classification is necessary in order to determine the duty rate applicable to the imported goods.

Customs Union: An agreement between two or more countries to eliminate tariffs and other import restrictions on each other's goods and establish a common tariff for goods imported from other countries.

Cut-Off Time: The latest time a container may be delivered to a terminal for loading on a departing ship or train.

Date Draft: A draft maturing a stipulated number of days after its date, regardless of the time of its acceptance. Unless otherwise agreed upon in the contract of sale, the date of the draft should not be prior to that of the ocean bill of lading or of the corresponding document on shipments by other means.

DDC (Destination Delivery Charge): A charge added by ocean carriers to compensate for crane lifts off the vessel, drayage of the container within the terminal, and gate fees at the terminal.

***Del Credere* Agent:** One who guarantees payments; a sales agent who, for a certain percentage in addition to her sales commission, will guarantee payment by the purchasers of goods.

Delivery Order: An order addressed to the holder of goods and issued by anyone who has authority to do so, that is, one who has the legal right to order delivery of merchandise. It is not considered a title document like a negotiable bill of lading. It is addressed and forwarded, together with the dock receipt, if any, to the transportation company effecting the transfer from the pickup location to the shipside pier.

Demurrage: Excess time taken for loading or unloading of a vessel that is not caused by the vessel operator but is due to the acts of a charterer or shipper. A charge is made for such delay. See "Lay Days."

Destination Control Statement: Specific words (legend) inserted in a commercial invoice and bill of lading prohibiting diversion of destination for exported goods subject to U.S. export control laws.

Devaluation: An official lowering of the value of a country's currency in relation to other currencies by a direct government decision to reduce gold content or to establish a new ratio to another agreed standard, such as the U.S. dollar. Devaluation tends to reduce domestic demand for imports in a country by raising their prices in terms of the devalued currency and to raise foreign demand for the country's exports by reducing their prices in terms of foreign currencies. Devaluation can therefore help to correct a balance of payments deficit and sometimes provide a short-term basis for economic adjustment of a national economy. See "Revaluation."

Discrepancy: The failure of a beneficiary of a letter of credit to tender to the advising bank the exact documents required by the letter of credit to obtain payment.

Distributor: A person who purchases goods for the purpose of reselling such goods. The distributor is distinguished from an agent because it takes title to the goods, assumes the risk of loss or damage to the goods, and is compensated by marking up the goods on resale.

Dock Receipt: A receipt given for a shipment received or delivered at a steamship pier. A dock receipt is usually a form supplied by the steamship line and prepared by the shipper or its freight forwarder. When delivery of a shipment is completed, the dock receipt is surrendered to the vessel operator or his agent and serves as the basis for preparation of the ocean bill of lading.

Documentary Bill: A draft (bill of exchange) accompanied by other documents required by the buyer for payment, for example, the bill of lading and inspection certificate.

Documents Against Acceptance (D/A): Instructions given by an exporter to a bank or freight forwarder that the documents (usually a negotiable bill of lading) attached to a draft for collection are deliverable to the drawee (importer/purchaser) only against her acceptance of the draft. The actual payment will be made by the purchaser at some agreed-upon time or date specified in the draft after acceptance. See "Uniform Rules for Collections."

Documents Against Payment (D/P): A type of payment for goods in which the documents transferring title to the goods (negotiable bill of lading) are not given to the purchaser until he has paid the value of a draft drawn on him. Collection may be made through a bank, a freight forwarder, or some other agent. See "Uniform Rules for Collections."

Draft: A negotiable instrument wherein a drawer orders a drawee to pay a fixed amount of money (with or without interest or other charges) described in the draft, payable on demand or at a definite time. It must be payable "to order" or bearer, and it must not contain any other instructions, conditions, or orders except an order to pay money. A draft is commonly drawn by an exporter (seller) on the purchaser (drawee) and delivered to a collecting bank or freight forwarder for presentation to the purchaser. See "Bill of Exchange."

Drawback: Import duties or taxes refunded by a government, in whole or in part, when the imported goods are re-exported or used in the manufacture of exported goods.

Drawee: A person (usually the purchaser of goods) ordered in a draft to make payment.

Drawer: A person who makes, creates, or issues a draft and instructs a drawee to make payment to the drawer or another person ("pay to the order of").

Drayage: A charge for delivery of goods or pickup of goods from docks or other port terminals.

Dumping: Under the GATT Antidumping Code (to which the United States is a party), the export sale of a commodity at "less than normal value," usually considered to be a price lower than that at which it is sold within the exporting country or to third countries. Dumping is generally recognized as an unfair trade practice that can disrupt markets and injure producers of competitive products in the importing country. Article VI of GATT permits the imposition of special antidumping duties against "dumped" goods equal to the difference between their export price and their normal value in the exporting country.

Dunnage: Packing material consisting mainly of rough pine board used as flooring for the ship's hold before loading is begun.

Duty: The tax imposed by a customs authority on imported merchandise.

Embargo: A prohibition upon exports or imports, with respect to either specific products or specific countries. Historically, embargoes have been ordered most frequently in time of war, but they may also be applied for political, economic, or sanitary purposes. Embargoes imposed against an individual country by the United Nations— or a group of nations—in an effort to influence that country's conduct or its policies are sometimes called "sanctions."

Embassy: The chief diplomatic office of a foreign government in the exporter's country, usually located at the capital city of the exporter's country.

Entry: The formal process by which goods are imported into a country, consisting of the filing of documents with the importing country's customs service and the payment of customs duties. Various types of entries are used in different circumstances, such as consumption entries, warehouse entries, immediate transportation entries, and transportation and exportation entries.

Escape Clause: A provision in a bilateral or multilateral trade agreement permitting a signatory nation to suspend tariff or other duty reductions when imports threaten serious harm to the producers of competitive domestic goods. Such agreements as the North American Free Trade Agreement contain such "safeguard" provisions to help firms and workers that are adversely affected by a relatively sudden surge of imports adjust to the rising level of import competition.

European Union: A monetary and political union entered into in 1992 in Maastricht, Netherlands, by twelve European countries; twenty-seven countries are now members.

Examination: The process by which the customs authorities of an importing country inspect the goods identified in the customs entry documents and confirm whether the goods are the same as those described in the documents and whether the goods are eligible for entry.

Exchange Controls: Government regulations rationing foreign currencies, bank drafts, and other instruments for settling international financial obligations by countries seeking to ameliorate acute balance of payments difficulties. When such measures are imposed, importers must apply for prior authorization from the government to obtain the foreign currency required to bring in designated amounts and types of goods. Since such measures have the effect of restricting imports, they are considered non-tariff barriers to trade.

Exchange Rate Risk: The possibility that an exporter (seller) will receive less value (for example, fewer U.S. dollars) than it is expecting in a sales transaction. This arises because exchange rates are generally floating rates, and if the exporter (seller) agrees to accept payment in the purchaser's currency (for example, yen) and the value of the yen vis-à-vis the U.S. dollar fluctuates between the time of price quotation and the date of payment, the exporter (seller) may receive more or less in U.S. dollars than it anticipated at the time that it quoted its price and accepted the purchase order. Sellers and purchasers may agree to share the exchange rate risk in their sales agreement.

Exchange Rates: The price at which banks or other currency traders are willing to buy or sell various currencies that a buyer may need in order to make payment. For example, if a contract for sale is in U.S. dollars, a purchaser in a foreign country will need to purchase U.S. dollars from a bank or currency trader in order to make proper payment. Usually, the exchange rate floats or fluctuates based on supply and demand, but it may also be fixed by government regulation.

Export License: A permit required to engage in the export of certain commodities to certain destinations. In the United States, such controls are usually determined by the Department of Commerce, Bureau of Export Administration; the Department of State, Office of Defense Trade Controls; or Department of Treasury, Office of Foreign Assets Control. Controls are imposed to implement U.S. foreign policy, ensure U.S. national security, prevent proliferation, or protect against short supply.

Export Quotas: Specific restriction or ceilings imposed by an exporting country on the value or volume of certain exports, designed to protect domestic consumers from temporary shortages of the goods, to bolster their prices in world markets, or to reduce injury to producers in importing countries. Some international commodity agreements explicitly indicate when producers should apply such restraints. Export quotas are also often applied in orderly marketing agreements and voluntary restraint agreements, and to promote domestic processing of raw materials in countries that produce them.

Export Trading Company: A corporation or other business unit organized and operated principally for the purpose of exporting goods and services, or for providing export-related services to other companies. The Export Trading Company Act of 1982 exempts authorized trading companies from certain provisions of the U.S. antitrust laws and authorizes banks to own and operate trading companies.

Factoring: A procedure whereby an exporter (seller) that is selling on open account or time drafts may sell its accounts receivable or drafts to a factoring company, which will make immediate payment of the face value of the accounts receivable less some discount amount to the seller and will then collect the amounts owed from the purchasers at the due date for payment.

FEU (Forty-foot Equivalent Unit): A measurement of container capacity.

Fixed Exchange Rate: The establishment of a price at which two currencies can be purchased or sold, set either by government regulation or in a sales agreement between a seller and a buyer. In such cases, there is no exchange rate risk because there is no exchange rate fluctuation between the date of price quotation and the date of payment.

Floating Exchange Rate: A condition where the governments issuing two different currencies do not legally regulate the price at which either currency can be bought or sold. See "Exchange Rate Risk."

Force Majeure: The title of a standard clause often found in contracts for the sale of goods or transportation exempting the parties from liability for non-fulfillment of their obligations by reason of certain acts beyond their control, such as natural disasters or war.

Foreign Assembler's Declaration: Under U.S. Harmonized Tariff Section 9802.00.80, an importer may pay reduced customs duties when importing a product that has been assembled abroad from U.S.-origin components. The foreign assembler must provide a declaration that is endorsed by the importer certifying that the assembly operation meets the regulatory requirements. If Customs agrees, the U.S. importer pays duty only on the foreign-origin materials, labor, and value added after deducting the U.S.-origin materials exported for assembly.

Foreign Corrupt Practices Act: A U.S. law prohibiting the payment of anything of value to a foreign government employee in order to obtain or retain business. The law also prohibits the maintenance of "slush funds" for such payments.

Foreign Sales Corporation (FSC): A company incorporated in Guam, the U.S. Virgin Islands, the Commonwealth of the Northern Mariana Islands, American Samoa, or any foreign country that has a satisfactory exchange-of-information agreement with the United States and is utilized in an export transaction. Use of an FSC in export sales transactions permits a U.S. exporter to exempt a portion of its export profits from U.S. income taxation.

Foreign Trade Zone: An area where goods may be received, stored, manipulated, and manufactured without entering a country's customs jurisdiction and hence without payment of duty. Outside the United States, it is usually called a "free trade zone."

Forward Exchange: A market offering various currencies for sale where the sales price of a currency is quoted and sold based on delivery of the currency to the purchaser at some date in the future, for example, the due date when the purchaser must make payment of a time draft. Purchasing currency in forward contracts is one method of eliminating exchange rate risk.

Foul Bill of Lading: A bill of lading issued by a carrier bearing a notation that the outward containers or the goods have been damaged. A foul bill of lading may not be acceptable for payment under a letter of credit.

Free In and Out (F.I.O.): The cost of loading and unloading of a vessel that is borne by the charterer.

Free of Capture and Seizure (F.C.&S.): An insurance clause providing that a loss is not insured if it is due to capture, seizure, confiscation, and like actions, whether legal or not, or from such acts as piracy, civil war, rebellion, and civil strife.

Free of Particular Average (F.P.A.): The phrase means that the insurance company will not cover partial losses resulting from perils of the sea except when caused by stranding, sinking, burning, or collision. American conditions (F.P.A.A.C.): Partial loss is not insured unless it is caused by the vessel's being sunk, stranded, burned, on fire, or in collision. English conditions (F.P.A.E.C.): Partial loss is not insured unless it is a result of the vessel's being sunk, stranded, burned, on fire, or in collision.

Free Out (F.O.): The cost of unloading a vessel that is borne by the charterer.

Free Port: An ocean port and its adjacent area where imported goods may be temporarily stored and sometimes repackaged; manipulated; or, under the laws of some countries, further processed or manufactured without payment of customs duties until the merchandise is sold in the country or the time period for exportation expires.

Free Trade: A theoretical concept that assumes that international trade is unhampered by government measures such as tariffs or non-tariff barriers. The objective of trade liberalization is to achieve "freer trade" rather than "free trade," it being generally recognized among trade policy officials that some restrictions on trade are likely to remain.

Free Trade Area: An arrangement between two or more countries for free trade among themselves while each nation maintains its own independent tariffs toward nonmember nations.

Free Trade Zone: See "Foreign Trade Zone."

Freight All Kinds (FAK): The general transportation rate for a shipment of multiple types of merchandise.

Freight Collect: The shipment of goods by an exporter (seller) where the purchaser has agreed to pay the transportation costs and the transportation carrier has agreed to transport the goods on the condition that the goods will not be released unless the purchaser makes payment for the transportation charges.

Freight Forwarder: A person who dispatches shipments via common carriers, books or otherwise arranges space for those shipments on behalf of shippers, and processes the documentation or performs related activities incident to those shipments.

Freight Prepaid: An agreement between the seller and a buyer that the seller will pay for the transportation charges before delivery to the transportation carrier.

Full Set: Generally used in reference to bills of lading. Where a steamship line undertakes to transport goods, it issues a sole original or full set (generally three copies, which are all originals) of the bill of lading. Where the bill of lading is negotiable, the steamship line is authorized to make delivery as soon as any person presents one original bill of lading at the destination.

GATT: The General Agreement on Tariffs and Trade. This is an international treaty that has now been superseded by the World Trade Organization. A number of agreements negotiated under GATT continue in force, such as the Valuation Code, the Antidumping Code, and the Subsidies Code. See "World Trade Organization."

General Average: A deliberate loss of or damage to goods in the face of a peril, such as dumping overboard, which sacrifice is made for the preservation of the vessel and other goods. The cost of the loss is shared by the owners of the saved goods.

Generalized System of Preferences (GSP): The United Nations program adopted by the United States and many other countries and designed to benefit less developed countries by extending duty-free treatment to imports from such countries. Sometimes certain countries or products are "graduated" and are no longer eligible to receive GSP benefits.

General Order: Merchandise for which proper customs entry has not been made within five working days after arrival is sent to a general order warehouse. All costs of storage are at the expense of the importer.

Gray Market Goods: Products that have been manufactured and sold by the inventor or duly authorized licensee that are being resold by purchasers into geographical areas not intended or authorized by the original seller. Depending upon the laws of the countries involved, gray marketing may be illegal, encouraged, or regulated. Sometimes economic incentives for gray marketing occur as a result of a manufacturer selling the products to different trade channels at different prices or due to fluctuating exchange rates.

Harmonized Tariff System (Codes): The system adopted by most of the commercial countries of the world in 1989, classifying products manufactured and sold in world commerce according to an agreed-upon numerical system. Common international classifications facilitate balance of trade statistics collection, customs classification, and country of origin determination.

In Bond: The transportation or storage of goods in a condition or location that is exempt under the customs laws from the payment of customs duties for the time period that is allowed by law for transportation or storage. Transportation or storage in bond may be effected by transportation carriers or warehouses that have posted a bond with the customs authorities guaranteeing payment of all customs duties in the event that the goods are improperly released without the payment of customs duties by the owner of the goods.

Inchmaree Clause: A provision in an ocean casualty insurance policy covering the assured against damage to the owner's goods as a result of negligence or mismanagement by the captain or the crew in navigation of the ship or damage due to latent defects in the ship.

Incoterms: A set of sales and delivery terms issued by the International Chamber of Commerce and widely used in international trade. These terms, such as "ex-works," "CIF," and "delivered duty paid," set out in detail the responsibilities and rights of the seller and purchaser in an international sale transaction. See also "Convention on Contracts for the International Sale of Goods" and "Uniform Commercial Code."

Indent Merchant: One who assembles a number of orders from merchants in his locality, such orders being placed with foreign manufacturers by the indent merchant for his own account. He assumes the full credit risk and obtains his commission from those for whom he orders.

Insurable Interest: The legal interest that a person must have in goods in order to be covered by insurance. For example, in an international sale under the Incoterm "ex-works," delivery and risk of loss for damage to the goods passes to the purchaser when the goods are loaded on and leave the seller's factory or warehouse. If the seller has already been paid for the goods at that time, the seller no longer has any legal interest in ownership or payment and cannot receive payment under any insurance coverage that the seller may have, such as a blanket insurance policy covering all sales.

Intellectual Property: Ownership conferring the right to possess, use, or dispose of products created by human ingenuity, including patents, trademarks, and copyrights. These rights are protected when properly registered, but registration in one country does not create rights in another country.

Invisible Trade: Items such as freight, insurance, and financial services that are included in a country's balance of payments accounts (in the "current" account), even though they are not recorded as physically visible exports and imports.

Invoice: See "Commercial Invoice" and "Consular Invoice."

Irrevocable Credit: A letter of credit issued by the purchaser's bank in favor of the seller that cannot be revoked without the consent of the seller (who is the beneficiary of the letter of credit). Under the Uniform Customs and Practice for Documentary Credits (No. 500), all letters of credit are irrevocable unless specifically stated otherwise on their face. This protects the seller against the risk of non-payment due to revocation after release of the goods to the buyer or the buyer's agent.

ISO 9000: A series of quality control standards promulgated by the International Standards Organization.

ITAR: See "Arms Export Control Act."

Jettison: The act of throwing the goods off a steamship into the ocean to lighten the ship in time of peril. It may occur as a way to save a sinking ship or through illegal or improper action by steamship employees. Certain jettisons are covered by insurance or general average, but others are not.

Lacey Act: The Lacey Act was originally enacted in 1900 to protect wildlife, fish, and plants. Recent amendments to the act were enacted to prohibit illegal logging and require importers to file a certification on the source of any plant products or products with plant components.

Lay Days: The dates between which a chartered vessel is to be available in a port for loading of cargo.

LCL: Less than a full container load.

Legalization: A procedure whereby an embassy or consular employee of the purchaser's country located in the exporter's (seller's) country signs or stamps an export document, for example, a commercial invoice, in order to enable the goods to be admitted upon arrival at the purchaser's country.

Letter of Credit (L/C): A formal letter issued by a bank that authorizes the drawing of drafts on the bank up to a fixed limit and under terms specified in the letter. Through the issuance of such letters, a bank guarantees payment on behalf of its customers (purchasers of goods) and thereby facilitates the transaction of business between parties who may not be otherwise acquainted with each other. The letter of credit may be sent directly by the issuing bank or its customer to the beneficiary (sellers of goods), or the terms of the credit may be transmitted through a correspondent bank. In the latter event, the correspondent may add its guarantee (confirmation) to that of the issuing bank, depending on the arrangements made between the seller and the purchaser. Letters of credit may be revocable or irrevocable depending on whether the issuing bank reserves the right to cancel the credit prior to its expiration date.

Letter of Indemnity/Guaranty: (1) A document issued by a shipper to a steamship line instructing the steamship line to issue a clean bill of lading even though the goods are damaged, and agreeing to hold the steamship line harmless from any claims. (2) An agreement by a beneficiary of a letter of credit to hold a bank harmless for making payment to the beneficiary, even though there are some discrepancies between the documents required by the letter of credit and those presented by the beneficiary. (3) An agreement by an exporter and/or importer to hold a steamship line harmless from any claims that may arise as a result of the steamship line's releasing goods where a negotiable bill of lading covering the goods has been lost or destroyed.

Lighterage: The cost for conveying the goods by lighters or barges between ships and shore and vice versa, including the loading into and discharging out of lighters.

Liner Service: Regularly scheduled departures of steamships to specific destinations (trade lanes).

Liquidation: A U.S. Customs term of art describing the official final determination by the customs authorities of the classification and value of the imported merchandise. For example, any importer, by posting a customs bond, may obtain immediate delivery of merchandise by classifying the imported product and paying customs duties at that time. The importer's classification and value, however, are not binding on U.S. Customs and Border Protection, and within an additional period of time, for example, three to six months, Customs will make its own analysis of the goods and determine whether or not it agrees with the classification, value, and duties paid.

Long Ton: 2,240 pounds.

LTL: A shipment of less than a full truckload.

Manifest: A listing of the cargo being transported by the transportation carrier.

Marine Extension Clause: A provision in an ocean casualty insurance policy extending the ordinary coverage to include time periods where goods have been received for shipment but not yet loaded on a steamship and have been loaded off the steamship but not yet delivered to the buyer, and periods where the ship deviates from its intended course or the goods are transshipped.

Marine Insurance: Insurance that will compensate the owner of goods transported overseas in the event of loss or damage. Some "marine" insurance policies also cover air shipments.

Marine Surveyor: A company or individual that assesses the extent of damage to cargo incurred during ocean transportation. Such survey reports are necessary in order for insurance companies to make payment to the beneficiary of the insurance policy.

Marking Laws: Laws requiring articles of foreign origin and/or their containers imported into a country to be marked in a specified manner that would indicate to the purchaser the country of origin of the article.

Mate's Receipt: Commonly used in Europe, a document similar to a dock receipt. A mate's receipt is issued by an employee of a steamship line, usually at the wharf or pier where the goods are received from the transportation carrier delivering the goods to the port. It evidences that delivery was made by the ground carrier. The steamship line will prepare the bill of lading based on the information in the mate's receipt.

Maturity: The date on which a time draft must be paid.

Measurement Ton: An alternative way of calculating the transportation charge for articles that may be unusually bulky or light. The steamship line ordinarily will charge the higher of the actual weight or a calculated or constructed weight based upon the dimensions of the goods being transported.

MERCOSUR: A common market established by Argentina, Brazil, Paraguay, and Uruguay.

Metric Ton: 2,200 pounds.

Minimum Freight: The minimum amount that a transportation carrier will charge for transportation. Because such minimum charges exist, freight consolidators provide the service of aggregating small shipments so that lower freight rates can be obtained, which are then partially passed back to the shippers.

Most Favored Nation: An agreement in a treaty or in a sales contract whereby one party promises to give to the other party benefits at least equal to the benefits that party has extended to any other country or customer.

NAFTA: North American Free Trade Agreement, a trade agreement between the United States, Canada, and Mexico allowing for preferential duty rates on imports that meet the criteria.

Negotiable Instrument: A document containing an unconditional promise or order to pay a fixed amount of money with or without interest or other charges described in the promise or order if it is payable to bearer or order at the time it is issued, is payable on demand or at a definite time, and does not state any other undertaking or instructions in addition to the payment of money. Examples of negotiable instruments include checks and drafts.

Negotiation: A transfer of possession of a negotiable instrument, whether voluntary or involuntary, for value received by a person to another person, who thereby becomes its holder.

Non-Negotiable: A document that is incapable of transferring legal ownership or rights to possession of the goods by transfer or endorsement of the document, for example, a railroad, sea, or air waybill.

Non-Tariff Barriers: Obstacles to selling or importing activities other than the customs duties assessed on imported goods, for example, inspections that delay importation, foreign exchange controls that make payment difficult, foreign language labeling regulations, buy national policies, product standards, and quotas.

Non-Vessel-Operating Common Carrier (NVOCC): A cargo consolidator of small shipments in ocean trade, generally soliciting business and arranging for or performing containerization functions at the port. The NVOCC is recognized by the Federal Maritime Commission as a common carrier that does not own or operate steamships, but that publishes tariffs after having filed them with the Commission and becomes the shipper of the goods.

Notify Party: The person listed on a bill of lading or other document that the transportation carrier is supposed to notify upon arrival. A notify party may be the purchaser of the goods, a foreign freight forwarder or customs broker, or a bank or other party, depending upon the terms of the sales agreement and the agreement relating to payment for the goods.

On Board Notation, On Board Endorsement: A legend, stamp, or handwritten statement on the face of a bill of lading issued by a steamship line certifying that the goods have actually been loaded on the ship. Often letters of credit will specify that the goods must be on board before the expiration date of the letter of credit in order for the exporter (seller) to receive payment under the letter of credit. See "Received Bill of Lading."

Open Account (O/A): A sale payable when specified, that is, R/M: return mail; E.O.M: end of month; 30 days: thirty days from date of invoice; 2/10/60: 2 percent discount for payment in ten days, net if paid sixty days from date of invoice. Unlike a letter of credit, there is no security or bank guaranty of payment.

Order Bill of Lading: Usually, "To Order" bills of lading are made to the order of the shipper and endorsed in blank, thereby giving the holder of the bill of lading title to the goods being shipped. They may also be to the order of the consignee or the bank financing the transaction. Order bills of lading are negotiable (whereas straight bills of lading are not).

Orderly Marketing Agreements (OMAs): International agreements negotiated between two or more governments in which the trading partners agree to restrain the growth of trade in specified "sensitive" products, usually through the imposition of export or import quotas. Orderly marketing agreements are intended to ensure that future trade increases will not disrupt, threaten, or impair competitive industries or their workers in importing countries.

OSD: A notation on a carrier receipt or bill of lading signifying "Over, Short, or Damaged."

Packing List: A document describing the contents of a shipment. It includes more detail than is contained in a commercial invoice but does not contain prices or values. It is used for insurance claims as well as by the foreign customs authorities when examining goods to verify proper customs entry.

Particular Average (P.A.): A partial loss or damage to cargo that solely affects "particular" interests. These damages or partial losses are not shared by other interests but are excepted in the ocean carrier's bill of lading. Therefore, unless negligence is involved, claims under particular average cannot be directed against the steamship line.

Passport: An official document issued by a country authorizing one of its citizens or legal residents to leave the country and to be readmitted to the country upon return. See "Visa."

Performance Bond: A guarantee issued by an insurance company, surety company, or other person acceptable to the beneficiary guaranteeing that the applicant (for example, a seller of goods) will manufacture and deliver the goods to the purchaser in accordance with the specifications and delivery schedule.

Perils of the Seas: Conditions covered by marine insurance, including heavy weather, stranding, collision, lightning, and seawater damage.

Permanent Establishment: An office, warehouse, or place of business in a foreign country that may cause its owner or lessor to be subject to income taxes in that country. Under the common international tax treaties negotiated between countries of the world, profits made by a seller are not taxable in the buyer's country unless the seller also has a permanent establishment in the buyer's country that has played some part in arranging the sale transaction.

Pickup Order: A document used when city or suburban export cargo has to be delivered to a dock, or for pickup of goods from storage places.

Power of Attorney: A legal document wherein a person authorizes another person to act on the first person's behalf. It may be issued to an attorney-at-law or to any person and authorizes that person to act as an agent for the issuer of the power of attorney for general or limited purposes.

Preshipment Inspections: A procedure whereby a buyer, through an independent agent such as an inspection company, will examine the goods being purchased prior to exportation by the foreign seller. These examinations may be for quality alone or, in some cases where the buyer's government requires it, the inspection company may require information on the value of the goods.

Product Liability: The responsibility of a manufacturer and, in some cases, a seller for defects in goods that cause injury to a purchaser, user, or consumer of the goods or cause damage to the purchaser's business.

Pro Forma Invoice: An abbreviated invoice sent at the beginning of a sale transaction, usually to enable the buyer to obtain an import permit or a foreign exchange permit or both. The pro forma invoice gives a close approximation of the weights and values of a shipment that is to be made.

Provisional Insurance: Temporary insurance issued by an agent of an insurance company covering a temporary time period until the actual insurance application can be reviewed by the insurance company and the insurance policy issued.

Quota: A limitation or restriction on the quantity or duty rate payable on imported goods. See "Absolute Quota" and "Tariff Rate Quota."

Received Bill of Lading: A document issued by a steamship company acknowledging that it has received delivery of goods to be transported at some later time, usually on the first available steamship going to the destination specified by the shipper. Since the goods are not yet loaded on board, there is no guarantee that the goods will be shipped in the near future, and, therefore, such bills of lading are generally not acceptable if presented by a seller for payment under a letter of credit that is about to expire.

Recourse: The right to claim a refund for amounts paid to a payee. For example, a factoring company may purchase accounts receivable from an exporter (seller), pay the exporter a discounted amount, and collect the accounts receivable as they become due from the purchasers of the goods. If the purchase of the accounts receivable by the factor is with recourse, if any of the purchasers fails to pay, the factor has the option of pursuing the purchaser or claiming a refund for that amount from the exporter (seller) from whom the accounts receivable were purchased.

Remittance: A payment, usually from one collecting bank to another, for example, under a documentary collection. However, a remittance may also include payments directly by the purchaser to the seller.

Revaluation: A government action whereby its currency is valued upward in relationship to another currency. See "Devaluation."

Revocable Credit: A letter of credit issued by a bank that is subject to revocation by the applicant (purchaser of the goods) at any time. Under the new Uniform Customs and Practice for Documentary Credits, No. 500, letters of credit are irrevocable unless expressly stated to be revocable.

Revolving Credit: An agreement by a bank issuing a letter of credit with the applicant (purchaser of goods) that as soon as the purchaser makes payment for a particular shipment or amount of goods to the seller, the bank will automatically issue a new letter of credit covering the next shipment or the amount agreed upon between the applicant and the bank.

Royalty: An amount paid by a licensee to acquire certain rights, for example, a lump sum or an ongoing amount to manufacture or sell goods in accordance with the licensed patent, trademark, copyright, or trade secrets. In some situations, royalties paid by the purchaser of goods to the seller of goods must be included in the dutiable value of the goods.

Sales Agreement or Contract: The agreement, oral or written, between the exporter (seller) and the importer (purchaser) describing the terms and conditions upon which the seller and purchaser will execute the sale and describing the rights and responsibilities of each party.

Schedule B: A classification system based on the Harmonized Tariff System applicable to U.S. exports.

Section 301 (of the Trade Act of 1974): A provision of U.S. law that enables the president to withdraw duty reductions or restrict imports from countries that discriminate against U.S. exports, subsidize their own exports to the United States, or engage in other unjustifiable or unreasonable practices that burden or discriminate against U.S. trade.

Selling Commission: Money or compensation paid by the seller of goods to the seller's agent for services performed by that agent, such as identifying prospective purchasers and assisting with export of the goods. If the amount of the selling commission is charged to the purchaser of the goods, it will usually become subject to customs duties in the country of importation.

Service Contract: A contract between an ocean carrier and a shipper or a shippers' association, in which the shipper commits to a minimum quantity of freight for transport within a fixed period of time and the carrier discounts its usual transportation charges and guarantees levels of service, such as assured space and transit time.

Shippers' Association: A group of exporters who negotiate with transportation carriers for lower freight rates by committing their aggregate volume of cargo.

Shipper's Export Declaration: A form required by the Treasury Department for shipments over $2,500 ($500 for mail shipments) to all countries except Canada. It is completed by a shipper or its freight forwarder showing the value, weight, consignee, designation, Schedule B number, etc., for the export shipment.

Shipper's Letter of Instructions: A document issued by an exporter or importer instructing the freight forwarder to effect transportation and exportation in accordance with the terms specified in the letter of instructions.

Shipping Conference: Steamship lines establishing regularly scheduled service and common transportation rates in the same trade lanes.

Shipping Permit: Sometimes called delivery permit, a document issued by the traffic department of an ocean carrier after the booking of cargo has been made. It directs the receiving clerk at the pier at which the vessel will load to receive from a named party (exporter or forwarder) on a specified day or time the goods for loading and ocean shipment measurement.

Ship's Manifest: A document containing a list of the shipments making up the cargo of a vessel.

Short Ton: 2,000 pounds.

Sight Draft (S/D): Similar to cash on delivery, a draft so drawn by the seller as to be payable on presentation to the drawee (importer) or within a brief period thereafter known as days of grace. Also referred to as a demand draft, a sight draft is used when the seller wishes to retain control of the shipment until payment.

Single Administrative Document: The document now used throughout the European Union to effect exports and customs clearance among member nations and external countries.

SL&C (Shipper's Load and Count): Shipments loaded and sealed by the shipper and not checked or verified by the carrier.

Special Endorsement: A direction by the payee of a draft specifying the name of an alternative payee to whom the drawee is authorized to make payment after delivery of the draft to the alternative payee.

Specific Duty: A tax imposed on imported merchandise without regard to value. It is usually based on the net weight or number of pieces.

Spot Exchange: The exchange rate that exists between two currencies for immediate purchase and sale.

Stale Bill of Lading: A bill of lading that has not been presented under a letter of credit to the issuing or confirming bank within a reasonable time (usually twenty-one days) after its date, thus precluding its arrival at the port of discharge by the time the vessel carrying the shipment has arrived.

Standby Credit: A letter of credit issued by a bank that is payable upon a simple certification by the beneficiary of the letter of credit that a particular condition or duty has not been performed by the applicant for the letter of credit. For example, an exporter (seller) may have to apply for and obtain a standby letter of credit issued in favor of the purchaser when the purchaser is a foreign government to guarantee that the exporter (seller) will perform the sales agreement and deliver the goods in accordance with the delivery schedule. This is to be distinguished from a documentary letter of credit, where the purchaser is the applicant and payment is made by the bank issuing the letter of credit upon presentation to the bank of certain specified documents, such as bills of lading, insurance certificates, inspection certificates, and weight certificates.

Stevedoring: A charge, generally so much per ton, agreed upon between the ocean carrier and a stevedoring, or terminal, operator covering the allocation of men (longshoremen), gear, and all other equipment for working the cargo into or out of the vessel, under the supervision and control of the ship's master.

Stowage: The placing of cargo into a vessel.

Straight Bill of Lading: A bill of lading in which the goods are consigned directly to a named consignee and not to the seller's or buyer's "order." Delivery can be made only to the named person; such a bill of lading is non-negotiable.

Strikes, Riots and Civil Commotions (S.R.&C.C.): A term referring to an insurance clause excluding insurance for loss caused by labor disturbances, riots, and civil commotions or any person engaged in such actions.

Stripping: Unloading (devanning) a container.

Stuffing: Loading a container.

Subrogation: The right that one person, usually an insurance or surety company, has after payment to the beneficiary of the insurance policy, for example, for damage to goods, to pursue any third party against whom the beneficiary would have had a claim, such as the person causing the damage to the goods.

Sue & Labor Clause: A provision in a marine insurance policy obligating the assured to do those things necessary after a loss to prevent further loss and to cooperate with, and act in the best interests of, the insurer.

Surveyor: A company or individual that assesses the extent of damages to cargo incurred during ocean transportation. Such survey reports are necessary in order for insurance companies to make payment to the beneficiary of the insurance policy.

Tariff: A duty (or tax) levied upon goods transported from one customs area to another. Tariffs raise the prices of imported goods, thus making them less competitive within the market of the importing country.

Tariff Rate Quota: An increase in the tariff duty rate imposed upon goods imported to a country after the quantity of the goods imported within the quota period reaches a certain pre-established level.

Tax Haven: A country that imposes a low or no income tax on business transactions conducted by its nationals.

Tender: A solicitation or request for quotations or bids issued by a prospective purchaser, usually a government entity, to select the supplier or seller for a procurement or project.

Tenor: The term fixed for the payment of a draft.

TEU (Twenty-Foot Equivalent Unit): A measurement of container capacity.

Theft, Pilferage &/or Non-Delivery: A type of risk that may be covered under a transportation insurance policy either within the terms of the main coverage or by special endorsement and payment of the corresponding premium.

Through Bill of Lading: Also called a combined transport bill of lading or intermodal bill of lading, a document issued by the transportation carrier that thereby agrees to effect delivery to the required destination by utilizing various means of transportation, such as truck, railroad, and/or steamship line.

Time Draft: A draft maturing at a certain fixed time after presentation or acceptance. This may be a given number of days after sight (acceptance) or a given number of days after the date of the draft.

TL: A truckload shipment.

Total Loss: A situation in which damaged goods covered by an insurance policy are adjudged to have no commercial value and their full value will be paid under the insurance policy.

Trademark: A brand name, word, or symbol placed on a product to distinguish that product from other similar types of products. The right to sell products under a trademark is regulated by the laws and regulations applicable in each country of sale.

Tramp: A steamship or steamship line that does not adhere to a shipping conference and, therefore, is free to charge whatever transportation rates and to sail in any ocean lane it desires.

Transferable Credit: A letter of credit in which the applicant (purchaser of goods) has authorized the beneficiary of the letter of credit (exporting seller of the goods) to transfer its right to payment to a third party, for example, the manufacturer of the goods being sold by the exporter to the purchaser.

Transfer Pricing: Sales of goods between sellers and buyers that are affiliated, for example, by common stock ownership. In such cases, the price may be artificially increased or decreased to vary from the price charged in an arms-length transaction. As a result, income tax and customs authorities may readjust the price.

Trust Receipt: A document signed by a buyer, based on which a bank holding title to goods releases possession of the goods to the buyer for the purpose of sale. The buyer obligates himself to maintain the identity of the goods or the proceeds thereof distinct from the rest of his assets and to hold them subject to repossession by the bank. Trust receipts are used extensively in the Far East, where it is customary to sell on terms of sixty or ninety days, documents against acceptance. The collecting bank permits buyers of good standing to obtain the goods, under a trust receipt contract, before the maturity date of the draft. In some countries, warrants serve the same purpose.

Unconfirmed Credit: A letter of credit issued by the applicant's (purchaser of goods') bank, usually in the purchaser's own country. See also "Confirming Bank."

Uniform Commercial Code: A series of laws applicable in the United States governing commercial transactions, such as sales, leasing, negotiable instruments, bank collections, warehousing, bills of lading, investment securities, and security interests. See also "Convention on Contracts for the International Sale of Goods" and "Incoterms."

Uniform Customs and Practice for Documentary Credits (UCP): A set of international rules and standards agreed upon and applied by many banks in the issuance of letters of credit. The most recent edition (No. 600) went into effect on January 1, 2007.

Uniform Rules for Collections (URC): A set of international rules and standards agreed upon and applied by many banks when acting as a collecting bank in a documentary collection. The most recent edition (No. 522), published by the International Chamber of Commerce, went into effect on January 1, 1996. See "Collecting Bank."

Unitization: The consolidation of a quantity of individual items into one large shipping unit for easier handling.

Usance: The time period during which credit is being extended and during which the purchaser of goods or borrower of monies must pay interest.

Valuation: The appraisal of the value of imported goods by customs officials for the purpose of determining the amount of ad valorem duty payable in the importing country. The GATT Customs Valuation Code obligates governments that are party to it to use the "transaction value" of imported goods—usually the price actually paid or payable for the goods—as the principal basis for valuing the goods for customs purposes.

Value-Added Tax (VAT): An indirect tax on consumption that is levied at each discrete point in the chain of production and distribution, from the raw material stage to final consumption. Each processor or merchant pays a tax proportional to the amount by which she increases the value or marks up the goods she purchases for resale.

Visa: (1) A stamp put into a traveler's passport by officials of an embassy or consulate authorizing a traveler to enter a foreign country. (2) The document issued by an exporting country allowing the export of products subject to an export quota that is in effect in the exporting country.

Voluntary Restraint Agreements (VRAs): Informal arrangements through which exporters voluntarily restrain certain exports, usually through export quotas, to avoid economic dislocation in an importing country and to avert the possible imposition of mandatory import restrictions.

Warehouse Receipt: A receipt given by a warehouseman for goods received by him for storage. A warehouse receipt in which it is stated that the commodities referred to therein will be delivered to the depositor or to any other specified person or company is a negotiable warehouse receipt. Endorsement and delivery of a negotiable warehouse receipt serves to transfer ownership of the property covered by the receipt.

Warehouse to Warehouse Clause: A provision in a transportation insurance policy extending coverage from the time of transport from the seller's place of business to the purchaser's place of business.

War Risk Insurance: Separate insurance coverage for loss of goods that results from any act of war. This insurance is necessary during peacetime because of objects, such as floating mines, left over from previous wars.

Wharfage: A charge assessed by a pier or dock owner against freight moving over the pier or dock or against carriers using the pier or dock.

With Average (W.A.): An insurance coverage broader than F.P.A. and representing protection for partial damage caused by the perils of the sea. Additional named perils, such as theft, pilferage, non-delivery, and freshwater damage, can be added to a W.A. clause. Generally, however, damage must be caused by seawater. A minimum percentage of damage may be required before payment is made.

World Trade Organization (WTO): The World Trade Organization consists of 123 signatory countries. The Uruguay Round of negotiations resulted in the formation of the

WTO and in numerous agreements relating to the reduction of tariffs and non-tariff barriers to trade. The WTO supersedes GATT, but a number of agreements reached under GATT, such as the Valuation Code, the Antidumping Code, the Subsidies Code, and the Agreement on Government Procurement, continue in revised form under the WTO.

York Antwerp Rules of General Average: An international treaty prescribing the conditions and rules under which damage to a steamship or to goods will be shared by the other owners of goods on the steamship.

Index